AN APACHE LIFE-WAY

PLATE I

CHIRICAHUA CAMP

AN APACHE LIFE-WAY

THE ECONOMIC, SOCIAL, AND
RELIGIOUS INSTITUTIONS OF
THE CHIRICAHUA INDIANS

By

MORRIS EDWARD OPLER

COOPER SQUARE PUBLISHERS, INC.
NEW YORK
1965

TO

ELSIE CLEWS PARSONS

ABLE ANTHROPOLOGIST, HELPFUL CRITIC, AND

GENEROUS SPONSOR OF THE WORK OF OTHERS

Copyright 1941 by The University of Chicago
Copyright Reassigned to Morris E. Opler 1956

Published 1965 by
Cooper Square Publishers, Inc.
59 Fourth Avenue, New York, N.Y. 10003

Printed in the United States of America

Library of Congress Catalog Card Number: 65-23533

PREFACE

I HAVE tried to fashion an account of the Chiricahua Apache that will be real and convincing for readers of Western European extractions and traditions. Often the anthropologist begins with the reactions and behavior of the average adult of the culture he has studied. The descriptive details then seem so far removed from anything we, the products of another lifeway, know, that an atmosphere of exotic contrast is created, and the relevance of the material for us and for our problems fails to emerge.

Consequently, I have endeavored to show how a person becomes a Chiricahua as well as to indicate what he does because he is a Chiricahua. Events are introduced in the order in which they are experienced in the course of the normal Chiricahua Apache life-cycle. The attempt has been made to convey an appreciation of first awareness to the culture, of initial contacts with its precepts, of the steady pressure by which it shapes its carriers, and of the adjustments to its demands, obligations, and satisfactions which the individual accepts. I have sought in this manner to shift the emphasis from strange externals to more familiar and important processes and purposes. I have wanted the average Chiricahua to be an intelligible and sympathetic figure, not in the sense that the reader approves or disapproves all his ideas and actions, but in the sense that the reader understands what he has become in terms of what he has experienced. My principal concern in this book has been with what is socialized and not with personality differences. Consequently, materials pertaining to the individual as such are stressed only when it is important to show the range of variation which the culture permits at particular points.

To trace, painstakingly and sensitively, the introduction of an individual to the formal requirements and implications of his culture requires more than a superficial treatment. It was necessary to make the study as "complete" as possible—not in any ethnologically utopian sense but in the practicable, attainable meaning of an inquiry many sided enough to satisfy the reader that no important aspect of thought or behavior had been left entirely unexplored.

Moreover, since it was the socialization of the Chiricahua which was to be examined, I felt that not only the sequence of events but the contexts in which they are placed should be faithful to the Chiricahua view. In order to keep the emphases as the participants feel them, it became necessary to separate items which might have been brought together by some other classification and to unite data which would have been scattered in response to a more conventional topical treatment. Thus, many varieties of religious experience have been introduced before any thorough explanation of religious ideology is attempted, simply because these impressions of the supernatural are communicated to the child long before he is in a position to rationalize their significance. Again, raid and warfare are subsumed under the maintenance of the household, not because of any notions of my own concerning the nature of these activities, but because, at the period described, the Chiricahua considered the raid a legitimate industry and trained faithfully for its proper fulfilment with this in mind.

It is my feeling that the most successful ethnographic study in terms of what it honestly establishes is the one in which the writer intrudes least upon the scene. It is a solemn responsibility to act as one of the few links between the world of letters and a way of life which has bounded the happiness and sorrow of thousands of individuals for hundreds of years. In determining how and when and where the basic understandings and persuasions ordinarily come to the individual consciousness, the primary source must be the testimony of the people involved. It has been part of my method, therefore, to describe the culture in its own terms, to employ the comments and explanations of informants wherever they seem pertinent. I have preferred to use my own observations as research leads by means of which to elicit descriptions and experiences from Chiricahua friends rather than to

employ them as final statements. The picture of external movement is essential, but the attitudes and evaluations that surround overt behavior are quite as important. These imponder-
ables of context the informant can best supply.

It is my hope that a volume which depicts the development of
the individual in relation to society, which draws so heavily from
source materials, and which emphasizes the functions of institutions in context will be of interest not only to professional anthro-
pologists but also to educators, child psychologists, sociologists,
and to all those sincerely concerned with the comprehension of
the human scene. With this larger potential audience in mind,
native words have been translated into English where this could
be done and technical terms have been avoided.[1] Because Dr.
Harry Hoijer will soon have available a Chiricahua Apache dic-
tionary, no glossary is included. For specialists, kinship materials are given in an appendix. Native names, unpronounceable
to the average reader in the original and often cumbersome in
translation, have been reduced to initials. An additional reason
for this is that many of the references are of an intimate or
religious nature, and the information was often given with the
understanding that identities be masked. Exceptions are made
in the case of Geronimo and several other former leaders who
have become historical figures. Summaries of legends and references to mythological subjects are based on my own collection
where other sources are not acknowledged.

This volume, besides describing the aboriginal life of the Chiricahua, is the first of a series of monographs which will character-
ize and compare the cultures of four Apache tribes of the American Southwest and the adjoining region of Old Mexico—the
Chiricahua, Mescalero, Lipan, and Jicarilla. I have gathered material, also, concerning the present status and adjustment of the
Chiricahua Apache. But most of these people now share a reservation in New Mexico with the Mescalero Apache. Consequently, in order that the acculturation of the inhabitants of the
Mescalero Reservation may be treated as the logical unit it is,

---

[1] For the few Chiricahua words retained, the orthography recommended in
the *American Anthropologist*, Vol. XXXVI, No. 4 (1934), has been followed.

I am withholding most of my comparisons of the old and the new until the Mescalero Apache have been described as well.

In bringing this segment of the project to completion, my obligations to institutions and friends are many. The Department of Anthropology and the Social Science Research Committee of the University of Chicago, the Council for Research in the Social Sciences of Columbia University, the Laboratory of Anthropology of Santa Fe, the National Research Council, the Office of Indian Affairs, the Social Science Research Council, and the Southwest Society, by field fellowships, financial assistance, and other courtesies, enabled me to remain in contact with Chiricahua informants for a total of approximately two years during the period 1931–37. The Social Science Research Committee of the University of Chicago has made possible the preparation and publication of the study at this time.

Dr. Ruth Benedict, Dr. Regina Flannery, Mr. Paul Frank, Dr. John Gillin, Mr. M. R. Harrington, Dr. Jules Henry, Dr. Harry Hoijer, Mrs. Edith Rosenfels Nash, and Dr. Sol Tax, as members of the summer field party of 1931 of the Laboratory of Anthropology of Santa Fe, or in other capacities, gathered Chiricahua data which they have generously put at my disposal. The materials of these co-workers have corroborated and extended my own information at many points and have been of signal value throughout. In addition, Dr. Benedict and Dr. Hoijer have read and criticized the manuscript. The last named has also given inestimable assistance in the translation of Chiricahua terms. Others who have read the manuscript in whole or in part and who have furnished valuable suggestions are Dr. Edwin R. Embree, Dr. Elsie Clews Parsons, Dr. Russell M. Story, Mr. Laurence Stutsman, and Mr. Richard Waterman. Mr. Thomas Miles, photographer, and Audrey Waterman have aided in the preparation of illustrative materials. Professors E. F. Castetter and A. L. Hershey have helped me in the identification of plant specimens.

I am indebted to the Claremont Colleges Museum, the Denver Art Museum, the Museum of the American Indian, Heye Foundation, the Laboratory of Anthropology of Santa Fe, and the

United States National Museum for photographs of Chiricahua subjects and artifacts.

Over thirty Chiricahua Apache, representing all three bands, have contributed to the field notes which have gone into this volume. Of these, a number who assisted for prolonged periods deserve special mention: John Allard, Duncan Balachu, Alfred Chatto, David Fatty, Paul Gadelkon, Martin Kayitah, Samuel E. Kenoi, Arnold Kinjoni, Charles Martine, Daniel Nicholas, and Leon Perico. John Allard, Samuel E. Kenoi, and Daniel Nicholas acted as interpreters as well as informants, and their interest and help far exceeded the ordinary requirements of their task.

My final acknowledgment is to my wife, Catherine Opler, associate in the plan and in the labor, without whose help and faith and lovely presence nothing else would avail.

MORRIS EDWARD OPLER

CLAREMONT COLLEGES
CLAREMONT, CALIFORNIA
November 1940

TABLE OF CONTENTS

LIST OF ILLUSTRATIONS

PLATES

FIGURES

LOCATION AND HISTORICAL SKETCH

THIS volume describes the culture of an Apachean-speaking tribe of the American Southwest as it existed during the youth of the older informants from whom data were collected. The Chiricahua were already horsemen and possessed their first firearms, but tribal life had not yet been disrupted by hostilities with the Americans.

The territory which they controlled during this period was extensive and is not easy to define accurately. They ranged through southwestern New Mexico, southeastern Arizona, and the northern parts of the Mexican states of Sonora and Chihuahua. The Rio Grande acted as the eastern boundary. Occasional journeys and raids brought them as far north as the pueblo outposts of Laguna, Acoma, and Zuñi, but ordinarily they did not stray much farther north than the present site of Quemado, New Mexico. The western limits of their country can be roughly indicated, from north to south, by the present towns of Spur Lake, Luna, Reserve, and Glenwood in New Mexico, and by Duncan, Wilcox, Johnson, Benson, Elgin, and Parker Canyon in Arizona. To the south an undetermined area in northern Mexico was also under their control.

The Chiricahua bands were three in number. The most eastern and northern band, whose territories joined those of the Mescalero Apache at the Rio Grande, controlled almost all the Chiricahua territory west of the Rio Grande in New Mexico and has been given a number of names throughout the literature. Those occurring most frequently are Warm Springs or Ojo Caliente Apache, Coppermine Apache, Mimbreños Apache, and Mogollones Apache. The Chiricahua name for this band is čîhéné, "Red Paint People." In historic times this band has been led by Mangus Colorado, Victorio, Nana, and Loco. From historical records and the accounts of informants, the local groups and camp sites of the members of this band can be traced to the

Datil Range, the vicinity of Rito, Hot Springs, Cuchillo, and the Black, the Mimbres, the Mogollon, the Pinos Altos, Victoria, and Florida mountain ranges. For convenience I have called the Red Paint People the Eastern Chiricahua band.

To the south and west of the Red Paint People, ranging through the portion of southwestern New Mexico west of the Continental Divide and through southeastern Arizona, a second Chiricahua band, called čóǩánéń, whose name does not yield to linguistic analysis, was to be found. This is the band to which the term "Chiricahua" was first applied. It was this band, often called in the literature "Cochise" Apache after their leader, Cochise, which held Apache Pass, and with which the government had a great deal of trouble during the Indian Wars. The most famous of the strongholds of this band, which I have named the Central Chiricahua band, were the Dragoon Mountains, the Chiricahua Mountains, and the Dos Cabezas Mountains.

The third and southernmost band of the Chiricahua, called in the native tongue, ⁿdê'ìⁿdà·í, "Enemy People," stayed almost entirely in what is now Old Mexico. I shall refer to this group as the Southern Chiricahua band. During the last half of the nineteenth century difficulties with the Mexican soldiery drove them north, where they speedily came into conflict with settlers and United States government forces. After that they were harried from either side of the border until Geronimo's surrender in 1886. Geronimo himself was born a member of this band. Mention of this tribal subdivision in the literature is made under the names of Southern Chiricahua and Pinery Apache. Reference in the literature may be found to their leader, Hǫ́· whose name has been variously written as Who, Whoa, or Juh. The Sierra Madre and the Hatchet Mountains were familiar landmarks of this band.

With the appearance in numbers of white settlers, the affairs of the tribe took an unhappy turn. About 1870 the Ojo Caliente Reserve in western New Mexico was established for the Eastern Chiricahua band. In 1872 similar provision was made for the Central Chiricahua and the Southern Chiricahua. Because part of their range lay in Old Mexico, it was particularly difficult to

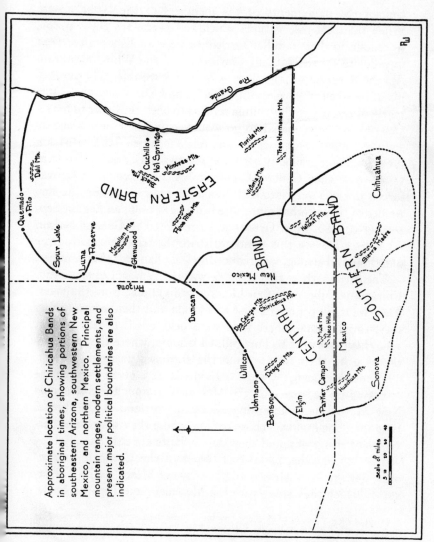

FIG. I.—Map showing approximate location of Chiricahua bands in aboriginal times

control the movements of the members of the latter group. When the local reservations which had permitted these people to remain in their familiar territories were abolished after 1875 in order to concentrate all Chiricahua on the White Mountain Apache Reservation, the stage was set for trouble. The antagonism between the Western Apache and the Chiricahua was marked, and many Chiricahua refused to obey the order to move. Others who were forced to go would leave their new home as soon as military supervision was relaxed. Out of this situation grew a number of bloody incidents and two major military operations—one when General Crook, in his campaign of 1883, was forced to cross over into Old Mexico in order to obtain the surrender of these Indians, and the last in 1885–86, ending on September 5, 1886, when Geronimo surrendered to General Nelson A. Miles.[1] During this period of strife the tribe, normally over one thousand strong, was reduced to less than half that number.

The aftermath of this struggle was the removal of the entire Chiricahua tribe, over four hundred individuals, from the West. They went, as prisoners, first to Florida and then, after a short stay, to Alabama, where they were held until 1894. In that year they were sent to Fort Sill, Oklahoma, where they were retained until their release from the status of prisoners of war. This occurred in 1913, when individuals were given their choice of taking up residence on the Mescalero Indian Reservation of New Mexico or of accepting allotments of land in Oklahoma. Less than one hundred chose to stay where they were. The survivors of this group and their descendants are still living in the vicinity of Apache, Oklahoma. Most of the Chiricahua, however, went to New Mexico and now live at Mescalero on a reservation which they share with the Mescalero and Lipan Apache.

[1] For a longer account of these troubles, from the native point of view, see Opler, "A Chiricahua Apache's Account of the Geronimo Campaign of 1886," *New Mexico Historical Review*, October, 1938.

CHILDHOOD

AT THE first signs of pregnancy a woman takes immediate steps to insure the safe delivery and good health of the developing child. To prevent injury to the fetus, she refrains from sexual intercourse as soon as the menses stop.

The food restrictions she observes are not onerous. She eats sparingly of fat meat lest the child become too large and delivery be difficult. She avoids eating animal intestines, a food associated with stillbirths in which the child is strangled by the umbilical cord. Piñon nuts are shunned also, for they cause the child to "have fat all over," thus prolonging delivery.

An important restriction is the injunction against riding a horse; "the shaking is not good for a pregnant woman." This rule became extended in later days to include riding in wagons. The woman also avoids ceremonies where masked dancers appear, for the sight of the hooded figures "hurts both mother and child. The child might not come out and might kill the woman." Some prospective fathers are just as careful about this, because the impersonator has "a hood over his head and the child may be born with a caul over its face." Others hold that the rule concerns the mother only and that the father can look at the masked dancers and can even act as a masked dancer, providing all signs of this role are entirely erased before he returns home.

The pregnant woman refrains from excessive walking, from lifting heavy burdens, and from sitting up for long periods. She is urged to take sufficient rest. The consideration with which she is treated reflects the great love of children that characterizes the society. "A woman about to become a mother is treated extra nice, just like a child." Yet the performance of ordinary household tasks is considered beneficial to her throughout this period, and laziness and self-pity are ridiculed. "They say that when you sit on the child after the fifth month it will be harder for you. The child gets in the right position for coming out if you move around. The more you are a coward about it, the worse it will be for you."

Little attempt is made to control the sex of the expected child. Whether or not such control is possible is a moot point. One informant told of "a ceremony which causes them to have a boy or a girl. It is performed right at the beginning." The man was unable to supply the details, however. On another occasion the same person stated that, if a man scrapes his foot over the four sides of the woman in labor, a boy is born; but, if a woman touches the four sides with her hand, the baby is a girl. Most commentators discount these claims:

> There are lots of people here who would control it if they could, like D., who has all boys and wants a daughter.

> Whether it's a boy or a girl is in Yusn's[1] power; that's the way I look at it. Some shamans say they can control it, but I believe there is nothing to that.

However, the activity of the child during the prenatal period furnishes a clue to its sex. A fetus which "has lots of life" is presumed to be a male; a less active one, a female. Estimates of the length of pregnancy are approximately accurate.

It is essential for the expectant mother and her husband to avoid acrimonious clashes with others. "A pregnant woman has to keep out of fusses with other women because many are witches, and, if she quarrels with them, they may harm the child. The husband has to be careful of witches, too, when his wife is pregnant."

At the onset of labor pains close female relatives of the woman attend her. Her mother, her mother's sisters, her mother's mother, and her older sisters are members of the relationship group from which assistants are most likely to come. If the husband's family lives near by, his mother or sister may be present. When a woman skilled in midwifery is numbered among these relatives, no outside help is asked. Otherwise the service of a woman who has special ceremonial and practical knowledge is sought. Such a woman is often selected on the basis of "the good luck

---

[1] A deity known also as Life Giver.

she has had in bringing babies into the world." If she has "a family of fine children of her own," it is a happy augury. Very important is her right to perform a ceremony, to pray and sing and treat the newborn infant ritually. It is not absolutely essential to have such a "ceremonial" woman in command at this time, but, since success in life depends so largely on ritual preparation, she functions in a majority of births. This woman is well paid for her services; some valuable property, often a horse, is her reward.

When the time for delivery draws near, the husband leaves the home. Unless an emergency arises, he cannot be present at the birth, for relatives of his wife to whom he stands in a relationship of respect and avoidance are certain to be there.[2]

There is no definite rule which bars other men from being present. In fact, they are sometimes asked to attend in emergencies. But usually "men don't come to a birth because there are so many women around, and a man would feel funny." Another factor which discourages their attendance is that discharges from the woman's body at childbirth are to some extent equated with menstrual blood, from which a man can contact painful swelling of the joints.

During delivery the woman kneels with legs apart before an oak post which she uses to steady herself. Assistants hold her arms if she requires aid. To facilitate the birth, the genitals may be bathed in water in which the pounded root of a plant (*Eriogonum jamesii*) has been boiled. A similar decoction will be used after the birth to insure rapid healing. To speed birth, four small, light-colored pieces of the inner leaves of narrow yucca may be swallowed with salt, one after the other. The midwife massages the woman's abdomen downward and receives the child. With a long black flint or with a sharp edge of a length of reed or yucca leaf, she cuts the umbilical cord about one and one-half inches from the baby's navel and knots the end or ties it with a strand of yucca-leaf string. If the child does not cry or breathe at once, cold water is dashed on its body. When a baby is obviously alive

[2] For an account of these observances see pp. 163–81.

but does not cry or cry loudly, that child "will grow up to be strong."

Following a normal delivery, the midwife washes the infant in tepid water at once and places it on a soft robe. In some cases a plant (*Parosela formosa*) is added to this water "to keep the child from crying." She rubs a mixture of grease and red ocher over the baby's body to keep the skin from getting sore. Next she strews pollen or ashes to the directions in clockwise circuit beginning with the east and holds the blanket and the child to the directions in the same order. Prayers and practices which mark her individually owned rite accompany this procedure. Meanwhile, others minister to the mother. Particular care is taken in cases of prolapse of the uterus to see that the organ is pushed back into place properly.

The afterbirth is gathered together in the robe or piece of old clothing upon which the woman has knelt. With it is put the umbilical cord. These must not be burned or buried. If they are buried and then dug up and consumed by animals, the child is harmed. The approved method of disposal is to place the bundle in a fruit-bearing bush or tree "because the tree comes to life every year, and they want life in this child to be renewed like the life in the tree." Before final disposal, the bundle is blessed by the midwife. To the tree she says, "May the child live and grow up to see you bear fruit many times."[3]

At the time of the birth ceremony a name may be suggested for the infant, often by the midwife. However, when nothing unusual marks the birth or distinguishes the newborn baby, the naming may not take place for two or three months. Even when a name is immediately conferred, there is little reason to think that the child will bear it long.

When my daughter was born, the midwife gave her a name, but it did not catch on. Then my wife called her "My Daughter." All the others around our camp now do so too. Later, before she is ten or eleven years old, we will give her another name. This is a Chiricahua custom. The baby name is outgrown. One child, for example, is called "Ugly Baby." But she will not be called

---

[3] One informant claimed that the cord is retained and later eaten by the child, but no verification of this was obtained from others.

this later on. Later the child will be named according to circumstances; something about the child will suggest a name. Once in a while the first name is kept because it fits so well that the person "wears" it all the time.

Since the name relates to personality traits or to events, it is not necessarily a clue to the sex of its bearer.

When labor is excessively difficult or long delayed, and especially when sorcery is suspected, appeal is made to men or women who carry on still other ceremonies. One elder described such a rite which he had performed over a young woman. She had been in labor for about eighteen hours, and it was feared that "the baby would have to be killed and taken out in pieces to save her." In response to an urgent request from her relatives, the old man hurried to the camp with a helper. He prayed and drew a cross of black mineral substance on his helper's hand. He then directed his assistant to put his arm around the woman's body at various places and to press her gently while he began a ceremonial song of four verses. At the end of the second verse a boy was born—"born before I got through with one song." Great claims are made for these childbirth ceremonies and for these practitioners. "As soon as they touch the woman who is having a hard time, everything is made easy for her."

Nursing begins "as soon as the mother has milk." The colostrum is not differentiated from the milk secreted later. Concerning frequency of feedings, it was said, "I have seen that, when women have babies, as soon as they cry the mothers give them the breast." "The women boil up lots of bones and make a soup right away. They say that makes lots of milk and pure milk." If the mother's milk does not flow at once, the child is not fed the first day. If she is unable to nurse the child on the second day, it is given a little water. Should she still lack milk on the third day, the child is nursed by a mother's sister or other close relative.

From the mother a Spartan attitude is expected. "Women didn't lie around as they do now; they got up soon afterward." "I saw T.'s wife. She has had many children. Today she has a baby; tomorrow she is around doing something. Some lie down for an hour maybe. The next day they are up." But most con-

finements last from a few days to a week. Moreover, the ceremonies for difficult childbirth and the many medicines in use for
ailments resulting from childbearing suggest that the woman
does not always have an easy time.

After the birth of her child, the woman ties a rope or a strap
around her waist "so that her stomach will not sag." She wears
this until she feels strong once more.

Despite the roving life, there is an attachment to the place of
birth. A child is told where he was born; and, when he is again
brought to the vicinity, "they roll him on the ground to the four
directions. They don't make a special trip for this, but they do
it if they happen to be there. This is done even if the child is
getting big." Adults as well as children have been known to roll
in this manner upon returning to the birthplace.

CRADLE DAYS

Normally, the fourth day after birth is the occasion for a cradle ceremony, although sometimes the rite is delayed for a few
days more. The immediate family may include an old man or
woman prepared to perform it, or the midwife may know the
rite and accept the task. Depending on the "way" of the shaman
who officiates, the ceremony will be elaborate or modest. A poor
family is satisfied to obtain a shaman whose ceremony is pruned
to essentials, while a wealthy family may make more of a display
of the event. Not infrequently the selection of the practitioner is
related to the web of human relations—to friendships, to bonds
of blood, to desire for gain.

There's a shaman, my relative. And there are some people who have a new
baby. They are well-off people; they have much property; they have horses and
buckskins and bring in lots of deer. My relative has nothing like this, though he
is a shaman. He is poor. I notice that this wealthy family with the new baby
has lost several babies before this.

I go to them. I say, "You people have a new baby. I notice that you have
lost several children. My relative is a good shaman. He knows something to
keep the child well. You go to him and ask him and he will put up a ceremony
for you. But don't tell him who told you about his ceremony."

Those relatives of the little child talk it over. One says, "I'll give a gun for
that ceremony." Another says, "I'll give two blankets." Another offers a horse
or a buckskin.

One of the relatives goes to the man who knows the ceremony. He says, "We have been unable to bring up our children. We need you to help us."

My relative sits there. He just makes some kind of sound in his throat first. Then he says, "Well, I'll do it. But I need a buckskin with a piece of turquoise tied at the middle of the head and a yellow horse. Give two other things, anything you wish, just so it makes four, a set of four."

They get these things together and bring them to him, and the ceremony takes place.

Once he has accepted the task, the shaman busies himself with the construction of the cradle. With prayers and ritual, oak, ash, or walnut is gathered for the ovate frame, and sotol or yucca stalk for the cross-pieces that will form the back of the cradle.

For the back part of the cradleboard, the cross-pieces are of sotol if the cradle is for a boy, and of narrow-leafed yucca if it is for a girl. The sotol, which is jagged edged along the leaf, is called the boy, the "he"; the yucca is called the girl, the "she." These plants are brother and sister, we say.

This sex distinction, however, is not acceptable to all.

A canopy to shield the child's face is made of the stems of red-barked dogwood, mock orange, or Apache plume. A piece of ash connects the frame and the canopy, and ash or oak is used for the footrest. The bedding is of wild mustard, and a pillow of *Solanium trifolium* prevents excessive movement of the head. The buckskin covering for the frame is usually colored with yellow ocher. In the buckskin which covers the top of the canopy, symbols are cut which sometimes have sex value. The girl's cradle is usually decorated with a full moon or half-moon; the boy's cradle, with a cross or four parallel slits.

Some feel that cradleboard materials may be prepared in advance but that, once actual construction has started, the work should be finished the same day. Others permit the outer frame to be made on one day and the cross-pieces and canopy on another. Still others have no strong conviction about the length of time to be allotted to the process as long as the cradle is ready when it is needed. It is assumed that all steps in the construction have been accompanied by prayers for the welfare and long life of the infant. The shaman ties protective amulets on the cradle—bags of pollen, turquoise beads, and pieces of lightning-riven wood.

The public part of the ceremony begins in the early morning before relatives and neighbors. The shaman may confine his own part to prayer and the giving of commands to an assistant, or he may perform the ritual acts alone. The child is marked with pollen or specular iron ore, and pollen is thrown to the directions. One practitioner places four dots of pollen on the face of a boy for whom he is officiating and traces a line of pollen across the bridge of the nose of a girl. The cradle, and sometimes the child, is held to the cardinal directions, beginning with the east and proceeding in the clockwise circuit. It is the "way" of one shaman to hold up both child and cradle if the ceremony is for a boy but to gesture with the cradle only if the infant is a girl. Finally, the cradle is faced to the east, and, after three ritual feints, the child is placed inside. A feast and social occasion follow. According to one informant, a child may later address a parental or grandparental term to the person who lifted him into the cradle, even though no actual relationship exists.

This rite is essentially a prayer that the child be spared to occupy the cradle in the future, for it is not until a month or more has elapsed and "the neck is strong enough so that the head does not hang limply" that the child is kept continuously in the cradle. After that, the mother carries the cradle by a tumpline passing across her chest or, more infrequently, over her forehead. Even when she travels on horseback, she often carries the cradle strung across her hip by the carrying strap and suspended over the side of the horse.

To the amulets and pendants supplied by the shaman the mother generally adds some of her own. The right paw of the badger, with grass substituted for the bone, is hung on the cradle to guard the child from fright. Such protection is important, for fright lies at the root of a number of serious illnesses. Hummingbird claws and pieces of wildcat skin also act as cradle charms. To ward off colds and other sickness, a length of cholla wood is often tied on the cradle. When anything is wrong with the child, a growth found on the creosote bush is suspended from the canopy. It is a general rule that no one may step over a child or a cradle.

PLATE II

United States National Museum

CARRYING THE CRADLE

When the baby is from a week to a few months old, his mother or his maternal grandmother pierces his ears. To do this she applies something hot to the ear and then punctures it with a strong thorn or a sharp bone. The child learns "to hear things sooner" and obeys more quickly if this is done promptly. "When the ears are not pierced, the child cannot be controlled; he will be wild and go to the bad. It is believed that children grow faster too if this is done." Pendants of white beads or turquoise are strung from the ears of very young children, and this mode of ornamentation continues throughout life.

Sexual intercourse between a man and his wife is not resumed until the child has been weaned. During this period of almost three years the couple is expected to remain continent. Actually, some men contrive to "sneak around" and "find easy women" with whom to have relations. But social pressure operates to enforce this rule of continence strictly in the majority of cases. A man so importunate as to demand connection with his wife too soon is subject to sharp criticism and is said to have acted "against" his growing child. "There is a man whose child is not walking yet, and his wife is pregnant. The Indians think he is no good. We are ashamed to have a second child on the way before a first is weaned."

Because the mother's milk supply has been stopped or altered by her new pregnancy, the nursing infant is "starved" and upset and is likely to become a weakling. In such an emergency another minor rite is arranged:

There's a hair-cutting ceremony that I'm going to tell you about. Let us say a child is only a year old and the mother is pregnant again while that child is still nursing. Then the little child that is only a year old is sick; it has stomach trouble. Something must be done for that child.

When this happens, the mother usually takes the child to an old woman or someone who knows what to do. This old woman cuts the child's hair and puts red paint over the child's body. Then she gives it some kind of medicine.

Polygyny, though it is not widely practiced, exists, and a man with more than one wife "is in a good position, for when one of his wives is pregnant or has a nursing child, he can go to the other."

Once the child is old enough for the cradleboard, it becomes his almost permanent home for a number of months. This continuous stay in the cradle causes a slight occipital flattening of the head. The baby is laced in tightly and is removed only occasionally. He may even be left in the cradle while he is nursed. He does have to be taken out when the soft grass, moss, or pulverized wild-rose bark, used as padding and as absorbent material for the discharges, needs renewing. To prevent chafing, the child is dusted with powder scraped from the bark of the heart-leafed willow. A very young child is bathed in a decoction obtained by boiling the plant *Drymaria fendleri* "to make the skin strong."

As the child becomes more active and restless, beads and jingles of various kinds are strung from the canopy to engage his attention. After he is six or seven months old he is allowed more time outside the cradle and crawls vigorously around the camp.

During this crawling stage the child must be carefully watched, lest he come in contact with baneful substances which can cause sickness—worms, certain insects, and feathers from evil birds such as the owl or the crow. Dogs are considered particularly inappropriate in a camp where there is a small child.

If you have a little child crawling around and suddenly a dog barks at it and scares it, they say that the fright will go inside that child and make its heart sick. So they don't like dogs around much. If you have one, some man might come along and say, "Why do you have that dog around? Don't you know it is no good? It might scare your children and make them sick."

When a child is stillborn or dies while it is being carried in the cradle, its body is hastily buried in a talus slope and is covered by rocks, branches, and earth. The cradle, if it has already been made, has a different destination:

They take the cradle and cut it so it will be recognized; cut slits in the buckskin, for instance. They hang it up in a tree which stands to the east of the encampment where the death took place. No one will dare to touch it. It is forbidden to touch it. If the cradle is still around the camp, it is hung out at the child's death even though the child is already walking when he dies. Sometimes the cradle is put in a place in a bluff.

Occasionally, a cradle is burned at the death of the child. This alternative usage conforms to the customary death practices, for all of an adult's combustible possessions are ordinarily destroyed by fire at his demise.

A still serviceable cradle, if the child for whom it was made is alive and healthy, may be used for a newborn sibling of the same sex. Nevertheless, a cradle ceremony is held for the new baby. The more usual practice is to fashion a separate cradle for each child.

There are no conventionalized cradlesongs, but the mother often croons some such improvised lullaby as, "Little baby, go to sleep again." "Sometimes it goes way up and makes you feel sorry for the baby. It almost makes you want to cry." To quiet a fretful child, a man or a woman swings the cradle and sings a vigorous tune accompanied by such words as:

> This, my little baby!
> This, my little baby!

FIRST STEPS

Life is conceived as a path along which individuals must constantly be helped by ritual devices. This trail must be followed exactly as the heroes of mythical times are said to have journeyed along it. It is appropriate, therefore, that the baby's first steps should be ceremonially celebrated.

Since this rite is purely symbolic in nature, it may occur before the child actually begins to walk or some time afterward. It will not take place until the child is at least seven months old, and it has ordinarily been held before he is two years of age. On this occasion the infant dons his first moccasins, an aspect of the rite which gives it its name, "Putting on Moccasins." As in the other rites, practitioners who "know" this particular ceremony must be hired. Depending on their "way" and the wealth and importance of the family sponsoring the occasion, the ceremony will vary in detail. The account that follows summaries the basic pattern.

There is a ceremony held over a child when it just begins to walk. . . . . Men and women who know how may carry on this ceremony for the child. They get the power through Child of the Water [the culture hero].[4] It is done to keep the child healthy and strong, and because Child of the Water, when he started to walk, had a ceremony like this one.

The family . . . . has to have a lot of meat and fruit ready. A feast is announced just like the one held at the girl's puberty rite. Many are invited. When a boy goes through this ceremony, they call him Child of the Water. When a girl goes through it, they call her White Painted Woman [the mother of the culture hero]. Every child should go through it.

When my son first began to walk, he had a good ceremony. T. and Old Man D. carried it out. They had power from Child of the Water.

D. directed my wife in the making of the buckskin outfit. It has to be made from the skin of a black-tailed buck for a boy. In D.'s ceremony just a shirt and moccasins are made for the boy. For a girl the outfit has to be made from the skin of a black-tailed doe. Crescents and stars and crosses were the designs. The same designs are used on the girl's clothes when the ceremony is for a girl.

They wait for the new or the full moon before beginning this ceremony. This time they waited for the new moon. They start just as early as they can. Early in the morning many came to the place where I lived. We had plenty there for them to eat. We had presents for everyone, too—fruit and tobacco and other things. J. B. helped me with this because he wanted the ceremony held. He is a relative on my wife's side. My father-in-law brought some of these things too, and his sisters helped also. My wife's sisters helped with the cooking.

They had a big hoop-and-pole game[5] going there too. P. and others who knew the ceremony well were off playing this game while they waited for the feast that was to follow.

After some prayers T. marked everyone with pollen. He put some on the head and above the nose of both men and women, the way they do at the girl's puberty rite. This was done just before sunup. At sunrise he took the boy and lifted him toward the east, raising him four times. He did the same to the south and the west and the north. Then he set him down.

With pollen he made footprints on a piece of white buckskin just as White Painted Women made them in the story of the killing of the monsters. We took the boy. I was holding him on one side, and T. was on the other. We led him through these footprints. T. said a prayer about Child of the Water and his first step just as the boy took the first step. He said another prayer for the second step and went on until four prayers and four steps were over. Then the boy took four steps by himself. As he did so, they said, "May he have good fortune." Now we turned the boy clockwise and brought him back, and he walked the four steps in the same way again. Four times we walked him like this. Then we

4 Actually the rite can be obtained through other sources as well.

5 For a description of the game see pp. 448–50.

took him in a clockwise circle four times. After four prayers, T. sang four songs. Then we sat down.

Next T., and after him all the others, marked that little boy just as the girl is marked in the puberty rite. After that, T. prayed, took a drum, beat it four times, and started to sing. All those who knew his songs helped with the singing. Four songs were sung before he stopped. They were about Life Giver [another name for Yusn], White Painted Woman, and Child of the Water, of how the earth was made and how the fruit grew, of how Child of the Water was born and reared under the fire and how the monsters were killed.

Now prayers were said by D., and another set of songs began. The people were dancing in there, women and men, boys and girls. They danced in place. The women uttered that call of applause[6] when the names of Child of the Water and White Painted Woman were mentioned.

There were two more sets of prayers and songs. D. said the prayers. They had me sit in the center with the boy, and they all danced around us. The boy was not bashful. He danced up and down and looked around. He was only about a year and nine months old.

D. and T. said the last set of four prayers. When the people playing the hoop-and-pole game heard about this, they all came up, for they knew we had presents there to give and that the end of the ceremony was near.

D. picked up the moccasins. He put pollen on them and lifted them to the directions. He put pollen on the boy's foot and put the right moccasin on first, then the left. "Now you can run," he said. The boy put his foot right in; he was glad to do it. Everyone said, "He's just like his father."

Finally the presents were blessed. D. and T. put pollen all over the baskets of fruit and presents, and a man began passing out these things to the people. He gave some to D. and T. first. He gave them tobacco. Then sweets were passed to the children. Then other gifts were distributed. After this was over, the big meal began. They feasted that day. That night T. lifted the boy up to the moon from the four directions so that he would grow tall.

SPRING HAIR-CUTTING CEREMONY

The spring, usually the spring following the first-moccasins ceremony, "when everything is starting to grow and the grass is coming up," is chosen as the appropriate time for a brief hair-cutting rite. The child is brought to a shaman who "knows" supernatural power useful in safeguarding and training children. The man or woman selected must have thick hair. "If a man performs this ceremony and the child grows up to be a fine one, other parents come to him."

---

[6] A high-pitched call of the woman, signifying reverent or ceremonial applause.

The minutiae of the ceremonies differ, but a composite description, distilled from some half-dozen separate accounts, reduces to the following elements. Pollen from cattail or from one of a number of other sources is applied to the cheeks and head of the child four times and scattered clockwise to the cardinal directions. Then his hair, with the exception of one or more locks, is closely cropped. Meanwhile the shaman prays for his long life and good health. The shaman may cut off a lock of his own and mix it with the shorn hair, saying, "May this child's hair be as thick as mine." The hair is usually placed in a fruit-bearing tree with this prayer, "May many seasons come and the child live long." The pollen on the child's face is not removed but is allowed to wear away. Each boy and girl should undergo this ceremony at least once. Ideally, the rite should be repeated for four successive springs, with the same individual officiating.

It is about this time that weaning takes place. Gradually, as teeth appear, the child is introduced to light foods so "it will not be so hungry and demand the nipple so much." Sometimes the baby is simply forced away from the breast and given to understand that he must henceforth depend on other food. More often something sour or peppery, like chili, is put on the nipples. The child is told that the milk "is this way now" and rapidly loses interest in nursing.

SURROUNDINGS

The household into which the child is born is one of a cluster of elementary families related through the maternal line. Near an older man and woman reside their unmarried sons and daughters, their married daughters and the sons-in-law, their daughters' daughters (married and unmarried), and their daughters' unmarried sons. The number of separate dwellings varies according to the size of the group and the ages and marital status of the individuals involved. Each daughter, upon marriage, occupies a separate dwelling with her husband. Ordinarily, an unmarried son lives in his parents' household, but an adult unmarried son might have his own adjoining dwelling.

It is with the members of this maternal extended family that the child has his earliest and most meaningful contacts. In his own household live his parents and his brothers and sisters. Only adoption or exceptional circumstances bring others into the home. Within easy reach are the maternal grandparents, the mother's sisters and their husbands and children, and the mother's unmarried brothers.

The child is not entirely cut off from other contacts. The extended family from which his father has come may be located in the same vicinity. Then the paternal relatives will see him often and show great affection for him.

Kinship is reckoned bilaterally. There are no special modes of address or obligations owed to maternal relatives which are withheld from paternal relatives. That the mother's kin figure so prominently is a mechanical reaction to the rule of residence and the scattered and isolated state of the extended families rather than to any theories concerning the closeness or remoteness of particular lines of kin.

The adult men the child sees are dressed in long-sleeved buckskin shirts, with rounded neck opening and with fringe at the shoulders and at the lower ends of the sleeves. They also wear broad loincloths of the same material which fall to a point just above the knees in front and hang in back "just high enough so they won't be stepped on." For footgear they have knee-high moccasins with uppers turned down in folds. These folds are convenient places in which to carry knives or small objects. Often an upward-curving, disk-shaped piece about an inch and a half in diameter projects beyond the toe. This is really a portion of the rawhide sole which has been pounded, moistened, and sewed into position at either side. When it dries, it stays fixed. This projection is found most often on moccasins made for special or dress occasions. "The upturned toe is for decoration only; it's of no special use. In fact, a person sometimes trips on it."

The high boot is the characteristic type, but, when buckskin is scarce, low-cut moccasins suffice. Sometimes high moccasins are worn in cold weather and low ones in summer. Among the members of the Eastern Chiricahua band, but not the Southern and Central Chiricahua, the low-cut moccasins are used almost as frequently as the others. In the two bands which favor the high moccasin, the possession of a pair of this type is a point of prestige: "The moccasin is worn high when you are able to have this kind. All people of influence had them this way." The seam line at the foot, especially on "dress" moccasins, is often painted red, the upturned portion of the toe may be variously painted, too, and sometimes the folded portion of the upper or the entire moccasin is colored with yellow ocher.

When the man is out hunting, raiding, or fighting, he wears a belt of buckskin or rawhide to which a knife sheath is attached, but in times of peace he seldom takes the trouble to don this when he is around camp.

After the spring ceremony the hair is allowed to grow. "We all wear long hair. A person doesn't dare cut his hair off with a knife. He has to take good care of his hair. To cut it brings bad luck. The only time you do that is when a member of your family has died." A man leaves his hair unbraided. He pushes it to the sides, out of his eyes and over his shoulders, and it is held in place by a band which crosses his forehead.

Yucca root, pounded, is used for shampooing the hair. "After washing the hair, they use fat on it to make it stick together. Also marrow from the shinbone of a deer is used for this purpose."

The faces of the men are smooth; all facial hair is plucked with the fingernails as soon as it is noticed, because "the Chiricahua don't like whiskers." There are exceptions, of course. "There is one man who has let his beard grow for good luck. He told me that when he was young he had a dream that he would have good luck if he let his beard grow. He is over sixty years old now and still has a moustache."

At times of dance and celebration a mixture of grease and red ocher is rubbed on the cheeks, and there are other face paints. "Paint is used for decoration when there is any gathering or dance. It can be put on at any time. Sometimes a person puts circles on each cheek; sometimes some other markings. A few put a streak of sticky mescal juice on each side of the face."

In addition to decorative face-painting, there is a great deal of painting for ritual reasons. The coloring of the patient's face by the shaman (often with sacred substances such as pollen, specular iron ore, or white clay) is one of the important elements of the ceremonial pattern. Thus the child becomes used to seeing individuals whose faces are marked with lines of white clay or whose cheeks are decorated with symbols of the sun, moon, stars, or various constellations.

The men tattoo themselves but limit the area to the inner part of the arms "because there is more flesh there and it is more tender." The colors used are red and blue-black. The red is obtained from red ocher or the juice of ripe prickly pears; the black, from charcoal. The material is laid on the skin, moistened, and punched in with a cactus thorn. Typical designs are stars, constellations, and zigzag lines symbolizing lightning. Sometimes these relate to the shamanistic rites of the individual. For instance, one man who claims power from lightning has tattooed markings representative of his tutelary. But most tattooing is merely decorative. In time the designs lose their sharpness and after many years can scarcely be distinguished.

The men have earrings, necklaces, bracelets, bandoleers, and pendants. Turquoise and white shell beads are worn. "The 'ancient people' [prehistoric Pueblo inhabitants] gave us the turquoise. These people were careless with the stones, and the Chiricahua pick them up." Beads are also made from the segments of a long root (*Hilaria cenchroides?*) and from the seeds of the mountain laurel. Many of these ornaments are primarily of religious and protective value.

Abalone shell, too, is used in ritual contexts and is frequently worn. "People cut out a piece, drill a hole through it, and wear it. Often they are directed to do this by a shaman after he has cured them. The shaman himself might give the abalone to the patient. A piece of it is often fastened right to the hair."

A sachet of mint may be worn, particularly by young men who wish to make themselves attractive to the girls.

The woman wears a two-piece dress of buckskin—an upper garment and a medium-length skirt. High-topped moccasins (women never wear the low-cut type) complete the costume. These moccasins often have the upturned toe.

Young women, and many middle-aged women too, part the hair, draw it together at the back, wrap it up in a knot at the nape, tie it, and cover it with an hour-glass-shaped hide form. Older women tend to wear their hair hanging loosely; "but, if it is in their way, they fix it up too." As a woman advances in age, she devotes less attention to hair-grooming, though there is great individual variation in the time at which these changes take place. Though some rather young women have the hair loose, a really old woman is never seen wearing the hair form.

Face-painting of women follows the conventions noted for men. Women tattoo also. In addition to tattoo markings on the arms, they place a dot on either cheek and often a figure, such as a circle or a wavy or serrated line, on the forehead. One informant insisted that the facial tattooing of the women is an innovation.

Women, like men, make lavish use of pendants and ornaments of stone, shell, and other materials; and many of these objects, too, are really amulets.

Very young children, particularly when the weather is mild, are burdened with little or no clothing. They play around the camps happy and unkempt. "It seems as though washing their hands and washing themselves is foreign to them." When clothes are made for them, the garments are modeled after those worn by adults. Sometimes a child's hair is gathered at the sides and "tied in two bundles." But most often, until the girl assumes the hair form and the boy the headband, the hair is left to hang loosely. For protection from the sun, both young people and adults wear wreaths of fresh willow.

The home in which the family lives is made by the women and is ordinarily a circular, dome-shaped brush dwelling, with the floor at ground level. It is seven feet high at the center and approximately eight feet in diameter. To build it, long fresh poles of oak or willow are driven into the ground or placed in holes made with a digging-stick. These poles, which form the framework, are arranged at one-foot intervals and are bound together at the top with yucca-leaf strands. Over them a thatching of bundles of big bluestem grass or bear grass is tied, shingle style, with yucca strings. A smoke hole opens above a central fireplace. A hide, suspended at the entrance, is fixed on a cross-beam so that it may be swung forward or backward. The doorway may face in any direction. For waterproofing, pieces of hide are thrown over the outer thatching, and in rainy weather, if a fire is not needed, even the smoke hole is covered. In warm, dry weather much of the outer roofing is stripped off. It takes approximately three days to erect a sturdy dwelling of this type. These houses are "warm and comfortable, even though there is a big snow."

The interior is lined with brush and grass beds over which robes are spread. Household equipment is utilitarian and minimal. Basketry receptacles include coiled shallow trays, large twined burden baskets for gathering wild foods, and pitch-covered woven water containers. There may be a few clay pots, unpainted and only occasionally incised. There are gourd cups and hide, gourd, and wooden dishes. Surplus food and clothing are stored in undecorated, envelope-like hide receptacles (parfleches). Ready for use are a metate and a cigar-shaped mano (as often as not of ancient Pueblo manufacture), stone and bone pounders, an awl, rawhide or horsetail hair ropes and tumplines, a fire drill, and combs made of dried and folded grass or mescal leaf.

In or around the camp are objects connected with horsemanship—saddles, bridles, bits, quirts, and saddlebags. Conspicuous, too, are weapons of war and chase—the bow and arrows, quiver, bow cover, shield, wrist guard, spear, sling, flint knives, and clubs.

Ceremonial objects—the pottery drum, a deer- or elk-hoof rattle, buckskin bags of pollen and other sacred substances, and the particular paraphernalia attached to the rites of the individuals of the household—are present but are less likely to be displayed.

The dwelling may contain a musical instrument or two not

necessarily connected with ritual, a one-stringed violin (probably inspired by European models), and more infrequently a flute.

The elaborate system of affinal avoidances makes it expedient to allow some space between the home of the man who joins the encampment and those of his wife's relatives. Therefore, a distance of two or three hundred paces may separate two dwellings. Each family is afforded privacy, yet relatives and neighbors are near enough in case of danger. The comparative independence of each home is further safeguarded by the nature of the country, by natural barriers which often conceal one dwelling from the next, even though the distance which separates them is not great. Because these people raid surrounding groups as a regular course, they have reason to fear retaliation and therefore seek to conceal their habitations as much as possible. Desirable locations must be near enough to streams and springs to insure an adequate water supply and close to the highlands so that foes can be led into a fruitless and wearying search through the hills.

The possessions, the materials from which they are made, and the uses which they imply make it plain that the food economy is based on the wild animals and plants of the region and that the people must be ready to follow a seasonal food quest and to remove to a new locality when it becomes apparent that hunting or gathering is more rewarding there. A popular folk tale, explicable in terms of this life, tells how a man becomes separated from the members of his family and seeks to rejoin them, passing camp site after camp site which they have abandoned, until he finally overtakes them. Other accounts describe the frequent movements of the people, with those who have no horses carrying their goods and their children.

Sometimes a single household goes off alone on an economic errand and even remains by itself for some time. But, ordinarily, the extended family breaks camp and moves as a body. It can, therefore, be called the smallest unit prepared to maintain a separate economic existence for any length of time. Thus, even in the midst of the nomadic phase of his life, the most significant social bonds remain undisturbed for the individual.

Despite constant movement, population tends to concentrate

at points advantageous for defense or economy, and the people who live in one vicinity are known by a name referring to the natural feature which marks the area. Often the members of the extended families concerned are, or become, loosely affiliated through intermarriage, but the bonds between them need not be more than those stemming from proximity of residence and the common local name. These extended families which recognize some natural feature as their home or base and share a common name which attests to this can be referred to collectively as a local group. The extended families of a local group may be separated from each other by some distance. A ridge or a mountain spur may intervene, or one camp cluster may be on one side of the mountain which acts as their common locus while a second extended family inhabits the other side. Nevertheless, all are within relatively easy reach of one another and can be quickly contacted for social, military, or religious events. Normally, the contacts afforded by the three segments which have been outlined—the elementary family, the extended family, and the local group—monopolize the experiences of the first years of the child.

EARLY TRAINING AND DISCIPLINE

The rearing and training of children are among the most serious of adult preoccupations. Supernatural help is sometimes sought for these purposes. Though the guidance received from his relatives is criticized if a child grows up to be worthless, he is not exempt from effort of his own. In the training process the child's co-operation is necessary, and an interest in the fundamentals of the folkways is deemed an essential step to informed adulthood.

The child grows into the meanings of his culture gradually and not without amusing misinterpretations. One informant recalled his first sight of the masked dancers. Noting that they wore kilts, he asked a man who stood near by if they were women and was abashed to receive a negative answer. No other explanation was offered, and he was too shy to inquire further. It was some time before he began to understand the character of these dance groups.

Another episode concerns a small boy who had just become aware of the "polite form" of speech, that indirect mode of address in use between affinal relatives who must conduct themselves with restraint when they are together. He approached his grandmother's home where there were visitors before whom he was too bashful to appear and, in this most formal manner, asked if the guests were still inside. He was, of course, greeted by laughter. He did not realize until later that he "was doing what a son-in-law does who thinks his mother-in-law is in a certain place and wants to make sure before he goes in."

A comparable mistake was made by some little boys at a girl's puberty rite. During the ceremony the adolescent girl runs around a basket tray placed to the east of the ceremonial structure. In her path, that the benefits of the ceremony may accrue to them also, run young boys and even old men. "When the girls ran around the basket, we boys were expected to run after them. At first, we thought it was a real race, and several of us beat the girls. Then one old man told us that it was not the way, that we were not supposed to pass them, so we stayed behind the other three times."

Even when the cultural ethic has been unmistakably indicated, a youngster may lag in conforming to it. One man was reluctant to talk about death or burial, for horror of such topics is great, but he confessed that this had not always been his state of mind:

I remember that whenever a funeral procession was passing by we were told not to look at it. But we did look at it whenever the old people were not around.

I once asked my grandmother where they were taking a dead man who was being carried away. She told me not to look at the procession. Then she told me that they were putting the man away; that he couldn't walk, or dance, or eat, or sing by himself any more; that they were putting him under the ground.

"But if they are putting him under the ground, how will he keep the dirt out of his eyes?" I asked. She explained to me that he was all fixed up so that no dirt would get in his eyes. It was the first time I had ever thought about death. I began to ask more questions of my grandmother, but she told me that he couldn't come back any more and to stop talking about it.

A few days later we children played funeral. We killed grasshoppers and buried them.

I wasn't afraid until I was about seven years old. Then I learned about ghosts, and from that time on I was pretty much afraid.

The memory of training is synonymous with the consciousness of self:

As far back as I can remember my father and mother directed me how to act. They used to tell me, "Do not use a bad word which you wouldn't like to be used to you. Do not feel that you are anyone's enemy. In playing with children remember this: do not take anything from another child. Don't take arrows away from another boy just because you are bigger than he is. Don't take his marbles away. Don't steal from your own friends. Don't be unkind to your playmates. If you are kind now, when you become a man you will love your fellow-men.

"When you go to the creek and swim, don't duck anyone's children. Don't ever fight a girl when you're playing with other children. Girls are weaker than boys. If you fight with them, that will cause us trouble with our neighbors.

"Don't laugh at feeble old men and women. That's the worst thing you can do. Don't criticize them and make fun of them. Don't laugh at anybody or make fun of anybody.

"This is your camp. What little we have here is for you to eat. Don't go to another camp with other children for a meal. Come back to your own camp when you are hungry and then go out and play again.

"When you start to eat, act like a grown person. Just wait until things are served to you. Do not take bread or a drink or a piece of meat before the rest start to eat. Don't ask before the meal for things that are still cooking, as many children do. Don't try to eat more than you want. Try to be just as polite as you can; sit still while you eat. Do not step over another person, going around and reaching for something.

"Don't run into another person's camp as though it was your own. Don't run around anyone's camp. When you go to another camp, don't stand at the door. Go right in and sit down like a grown person. Don't get into their drinking water. Don't go out and catch or hobble horses and ride them as if they belonged to you the way some boys do. Do not throw stones at anybody's animals.

"When a visitor comes, do not go in front of him or step over him. Do not cut up while the visitor is here. If you want to play, get up quietly, go behind the visitor, and out the door."

The foundations for the sexual division of labor are early laid:

"Your work will be to make baskets and to build fires, my daughter. Keep busy like your mother. Watch your mother as she is going through her daily work. When you get older, you will do the same things. It doesn't hurt you to pick up little sticks of wood and carry them in. Stay here by the fire. Watch your mother and see what she is doing around the camp."

When my mother and father talked to both my sister and me, they would say, "This means you. This means you," pointing to each of us. And many times my father would say to my sister, "There are things which can be told to you by your mother, and you can learn all the time. I have to train this boy. Of course, he may not hear part of the time, but I have to tell him what he should do, what he has to go through."

All adults feel the responsibility for furnishing the child with information appropriate to his age and sex:

The boys watch the men when they are making bows and arrows; the man calls them over, and they are forced to watch him. The women, on the other hand, take the girls out and show them what plants to use for baskets, what clay for pots. And at home the women weave the baskets, sew moccasins, and tan buckskin before the girls. While they are at work, they tell the students to watch closely so that when they reach womanhood nobody can say anything about their being lazy or ignorant. They teach the girls to cook and advise them about picking berries and other fruits and gathering food.

Not much importance is attributed to distinctions of status, but there are band and local group leaders and their families who are conscious of their position and good birth:

The word [good status] includes the idea that they are better educated in the Indian way. More pains are taken with such children; they are kept out of mischief more. They should not resent things easily. They are supposed to be better bred. Quarreling should be beneath them. That is why, when a man is unreasonable or insulting, they say, "Even though you are of worthless stock, you should try to hold yourself back." I hear lots of boys of good families being instructed by their parents. They are told to act accordingly. I heard one girl called down by her father for gossiping. She was told that those of her family did not do this and that she was acting like a trashy person.

"These people," said another informant, "don't want their children to get in any mixup; they are jealous of the reputations of their sons and daughters." So important did training in childhood loom to this man that he added: "A leader's son never fails to make good, for he is trained and advised from boyhood up to manhood."

The difference in social atmosphere with which various families surround the child has been noted thus:

At our camp my father and mother used to say, "Respect whoever comes to your camp. If it is just at mealtime when they come to your camp, just tell them to sit down. Then feed them first." Most of these Indians are this way.

But there are great differences among different families. I've noticed it. A man might have visitors at his home just about mealtime. His wife might cook a big meal. Generally, she would serve the visitor first, even if the visitor was a woman. After the visitors had gone, the man might get after his wife and ask her, "Why should you feed those people first? Why didn't you feed me first?"

If a visitor happens to hear of this, he will say, "I'm sorry I went over there. I didn't know that man was like that. I won't go over there any more."

The child must early be made sensible of certain dangers and must learn to be quiet at a command. Enemies often lurk perilously near, and the encampments may suffer severe loss before help can be summoned. Often a child's first memories have to do with threats concerning a dread and shadowy being who preys upon noisy or disobedient children. "The word *gode* is enough. They don't try to describe him. The children become afraid of the word."

Another sound which the child learns to respect is the call of the poorwill. This bird is known by the same name as the masked dancers, for it is thought that the call of the poorwill resembles the traditional call of the dancer as he approaches and "worships" the fire.

When I was a boy, there was a bird that sang only at night. We were told that its song was the voice of the clown of the masked dancers who took bad children. We were pretty quiet and well behaved when we heard that song at night. I realize now that the song is pretty, but when I was a child it frightened me and I disliked it.

This masked-dancer clown, or Gray One, is one of the terrors of childhood. "The clown is going to put you in a basket and carry you off somewhere. Say this to a little child and he is going to mind right away."

The threat of the clown is maintained as long as possible to keep the children out of the way of prowling enemies and predatory animals. When warnings of the clown's arrival lose their efficacy, Gray One himself may "appear."

Suppose now that children are playing out there and won't mind at all. All right! The parents will say, "Let's scare those children."

They go way around through the woods somewhere. Maybe a big fat man goes out there with them, and they put white paint on him. They make him look like the clown. Well, he goes over to the other side of the place where those children are playing in the brush. He takes a little switch or a stick along with him. Then, when he is about twenty yeards away, he shows his face, and one of the boys or girls sees it and starts to run. Then the rest look and see the clown coming. The children cry and run back to camp. And the clown will be running after them, trying to hit them with the stick, throwing stones after them, but being careful not to hit them. I'll tell you, those children will not go far from camp any more!

Clowns accompany the masked dancers at the girl's puberty rite, and parents of disobedient children, taking advantage of the fears already engendered, arrange to have Gray One "get after" their youngsters at this time.

The child is silenced, too, by dark forces, as fearful to adults as to him:

From the earliest time I can remember I was afraid of the owl. It was not until much later that I knew why—that I knew the owl can cause evil influence to a person. When I was bad, my mother would make me listen to the hooting of the owl. "Listen to that!" she would say, and I would settle down and be quiet. She told me it was a bad animal and would catch me if I were bad.

The clue to the abhorrence for owls emerges in another account:

It was taught to me in camp when I was small that ghosts and owls are related in some way. At night you go out in the woods over there by yourself. If you are a full-blood Chiricahua, you have been taught ever since you were a small child, "Don't ever throw anything at an owl. Never mock an owl. They are dangerous. They are ghosts." If you are out in the woods on a dark night after you have been taught in this way what owls are and you hear them close to you, you certainly are frightened. In those days they claimed Indians used to get very sick from owls, and some shamans had to work to get them well.

Other devices for subduing unruly children are used:

There was an old man whom I did not like. He used to chase me and catch me whenever he saw me. So, when I was bad, my mother used to say that this old man was coming for me or that she was going to give me away to him.

Sometimes the old man comes to see the recalcitrant child at the parents' request:

When a child is mischievous, they call an old man who looks fierce. He is no relative. The old man limps in with a sack or blanket in his hand. He acts angry and shouts, "What's the matter?"

The father and the mother sit there. They say, "This boy won't obey. He is always fighting. You can take him and do what you wish with him. You can cut off his head or sit on him. We don't care. We aren't going to put up with him any longer." The boy begins to cry.

The old man says, "So, you won't obey? I'm going to check you off right now." The boy cries louder.

"Now stop that! Listen to me. Come over to me or I'm going to get you." The child is frightened. He tries to crawl behind his father, his mother, or his grandmother. But they act as if they have given the old man the privilege to do what he wants with the boy, and they push the boy forward. Then the old man grabs him and struggles with him. He puts him in the sack and says, "Are you going to behave?"

After that the boy is prompt and behaves. If he won't get wood, his mother says, "All right, I'll call the old man." Then he goes for the wood at once. After the old man works on him like this two or three times, he comes to be a good boy.

These old men look fierce and funny. The children are afraid of them. The old man is never the grandparent. It is always an outsider. The grandparent is there with the parents to see the child get his lesson.

Cowing children by reference to ill-favored old people is not to be confused with a manner of joking practiced for another purpose:

An old woman might joke with a little boy, calling him her husband, telling him, "I'll be back tonight and see you," and making all kinds of funny remarks. Here is what is behind it. They say that when an old person jokes like this it will give long life and good luck to a little child. But [for an old person] to joke about this concerning someone of the child's age is not good. It's against the child.

I've been joked at like this. My aunt [a mother's sister; the child's mother had died] used to play this trick on me. She picked out an old woman who was as ugly as anything. She used to say, "I've brought you up and you've got to do what I tell you. You must marry that old woman." The old woman, when she came around, would say, "I missed you last night. Come over to my place and I'll cook for you."

But they never mention relatives when they joke in this way. To do that will give the child bad habits and bad ideas. If you fool like that with a grandmother, you'll get used to being free with relatives. You'll see your own sister over there and have relations with her. You'll turn into a witch. To encourage joking about marriage with relatives is just like teaching your daughter to play cards all the time or to drink whiskey.

To return to other disciplinary measures:

For crying children we have some kind of covering. We do not whip the child if we can help it. We put the covering over the child's head and hold it that way until he stops crying. We do this to little children, do it several times until they stop crying. The little children do not like to have anything over their heads. That is one punishment.

Another punishment for crying is to pour a little cup of water slowly on the child's head. It is cold and the child stops. Then we get another cupful and ask, "Going to cry again?" The child says, "No."

But the parent is usually gentle with the child. "If you love a child, it is awful to hear him cry or to have other children angry with him. You want to play with him and please him." Therefore, forceful measures of any kind are avoided where threats will gain the desired end. "We tell children we will put them in a sack if they are not good. I told it to mine. I never did it though."

Instead of punishing a child for enuresis, other means are used to treat the difficulty. "If a child wets the bed, we put a bird's nest there and let him wet it. Then the nest is thrown to the east, and the child won't wet the bed any more."

Another ceremonial aid in child-training calls for the assistance of the adolescent girl at the time of her puberty rite: "If a child, a boy or a girl, is mean, they bring it to one of the girls. She takes pollen and hits him on the mouth four times with it. Then he can't talk evil any more and will be good."

Thoughtless children who are a nuisance to their elders are chastised in subtle ways. One of the most popular is to send an ill-mannered boy on a wild-goose chase. This is a favorite device of story-tellers. The old man bides his time; then, at a convenient stopping-place he picks up his tobacco pouch as though he is going to smoke, assumes his most innocent expression, and

. . . . says to this boy, "You get 'that with which one smokes' for me. I want to smoke with it and I left it over at the next camp." There is no such thing as "that with which one smokes." He just sends the boy to get rid of him.

When the boy gets over to the next camp, the man there tells him, "Go over to So-and-so's place. I just sent it over to him." Sometimes a boy chases it all night. Then another boy cuts up, and that boy is sent over to see what happened to the first one.

"The Chiricahua loves his children and does not like to whip them"; but, when other methods fail, he resorts to corporal punishment. "Parents never whip their children unless they won't get up and run a race or something like that. Parents try to make men of them, and some punish them for not minding."

Though most parents exhibit self-discipline, there are instances where tempers are completely lost. Of the conduct of one woman it is reported, "I have seen her knock her little boy around like a ball. Every time he got up, she would knock him down again." Coolness between one father and son goes back to the time, in the words of the latter, "when he used me just like a slave. He whipped me, made me work, and kept me around the house." Similar difficulties have arisen between another father and son because of the father's severity.

E. is a pretty hard man with his wife and children. You see that stick he carries. Well, he is always poking those children with it, and they keep away from him as much as they can. His oldest boy is at Whitetail now. At night he stays in an old shack there. The place where he stays is all caved in. The boy has no blankets there but just sleeps between two old mattresses. The father is trying to get him home, but the boy won't come because he was treated in such a mean way. Not long ago his father tried to hit him with that stick. The boy took the stick away and hit his father on the head instead, and then he went off to Whitetail.

For serious breaches of etiquette or morals the adult in a position of authority takes direct action. A child who impolitely refused a gift quickly learned this:

My grandmother asked me about it. I told her that I had refused it. Then she gave me a good box on the ear, for it is very impolite according to the Indian custom to refuse anything that is offered. If someone gives you a gift, you must take it, no matter what his station in life is. The lower he is, the more quickly you must take it so as not to hurt his feelings.

At a later period, for sexual intercourse, the girl may be whipped by her father, sometimes publicly, with a rope or a stick. The parent expresses himself strongly during the chastisement, reminding her of the good advice she has disregarded and of the wrong she has done the family. The public nature of the punishment acts as a lesson to other girls. The girls "cry loud and long, and the neighbors around usually watch."

Parents who do not wish to whip their boys find other ways of correcting them:

The parents don't like to strike their bigger boys. They get some other fellow to punish him. If a boy doesn't obey and is rough and fights all the time, they take him to the hoop-and-pole ground. His father says, "We'll see how tough you are!" He drags the boy over there. Other men are there with boys. Always there is a big crowd of men and boys at the grounds.

The father calls out, "Here is my boy. He's always in trouble. Let's see how bad he really is. Is there any other troublesome boy here?"

Perhaps some other father has a boy who needs a good lesson. He brings his boy forward. Maybe those two boys don't want to fight. The men hit them with sticks until they begin. They are both troublesome boys. No one cares who wins. The parents want them to get beaten up. The father keeps matching his boy up against others until the boy gets a good licking. Then he takes him home.

He says to the boy, "Are you hurt? Does it hurt? We want you to go through life without getting hurt. We want you to obey and to listen to our good words. But you try to run us and make trouble. Now you've been licked. You see that you are not such a man as you think. If you can't behave, we are going to take you out and make you fight a boy who is still bigger."

Yet there is greater dependence on advice and traditional stories for guiding the young than on physical coercion. The tales are particularly important in this connection. Some have no other point than to rationalize usage or belief. A child who is reluctant to "feed" his legs, that is, to rub grease on them after eating, is reminded of the story of the man who fed only his stomach and was told by his legs, "Run with your belly!" when he appealed to them to carry him out of danger.

Narratives of personal experience are also used to instruct the young. Once when some boys were showing insufficient interest in the running they were supposed to practice, an old man called them over and offered them the following counsel:

Boys, I'm an old man and funny looking now, and you all laugh at me. But there's one thing I always took care of, and they are pretty good still. I mean my legs. And you can learn that from me. My legs have saved me many a time.

Once I was out with a bunch of men. I stopped behind for a few minutes and they went ahead. I ran right into a bear there. That bear took after me. He was right behind me when I started running. But by the time I caught up with the others I was way ahead of him. I outran that bear. If I hadn't trained and kept myself a good runner, I would have been killed right there. So you boys ought to practice some running.

Many of the important myths can be told in winter only, and so the long winter nights are often enlivened by story-telling sessions. These occasions are not arranged for the exclusive benefit of the children, but, when children are present, special care is taken by the raconteur to point the moral. Such instruction is not always taken in good spirits. "My father told me many stories, but sometimes I got very sleepy. Sometimes I got contrary and wanted to go to bed," an informant admitted. Usually, however, the children look forward to these evenings and often beg a grandparent to arrange one.

The most important story a child hears at this time is that of the birth of the culture hero and his victorious encounters with the monsters. Familiarity with this account is a necessary background for much ritual. Parts of the story are dramatized in the girl's puberty rite. Ceremonial songs and many ritual touches refer to the protagonists of this legend. Grama grass, for example, appears in ceremonial contexts because Child of the Water used it for an arrow in his encounter with Giant, one of the monsters. Other stories of the culture hero and his mother further acquaint the child with their holiness and the great respect he owes them.

Scarcely less important is the set of stories devoted to the Mountain People, supernaturals inhabiting the interiors of sacred mountains. These Mountain People, who are impersonated by the masked dancers, are described in the legends as potential sources of supernatural power and as protectors of the tribal territory.

Most appreciated by the young people, however, is the Coyote cycle, a series of episodes of the pranks of the trickster. Coyote violates all the social and sexual conventions of the society, and this permits the narrator to contrast "Coyote's way" with more approved conduct. Coyote stories "make a child sleepy," and so it is often necessary to tickle his nose or tap him lightly on the head in order to keep him awake. Through the Coyote tales the child gets some hint of the imperfectibility of man and of the inevitability of moral turpitude in the world. "Coyote stories are used as a lesson. And they still blame Coyote today for the foolish things humans do."

Other tales serve to imbue the child with the proper attitudes toward baneful or helpful animal life, toward supernaturals, and toward neighboring peoples.

The child's first religious instruction centers about reverence for the principal supernaturals and emphasizes the virtues of humility and gratitude. "At our own camps, when a child is old enough to understand his parents, they begin to teach him to be religious, to use religious words, and to know Life Giver, Child of the Water, and White Painted Woman."

The child soon comes to sense that specific favors are the result of the activity of other powers. There are no stories to record the deeds of Life Giver, but there are numerous tales to explain the part of other supernaturals in origins and possessions. For instance, according to tradition, daylight was acquired as a result of the moccasin or hidden-ball game played between the birds and the four-footed animals. Even the origin of man is not attributed to the nominal creator in the myths; what hints there are (and these creation elements may be of European origin) seem to credit Child of the Water with the act.

The child is given very little in the way of a formalized conception of the universe:

If we aren't shamans or have no supernatural power, we have no basis to stand on in saying how far from us the clouds are or how far away the sun is. A person like myself will tell you that rain comes from the clouds, because I have no vision about it. But others will say their power causes it. I don't know just where to begin or what to believe.

In other words, one person claims to know more than another concerning those aspects of nature which his personal power touches, but, since no adult should presume to conviction about the prerogatives of his fellows, the child hears no unified philosphy of nature.

THE DANGERS OF CHILDHOOD

With age the individual becomes "toughened" against the assaults of malevolent forces; but the child is almost defenseless before them. While adults ordinarily have protective ceremonies and guardian spirits to warn them of danger, children are less shielded in this way. Because of his precarious position, the child is constantly guarded by minor rituals and devices. From these he gains his first impressions of the forces opposed to his welfare and of the ceremonial usages that benefit him.

His first attendance at the girl's puberty rite is likely to be an unforgettable occasion. He is brought forward that his face may be painted with pollen by the girl. To insure his health and growth, she may pick him up and hold him to the directions, and, if he is small for his age, she may be asked to place her hands under his chin at the neck and lift him.

So that a child may grow tall he is lifted four times to the new moon. He is warned never to urinate in an anthill, lest he have bladder stones. That he may not become lonesome in the absence of a departing relative, the traveler wets his finger with saliva and touches it to the child's face. If, nevertheless, he does get lonesome, a basket is placed four times over his head. When their father is on the raid, the children are urged not to throw the wood for the fire around carelessly, lest their parent become confused about the direction to take. When a child loses a tooth, he is counseled to say, "I hope I have another tooth," and to throw it to the east or to tie grama grass around it and throw it to the sun; that witches may not retrieve it and do him harm, he is told to dispose of it at some remote spot. The child is also advised not to watch masked dancers being decorated and never to call the name of an impersonator whom he may recognize. To safeguard him against sickness, a fringed buckskin amulet containing a growth from the creosote bush may be strung around his neck. Such practices, solemnly advised by his elders, impress the child with the efficacy of magical aids and with the proximity and power of the forces against which they are pitted.

During this early period, too, the child learns of the evil animals and the natural agencies toward which he must exercise special care. "Drop that feather!" someone may call as he stoops to pick up a buzzard feather. Or the nature of a disease resulting from contact with Snake is explained by one who has ceremonial power from it and knows its ways. A person with such knowledge often takes measures that protect the children of the vicinity:

In the summer when the snakes came back and the parents were afraid that the children would be bitten, this woman used to call many children together and sing for them, and she would put a cross of pollen inside each moccasin for them. She told them not to call Snake too much or it would come and not to look for it or they would see it. She would make a buckskin string with two pieces of turquoise tied to it and give it to anyone who was afraid of the snake. That one had to wear it on the right foot below the ankle.

It is quite as important that the child understand the ways of the cloud-dwelling Thunder People whose arrows are chipped flints found throughout Chiricahua country. The children are directed to make a respectful spitting noise when the lightning flashes and to refrain from eating during a storm. Sage is pointed out as a protective plant which may be worn in the hair during a storm. Nothing red should be displayed at such a time, they are told, for red is associated with the lightning flash and may draw it.

While the child is very young, adults take the proper steps to protect him from danger. But, as he grows old enough to understand ideas and to react consistently to them, more responsibility for his own safety is transferred to him. Thus, quite small children not only depend upon the amulets provided for them but pick and wear the sage which wards off the lightning, dispose of a loose tooth, and extend due respect to masked dancers. Advice and guidance are freely given, but the response which constitutes growth and fulfilment is, as far as possible, elicited from the child himself. The prevailing theme in things nonritual as well as ritual is that the youngster must learn to do for himself tomorrow what is done for him today.

Since most ceremonies are curative rites and are of frequent occurrence, it is almost inevitable that, while the child is still very young, he will witness a full-length ceremony. Very often the first shamanistic performance a child remembers is one in which he was the patient:

At this time, when I was about six years old, I saw the first ceremony I can remember. It was given for me. I don't know what was the matter with me, but at that time I was very slim and underweight, and it may have been for a general run-down condition. I know I was taken to the shaman's house. I was lying on a bed in the middle of the room. My grandmother was there. My mother, but not my father, was there. My father couldn't be there because my mother's mother was present. Other people whom I did not know were sitting around. The man who was curing me sang. Later on I was told that he had forbidden me to eat the head and liver of any animal. Whenever they had liver after that, they had something else for me. At big gatherings where there was head, I would not eat any of it.

Another man describes the first ceremony he recalls:

My father once cured me with his ceremony. I was a pretty small boy. I can hardly remember it. My father says that I must have been about six years old. Maybe I was seven.

I got very, very sick. My mother and my father thought I was going to die. This was out in the mountains. Of course, my father knew in his own way how to use his power and cure people. So my father went to work on me during part of the day and a good part of the night, I know. While he was carrying on this ceremony for me, I went blind, completely blind.

Well, he got me a little better from my sickness, but after I got well I was blind. It seemed as though my eyes were back in my head, and they hurt badly. It looked as though a different sickness had come over my eyes. It was just as though something was turning way back in my head.

My father was very good at the masked-dancer ceremony. He just made a mask and horns [frame or uprights surmounting the mask] and decorated them as though they were going to be put on a dancer. He made the sticks too [wooden wands carried by the masked dancer].

He had the mask in his right hand and was shaking it in front of me. He was singing those ceremonial songs. Every time he sang a song he held that mask to my head this way and that, to my eyes and all over me. I was half-sitting up, on a slant. I couldn't see, but I knew what he was doing and what he was saying. I remember it.

And my father was crying part of the time; I could hear him. He said, "Why not punish me this way? I've lived here many years on earth. I've seen what it looks like. I know how hard it is to live through this world. Don't kill that poor little child. He didn't harm anyone. I love him. Don't let him go. I want him to live to an old age in this world." He said, "If you want to kill anybody in this family, kill me. Take me. I know you can help me relieve this poor child from his sickness, and there's no reason why you should act this way to me." He was angry about this, angry at his own power. I heard him arguing with his power. He tried pretty hard. "Well," he said to his power, "if you aren't going to do what I want you to do, if you're going to have your own way all the time, you might as well stop talking to me from now on." He was scolding his power.

After a while he said, "Here's an eagle feather, son. I'm going to try this eagle feather; my power wants me to try it. Because you went blind, your eyes are going to go back, then the sickness is coming out. It's going to pop out and it's going to kill you. This is my last chance for you. If this doesn't work, I'm going to give up all hope." He said he saw it in a vision, a spirit talked to him. I don't know who was talking to him. I couldn't have seen if someone had been there. My mother didn't see anyone and she was sitting there. But he knew what he was doing, I guess.

He said, "If this eagle feather doesn't stay on you, you've got no chance. If it stays on you, it will show that you are going to get your sight back and get well. It will tell us right here, one way or the other."

He opened my shirt. He put that feather right here on my chest, just touched me lightly with it. I could feel it; it was sticking right on my chest. How he did it my mother never knew; I never knew; but he knew.

I must have been blind two or three months. Then about the fourth month I was just beginning to get my sight back. Then I recovered.

A third account is that of a ceremony presided over by Geronimo, the well-known leader, and attended by the informant as a young child:

The first ceremony by Geronimo I saw was one for an older man. Some coyote or dog had made him sick.[7] One boy got hold of the news that the ceremony was going to be held, and we learned of it through him. We asked Geronimo if we could attend. He said it would be all right but told us we could not scratch ourselves or make any noise.

The ceremony began in the evening, as soon as it became dark. It took place in an arbor outside Geronimo's home. There was a fire. Geronimo and the patient were on the west side of the fire. Geronimo sat facing the east, and the patient lay stretched out before him. Some older people were there. They were mostly relatives of the sick man. But it would have been all right for anyone to come in and watch. We sat in circular fashion in the back of the shelter. But the space to the east was left open, as always happens at a ceremony.

Geronimo had an old black tray basket before him filled with the things he used for the ceremony. He had a downy eagle feather in it and an abalone shell and a bag of pollen. All these things were wrapped up in a bundle before the ceremony began.

He rolled a cigarette and puffed to the directions first of all, beginning with the east, puffing just once to each direction. Then he threw the cigarette away. After smoking, he rubbed the patient with pollen. He dropped pollen on the patient, just on certain parts of the body. He prayed to the directions as he did this. These prayers referred to Coyote and were on the same order as the songs which followed.

He started to sing. There were many songs, and the songs were about Coyote. They told how Coyote was a tricky fellow, hard to see and find, and how he gave these characteristics to Geronimo so that he could make himself invisible and even turn into a doorway. They told how the coyote helped Geronimo in his curing. Geronimo accompanied his singing with a drum which he beat with a curved stick. At the end of each song he gave a call like a coyote.

When the evening star was halfway between the horizon and the zenith, Geronimo stopped singing. This is the Chiricahua midnight. The ceremony lasted four nights. The same prayers, songs, and procedure were gone through for the four nights. I know that Geronimo had ghost power too. That night he

---

[7] Note the implication that dog and coyote sickness are treated by the same ceremony.

told some of the boys that he was going to give another ceremony for a patient on another night, this time for ghost sickness, and that they might attend if they would promise not to scratch themselves.

As a result of such experiences the child learns to anticipate the curative function of ceremonies, the claims of shamans, their pattern of prayers, songs, and manipulation of sacred objects. He becomes sensible of the close rapport between the shaman and the power source, of the mingled flattery, pleading, and threats which mark the attempts to force the supernatural world to respond to the needs of man. He becomes aware of the sources of disease—snakes, bears, coyotes, ghosts, witches; of the implicit homeopathic feeling that snake sickness, for instance, requires the services of a snake shaman. He gets some hint, also, of the multiple ceremonies which such a shaman as Geronimo possesses, and he learns of the restrictions associated with ritual.

The beliefs and ceremonial usages associated with the related concepts of death, the ghost, and the owl are very early transmitted to the child by older relatives. "When I was little I never gave any thought to death. But once I got very sick. My mother thought I was going to die. She told me that I could not come back if I died. This was my first scare. Since then I have been afraid of death."

Often a child's awareness of death begins at the demise of some relative. Then his name may be changed because the dead person had spoken it so frequently that its use would recall the deceased to mind. Or his hair may be cut and his appearance thus altered. At the time of a close relative's burial, a child's clothing is discarded and replaced, for nothing must be left as it was before death. Efforts are now intensified to protect the child from supernatural harm; ashes are strewn upon him and around his bed to discourage the approach of ghosts, and he is thoroughly incensed with smoke from burning sage, called "ghost medicine."

Whether or not the child is curious about the meanings of death practices, they must be explained to him, for it is socially dangerous to permit individuals, however young, to remain in ignorance of them:

When I was little I was told about death. According to what I was taught as far back as I can remember, when someone died he would never come back to this world; he was gone. I was told that I must therefore never again call his name, for I might accidentally say his name in the presence of his parents or other relatives and they might scold me for it or slap my mouth. The parents taught the children that it is an insult to another person to call the name of his dead relative. If I was a little fellow and didn't know any better, someone might have slapped my mouth; then the families might have been angry, and there might have been trouble.

I was told that you never watch burial parties just to see what is going on. Men and women show that they sympathize with those people who are carrying their relative to the mountains by getting out and crying when they go by, even though they are not related. You should never watch unless you are crying like this for them. Children should not watch at all.

At first, little attempt is made to enlarge upon the precise place of the owl in the death complex. But, as the child grows older, the nexus between ghost and owl is clarified:

When I was young this is what I heard the old Indians say about ghosts and owls. They said that owls are part of ghosts. A night or so after a death you hear an owl close to the camp where the person died. Not only in that camp but in other camps near by the people hear that owl calling. They say, "That person is back over there again!"

They claimed that if the dead man had a horse left alive there, or if any of his clothes were there, he would come back every night until his possessions were destroyed. He would come back after his things. If you had not destroyed what belonged to the dead man, the things he had had his hands on during his life, the owl would come every now and then, perhaps often, they said. Then it might bring sickness or bad luck to that family. That's the way I heard it long ago.

And so to prevent sickness, if an owl cried around the camp, they set fire to a stick of wood, carried it outside, and threw it in the direction of the owl. Then it stopped [hooting].

In the following excerpt an informant recalls the manner in which his father sought to satisfy his curiosity concerning the destination of the dead:

I asked, "Suppose I die. Where would I go?"

My father said, "When a man dies he is just like any human being and is just transferred to another state. He is in another world. There are mountains and rivers there as there are here." He called it the underworld. He said, "The habits you have on earth are carried with you. If you are a bronco-buster on earth, you would be a bronco-buster in the other world. If you play hoop and pole on earth a great deal, you play that game all the time in the underworld. Whatever a person is accustomed to do on earth he will be doing down there."

One of the reasons for telling the child about the underworld is to warn him of the machinations of ghosts who strive to lure him thither:

> This is what I learned from my older relatives. The ghosts are supposed to go around in the early part of the night and then again when it gets on toward morning, from about two o'clock on. That's the old Chiricahua belief.

> Toward morning a person will be dreaming. He dreams that ghosts are bothering him. He dreams of the underworld and the people there. Some of them he knows, some he doesn't know. He sees the beautiful land. They offer him food, a piece of yucca fruit or bread. When I was small my father and the older people told me that if I dreamed this I should not accept the fruit, for, if you accept it, it means that you are going to die and go to that place yourself.

The fear of the departed, and especially of departed relatives, plays a conspicuous part in adult life, in ideas of witchcraft, in aspects of social organization, and in shamanism. The basis for this is solidly laid in childhood:

> I was pretty thin when I was a child. . . . . . I used to be very much afraid too. I was influenced a great deal by the Indian beliefs about ghosts and used to get scared at night. I'd go over to someone else's bed and force myself upon him. Often I'd wake up screaming in the middle of the night, thinking I had seen someone near my bed. I'd dream of ghosts. A face would be bending over me, laughing. It would be just an outline, no features showing.

> . . . . I always had a tendency to look back and see if anyone was following me when I was out at night. This is what the Chiricahua call being influenced by ghosts; I must have been suffering from ghosts.

Sometimes the child's panic reaches such proportions that a ceremony must be conducted over him:

> Once when I was a boy we children were playing out at night. As I was coming home I felt that someone was touching me. I became frightened, ran home, fell in the door, and became sick. They performed a ghost ceremony over me. The shaman worked a fire drill. The first sparks that came he put in my mouth.[8] I came to my senses. Then the shaman prayed and finally he sang. I was small and do not remember more of the details.

There are cases where a child's ailment, though the symptoms are not so transparent, is finally interpreted as ghost or "darkness" sickness (to use the approved euphemism) and dealt with

---

[8] An evidence of the opposition of fire and the ghost (owl) which is believed to exist.

accordingly: "I walked in my sleep and I talked, too, while I walked. My father knew a ghost ceremony. He sang for me and I stopped."

No less memorable is a child's first acquaintance with witchcraft. For his own protection this knowledge concerning people who use supernatural power for evil ends must be communicated to him as soon as he is able to absorb it.

You have to hide from witch people all the time and must not go too near them. That's what parents tell their children. "Don't go near that man. Don't go around his camp. Don't let him see you. Don't be too free and happy in his sight. When you pass a witch don't look toward him. Don't pay any attention to him. . . . . If they talk to you, answer. If not, pass them by and keep out of their way. If you have something pleasant to tell them, do it; if not, pass them by without a word."

Even ordinary instruction concerning personal cleanliness is influenced by the same considerations:

Children were taught, "When you have to defecate, don't do it on the path where people pass." So they would go way out. . . . .

It is because of witchcraft that we are so very particular about it. Suppose a witch or his wife or child should step on it. There is no telling what he might do about it. He might witch you for it.

Gradually notions of witchcraft intrude into the life of the child:

I remember that I knew about witches at a very early age, when I was four or five years old. I was eight when I learned that S. was a witch. My grandmother told me so. Also I heard other children say it. One time he came to N.'s encampment. We children ducked around the home because they said he was a witch. I heard one man talking and saying that S. had tried to get married a number of times, but that he was always refused because he was a witch. They told us to keep out of his sight as much as possible, to refuse any gift from him, and not to let him do anything queer to us. Also we were told to treat him with respect when we met him so that he wouldn't do anything harmful to us. We were told not to offend him in any circumstances.

The children were afraid of him, and when I was with them I acted this way too. But really I was curious. I wanted to learn more about this man. So when I was a little older I went to his place. I didn't let anyone see me. I went by a roundabout way. I went during the day. He was lying on the bed, singing a social dance song. He told me to come in. I expected to see something, to find some proof of his witchcraft. But I failed to see anything. He seemed just like a normal man to me that first time.

He didn't act as though he was surprised to see me. He stopped singing and asked me to sit down. He just talked in a social way. I don't think he suspected the reason for my visit. I asked him for a smoke. At first he hesitated. He asked me if I was allowed to smoke. I told him that my aunt let me smoke. Then he gave it to me. It is unusual for an older man to give a boy a smoke. A boy wouldn't ever ask an old Indian for a smoke; he wouldn't dare. I stayed with him for about an hour. When I left I still thought he was a witch, though I had no reason for it. I just thought he hadn't revealed himself.

The first few times I went to visit him I took pains not to be seen by others. At first I thought it was something daring to do, but after a while it wore off. Even when I was visiting him openly by myself, I used to avoid him when I was with the other boys.

I took precautions while I was going to him though. I was afraid of being witched. I didn't accept anything from him. Once I refused something, though I needed it badly. I wouldn't eat there either. If he offered me food, I always explained that I had just eaten and wasn't hungry. I did take smokes though. I wanted them pretty badly, I guess, because he could have done more harm through tobacco than through food, since tobacco is used in ceremonies. I never found out why he was suspected or met anybody he was supposed to have harmed.

PLAY

It would be a mistake to suppose that childhood is little more than an unhappy introduction to notions of death and witchcraft. Fears exist, but the normal youngster devotes far less attention to these alarming subjects than he does to his playmates and games.

The children are amazingly resourceful in exploiting the possibilities of their natural surroundings in play. Little girls, and sometimes little boys, make beads from wild-rose hips, ground cherries, and the scouring rush plant. Pine needles serve for earrings and bracelets. The girls fashion dolls from panic grass and string together ground cherries to form little figures. They then make, on a tiny scale, substitutes for all the possessions they observe in their own households. Small toy homes are constructed from a number of plants. Ferns yield pillows, blankets, and beds for the dolls. From the Jacob's-ladder are shaped little dresses for the doll, and these dresses are decorated with "jingles" of side-oats grama grass. Even a miniature of the food staple, mescal, has been found, and so the dolls go forth industriously to gather "doll's mescal" (*Androsace pinetorum*). Food is generously provided at these toy encampments, wild peas often serving as the main dish.

Not all the toys that the children make meet with parental approval: "We used to take a flat stick, make a hole through it, put a string through this hole, and run with it. It makes a noise. Our parents did not want us to do this. They would always scold us when we did it. They said it brought the wind." Besides this rhombus or bull-roarer, the children make another object somewhat similar in effect: "There is another noisemaker. We use a piece of hide, cut two holes in it, and put a string through. Then we wind up the string and pull it. It makes a noise. A good many of the old people don't like it. They say it will bring wind too."

The boy whips pellets of mud, lightly stuck at the end of a willow branch, at birds and achieves considerable accuracy with this weapon. He soon learns to make good use of the sling, a diamond-shaped piece of hide to which one looped and one un-looped side thong are attached. The hide is folded over upon itself, incasing a stone which is projected when the sling is swung forward. A piece of elderberry, ash, reed, or walnut from which the pith has been removed, or through which a hole has been worked, is made into a popgun by tamping one end and forcing another piece through until the tamp flies out with a loud report.

Many a child has learned to braid with wild iris, candy grass, or clover. Little girls pass the time pleasantly making a long string of the leaves of *Dalea dalea* and then arranging it in several strands with leaves interlocking. From the virgin's bower plant and a species of aster the children obtain toy hats, and *Vicia* is employed as a dancing robe. The four-leafed clover is considered lucky, and the children have contests to see who can find one first. They blow into the choisey flower to make a sound that is likened to the call of the fawn. The name of the plant is, accordingly, "that which cries like a deer's child." Beard-tongue buds are picked and popped. "Bird tracks" are made in the sand with Bermuda grass, and a leaf transfixed to Bermuda grass "feet" is called a bird.

There are practical jokers, even among the children, who throw clinging or mildly irritating grasses (*Nama hispida* is one) at someone or hide them in his bed.

The children of an encampment organize expeditions to search for certain delicacies which are not plentiful or valuable enough to figure in adult food economy. Ground cherries, the red fruits of the nipple cacti, and willow buds are gathered, and cottonwood buds are chewed like gum. The search for honey provides another diversion:

> When I was a boy, so long ago I can hardly remember it now, there was a certain bee we used to get. When it collected honey the children caught it, split it open, and sucked out the sweet stuff from the body. They didn't eat the whole thing. Only children did this. I never saw grown-ups do it.

When hives are found in the trees, a smudge fire is started under the tree and the bees are smoked out. A cliff hive is dislodged by well-directed shots from slings. For a ground hive another method is employed: "When the hive is in the ground a boy stands over the small hole and lets the bees out one at a time. Others kill each bee as it comes out. When all the bees are killed, they dig out the hole and eat the honey."

To the stock of playthings which the child makes for himself are added toys given him by his parents or other relatives. Little girls are presented with buckskin dolls filled with grass,[9] toy cradles, water jars, and burden baskets. For the boy the obvious plaything is a small bow and some arrows made of ocean spray, mock orange, snowberry, willow, service berry, or *Edwinia americana*. As a blanket for her doll cradle the girl uses a cottontail rabbit skin. A rabbit-skin cap, with the ears left on, is made for the little boy.

The older boys and girls enjoy swimming, a sport which a child begins to master at about the age of eight. A practical purpose is credited to another activity:

---

[9] These dolls are not supposed to approximate the human form too closely, for anything that has great likeness to a human being but is not animate is suggestive of a corpse. The mothers would not, at first, allow their children to have dolls of European type, claiming that they were "too natural."

We used to chase birds and butterflies. We would let the butterflies go after catching them. Both boys and girls did it. The old people said it would make us fast runners. In wet weather we could catch big birds. Their wings get wet in the rain and they can't go fast.

An unusual type of recreation involves the bat:

The boys used to build a fire at night. When the bats came by, they would throw their moccasins at them. They would get them in the moccasins and kill them. That's how the Indian boys used to play at night.

The children imitate many of the social and ceremonial practices of their elders:

During this time Old Man J., a lively old man, used to come out and sing for us while we danced the masked-dancer dance in the evening. The old people would be there and watch. We didn't dress up. The old people didn't allow us to dress up, for it was said to bring evil influence. The songs which were sung were N.'s songs. J. would ask him if it would be all right to sing these songs, and N. would tell him to go ahead.

Actually the boys learn much more than the steps and songs of the masked dancers on these occasions. For instance, the exchange between the two old men must have impressed upon them that ceremonial songs are personally owned and that permission must be obtained from the owner before using them. When the children are playing masked dancer away from the camps, they sometimes violate the rule about wearing costumes and make headdresses to wear and wands to carry.

Social dances are of increasing interest to the children as they grow older. "We used to dance the circle dance too, just the boys. Sometimes the old men would join in and sing for us. They certainly had a good time watching us."

The children organize elaborate and dramatic imitations of adult occupations. They hunt, with tall grass as the woods and playmates for the game animals. They go scouting and defend themselves against enemy attacks, using spears made from sunflower and lupine stalks.

Boys and girls play house in a realistic manner. They build small homes modeled after the regular residences (often making them large enough to enter), play man and wife, entertain visitors to whom they extend the amenities, and arrange feasts with provisions concocted from sticks and mud:

The girls see that at home the mother has a cradle and is carrying a baby around. So they play mother sometimes with an Indian doll and cradle made by their mothers. The girls carry the cradles on their backs as their mothers do. And the boys pick up their little arrows and hunt birds just as if they were hunting deer. All the Indian children play just the way their parents live at home. The children build little brush homes.

In this domestic play no overt sexuality is involved. The simulation of the husband-wife relationship is confined to an imitation of the industrial pursuits of the adults. The absence of more direct sexual experimentation is to be explained, doubtless, by the fact that boys rarely continue to participate in this form of amusement after the age of six or seven. It is then that little boys become eager to join older male companions in hunts for small birds and mammals and to engage in play not considered appropriate for girls. This pleasure in manly affairs is strongly encouraged by the elders. From the exciting hunts, arrow games, and mimic battles of childhood the boy plunges into the rigors of his training period. Thus he is absorbed in masculine concerns and diverted from contacts with girls until the onset of physiological maturity again awakens him to an interest in them.

Besides playing in the brush houses built for daytime games, the boys sometimes construct beds in trees for "camping out" at night.

You find a forked branch in a tree right by your camp. It should not be too high; you want a place close to the ground. You can put cross-branches there and fix it up nicely. Then you can sleep there. The boys did it mostly. I used to do it. We did it in the summertime, just because we liked it, because we liked the fresh air.

For the grown man the hoop-and-pole ground, from which the women are barred, is a favorite retreat where things strictly masculine are discussed. To play the hoop-and-pole game, two men slide poles after a hoop; the object is to make the hoop fall upon the butt end of the pole. Pole and hoop are marked with incised bands, and, according to the relationship of these bands after the throw, a count is made. The game has definite ceremonial overtones. It is well for a man to be an expert player, for lively betting attends every contest. Boys are eager to learn this game:

It is dangerous to make the hoop and pole unless you know how. Not every-one can do it, though there are many who have the right. . . . . Suppose a man knows how to do it. He will be making hoop-and-pole sets for all the men. I am a little boy there, let us say, and he is very kind to me. So I beg him to make a set for us boys, a little one.

He goes ahead and does it, does it with his own ceremony in such a way that it will not harm me. He doesn't want it to harm the children with whom I play either, and so he makes it in a ceremonial way. I suppose he prays over it, but I never watch him. He makes a little one, just the same as the regular ones, only smaller. When he hands it to me, he says, "All right, now you can play with this."

The men take their hoop-and-pole sets out where there is level ground and play there, far from the women. The women know about it and won't go over there. The children never go around the regular grounds either. Even when the men are not playing, the little boys do not go around there. When the little boys play at their hoop-and-pole game, the girls have to keep away.

When a man makes a set for little boys, he instructs them in the rules for counting and keeping score. The men like to watch the little boys playing. Many men will go over where the small boys are playing and stand in groups and watch. Some men count for each side, and all the boys stand there taking lessons. When the men direct the boys in this game, they tell them it is a gambling game. They say, "If you get to be an expert in this, when you get to manhood you can win horses, weapons, everything."

As soon as the boy is provided with a bow and arrows he spends a great deal of time gaining accuracy in handling them. Arrow games are an effective means to this end, and the boy has a variety of them from which to choose. "You are there all day long. Sometimes you don't care to eat, you are so interested." The arrows used in play "are just common ones made with any feathers—bluebird feathers, flicker feathers, feathers from any kind of bird the size of a robin or larger. Some of them are well made; you can shoot big animals with them if you have a good bow. They put three feathers on the shaft."

The simplest form of arrow game is shooting for distance, the winner collecting the arrows of his outdistanced playmates. Shooting for accuracy takes a number of forms. In one game a boy shoots his arrow into a bank, and his companion shoots after him, trying to touch or "cross" the arrow of the first boy. Should he succeed, he takes both arrows, and the loser has to send another arrow into the bank as a target. When the one who is shooting misses, he must offer one of his arrows as the target.

The youngsters play their games shrewdly:

I have about five arrows and my bow. A boy of my age asks me to play. He has a bunch of arrows too. He is good at playing this arrow game. Of course he wants my arrows. "All right," I say, "how do you want to play?"

About fifty feet apart stand two banks with a hollow between. He says, "You have more arrows than I have; you shoot first. Shoot your arrow from that bank into the other bank." We decide who should shoot first. Maybe he shoots first and his arrow sticks in the bank over there. Then I shoot. I try to shoot so that my arrow crosses or touches his. Sometimes there is a dispute. He says, "It doesn't touch!" and I say, "It does!" We try to look between the arrows and get down under them to see if they touch. But pretty soon we settle it. When I cross or touch his arrow, I walk over there and take it. He shoots another arrow, and I shoot and get it again. I begin to stick my arrows in the ground.

I always use one arrow, my best arrow, to cross his. All arrows don't shoot well, and so I use my good arrow to get his arrows. Pretty soon I miss. So it is my turn to shoot into the bank and let him try for my arrows. I take the worst arrow I have, so if he gets it, I will not lose much.

The game keeps up until one fellow gets all the arrows or we get tired.

In another shooting contest the first arrow is shot in such a way that it will stick in the ground when it falls. This arrow can be won only when its feathers are touched by those of a second arrow.

Boys also shoot at a target of twisted grass. The one who hits the target throws it up and tries to pierce it with an arrow before it touches the ground. If he does this twice in succession, he earns the arrows that others have unsuccessfully shot at the target. Again there are a number of modifications of this particular game. One variant is to make a target of yucca or other material, leaving a central hole. The boys attempt to shoot their arrows through the hole. The one who first succeeds in doing so a specified number of times wins whatever has been bet.

Another pastime is the "sliding arrow game." Here the arrow is slid by hand along the ground, point foremost, at any level place. The object is to touch the feathers of an arrow with the feathers of a second arrow which is slid after it. This game develops a steady hand and a good judgment of distance.

A game like blindman's buff is played with an arrow as the

prize. Someone is blindfolded, and an arrow is stuck in the ground far from him. If he finds the arrow, he is allowed to retain it. "They sometimes stick several arrows in the ground. If he finds one, all the rest belong to him."

Children play a game that may be likened to "heads and tails," using a bone with sides distinguished from each other by shape or color. Sometimes the bone is spit upon and the sides are called "wet" and "dry." If the side he has named shows uppermost, the player in possession of the bone wins the throw and retains the bone. Otherwise the bone changes hands. Today the game is played with a metal knife that has a handle rough on one side and smooth on the other.

In an exciting ball game a member of one side throws a buckskin ball to a member of the opposition who is standing with his team mates in a large circle or safety zone. This individual hits the ball with his hand, and he or one of his team mates must then run to another safety zone some distance away. The side of the thrower tries to retrieve the ball and hit the runner with it before he reaches the other circle. Should the runner be struck, his opponents make a rush for the safety zones, while he and his helpers try to recover the ball and strike one of the other team with it before he gains the circle. After the exchange, when the "ins" and "outs" are decided, the round of pitching and batting starts again.

The boys sometimes make clay marbles and dry them in the sun or near the fire, but often round stones are used instead. In one marble game a row of holes is scooped out. The order of play is determined by seeing who can roll a marble closest to a line. The object of the game is to roll the marble into each of the holes. A successful play for the first hole entitles the player to try for the second. When the row of holes has been traversed, the player must play in the opposite direction and come back to the starting-point. The first one to accomplish this is the winner. Instead of throwing directly toward a hole, a player is entitled to try to knock a competitor out of the way. If he strikes the marble at which he aims, he is allowed another throw for the hole.

Another marble game calls for four players, sitting around a hollow square, one on each side of it. Two teams are involved. Partners sit across from each other. A member of one side places a marble in the center. A player of the opposition tries to knock this away with one of his own. Should he succeed, his partner retrieves both marbles, and his opponent must place another at the center as a target. As long as this central marble is knocked away, it must be replaced by the side furnishing it. When a player misses, he substitutes a marble of his own, and the game continues.

Hide-and-seek, tag, foot races, tug-of-war, and wrestling contests are all popular. To begin a wrestling match, the rivals clasp each other around the waist. At a signal each tries to down his opponent. Almost anything is permissible, tripping included. If one wrestler is off his feet, no matter which part of his body touches the ground, and the other is still standing, the match is over.

Little girls are skilful at a game comparable to jackstones. "Four or five girls from about seven to fourteen years of age usually play together." One way of playing is called "those which pass each other again and again." Four stones are juggled while the girls walk along until a certain mark is reached. In another type of "rock game" an attempt is made to pick up four stones successively with one hand and put them on the back of the other while a fifth stone is repeatedly thrown in the air. The stones are arranged in a row on the knuckles, starting from the right and going to the left until each of the four knuckles is covered. "Throwing between fingers" describes a variant in which the stones are put, one by one, between the fingers, while the fifth stone is tossed up. Next the palm is turned up, and the stones are removed one by one. Another way is to cup the palm and put the stones in it, one at a time. Although these games with the stones are typically girls' pastimes, little boys occasionally play them too.

Boys whip a pointed wooden top with a sinew string. The making of cat's cradles or string figures furnishes year-round recreation for young and old of both sexes. There are many forms of these figures. One, after great elaboration, comes to a surprise ending by collapsing completely. Another represents the bow, and still another a house.

The children seldom attempt such adult pastimes as shinny, the stave games, and the moccasin game. They watch their elders play them, however, and become conversant with the principles involved.

THE CHILD AND HIS KIN

The social world to which the child is first introduced consists of a well-organized group of kin. The significant events of his life will be planned and made possible by his blood relatives. Should a person be wronged, his relatives act for him and with him; should he be accused, they shield him from vengeance. If a man dies with grievances unavenged, his relatives perpetuate his quarrel in a feud between families. It is they who have the responsibility of his death rites and who mourn for him.

Kinship is counted bilaterally, through the mother and through the father equally.[10] It is impossible to get any convincing assurance that one kind of relative is necessarily "closer" than another. The expressions on this point seem to be reflections of personal feelings rather than instances of the operation of any rule.

All blood relatives are supposed to be generous and loyal, and, in times of crisis, the appeal of a blood relative of any degree is difficult to ignore. Nevertheless, differences of age, sex, residence, and remoteness of connection become inevitably registered in patterns of behavior.

The parent-child relationship.—The parents take primary responsibility for the support, proper rearing, and ceremonial protection of their children. The influence of the child-parent bond is present in many forms of behavior. A man often begs for supernatural power, for "something to live by," because of the need of his children. One who makes a request for help, material or spiritual, greatly strengthens his plea if he supplicates in the

[10] For the kinship terms and a diagram of the kinship system see the Appendix.

name of the child of the one he is addressing. In discussing anyone, great care is taken to say nothing critical or abusive concerning him before his parents or his children. One man told of a
series of fights he initiated by uttering the remark, "Your father
is messy around the ankles." He knew very well in advance
what the consequences of that observation would be. In a Coyote story the trickster, after being skinned and jeered at for having a "red shirt," retaliates against his tormentors by shouting,
"It's your father who has a red shirt!"

Despite the affection and regard which mark the parent-child
relationship, it must not be forgotten that discipline and authority are the prerogatives of the father and mother. The daughter,
especially, is conditioned to lifelong obedience to parental edicts.

Four terms, the equivalents of father, mother, son, and daughter, serve to express the parent-child relationship. The term for
father can refer to no one else. The mother, likewise, is distinguished from her siblings. The parent-child terms differ from
others of the kinship system in two particulars. First, they are
not self-reciprocal; that is, the same term that is addressed to
the son by the father cannot mean father when the son is speaking. Second, each term expresses one relationship only and is
not extended to include collateral relatives.

Uncle, aunt-nephew, niece relationships. Of tremendous importance in the child's life are the maternal uncle and aunt. The
mother's sister is likely to be present at the child's birth. She
may volunteer to nurse the baby if she has milk and the mother
has not enough. She is a permanent member of the mother's extended domestic family. A girl will have intimate contact with
this relative throughout life; a boy, at least until his marriage and
departure from the encampment. In case the mother dies, this
woman may be called upon to adopt or care for her sister's children. She may elect to marry their widowed father[11] and so become their stepmother. Or, since sororal polygyny is practiced,
if she is younger than her sister, she may become the second
wife of her sister's husband and, by a different route, attain the

[11] See pp. 421–25.

position of stepmother to these youngsters.[12] Her very closeness to her sister, the fact that these girls have played and worked together since childhood, establishes her interest in the development of her sister's children. The chances are that she will perform protective ceremonies for them, that she will give them food and presents, that they will be frequent visitors in her home, and that she will offer them economic assistance in times of need. At the puberty rite of her sister's daughter, she will give generously of her labor and provisions. When her niece is about to marry, she will doubtless act as one of the group of relatives who passes on the desirability of the union; she will help erect the dwelling to which the husband will be brought; and she may furnish household necessities. When her nephew marries, her household will contribute to the gifts to be presented to his bride's relatives. The degree to which she participates in the instruction of her sister's children will vary with her own proficiency. If she knows a great deal about the medicinal value of plants, it is quite likely that she will transmit that information to her sister's daughter as well as to her own girls.

Somewhat different are the relations between the child and the mother's brother, for he resides with the extended domestic family only until he marries. If he is considerably younger than the mother, he may be around during the entire childhood of the individual; if he is older or near her age, he may depart while the child is yet very young. But even after he leaves the encampment through marriage, he frequently visits his parental home. At first, to his wife's relatives, he is a stranger and an unproved acquisition. He is bound to many of them by obligations of avoidance, restraint, and economic assistance, but the warmer bonds of kinship and prolonged common residence are lacking. Therefore, until he has children of his own and his status among his wife's relatives is established, he is likely to keep in closest touch with his own blood kin. There is a good deal of restraint

[12] When a woman marries her deceased sister's husband or becomes her sister's co-wife, the stepmother term may be used as a self-reciprocal between her sister's children and herself, or the mother's sister term may be continued. The first is the more common practice.

between the mother and her brother, for siblings of opposite sex, especially after puberty, must show great respect and decorum when they are together. Consequently, the maternal uncle best shows his affection toward his sister by the interest he takes in her children. There is frequent reference to his instruction of his sister's child, especially of her son, to his economic help at many of the crises, and to his constant friendly contact with his nieces and nephews. There is always the possibility that the mother's brother will marry an unrelated woman from the same local group in which he has grown up and will continue to live near his blood relatives.

Mother's siblings are addressed by one term, a self-reciprocal. Thus the mother's brother, the mother's sister, the sister's son, and the sister's daughter are all subsumed under the same kinship term. In a secondary sense this term may be addressed to other relatives, to any cousin of the mother, no matter how distantly related, and reciprocally to any female cousin's child.

In normal circumstances the father's sisters and brothers will never be members of the same extended family as the child, though they may be living in the same local group or vicinity. Since their primary ties are with other family units, they have less contact with a child than the maternal relatives. In spite of this, they demonstrate a lively interest in him. This is particularly true of the father's brother. As long as brothers inhabit the same camp they are inseparable, and their interest in each other and in the family line does not cease at marriage. Brother's children are blood kin, and such kinship imposes a solidarity which cannot be denied. "H. is my brother's daughter. No matter how far away she is, if I am sick she comes and helps around camp. But I have helped her as much as she has helped me. I feel that those related in this way should show a lifelong faithfulness to each other in any emergency and all the time."

The fate of brothers is further linked by a levirate arrangement which entitles an unmarried man to take his deceased brother's wife and place if he and his relatives so decide. This means that a man may in time become the stepfather of his brother's children.[13] At all the significant occasions when the maternal relatives offer personal or economic assistance the father's brother contributes also.

The father's sister normally has a family and duties of her own, her brother has passed from the extended family to which she is attached, and the sororate-levirate forms can have no effect upon her future position in respect to her brother's offspring. But the restraint relationship which has existed between this woman and her brother implies lifelong consideration. No better way of responding to this exists than generosity toward the brother's children. Moreover, a man who is in difficulty with his affinal relatives, angered over his wife's behavior, or divorced is likely to return to the extended family in which he was reared. His sister is one of the members of this social group, and her counsel is of great moment in the formation of decisions. These strong ties of consanguinity are felt by the woman to include her brother's children as well.

One term means father's brother and father's sister and is extended in use to include father's cousins, male and female. The same term, used as a self-reciprocal, designates a brother's child and, in an extended sense, a male cousin's child.

Brother-sister and cousin relationships.—The terminology employed to express the sibling, cousin relationship departs in principle from other sets. There are two self-reciprocal terms in use, but, unlike the other kinship terms, they imply sex difference or similarity between the speaker and the person addressed. *Šikis* literally signifies "sibling or cousin of the same sex as myself," and *šilah* carries the force of "sibling or cousin of the opposite sex from myself." Thus, when a woman says *šikis*, she is speaking of a sister or female cousin; when a man uses the same term, he has in mind a brother or a male cousin. Conversely, when a man says *šilah*, he is referring to a sister or a female cousin, and when a woman employs the same term, she is indicating a brother or a male cousin. The *šikis* term can be said to link relatives of the

[13] In that case a stepfather-stepchild term may be substituted for the father's sibling term (see n. 12, p. 56).

same generation and sex; the *šiłah* term, relatives of the same generation but of opposite sex.

From the comments and practices of his elders the child soon discovers that his *šiḱis* is designed to be his companion in experience and adventure, his confidant, his defender against misrepresentation or direct attack. The everyday stream of events steadily contributes to his conception of how two brothers or two sisters should act toward each other. His own mother and her sister sit and sew or go after fruit or mescal plants together. His father and his father's brother often act together in matters of raid or warfare. When the extended family is foraging or camping by itself, the children who are thrown together in play, in story-telling sessions, and in training are necessarily brothers, sisters, and cousins. Because of the sexual division in industry and social life, the child is often left with his *šiḱis* as the available partner for play. The close identification of *šiḱis* persists throughout life. This fact makes reasonable the sororate-levirate institution. If anyone is wronged or murdered, it is likely to be his *šiḱis* who demand retaliation.

Quite different is the *šiłah* relationship. Everyone is expected to be slightly reserved to all relatives of the opposite sex, whatever their age. Not even the father and his young daughters escape this feeling: "I still kiss my daughter [age six], but I doubt that I will when she is ten, and of course not after she has reached the age of puberty." This restraint becomes heightened between relatives of opposite sex of the same generation.

Brother and sister are so carefully trained to be reserved when they are together that any inclinations to exhibit overt sexual interest in each other are almost certain to be repressed. There is the possibility, however, that young men and women more distantly related will meet and become intimate. The term *šiłah* stands as a barrier against this, for a female cousin is terminologically classified by a young man with his sister and is just as forbidden to him. Very often the precise relationship is difficult to trace, but, if the young man knows that either of his parents addressed one of the girl's parents as *šiḱis* or *šiłah*, his attentions to that girl are illicit.

The child is psychologically prepared for the *šilah* relationship by the comments, stories, and actual behavior of adults: "Your father and mother, when you and your sister are both at home, do not say any wrong word. They are very careful." Thus the child, as soon as he is old enough to appreciate the cross-currents of social attitudes, becomes aware that the appearance of a *šilah* compels a certain decorum in speech and action.

A Chiricahua man and woman related in this way hardly speak to each other. Cousins, or a sister and a brother, could not even go out walking together. They can't joke much. Something holds them apart, so that they don't get too familiar. They aren't lectured about it when they are young. They just sense it and see it; it is taken for granted.

I notice the restraint in my own wife's family. My wife's *šilah* [father's brother's son] doesn't stay long when my wife is around. He has never been known to joke with her. He will with me. She takes the attitude that she wants to serve him when he is around. She acts in a formal way as if she wanted to serve him and please him. This man has a sister who is quite free with my wife. They are just reserved to the opposite sex.

In the old days those [a boy and a girl] who had the same father and mother hardly spoke to each other. They would sit there and wouldn't say anything. They talked to the father and mother in each other's presence, but not to each other. If joking [risqué] goes on when they are both there, one of them has to go away to show respect.

If you come where your sister is alone, you put disgrace on the whole family. If the mother and father aren't at home and the sister is alone, you must leave the camp. You must stay somewhere else. You must go to the sunny side of a hill or in the shade and sleep until your parents come home. Also, when the whole family is together, you must show respect for your sister. This feeling begins when you are about six or seven years old, when you are just big enough to understand what is being said to you. At that age you can still play with your sisters because perhaps you have no other playmates. But after you are fourteen or fifteen, you don't play with your sisters any more. In the old days a boy would not even accompany his sister to an Indian dance.

Many households where there are older children find it convenient to erect an additional shelter where the boy can stay if he should find his sister the sole occupant of the family dwelling.

Brothers and sisters feel so uncomfortable in each other's presence that they do not court situations which will throw them together. But they are members of the same household, and it is not possible for them to practice total avoidance, considered the ultimate in respect and reserve. The possibility of complete avoidance does exist for cousins of opposite sex, however, since they are of different households. One man who was asked how he would demonstrate his respect for his female cousin answered, "A boy shows his respect for a girl cousin by not visiting her."

From this conception of cousin relations it is not a great jump to total avoidance, and we find that some persons, though by no means all, do practice such avoidance. This is the only instance in which a true blood relative is avoided, though the married man responds to one of the most inclusive lists of affinal avoidances on record.

Avoidance of cousins of opposite sex "starts when they are old enough to understand such things, when they have grown to maturity, and lasts all their lives."

Šilah who are cousins, not sister and brother, sometimes hide from each other. R. hides from J.; they are cousins. They cannot see each other at all. It wouldn't be done between sister and brother, or between two boy cousins or two girl cousins. Cousins do it because they love each other very much and wish to show their respect. After they start it, they are very careful what they say about each other, for their relation is one of respect, like that of a man to his mother-in-law.

J. and S. are cousins. They have hidden from each other all their lives. When cousins do this, they give presents to each other in the beginning, and after that they help each other all the time. They hide from each other from that time on just as a man hides from his mother-in-law. Either the man or the woman can start it. You can't hide from a sister or an aunt. It is only between cousins of opposite sex that this is done, not between two men or two women. You cannot arrange with a cousin to use the polite form only;[14] it must be hiding or nothing. Of course, if you must speak to your cousin who hides from you, you might stand behind a tree, and then you would use polite form in talking to her. K. and Mrs. C. were cousins who hid from each other too.

I had a cousin. Just because she liked me, she wanted me to do it. I had been away to school. When I got back, she gave me a saddle and bridle. Then she asked me to hide from her. I said, "No." I told her I had been to school, that I didn't want to go the old way, that maybe the government would get after me if I did. So she said, "All right." This was about 1897.

[14] For an explanation of polite form see pp. 171–81.

If you hide from your cousin, then anything she has, whether it is money or property, or anything else, she will give to you. You can't refuse a request from a person who hides from you. And it's the same for you if she needs anything.

Since cousin avoidance is voluntary, where it will lead to complications or where the individuals concerned are likely to be thrown together constantly, it is seldom begun.

If marriage between cousins is prohibited, is it not difficult, in view of the small population, for a young person to find a suitable mate? Sometimes this problem does arise, and young men have been known to journey far from their homes for the purpose of making contacts which could lead to marriage. That the issue does not become more serious is due to two factors: the mobility and extensive range of these people and their anxiety to eliminate all mention and memory of the dead. Because of the first factor, families, except for nuclear groups of very close kin, tend to move apart and lose contact with each other. And because the names and antecedents of the departed are seldom mentioned, connections between remoter kin are soon forgotten when the families are separated.

When circumstances warrant, the cousin avoidance may be terminated and the more ordinary manner of behavior toward a relative of this degree resumed. The details of the procedure are the same as those governing the abrogation of affinal avoidance.[15]

Grandparent-grandchild relationships.—The wish for long life and old age is constantly expressed in prayer and ceremonial song. The staff on which the old person leans has become a symbol of this concept. As one commentator wryly observed: "They pray for the old age staff. They say, 'Let me be old, let me have the old age stick.' If you have the old age stick that means you have reached a long life. But when they get it, they don't like it."

It is considered a good omen if an old person blesses a child or performs a ceremony over him, for even as this individual's power and ceremony have preserved him to a ripe age, they may protect the child for a generous time span. The same notion is present in the preparation of the first cigarette. "A person's first

15 See pp. 174–75.

cigarette was rolled by an old man or woman. This was done so the person could reach the age of the one who rolled it. The old person prayed and lit it for him."

Age brings prestige, if it is ever to come to an individual. The band leaders are chosen from the most forceful heads of local groups; local group leaders are the most authoritative voices of extended families. Few men who have not lived long enough to rear a large family and to see their daughters marry well head extended families. With his children and grandchildren around him and sons-in-law to do his bidding, a man may establish important alliances and gain political and economic stature. That older persons figure so prominently in the ceremonial and political life is significant for the grandparent-grandchild relations.

The rule of matrilocal residence permits constant contact between the child and his mother's parents. These kin are usually the oldest and, while they retain their vigor, the most respected members of the extended family. The family is the realization of the line they have founded. Their daughters and unmarried sons owe them obedience and deference, and their sons-in-law are bound and subordinated to them by strict social and economic rules.

The maternal grandparents concern themselves in countless ways with the child's development. They are constantly consulted by their daughter on problems of child-rearing. They are present at the first ceremonies held for the baby and contribute whatever is needed for these occasions. It is often one of these grandparents who acts as the cradle-maker and shaman of the cradle ceremony. They may suggest a first name for their grandchild. Their home is always open to him, and it is not unusual for him to sleep there. If his mother dies and his father leaves the extended family because it cannot offer him a suitable mate, the maternal grandparents are likely to rear the child.

My father was left an orphan at about six years of age and was brought up by his grandparent. It was his mother's father who took care of him. This man lived in Chiricahua country. My father lived there with him until he was twelve or fifteen years old. He was with the old man all the time. When he told about it in after years, he said he often wondered why this old man took such an interest in him. He often wondered if he was worth it, worth having so much attention paid to him. My father said the old man was kind to him, was always gentle with him, and used to advise him. He took more trouble with him than other relatives did.

The maternal grandparents, who are the approved raconteurs for the children of the extended family, function to a considerable degree as teachers, for a good deal of instruction for the young comes obliquely through stories.

The influence of the maternal grandparents is not limited to oral instruction. While the younger men are hunting or raiding and the younger women are away gathering food or getting wood and water, the care of the children and the performance of camp tasks fall to the older people. The grandfather makes arrows, ropes, and many other objects. Often his grandson watches him or even assists him. The grandmother cooks, sews, and weaves baskets, occasionally pausing to explain her methods to her granddaughter.

Ceremonial knowledge may also be received from the grandparent. Many rites result from personal experiences with the supernatural, but a certain number are passed along to others by those who have had such individual encounters. When a ceremony is transmitted, it is most often taught to a relative. Usually a shaman is reluctant to reveal his secrets until he feels that the end of his life is near and that his ceremony will perish with him unless a successor is found. Thus there is a tendency for very old persons to seek younger relatives as their understudies in things ceremonial. The grandchild often proves a promising candidate, especially if he is not too young during his grandparent's declining years.

The paternal grandparents usually cannot hope for a great deal of contact with their son's child. At marriage their son has left their encampment, and his obligations are to his wife's relatives. Yet when it happens that the father's parents do live near the extended family into which their son has married, they take pleasure in being with their grandchildren and may even rival the maternal grandparents in solicitude.

Four kinship terms, one for each grandparent, label the grandparent-grandchild relationship. Since they are used as self-reciprocals, one term, in its primary sense, stands for mother's mother and also, when a woman is speaking, for daughter's child; another indicates father's mother and likewise, when a woman is speaking, son's child, etc.

It is a feature of this kinship system that siblings and cousins of the grandparent are addressed by the same term as the grandparent, regardless of sex. For example, the term for mother's mother also designates her sisters, brothers, and cousins. Reciprocally, the brothers or sisters of a woman will address this same term to their sister's daughter's child, male or female.

For the great-grandparent–great-grandchild relationship the terms of the grandparent-grandchild set are utilized. There is no strong feeling concerning the functions of the great-grandparents and no specialization of terminology. If they are active enough to participate in social, economic, and ceremonial matters, they are treated much as are grandparents. It is the duty of children to support old people who are so far past their prime, and members of the great-grandparent generation receive the extra consideration to which their extreme age entitles them.

CHILDHOOD'S END

Childhood is, strictly speaking, a period of preparation for adult standards. The view of the world is not softened for the young beholder. The child and the adult often listen together to accounts of the rigors of the hunt, of the hardships and glories of war, and of the cruelties of the enemy. "As soon as I was old enough to know," said one informant, "I was told who were our enemies." Another man prefaced an exceptionally vivid description of a war dance with the remark, "When I was just old enough to understand and remember it, I saw them go through this performance."

The child is early introduced to the goals and values of the society. An old man mentioned hunting as one of the first experiences he could recall. He was with older children who were shooting birds with slings, and he followed them around to see what they were doing.

Boys begin their interest in horsemanship while they are still very young:

The Chiricahua would hobble their horses way off in the woods. A boy would play with the horse when no one was watching. Children from seven years of age and on would go and learn by themselves when the older people didn't even know about it. There were always some gentle horses for the boys to ride. I would crawl on a horse when I was about seven. I used to put my foot on his leg, get hold of his mane, and crawl up on his back. Sometimes I fell off again, but after a while I would get on the horse's back.

When the boy is sufficiently strong to handle a bow and arrows, some member of the extended family—the father, the mother's brother, or the grandfather—provides him with them and gives him the necessary advice.

When I was small I didn't know how to make a bow and arrows myself. My father said, "First, I'm going to make you learn how to hunt." He made a bow and arrows for me. Children use a small wooden arrow with a wooden point, but they can shoot a long way with it, for they have a good bow.

My father said, "Go ahead, son, and shoot birds and squirrels and any small things. But, before you try, I must tell you that these little birds and animals are not tame. They see you just as soon as you come in sight of them. The squirrels, as soon as they see you come anywhere near them, run away. You must see the squirrel before it sees you. You can't just run up to squirrels and shoot them, because they are wild. If you have to crawl to get where your arrow can hit a squirrel, do it.

"A bird is the same way. If he is over there on a limb, you must come around so that you can get within range of him. Part of the time you must crawl, because he is watching, and in that way you can get within range and shoot him. In hunting you must go very slowly and softly, not rattling stones with your feet or making rocks roll down a steep place. Go carefully; creep up to your game.

"It will be just the same when you hunt deer. Then you will still have to go slyly and carefully. Deer can see you before you see them. The deer places himself where he can see very well. You must look for him. You must go slyly up to him as if you were a fox. It's the same if you are hunting antelopes or any other animals; you must be very cautious."

That is the teaching for a little boy when he is given a bow and arrows. So I did these things, and it worked out exactly as he said.

Most adults, when they present the boy with his first bow, advise him to swallow whole the raw heart of the first kill he makes to guarantee continued abundance from the hunt.

But no amount of good advice will prepare a youth for hunting and raiding unless he reaches a high point of physical fitness. At first it is the members of the immediate family who urge the boy to undertake special exercises. Such pressure begins when the boy is anywhere from eight to twelve years old, depending on his size and the attitudes of the members of his family.

Now the next thing [after learning to hunt] was getting up before daylight. My father said, "Be up; be up before daylight and run up the mountain. Run to the top of that mountain and back before daylight. You must do it, and I'm going to make you do it. It will be better for you to do it in your own way, but if you don't, I'll force you to do it."

I asked, "What if the clown should see me? Is he everywhere?"

"My son, that time the clown frightened you it was only I dressed up. You were a little boy at that time. You would not obey. There is nothing to be afraid of. That is the way little children are made to mind. Now you are big enough to handle a bow and arrows. Now I am going to train you so that when you get to be a few years older you will be almost as good as any man. Your mind will be well developed. Your legs will be developed so nobody can outrun you. You will be able to keep up with others when you are running long distances. Getting up early in the morning, running to the top of that hill and back will give you a strong mind, a strong heart, and a strong body."

Physical fitness is considered by some parents even more vital for survival than the assistance of relatives.

If my son is strong, when he is about eight or ten years old I must give him his lesson. It's like breaking in a mule. . . . . He must get up before sunrise.

The father talks to his son. "My son, you know no one will help you in this world. You must do something. You run to that mountain and come back. That will make you strong. My son, you know no one is your friend, not even your sister, your father, or your mother. Your legs are your friends; your brain is your friend; your eyesight is your friend; your hair is your friend; your hands are your friends; you must do something with them. When you grow up you live with these things and think about it.

"Some day you will be with people who are starving. You will have to get something for them. If you go somewhere, you must beat the enemy who are attacking you before they get over the hill [i.e., escape]. Before they beat you, you must get in front of them [i.e., best them] and bring them back dead. Then all the people will be proud of you. Then you are the only man. Then all the people will talk about you. That is why I talk to you in this way. If you do all these things and you stay among the people, they will all like you—your brother, your sister, your uncle. All the camps will talk about you. They will call my name and say my son is fine and does good work. Then we will be proud of you. If you are lazy, the people will hate you."

Soon the boy is requested to care for the horses. He is told that he should carry a pack on his back while he is running. To prove his endurance, he may be ordered to stay awake continuously for a day and a night or even longer. An inevitable incident of this training period is the icy morning plunge.

There was a creek deep enough for a boy to jump in. In the fall of the year the water was frozen a little. The creek was about a mile away. My father said, "Son, get up, and before you build a fire, take everything off except your breech-cloth, run to that creek, and jump in the water. If the ice is thin enough, you jump in so it will not cut you. Go ahead! Jump in!"

Many boys used to put water on their heads and make believe they had jumped in. And some of the boys used to throw water over themselves before they went in, but their parents would find it out. If a boy wouldn't do it, his father would get a whip, call the boy to him, and say, "You go over and jump in!" So the boy would go to escape a whipping.

Afterward we would come back soaking wet, but we were not allowed to come up to the fire. We just had to take a covering and wrap it around ourselves.

Nor does this exhaust the ingenuity of those in charge of the boy:

There is a small tree. My father takes me out there. He says, "Fight that tree!" I go over there and hit the tree with both hands. Perhaps it hurts and I will have sore hands the next day. Then there is a tree with a limb about as big as my arm sticking out just about high enough for me to jump and catch it. My father says, "Break that limb." And he is standing there watching me fight it. Some limbs are pretty hard to break, but he is going to stand there until I break it.

A variation of this type of strenuous exercise is to have the boy uproot small trees or pull long poles from the ground.

One of the devices of winter training is to send the boy out early in the morning to roll a ball of snow. He is told to push it until he is called.

As the youth progresses in his training, guard and scout duties fall to his lot:

If older men are going away, they leave a young man to watch camp and guard the women and children. They say to him, "Camp up high. Get up early. Go up on a hill and watch. Go out and hide in the brush and look for tracks." That's what they told me.

They told me, "Don't eat too much in the day. Eat just enough so that you keep your strength. If you eat too much, you won't be able to run. But in the night eat well, for if the enemy does come you can hide yourself because of the dark and get away."

Facial hair is greatly disdained, and its growth is usually attributed to disobedience of some kind. There is a test of self-discipline related to this:

My father used to tell me, "When you are old enough to go in the creek and you are in training, every now and then walk straight into the water until it reaches the place under your nose where a moustache would begin. But if you drink the water or get it in your nose or mouth you will have a moustache." I tried this several times just for fun. The older people warned us not to let the water in; they didn't want us to have moustaches. They said that if we smoked while we were little we would get a moustache too.

The last sentence of this quotation calls attention to another matter concerning which the boy receives instruction at about this time. Smoking is the prerogative of the warriors and of the older women:

They tell a boy that he will have to catch a coyote first before he can smoke, but they mean it just as a joke. Some try it, of course; that's what they tell the boys to do it for, to see them try something that no boy can do. It's just like sending a boy for the thing they call "that with which one smokes."

Among older men the admonition is used in jest: "Not long ago when I lit a cigarette an old man said to me, 'When did you catch your coyote?' I told him, 'I've never done it, and I don't believe you ever did either.' He only laughed." To smoke during the boyhood or the training period is said to make a boy "lazy and no good at work."

Gradually the boys become inured to the demands made upon them and even devise tests of character for themselves. To demonstrate their bravery, they place dry sage or the pith of the sunflower stalk on their skins, ignite it, and let it burn to ash. Even though they are burned severely enough to show a scar years later, they must not flinch.

The training described thus far is entirely in the hands of the immediate family, but, when the youth reaches the age of puberty, this hardening process takes a more formalized turn. The father lets his son know that momentous days are ahead: "There are harder things to be learned later. When you are a little older,

I will continue to make you get up early in the morning just as you do now, but you will have to do more than that. You will become a raid and war novice."

The term that has been translated here as "novice" denotes the status of a youth who is advanced enough in his training to enter the final phases of preparation for actual raiding. Some informants use the word only to refer to the participant in the four raid or war expeditions which elevate a youth to the full status of a warrior.

The initial training of the novice (using the word in the less restricted sense) does not differ greatly from what has gone before:

When I was a boy they began training me as a novice. To be a novice means that you cannot disobey but must train yourself as your elders say. . . . . Many a young boy at fourteen was as well trained and dangerous as a soldier.

My father did his best to train me just as he had been trained when he was a young boy. He gave me all the ceremonial training he had once been through himself too. When I was ten or twelve years old he began to teach me and was very strict with me.

He would say to me, "You must have your arrows and your bow where you can grab them. Keep your knife beside you. Have your moccasins ready. Be on the alert in peace or in war. Don't spend all your time sleeping. Get up when the morning star comes out. Watch for that star. Don't let it get up before you do." That is the kind of teaching a boy gets when he is a novice.

The reference to "ceremonial training" suggests that more than purely practical measures are involved. The parents pray for their son's success and future safety, and he may be taken to a shaman whose ceremony is known to be of special benefit to novices. "The shaman prays that the boy may be free from harm. A yellow light shines on the boy's head. It follows the boy and makes a circle back to the shaman. That means that the boy will come back safely. The shaman smokes and sings."

"At about fourteen years of age the boy starts hunting with the men." Usually an older man who "knows" a great deal about deer goes along and marks the tips of the young hunter's moccasins with blood from the kill.

At the conclusion of the training period, some boys, to insure their competence in horsemanship, are brought to shamans who perform ceremonies for them originating in supernatural experiences with Bat; for the bat, because of its habit of clinging to objects, is associated with riding ability.

Sweat-bathing is utilized as an aid to fleetness: "Sometimes boys are put in a sweat lodge to make them good runners. They come out and run for about a mile; then they go in again if they wish. It makes them longwinded." In another account it is said that the young men emerge from the sweat lodge and run "while they are still warm." "If a man is training for running, he should keep away from women and should not drink or smoke." However, there is no taboo on the presence of women where youths are practicing running.

As the boy's training advances, the circle of those who are interested in his progress steadily enlarges.

I was a small boy, about nine years old, when I saw this. I remember it well. Many boys in my time saw what I'm going to tell you about. It was just before Geronimo's last war, about 1884 or 1885.

Old Man C. had an orphan boy. He was rearing and training that boy. He had taught him how to ride well. The boy was about fifteen or sixteen years old and was well trained as a warrior. He knew how to shoot an arrow, how to use a sling, how to shoot with guns. He was a good hunter; he could shoot deer. He was as good as the average man, though he was just a young boy.

One man had made tiswin [a weak beer made of maize]. C. went to a crowd of men who were drinking. He said, "I've got a boy. I am his uncle. The boy can ride any horse bareback without a rope on it."

"Well," one man said, "we all like to see things like that. We will bet you two big jars of tiswin. You get that boy; let him ride down that steep hill bareback."

In those days one jar of tiswin was worth a horse, and a horse was very hard to get. That much tiswin was worth a belt and cartridges, or a gun and belt. Guns were hard to get in those days too. So C. told the man, "Give your horse to him. Any side of the hill you want to have him ride is all right."

Nobody knew then that this boy was so well trained. C. had been out training him somewhere away from the rest of the people. The man took the bronco on the side of the hill, and the boy was called over there. The horse had a rope on but no saddle.

Just as soon as C. spoke, the boy would do what he said, whether it was dangerous or not. That boy rode the horse down the hill just like nothing! The horse pitched all around with him but could not shake him off. So C. got the tiswin, and he was drinking and got feeling good.

In those days the warriors never went without their guns. They always carried their guns and belt no matter how close they were to camp. Awake or asleep they were never without their guns. After this ride C. wanted to show those people just how he had trained his boy. They were on the sandy side of the hill. Nobody was on that hill.

C. told the boy, "Take your shirt off so that you'll have no excuse of something to trip over." All the men watched from the side. C. told the boy to stand on a gentle slope. He stood about fifty feet away from the boy.

C. took his gun and put cartridges in it. He is a sharpshooter; he shoots from the hip. He said, "All right, you start! You go down there."

The boy began to dodge and run. C. began to shoot. You could see the dust flying all around that boy, but he didn't get hit!

The boy is constantly reminded that this training must serve him for the raid and warfare situations which he will face.

The parents and grandparents all advise the boy. They tell him to run up hills so that in emergencies he can get along by himself, for in wartime, they tell him, nobody will go back for him, and he must keep up.

They advise the boys that in case of war they should have a strong feeling that they will overcome the enemy; they tell the boy that the enemy is as frightened as he is; and that, if he puts on a brave front and charges, the enemy may run. And they tell the boys that, after coming home from a successful battle, their relatives and friends will be proud of them. Cowards are talked about, told nasty things before their faces, and are in disgrace. A girl would not marry a lazy or cowardly man because the women say he wouldn't be a good provider. The boys know all this.

As time goes on group tactics assume increasing importance in the physical education of the novice. Where there are a number of boys of the proper age in the local group, they are brought together frequently for the training tasks.

Suppose I have a boy in the group. I give him equipment and tell him to go out there. The boys line up, ready to run. Maybe two men go along and see that the boys don't stop running. Then along comes a man with water in a little container and says, "Take a mouthful, but don't swallow it; hold it in your mouth. You are going to run four miles with this water in your mouth."

They all start out, not running full speed, but trotting. When they come back they are inspected. Each man inspects his boy to see if he still has the water in his mouth. He says, "All right, spit that water out." If the boy swallows the water on the way, the trainers see that he doesn't do it a second time.

Now one old man from the group of camps [extended family] might say, "I have a fine boy. He is hard to beat." Then perhaps my father would say, "I have a good boy. Bring your boy in." In they come. Everybody is around. The other boys who are novices are there too, waiting. They match these two, and the fighting begins. Maybe they are both crying. They fight until they bleed, until one of the boys says, "Enough!" Then he is whipped.

Then another day is set. A different boy is matched with the one who won the first fight. When it comes to one of these fellows, they tell him, "Well, it is your turn to fight him now." I have seen some poor boys who had to fight the winner, cry before they got out. Before they started they knew they were going to be beaten, but they had to go through with it whether they were good fighters or not.

Then they take eight boys, all of about the same size and with about the same amount of training and give them slings. They take them to a flat place where there are many stones and where all of them can see each other. The trainer says, "All right, four of you boys go on the other side, four stay on this side. This is going to make you quick; this is to develop you in speed."

They have to pick up the stones and sling them at each other, one side against the other. They have to learn to duck and dodge and keep from being hit. They are taught to throw at each other and to hit each other. If a stone hits you in the head, you are gone; if it hits you in the arm, it may break a bone. You have to jump aside and dodge in order not to get hurt. C. has a scar over his eye from a sling fight of this kind.

After so much sling-fighting they are beginning to be a little like warriors. Next they make small bows and arrows. The boys divide into equal sides again and take their places about fifty feet apart. They use small arrows; but, if these arrows hit you, they stick into you. They are of wood, sharp pointed. The trainer says, "All right, you boys go out there and fight." And I tell you they have fun too! They hardly ever hit each other. But I remember one boy in the crowd at Carlisle who had been shot in the eye, and it put his eye out.

Then they take them out again. They have the boys race without any water in their mouths and without carrying anything, in order to see which are the best two runners. Maybe they run to a little tree, around it and back again, about 800 paces. The next day they run about a mile around another tree. A man on horseback follows on each side. They try that twice to see who can run. Then they select two boys. They cut two switches, each about three feet long, and give them to these good runners. These two run ahead as usual and they whip the last boy in.

A mimic contest in which stones are parried with round shields is described and also wrestling matches in which "the idea is to throw an opponent down before you get hit or kicked."

The boys are anything but docile, even in regard to their trainers: "Sometimes when they have an older person to run along during racing to lash those who lag behind, one or two boys jump on him and struggle with him. This gives the others a chance to get far enough ahead so they won't be bothered."

Practice in handling and riding horses under all conditions is a regular part of the training. The boy is taught to ride bareback, to control the horse with only a rope around its nose, and to ride down a steep incline, picking up objects from the ground as he goes. He is also judged as he rides full speed toward a barrier and tries to halt his horse just before reaching it, or jumps the horse over hurdles.

One of the last activities of this phase of the training is a cross-country run. The route that is to be covered is laid out. There are no long halts, and the boys try to refrain from eating for the two days of this journey. Not until the afternoon of the second day may they kill animals for food. The boys do not sleep until the race is over. A variation is to make a group of boys walk all night to see if they can withstand fatigue.

The boys who achieve a position of superiority during this training period rise to pre-eminence in their age group. The tasks which lie ahead are close enough in spirit to those in which they have already excelled so that their futures are reasonably assured. The foundations of status recognitions are laid in the training period, therefore.

Paternal affection is reinterpreted when the training period begins. No longer is it indulgence. "Because a Chiricahua parent loves his child," he insists upon duties which are often painful, for in his opinion this is the only way "his son will eventually make a living." There is no rancor involved; certainly no conscious cruelty or sadism.

This attitude penetrates deeply to the core of all response and behavior. Demonstrativeness is considered unbecoming; what cannot be translated into action need not be protested. Since stoicism and strength are underlined, displays of personal consideration and "softness" must be repressed. Only at times of crisis and of great grief, in appeals to the supernatural, or during mourning do the people permit the emotions full expression.

The girl's destiny as a dutiful wife is made very clear to her while she is still a child. The father may say, "We want to rear you well so people won't talk about us; we want to get something out of your marriage, so we want to take care of you."

Women school the girls in obedience "so that their husbands won't hear saucy words from them."

The girl's training is less formalized than that of the boy. It amounts to a greater and greater association with the duties of her mother, older sisters, and other female relatives, until she attains adult standards in the quality of work she can perform.

At this time, when the little girl is first learning to do women's work, her hair is done up in the style worn by young women:

In the old days the young woman had her hair done up. She took it in one bunch and wrapped it up in back. Then she put a hair ornament on, and it covered the knot of hair and was tied in the middle. The hair ornament was made out of buckskin or cowhide. It had to be stiff. In my day they covered the hide with cloth. The color was usually red. . . . .

The hair ornament was put on as soon as the girl was ten or twelve years old. It had nothing to do with the girl's feast [puberty rite]. There was no ceremony connected with it that I know of. The mother would make it. The only thing I know about it is that they said anyone who had the hair done up that way would have very long hair, for it would grow long while it was done up that way. They told this to the little girls, and it was generally true.

One of the earliest tasks given the little girl is the care of still younger members of the family. She is also instructed in the use of the tumpline and is expected to help bring in wood and water.

These simple household tasks are supposed to be shared by children of both sexes, but the boy is hardly old enough to be of appreciable assistance when he senses the sexual division of labor: "After my father was gone I worked a little around the house, getting wood, carrying water, and helping my mother. I was ashamed to do that though. It was woman's work. The other boys used to pass by and see me and make fun of me." It is not long before the boy has to be released entirely from such duties to follow his companions in their training and sports. But the girl is encouraged to continue and intensify her interest in household affairs.

However, like the boy, she must train herself to be strong and vigorous. She is told to rise early, to run often, and to shun no hard work. Tales are frequently told of girls so fleet that they rival boys in races. Such swiftness and strength are necessary, for girls must be able to get quickly to safety in case of attack on the camp. Girls who are good runners even aid boys and adults in one form of hunting, the rabbit surround. All close in on a circular area, beating the brush to drive the rabbits toward the center and club or shoot them.

But the young girl's principal concern is to assist the women in those tasks not beyond her strength and to receive continual instruction from them. They indicate to her the plants useful for food, artifacts, and medicine and teach her to gather materials and to dry, store, and prepare them. "A girl is taught to sew moccasins, weave baskets, make clothing, and cook. Her mother and grandmother begin to teach her as soon as she is old enough to understand, and by the time she is fifteen she is well educated."

MATURATION

WHILE the child is very young and is still unable to comprehend the social forms which differentiate one class of relationship from another, he is little inhibited. But with his introduction to the ideas clustering around the sibling and cousin relationships comes the first pressure toward reserve between the sexes. Soon this trend is fortified by the increasing separation of boys and girls for play and amusement. Since the youngster is with members of his own sex so much of the time, the feeling of shyness when he is in the company of the other sex becomes pronounced.

The parents try to instil the proper attitudes regarding personal matters: "When the children are about six years old, they begin to notice things, so the parents are very careful to urinate and to have sexual intercourse in private and to speak carefully. The children thus grow up the way they are supposed to." What cannot be concealed from the child, he is taught to ignore. Thus, a young man, in telling of serious temptations which he had successfully withstood, could explain: "My early training helped me. For I was brought up in Indian camps where it is hard to be private and where we were trained to pay no attention to such things."

There is a definite etiquette of modest deportment. The girl is taught to sit with her legs close together, flexed back and to one side, so that her genitals will never be exposed. Children of both sexes are told to leave the dwelling quietly without reference to their errand when they go to the brush. If some explanation is necessary, a simple, "I am going out," is the customary phrase. This modesty becomes habitual and extends to all situations.

Older boys went swimming in the creek too. The girls would not go swimming then. The bigger boys didn't go over where the girls were swimming because the girls were naked. When I was about fourteen years old or so, I kept apart from the older girls. I became ashamed then.

77

Premarital chastity is expected in the girl. The maidenhead is considered the proof of virginity. A marriage may be abrogated if a bride is found to have been unchaste, and a girl who is deserted for this reason brings disgrace to herself and her family.

But, because of the heightened round of physical activity at about the time of adolescence and the encouragement of early marriage, premarital sexual activity does not become a serious problem. Of great importance, also, is the existence of separate spheres of activity for men and women. This dichotomy tends to draw the child's interest away from situations which involve the other sex and causes him to seek recognition, rather, in those outlets unequivocally masculine or unequivocally feminine.

An Apache boy is trained not to pay too much attention to the women. It is not considered manly. The Apache girl is expected to be reserved, and a show of affection in public between the sexes is laughed at. This training becomes a part of the Apache's thought. He sees it all around him. He notices who is laughed at and who is thought well of, and why. This bashfulness, the unwillingness openly to show a lot of feeling for one of the other sex, is carried right through. It comes out in courtship. It comes out even in marriage.

Of an aberrant girl who violates the conventions in this regard, the following criticism was offered:

Unlike most Chiricahua girls, she is not bashful. If she came in the room here, she would start talking to you. Lots of the old Indians hold this against her. It is considered too forward for a boy to walk up to a girl and start talking a lot. But when I see this girl I go up to her and start talking. I wouldn't dare do that with any other woman. She will hail someone at a dance before a lot of other people. Many of the older people do not like her for this.

Since casual contact between the sexes is discouraged, any overt signs of friendliness between men and women suggest the desire for intimacy. Once when an informant had gone to some trouble to reach a man's camp, he declined to wait there for his friend who was expected back in a short time, saying, "Well, it wouldn't look well if C. came and found me here with these women. C. and I are great friends, and I wouldn't want him to think anything bad of me."

"The feeling is that a man should go his way with his friends and a woman her way with her friends." Anything else is effeminacy on the man's part, forwardness on the woman's. These are barriers to intimacy which it is very difficult for the youth to surmount before he is ready to enter into a marriage relationship arranged and approved by his elders. Ordinarily, before maturity and the time for marriage, the boy is so busy proving himself a worthy competitor among men, and the girl is so engrossed in establishing herself as a competent worker among the women, that there is limited need to gratify the primary sex drive. There is no use for prudery or continence as such, but there is a definite concept of normalcy in the relation between the sexes which subordinates the sexual drive to other concerns.

Sexual precocity is rare and sternly discouraged. The one account of such misbehavior which was obtained was that of a seven-year-old boy charged with trying to throw down little girls and molest them. The mothers refused to allow their children to associate with him. An informant, when he was questioned about sexual play among children, claimed that he had never heard of children engaging in sex games but added that, if two children had been caught at "such a thing," the parents "would certainly have whipped both of them."

That masturbation occurs infrequently among the children has been asserted by a number of informants:

> There is no masturbation among the Chiricahua boys. It is against the Apache nature to handle the private organs. There was one boy, a Comanche, who did it and advised J. and me to do it. We thought it a shameful thing to do. I can hardly believe that it is so common among the Whites! It is not done by the Chiricahua. We children were never warned against it. It never was mentioned, thought of, or considered.

Another old man disclaimed knowledge of it, insisting that his people "never thought along that line." "Way back the Chiricahua didn't know what masturbation was," another man declared. However, one informant who had "never heard of masturbation or anything like that among the men" said he had heard of girls masturbating with sticks. A traditional story is told of a woman who abused herself with a cactus plant from which the outer covering had been peeled.

Berdaches rarely appear and are far from pampered or encouraged when they do. They are not mistreated, but they are

privately ridiculed. Perversion seldom occurs and is not coun-
tenanced; it may even be equated with witchcraft.

The elders do not rely entirely on implicit attitudes and the
demands of the training process to guard their children from undesirable sex scrapes but provide continual supervision as well.
When an unmarried girl goes to social dances, she is accompanied
by an older relative. Or she herself may be put in charge of a
younger child so that she will not have time for an assignation.
Her mother is strict and watchful. She tells the girl not to permit any intimacies from men or boys before her marriage and
warns her about bearing unwanted babies. "A girl who goes
wrong is usually one who has no close relatives, no mother, father, grandparents."

The mother, the grandmother, or some other female relative
gives the girl counsel as the time for her first menses approaches.
She is told that menstrual blood is dangerous to men and is instructed how to keep clean. She is encouraged to endure bravely
the possible accompanying pain, for "as long as she acts like a
child she is going to have a hard time at menstruation."

It is at this time that the girl may have a ceremony performed
over her which results in sterility:

No woman should be sterile. There is no excuse for any woman not to have
children. That's the way my people talk and feel about it. The trouble is that
those who are sterile have been ruined right when they came of age, about the
time when they had their first flow. A girl's own mother might have a woman fix
it so the girl won't have children. The father won't know anything about it.
Sometimes the mother, who has had children and knows the pain and hard time
of it, doesn't want her daughter to have children. There are women right now
who know this kind of thing. S. and B. have had no children, and this must be
why. Those who made us made every woman to have children without exception
if not interfered with.

Often a similar charge is directed against a jealous shaman
who has been called for some other service but who has taken
advantage of the opportunity to injure the girl:

We didn't have children for the first five years. We didn't try to prevent it.
Then my wife found out that when she was young and sickly an old woman gave
her some medicine. She didn't know it at the time, but it turned out to be
medicine to prevent children. Some Indian women do this just for meanness.

Her grandmother told her this. It was the same with her sister. Her sister had a child, but it took a long time.

The boy is exempt from the strict supervision to which the girl is subject. They "warn the boy about having a bad reputation. Boys are instructed all right, but you can't keep a boy back."

Yet there are a number of dangers against which the boy has to be warned. He must be advised that contact with menstrual discharges will make his joints swell and ache. He must also be told that "sometimes boys have sexual relations with old women; that is why they die." Because unmarried girls are so sedulously restricted, there is always the possibility that a youth may thus jeopardize his health:

Sometimes a boy would go around with an old, experienced woman. Bad blood gets into him from these bad women. He gets arm aches and leg aches. Sometimes he gets aching all over like this before he is thirty years old; sometimes he is dead from it before he reaches this age.

This is because he is giving his richest blood [semen] to these older women and getting nothing in return but their diseased blood [vaginal discharges] which they got from having intercourse over a long period of time with other men, some of them sick and old. The people laugh at a young fellow who does this. He gives his young, good blood and prolongs and saves that woman's life.

I know a woman like that. She is an older woman who has been having intercourse with all kinds of men. J. was a young man. He became intimate with her and was very sick almost at once. She is still living and still doing it. The young men just shorten their lives by going with women like this. The bad blood that they get from such women comes out in lumps and sore joints.

It is usually the father who counsels the boy in these matters; often he adds frightening details:

I was taught by my father, "Don't do anything to any woman. They have teeth in there. They bite off your penis. And some have diseases." I've heard many parents say the same thing to boys.

Once my father gave me something sweet. He said, "You like this. You like to eat it; it tastes good. You like to live and be well. Then keep away from girls and women. Don't have anything to do with them. They have teeth and will bite off your penis."

Finally I asked some older boys about this. They told me, "No, the old people just tell that to you to scare you. There isn't anything to it. When you get a good thing, don't let it go. If you live long enough, you're going to do it anyway, so you're just going to be the loser if you let a good chance pass."

THE GIRL'S PUBERTY RITE

The scene and the actors—The girl should come to her first menses and her puberty rite a virgin. The proper performance of the ceremony is supposed to grant long life to the singer as well as to the girl, and it is dangerous for a practitioner to sing for a girl who has been "spoiled," for his life will thereby be shortened. When a girl who is about to pass through the ceremony is discovered to be unchaste, she is fortunate if she is not cast off to fend for herself.

First menstruation is an important transition point in the girl's life. Before this physiological event and her puberty rite, she is called a girl; afterward the term "woman" is applied to her. Before the rite she is not eligible for marriage; afterward she is considered of marriageable age.

The rite itself has become the focal point for a complex of events—social, economic, and ritual. The term for this interwoven pattern of activities is simply "a ceremony has been set up." Of a girl who is nearing maturity, it is said, "She is one through whom the people are going to have a good time" (i.e., a ceremony and a social occasion). If a girl who is about to enter womanhood falls sick and the shaman who is hired to cure her finds evidence of witchcraft, it is attributed to the jealousy of some evil person. Additionally, it is considered an affront "out of meanness" against all the people. Should the identity of the evildoer be discovered, the ire of the entire community is directed against him.

Normally, every girl is the center of such a rite. "A girl who does not go through this ceremony is not discriminated against, but it is thought that she will not be healthy and will not live long." Only a girl who is "poor in relatives" passes through this phase of her life-journey without the proper ceremonial help and the accompanying popular recognition.

Preparations for the rite begin as much as a year or more before the first menses:

They can go out and get deer [in preparation for the rite] at any time, and they can have the feast at any time of the year. They store things away for it. They notice that their girl is getting to be a young woman, and so they begin to get things ready for the ceremony. They get their in-laws to help at this time.

These preparations tax the resources of any one family. Therefore, because of the pleasurable public aspects of the rite, individuals outside the relationship group may lend aid, and its approach is a signal for exceptional generosity in many matters.

> The man who's with you [on the hunt] is ruling you. He tells you what he
> wants and takes it. But many times it happens this way: if you were out with a
> thoughtful man and you had a daughter who was going to have a feast next
> summer, this man you're hunting with might say, "Your daughter is going to
> have a feast, and you haven't enough buckskin. You keep all the hides." He
> would do that because maybe that might be your last chance to get buckskin.

Buckskin is needed for the ornamented dress which the girl
will wear during the rite. At least five skins are required: two
for the upper garment, two for the skirt, and one for the high
moccasins. This clothing follows the ordinary dress in cut, but
only choice materials are used, and the garments are decorated
with special designs. The girl's mother, her grandmother, or
some other close female relative may work on this clothing; but,
if no one in the family has the requisite skill, an outsider may be
hired. The maker proceeds carefully and according to prescribed
rules. Doeskins or buckskins may be used, but the tail suspended from the jacket must be that of a black-tailed doe. For the
upper garment the skin side faces outward; for the skirt the flesh
side is out.

The garments are decorated with designs symbolic of the
forces which will be supplicated on behalf of the girl. The morning star and the crescent moon may be represented, as may a
stepped design symbolizing the dwelling. Circles indicate the
sun, and fringes streaming from their centers, the sunbeams.
Connected arcs stand for the rainbow. Before the dress is finished all parts have to be colored yellow, the hue of pollen. Yellow ocher may be rubbed on, or the buckskin may be dyed in a
liquid prepared from algerita roots.

The dress must be blessed as well as beautifully finished:

> While it is being made they have someone sing for it. J. [a man] used to do it.
> But this singer is usually an old woman. She sometimes sings over it during two
> months. The family has to give her a great deal for these services. Sometimes
> the woman who makes it ties amulets on and sings for every string.

During the ceremony the girl is constantly attended and advised by an older woman. Because this woman punctuates certain moments of the rite with a distinctive, high-pitched cry, one name for her is "she who makes the sound." The first use of this cry of applause is attributed to White Painted Woman when her son returned to her after vanquishing the monsters. The helper is also known as "she who trots them off," a reference to the ceremonial run on which she sends the girl. For the sake of convenience she will be called "the attendant" in these pages.

The role which the attendant plays in the girl's puberty rite amounts to a separate ceremony which fits, like part of a mosaic, into the ritual whole. These women, when they become too old to carry on their duties further, teach their lore to others and thus perpetuate the office.

Unlike the rites of shamans, the ceremony of the attendant is knowledge which was granted humankind by the supernaturals in the beginning. No personal experience is at its root, and it is simply learned by one woman from another. Once it is learned, it is, however, an individual possession. The woman must be personally approached and asked to lend her help, and she may even refuse to participate. She must always be rewarded if she does perform the function.

The place of the attendant, then, is somewhere between the purely individualistic shamanism which predominates in the religious life and true priestcraft. Even here a suggestion of the purely shamanistic premise persists, for women who "know" a ceremony from the moon or who have had a supernatural experience with White Painted Woman are thought to carry on this ceremony with best results. Although exceptions are reported, the attendant is most often a woman of advanced years, in keeping with the custom of having elderly practitioners carry out ceremonies for younger people.

Within reach of any large encampment are women who have the right to act as the girl's attendant. "The choice of the woman who attends the girl is up to the parents. They can choose any woman they want." The understanding with the attendant is reached well in advance:

When they are just beginning to talk about the ceremony, the girl goes to the woman who is going to take care of her. She brings an eagle feather to this woman. The girl holds the butt end and motions four times with the tip end of the feather toward the woman. The woman takes it the fourth time. Then the woman will take care of the girl. She will rub her and push her out to run.

Right from this time the girl calls that woman "mother," even though she is no relative, and this woman calls the girl "my daughter." And they give each other presents throughout life.

The most conspicuous ritualist of the ceremony is one who will be called "the singer" because it is his primary task to superintend the erection of the sacred shelter in which the songs of the rite are chanted and to sing the songs.

The role of the singer also hovers on the border line between shamanism and priestcraft. He does not depend on a personal supernatural encounter for obtaining his songs, nor does he believe that he can intercede for the benefit of the girl through impromptu appeals to supernatural forces with which he is in special rapport:

I became a singer just through experience. I was interested. Every chance I got I sat inside the tepee and sang the songs. I went to the ceremony every time and learned the songs. I connected myself with this ceremony over forty years ago and learned it from the ground up. I approached one of the men who conducted the ceremony and asked for help. The one who is learning to be a singer gets instruction right at the ceremony. When he has enough experience, he conducts it himself. It is very simple. The prayers don't take long to learn. In the course of two or three ceremonies, even, the songs can be learned. I gave no payment to the one who instructed me.

The fact that no payment passed between this man and the one who taught him the songs is convincing proof that the songs are not a personal shamanistic possession but are conceived of as the sacred property of the people as a whole. A shaman seldom parts with his ceremony unless appropriate payment is made both to him and to the supernatural source involved.

In the selection of the singer the greatest forethought is exercised:

Well, suppose you were an Indian here and you had a granddaughter who was growing up. You would come around and say that you wanted your granddaughter to be White Painted Woman. You know me very well, and you say to me, "There are three or four men who know how to sing for this ceremony. Just between you and me which one of these men do you think should sing for my granddaughter? Which one should I make my friend?"

And right there you want to be very careful. If you choose one of these men, you are brother to him all your life, even if you are not related to him. You call him friend, but you think just as much of him as you do of your brother. He thinks of your children as his children. After the ceremony is over, you give each other some valuable things—saddles, horses, anything that is worth something. When a man is poor, he gives what he can; it doesn't matter. They do that as long as they live. They might come out equal in giving things to each other.

Then I think about it and say, "You take B. for your granddaughter."

If you choose him, he will be there to see that everything is done right and he will be in there to bless your granddaughter in his way. He blesses all the people when they are putting pollen on the girl. Right in that tepee he asks for good in life for your granddaughter, for all good things, for long life. That's what the ceremony is for. It's up to the man that you choose to have the girl do the things that have always been done in this ceremony. He directs things.

In the minds of individuals the singers are graded according to considerations of friendship and faith. Some singers are thought by their admirers "to know the songs better and to know more about the ceremony." Others watch the fates of the girls for whom particular men have officiated.

I can't say which is the best. The girl my father sang for is still living and is healthy. Many girls die. The ceremony is held so that the girl will grow up and be strong, so you must watch for that. For the girl's puberty rite the Eastern Chiricahua and the Central Chiricahua singers sometimes teach different things. Whatever the singer in charge tells you to do, you must obey. You must follow his directions.

The singer is a free agent as far as obligation to participate in any specific ceremony is concerned:

S.'s mother-in-law was one of the feast-givers. She was talking about the preparations they were making. Just at this time W. [a singer] came up. She spoke to him, asking him to sing for her girl. She called him "brother" and pleaded with him. She said, "I am old and crippled and had to wait to see you. I had no way to get to see you before."

W. just sat there for a long time and said nothing. Then he said, "It looks as if you were waiting for me to come around so it would be easy for you to ask me." He acted as though he wasn't going to do it.

The singer takes his task seriously: "I was singing for C. I took care of her. All my thoughts and efforts were for that girl during the ceremony."

The girl feels good toward the man who sings for her too. She gives him presents now and then. She has to give the man a horse and saddle at the end of the ceremony. Usually he gets a good buckskin and blankets too. The father of one of the girls who recently went through her ceremony had only one good horse, but he had to give it to the singer. It's that gray one that B. [the singer] rides now. He had to do it according to the Indian way.

For the girl, her relatives, and a few serious-minded individuals the ceremonial aspects of the occasion will be of most significance. But for most of the guests the feasting, the social dancing, and the performance of the masked dancers will be the greatest attractions.

The masked dancers are men dressed and decorated to represent mountain-dwelling supernaturals. The dancers themselves possess no power and no ceremony. But the one who "makes" them, who fashions the masks they wear and paints or directs the painting of their bodies, is a shaman who controls a most important ceremony. The primary purpose of the masked-dancer rite when it is not associated with the celebration for the adolescent girl is to ward off epidemic and evil or to cure illness that has been contracted. When it is so used, its performance is a most serious matter. However, these same masked dancers have become one of the standard sources of entertainment of the girl's puberty rite. Early each evening they appear, and, while they may bless the camp initially, drive away evil, or even perform some cures privately on request, their main function is to engage in several spectacular dances for the noisy approval of the onlookers.

The girl's relatives must secure the co-operation of a masked-dancer shaman:

A month or more before the ceremony the ones who are giving the feast start thinking about the man they are going to get to paint the masked dancers. They say, "Let's ask the old man."

One of them goes to the old man and says, "I'm giving a feast and want you to work for us. I don't want you to refuse." If the old man promises, it is all settled. The relatives of the girl will begin talking to him, perhaps it will be her uncles or aunts.

I've seen it done this way, too. Suppose there are a lot of camps together. A man whose girl is going to have her ceremony would come out and say, "All you people, listen! I'm going to give a feast for all you people. I need your help. I want all you men who know the ceremony of the masked dancers and you men who know songs to help. I'm paying for your good time. I'm having plenty to eat for all of you. I'm a poor man, but still I'm doing this. Let's all help and have a good time."

Then anyone who knew the ceremony of the masked dancers and felt like it could paint dancers for him. Afterward he might ask more definitely to be sure he'd have somebody. He would go to a man and say, "You know the ceremony of the masked dancers; you help me this time."

If no one comes up to my father to ask him to do it, he won't do it. I have seen him just let it go. He can see more at the feast grounds, have his meals like anyone else, and have a better time than he can spending his time at his camp painting dancers. I think that many times it looks as though the old man doesn't want to do it. But these feast-makers ask in such a way that he can't refuse. Sometimes he goes away, and when he comes back there is someone waiting for him, begging him to help.

When they asked him to do it, my father used to complain. He said, "Those people ask me to paint masked dancers. But they don't help me out with the equipment. They don't know how much work it is doing this for four days. It's tiring. They don't help as they should." Then the people who were giving the feast had to scurry around and get equipment if my father was short of things. They sometimes had to ask other people for buckskin and things that were needed.

There was S. He said to my father, "I want you to help me out; paint those masked dancers for me." His girl was going to be White Painted Woman [that is, was going to have the puberty rite performed for her]. Then my father said, "All right, but you must do your part. You must feed my dancers. It is hard work. You must feed them in the morning, at noon, and at night." S. said he would do it.

So my father went out. He tried to get the right men to dance for him. He came to me. I didn't want to do it. He asked another man, a good dancer, and he said "No" this time. Then the feast people had to help out. My father went back to them and said, "I'm willing to help, but I can't get enough good dancers." He referred the whole thing back to them.

Then they came to me and pleaded with me. "We'll give you a whole side of the ribs and your wife can get all the food she wants down at the place where we are cooking for the crowd." And they offered me something else valuable, too.

Some of them come up in a pitiful way and say, "I'm a poor fellow. This feast is for everybody. You can dance better than anyone else." So you have to sympathize with them sometimes. If they just have to have you and it looks as though you are not going to do it, they call you "brother" even though you're no relation to them. They say, "Don't refuse!"

The relatives have been watching those painters of masked dancers. They notice who makes good designs and turns out the best dancers. The dancing is just to make the celebration lively though. The masked dancers do not affect the health of the girl by their dancing.

The singer will need eagle feathers, a deer- or elk-hoof rattle, and a supply of pollen, white clay, red ocher, and specular iron ore. Required for the ceremony also are a basket tray, usually made from the black outer covering of the unicorn plant; skins on which the girl will kneel or lie during certain parts of the ceremony; and other ritual objects. If the singer or attendant does not have these at hand, the girl's parents must make or procure them.

The origin of the rite.—White Painted Woman is usually credited with the establishment of the puberty rite. Often associated with her in this undertaking is her son.

It was not until Child of the Water was rid of all the monsters and evil things, until there were many people and the different tribes began to be seen, that the big tepee [girl's puberty rite] was known.

There was a woman who had a daughter who was almost grown. It was time for her to have her first flow. Then Child of the Water and White Painted Woman showed them what to do; this good time was given to the people.

They gave a little feast this first day when she menstruated. Then, after this first day, the relatives of this girl went out and hunted and got everything together so that they could give a big feast. They did this in the fall when there was plenty of fruit and many good things of all kinds. They got a man to sing for her in the tepee. The best masked dancers were got ready. They made them, not in camp, but way off in the mountains and led them in. The spruce trees were cut down for the tepee.

Then, when all was ready, they let many know, and they came from far places. All were invited. The celebration was held for four days. The people had a good time at the dancing. First came the masked dancers. Child of the Water and White Painted Woman gave the people the round dance to enjoy, but this was not to begin until after the performance of the masked dancers was over. After that came the partner dances.

The last two nights the masked dancers remained on the grounds until all the dancing was over. Even the masked dancers took part in the social dancing with their masks pulled to the top of their heads. And the clown was there. The clown, too, danced with women who wished to dance with him. He carried his headdress.

Important incidents of the rite and their respective order are foreshadowed in this narrative. In another account major honors for the establishment of this ritual practice go to White Painted Woman:

White Painted Woman said, "From here on we will have the girl's puberty rite. When the girls first menstruate, you shall have a feast. There shall be songs for these girls. During this feast the masked dancers shall dance in front. After that there shall be round dancing and face-to-face dancing."

Other information, however, emphasizes the importance of the culture hero for this ceremony. "They do this ceremony according to the way Child of the Water directed them," said one spokesman; and another asserted that the culture hero "is the founder of this whole thing."

The pubescent girl herself is identified with White Painted Woman. During the four days and nights of the rite and for four days thereafter the girl must be addressed and referred to only as White Painted Woman. Her dress and decoration are meant to duplicate the costume which the benefactress of the tribe wore during her stay on earth. The very name, White Painted Woman, is symbolic of the body paint with which its first bearer was designed. At one point in the ritual the initiate is painted with white clay so that the promise of her name may be actualized. Throughout the songs and the prayers the girl is likened to her divine namesake; the structure that has been erected is described as "the home of White Painted Woman"; and, as an informant has put it, "the young girl is the image of the real one." This may explain the control over the weather and the curative functions of the adolescent at this period.

The "little" rite.—The physiological fact of first menstruation is cause for great rejoicing on the part of the family of the girl and is so important that reference is made to it by a different term from the one which means "regular monthly flow." Even though all is not in readiness for the prolonged ritual and celebration, the family and close neighbors gather for a feast and token ceremony, to be followed at a later date by the complete round of ritual.

They had a little ceremony for E. It was held at her parents' place. Quite a few people came down. There was a feast and social dancing. The girl was called White Painted Woman for the day of the little ceremony. The ceremony for the girl, who is about fourteen years old, came about noon. She was dressed in an uncolored buckskin costume without much design on it. I don't think it is finished yet. Mrs. S. acted as "she who trots them off" [the attendant] for her. W. sang.

About noon Mrs. S. came out, bringing a buckskin. A little later the girl came out. She came directly to the buckskin, and Mrs. S. put her down and rubbed her. Then Mrs. S. made four tracks with pollen on the buckskin. W. sang and led her through the four steps, one song for each step. Then the basket with the bag of pollen and an eagle feather in it was put to the east. She ran around it clockwise and returned to her place. She did this four times. Each time the basket was brought nearer. As she came in the last time, tobacco, fruits, and other presents were thrown into the air just as soon as she got back on the buckskin.

Then she marked W. with pollen, marked him across the nose. He marked her the same way. Next she marked the women and children and they marked her. She marked them across the bridge of the nose also. Then the men came. She marked them on the side of the face. After that she picked up the buckskin and shook it to the directions, beginning with the east. Then more presents were given out.

The procedure just described is a much-reduced version of the full rite. The order of events is altered to compress the activities of many days into the hours of one morning, but the incidents enumerated offer a good inventory of the significant elements.

Final preparation and the beginning of the rite.—The ceremony is usually held outside the permanent encampments at a level spot in a clearing selected by the family sponsoring the event. Some days before the exercises are to start (often four days for ceremonial emphasis) the girl's family repairs to the grounds to get everything in readiness.

One of the first acts is to erect the "cook shack," a long, rectangular, leafy shelter to the south of the place where the principal ceremonial structure will stand.

Meanwhile news of the approaching ritual has spread. Members of the local group to which the girl's family belongs and visitors from near-by local groups of the same band gather. If the ceremony is well advertised and the site is near the dividing-line between bands, persons from these neighboring bands may attend. This is a ceremony at which all members of the tribe feel welcome:

All the Indians enjoy the feast—poor and rich, the able-bodied and the lame and blind. This feast has been handed down for many, many years. . . . . All the singing is supposed to work out the future life for the girl in order . . . . that she have long life. The songs bring good luck. The ceremony works good luck for everyone that takes part in it and good luck for the old people during the time of the ceremony, also good luck for the spectators. They sing and pray for all.

The visitors build temporary camps to the south, west, and north of the space reserved for the ceremonial tepee. A long lane to the east must be left unobstructed.

At the beginning of the ceremony, custody of the girl will pass into the hands of the attendant and the singer. But before this the girl is reminded by her parents of the seriousness of her role and is advised to be obedient and cheerful. However, these ideals are not always attained.

> Some of the girls are bashful. They have a time with them! They had a time with them in the old days too; I've heard stories about it. Some girls had to be whipped before they'd go through with it. Some of them got scolded before everyone. . . . . They talk to her, tell her to be good, but the girl gets mean sometimes.

The exact manner of deciding when the ceremony shall begin is subject to some variation. According to one account, the proper starting-point should fall four days after the onset of menstruation. Most informants agree that the rite may begin "when everything is ready." Some see a tendency for the group in charge to set the time for fall, "when food is plentiful," although theoretically the ceremony may occur any time of the year.

Before sunrise of the first day the girl washes her hair in yucca-root suds. Then she presents herself before the attendant, either at a special shelter erected for her care or at the home of the older woman.

> The attendant first puts pollen on the girl's head and face and across the bridge of her nose before anything starts the first morning. Then the woman prays over her that she may advance to good womanhood. From then on her womanhood begins. No man is allowed to go in there at this time.
>
> Then the woman arranges the girl's hair and dresses her, beginning with the right moccasin, then the left, and continuing up to the head. She ties two eagle feathers at the back of the girl's head. The girl always faces the sunrise while this is being done. The woman prays for the girl while she is dressing her, and some even sing if they have songs and the girl wants them sung. The men do not say much about this dressing. This is the woman's part, and men are not supposed to say much about it. When the girl is all dressed, it is all right for a man to see her. After the dressing you have to call the girl "White Painted Woman."
>
> The girl must not eat anything up to now. Then, the first day, when the girl

is dressed but before she has eaten anything, the woman gives her yucca fruit with a cross of pollen on it. She first holds it to the directions, motions three times toward the girl with it, and puts it in her mouth the fourth time. This is to give her a good appetite; if she is fed with Indian fruits and piñon nuts and all the good things at this time, the girl will have a good appetite throughout life.

The attendant now advises the girl:

She tells her how to drink water through the tube [of carrizo, suspended from the fringe of the dress on the right side], how to scratch herself with the stick [from a fruit- or nut-bearing tree; the scratcher hangs on the left side of the dress]. She tells the girl that she must not scratch herself with her nails, because, if she does, it will leave scars, and that she must not touch water with her lips but must use the tube for eight days or it will rain.

She tells the girl not to eat too much, because she must stay in the tepee most of the time, and she shouldn't go out in the brush much.

She tells the girl that she mustn't go around except where she is told she can go, that she should stay in the tepee most of the time for the four days of the ceremony and then for four days afterward, until she takes these clothes off.

The woman tells the girl not to talk much during this time and not to laugh, because her face will be old and wrinkled before her time if she does. And she tells the girl that for the ceremony and for four days after it she should not wash. She has pollen on, and if she should put her hand in water and wash it off, it would rain like anything. She tells the girl that if it rains and she goes out in it, that will make it rain harder. If the girl gets wet, it will be rainy and spoil the good time of the people. She must not even go to a spring or look up at the sky, for the rain clouds would gather if she did.[1]

And these old women talk to the girl about cooking and women's work too. They tell her to think what it means and to believe what the singer tells her, for, if she does not believe, it will not do her any good. And the girl is told to mind and not to make fun of anyone. She is told that she must not get angry or curse anyone till the ceremony is all over for her, till the eight days are over. For the Chiricahua believe that the disposition a girl shows at the time of the ceremony will be hers all through life. If she gets angry, she is going to be mean the rest of her life. They say, too, that if a girl doesn't mind at this time, bad weather comes. If she is pleasant and goes through the ceremony well, she will always be that way.

And it seems to me that it turns out this way. There's my wife. She went through the ceremony very well, obeyed, and was good. You take C.; she was mean and balky when she was going around that basket. Today she's very mean. My wife went through first, a year or so ahead of C. Then C. went

---

[1] One informant stated that the singer may not wash his hair during the rite, presumably to prevent rainfall.

through and wouldn't do anything. And now she's cross, has a bad mouth and a high temper. But she's a good-looking woman all right!

And if the girls are not of good disposition and balk, it harms not only themselves but causes it to rain and spoils the good time of all the people. That's what happened at the last ceremony, and that's why part of the dancing was spoiled. So we try to keep the girls in good humor and coax them.

After eating and listening to the old woman, the girl is ready and comes out. From here on all the people see what happens.

In spite of general similarities, the rituals of various attendants differ in detail. The prayers show minor divergences. One attendant feeds the girl throughout the four days of the rite; another asks the singer to do this. Some attendants sing for the girl, though most of them only pray. One attendant washes the girl's hair the first morning instead of having the initiate do it.

The erection of the ceremonial structure.—While the attendant is dressing the girl, the singer directs the building of the tepee-shaped ceremonial structure. Male relatives of the adolescent bring to the grounds four freshly cut young spruce trees, thirty to thirty-five feet long, from which all but the topmost boughs have been trimmed, and some oak boughs and yucca leaves.

At sunrise the singer requests the girl's male relatives and some of the visitors to arrange and erect the main poles. The trees are laid on the ground in clockwise order with butts equidistant from a central point and tips extending outward. The first to be arranged is the east pole. A second pole is laid with tip pointing to the south, a third lies to the west, and a fourth to the north. At the base of each pole a hole is dug. The singer sprinkles pollen on the poles from butt to tip. Then near the leafy tip of each, in clockwise order, he ties a spray of sage and some snakeweed. To the east pole a bunch of grama grass may also be tied, and at its top two eagle feathers are so attached that they will blow freely. This is to guarantee that "nothing is to happen while the tepee is up, that no poles shall fall." To this same pole a long rawhide rope is affixed.

After a prayer has been said, knots of men lift the poles, sliding the butt ends into the holes prepared for them. As the poles

PLATE III

ERECTING THE CEREMONIAL STRUCTURE

are held erect, an assistant shakes an animal-hoof rattle,[2] and the singer begins his first chant. These opening songs are known as "dwelling songs." The first song "is about all the four poles. It is about the black horse, the stallion, the four horses, because in this ceremony a horse is given on the last day." Much of the vocalization is meaningless refrain, for the substance of ritual songs and prayers is largely implicit. But the prayer portion can be translated:

> Killer of Enemies[3] and White Painted Woman have made them so,
> They have made the poles of the dwelling so,
> For long life stands the blue stallion.

> Here Killer of Enemies and White Painted Woman have made them so,
> They have made the poles of the dwelling so,
> For long life stands the yellow stallion.

> Here Killer of Enemies and White Painted Woman have made them so,
> They have made the poles of the dwelling so,
> For long life stands the black stallion.

> Here Killer of Enemies and White Painted Woman have made them so,
> They have made the poles of the dwelling so,
> For long life stands the white stallion.

From the structure to the south, where she is caring for her charge, the attendant cries out in reverent applause when the names of the supernaturals are mentioned. Throughout the rite, whenever reference is made in the songs to Killer of Enemies,

[2] From one informant, a Southern Chiricahua man, comes an assertion that a gourd rattle may be used in the girl's puberty rite in substitution for an animal-hoof rattle. He said: "A gourd rattle as well as the deer-hoof rattle can be used when the ceremonial tepee is being put up. This is the only time it is used; just the tepee singer has it. There are four small holes on each side of it. That is what makes the sound perfect. It has no design." All other informants state that only the animal-hoof rattle, made of four or more hoofs, usually tied to a length of wood, is used.

[3] For most of the Apache people of the Southwest, Killer of Enemies is the culture hero, and Child of the Water is a subordinate brother or companion. The Chiricahua have reversed the positions of these two; indeed, some Chiricahua have eliminated Killer of Enemies altogether and claim that the name is a synonym for Child of the Water. The older heritage persists, however, in the songs of the girl's puberty rite, which mention only Killer of Enemies. The Chiricahua simply accept these references as concerned with Child of the Water.

White Painted Woman, Sun, or turquoise, she will utter this call.[4]

During a second "dwelling song" the poles are lowered until their tips meet:

> The home of the long-life dwelling ceremony
> Is the home of White Painted Woman,
> Of long life the home of White Painted Woman is made,
> For Killer of Enemies has made it so,
> Killer of Enemies has made it so.

Quickly, when the tops of the four poles meet, the rope hanging from the east pole is wound around the others, and the framework is secure. Now the women come from the community kitchen, bearing receptacles filled with mesquite beans, boiled meat, mescal, yucca fruit, and other food. They set these in an east-west line before the entrance, and, after pollen crosses have been sprinkled over the top of each by the singer, everyone gathers to eat. The conspicuous display of food is symbolic of plenty and of the favor of the supernaturals: "Child of the Water told the Apache to carry food into the ceremonial dwelling, to grab at it, play with it, and eat it. That's why we do it; it is his command."

After the meal the ceremonial structure is quickly finished. The central fire pit is dug to the accompaniment of more songs. The oak boughs are tied horizontally to the poles, but an opening is left to the east. Women bring to the entrance spruce needles for the floor, and these are arranged by the singer and his helpers. The ceremonial home of White Painted Woman is now ready.[5]

---

[4] While it is the primary responsibility of the attendant to call thus, other women may join her: "Women, when White Painted Woman, turquoise, or sacred things are mentioned, have the right to make that call. This is true of any ceremony, not just the puberty ceremony. Also they can give that cry when the masked dancers approach, when they just begin to trot in from the east and the jingle of their pendants is heard. Any mature woman can do it, but old women do it mostly. They do it because of the religious feeling they have toward the Mountain People."

[5] The Mescalero Apache, with whom the Chiricahua now share a reservation, use four main poles of spruce and eight others—twelve in all—for the ceremonial structure. They also build the tepee with a runway of eight smaller spruces, four on either side, stretching eastward from the doorway. The Mescalero and Chiri-

PLATE IV

United States National Museum

GIRL DRESSED FOR PUBERTY RITE

The conclusion of the events of the first day.—The attendant now comes forward, followed by the girl. Both are marked with pollen across the face and on top of the head. At the southeast of the structure the woman lays the skin of a four-year-old black-tailed deer. On this the girl kneels. Before her the attendant places a coiled basket tray, made of the unicorn plant, filled with bags of pollen and with ritual objects.

The attendant is the first to come before the girl. She offers pollen to the directions and then paints the girl with it, marking her from cheek to cheek across the bridge of the nose and along the part of the hair. The girl marks her in the same way. A line of persons forms to the south and files past the girl to paint her with pollen and to be painted in turn. "We motion to the directions and then put pollen on her face. She does it to us. If she is a good girl, we'll have good luck then." Mothers bring forward their children to be blessed, painting the girl for them but allowing them to receive pollen from her.

Definite curative powers are attributed to the girl:

Painting the girl and being painted by her are thought to cure sickness. Some years ago there was a girl who was deformed pretty badly. Her buttocks stuck out in back, and her chest forward. She went through the line with the others. Then the old woman, the girl's attendant, massaged her. A little while later she began to straighten up and finally got entirely well.

---

cahua act together now to hold the puberty rite. Most Chiricahua informants claim that their tribe used a four-pole tepee without runway. But a number of spokesmen have mentioned either the twelve-pole structure, the runway, or both, as aboriginal Chiricahua features.

In a tale told by an Eastern Chiricahua mention is made of a "big tepee" for which the "poles were of spruce and there was a runway of trees on either side."

Another Eastern Chiricahua said: "We used the tepee for the girl's puberty ceremony and had the same number of poles as are used here. I never saw one with four poles only among my people. There were four main poles."

A Southern Chiricahua claims the twelve-pole tepee for his people, but rejects the runway: "These Chiricahua never used the tepee except at the time of the girl's ceremony. Then they would put up four poles. Then they had eight more to make twelve, just as is done here at Mescalero. They didn't have the runway of small trees to the east. I never saw a Chiricahua have this before coming here."

Yet a four-pole ceremonial structure is specifically mentioned by other informants of these same bands. We may suspect, therefore, that there was a great deal of local variation among the Chiricahua in respect to these details.

When no more come forward, the attendant places the girl face downward on the buckskin with her head to the east and "molds" her, working from her head to her feet and from the right side to the left:

The girl is rubbed so that she will have a good disposition and be good. The old women who do it have that as special work. The woman attendant is praying as she does this. She is saying, "May this girl be good in disposition, good in morals. May she grow up, live long, and be a fine woman." The molding also makes the girl straight and supple.

The girls are massaged to give them good health and strength and to straighten out their lives and make them long. . . . .

The girl rises, and on the buckskin the attendant outlines four footprints in pollen. Through these the girl walks toward the east, right foot first, "so she will walk on a trail of pollen, so that her way will be fortunate and healthy." The pollen is from trees that bear fruit and nuts.

Next the basket tray, containing bags of pollen and ocher, a deer- or elk-hoof rattle, a bundle of grama grass, an eagle feather, and other ritual objects, is placed about thirty paces to the east. When all is ready the attendant "pushes her out to run," and the girl trots clockwise around the basket and back that "she may live long." As she runs, the attendant again utters the call.

Old men and young boys run after the girls when they go around the basket. They pray as they run. Sometimes the very old men do it. They pray to White Painted Woman. These old men ask for strength, for long life. The young ones ask for long life or anything good. Any way they want to pray is all right. I ran like that when I was a boy. I asked for long life and good health. The older people told me what to do and what to pray for. They say you get long winded when you do this.

At the end of the first run the basket is brought nearer the ceremonial structure. Three more times the girl runs, and before each run the basket is brought westward. When the girl reaches the buckskin after the last run, she picks it up and shakes it to each direction in clockwise order, beginning with the south, "to send to the directions all sickness and disease that might harm her."

During these events, women of the adolescent girl's family

have brought baskets of fruit and nuts to the rear of the hide upon which she has stood. They throw these presents upon the hide, and a scramble ensues. Thus the cycle which began when the pollen footprints were drawn has been completed symbolically; the fruits have followed the pollen and the season of growth. In the good-natured din and confusion the girl and her attendant retire. The girl has custody of the singer's rattle until evening. It is noon before this opening ritual is concluded, and more food is now distributed.

The afternoon is devoted to social activities—dancing in the open space to the east of the ceremonial structure, singing, racing, and visiting. Men gather at the hoop-and-pole ground, while the women play the stave game. The girl's parents move about among their guests, and grateful visitors seek them out to comment upon their hospitality and "to say they are thankful that this daughter has grown up to have the ceremony." "The feast-givers are shown respect, and all obey them. Nobody ever breaks this rule."

Ordinarily, the girl's ritual obligations are over until evening, but she may be requested to treat the very young during the day:

The Chiricahua believe that it is good luck for a child or a baby if a girl who is White Painted Woman lifts it up. At any time during the ceremony the girl can take a very young child, pick it up under the arms, and hold it to the directions. This is done to give the child long life and good luck.

She also helps the infirm:

If your arm is crooked, go to the girl at the time of the ceremony. She can work it and make it straight. She picks up children by the neck too. It is good for them. They tell me to let one of the girls work on me. [This man has a crippled arm.] I go there, but there are lots of people in there, and I back out every time.

In the late afternoon of the first day the adolescent girl or the singer, using a fire drill, lights a fire in the ceremonial structure. This fire is to be kept alive during the course of the ritual or, at least, during the nights. Sometime in the afternoon a great pile of firewood is stacked to the north side of the ceremonial structure. This will be used for the fire around which the masked dancers will perform.

The masked dancers.—As the sun starts to go down, the painting and the dressing of the masked dancers begin. The men who have agreed to dance make their way to a brush shelter erected quite a distance from the ceremonial grounds, for it would be dangerous to the people, and especially to the women and children, to have them "made" in the vicinity of the camps. Since the dancers are impersonating mountain-dwelling supernaturals, a place in the foothills surrounding the level dance ground is most likely to be chosen. There the masked-dancer shaman waits with dancing costumes and paints. The shaman rarely paints the dancers but directs his helpers and prays and sings, accompanying himself with a buckskin-covered pottery drum. Upon this he draws figures, such as that of the sun, in pollen "to keep his voice from becoming hoarse."

The shaman may have some difficulty in assembling a dance group, for the supernatural impersonator must obey irksome restrictions:

You shouldn't wash the paint off. It sweats off while you are dancing and when you put your shirt on. It is just clay and charcoal. Perhaps the second night there will be just a faint mark left from the paint of the night before. When the next paint goes on fresh, you can't tell that there was any paint on there before. If you do have to get some off, you rub it but do not wash it off, for if you wash, it will cause a big rain to come.

Mistakes during the dance are most dangerous:

Not many men want to dance; it can cause evil influence. They fear to get into this costume just as they fear a coyote. If the dancer makes a mistake and doesn't do things according to the ceremony, he will get sick. It is dangerous for one dancer to touch another who has been made by a different shaman. The power of one masked-dancer maker may be stronger than that of the other and cause some disaster to a dancer. It sometimes causes a spasm [paralysis] in the mouth, or trouble with the ear or eye, or a swollen face. Then the only way is to go through a ceremony and have the masked dancers blow the sickness away.

The dancer must be quite as particular about other points. If he should place the mask over his head without the proper ritual gestures, he is likely to go mad. He must show proper reverence as well:

One time I was dancing for D. Three of us were dancing—S., T., and I. It was S.'s first time. He was speaking in English, cursing while they were painting him. You know he is just like a mocking bird; he doesn't respect anything.

PLATE V

Museum of the American Indian, Heye Foundation

A MASKED DANCER

The old man said, "Look here, that kind of talk doesn't go here! You men should be praying in your hearts. Pray for all the good things. Be saying, 'Let me be a reliable masked dancer. Let me be reliable in life.' That's what you should be doing while you are in this brush hut."

Just as soon as the old man stopped talking, there S. was again, cursing. Well, we went out, the three of us. We came toward the fire. The last minute S. was putting on the mask. He couldn't get it on. He said, "I can't get this damn thing on! How does this damn thing work?" I told him, talking softly, "Don't talk that way." You can't talk in a loud voice when you are in the mask. "Have some manners!"

The old man heard and said, "Hey, what are you doing? Now if anything happens to you, you'll say you are witched, but I warned you." S. said, "Oh, I always forget."

We went out to the fire. The first time we approached the fire, S. bumped into me. I heard him laughing. Every time we went around and started toward the fire he bumped into me. I said softly, "Keep your distance and be careful." I was leader. He was right behind me.

All of a sudden I noticed S. was putting his hands to his head. He just took his sticks and pressed them to his head. Then I saw him break out of line and run away from the fire. He ran right to his camp, pulling off his mask. His camp was just a little way from the grounds. They found him there crying and yelling and rolling around.

Pretty soon they sent a message to D. "That man who danced for you is pretty sick," they told him. The next time we came out from the fire, D. came to us. "We'll have to go right over and see that boy," he said. So we went over. S. was just like out of his head. He was rolling around, trying to stand on his head. They couldn't hold him down.

D. told me to work on him, because I was the leader. T. came behind me in the dancing, but I was the only one that touched S. The old man was singing his songs and praying while I was working on S. First I came toward him from the east. The fourth time I crossed my sticks over his head. Then I grabbed his head in both hands and shook it, shook it hard. You can't be gentle with them. Besides I was angry at missing the dancing over there at the grounds all because of his foolish talk. He yelled, but I pulled him around good. I did this from the south, west, and north too. Each time I shook him we made the masked-dancer call, and then I blew his sickness away to the four directions, beginning with the east.

After I finished, D. said to him, "Now you're all right; nothing is the matter with you. Get up, no matter how you feel, and follow these men." So S. followed us, and we went around once and then went toward the east.

"All right," said D., "you fellows go back and dance. He will be better now. He will be over there at the feast pretty soon."

So we went back. While we were dancing I watched for S. I looked around every once in a while to see if he was there. Pretty soon I saw him there, laughing and clapping his hands, having a good time. It was just about an hour after we had worked on him. I don't know what made that fellow well. I didn't do it. I just followed D.'s directions. It wasn't I but it was D.'s power that did it. The old man knew what was wrong with S. and how to cure him.

As this story indicates, whenever the dancer gets into difficulty because of his participation, it is to the masked-dancer maker that he must turn. Said one of these shamans, "If a dancer who is working for me gets a pain in his foot, I put a feather on his foot, and it goes away."

The dancer must observe suitable modesty and remember that he is but an instrument of the rite and not its owner:

One man got into trouble from this. He danced three or four times. Then he made his own outfit and carried it on, though he had no right to the ceremony. Soon his baby got sick, and no one could cure her. When she died she made the masked-dancer cry and held her hands outward.

When I asked a man who had acted as a masked dancer to sketch the designs which had been put upon him, he replied that he was not sure he could do this. Later he refused entirely, saying, "I asked T. if I could draw his masked dancers, and he said, 'You'd better leave those Mountain Spirits alone,' so I can't do it."

The subordinate role of the masked dancer is emphasized in another statement:

If I learned that song without getting the whole ceremony, without having the whole thing turned over to me, if I didn't get it in a spiritual way, it wouldn't do me good. If I painted a man, I might do it in this same way, but it would just make both of us sick. I can pound on the hide and sing the refrain with the chorus, but I shouldn't sing the words of the prayer in the [masked-dancer] song if it isn't mine. The dancer is just in there working for the one who knows the ceremony. I can't tell, just because I danced for him, whether R.'s masked-dancer ceremony is good. He has a good outfit all right.

A man must have natural aptitude to become a successful dancer:

According to my understanding about being a masked dancer, it comes like anything else. After you do it once the feeling for it comes to you if you are the right kind for it. I did exactly as I was told, and right from the first time I was almost as good as the best dancer. I ran around that fire all night long. Right from the beginning I was getting better every night. And I was dancing with old-timers. People hardly knew the difference between me and those other dancers.

On the other hand, you take N. over there. He's a well-formed man and should be a good dancer, but he has no natural inclination to be a masked dancer. You have to be in special physical condition to do this dance, like in prize-fighting.

Despite the dangers there are many factors which induce men to become masked dancers and insure their continued enthusiasm for the art:

If you have never taken the part of the masked dancer, the first time you put on the mask you feel awkward. I must have been twenty-five years old the first time. They were going to have my brother dance. They were starting to mark him with paint. I was riding a horse and came up to them. Someone said, "Here's a better one; he's older." My brother put on his clothes. I didn't want to dance, but they begged me to, so I did. My father was painting four. He is supposed to make four. Sometimes he only gets two or three men; but he won't do it with one.

My father said, "My son, I want to tell you some things before you start, for this is your first time. Putting this mask on and getting everything on tight is going to feel awkward. When you are led out to the fire by the leader, there is going to be a big crowd of people, but they don't know who you are. Don't be bashful. This is your first time, and the way you dance now is going to influence all the dancing you ever do. If you act bashful when you start to dance, that habit is going to stay with you. If the other dancers are lively and are trotting around there like wild steers and you drag and aren't lively, you'll always dance like that. The leader is the one who is the best dancer. Watch your leader, Y. Watch how he holds his hand up and do as he does. Don't watch the last man." And my father said, "You must dance four nights the first time you are in this work."

Y. talked to me before we went out. He said, "Take short steps. Don't spread your legs. Don't have your head down. Look at your sticks. Keep the horns of your headdress in line."

When you get over there and start to dance, you must be singing for yourself, humming a little. Y. told me to do it, to learn this way. You don't have to do it later when you know how. I asked my father if this was the way to learn to be a good dancer, and he said "Yes." No one can hear you in all that noise. I learned many songs this way.

I danced for my father for several years, for T., for D., and for M. All these people do it about the same but have different designs. They do the way my father does. They sit there singing and praying while the dancers are painted.

They pay the very best dancers. They might send for a dancer who was thirty miles away. Then they would have to pay him. I was sometimes paid.

Sometimes I'd want to dance all right, but I would hesitate a little so that they'd pay me. I'd say, "Oh, it's too much work, too hard." P. paid me when his daughter went through the girl's ceremony. I said I didn't want to do it.

They came for me several times. Finally P. came. He said, "My friend, I want you to do it. Dance, and the first time the masked dancers come to the fire, I'm going to show you what I will give you." So we were coming to the fire. I was the leading dancer. P. came to us. He put up his hand and gave me a big present.

The virtuoso among dancers is sometimes particular and demanding concerning the conditions under which he will lend his services:

When I was a leading dancer, I wanted a long stick so that I wouldn't have to bend to place it on the ground. That's the teaching I got from my father and from the leading dancer. When I wanted to make it short, I'd grab it in the middle. So if they gave me a short stick, I'd throw it to another dancer, and they'd make a long one for me. Each dancer always carries two sticks.

I always wanted a new mask. During the winter I might notice that another had used, in a curing ceremony, the mask I usually wore. Then in the spring or summer they would want me to dance. I would say, "I want a new mask. I'm not going to have someone else in my mask. They sweat in there, and it's dangerous and gives diseases."

The experienced dancer takes delight in mastery over the minute details of his calling:

Then my father would make me a new mask. He would put the buckskin over my head. "Where are your eyes?" he would ask. I would tell him to make the holes, not at my eyes, but over my eyebrows. He would mark it and make the holes there. Y. told me it should be done this way because the buckskin stretches. Then, when the buckskin is pulled down, it will be just right.

"How do you know the holes should be high?" my father asked. "You told me to follow Y. and that's what he told me."

"That's good," said the old man. "Some dancers tell me to put the holes just at their eyes. Then they go digging at the holes with their sticks, trying to make them bigger, when they are going around the fire."

Within his own sphere the masked dancer is relatively independent:

Sometimes there are sixteen masked dancers at the feast grounds. The best men don't want to dance out there where it's crowded. They can't dance well then. You can come in and dance and go out about four times and then you can stop if you want to. You don't have to ask the shaman; you just go over to the place where you were painted and leave the equipment there. Sometimes the old man will ask when he sees you the next day, "Why did you stop so soon last night?" You just make some excuse. When you quit, you come back and watch the dances.

When you're out there in the woods resting between dances, the people call for the dancers. You don't have to pay any attention. You come back when you want to. While you are out there, you can take up the mask and smoke cigarettes. It's all right. You are just entertaining the people. You don't have to keep away from women during the four nights of the dancing either.

There is great rivalry for the leadership of the masked-dancer groups:

I was dancing for T. once. E. was going to lead. I was going to be second in line. While we were being painted, E. said, "Watch me. I'm the leader, and the leader is supposed to be the best dancer." I just laughed.

They finished painting us, and T. said, "All right, go ahead." It was dusk by this time. We were late, for the fellows had been late in getting there. We could see the big fire over at the feast grounds. So E. started off. His mask was down over his face. He must have been blinded by the fire, for before you know it he went off the bank and into an arroyo! You could hear him go down, and then he was down there grunting. I had thought he was going wrong. I had the front of my mask pulled up. I knew how to wear it and could pull it up and still have it stay on.

I just laughed and laughed when he went down. I said, "Hey, leader, I can't follow you there." T. went down and got him. He was skinned and the horns of his headdress were broken. T. said, "You fellows go on and dance," and so we went on.

The next day I saw him standing there holding one arm. The news got around, and the people were laughing and calling, "A masked dancer fell in the arroyo! A masked dancer fell in the arroyo!"

Accomplished dancers, in spite of the strenuous nature of the task, are reluctant to withdraw even when they grow old. "E. still dances. They have to pull his skin smooth to put the paint on. It is the same with H.; they have to stretch his skin. But they don't want to give it up."

If a dancer wishes to become a ceremonialist of this rite, his experience as an impersonator "makes it easier for him to learn." One prominent masked-dancer shaman, describing how readily he had mastered the details of his calling, said: "I learned so fast because I had been a dancer right along."

While the masked dancers just described are being painted, another type of impersonator, the clown ("Gray One," "Long Nose," or "White Painted"), is being prepared also:

He wears a mask of scraped rawhide. Sometimes they make it with a big nose or big ears. He wears only moccasins and a gee string. The rest of his body is bare and covered with white paint. They say that it is good to be a clown before you dance as a masked dancer. Then you get used to the dances.

When the masked dancers are out there just for the good time of the people, it isn't necessary to have a clown with each set of dancers. Sometimes the shaman doesn't even paint a clown. He doesn't worry about it. If someone wants to be one, all right; but he doesn't ask anyone to do it. If someone wants to, he says, "All right, get your own equipment then." The clown is not counted in the set. A man may paint four others and a clown. But when they are dancing to cure sickness, the clown is supposed to be the most important dancer. The old man told me that the clown has more power than any other masked dancer.

The clown won't talk to the people when he's dancing at the time of the puberty rite. He only motions. He's just there to make fun. The people give him directions, and he goes and does what they say and makes a fool of himself just for the fun of it. He will roll on the ground if they tell him to. He dances all over. He may be in the lead or he may come last. He has no special position. It is not dangerous to touch a clown as it is to touch another masked dancer.

The clown is the servant and messenger of the masked dancers. You notice that he runs over to the group of men who are singing for the dancers and bends down and says something. He is saying, "The dancers out there [resting in the woods] want to smoke and they need tobacco," or, "They want you to sing a 'high-step' dance song for them."

If you are a masked dancer, you can tell the clown to deliver a message for you. He goes among the people; it's all right for him to do it. People are all saying, "There's the clown. What is he after?" He gets near your man. Then he leans over quickly and delivers your message. And he's gone like a flash.

When I was a dancer, I used the clown. The girl I sent a message to is still living here. Just as we were going out from the fire I motioned to the clown, and he followed me. I told him, "See that girl by the wood pile. Tell her that I want to see her over here when the next dance begins." Pretty soon I saw the clown going toward that wood pile. He talked to my girl.

The next time they danced, I didn't go in. I went to the place where I was going to meet the girl. I had my mask on, and people I met couldn't see who I was. I was waiting there. Pretty soon I saw a girl coming. I jingled my costume to let her know I was there.[6]

To continue with the account of the preparation of the masked dancers. The men who are to dance, strip, don the kilts and moccasins, and stand or sit facing the east. The shaman puffs a preliminary cigarette to the directions while he recites an extemporaneous prayer such as this:

Under the heavens to the east, inside Big Star Mountain, can be seen the great Black Mountain Spirit. His body has been designed and the uprights of his

---

[6] It is dangerous to touch, speak to, or point at a masked dancer only when he is dancing or actually impersonating a supernatural.

headdress have been made with the big star. Against these diseases I use the sound of the Mountain Spirit rattling his headdress as he dances to the fire. By means of it I walk the earth. It drives all evil away. With it I perform this ceremony. With this I walk. That is all.

"They always start to paint the leader first. It doesn't matter who is finished first though." Helpers apply the paint with sticks which have been pounded, softened, and sometimes turned back at the end. Even the finger is used if the work has to proceed quickly. The helper, who has seen the masked dancers of this shaman perform many times and may have acted as dancer for the shaman himself, is usually familiar with the designs. What information he lacks is supplied by the shaman. Often masked dancers assist in painting each other.

Anyone can help the shaman paint the dancers. The shaman sits there and tells them what to do. Sometimes he paints too. When he has several men around, he will have everybody working on them. He will be singing and praying while they do it. I've never asked about this part. They start painting in the late afternoon. It takes some fellows longer than others. It doesn't make any difference whose masked dancers are first on the grounds below.

I painted masked dancers once. I was already painted myself and ready to go out. They were a little behind. I just went over and put the marks on one of the fellows to help out. I went ahead and did it while the shaman was there singing.

During the painting the shaman sings, beating a pottery drum with a curved drumstick. Should these songs not be sung in the right way, "the masked dancer would fall down like a man knocked out by a blow if he should touch another masked dancer down on the grounds." According to one masked-dancer shaman, his songs "call on the Mountain Spirits to give the dancers endurance," and so his dancers are able to "stay in there a long time."

These songs which accompany the painting of the dancers are sung as memory and convenience dictate. The allusions in them are to the themes associated with the ceremony, to the "holy home" where the ritual was learned from the resident Mountain Spirits, to the sounds made by the pendants of the headdress and kilt as the dancers trot to the fire, to the cardinal directions from which the Mountain Spirits guard the Chiricahua against all sickness and danger. The prayer or softly and quickly uttered recitation which separates the choruses can be freely translated as follows for one of these songs:

> Inside the holy home
> At the place called "Home in the Turning Rock,"
> The Mountain Spirits, truly holy,
> Rejoice over me to the four directions
> And make sounds over me.

The words of another of these songs show a forceful and vivid imagery:

> In the middle of the Holy Mountain,
> In the middle of its body, stands a hut,
> Brush-built, for the Black Mountain Spirit.
> White lightning flashes in these moccasins;
> White lightning streaks in angular path;
> I am the lightning flashing and streaking!
> This headdress lives; the noise of its pendants
> Sounds and is heard!
> My song shall encircle these dancers!

When the body-painting is finished, the dancers eat the generous meal provided for them by the feast-makers. It is nearly dusk now, and soon the great fire will be kindled below and the people will gather to see the entrance of the masked dancers.

While the shaman chants another set of four songs, the dancers line up in a row facing the east, headdresses in hand, praying and asking to be blessed. Of one of these songs the informant said:

I'm going to sing an old song. It's very valuable. It is sung when the masked dancers are standing there, painted, dancing in place, and ready to go out, shaking their headdresses. This song is called "Earth's Song." It is sung very slowly.

> Thus speaks earth's thunder:
> Because of it there is good about you,
> Because of it your body is well:
> Thus speaks earth's thunder.

As these songs are sung, the impersonators gyrate clockwise, uttering their call at the mention of the Mountain Spirits and motioning with their headdresses to the directions. The buckskin masks have been moistened so that they will be pliable. At the conclusion of the singing, the dancers, including the clown if

PLATE VI

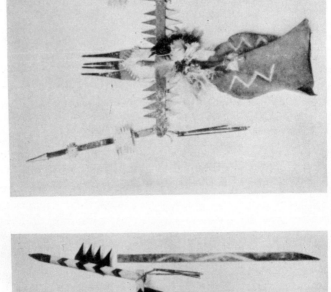

HEADDRESSES OF THE MASKED DANCER

one is present, spit into the masks four times, make three ritual feints toward themselves with the headdresses, and draw the masks over their heads the fourth time. Now they are ready to move in single file down the hillside, led by their most experienced dancer.

As they depart, they present a colorful spectacle. They wear high moccasins (with upturned toe) and buckskin skirts. These are colored yellow. The skirt is held in place by a broad belt; and from the skirt are suspended pendants of various kinds.[7] The arms and upper part of the body, with the exception of the face, are entirely covered with paint. Black, white, and yellow are most used; blue appears occasionally. The motifs most frequently employed are narrow bands of contrasting color, a branching design to stand for cactus, a saw-toothed element, a stepped line, a zigzag line, the triangle, the Greek cross, a pattée type cross, and a four-pointed star. These designs may remain the same all four nights, the same design may be used the first and third nights and another the second and fourth nights, or different designs may be painted each evening. Occasionally, the painted designs on the leader vary slightly from those of the others. The dancers carry painted wooden sticks in each hand; one or both of those carried by the leader may have a cross-piece at the handle. Long, narrow, buckskin streamers with eagle feathers attached are tied just above the elbows.

The mask is a buckskin hood which fits snugly over the head and is gathered at the neck by a drawstring. Two tiny holes for the eyes, and one sometimes cut at the mouth, are the only openings. These hoods are usually painted black but are also seen in yellow, in blue, or in two tones. When they are not a solid color, they may show such design elements as have been mentioned for the body. On the mask, at the forehead or nose

[7] Today, small cone-shaped jingles of tin have taken the place of these on the dance kilts, the dress made for the pubescent girl, and on other objects (awl cases, buckskin bags, burden baskets, etc.). To make these tin jingles, the metal is cut to proper size, placed over a depression in a board, and smartly struck at the median point. This curls the two sides, and it is then an easy matter to press them together with the fingers to form the cone, which is attached to the garment on a length of fringe.

region, may be suspended a piece of abalone shell or turquoise. One shaman employs the shell "because abalone has strength, and the masked dancers should have the same strength as the abalone."

At its top the hood is attached to the horns[8] or uprights by spreading prongs of a piece of oak which has been split, soaked in water, and heated until it could be worked. At its upper end this piece is connected to the yucca or sotol frame which rises above it. A bunch of turkey feathers or some green juniper is tied at the point of union. The superstructure of wooden slats looks like a great, squarish candelabra balanced on the top of the dancer's head. It is essentially a horizontal bar to which vertical pieces approximately two feet high have been attached at the two ends and in the middle. From each end of the horizontal support hang two or four short lengths of wood called "earrings." These strike against one another, making a sound that has become a symbol for the approach of the dancers. From the tops of the vertical pieces float downy eagle feathers. The colors of the uprights are black, yellow, and green (blue);[9] red "would be used only by a witch on a masked-dancer horn."

The shaman, drum in hand, may accompany his dancers to the edge of the clearing. Then, often, he will join the group of men who have gathered at the north of the ceremonial structure to sing for the masked dancers.

But the entrance of the dancers may be delayed still further, for they are often called upon at this time to cure. Yet the fiction of their purely social function at the puberty rite is maintained by having what serious ritual they attempt remain a private matter, unguided by the sponsors of the ceremony:

[8] That the headdress should be called "horns" is of special interest, in the light of the fact that Mountain Spirits are associated with the protection and guardianship of game animals, the most important of which have horns.

[9] Juice of the yucca leaf is mixed with charcoal, yellow ocher or a decoction from algerita root, and soft turquoise to obtain these colors. The addition of the yucca juice makes the difference between the impermanent paint used on the bodies of the dancers and the fixed color with which the headdress and sticks are painted. Green and blue are not terminologically differentiated.

Sometimes, before the masked dancers go out to the fire, people come for help to the place where they are being painted. They come of their own accord. I never liked to work at this, but I couldn't say "No." When you're all dressed up and someone comes, and the old man tells you to help them, you have to do it. You can't say "No." It wouldn't be right.

The general rule is, according to the way some shamans do it, that the leading dancer blows the disease away. I've done it myself. The others dance behind the leader as he approaches the sick one from the directions, but they don't touch the sick person. It seems that the shamans feel it will be better and quicker if the leader does it instead of all the dancers. Some dancers are beginners. They might mix things up. But some shamans require all the masked dancers to work on the sick one and blow the disease away. This takes longer.

It takes about fifteen or twenty minutes for one man to go through it. While we are dancing, the shaman smokes, prays, and sings. He makes a regular little ceremony. If the patient does not get better that night, he comes back the next night.

Not all the curing occurs at the place of preparation. Sometimes arrangements are made by sick persons or their relatives for the services of the masked dancers at one of the camps below.[10]

If we were down by the fire and someone was sick, we'd cure him with this song [a masked-dancer song used for curing or for the painting of the dancers] off to the side of the grounds.

First the sick person or a relative would have to request the ceremony from the leader of the masked dancers. He has to throw pollen to the directions, put pollen over the masked dancer's right foot, and come up and around his body to the left foot with it. If it is a woman who is sick, she puts a piece of abalone on his foot. It is tied to a string and has an eagle feather with it. A man puts a piece of turquoise with an eagle feather there. The shaman doesn't take this and keep it; the masked-dancer leader keeps it. I had a whole bunch of them. Some other shamans, like T., take it themselves. But that was not the way of the one for whom I danced.

This stone and feather can be used back. If I sympathize with someone who is sick, I give it to him, providing he uses it to ask the man for whom I dance. I give it to him and tell him how to use it.

When all the ceremonies for which requests have been made are concluded, the masked dancers make their way to the dance

[10] In the summer of 1931, at a girl's puberty rite, I witnessed such a ceremony performed over a youth who was becoming increasingly deaf. The rite took place at the edge of the dance clearing, just to the south of the central fire, before the impersonators began to dance for the people.

arena. Sounding their call, they burst into the open space from
the east at a trot and circle the fire. They are greeted by the cry
of the women and the prayers of the devout.

.... They would come down at night carrying a big light. .... When they
first came down the hill, even if the camp were a large one, they used to go around
to each home and not miss a single one. Just as soon as the people saw them
coming they began to pray. .... "Men of the Mountain,"[11] they would say, "I
wish you would protect me. If anything comes to hurt me, stand in front of me
and help me."

First the dance group "worships the fire" from the directions:

This is what the old man told me when I was the leader of his dancers. "The
first time you come in and go to the fire, go around it four times. Then approach
it from the east. When you get within about eight paces of the fire, just when the
light begins to shine on you, sound the masked-dancer call. Then go around the
fire once. Stop at the south, go toward the fire, sway and make the call in the
same way. Do the same from the west and the north. Next come back where
you started from, the east, and worship the fire again from there."

Sometimes the ceremonial structure is circled and "blessed,"
each pole being approached in clockwise rotation by the single
file of dancers and clasped by the leader. Then the dancers trot
off to the east and vanish in the darkness. On their way through
the camps they may dance back and forth before a dwelling
where there has been sickness or trouble. The entire encampment may be circled, and sickness frightened away by gesticula-
tion and blowing.

With the arrival of the dancers, the restrictions applicable to
the onlookers come into force. No one may address or call the
name of an impersonator whom he recognizes; no one may point,
with hand or lips, to a masked dancer; nor may anyone touch a
dancer when he is in costume. "If you don't worship them in the
right way, you should be frightened." However, neither men nor
women confuse the impersonators with the actual Mountain
Spirits. "The dancers do not turn into the real Mountain Spirits
while they are dancing. They stay men but just get more
strength." The restrictions are obeyed, not from fear of the

----

[11] A term for Mountain Spirits indicating greatest respect and used when
supplicating these supernaturals or when there is reason to fear them.

PLATE VII

a) Masked Dancers Coming Down from the Hills at Dusk

b) Worshiping the Fire

power of those dancing, but because "the real Mountain Spirits could bring on sickness or death if these things were violated."

The added strength of the masked dancers is attributed to the costumes they wear:

> The costume gives the dancer strength. He doesn't get tired. There are no holes near the nose for breathing in the masks. The man wearing the mask is fighting for breath. When he gets tired, he runs his sticks around his body and then flourishes them in the air, and in this way he rids himself of his tiredness. If it was not for this, he couldn't last through one song.

When the masked dancers return, a knot of men assembled just northeast of the entrance of the ceremonial structure is ready to beat out the measure of the songs with stout sticks on a thick piece of rawhide. Others hold buckskin-covered pottery drums which they will strike with curved drumsticks.

From the east the masked dancers spring into the glare of the firelight and move swiftly around the fire:

> When the leader of the masked dancers throws his arms wide, this means to the singers that they are to begin. The men at the rawhide know that this is the signal. If they don't start to sing, the dancers go past them, then turn toward them and repeat the gesture. If they don't start then, the dancers can leave the grounds if they want to. Many times I have done that. I figured, "Well, I'm not going to let them just watch me! It's no use to run around here without any song." Sometimes, as you come toward the rawhide after blessing the fire, they start right in. Then, as you go past, you cry, "Hoo-hoo-hoo!" which is just like saying, "That's fine! That's what we want!" The masked dancers can't talk but they make that sound. It means, "Go ahead and sing." I was told to make the masked-dancer call when turquoise, abalone, cloud, Mountain Spirit, White Painted Woman, and other holy things and people were mentioned in the songs.

The songs to which the dancers perform at the feast grounds are not the same as those to which they were painted but are associated with definite dance steps. The shaman may know and use both kinds of songs, but just as often another person will lead the singing during the evening. The relatives of the adolescent girl have to make sure that some qualified person will be present to perform this function.

> I am an official singer for masked dancers. The parents of the girl will ask me to sing at their feast. They pay me. I will be singing for one family. I learned these songs. I sat in and gained experience. No one else would sing my songs. It's not done.

It is the privilege of the singer to begin the song and to recite alone the prayer or half-spoken, half-chanted portion interspersed between the nonsense-syllable refrains. At the refrain the other members of the chorus join in heartily again, and so these songs give the impression of great bursts of melody, suddenly hushed and as suddenly resumed and swelled. When a singer of these songs grows tired or feels that he should make way for another, he relinquishes his post and joins the chorus, while his successor contributes other songs. The songs of any individual are well known to those of his region, so that it is always possible to bring together a chorus.

The songs are classified in three groups, each related to one of three types of dance: the "free step," the "short step," and the "high step." The dancers, and especially the leader, must be able to recognize a song at once and enter upon the proper step.

The performance always begins with a free-step song, so called because it imposes less formal restrictions upon the actions of the dancers and allows more exhibition of individuality than either of the other two. When he hears this music, "a man uses his own judgment and dances according to his feelings." The best performers contest in the firelight for the rolling, throaty call of approval of the audience.

The prayers of the free-step songs are similar in theme to those of the songs sung when the dancers are painted:

I

At the place called "Home in the Center of the Sky,"
Inside is the home's holiness.
The door to the home is of white clouds.
There all the Gray Mountain Spirits
Rejoicing over me
Kneel in the four directions with me.

II

When first my power was created,
Pollen's body, speaking my words,
Brought my power into being,
So I have come here.

After the first, free-step, masked-dancer song, "they switch around, singing the songs of the different steps so that the masked dancers don't get tired." A second type of song is that which accompanies the short step. The words of these songs are much like those of the free-step songs, but the rhythm and mode of execution of the step are different. The dance is marked by bodily rigidity, studied posturing, and short, terse steps.

The third kind of song is that to which the dancers perform the high step. The prayers of these songs reveal nothing new. But the dance step itself departs widely from the others. As soon as the dancers recognize the character of the song, they form a circle around the fire, facing away from it, and dance with vehemence, throwing first one leg and then the other forward and upward. The dance is much like the Russian *trepak* except that the performers do not squat so low during its execution. Although this dance is the most spectacular of the three and is constantly requested by the audience, it is so difficult that it is performed much less often than the other two.

Despite the excitement and the rivalry the potential dangers for the participants are never forgotten. If two dancers collide, especially if they have been painted by different shamans, and one drops a stick, he dare not pick it up at once. He will stagger around as if dazed until his companions, lining up in single file, "worship" the wand from the directions and the leader picks it up and returns it to him.

Inside the ceremonial structure.—While the exhibition of the masked dancers is at its height, another phase of the rite, more closely associated with the fate of the pubescent girl, is quietly unfolding.

Sometime during the early part of the night the singer makes his way to the place where the girl and her attendant await him. The girl hands him the rattle that was intrusted to her. He extends an eagle feather toward her, and she grasps the tip of it with her right hand. He shakes the rattle and walks slowly backward, singing:

> They move her by means of the finest eagle feather,
> By means of it White Painted Woman walks into her home.

A singer has described this act: "In the evening when the girl first comes out to dance, I lead her with the eagle feather. There is one song to lead the girl in with. I go a little way and sing it again. The fourth time I go right in and put the girl in the corner."

But before they enter, the attendant, who has followed them carrying an untanned hide, and who has given her call of applause at each of the four stops, hurries to the rear of the structure and spreads out the skin. She is followed by the girl, who skirts the fire clockwise (as must always be done when entering or leaving the ceremonial structure) and sits or kneels on the hide, facing the east. If she sits, her legs are flexed under her to the side. Her trunk is held erect, as it should be as long as she remains in the holy place. The singer squats close to the fire, at the south. Behind him sits the attendant, near the center of the south wall. Relatives of the girl and visitors pass clockwise about the structure and make their way to the west. Some latecomers sit in the doorway.

The singer, before going after the girl, has arranged a number of ritual objects. At the main pole of the south he has tied (or stuck into the oak boughs), butt end toward the east, a length of oak wood which is called the "age stick." This, the symbol of long life, stands for the cane his charge will use in her old age. It will serve him as a fire poker and as a support while he sings. On the same pole hangs a fuse of shredded juniper bark tied with yucca strands. This fuse, representative of fire and the hearth, he will use to ignite the ceremonial cigarettes he smokes. On the pole, too, is a grama grass brush which will be used "to brush off evil influences" from the girl and to apply white paint to her.

The singer unfastens these objects and brings them to the fireside. After the ceremony of the first night he will return them to a main pole, this time to the one at the west. In the same way he will continue to move them in sunwise rotation each night until, at the beginning of the fourth and last night, the ceremonial circuit will be completed, and these objects will be found on the east pole.

At the edge of the fire other objects have been arranged. The fire pit is flanked at each cardinal point by a flat rock painted red on top. These "stand for" the mescal or century plant, a food staple, and act as a prayer that the girl may find and prepare an abundant supply of mescal in the course of her life. A stone bowl, the mortar for the paints of the ceremony, is set toward the east this first night. This, too, will be moved each night.

The singer rolls a cigarette, lights it with the slow fuse, and smokes and prays. His voice is hardly audible. The attendant, using the same fuse, also offers smoke ceremonially. Then the singer starts to shake the hoof rattle which he holds in his right hand and begins his first song.

The songs of this ceremony are in reality a journey in which the girl is brought to the holy home and from there is conducted symbolically through a long and successful life.

We think of a woman's life as blocked out in parts. One is girlhood, one is young womanhood, one is middle age, and one is old age. The songs are supposed to carry her through them. The first songs describe the holy home and the ceremony. Later come the songs about the flowers and the growing things. These stand for her youth, and as the songs go through the seasons the girl is growing up and reaching old age.

At the conclusion of a song the singer explained:

This song is about flowers. We are taking this girl through a beautiful life. This is the conception of a beautiful life for the Apache. We take the girl through beautiful lands, past flowers, through seasons with their fruits. The translation doesn't mean much, but there is a great deal to it if you think about it.

There is a general tendency to move, as the songs continue, from the more remote and abstract qualities to the growing things of the earth.

The big ceremony starts with songs of the sun, the moon, and such things. Then comes the earth. Then the songs are mostly about the earth and the things that grow on it, about the fruits, the trees, the plants; about even the children. Nothing is left out. . . . .

. . . . On the fourth night the songs deal with all the different grasses and carry them through all the different stages of development, from spring to winter. Then by morning we are through.

The songs belong to two general groups, and each kind of song is accompanied by a different dance. Most numerous are the "shuffling-step" songs, and, when these are sung, the girl stands, raises her arms upright from the elbows with palms outward, holds her feet close together, and moves from left to right and right to left by alternately pivoting on her toes and her heels. The second type of song calls for an "in-place" step and provides rest from the exertions of the first type. In its performance the girl sways in place with her hands on her hips.[12]

Because of the repetition of its verses, each song is long, and the shuffling step is very tiring. But, whenever the girl is weary, she may stop and kneel, even though the song is not finished. The singer makes no attempt to test or to overtax her.

The singer watches the girl and uses his judgment. The idea is not to let her get too tired. There is the dance the girls do with their arms up. The word for it means "shuffling," sliding to a place as a horse does. They sing about six songs of this kind and then change to the one where the girl dances in place with her hands on her hips. The singer tells the girl which dance to do if she does not know. They sing fewer songs of this second kind. These are just to rest the girl.

Every fourth, sixth, or twelfth song may be set aside for a "smoking song," after which the singer smokes or prays:

After about six songs they have a smoking song. They smoke after this song; all those inside can smoke then. There is no dancing during the smoking song. The girl can rest; she can kneel but cannot sit. She must have her body erect. There are many of the smoking songs. After this they start singing and dancing again.

The initial song of the first night is of the shuffling-step type. "This is the first song sung. It is the home's own song, the first one sung when they are in there." The second song, also of the shuffling-step variety, simply repeats between refrains these words:

> I have walked well
> Into the home of White Painted Woman.

Now follow songs of the singer's choosing, fixed only in accordance with the general pattern already outlined. No definite number of songs need be sung during the night. One singer remarked:

---

[12] An informant described a third step, which he claims was formerly danced by the pubescent girl. "It is called 'walking around.' The girl has her arms up and her elbows pointed down. She walks forward, turns toward the south, and comes back, doing this four times. It's mostly to rest and relax." This step is not performed now.

"In summer I sing fewer songs because the nights are short. In winter I sing more." After the introductory numbers, the songs are arranged in groups of fours. The songs of each group are called "siblings of the same sex" because, in passing from one to another in a set of four songs, an alteration of a word or two of the prayer may be the only discernible change.

Throughout the dancing the attendant remains in her station at the south. Whenever, in the course of the singing, the names of supernaturals or sacred substances are mentioned, she raises her voice in the call of applause.

The songs of the ceremony are too numerous to reproduce in full, but a few of different types, representative of the first night's repertory, are here given in free translation. First are two shuffling-step dance songs:

I

Killer of Enemies, source of long life,
White Painted Woman has come inside;
She grows up by means of it.

II

The spruce home of White Painted Woman is built of long life,
By means of a home built of this she has gone inside,
By means of her power of goodness White Painted Woman has come to her,
By means of it the words have gone inside.

Of the in-place dance songs the following two examples are offered:

I

I come to White Painted Woman,
By means of long life I come to her.
I come to her by means of her blessing,
I come to her by means of her good fortune,
I come to her by means of all her different fruits;
By means of the long life she bestows, I come to her;
By means of this holy truth she goes about.

II

I am about to sing this song of yours,
The song of long life.
Sun, I stand here on the earth with your song;
Moon, I have come in with your song.

The translation below indicates the character of the third type of song—the smoking song. Often, when the men who are sitting just outside the structure singing and drumming for the masked dancers hear one of these songs, they also pause to smoke.

> The time for smoking has come.
> With the sun's tobacco let all be made pleasant.
> From here on let good constantly follow,
> From now on let many old men and old women rejoice;
> Let them come back to many ceremonies like this;
> Let all the girls be happy;
> Let them know many ceremonies like this;
> Let all rejoice;
> Let all the boys rejoice;
> Let them attend many ceremonies like this.

The dancing within the ceremonial structure is brought to an early close the first night. Sometimes the masked dancers are still circling the fire as the singer, the attendant, and the girl file sunwise from the holy home. If this is the case, the girl may be asked to shuffle around the fire in the wake of the masked impersonators before leaving for her camp. Meanwhile the attendant has gathered up the hide, the rattle, and the feather and will keep them until they are needed on the following night.

The social dancing.—If the masked dancers have not left before the girl has concluded her dance within the ceremonial structure, they disappear for the night soon afterward. But the evening's activities have scarcely begun for the visitors. Social dancing is closely associated in the popular mind with the ceremony, for this is one of the few occasions which brings together enough people to make it possible. The dances take place every night and must follow an invariable order.

The songs for the social dances contrast markedly with the sacred music:

> With the social dance songs it is different. They don't belong to any one person. Anyone can sing them. Anyone can make up his own, and, if it is a good one and the people like it, he and others will keep singing it. Anyone can join in these songs if he knows them, even in the part with the words. These songs are funny. You can say almost anything in them.

A dignified old man, when he was working out the details of some music, indicated the great difference between the social dance songs and the ceremonial songs:

> I want you to keep these [girl's puberty rite] songs private. I am not a foolish man and do not sing these songs easily. Some of the Indians might not like it. But the social dance songs are all right. I don't care what you do about them.

This is the way two composers of social dance songs went about their task:

> Y. and I made up a couple of these songs. We worked them out together. I went over to his place, and we patched them up. First he'd sing a little and then I'd sing a little, and we'd agree on it and work it out. We practiced. Then we sang them at the last girl's puberty rite. All the people liked them. The word part of one goes like this:
>
> > Young woman, young woman,
> > We've been very intimate,
> > But now stay away from me.

Another composer sang his own song and some others from which he had drawn his inspiration:

> I took some old songs and chose a little from one and a little from another. I used about three and worked one new song out of them. I did it while I was away on a trip. Then I sang this song at the ceremony when I came back. At the last ceremony I sang it for four nights straight. All the people said it was a good song.

But by no means are all these songs recent compositions or modifications. Many old favorites continue to be as popular as ever:

> Some of the songs for this are very old. I'll sing one for you. It's very old; perhaps two hundred years old. When I was just a little boy at Fort Apache fifty years ago, just old enough to listen to singing, I heard it. There was one very old man who sat by a fire working on arrows and singing it. And while he sang it he was crying. This song reminded him of the times when he was a young man. That's why I think it is so old. It goes like this:
>
> > Young woman, you are thinking of something,
> > Young woman, you are thinking of something;
> > You are thinking of what you are going to get:
> > That man of whom you are thinking is worthless!

This comment suggests one of the greatest appeals of the social dance songs—their associations. The occasions when they have been heard and learned are memorable points in the individual career—moments of travel, adventure, and courtship:

This is the song to which my wife and I fell in love. It's not much of a song; but I thought a lot of it and so did she. N. was singing it. It is his morning song. I went out with her under the piñon trees and I sang this song to her during the days of the feast. I've had this song for my favorite ever since. It reminds my wife and me of that time.

The few words of a social dance song are rich in implication. Once an old man dismissed American songs with a contemptuous, "There isn't much singing to them; it's all words!" Doubtless he was thinking of the more subtle technique of his people, by which, with a few well-chosen words and a wealth of inner meaning, a dozen youths can be made to hang their heads.

As soon as the masked dancers have departed for the night, the first of the social dances—the round dance—begins. Several men holding pottery drums come together. Others form a compact knot around them, and this group, their arms around each other's shoulders, circles the fire clockwise. One man, ordinarily one of the drummers, begins a song, and the others join in. Now women step out and stand at the side of the singers, forming a circle. Sometimes the circle incloses the singers. The dancers face the fire and shuffle sideways, clockwise, in time to the music.

In the round-dance songs such words as "Stoop," or "Faster," may be the only words, and the dancers are expected to follow these commands. Others may contain only a short phrase or two, but these few words satirize common foibles and provoke general amusement. In a certain round-dance song one question is simply repeated over and over:

What belongs to us?

This seems enigmatic to an outsider, but it is fraught with meaning to the dancers:

This is a round-dance song. "What belongs to us?" Where are our possessions? We haven't got anything. That is what this song means. Many people get married but haven't anything. What is going to be ours when we get married? Suppose I am dancing. I want to marry a girl though I have nothing. Then I'll be ashamed when they sing this, as lots of boys are.

Another of these songs derides the marriage of a young girl to an ill-favored old man:

She married an old man
With big buttocks!

PLATE VIII

THE ROUND DANCE (THE CEREMONIAL STRUCTURE IN THE BACKGROUND)

The domestic intruder receives mention:

> He asks me what happened
> To his wife!

For the young people who are planning an assignation, a song has this reminder:

> Wait for me
> At the high bluff over there.

One song has to do with those who have become acquainted at the feast and soon must separate:

> You will go back to your distant home;
> We will be lonesome.

At midnight, often at the time when the second social dance of the evening is about to get under way, food is again served.

I have called the second dance of the night the "partner" dance:

After the circle dance, the men get in a group by the fire and the women go around and choose partners. A woman pulls at a man's clothes or pokes him if she wants him for a partner. Then he has to dance.

It's a general rule that the man has to pay the woman something if he dances with her. He pays after the four nights. If you haven't got anything, you tell the woman the first night so she can choose someone else. It is understood that if you dance with a woman you have something for her. It's not that you have to pay if you dance, but it's just too bad if you don't. Everybody talks about you. The girl will tell everyone. She will say, "That man is no good; he didn't pay." All the girls will say this then.

The girl dances with the same man for the four nights. It is right then that they fall in love. A girl chooses a boy she likes. I got acquainted with my wife this way. I danced with her. That's what these dances are mostly for.

To execute the partner dance, a man and woman remain in the same line but face in opposite directions. The man's left arm is opposite the woman's left arm, or his right arm is opposite her right arm. The couples, who are scattered here and there, dance forth and back in relation to the fire, about four steps one way and then four the other. Occasionally, two women tap the same man and then he must dance with both and must finally pay both.

Blood kin and affinal relatives, including husband and wife, may not dance together. "You have to be sure you are not related. Sometimes a man makes a mistake and asks a girl who is his kin to dance with him. She says, 'No, you are related to me.' "

There is a definite etiquette attached to the partner dance:

Some touch or link arms. A very prominent or dignified man would not touch a woman during the dance though. He wouldn't get familiar. A man who dances politely will have his hands locked over his breast. It shows that the man is not bothering the woman. N. [a prominent Chiricahua] always danced with his hands locked over his chest.

An unmarried man may dance with a married woman, or the other way around. It is all right to talk to your partner while you are dancing.

The songs of the partner dance do not differ materially from those of the round dance.

> We will go to the last home.

are the only words of one. Its inner meaning is somewhat more complex, however: "The song means that perhaps your camp is the one far from the feast grounds and that after the dance you two are going over there together."

In another song of this type ridicule is heaped on the young man who is enamored of an older woman, the mother of children:

> When there is a gathering for the ceremony, sweetheart,
> I will take care of your baby for you,
> I will take care of your baby for you.

Still another runs as follows:

> Oh, Mescalero maiden, don't be afraid;
> They are already gossiping about us,
>   But don't be afraid.
> They who speak so chew rocks;[13]
>   Don't be afraid.

The songs of the third and last social dance of each night of the puberty rite may appropriately be called the morning-dance songs, since the dance they accompany begins several hours before dawn and continues until daybreak.

Toward morning the songs change, and the men and women separate and get in two lines facing each other. The lines are pretty far apart, and the partners of the dance which has just ended are right across from each other. When the sing-

---

[13] That is, "are envious"; witches are often said to "chew rocks."

ing starts, the lines come toward each other, stopping a few feet apart, and then separate. They go back and forth like this. The singers are in a line with the men and go back and forth with them. This dancing goes on until sunrise.

The round-dance songs and the partner-dance songs may or may not have words, but the songs of the morning dance always have words. These morning-dance songs are the favorites. "The morning songs, the love songs, sound beautiful. They are high pitched. We like them best of all. People just fall in love there singing them."

Some of these compositions well earn the name of "love song" which informants have given them:

I

I see that girl again,
 Then I become like this;
I see my own sweetheart again,
 Then I become like this.

II

Maiden, you talk kindly to me,
 You, I shall surely remember it,
I shall surely remember you alone,
Your words are so kind,
 You, I shall surely remember it.

A reproachful note is struck in one of these songs:

My sweetheart, we surely could have gone home,
 But you were afraid!
When it was night we surely could have gone home,
 But you were afraid!

Of the manner of singing the following somewhat acrid song a commentator said:

The song is really sung by the men all the way through. But the men take the part of the women and then of the men. As they dance together, the men take the part first of one and then of the other. When the men are singing the part of the men, they change the word "man" in the song to "woman."

Man from a distant land,
Why do you talk to me?
Why do you talk to me?
Why do you talk to me?
What have you done for me
But just talk to me?

Another morning song purports to be a passage between a man and a woman who is endeavoring to hide her age so that she may have a good time:

> They tell me you are old:
> I, I don't think so.

Then there are the lines depicting the confusion of two young friends who cannot bring themselves to separate:

> Woman from a far land,
> Give me your moccasins that I may be going.
> Man from a far land,
> Give me your moccasins that I may be going.

At dawn those who have remained up all night disperse for a few hours of rest. There will be no morning ceremony to rouse them, for the puberty rite proper of the second day is not resumed until nightfall.

Events through the fourth night.—During the morning and afternoon of the second day visiting, feasting, gambling, and sporadic social dancing take place. The girl has no special duties during the day, although she must be mindful of her general restrictions. If she becomes restless, she may be permitted to walk toward the hills or to join in the daytime social dancing for short intervals.

At dusk the events of the preceding evening are repeated without significant variation. The central fire is renewed, the masked dancers appear, the pubescent girl is led to the ceremonial structure, and later in the evening the same social dances, in identical order, are again performed.

In outline the third day and third night differ in no essential way from the second day and night. The activities of the fourth day, moreover, follow closely those of the second and third days.

But the fourth night of the ceremony departs in several important respects from what has gone before. The first events are the familiar ones. At dusk the masked dancers appear and repeat their performance. And, as before, when the masked-dancer display is at its height, the singer leads the girl to the ceremonial structure. This time, however, he brings with him a bundle of narrow sticks of mock orange wood. Beginning at the southeast and moving clockwise around the fire pit, he erects one stick for every song he sings this fourth night, until the fire pit is surrounded except for a space to the east that must remain open. After every set of four songs has been sung and the corresponding four sticks have been set up, a fifth, shorter length of wood is placed horizontally on the ground between this set and the one to follow. This horizontal piece represents a smoking song presumably: "When I lay the stick down, there is a song about smoking that goes with it. The song comes first, then I put the stick down, then smoke, then pray, then go on to the next set." For the first three nights the singing and dancing within the structure cease at midnight or before. But this night they continue until daybreak.

The songs of the second, third, and fourth nights to which the girl dances are a continuation of the life-journey pattern. In order to indicate the sweep of this ritual progression, a number of songs, arranged roughly in chronological order in respect to the rite as a whole, are introduced. The first, a shuffling-step song, has to do with the birds:

> White Painted Woman commands that which lies above,
> Killer of Enemies commands,
> By means of long life they command.
> From the mouth of the chief bird
> Yellowness emerges by means of it,
> By means of it yellow emerges from your mouth.

The girl's necklace, symbolic of lifelong wealth, is celebrated in a shuffling-step song:

> The words of Killer of Enemies, good through long life,
> Have entered you;
> They have entered you by means of your necklace;
> Your necklace has gone into your body,
> For its power is good.

Of the next song, which he called "She Sleeps with It," the singer said:

In this song the girl is taken through the sleeping period, through a rest period. We take her through all experiences with these songs.

> White Painted Woman's power emerges,
> Her power for sleep.
> White Painted Woman carries this girl;
> She carries her through long life,
> She carries her to good fortune,
> She carries her to old age,
> She bears her to peaceful sleep.

The growth of the things of the earth is emphasized in many of the songs. This one tells of the grasses:

> By means of the ceremony I have gone to White Painted Woman,
> I have gone to the source of long life created of goodness.
> White Painted Woman, her grasses are striped with yellow,
> Killer of Enemies spoke thus;
> White Painted Woman, her grasses are much striped with blue,
> Killer of Enemies, his grasses are much striped with red.

Periods of life are commemorated:

> White Painted Woman has reached middle age by means of it,
> She has reached middle age by means of it,
> By means of it she has entered long life,
> She has reached middle age by means of it.

The last years of life are referred to symbolically in song in terms of the "old age staff":

> He made the black staff of old age for me,
> He made the road of the sun for me;
> These holy things he has made for me, saying,
> "With these you will grow old."
> Now when I have become old,
> You will remember me by means of them.

If this selection is allowed to represent the song cycle as it unfolds through the four nights, the events which take place in the interior of the ceremonial structure until sunrise of the fifth day have been indicated.

On the fourth night the masked dancers have an additional and interesting role:

On the last night the masked dancers come out and stay all night. They do their own dances until ten or eleven o'clock. Then comes the round dance. They save about four good masked dancers, keep them fresh. These go around for about an hour and chase all the people out to dance. They even chase them from their camps and get them out of bed. They bring out the girls and make them dance. The masked dancers do not push the people toward the dance grounds with their hands. They just make the noise and motion with their sticks. They get a girl and give their cry and bring her out. I have gone after them this way. Toward morning even the girl for whom the feast is given can be brought out to dance.

The restriction against speaking lapses for the masked dancers at this time:

The masked dancer asks a girl, "Who shall I get for you to dance with?" The girl says, "That man by the fire." So the dancer goes over there and pulls that fellow. The man never pulls back. He has to go and dance.

The relaxation of the masked dancer's semisacred role goes even further:

The last night the masked dancer can dance with any girl if she chooses him, and this girl has to be paid. But the feast-maker has to pay her for him. The masked dancer has been helping him all night, so of his own accord the feast-giver walks out there and pays the girl. I have seen that happen many times.

Every man has to compensate his partner at the close of the dancing:

One time everyone was paying but one man. He had nothing with him, but he must have had some horses over at his camp. This man walked around there and picked up a dry ball of horse dung. He walked back to the place where the other men were paying the women. He went to the girl he had danced with and right before the crowd he handed her the horse dung. Even in those days very few knew the meaning of this. Horses were very scarce then, and it was pretty hard to part with a horse and give it to anybody.

The girl receiving the horse dung didn't know the meaning of it. She took it home to her people, to her camp. She told her father and mother, "This is all I got!"

Her father was an old man and knew what it meant. He told her right away, "That's more than the other people got over there. That means a horse; that man means he is going to give you a horse." Sure enough, that came true.

Upon the givers of the feast falls the responsibility of seeing that all participants are satisfied with their rewards: "If a girl is not paid and the boy runs away, she can go to the ones giving the ceremony or to someone in authority there and protest. This has been done." As a final gesture of appreciation toward those who have helped make the social aspect of their ceremony a success, the hosts "give a personal present to the women who dance until sunup."

Conclusion.—The final events of the rite should take place in the sun's rays and, if the sunrise is obscured by clouds, the people wait patiently for the emergence of the first beams. As the eastern skies become lighter, twelve songs, familiarly known as "stop" songs, close another chapter of the ceremony. One of the last of these, heralding the appearance of the sun, simply repeats over and over:

> The sun, emerging,
> Says to me, "My grandchild."

The last of this series is a graceful apotheosis of the life-journey upon which the adolescent girl has embarked:

> You have started out on the good earth;
> You have started out with good moccasins;
> With moccasin strings of the rainbow, you have started out;
> With moccasin strings of the sun's rays, you have started out;
> In the midst of plenty you have started out.

Now the girl faces the east, kneeling on the hide. The space to the east of the ceremonial structure is cleared of all loiterers:

They won't let anyone, even a dog, go across between the sun and the ceremonial structure on the last morning. They say that anyone who does this will get sick and die. I believe it. T.'s daughter didn't think and went across once just as the sun was coming up. She died soon afterward.

The sticks which have been erected around the fire pit during the singing are gathered up in clockwise direction, tied in a bundle, and deposited in the coiled basket tray containing the other ceremonial objects.

The singer faces the east with the basket before him and sings four songs. Everything is taken out of the basket except white clay. Then the singer faces the girl and puts pollen first on his own face and head and then on her head. Meanwhile the attendant has mixed water with the white clay in the basket. After another song, the singer paints a line of white and red on the girl's face. Again he turns to the east. He hands his rattle to a man who comes forward to assist him.

He dips his right forefinger into the red paint, holds it up, and sings the "Red Paint Song." Using a splinter of wood to trace the rays, he draws a sun symbol on the palm of his left hand in pollen, red ocher, and specular iron ore. While he does this, he sings a song, "a long one because it takes a long time to put that design on":

> Now I'll make long life of the sun's rays,
> Now I'll make long life of the sun's pointed rays,
> I'll make peaks extending outward.
> The rays of the sun and long life are made of pollen,
> The points of the sun and long life are made of pollen,
> The points of the sun and long life are made of specular iron ore,
> The rays of the sun and long life are made of specular iron ore,
> The rays of the sun and long life are made of blue paint,
> The points of the sun and long life are made of blue paint,
> The rays of the sun and long life are made of red paint,
> The points of the sun and long life are made of red paint,
> The rays of the sun and long life are made of white paint,
> The points of the sun and long life are made of white paint.

The completed sun symbol is held up to the advancing shafts of light as the singer chants:

> That which comes has come well out,
> In here it has come.

Again the singer faces the girl. He touches the painted hand to her body at various places, circles her head clockwise with it, and finally obliterates the symbol by rubbing it over her head just as the rays of the sun shine upon her. At this time, too, the singer ties a piece of abalone shell or turquoise to the girl's forelock.

The eagle feather with which the girl has been led to the inclosure each of the four nights has been thrust into the bundle of grama grass. The singer uses the stems and the quill of this bundle as a brush to paint the girl with white clay. First he paints the right side and then the left side of her face, next her right arm below the elbow and her left arm, and finally her legs from the moccasin tops to the knees. This is a signal for the onlookers to press forward. With the materials left, the singer marks them on various parts of their bodies as they file past him.

When no more come, he returns to the girl, removes the eagle feather from the improvised paint brush, and extends the tip toward her. She grasps this, arises, and follows him as he walks backward, sháking his rattle and singing. Before they reach the front of the ceremonial structure, he has paused four times and sung two songs "about walking along the place of many fruit trees."

Meanwhile the attendant has replaced the ritual objects in the basket. She lays down a buckskin, head to the east, and places the laden basket before it. When the singer and the girl pause at the hide, the eagle feather is added to the tray's contents.

No sooner have the singer and the adolescent left the ceremonial structure than containers of food are brought and placed in a straight line extending east of the fire pit. The singer marks each food receptacle with a pollen cross, and the people eat.

After the meal the men begin to dismantle the ceremonial structure, stripping the oak boughs from the sides and leaving the framework, the four main poles, standing alone.

A "trail" of pollen and specular iron ore is now prepared for the girl. Working from west to east, the singer outlines four footprints on the skin, the first in specular iron ore, the second in pollen, the third in specular iron ore again, and the fourth in pollen. Slowly, as her guide sings, the girl leads with her right foot and walks along this ceremonial path. At the end of the fourth verse and fourth step she stands at the head of the hide. Children, old people, and the infirm then walk along this same path.

Now the attendant takes the basket tray and, as was done the first morning of the rite, places it twenty-five or thirty paces to the east. At a word from the singer, the adolescent runs to the basket, circles it clockwise, and returns to the starting-place. The call of the attendant is heard as she runs. After the run the basket is moved westward. For two more runs an identical procedure is followed, but on the fourth and last run, the girl completely circles the basket, bends low to pick up the feather from it, and trots east once more to some designated point. She circles it clockwise and heads westward once again.

The last run is made so that the girl will be strong, so that she will be a good runner and have a good heart [i.e., be brave]. Some used to run about a quarter of a mile to the east this last time. Because of this some girls became as good runners as men in the old days. If they have far to go, they do not have to run all the way. They can alternate between walking and running.

As the girl approaches the ceremonial structure for the last time, the attendant calls; the main poles are pushed to the east; and, as favors are tossed in the air and the children scramble for them, the girl makes her way to the encampment of her parents.

The temporary camps that have been established for the period of the rite begin to disappear. The poles of the ceremonial structure lie unmolested; they may not be used for firewood.

The girl's family stays on the grounds four days after the ceremony ends. During that time the girl can't wash and has to wear her costume. She must use the scratcher and reed for these four days too.

The girl has still another ritual duty to perform:

The little ceremony where the girl gives the horse takes place four days after the close of the big feast. A horse, any kind of a horse, is required. It always was so and has been handed down. She is still dressed in her costume. She walks the horse to the singer. That ends it. Her part is now over.

On the morning of the ninth day "before the sun comes up, the woman who cares for the girl [attendant] prepares yucca root and warm water and washes the girl's hair and entire body."

The prevailing tone of this ceremony is one of pleasure and promise. The physiological aspects of maturation are little emphasized. The behavior restrictions imposed upon the girl are not irksome, and their violation brings no really dire consequences. She is not isolated but achieves recognition as the central figure of a major social and ritual event during which she is likened to a supernatural being. Her formal introduction to adult status is accomplished in the midst of abundance, ritual safeguards, and festivity; therefore, she has little desire to return to the status which preceded the recognition accorded her.

Many heterogeneous elements combine to produce the girl's puberty rite. The singer, the attendant, the masked-dancer shaman, the dancers themselves, the musical accompanists for the social dance songs—all possess individual prerogatives which are not subject to call. The participation of these persons can only be guaranteed by separate arrangements between them and the sponsors of the ceremony. Various aspects of the rite, such as the masked dancing and the singing within the ceremonial structure, have but the loosest relations to one another from a purely logical point of view. Yet everyone regards the ritual as a unity and accepts that somehow all the necessities will be secured and the integration achieved in time-honored fashion. No threat to individual rights is made, and there is no danger of reprisal for failure to respond. The motive force is primarily psychological. Because the people at large share in the blessing of the girl and because the ceremony provides them with an eagerly awaited social occasion, to take part in the total round of activities becomes almost a public duty.

THE NOVITIATE FOR RAID AND WAR

When the boy reaches the age at which the girl is elevated to womanhood, he is still undergoing the hardening process. Tasks allotted to the young woman can be graduated according to her strength, but the young man on the raid must cover the same distance and suffer the same hardships as the sturdiest member of the party. Therefore, his social maturation is slower.

At about his sixteenth year the youth approaches manly standards. Yet he is not permitted to plunge recklessly from raiding games to the dangerous reality of stealing the horses of the enemy. Instead, he must serve an apprenticeship on his first four raiding or war expeditions. During this period, though he is exposed to a minimum of danger, he acquires the experience which will enable him to undertake with confidence the hazards of war. This novitiate constitutes the conventionalized mechanism through which the youth reaches adult status.

Before a boy is accepted as a novice, he learns how to care for himself on the march, especially what to do if he should become separated from the others:

My relatives and the older men told me, "If you are going on a journey from here, have the women pound meat and fat for you, enough for a week. Take water. Then at sundown, just when it is dark enough so that you can't be seen in the distance, start out. Try to make it across the flats and to the mountains on the other side by daybreak. Then get in the brush and look around. Keep in the brush until night and then start out to the next mountain range. Don't go across flats in the day. Only travel day and night if you are in the mountains."

About water they told me this: "If you don't know where there is water, get up on a high place and look for the green spots. Where there are trees and green grass growing, there you will find water. Don't go to it in the day though. Enemies look for you there. No matter how thirsty you are, wait until night comes. Then go there, drink, and fill up any water container you have brought with you."

Also they told me to go to sleep in a place from which I could get to cover quickly. And they told me, "Even if it is a hot day, don't go to the deep shade. Go under a little bush in the open or under grass. The first place a Mexican or another Indian or a wild animal looks when it comes along is in the shade, and there you are. If you are in the tall grass and hear something, just pick some grass up, hold it before you, and look through it. Then it will be hard to see you, especially from a distance. If you are out where the brush is heavy and you want to conceal yourself without moving, just take a branch which is to the right or left and pull it in front of you."

I was spoken to in this manner also. "If you see someone in the distance and don't know who it is, pick out a place from which you can get to cover easily but which is in the open and visible from this cover. Take grass and make a fire and put evergreen on to make a heavy smoke. Then put it out at once and run to the place from which you can see well. The person will come over to the place where the fire was, and you can tell who he is. You are in a good place from which to strike or get away if he is an enemy, and you can go to him if he is a friend.

"If you are lost or want to find someone, make a fire and a smoke and put it out. Look around then. Your friends will make one too and then you'll find them. If you want someone to follow you, send up smoke and at the place put a notched stick pointing toward the direction in which you went. Your friends will find it. They will come in to your people and say, 'The fire looks as though it was made two or three days ago; we'd better follow at once.' "

They told me how to camp out in bad weather too. They said: "In winter try to find a tree with wide branches, for there will be less snow under it than in other places. Rake away what snow is there. Find a dry spot, cut branches, and pile them on it, and put your robe on them. Sleep near a fire there. Build the fire on top of the ground if you are not going to stay long. If you are going to camp there for some time, dig a pit."

There is no definite age at which a boy must join his first expedition: "When a boy is old enough, he volunteers." Though there is no compulsion to participate, the physically fit who wish to enjoy material benefits can hardly choose another course. Because of its practical and ceremonial extensions this apprenticeship is indispensable to successful warfare, and the man who has not undergone it is not cheerfully received by members of a raiding party he seeks to join. "Some do not volunteer. They are looked down upon. They cannot go on the warpath." Yet the youth who is unprepared is not goaded into premature participation. "If a boy thinks he can't stand it, he doesn't go." Nor does any boy start out ignorant of what he faces: "When a boy wants to volunteer, his relatives tell him of the hardships and dangers. If he still wants to go, they let him."

Once a boy has declared his intention of becoming a novice, he receives advice to guide his conduct during the four expeditions:

The first four times are important because, if a man shows himself to be unreliable and disobedient these first four times, that will remain his nature throughout expeditions and battles. The boys are told this, and they try to be at their best during this time. So they don't cause much trouble.

While you are a novice you have to watch out for your morals. If you are loose when you come back from one of these expeditions and have a lot of sexual intercourse, it will be your nature through life. Boys are instructed from the start about this. These things are impressed on them: "Don't be a coward; don't be untruthful; don't eat too much when you come back to camp between raids, or that will be your nature." So during the entire period the boy puts out his best [effort] and behaves his best.

One informant testified that the necessary information was imparted to him by his father. Another claimed that "a relative teaches the boy; a special man is not needed." Yet from still other accounts it is clear that shamans whose rites center about the location and frustration of the enemy and the granting of invulnerability in battle often prepare the youths for these journeys. Their selection is logical, for "these shamans, the 'bow shamans,' also make the jackets and other things which protect a man in battle." Often a number of young men of the same age are put in the care of one shaman.

All the volunteers are gathered and instructed by the shaman. They are taught the words and how they should conduct themselves. They are given a general outline of what they should do. It takes just a few days to learn.

The inexperienced boys who are on the raid for the first time have a certain kind of hat. And they are the only ones who have the drinking-tube along. The drinking-tube has a scratching-stick attached to it; that is, on the same cord. This scratching-stick is about five inches long and is made from the wood of any tree that bears fruit.

The shaman in charge of the boys makes the hats for them. There is no payment for this. It is like an issue[14] to the boys that comes automatically. This comes from a certain kind of shaman who has to do with war. The drinking-tube is given by the same person and is issued in the same way. The shaman has prayers to the directions. He throws pollen to the directions as he makes these things. The tube and the scratcher have a lightning design on. When the boy comes back, he returns the hat, scratcher, and tube to the shaman. The shaman can use them again for others.

"One who is a novice is different from the others." The difference is in the first instance a ritual one: "The older men treat the novices reverently because these young men are on one of their first raids and there are restrictions upon them." Like the pubescent girl, the novice is identified with a supernatural. "On the raid and warpath the men call the novice Child of the Water." Sacred aspects are further emphasized by behavior and food restrictions:

The novice, when he first gets the tube and scratcher and goes out with the others, cannot turn around quickly and look behind him. He must glance over his shoulder first. And in facing the other way he has to turn toward the sun first, the way they throw pollen. Bad luck would come to the party if this was not done.

If the boy does not use the scratcher, his skin will be soft; the flesh will be no good. He has to use the tube for all drinking. It is a rule that is put upon the boy. If he does not use the scratcher and tube, his whiskers will grow fast.

There is also a very strict rule against a novice having sexual intercourse while he is out.

Another thing: he must use the words that have been taught him. If he disobeys in this, he will be very unlucky.

Novices are not allowed to eat warm food, but must eat it cold. If they have to cook the food, they must let it get cold before they eat it. If the novice eats warm food, horses will not be worth anything to him. He is not allowed to eat entrails either. If he eats entrails, he will not have good luck with horses. Meat from the head of an animal is forbidden to him also.

To these rules various informants have added others. The novice should not gaze upward when he is on the raid or a heavy rain will come. He is not supposed to laugh at anyone, no matter how amusing the situation. He must speak respectfully to all the men and must not talk freely or obscenely about women. He must stay awake until he is given permission to lie down; to go to

[14] The Chiricahua refer to rations and goods distributed by reservation officials and the military as "issues."

sleep before the others would show indolence and would cause all the members of the party to be drowsy. The novice is cautioned against eating heartily lest he become gluttonous, and he is forbidden to eat choice parts of the meat or anything from the inside of the animal. When captured stock is killed on the return journey, the tough neck part is set aside for him. Also the ban against anything from the inside of an animal is then relaxed, and novices may be fed lung so that the stock will not become exhausted before the party reaches home.

Although his conduct is so important for the success of the expedition, the novice is obliged to gain his practical experience in a subordinate capacity:

They take the novices four times for the rough work but won't let them fight. It is to toughen them, they say.

The novices have to get the water and wood and do the heavy work around the camp when the men stop for the night. The men order them around pretty much. They must get up early in the morning and build the fire and care for the horses if there are any along. They are told, "Go over there and get those horses," and they have to go pretty fast. They have to do the cooking and make beds for the men. Sometimes they carry provisions for the men too. The men make these boys stay up on guard. They are the only ones who do guard duty.

The words which the boy learns and which he is instructed to use during his first four raiding journeys constitute a vocabulary of circumlocutory elements which replace ordinary forms of speech: "They had ceremonial words. Just the novice used them and only while he was out on the raid. The old men taught them these words and said, 'This is the novice's talk.'" In the raid or war vocabulary the term for heart becomes "that by means of which I live"; the customary word for pollen is replaced by a form which can be translated "that which is becoming life"; the owl is referred to as "he who wanders about at night," etc. Approximately eighty forms belonging to this special vocabulary have been collected. It is probable that the vocabulary was never a great deal more extensive, for the novice continues to designate most objects in the usual manner.[15]

[15] For a full analysis of the vocabulary see Opler and Hoijer, "The Raid and War-Path Language of the Chiricahua Apache," *American Anthropologist*, October–December, 1940.

Although the novices are expected to share the hardships of the journey, they are guarded from actual physical danger. The loss of a novice reflects upon the leadership of the raid, for the youth is under the protection of ritual and is present primarily for experience.

But raiding in enemy country is hazardous work at best, and sometimes the raiders, when they go forward on a particularly dangerous mission, must leave the novice at a distance so that he will not be drawn into battle. Then, if they encounter difficulties or superior forces, they may be unable to reach him again. Novices deserted in this way have perished or have suffered great hardship before reaching their homes.

Not all boys who begin this apprenticeship pass through it successfully. "If a boy is unreliable and doesn't show improvement, they don't take him out any more. They just drop him."

No special raiding parties are organized for the convenience of the novice. "The boys are taken on when there is trouble and many raids take place; then they get through in a hurry." Depending upon the needs of the encampments and the state of intertribal relations, as much as a year may elapse between the first and the fourth journeys.

Unless there is sharp criticism of the young man's conduct on the last journey, when he returns home he belongs to the ranks of the men. Of him it is said, "He has just moved up to adulthood": "It means that he has arrived at the point where he is a real man. He doesn't have to stay at home. He is free to do what he will and to have his own views. He can smoke now, and he can marry."

When the next raid or war party is announced, this new adult may participate in the war dance and commit himself to the undertaking on a different basis: "The fifth time the restrictions are off; there are no obligations to rule the young men. After the first four trips, after the apprenticeship, these youths are put first in battle to try them out. The fifth time out they are expected to be in the front ranks."

SOCIAL RELATIONS OF ADULTS

AN IMPORTANT element in the character of courtship and in the nature of premarital relations is a generalized negative set toward the easy display of emotion. The kiss, for instance, is considered too personal and expressive a gesture for adult or public use.

The mother and father kiss the children when they are playing with them and have them on their laps. But those who are grown up a little wouldn't kiss in anyone else's presence. When Chiricahua have not seen each other for a long time, they embrace. If you love someone, you embrace him and you say, "I'm glad to see you again." The women do the same thing, but they love one another so much they often sit down and cry. Maybe the last time they met one had a brother who is now dead, or something like that. A man might embrace his wife when he comes back from a long journey.

There is a feeling of inhibition in regard to intimate matters even between members of the same sex:

A grown person does not like to defecate or urinate before anyone else. If two men or two women are together, one will say, "I am going out." But if polite form of speech is used between these two, nothing will be said. The person just leaves. And a man would not make any explanation to a woman either.

Women do not want to be seen naked by other women any more than do men by men. Adults are reserved in these matters before one another. . . . . When a boy grew to manhood, he would not swim naked any more, not even before other men. The Chiricahua is very much ashamed about this. A grown man considers it a disgrace if another adult sees his privates. When a grown man goes in swimming, he always wears a loincloth or something. I have seen older men in swimming, but never naked.

Great dignity should be observed in speech:

I don't know the names of all the parts of a woman's genitals. Men don't usually talk about a woman's parts. If I talk like this, someone will say, "You're no man at all!" When X. [an aberrant in respect to sexually pointed speech whose case is considered below] talks, I don't know whether he means something on top or way in.

The reluctance to discuss intimate matters becomes intensified between individuals of opposite sex:

It is part of Chiricahua nature to be shy about such personal matters. It is almost impossible to talk to a Chiricahua girl about such things. Before I married my wife I never mentioned things of this nature [sexual] to her. Even after her father gave consent to the marriage we said nothing about it until we were living together. That is the old Chiricahua attitude. . . . . She belonged to the old school. I never kissed her or hugged her. We didn't even hold hands.

To give point to their ideal of restraint between the sexes, informants have repeatedly compared their own customs with those of other peoples whom they have lately come to know:

The young men I went around with attended the Comanche dances. The Comanche were the only ones that had any tribal life and dances still going. We really went to meet the Comanche girls, because they were the ones we had intercourse with.

You couldn't do much with the Chiricahua girls. If you began talking to them about such things, they just got mad and walked away. With the Comanche girls it was different, and we had no trouble at all. The Comanche men did not seem to resent the fact that we went around with the Comanche girls. It seems like a difference in attitude. I don't think it is because the Comanche were more degenerate or had had more contact with whites, because, as a matter of fact, I think the Apache had had more contact and more trouble with the whites and were more disorganized. It seems to me that it was a difference in attitude in treating the whole question. . . . .

Modesty and delicacy are ideals which some individuals fail to attain:

He is just a man with a dirty mouth. He's been this way ever since I have known him. Because he is always talking about these things some of the Indians call him "He Who Knows about It"; or they call him "Vulva," because he's always talking about that. You can't be with him for five minutes before he will start talking like this. I'll bet if we went right up now and asked him to tell something about the old times, he'd find some excuse for talking like this.

He goes right in to a place where he knows there are people who are ashamed before each other, and just the same he will say something so bad that all these people will have to leave. When the others who are there scold him about it, he says, "Well, I told nothing but the truth, didn't I?"

One time we were having a big council. He was sitting with the men, and his wife was over there sitting on the side of the hill with some other women. After a while she took her moccasins off. He noticed this. "Hey!" he called to her, "what are you doing?" "Oh, I've just taken my moccasins off," she said. "Well, you'd better put them on again," he told her, "or some of these men here will see your bare feet and get excited and go for you." His wife only laughed. She's used to that kind of talk. She's much younger than he is. She sticks to him because he's good support, I guess.

A second offender, a woman, was also adversely discussed:

That woman is a regular bulldog. She has a dirty mouth. She is awful, that woman! Everybody knows her. She will knock her husband about twenty feet, kick him, and call him dirty names. He doesn't do anything or say anything. He is very mild and doesn't stick up for himself. If you curse him, he will just laugh. Some do not like this about him.

One time my wife and I were visiting. There were about fifteen people present. This couple was there. My wife noticed earlier in the day that the woman was angry. When she saw her come in, she told me to go, because she knew that the woman would use all sorts of bad language. So I got out pretty quick. Later I asked my wife what the woman had done. She had backed her husband against the wall and given him an awful talking to right before all the people. She mentioned how big his privates were and everything.

Yet, despite these cases, the avowed canons of good taste generally prevail.

Concepts of courtship and sexual behavior are influenced by a manly ideal which slightly subordinates women and penalizes men for any open attention to them:

The Chiricahua men and women regard each other differently from the way the white people do. A man has a more honorary position than a woman. It looks to me as if the women try to serve the men and expect to do so. They show the men a little extra respect. That is why they let the men walk down the road ahead of them.

At a feast, such as a marriage feast, there is a special place for the men. The food is taken out and served to the men first. But there is no special place for the women. The women crowd around and eat what they can get and sit anywhere they can. But the women expect this. They do not think they are abused because of it. They would resent any other kind of treatment. If visitors come, they are served first, but the men visitors are served first of all. It looks as if men do not like to be thought of as coming under the influence of women.

We Chiricahua say, "Look at those white men! They go with their wives all the time. It looks as if they never get tired of them." We brag of the way we do, for we don't like to take our wives along. We have a better time when we are alone. Some of the fellows get together and talk and have fun for hours. We don't have such a good time if the women are around. The men might go to a social dance with their wives, but as soon as they get to the place they leave their wives and go with the men.

Courtship, elopement, and ideals of beauty.—Only shortsighted parents fail to plan and guide their daughter's future properly, for, with matrilocal residence in force, an undisciplined daughter or an improvident son-in-law may well be their ruin as they grow older and more dependent on the younger workers. Parents and close relatives owe a girl affection, the necessities of life, protection from natural and supernatural enemies, and proper training during her formative years. In return they expect gratitude from her for the sacrifices they have made, obedience, and stable conduct.

Unmarried girls are carefully guarded by their relatives:

They are pretty strict with girls after the puberty ceremony and before marriage. The girls are made to cook and sew. The mother, father, or brother attends them to or from a dance. Unmarried women, if young, are not allowed at a tiswin party.

In the words of another informant:

The girl was watched carefully by her folks. Because of this it was necessary to have someone approach the parents and speak for you if you wanted to marry a girl. It was almost impossible to court a girl. Men had to do it on the sly.

From this statement we see the strategic advantage to the parents of premarital control over their daughters. It brings suitors or their representatives directly to them, allowing them to choose their sons-in-law and to fix the terms of the agreement.

The same degree of supervision is not exercised over the son:

They are very strict with the girls. The girls are given general information by parents and relatives. The girls have attendants when they go to dances and they are watched in the home too. The parents are not so strict with the boys. The boys are given more freedom.

The absence of any approved period of courtship is emphasized in the account of a father who advised his daughter "not to go around with any man until she was married." An able informant summed up the matter by saying: "There is not much courtship. Marriage is usually arranged. The young people do not have much to say about it. The boy has the best of it. If he sees a girl he likes, he will go to his father and tell him."

Though no period of open courtship is institutionalized, there are ways for young people who are attracted to each other to meet:

In the old days it was considered shameful to go openly with a girl. If a man liked a girl, he would try to put himself in her way as much as possible without attracting notice. He would try to get to every social dance that she went to. That was the Chiricahua substitute for taking a girl out. It gave the young people a chance to meet. It gave the girl a chance to show whom she liked. If a girl chose the same man for a partner many times, you could be sure that that couple might get married. If a boy liked a girl and she showed him attention in this way, he might go to his father or his uncle or some other close relative and ask if he would try to arrange a marriage. Sometimes the boy would be turned down and sometimes not; he never knew.

D. is going through this stage now. He is in love with S.'s daughter. . . . . He doesn't do anything. He just goes to the store when he thinks she'll be there. He gets in a word or two. Then he goes one way and she goes another. He'll be watching every few minutes from the other side of the canyon. Pretty soon she'll come for water. He will be watching and will come to the place by a roundabout way, timing it to get there while she's there. Then he'll get in a couple of more words. Later she'll find some excuse to go off somewhere where he is, and so on.

Many understandings are reached following a military triumph. This is the time when spirits are high and when young men have won a stake which permits them to join the ranks of the suitors. "The Chiricahua turned their victories into a celebration, a dancing and marrying time. Lots of young men took advantage of the occasion."

The etiquette regulating the conduct of the married man and his wife's relatives makes elopement almost an impossibility. When it occurs, the affront to the girl's family is so serious that the offending couple is forced to live in isolation unless forgiveness and approval can be secured. "There are few cases of elopement. A girl who is not trained right might elope. Usually the couple doesn't come back to the girl's folks to live then but makes a camp apart."

But, even though their parents and relatives have much to say about the choice of a mate, the young people have their own standards of beauty and desirability and their own ways of influencing the issue. Concerning the physical traits in a girl which excite most admiration, and those which are least well considered, the following pronouncement is typical:

Girls with big lips, or a big nose, or with skin too dark; who are stooped or have big feet; who have a Roman nose or one too wide, or who have too long a

face—these are not considered good-looking. A full oval face is liked and medium height, not too tall. We like small hands and feet, but not too thin. A
plump, full body is best. Legs should be in proportion to the rest of the body and
not too thin. Mouth and ears should be in proportion to the rest of the face,
not big.

Premarital sex experiences.—Parents are not always successful
in bringing a daughter to marriage a virgin. Occasional cases of
rape have been reported.

Rape is classed as stealing. Sometimes a man is killed for this. It is more
serious to attack an unmarried than a married woman. If the person who did it
is found out, there is bound to be revenge by a member of the family who have
been wronged. This is individual revenge or revenge backed by a family. It does
not involve all the people.

If the woman is married, the husband has the right to do anything to the one
who mistreated her. The man's relatives may try to smooth it over for him.
Payment is often offered.

The girl, instead of being an innocent victim, may carry on a
clandestine affair. This is known as "night crawling," or, literally, "he crawls up to someone." One moonless night I was talking
with two men, one young and one old. The young man remarked,
"It's a good time for night crawling." The old man laughed, explained the meaning of the phrase, and added: "It's something
that used to happen in the old days too. The word was used in
the old times. But to do this was considered a disgraceful thing.
A man would be beaten if he was caught at it. When you do this
to a virgin, they kill your horses if you are caught."

If sexual relations between two young people are discovered,
the girl's family has suffered an economic loss. Should the young
man not be considered eligible by the parents, their anger is particularly aroused, for they have probably lost a chance to marry
their daughter worthily and yet cannot force a suitable match
from the intrigue. In this case "the parents of the girl have the
right to handle the boy. They won't demand payment. They
demand punishment, physical punishment." "When a girl goes
wrong, it is considered very serious. It is up to the girl's parents.
The man might be killed. Usually the couple is made to marry."
As the last sentence indicates, the average family is likely to
take the philosophical view:

They don't like it if there is sexual activity before marriage. If there is a child as a result of this, they make them marry. This kind of marriage is the same as any other kind. Polite terms are used between the in-laws, and presents are given to the father-in-law. They usually marry after the child is born, for a girl conceals her condition as long as she can.

In another account the possibility of flight to avoid the wrath of the family is mentioned, and there is a hint of retribution even in the case of a forced marriage:

Sometimes she went to another band to escape punishment. Nothing was done in the other band. Sometimes the boy and girl were forced to marry. When a girl of good family got into trouble, the two families talked it over, and they were married. But the man had to pay a horse because he had gone with the girl on the sly. The horse pardons the case.

Often pressure for honorable marriage comes from the relatives of the boy as well as those of the girl, for they are conscious of the wrong their kinsman has committed and are eager to avoid difficulties between the two families.

One night I was caught by another fellow lying with this girl. The next night several more caught me. The news spread. The relatives of the girl found it out, came to me, and asked me if it was true.

One of them said, "You've been going with my relative. You've been doing this all the time. Why aren't you a man and tell me you want to marry her instead of keeping her outside nights where it's cold and things might happen?" . . . .

My father, sisters, and brother knew nothing of this. I was sneaking. The girl's relatives told my parents, and my father told me that I should marry her. He said that I should let him tell the girl's relatives of my intentions so that they wouldn't feel bitter against me.

Her brothers and her mother, too, found out. They said to the girl, "You've been fooling around with this man. You'd better get married or else there will be talk against you." I really wanted to marry her and she wanted to marry me. I was just young and didn't have sense enough to do it right.

Of course, many assignations go undiscovered. The young people are capable of clever devices against prying elders. One girl, for instance, took advantage of the close family bonds and contrived to have a sleeping-place at home and another at her grandmother's. When she did not return to one of these beds, it was assumed that she was in the other. Often she was in neither place but in the encampment of her lover, a young widower.

Sometimes these affairs become a testing-ground for love and result in stable union. Such a case is the one cited below, where social dancing acted as a shield for a sexual adventure. The individuals involved have been happily married for many years now:

When I danced with her, I'd say, "What are we fooling around here for? We could be by ourselves." The next time she'd pull my sleeve, and we'd dance a little. Then I'd say, "Let's go." I'd go one way, and she'd go the other. We'd meet at a certain place.

Many problems arise when premarital sex relations result in pregnancy, especially if the man involved flees, denies responsibility, or is considered undesirable. The girl's kinsmen can no longer demand generous marriage gifts and will be relieved to find a man who will agree to support another's child. If a husband cannot be found for the girl prior to the birth of her baby, the public nature of the scandal and the necessity of provision for the child raise further issues. Therefore, resort is sometimes made to abortion, and illegitimate children are occasionally abandoned or destroyed at birth.

Herbalists give decoctions said to promote abortion. "There is a medicine used. You have to hire someone who knows how to make and use it." Mechanical means are also attempted:

They try to bring about abortion by pressing themselves over a sharp stick or stump, or by getting someone to press the stomach in a certain way. It was practiced in the old days, and it is practiced now. News of it always leaks out, though it is practiced in secret.

To perform abortion they press and massage the stomach. The girl shouldn't have anything to eat for several days.

Of the fate of an unwanted illegitimate child the following suspicion was voiced: "A certain man's daughter was in trouble a while back. She's just a young girl. They say her baby was born dead, but I think she killed it, or her relatives killed it in some way."

When illegitimate children are not disposed of, however, they are treated kindly. "Illegitimate children are often kept, and such a child is not discriminated against. It lessens a woman's chance for a good marriage if she has an illegitimate child, however." Illegitimacy may even be a spur to achievement:

An illegitimate child, when he realizes that he has no father, tries to make good in other ways, by bravery perhaps. There was a man in my group who was illegitimate but who rose to be a leader in war. He was recognized as a brave and good man and was respected. A man can rise from an illegitimate childhood position to wealth or even chieftainship if he has powerful friends.

Theories of conception.—Any discussion of illegitimacy raises the question of theories of conception, for the term for "bastard," literally, "child of many," is the verbal symbol of far-reaching notions.

Ideas of fetal development begin much like modern scientific dicta:

We believe that life is connected with a woman's egg. I've never heard them talk much about what there is there first from which the child develops. Everything has to start from eggs, I guess. Turtles and birds do.

Likewise the male seminal fluid is seen as a fertilizing agent. But here the parallel ceases:

I have heard the old men speak about it [i.e., semen] and say that it comes out of very rich blood. It is the very best, the richest blood. It is stored up in the testicles. Then it affects the feeling of all the nerves [creates desire] and it is the belief that it brings birth. It affects both men and women.

The Chiricahua believe that there is in the woman a pouch with her blood in it. When the man has intercourse with a woman, some of his blood [semen] enters her. But just a little goes in the first time, and not as much as the woman has in there. The child does not begin to develop yet, because the woman's blood struggles against it. The woman's blood is against having the child; the man's blood is for it. When enough collects, the man's blood forces the baby to come.

A logical extension of the "blood accumulation" theory is the belief that impregnation cannot occur as a result of a single sexual contact. Said a spokesman in reference to his first sexual experience:

One night when I was out with her, we got pretty excited. I handled her quite a lot. She resisted a little but not too much, and finally she let me do it. . . . . After we finished, I felt pretty ashamed. I took that girl back. I avoided her for quite a time. Later on I got over it and didn't avoid her, but I never took her out again or did anything to her.

I wasn't afraid that I had got her in trouble. I had only had intercourse with her once. Nothing can come of that. You have to do it with a girl twenty or even forty times to have a baby. There are cases where a baby has come sooner, but they are very rare. I believe this today. It is a general Chiricahua belief. I have seen it work out too many times to doubt it.

Acceptance of this idea reduces the fear of the consequences of an isolated sexual experience, but it dooms the unmarried mother to the stigma of having been repeatedly unchaste. The girl who claims that she is with child as the result of but one mis-step is simply not believed.

In another account the blood accumulation theory is worked out more precisely:

You have to have intercourse with a girl more than once to get a baby started. If you do it about three times a week, you will have a baby started in about two or three months. But it depends on the man and woman and on how much they do it. I know of a girl who had intercourse with a man many times in one night. If a girl did it at that rate, it wouldn't take any time at all to get a child started.

This theory of conception does not demand that the necessary semen be that of one man:

If a woman has intercourse with more than one man over a period of time, the child that comes will belong to both of them; each man contributes something to its physical makeup. The child will belong mostly to the man who has had most intercourse with the woman. If a woman has intercourse with many men and a child is born, the men say that each one has some small part in the child. Of a child of a loose woman one often hears a man say, "I have an elbow in there," or, "I have a foot in there."

It is believed that many men can be the father of one child. If a woman goes with several men, it is said that the child belongs to all of them. That is why an illegitimate child is so good-looking. He has the good points of all the men. And that is why the word for illegitimate child means "child of many." It can have parts from more than one man.

It is obvious from the last two excerpts that there exists a well-defined concept of heredity, based upon the continuity of the "blood" and its properties. This was made more explicit by a commentator who declared: "Children look like their parents. My oldest daughter looks like my mother, the old men tell me. My youngest daughter looks like her mother." This view is also expressed in joking. Thus, a young man was told by his friends that his big ears strangely resembled those of an illegitimate child whose parentage had not been fully accounted for.

Not long ago the idea that a child may have more than one father was introduced in a legal dispute. A man had been practicing polygyny with two sisters. Since plural marriages are banned by white edict, only one of these women could be registered as his lawful wife. When the other became pregnant, the problem arose of how to answer the queries of the agency officials. Finally, the woman blamed another young man for her condition, and, since he admitted having had intercourse with her three times, it seemed that he would be punished and be forced to support the baby. It was here that native doctrine was invoked. A legally minded brother of the accused man proved to the superintendent that the "secret husband" had been having relations with this woman and asserted that the child belonged "more to that man than to anyone else." It is doubtful that the superintendent understood the latter statement, but he was enough impressed by the testimony concerning the woman's irregular conduct to reduce the threatened punishment.

With the theory of blood accumulation goes a concept of blood exchange. The primary result of sexual intercourse is to add male blood to the store of female blood. The condition of the generative blood of the man is modified by his age and the state of his health. The blood accumulated within a woman has two special characteristics in addition. First, it is associated somehow with the menstruum. Menstrual blood is most dangerous to men; contact with it brings, at the least, rheumatic joints. Therefore, men fear it and avoid intercourse with menstruating women. Second, a woman's blood is in a special category because, if she is promiscuous, her augmented supply represents the contributions of many men of dubious soundness.

This fully explains the warning to young men against tampering with older women of bad reputation. Evidently, it is suspected that during intercourse the man's genitals may come in contact with the woman's blood and that any disease which it carries can be thus transmitted to him. Tuberculosis, for instance, has been considered communicable in this way:

In the time before my day and my father's day, the Chiricahua didn't know what tuberculosis was. They knew that sometimes a man's stomach got bad and he coughed up nasty yellow stuff that tasted bad. They said this came from smoking too much. The yellow in the tobacco just got in the stomach, and more and more accumulated until a person could spit it out. Sometimes a person got pretty bad and began to spit blood—have what you call hemorrhage now, I guess.

The Chiricahua thought you could catch this from someone who had it, and that you got it from having intercourse with someone who had it. So a man would be ashamed to admit that he was spitting blood or yellow pus for fear that someone would say he had had intercourse with a woman who had this.

The Chiricahua had remedies for this. Some used "narrow medicine" [*Perezia wrightii*] for tuberculosis.[1] But lots of them were ashamed and waited until it was too late to save them.

Love ceremonies.—Love ceremonies are carried on by some men and women for their own purposes or, upon request and payment, for others who seek them out. Though this type of ritual is not equated with witchcraft, "charmers" are seldom talkative about their art. The danger in wielding a love ceremony is that the person who is to be influenced may detect and resist the onslaught. "Often a love ceremony that fails or is improperly performed makes a person crazy. There is a ceremony to cure the effects of the love craziness."

Certain objects and motifs occur time and again in love ceremonies. The four-holed flageolet, made of carrizo, is one of these:

There were very few who played the flute. I've seen flutes played, but the Chiricahua didn't pay much attention to them. The flute must have come from the Western Apache. They use it a great deal. The Chiricahua feel that, when anyone is playing on the flute like that, it's not a good thing. It is connected with love magic, and they don't like it. Only people with love ceremonies use it, it seems.

Many charges concerning the possession of love power are undoubtedly inspired by rivalry and jealousy. Exceptional success in gaining the attentions of the other sex, or polygyny involving a man of but ordinary means, may lead to the same suspicion:

The hummingbird is ceremonially used. I think some use it in love ceremonies and to influence girls just as they use the butterfly. R., they say, knows this

---

[1] Tuberculosis can also be caused by worms. In a trickster tale, Coyote, wishing to deceive his family, tells them he has lung trouble and that they should leave him for dead if worms drop to the ground from his bed. That the "worms" may really drop, he takes spoiled meat to bed with him.

ceremony. He got a young woman with it. Everybody knows he influenced her. She chased him all around, day and night, when she was a young girl. He's much older than she is. That girl was very pretty and he was ugly. They think he used butterflies. They say that he has been helping some other people with his power too. I've heard young fellows talking about it.

And they talk about another man that way too. It shows. He has two wives, one in secret. He's not good-looking; he hasn't anything. That's how you know. Some suspected N. of having love power because he had two wives. Some even suspect C. They say he's got a pretty fair-looking wife and doesn't do anything. They say anything about you these days.

They think that the time to perform this ceremony is in spring or midsummer when the butterfly is out. Then it works easier.

In an expansive mood, one man revealed that in his younger days he was "so lucky with the girls that many said it was love power." He added, however, "I swear that I never had one little bit of this power."

But there are practitioners who do carry on such ceremonies:

There are people who can make others love you. Their work is not considered a disgrace like that of a witch. If you are a man, you go to one of them and say that you want a certain woman. You must pay these people.

In the ceremony they use the sun, the butterfly, and water. When they want to influence you, they splash water on you with the hand. Sometimes they have something shiny to flash in your eyes. Sometimes they take a piece of your clothing or your hair—something of yours is needed to work with. They sing to the sun. They think that the sun can stretch a net like a spider's net and catch a person in it.

I had a friend, an old man, who used to boast to me that he had such power. He married a young girl. I asked, "How did you get your wife?" He said, "I used power." I believed him because it looked queer to me. He was not good-looking either. He said that when he prayed to a girl he made her put on the nature of a butterfly. She would then fly here and there, take no responsibility, and have no worry about the future, and so you could make love to her.

The use of water is especially interesting, for the term meaning love power, while it does not yield to linguistic analysis in entirety, is evidently related to the word for water.

Concerning the reality of a love ceremony another informant said:

There was a man at Whitetail who knew the ceremony pretty well. He died about 1919. . . . . The old man, if I liked a girl, could be hired to get her for me. He would sing over the girl for me, and when he finished, the girl would come right in and sit down. Then she would love me forever and never leave me.

Women, as well as men, claim to control this power:

> T.'s wife has this ceremony. Once when she was full of tiswin she promised to show me what she knew about it. She sang one of the butterfly songs for me. I couldn't get on to it, for I heard it only once. In the morning when she was sober she changed her mind and wouldn't show me any more. In these ceremonies the caterpillar and rope are used with the butterfly. If the butterfly is put in your bed during such a ceremony, you're a "goner"; you are "charmed."

Another ramification of love power is its relation to deer ceremonies:

> The man who knows the ceremony of the deer is good at love medicine, they say. He gets any young girl. He will always be poor though. He never has anything but his loincloth, but the girl loves him just the same.

> If a person is under the influence of the love ceremony and eats meat from a deer's head, it will cause his own head to swell up.

The main outlines of the love ceremony are now clear. The desired one, lured by flageolet music, is to become as aimless and irresponsible as the butterfly and is to be enmeshed in a net of "ropes" of the sun (sunbeams, sometimes symbolized by pieces of cord). Contact with the person to be influenced is important. Water may be playfully splashed upon him; a beam of light may be directed toward him from some shiny object (another form of the sun motif); a sticky leaf may be flicked at him; a butterfly or a caterpillar may be dropped in his bed; a piece of his clothing or a strand of his hair may be secured.

The emphasis of the ceremony is upon disarming any contrary will and securing fast the one desired. This explains the seeming intrusion of deer power. The deer ceremony has broadly similar objectives—to induce the animal to be tractable and to hold it in a place from which it may easily be taken. By substituting an object of affection for the game animal, the deer ceremony becomes quite as effective for another purpose. But here a choice must be made. One who decides to use his deer ceremony for love rather than for sustenance will remain poor in material things.

MARRIAGE ARRANGEMENTS, MARRIAGE, AND RESIDENCE

Most marriages are arranged in terms of a conventional pattern in which the wishes of the families involved carry much weight. The early completion of the girl's training, the need of the encampment for additional young men, and the disapproval of premarital sex experience for women are all factors contributing to the tendency for girls to marry young. Therefore, "the girl is allowed to marry by Chiricahua rule after her ceremony, after her first menstruation."[2]

At the time of puberty the girl is given the advice necessary to guide her actions in caring for herself at the time of menstruation and in regulating her relations with men:

They tell the girls how to keep clean during menstruation. There are no restrictions on a woman at this time; she can eat any food and she can go around. But the girls are told to wear their old clothes during menstruation and that they must not leave them around. They are shown how to wear something like a loincloth with a pad at this time. The girls are also reminded of the effect of menstrual blood on men. They are told that it makes men paralyzed and deformed, unable to straighten their arms or legs. The girls are also told that they can ride mares but not male horses during menstruation.

And they tell a girl that she must stay pure until her marriage, that virginity is expected of a woman who has not been married before. They tell her that a man might leave a woman who is not a virgin, that the maidenhead is the sign of virginity, and if a woman is not proved a virgin by this means at marriage, a man would get angry and the marriage would be broken up.

The young man cannot look forward to so early a marriage, for he must first prove his ability to provide for and defend a family by participating in the four raiding parties.

Marriage is considered less a romantic venture than a solid economic arrangement, though personal and individual values are by no means totally eliminated:

Many of the old people think of marriage from the economic side. They advise a man to marry and have a home because they figure that the man will then be serious, will provide for his family, and get ahead. On the other hand, you can't disregard physical love either. Whether or not the old people think of this, the young ones do. I often hear people remarking that some boy has married just for love and wasn't sensible enough to take a girl who was a good worker and

---

[2] Some informants deny this and even complain that "the girls marry too young today," but the evidence of former early marriage is conclusive.

could provide a real home for him. Often they talk of foolish young people who don't think of practical things when they marry.

Sometimes the parents of the boy and girl arrange the match and only tell the principals when all arrangements are made. If a man is industrious, he has more chance to get a match, and the same is true for the girls. Some very ugly Indian men have gotten beautiful girls, not because the girls wanted them, but because the parents of the girl recognized their industry and insisted on the marriage. Old men who are rich sometimes marry very young girls in this way.

Often the prospective husband thoughtfully contemplates not only the young lady but the affinities to whom he will be so closely bound if he marries her:

Before marriage a man looks at the parents of the girl, at her industry, sees how strong and able to bear children she is, how congenial and sweet she is, and he decides on these grounds. Beauty of face is of little account. Industriousness is most important probably, but if a woman is mean and cranky a man would never have her, even if she was a good worker.

As might be expected from the important part that settled elders play in marriage arrangements, the decisions arrived at do not always conform to the wishes of the young people:

In one way of arranging it, the children are just matched up by the parents and relatives when they reach marriageable age. The two families might be friendly. When they tell the girl, sometimes she may not want to marry the man chosen for her. Sometimes they appeal to her or otherwise influence her against her will. As for the boy, maybe he knows the girl, maybe not. Perhaps he has never spoken to her but has seen her only at a distance.

It's not so easy as we've been making out. Sometimes a girl will run off rather than marry a man. Some girls are forced into marriage.

Girls are married to men many years older than they are sometimes, because their parents match them to wealthy persons. And some younger men marry rich widows. I notice that the older person is inclined to be very jealous in these cases.

This does not mean that true love matches are unknown, but such unions receive scant sympathy, especially when they turn out badly:

F. is a good example of a woman who went crazy over a man and still is that way. She can take more abuse than any woman I ever saw. Her husband has never done any work and never will. There's no chance of his making good. But she married him. Look how he has treated her! But she is wild about him right now. If it wasn't for her family, she'd be back with him now.

Though the parents and close relatives of young people are eager to have them confortably married and united to a family of standing, they are ordinarily willing to listen to any sensible conjugal plans which their charges may have. "After all, the final decision is usually left to the young people. They can be persuaded, but they can't be forced as a general thing. Such marriages do not last." And the young people, knowing their stake and place in the marriage arrangements, are not hesitant about indicating their preferences. The young man may be emboldened to ask a girl how seriously concerned about him she is. He may hint that if she will encourage such a move he will request his relatives to approach her parents about the matter. "Often the boy will tell his father or some other relative which girl he likes. He works through the family. He tells his father or his uncle to go to the girl's father and ask for her." Meanwhile the girl has revealed her affection for the young man to her mother or some other close relative and has paved the way for the reception of a representative of the suitor.

Theoretically, the young man's family is expected to take the initiative and approach the girl's relatives. In a good many cases, however, the relatives of a marriageable girl take a far from passive role:

She was a fine-looking girl. Her mother sent word to me by the girl's stepfather. "Any time you get ready you can marry my girl," she said. My intention was not to do it, but I gave no answer one way or another. A second time she sent word to me by the same man, saying, "I'll give you this girl. Why don't you say something about it?" My friend, a relative of the girl, said, "Why don't you marry that girl? Then we'll be together all the time."

They moved camp close to me. I was called over there by the stepfather. They had something to drink. They all got to feeling good. Then the mother asked me for the third time. She pointed to me and said, "You, I want you for my son-in-law. I want you to have my daughter."

I had never known the girl. She was good-looking and a good worker. But I didn't know whether she cared for me or would love me all of her life. I couldn't go just by what her mother said. I was drunk and not bashful. I told the old lady right to her face, "I have never at any time spoken to your daughter. I don't know whether she would care for me. By forcing her this way I don't think we'd have a home together very long. I'd rather get acquainted with a girl. I don't care what kind of looking girl she is as long as she gets on well with me."

The old lady answered me, "I'm the one who raised her. She's going to marry the man I want her to or she won't marry. You're the only man I want to have for my son-in-law." So the girl didn't have any chance to choose her own husband.

In another account the first move leading to the marriage of the narrator was taken by the grandmother of a girl whose parents were dead:

I went to her place that night. I had heard that the old lady had some tiswin. When I got there she told me to have a drink. As we talked she told me that I was single and needed a wife. She mentioned this girl and said it was worth two horses to get her. I had never seen the girl before. When I got home I started to think about it seriously. I talked it over with my relatives. An uncle of mine gave me a mule, and a cousin gave me a horse.

The next day I went to the home of a certain woman, a middle-aged woman. She was eating when I arrived. I called her outside and hired her to speak for me to this girl's grandmother. This woman lived just on the other side of a stream from the girl and her grandmother. The next day my go-between went to the old woman and asked her to give me the girl. The old woman demanded two good horses. My go-between thanked the grandmother and came to tell me what had been said. I gave her the horse and the mule to lead to the old woman, and the next day I went to the girl.

But regardless of the direction from which the first overture comes, it is the young man or his representative who must lodge a formal request with the girl's kin for consent to the union. Gaining this consent and perfecting the arrangements is a delicate undertaking, for nothing is more humiliating than a refusal when matters have gone this far. A suitor who is an older man, who is without close relatives, or who is independent of them may plead his own cause. A man may also speak for himself if he is courting a divorced woman. But making the request is considered a most unwelcome task, and the matter is usually intrusted to a go-between: "There is always someone who goes to the girl's relatives and tells of a man's good points. This is not a profession. They find someone who is interested in the boy and is willing to go to the parents of the girl. It can be a man or woman who does this."

Occasionally, it is the boy's father who acts in this capacity. "The boy's father will go to the girl's father and say, 'I have a boy who likes your girl.' He tells what the presents will be." The degree of formality depends largely on the relations between the two families. Where a kindly understanding has been established the boy's father feels least hesitant about assuming the initiative himself. But more frequently someone other than the parent is found for this duty:

The father does not always go to the girl's family. Another relative or friend will go, or the family may hire a man who is somewhat of a public figure and will know just what to do. The go-between is paid if the marriage goes through. He is given something valuable, like a buckskin or a horse, because what he has done is a very unpleasant task to the Chiricahua mind. Something holds a man back from this. I can't describe it.

A young man may have less trouble gaining the good will of his future parents-in-law than in finding a suitable spokesman to act for him:

So I said, "You're my uncle and I plead with you to get me fixed up. It's your duty." We talked back and forth like this for a few days. I told him it was very important to me. But he took it easy. He'd just smile and light a cigarette when I'd ask him. I felt like throwing something at him. After he lit his cigarette he'd make himself more comfortable. He just gave lots of excuses. He wouldn't do it.

It was bashfulness on his part that held him back. S. (the girl's father) is a pretty important man and hard to handle, and that held him back. Besides he didn't know how to talk along this line. You have to be pretty experienced. If you are refused you have to take it gracefully. You have to know how. There are lots of things that hold a man back. It's not just going up to a man and saying, "This boy wants to marry your daughter. What do you say, yes or no?" Sometimes a go-between has to get drunk to get courage up to speak.

The go-between must be prepared to cope with embarrassing situations such as this:

When D. started to go in there, the mother said, "Here's an old man who never comes to visit us. What's up?" She thought there was something wrong. D. said, "I have come over here to speak to you."

"What do you want to speak to us about?"

"I want to speak for your daughter."

Right away the old man, the father, said, "No, nothing doing!"

The old lady told him, "Keep still! You've got nothing to say. We are poor people, and everybody dislikes you. You need some good man to defend you, to keep flies off you. If there is any good man coming—I don't know who he is—but if it's a good man, he will be a big help to me. But you begin talking against him right away!"

D. said, "I am going to give you valuable property. That man will give you horses. But the way you start off is not right."

The old lady asked, "Who is this man?"

He's standing out there. He's my nephew. I love him. He's a good man for you. . . . ."

If the go-between is a relative of the suitor and a friend of the girl's family, he meets opposition by injecting a personal note that is hard to resist: "Sometimes the go-between would say, 'I want your daughter to marry this boy. He is my relative. From now on we will live as relatives.'"

It is an advantage "to get an influential person to talk for you." While the go-between is simply an agent, he takes his task seriously and believes his success is a measure of his persuasiveness. Should he be ungraciously received, he is likely to feel personal resentment. Consequently, it is more difficult for the average family to return a negative reply to a "public figure" than to an ordinary man. Forceful conversationalists are likewise in demand for this office. Sometimes a person gains a reputation in this field and may be asked to perform this service a number of times, but it is denied that there are any "professional go-betweens." Even affinal relatives may act for a young man: "I talked to my sister-in-law about a wife. I told her to ask a certain person for a wife for me. It took a long time."

A humorous story, illustrating the kind of temperament eminently suited for the task, is told of a man who has acted as go-between by request on a number of occasions and at least once without specific instructions:

J. got married through L. L. was always the life of the party. He was witty and loud spoken. He was a widower and J. was living with him. He was related to J. in some way. J. had been going with E.'s daughter for a long time. He intended to marry her anyway, but he had not done anything yet about it. Then L. was invited to a tiswin party at E.'s place. He got feeling good. J. and the girl were not there. While he was feeling good he got talking with Mrs. E. He said, "Now how about letting my relative marry your daughter?" Mrs. E. said, "That's fine!"

The next day L. woke up. He was the way people are after a party. "Oh, J.," he said, "now you are in for it!"

"What's the matter with you? You must feel pretty bad after that party," J. said.

"Well, J.," L. said, "you've been going around with that girl and now I guess you can go with her for the rest of your life. Yesterday I acted as a go-between for you and fixed it up for you to marry her. So we'll have to clean you up, and you'll have to leave me and set up your own home."

J. couldn't believe it was true, but the man had done it. And Mrs. E. had taken it seriously. But J. was glad anyway. He married the girl shortly after that. I sure joke with J.'s wife about this! I tell her that if L. hadn't got drunk, she never would have been married.

Usually the go-between leaves the young man behind to await the outcome of the negotiations and performs his work without the suitor's co-operation:

I went to K. He agreed to do it. I was to stay at his place and wait for him while he went out and talked to her father. He promised that he would hurry back as soon as he could. He was all dressed up in his best clothes.

I was pretty nervous while he was gone. I thought of the possibility that I would be turned down. I made up my mind that if I was turned down I would get out of that place just as fast and as quietly as possible.

By and by I saw K. coming. He was taking his time instead of hurrying. "Well! What did he say?" I asked him. "Prepare yourself for bad news," he told me. But I could see he was joking. He fooled around with me for a few minutes before he told me everything was all right. He told me then that the girl's father had agreed right away.

But when there is some uncertainty about gaining consent and the young man's personal assurances of good faith may be required in order to secure a favorable reply, the suitor accompanies the go-between and remains near by. Whenever possible the actual face-to-face encounter of a man and his potential parents-in-law is avoided, because, should consent be given, he finds himself standing in the presence of those whom he should not see.

When I went with D., who acted as go-between for me, I stopped at the door. I was not going in there. I would have a better chance if I stayed outside. D. told me, "Stay outside so that you will have more chance; for if you marry this girl, you will have to hide from her mother." J. [a rejected suitor for the hand of the same girl] had come right in with his go-between and made a fool of himself.

I stayed near by so that if they should say, "Well, let's hear from this man," I'd be there and could speak from where I was. I couldn't run right in there and show no respect. So I was standing near the door.

On request, however, the young man has to appear before the kin group of the girl he hopes to marry:

Suppose I want to marry a certain girl. A relative of mine goes over to her folks and speaks to them about it. They might say, "Send that boy over here."

I go over there. They tell me to sit outside, perhaps, and they talk to me from the inside of their camp. Or they might tell me to come in. I go in. They ask me what I intend to do. I give them a good talk, telling them that I will work for them, stay with them, bring in something to each one of them, and give so many horses to them too. Then, if they agree, one of the old ladies, a relative of the girl I am going to marry, may put a blanket over her head and walk out, saying, "I'm going to hide from this man." The father and mother do that too. They have to [i.e., practice avoidance]. There is no choice for them. The close relatives of my wife are all there and show what they intend to do. Those who are not there send word to me about hiding or speaking polite. Then I act that way toward them.

The presentation of gifts is a convention that is seldom violated. "A man must give a present to his wife's relatives or be disgraced; the woman is disgraced too if this is not done." It is expected that a chaste and dutiful girl will attract valuable gifts, and, in the words of an informant, "it's not much use asking for a woman in marriage if you can't give a present." It is one of the duties of the go-between to mention the gifts and to satisfy the girl's relatives that they will be adequate: "Whoever goes as go-between for the young man says, 'I want to ask you for your daughter. I'll give you so many horses, so many buckskins,' and he mentions whatever else he has been told to offer."

If an understanding between the families has been reached in advance and the visit of the go-between is merely a formality, he may take the presents with him and leave them as soon as consent is granted. More commonly, he returns later to deliver what has been promised. Therefore, the marriage gift is called "a burden has been brought." If the arrangement entails the giving of horses only, the prospective groom may simply turn them out to graze with those of his future parents-in-law.

There are no definite limits to the number of presents that may be promised, and the size of the gift has little bearing on the status of the principals:

The woman's status is not affected by the amount of the present. The man who gives a great deal is just thought of as a man who is able to give a great deal. It's considered all right, but he can't raise his position that way. About four or five horses with saddles would be a very big present. A horse or two would be normal and average.

It would be a mistake to interpret these presents as a "bride price." They do not entitle the husband or his family to any extraordinary control over the wife or her property. In fact, the control exercised by the wife's family over the husband is much more stringent than that to which the woman is subject, despite the total absence of any exchange gifts to the man's family. Moreover, these gifts or their equivalents are never returned, not even in cases of unfaithfulness on the part of the woman or of dissolution of the marriage tie.

The marriage gift functions as initial evidence of the economic support, co-operation, and generosity which a man owes his wife's close relatives. The promise of future assistance can even take the place of the gift on occasion, for it is said that a poor man, unable to muster wealth at the time he wishes to marry, might say: "I am poor, but whatever I am able to accumulate in the way of material things will be yours, for I will be here with you all the time."

The usual practice, after the presents have been received, is to "divide them up among the relatives." Kin of the girl who have contributed to her support and who have been consulted about the marriage arrangements, are sure to receive some part, if only a token offering.

As soon as a separate dwelling can be built and equipped, the young couple begin their married life together, without ritual or formalities:

A day or two after consent is given, the marriage takes place. As soon as everything is ready they start living together. The girl and her female relatives build the house. They put it up near the home of the girl's parents, for the young people usually go to live with the girl's relatives. The relatives of the girl usually furnish baskets and household equipment for the place, though sometimes the man's family may give them things with which to start out.

This emphasis upon matrilocal residence calls attention to one of the fundamental themes of the culture, for the organization of the economy assumes the presence and the closest co-operation of the sons-in-law.

A man feels under obligation to his father-in-law. He feels that he should hunt for him. Therefore, there was the tendency in the old days to go to the wife's people. A man's parents recognized this obligation too. They often said, "Well, that's what you married for. You'd better go over there."

Residence with or near his affinities is almost imperative for the man, for obviously it would be an insupportable burden for him to maintain a distant encampment of his own and still provide liberally for his wife's parents. Moreover, his identification with these affinal relatives is not without its reciprocal benefits.

At marriage a man goes to the camp of the girl's parents to live. We do this because a woman is more valuable than a man. We do it to accommodate the woman. The son-in-law is considered a son and as one of the family. The in-laws depend a great deal on him. They depend on him for hunting and all kinds of work. He is almost a slave to them. Everything he gets on the hunt goes to them. In return he has privileges with the property of his wife's people. He can get anything they have very easily. It is understood that he can call on them for aid. This relationship dates from the time of consent to the marriage.

Sometimes the arrival of the groom is the signal for a celebration at the encampment of the bride to which relatives and friends of the couple are invited. The expense and labor are borne by the woman's relatives, although the man's kin, if they live close by, may assist. The program is the usual one of games, feasting, and social dancing. The festivities continue through a day and late into the night.

After marriage the face of the world is changed for the young man: he removes to another residence, he becomes drawn into the orbit of a new economic constellation, and he becomes subject to the edicts and desires of new masters.

THE MAN AND HIS WIFE'S RELATIVES

Primary avoidances and the avoidance behavior pattern.—The regular terms for various affinal relatives are all forms of one verb—the verb "to carry a burden." There have been recent extensions of the meaning of this root, but in the older sense the burden to which reference is made seems to have been the proceeds of the hunt:

I can say to anyone, "I will bring in [carry in] deer for you," using this word. Friends have said this to me because I do not hunt much. I say to them, using the same word, "Yes, bring in the game for me." This does not imply any relationship between us necessarily. On the other hand, when it comes to marriage, we speak of one who marries into our family as "one who carries things in for me" in the sense of "one who goes out and kills and carries in game for me." The word means to me that in the old days a son-in-law would go out and kill game for his parents-in-law. The word implies to me that the man's business is to hunt in this fashion for me if I am the father-in-law. It is his obligation to do so forever.

It is not alone the father-in-law who calls a son-in-law "one who carries burdens for me." Every relative of the wife, no matter how remotely connected, is entitled to so address or refer to the husband. And the term with which he reciprocates is simply another form of the same verb which means "one for whom I carry burdens."

From the moment that consent to the marriage has been given, a relationship of total avoidance is established between the husband and certain of his wife's relatives. With these persons, avoidance is the unalterable rule and no choice is permitted. "Even if your wife's parents don't approve of the marriage, they have to be ashamed [practice avoidance] anyway." These obligatory avoidance affinities are: the wife's mother, her father, her mother's mother, and her father's mother. Thus, when the young man comes to his new home, there are at least three affinal relatives living close by (providing they are still alive) upon whom he may not look, and who may not see him. Even at the marriage feast this rule of avoidance must be respected. Avoidance makes necessary certain precautions in the arrangement of homes and obviates the possibility of a common meal for the larger relationship group, even though its members share the same larder.

A man lives near his in-laws and brings what he gets on the hunt back to them, all of it. His food is prepared there at his mother-in-law's place anyway. The camp of the young people is so arranged that the place of the parents-in-law cannot be seen; it might be behind some brush with the door facing the other way. The wife eats with her husband, though the food is usually prepared at her mother's home.

The bringing of food to the husband by the wife is termed "she sets something in a container before him":

This means the act of the wife in bringing to her husband food that has been prepared by her mother. The word is now jokingly used to lazy men in the sense of, "You want things pretty easy, don't you? You want things brought on a silver platter to you."

The adjustments which avoidance requires are a constant source of humor:

One day J. and I were in the trader's store. The baker was bringing in a tray of bread and rolls, holding it before him. We did not see him and were in his way. Someone shouted, "You, get out of the way! Do you think this is food being carried to an avoided person?" He said that because it looked as if the baker was coming to wait on us with a tray. Everyone laughed.

The difficulties of avoidance under all conditions give rise to a crop of "mother-in-law jokes" too:

We have stories and jokes about the mother-in-law. A man will tell how every time he wanted to cross a path or do this or that, his mother-in-law would always come into sight. It sounds funny when told by an Indian in the Indian language.

But, in spite of such levity, the obligation to avoid the designated affinities is solemn. The avoided person is called "the one to whom I do not go," and all kindly disposed individuals are expected to sound the warning, "Do not walk here!" when an individual is about to come into the presence of anyone from whom he "hides."

Sometimes by accident you meet a person you should avoid, nevertheless. Then you just duck away as fast as possible. When it happens, a man gets angry at himself sometimes. He says, "I should not have gone here." Or he might blame his mother-in-law and say, "She had no business being around here." It is a custom violated, and we do not like it.

The gravest objection is not to the proximity of the avoided relative or to the sound of his voice but to the sight of him:

If I do not hide from my wife's relatives whom I am supposed to avoid, they will call me a witch. If I run into the woman from whom I am supposed to hide and do it right along, she gets angry and calls me a witch. They say you'll get blind if you keep looking at these in-laws. This one tells the other relatives and they may try to chase me away perhaps. But I love my wife and want to stay on. Sometimes the Chiricahua had a little war among themselves about things like this, and someone would get killed.

The average person takes little risk of jeopardizing his sight or of being considered a witch:

Often a mother-in-law will not take part in a social dance if she thinks it will expose her to her son-in-law. The same with a feast; both will not stay around at the same time. Often a man has to duck away or go out the back way before a crowd of people when his mother-in-law comes. They keep it up today and have to be just as careful, although it is sometimes even harder now.

The husband is always conscious of the wishes and attitudes of the affinal relatives he never sees; "the man is ruled by them." Using his wife as messenger, they send him orders and hints of praise or censure. They know as much about his activities as if they shared his household, and he is correspondingly sensitive to their reactions. Said one man: "I know that if I had trouble with my wife, my father-in-law would stick up for her. Your father-in-law tells you to do something, and if you don't do it, you have your wife on your hands, scolding all the time."

A common device of the parents-in-law for communicating directions is to tell their daughter what they want done when they know her husband is within hearing. Once a man with whom I was working paused to tell his daughter that he wanted some rocks, which he considered a hazard to his home, removed. No mention of who should do the work was made. But the implications were clear, and the next day the son-in-law was busy at the task. Soon after, the older man discussed the state of the woodpile in the same impersonal vein, and the following day the son-in-law was chopping wood.

Much oblique communication passes between avoidance affinities when a situation warrants it:

You can't see your mother-in-law, but that doesn't mean that you don't think a great deal of her. Very likely she's the one you count on most in your wife's family. If you and your wife have trouble, maybe your mother-in-law will stand out of sight and pretend to be talking to the baby or someone else, and she will talk with you and try to settle the trouble you have been having. If she has stood up for you in this way, probably, even if you separate from your wife, you will continue to bring your mother-in-law food and things because you like her.

Sometimes the pretense of indirect discourse is dropped and an actual conversation between the two avoidance affinities takes place:

In cases of emergency, or if you have wronged your wife, your mother-in-law may approach near enough to speak to you. She usually comes at night, but if she comes during the day, she must be behind some object so that you cannot see her face.

Then, too, you may have to go and talk to her about important things. If you are separated from your wife and you trust your mother-in-law, you may get the help of somebody at your mother-in-law's camp to see that she is safely inside so you won't run into her. Then, standing outside, you may talk to her.

The father-in-law, too, may find it necessary to state his views directly:

I talked to that boy, her husband. I said, "I'm talking to you. This day means something. It shouldn't be wasted. This day means something to everybody. Every day means that you should bring in something to eat. Make it count; work and make something. If you have nothing to eat, your wife cannot cook anything for you. It's not your place to be angry at your wife because you don't have anything to eat. Look at her clothes. Many things rest on you. It's the man's duty to bring in the meat and clothes. You can't expect the woman to do that."

I said, "My daughter, it is your place to keep house. Keep everything neat about your place. Keep yourself neat the way you were when I was raising you. Wear good clothes. Keep your husband's clothes clean. Keep your fire going all the time. Quit running around nights and doing things as though you were single. Don't fuss at each other."

And I said to the boy, "A woman must be treated well because she feeds you; she's the only friend you have. Your mother and father can't treat you better than your wife does. That's the way I feel about my wife." I told him, "She's the mother of the whole thing, this life you have to go through, and you may have a long life."

When quarrels arise among a man's affinal relatives, it is to his advantage to be as neutral as possible, so that his relatives-in-law, and particularly his wife's parents, will not condemn him for intrusion into their affairs.

Now there's trouble at my place. My wife's stepmother told her that a cousin said something about her. So my wife hasn't gone over to visit that cousin for a long time. The cousin sees me and asks me why, but I make excuses and never say. But then my wife met this cousin and told her the truth. The next day this cousin came over to the stepmother and asked, "Did you tell that woman I said so-and-so?" The stepmother said, "No." So now the cousin says my wife made it all up. I thought it best to let my father-in-law know that I'm not taking sides, that I'm only an in-law here. He says that it's all right, he does not hold it against me. It's the nature of women, and we shouldn't bother about it, he says.

But it would be superficial to infer that the husband is constantly tyrannized by his avoidance affinities. They would be ill advised, indeed, to drive to divorce a man who is discharging his obligations to them satisfactorily. "The mother-in-law sticks up for the son-in-law in case of trouble if he is known to be a good man. The mother-in-law does not beat about the bush. She tells the person right out what is in her mind."

That the son-in-law can expect justice and consideration is illustrated by a case, phrased in terms of present-day economy, which preserves values operative in purely aboriginal times. The son-in-law here assumes a passive attitude, for it would be unbecoming of him to voice his own demands.

If one of the sons is lazy and the brother-in-law does all the work, all the herding, and, when they come to sell the sheep or to slaughter the animals, the son wants his proportionate share of the proceeds, his father will say to him, "My son, your brother-in-law did all the work. Now you want just as much of the profit as if you had worked. You must go and see your sister."

His sister says, "Take your bunch of sheep and put them in some other flock. Get someone who will herd your sheep for nothing! That's what you are looking for." The brother-in-law will sit by, keeping his peace.

Avoidance and honor comprise only one aspect of a man's obligations to his wife's parents; the other facet is the duty of economic support. "A son may help support the old people if he desires to, but the son-in-law has to support them."

If his father-in-law wants a son-in-law to do something, he has to do it. If he is given a bow and arrows, he has to go out. He is supposed to turn the whole deer over to his father-in-law and mother-in-law and not to take any unless they give it to him. The father-in-law and mother-in-law can share it with their neighbors if they wish to. The young man gives to his in-laws even if he is not ordered out to hunt by them.

This sense of identification with the economic activities of the wife's relatives begins immediately upon marriage. "There is something about it so that a man helps his wife's people." "As soon as a man marries he feels that he should work for his father-in-law and mother-in-law." The connection between this economic tie and the rule of residence is again emphasized. "It is usual to live with the wife's people. In the old days the boy had to work for his father-in-law. If a man killed two deer, he would give most of it to his wife's people." But so strong is the sense of economic obligation to the wife's parents that its dictates are heeded even when, for some reason, matrilocal residence is not maintained. One informant said, "Now I live a mile or so from my mother-in-law. I always want to help her though, for she is alone and getting old."

This assistance is accepted as a matter of course and is viewed as a right by the older affinity. "A man would come to a son-in-law for aid before he would approach anyone else, even his own brother." Requests made of a brother are a test of fraternal solidarity and are seldom refused, but they constitute a tax on the generosity of one who has obligations in other directions. To approach the son-in-law instead relates to a primary economic duty.

Although the son-in-law (because he is younger and more vigorous than his wife's father) is called upon for the most arduous duties of the extended family, he, too, derives benefits from the arrangement, for "he may take anything belonging to the parents-in-law, not because they are rich or poor, but because that is the rule."

Often, in the economic exchanges that follow a marriage, the son-in-law is by far the gainer. He may come to his wife's relatives as a young man without many possessions. The older members of the encampment which he joins may be wealthy and influential. Whatever of their goods he needs he may use freely, and the reputation of the family advances his interests.

It occasionally happens that an affinal relative takes advantage of the son-in-law. One man was considerably piqued because his mother-in-law, who had carried away untanned hides from his home with the understanding that she would keep some for herself and return the others tanned, had conveniently forgotten the latter part of the agreement. He was particularly irritated because nothing could be done about the matter, since it was his mother-in-law who was involved.

On the other hand, there are cases where a man has attempted to elude the claims of his parent-in-law:

This year I had to make J. help my other son-in-law put up my camp at the grounds of the girl's puberty rite. I asked him a first time, and he sent word that he was working. I knew he wasn't doing a thing. So I sent someone with word that he had to do it, and so he did.

The extensions of avoidance.—The list of four affinities from whom the newly married man must hide is only the theoretical minimum; he is likely to be called upon to avoid many more individuals. Where the possibility of choice exists, the decision concerning which of the alternatives is to be adopted rests with the wife's relative. All the close kin of the wife—of her own, her parents', and her grandparents' generation—may elect to request avoidance. The list includes siblings and cousins of her father and mother, her grandfathers, siblings and cousins of her grandparents, and her own siblings and cousins.

In practice the number is much reduced, however. With the exception of those for whom avoidance is mandatory, most of the woman's male relatives will require only the polite form of speech from the husband. Many of them will waive even this requirement. Seldom do a woman's relatives of her own generation exercise their privilege of requesting avoidance. Most cousins and many siblings make no attempt to inaugurate even polite-form usages. The man's affinities who are most likely to demand avoidance are the sisters of his mother-in-law. It would be an affront if they failed to do so. Female cousins of the mother-in-law may be satisfied with polite form, however, and where the cousin relationship is rather remote, all special usages may be ignored.

Those who have been mentioned thus far as persons with the right to ask for avoidance are consanguineous relatives of the wife. But a stepmother who is not the wife's blood relative may request avoidance of her stepdaughter's husband. Once a young man and I were about to seek shelter from the cold in a trader's store. My friend opened the door, then said quickly, "I can't go in there. There is someone in there I can't see." We stole in through another door and made our way to a storeroom. The woman whose presence had made necessary our devious route turned out to be the stepmother and no real kin of the man's wife. Of the circumstances surrounding this case my companion said:

I avoid my wife's stepmother and cannot look at her. She requested it through my wife. It isn't necessary that a man avoid his wife's stepmother, but she sent word that we were to avoid each other, and so I must do it. She could have requested polite form only if she had wanted to, and we wouldn't have had to use that either if she had not requested it.

In a number of other cases the stepmother has not requested the avoidance.

A man may be called upon to avoid those who have adopted and reared his wife, even though they are no real kin of the girl. The initiative comes from the foster-parents, and ordinarily none but the foster-mother and foster-father of the woman will be involved. Such cases are rare, however, for almost always some relatives survive to care for an orphan child.

Where avoidance is not obligatory, there are a number of factors which may determine the decision. The closeness or remoteness of the relationship to the woman through whom the affinal bond is established is one of these. Thus, a sister of the wife's mother would be more likely to request avoidance than would the mother-in-law's female cousin, though both have the identical right theoretically. And, if a "first cousin" of the mother-in-law makes the request, it will still occasion no surprise, for she is considered a close relative of the bride. But if cousins of the mother-in-law beyond this range come forward with the demand, personal, less explicit reasons are likely to account for it.

When the two kin are very good friends, avoidance is likely to be the choice, for it is a means of honoring the wife by according the utmost respect to her mate. Since so much depends upon the manner in which intimacy has developed in the course of the years among kin, the reality may differ from the theoretical expectations. A mother's sister who has not got along too well with her niece may ask for no more than polite form from that relative's husband, whereas a mother's female cousin who happens to have the liveliest interest in the young woman may exercise full rights in the affinity situation. Accordingly, the selection of avoidance, where a choice exists, is evidence of approval of the union and of the principals to it.

Just as friendly backgrounds operate to establish avoidance understandings, so do opposite circumstances make them less likely. Where hostility has existed between the husband and the wife's relative in the past, avoidances which are not obligatory will certainly not be requested.

If the new affinity has formerly been on most familiar terms with the wife's relative, it is felt that the intimate knowledge implied makes difficult the formal behavior of an avoidance obligation. Here, again, the polite form or less is deemed sufficient. Avoidance will also be waived when it is apparent that for some reason the two concerned are likely to be thrown together continually in situations where such behavior would be unfeasible.

Once avoidance has been established by choice, it is indistinguishable from avoidance begun automatically. Upon the marriage of his relative, the person who may exercise choice in respect to avoidance must come to an immediate decision. "There is no such thing as failing to avoid a certain relative-in-law for a number of years and then suddenly deciding to do it. The avoidance starts immediately after the marriage that makes it possible, or it does not occur at all." The decision to establish avoidance must be communicated to the relative at once, so that her husband will know what is expected of him and will not suffer the embarrassment of coming into the presence of one whom he should not see. If the husband and his wife's relative meet face to face before any notice is sent, it is very difficult to carry out the plan of avoidance:

B.'s wife is a distant relative of my wife. After I married I ran into her. I didn't know she was intending to hide from me. She didn't send any message to me. When she saw me she said; "I was going to hide from him, but now I'll just be polite in words" [use polite form].

The continuation or termination of avoidance.—Even after the death of the spouse through whom it was established, unless extraordinary steps are taken, avoidance continues. And if the widower marries a woman of another family, the avoidance obligations to his first wife's relatives still persist:

F. was married to M.'s daughter. She died eight years ago. There were no other girls for him to marry in M.'s family when his wife died. He married E.'s girl. He avoids both Mrs. M. and Mrs. E. now.

K. avoids my mother-in-law, who is his mother-in-law, too, by a first marriage. When his wife died there were no other available girls in the family. So he
married outside the family. Now he avoids B., his present mother-in-law, too.

I hide from my present father-in-law. My first wife's mother was living
until recently, and I hid from her too.

Avoidance of the wife's relatives commonly continues, also,
after the separation of the married pair. This is all the more re-
markable because, with divorce, the family of the woman loses
all real claim to the economic support of the former husband.

The perpetuation of the avoidance relations serves a number
of functions. It acts as a reminder that marriage is more than a
matter of sexual privileges; that it is, in addition, a commitment
of co-operation and respect between a man and a family—a commitment which death, remarriage, or divorce cannot entirely
efface. Also it encourages a man to remarry into the same family
after the death of his wife, for double obligations of this nature
loom as a burden to him. Finally, it deters divorce and remarriage into another family with the attendant obligations.

Termination of avoidance in any circumstances is strongly
opposed by some informants:

According to the old custom, the person who stops avoiding his in-law is a
witch. A man is a fool for stopping. I don't care if you are divorced; it goes on.
It could be stopped, of course. I could get angry and say to my wife's relative,
"Oh, I'm not going to hide from you any more." But what would people think of
me? I wouldn't do it. I'm a good Chiricahua. You can't do it gracefully. The
men in the three cases [of duplicate avoidance obligations following remarriage] I
have just given you are young fellows. One is thirty-two years old, one is also in
his thirties, the oldest is about forty. All were born under government supervision. If the young fellows do it, what do you think about the old fellows? They
wouldn't stop doing it. C. told me these forms go on and on.

And yet, under certain conditions, avoidance may be suspended or terminated:[3]

In an emergency, at the birth or death of a member of the family, in a case of
life or death, you can go over avoidance and walk right in to the place where your
mother-in-law or someone from whom you hide is. But it's not necessary to drop

---

[3] The procedure described at this point is also used to terminate the cousin
avoidances described on pp. 61–62.

polite form at this time. You can say anything you want in polite form. This may occur at a birth, when a woman labors so hard that some man who knows how to take care of her is needed. Then they overlook it.

Obligatory avoidances cannot be permanently ended while the woman because of whom the relationship was established is still alive. Even where avoidance was optional, "almost always the woman whose marriage had started the relationship would be asked first and her approval gained if she were still alive."

A man might have bad luck. One after another of his relatives might die. There might be a certain relative whom he avoids, but who he thinks might give him good advice and encouragement if he could talk matters over with him. So he tells his wife that he does not want to avoid her relative any more. If she thinks it is all right, he rolls a cigarette, takes a few puffs on it, and sends it to the relative with word that, after this, they should not hide from each other. If the relative takes the cigarette and smokes it too, it is all over, and they do not hide from each other after that.

The first move may come from either affinal relative:

There was an equal right for either the husband or the woman's relative to roll and send the cigarette. A man might say to his wife: "I no longer want to avoid your brother. I want to be with him and go with him and speak with him." If his wife approved, he would have her take over the cigarette. When the avoidance is broken off like this we say, "It has become again that one goes to him."

Cigarettes offered in this fashion do not have to be accepted:

When a cigarette was offered in this way to end an avoidance relationship, it could be refused, but this refusal would never show anger on the part of the person who refused. A man might say: "We have hidden from each other all these years. All this time we have helped each other and thought well of each other. I do not think our relations would be helped by this move. I would rather hide from you for the rest of my life."

Even when avoidance is abrogated, a measure of formality is retained. "If the two who are hiding from each other smoke a cigarette like that, they don't have to hide from each other any more. But they have to keep on with the polite form."

After the death of a man's wife and his remarriage, the obligatory avoidance observances between him and relatives of his first wife may be terminated:

If the family has no more girls he can marry and a man gets permission to marry out of the family after his wife's death, perhaps he will not want to avoid his first wife's father any longer. In that case he will take a cigarette and go through that ceremony. This happens a good many times. It happened with S. and P. not long before S. died. That was about six months ago. P. was S.'s father-in-law. They had been hiding from each other for over forty years. Six months ago they gave each other cigarettes in this way. After that you could see them sitting together talking, just like any other two men. The same thing happened between M. and K.

Personality conflicts in the avoidance relationship.—In spite of the absolute standards of good will which are supposed to govern the relations between a married man and his affinities, conflicts in interests and in personalities do occur. The wife is in continuous touch with her relatives, and any indignity she suffers at the hands of her husband is immediately known to them. The husband is in an anomalous position until his standing among his wife's kin is assured, for, although he is nominally considered the head of his household, he is subject to the strict scrutiny of his wife's relatives.

Irritations and resentments between affinal relatives sometimes erupt into open hostility:

R. was . . . . always abusing his wife. It led to a fight between him and the woman's stepfather. The stepfather was just like a bulldog. In the fight he bit R.'s finger off. He must have swallowed it, for they never found it. It was a jubilee fight, right on a moonlit night!

The older participant, the wife's stepfather, had never avoided his opponent. Therefore, the encounter did not involve a violation of the avoidance obligation. But in the heat of anger even that extreme breach of etiquette has been known to take place:

A man has just beaten up his mother-in-law. This man has avoided his mother-in-law and her sister. He has had trouble with his wife and has been separated from her. Now he has tried to get his wife to go on with him again. He went over to her place. Her mother was so angry at him that she came right over to the place where he was. They threw everything to the wind and began fighting. He beat her up. They won't even use polite form any more. They insulted each other and got kicked, so what's the use of polite form now? But this does not mean that the man will not continue to avoid his mother-in-law's sister. It depends on the individuals concerned.

Of another mother-in-law–son-in-law breach this account was given:

One man had serious trouble with his wife and her family. His mother-in-law helped his wife throw stones at him and drive him out of camp. She saw him that time! But now they are hiding from each other again. This happened about six months ago.

The last part of the quotation reveals the usual aftermath of such violent incidents. Ordinarily the principals are very contrite and are glad to have the episode forgotten.

Quarrels between son-in-law and father-in-law are likewise not unknown:

We were staying at the old man's place [the father-in-law's place]. They came after me. They had been drinking tiswin and were drunk. I heard them say, "We'll beat him up." They went out to the woodpile to get clubs to beat me with.

"I don't like this," I said to my wife. "I don't want to live here."

She said, "I can't help it. I'm afraid of my father. He's pretty bad."

I said, "The best man's going to get away from here!"

These three who were coming for me were all relatives of my wife; they all used polite form to me too. But they were sticking up for the old man. I got my ax. I was angry. They came for me. I came out of my home. I had the ax behind me. They advanced.

I said to the first one, "What do you want?"

"You are not the only man!" he told me.

I said, "You come any nearer and someone is bound to get hurt!" and I began swinging my ax. One of them is a coward. He backed out when he saw the ax. Another began asking, "What's he done?"

I told him, "Don't make believe! You've got a club in your hand, and you know what you've got it for."

Just then one of my relatives came. "What's the matter?" he asked. I told him. "If they're going to club you, they've got to club me too," he said. Then they backed down.

Once an informant asserted darkly that his mother-in-law was "no good." The only explanation of this unusual statement he would vouchsafe at the time was, "She comes around here and cusses me out." Little by little the details of the clash emerged. His later statement was this:

I was sitting in the agent's office and she came right up to me. "After this we will not avoid each other," she said. I guess she was angry at me about something. She feels pretty bad about it now, but I am not going to avoid her any more. She can hide from me if she wants to, but I am going on just as I am now.

But the actual cause of the quarrel had to be obtained from other sources and turned out to involve property of the woman which had been improperly disposed of by the son-in-law.

Polite form.—Polite form is a special third-person singular or plural form of the verb attached to every paradigm. There is an ordinary third-person form, and so linguists distinguish between the two by labeling the polite form the "fourth person." Since the polite form, though it can be used in direct address, is essentially a third-person form, it necessarily injects a note of indirection into any conversation in which it is employed.

The presence of an avoided person, if he is within hearing, must be discreetly ignored, and direct address to him is ordinarily ruled out except for moments of crisis. At these times it is the polite form of speech which passes between the two. Whenever one avoidance affinity speaks of another, and this is much more common, the reference must be couched in the fourth-person form.

Since the common set of terms for affinal relatives is derived from the verb "to carry a burden," and since every paradigm has a fourth-person form as well as a regular third-person form, it follows that there are two ways of saying "affinity who has married into my family"—one polite and one ordinary—and two ways of saying "affinity into whose family I have married." The two terms of this set which are expressed in the fourth-person form are the ones used to denominate affinities who are avoided or to address those to whom polite form is used. The other pair is used of or to affinities with whom neither avoidance nor polite form has been inaugurated.

There are two other words in use to designate affinal relatives with whom avoidance or polite-form usages have been instituted. They, too, are taken from verbs and are fourth-person forms. Unlike the words of the other set, these two forms indicate the sex of the person to whom they are addressed. The term which singles out the male to whom polite form or avoidance is owed literally means "he who is old" and in a primary sense has the connotation of father-in-law. The other, in use to or of women of a comparable category and carrying the primary meaning of mother-in-law, can be translated as "she who has become old." The use of the two affinity systems overlaps. For instance, the father-in-law can be referred to by the son-in-law as "one for whom I carry burdens" and also as "he who is old."

The question of whether polite form is to be required and the mode of notification are the business of the woman's relatives.

As soon as the relatives of the girl heard about it, those who intended to do so started to use the polite form the next time they saw me. They told me that I should use the polite form to them, and in that very sentence they used it themselves. So they really used it first.

Polite form begins immediately after marriage. Sometimes the individual tells you to use the polite form; sometimes he or she just uses it to you, and you must use it in return.

Perfect decorum must be maintained when two "who are ashamed in words" are together:

You can't pass water, defecate, or use smutty language when anyone to whom you use polite form is around. If one of them is in an embarrassing or ridiculous position, you cannot laugh at him but must leave the place immediately. You have to be careful of your language, too, when someone like this is around.

Ordinarily, names may be used in speaking of absent persons, but a stricter usage is observed by a polite-form affinity:

You don't call the name of a man to whom you use polite form. If you do have to mention his name, you have to add something, as "the one who is known as C." or "the one who is called C." Others can use his name before you though. Usually in referring to him you just say "the one who is an affinity to me."

It is evident that these observances are related to that same economic solidarity which exists between avoidance relatives:

I feel that if I needed some service or property I could ask it of someone to whom I used the polite form. I'd be sure of getting it. If I were having a girl go through the puberty ceremony, I might ask these people for help, and a man helps his wife's relatives meet the expense of a ceremony which his wife's relatives are putting on. You can take property privileges with anyone to whom you use the polite form. You can borrow property from them freely, for you know they will never say anything to you that is disrespectful. You have more rights in this respect than you would with your own family.

But in spite of convention, polite form, like avoidance, often masks repressed dislikes:

Some people, when they get drunk, will fight their own fathers. And they don't care if someone they have to be polite to tries to handle them. Even though they are supposed to be ashamed before a person, that isn't going to hold them down when they're drunk. Sometimes they don't like a person they are ashamed before in words, and then, when they are drunk, it comes out.

Theoretically, all adult relatives of the wife who do not automatically avoid her husband may request polite form of him. There are some of these relatives who will almost certainly ask for polite form and others who probably will not. Among the former are those who might have been expected to request avoidance, but who, for some reason, did not. Any other course would advertise the poor opinion they have of their relative or of her new mate.

But there will be more distantly related kin of the wife who have had little intimate contact with her. When such individuals meet the man for the first time after his marriage, they may indicate the unchanged nature of the association by speaking pleasantly to him in the ordinary way. Most likely they will address the in-law term, "one who carries burdens for me," to him, but it will be the "regular" and not the "polite" term of the set that they will use.

As in the case of avoidance, where latitude in the matter exists and polite form is chosen nevertheless, it may be accepted as an evidence of friendliness and approval:

A person who does not have to ask for avoidance or polite form but who does it anyway shows that he or she likes the relative and approves of the in-law. It shows approval of the marriage. I should be very proud, for many of the prominent men of the reservation use polite form to me.

The ages of some of the wife's relatives at the time of her marriage automatically prevent many polite-form usages (and avoidances too) from ever being established:

A person could not request polite form from another until he or she was old enough to understand the custom, that is, until about eighteen years of age.[4]

I don't talk in the polite way to S. He was little when I married his sister, so he couldn't ask for it. It's got to be started right away, so we have never talked in polite form all these years. . . . .

In fact, the relations established in lieu of polite form between a man and the younger members of his wife's extended family are

[4] The concept of the years of discretion, independence, and maturity has stretched with white contact. In purely aboriginal times an individual several years younger than the age mentioned would have been prepared to make decisions of this kind. But the substance of the statement would hold, doubtless, for preadolescents in aboriginal times.

likely to be really informal. These youngsters are among the few individuals of that group with whom the man does not have to exercise care in word and action, and he is soon on grounds of easy familiarity with them. This makes all the more impossible any establishment of future restraint relations with them.

The last statement implies another factor which controls polite-form decisions—the degree of past or present intimacy between the wife's relative and her husband.

If a relative of your wife doesn't want you to use polite form to him, perhaps it is because he likes you very much and wants to go with you as a partner. Then you'd have to sleep together when you were out camping, bathe together, relieve yourselves when you were together, and that would be all right only if he was not ashamed of you in words. If the polite relationship exists, you can't undress, urinate, or do anything personal like that in his presence. If you ever go out with your wife's brother on a hunt and there is only flat country around and no place to hide, the shame relationship would make it hard on you. So, often, the polite form is not entered into for practical reasons.

C. called my father "cousin" [father's brother's son, in this case]. I call C.'s daughter "cousin." When she married, I could have used polite form to her husband. Then he would have had to use it to me. But I did not want to, because we had been pretty intimate. He would have had to act reserved, and it was hard to put him in that position after what had taken place.

But, once it is started, polite form cannot be casually terminated. "If your wife's brother wants to change his relationship with you, your wife would object, and a thing like this might even break up the marriage. You can't quit or change in the middle."

In reference to the perpetuation of the polite form beyond the life-span of the connecting relative and after divorce, there are these dicta:

We use these forms and usages as long as these people to whom we are acting in this way live. Even if a man's wife dies, this goes on.

We keep up polite forms even after the death of the wife. In case of divorce, polite form continues too.

Polite form is terminated even less frequently than avoidance. If total avoidance becomes an intolerable burden, after a death or divorce it may be scaled down to polite form. But if polite form were discarded, there would be a return to familiar relations on the part of persons between whom restraint has been practiced for some time—an abrupt change of demeanor which most individuals do not care to invite.[5]

THE MARRIED MAN AND HIS BLOOD KIN

The formal obligations of a man to his wife's relatives are explicit and numerous, but he is seldom as isolated from his own relatives and friends as a bare recital of affinal relationships would suggest:

There is the word that means one household or home. If the group of related households is very small, if there is only one, or if there are only two or three dwellings in it, you might call this a household still, for we do not like to use the word "extended family" unless there are as many as five or six houses.

"Extended family" means a group of homes occupied by relatives. At the very least an extended family is a father and mother, their unmarried children, and the families of their married daughters.

Several extended families make up the local group. In most cases it includes families which are connected by marriage, and between whose members friendly relations signified by the term "friends we have become" are in force.

It appears, then, that it is not unusual for families whose members have intermarried to belong to the same local group, and often a married man may expect to have consanguineous relatives as well as affinities in the vicinity. One factor which explains why families united by marriage live in such close proximity is the absence, in general, of any obligation to marry out of the local group.

At our encampment we are really an extended family. My father-in-law is here with his father-in-law. I am here with my father-in-law. If my wife's sister marries, there will be another household. Since the people in such an extended family are all related, all the girls and boys of marriageable age are *šilah* to each other and can't marry. But a man doesn't have to go far for a wife, for there are many extended families near by from which he can choose a wife. Being in the same local group doesn't prevent a man from marrying someone. There has to be real relationship to prevent marriage.

This does not mean that a mate is always chosen from the same local group. Previous marriages within the local group may make this impossible: "Marriages like this went on between

---

[5] Yet polite form can be terminated to accommodate the sororate-levirate (see p. 424).

those who camped together all the time, until they became so intermarried that the younger people were really relatives, and then men had to go elsewhere for wives." And yet, the better chance of the young people of the same district to become acquainted, the fluidity of the local group over the years, and the tendency to forget quickly remoter kin who are deceased make it possible for many of the youths to find eligible mates in their own local groups and to strengthen the ties between the resident families.

Even when the extended families united by the marriage of their younger members do not reside in the same local group, they are drawn into closer understanding by these marital arrangements:

If a man of one local group marries a woman of another, his kin do not consider themselves related to his wife's people. But there is a relationship of mutual friendliness and help which is set up between the two families. If someone of the family of the boy is giving a tiswin party or a social dance, the members of the other family are sure to be invited. The relationship is expressed by this term, "friends we have become." If a person uses this of another, it is understood that they are friends because of the marriage of a relative of one to a relative of the other. This word can be used for other things. You can say, using it, "Because he gave me something, we have become friends," but in this case the reason for the friendship has to be expressed. If the word is used alone, it gives the idea of friendship through marriage.

N. is on especially friendly terms with D. and his family. He borrows their property and can get help there any time. Yet N. and D. are not relatives. They have no right to call each other anything. It is because N.'s sister married D.'s brother; their relatives have married. This is a good example of "friends we have become."

When two families whose members marry live in the same local group, the benefits of the new bond are not difficult to exploit. This is less simple when the families are separated by some distance. Consequently, there is a tendency for intermarried families to make the logical adjustments. "The family of a married man would be very likely to locate near the family of the girl he married, because they considered themselves bound by ties of friendship. They would all be in the same local group, camping in the same general region."

Obviously, this is no rule which can be strictly followed. Where a number of sons marry into separated groups, a choice has to be made if the family is to live near "friends." All that can be said is that residence in one place rather than in another may be determined by the presence there of a family with which friendly connections have been established through marriage.

The presence of his own kin in the same local group where he lives with his affinities assures the newly married man of the perpetuation of a good many past ties, as an understanding of the relations between the extended family and the local group suggests.

The local group is a cluster of encampments in one general locality. It is a division of the larger group, the band. The people in it all camp around some well-known spot from which the local group gets its name. Those who camp around Mora Mountain are called "People of Mora Mountain." This refers to all the people living together in this region. But within the local group there would be other divisions. All would not live at one place. Some would camp on one side of the mountain, some would camp on the other. Others might camp at any favorable spot near water. These smaller groups or camps are decided along relationship lines. That is, all the relatives and those who marry into a certain family live together.

These smaller units, the extended families, are referred to by means of the leading men in them. Thus, we speak of N.'s encampment, C.'s encampment. The local group is not a relationship group strictly, but the extended family does consist of relatives. If a person asks, "Who are you? To what people do you belong?" you give the name of your band. But if someone asks where you live, you say that you are one of a certain local group.

The local group tie is essentially one of residence and may be severed summarily:

The children are usually members of the local group to which the mother belongs, because a man is supposed to live near and work for his wife's people. When a man of one local group marries a woman of another, his direct affiliation with the first local group is over. He is now related by marriage to people in the second local group. But he has relatives in the first one, and in case of trouble or divorce he would go back there.

Further characteristics of the local group are summarized in this explanation:

The local group consists of a number of extended families living near some prominent family, that is, living around some family who has a good leader. This leader would be expected to lead the men of the local group when they go on a raid or engage in war. But each extended family has its own place to store food. And whenever a girl's puberty rite takes place, people outside the local group come too.

A great many families of a local group are related, but not all of them. Therefore, it does not necessarily mean that a man has to marry outside the local group. The families who make up the group shift constantly. A family will often go and attach itself to some other local group.

The women of a local group are the ones who would go to gather mescal together. Those who went would go and come from the main group. It might be that they'd split off into smaller parties which would later rejoin. It depends on how thick the mescal is in one place and how many people there are.

The members of the local group can go anywhere in the territory of their band, but they are out of place if they go into the territory of another band. An individual or family of the Southern Chiricahua band might join many Southern Chiricahua local groups in turn. . . . .

At the time of a big raid, men from more than one local group might get together, but those from each locality would stay around their own leader. He acted as a sort of captain for them. When they made camp at night, those from one local group would stay together. For boys' training, the young fellows of a local group are the most that would be brought together at one time.

Though allegiance to the local group is brittle and its composition is constantly changing, it does provide a common name, base, and leadership for its members and gives them the opportunity to engage in certain industries in common. In these matters it cuts across the boundaries of the extended family, and, if a married man has blood relatives in the same local group, it offers him the opportunity to co-operate with these kin for many purposes. This means that his horizon is never entirely limited to the interests of his affinities.

THE WOMAN AND HER HUSBAND'S RELATIVES

The married woman has no formal obligation to labor for her husband's relatives but is expected to carry on her industrial activities in company with her mother and sisters as a permanent member of the extended family in which she was born. Moreover, none of her husband's kin calls upon her to avoid them. To express approval, some of them may, however, use polite form in speaking to her.

Relatives of a boy can ask the girl he marries for polite talk if they think much of him. His own brothers and sisters and cousins can do this. The father and mother of the boy don't do this. They regard their son's wife as their own daughter. The brothers and sisters of both the father and the mother can do it though. But they don't have to. It's up to them.

Another quotation extends this information:

If she is asked to start it [polite form] with the boy's brothers, she can never marry one of them. The reason given for not using polite form to the boy's mother is that his mother may be required to be at the birth of the child of her daughter-in-law, and it would not be right for her to have such intimate dealings with the girl if she used the polite form to her. At the birth of a child, no one who uses polite form to the mother is around.

Other statements explain that the collateral relatives of the husband's grandparents but not the grandparents themselves, may request polite form. It appears that the classes of affinities that expect avoidance from the husband are the very ones which, in the woman's affinal constellation, refrain from making even the polite-form request. None of these polite-form usages is obligatory, it should be noted. This time the initiative comes from the husband's relatives. The same sets of terms are utilized; it is the young woman who is called "one who carries burdens for me" by her affinity and who calls her husband's relative "one for whom I carry burdens."

Again, the usage, to be effective, must begin at once. "I could have used polite form to my cousin's wife. It's too late now. I didn't start it from the beginning. My cousin could have used the polite form to my wife, but he didn't either."

In determining whether he will make the request for polite form of the wife, each member of the husband's relationship group is guided by considerations of age, degree of past intimacy, and closeness of connection to the linking relative—the same factors operative in the man's avoidance and polite-form obligations. Polite form between the woman and her affinal relative, once started, also is supposed to continue indefinitely, regardless of the disturbance of the union by divorce or death.

A woman's obligations to her affinities at marriage are slight compared with those to which her husband is subject, but their existence does serve to indicate that she owes consideration to her husband's kin and can never entirely eliminate them from her plans. Their claim upon her is most fully realized at the death of her mate when they can force her to accept a brother or a cousin of the deceased in his stead.

FOLK BELIEFS, MEDICAL PRACTICE
AND SHAMANISM

ALL items of belief are by no means of equal importance. They range in significance from the trivial to those basic for the ceremonies. Many of them are of no great moment and, indeed, may be uttered half in jest.

They say in the way of a joke that you get a rash from giving things and taking them back all the time. You have to put ashes on the rash, which is called "lice sew you up." If you are stingy, the person from whom you take things says, "I wish you'd get warts" [such warts should be cut off with sinew], or, "I wish you'd get the rash."

Sneezing, which indicates that "someone is thinking of you," may also be treated jokingly:

Upon sneezing, they say, "I am still here for you," or, "Sometime we will see each other again, sweetheart." Once two old men and I were together. One sneezed, and he made this remark. The other told him, "Nobody is thinking of you, you old fool! All that means is that you're catching cold."

Yet some regard the sneeze as an ominous sign and pray to the culture hero or exclaim, "May it be well!"

When the ear rings, "someone is talking about you," and young people think the speaker is one of their admirers. Some persons regard a frequent buzzing in the ear as a sign that good news will be heard; others say it is the calling of a dead relative. A burning sensation in the ear is a harbinger of cold weather.

Rings around the sun and moon indicate change of weather, rain, or snow. Rain will come if a horned toad or a snake is killed and turned on its back, if a dog rolls on the ground, if there is a good deal of drumming in the camps or much singing of masked-dancer songs. Smoke from a big fire kindled on a still night will cause clouds to gather. The crescent moon "is draining" when its tip is pointed downward, and rain falls. "A dark, heavy, pouring rain is male; a light rain when the horizon seems bright nevertheless is called female rain." To stop rain or snow, lice are hunted and tied to a rock with sinew; or an individual may draw a charcoal ring around his anus and lift his buttocks to the sky to bring the sun out. Sudden storms are regarded with fear. "If it doesn't look like rain, but then the wind and dust come up suddenly and it starts to rain, it brings news—bad news of death. If someone is very sick and this happens, it means he won't last. I have seen it happen."

Various things are seen in the half or full moon, the most common being walnut or cottonwood trees and a human face. Some persons think that watching the sunrise or sunset colors will cause sickness. Warts are also the penalty for pointing to heavenly bodies with the fingers; only the thumb may be so used.

Pulling out gray hair is said to make it grow faster; it is also held that one who brings water and drinks first himself will grow old quickly. It is forbidden to step over a person who is sitting or lying down: "If someone starts to step over you before he sees you, he has to go back. If he has already stepped over, he has to step back." Because it "may cause a severe pain in the stomach, food which is being cooked is not stirred with a knife." Eating frogs can result, it is thought, in bowlegs. Blood and tobacco are considered incompatible:

My people don't want any blood around when they smoke. If there is blood on the hands, they will get it off before they smoke. If a person has a knife with blood on it, he cleans it up or puts it away before he smokes. He will have bad luck otherwise.

Much of the cosmology is expressed in terms similar to the beliefs already enumerated. Thus, the pitching of a flour-laden burro explains the Milky Way; an earthquake is the crying of the earth over an approaching epidemic; eclipses, either of the sun or of the moon, warn of epidemics also and necessitate a masked-dancer ceremony to ward off the disaster; a shooting star points to an advancing enemy; of a cloudburst it is said, "The sky is old and has split there; when it is sewed up it will be all right."

Of greater significance than such beliefs is a diagnostic sign, a muscular tremor, which few fail to heed at some time in their lives:

This is the unknown force, the power, that causes the twitching of the flesh anywhere on your body. Some people have it near the eye, some at the foot, the shoulder, or on some other part of the body. The Chiricahua believe in this as an indication of what is going to happen. A man is starting out on a trip by horse. If he gets the tremor and it tells him not to go, he turns back until another day. It is often the determining factor in a person's life. It shows you some special event. A person may occasionally get it in various parts of the body, but he knows of a special place that has a meaning for him. Some believe in this more than they do in the shaman. To some this is the real power. People find out by experience what their tremor means.

I know that certain signs mean certain things. I get it under one eye. It means someone is going to die. I had it for two days at the beginning of the girl's puberty rite. Soon after the ceremony a woman died. I mentioned this to another man with whom I was walking. He said he had it there sometimes too and that it was a bad sign for him also. Just two weeks ago I had this sign for a long time. Now I learn that C.'s wife has just died. This trembling under the eye is a general sign, and all agree on its meaning. But I didn't recognize these signs for myself or notice that they were giving information to me until a few years ago. I had had this sign a great deal. I decided to study it and see if it was true. So I remembered whenever I had it, and, sure enough, someone always died a few days later.

. . . . Some people, when they have a bad sign, rub ashes on the place that is trembling. Or they say, "Whatever you are, don't let this thing come to pass." The ashes don't make my trembling stop.

Tribute is paid to the dependability of these signals by another informant:

Muscular shaking is recognized as "that which informs one" in some emergency. When a man is just about to do something that will cost him his life or property, or to make some great decision, if he knows the meaning of his muscular tremor, he will be warned. Some people pray to their muscular tremor. It is so specialized to some that they look upon it as a ceremony for themselves. Some people place more faith in it than in ceremonies.

When you have the shaking on the outside of your legs, it is recognized by everybody as a bad sign. For most people this holds good. A person must recognize what his own tremors mean though. You watch what happens after you get it and then you learn what it was trying to say to you. Pretty soon it is a sure thing to you. The inside of the legs is usually a good sign. If the muscle of the arm [bicep] twitches, it is said that the person will carry a great deal; he will be successful in war.

My good sign is over my right eye. When it is under my left eye, it is surely going to rain. In the old days, during the Indian Wars, when I was nervous and afraid, I would get a tremor on the inside of my leg. Then I would be at peace and go to sleep. It was my sign.

The warnings of muscular tremor served well in the strife of the seventies and eighties:

Once a bunch of Geronimo's band saw C. and his wife working in the distance. They planned to catch C. and force him to go with them. All of a sudden they saw C. and the woman drop everything, jump on a horse, and head back toward the reservation. Many years later someone reminded C. of this. They asked him what warned him. He said, "Oh, yes! I remember the time. I was working and all of a sudden I got a muscular tremor sign which I knew from experience meant, 'Something bad is going to happen. Drop everything!' So I did."

The most prevalent of these signs by far and the ones upon which there is greatest agreement are those which occur on the outside and the inside of the arms and legs and those which are felt above and below the eyes. But personal variation is common too.

While everyone knows of these signs, there is a marked difference in the amount of reliance which each individual places upon them. Most persons accept the warnings gratefully and try to fathom the meaning of unusual tremors to which they are subject. An occasional individual, however, goes beyond this and uses the tremor as a guide to all important problems and as a key to the solution of the perplexities of others who seek his advice. In a time of emergency he appeals to this phenomenon and waits for some sign to govern his actions. He may even have songs and prayers which he directs to the muscular tremor in anticipation of a reply.

P. believes in this more than in anything else on earth. He says he has lived to an old age with it. When he gets a quivering in the muscle inside the legs, it's very good. When it's on the outside of his legs, it's very bad. It's the same with the arms. Before any important thing he intends to do, whether for himself or for any of his friends in the tribe, or for the whole tribe, he has to ask his sign. He has lived according to the direction of these signs.

I have heard him say, "The sign does not come on just to give you a sensation. It means something. Many of you don't believe in it. I believe in it and I know the meaning of it. It has saved me trouble. Many a time, when I have had a bad sign, I have waited for a good sign before doing something. I have prayed for help to meet trouble when I have been warned. Then I wait for an answer. I get my answer by getting a good sign. Then I go about my affairs." And I know that he prays to Child of the Water and Life Giver about these signs.

This elaborate exploitation of muscular twitching and its use on behalf of others departs from the mere reading of diagnostic signs and impinges upon the realm of true ceremonialism.

"The dream and muscular tremor are about the same. They both tell the truth, whether good or bad." The implication is that specific dreams or types of dreams convey definite meanings. This, indeed, is the case, and the most common dream elements upon which there is general agreement are contained in the following summary:

To dream of fire is bad. If you dream of fire, the only thing to do to prevent something bad from happening is to get up right away and start a fire. This takes its place. It rubs it out. I did this down at my old home. I dreamed of a big fire. It was the middle of the night, but I got up, went down to the ditch with boxes, and fired them.

I got sick a few years ago. Before this happened I dreamed of my house. There was a big fire near it. It came close to the house and blackened one side of it. Now my one side is no good. If I had dreamed that the whole house burned, I'd be gone today.

To dream of water, of water overflowing, is just as bad. And there is no way to fix it when you dream of a big flood. I got sick before L. did. So he came to me and put pollen on me and prayed for me. He came and stayed with me that night. During the night I woke up. He was making noises and having a nightmare. He woke up and told me what it was about. He said, "I dreamed that a big flood of water came down the canyon. It came under my bed and washed me away." He died a little later. Fire and water are no good to dream of!

To dream of losing teeth is another thing. It is as bad as anything. And if you dream that buffaloes, bulls, or any kind of hoofed animals are running after you, it is bad. Something bad is going to happen to you then. I dreamed of that just before I got sick and I am not well yet. They say that, soon after you dream this, sickness is coming around you.

Dreams about yourself mean the opposite. If you dream you are going to be sick, that means you are going to stay well. If you dream that you are well, it's not good. I dreamed that I was well. That's why I stay the same way. If you dream that a snake bites you, that's good. It won't happen. If you dream that you die, it means that you will live a long time. If you dream that your father, mother, brother, or sister dies, it doesn't mean that one. It means that someone outside the family is going to die.

If you dream about summer, about everything green, about things growing and fruits and pollen, everything is all right.

In this quotation the speaker fails to include certain dreams that are consistently held to be most unfortunate, namely, dreams of the dead and of their return.[1] But from other sources this omission (owing perhaps to fear of dwelling upon such a dangerous topic) is repaired. "If you see a dead person in your sleep, you're not going to last long," said one informant. So feared are such dreams that special precautions are often taken to prevent them: "Clothing, especially moccasins and hats, should not be put above or under the pillow or about the head of the bed at night, for this causes dreams about ghosts."

The importance attached to dreams other than these varies from individual to individual:

Some people are very much guided by dreams. Some people are recognized as very true dreamers. But I have just ordinary dreams. All my dreams are about raids: I am always running away from Mexicans. I also dream a great deal about dances. I am always in there dancing. I recognize a Mescalero woman in there, and I am always dancing with her. Sometimes I am standing there and I wonder, "Why doesn't someone dance with me?"

My dreams run on the order of war. Long ago the government had Western Apache scouts to track down the Chiricahua. I dream that they are making a raid on my people. I am trying to get away from them. I climb into a tree, and then I always wake up.

Still another commentator disclaimed any reliance on dreams for himself. "I can dream plenty of things, some good and some bad, and I don't pay any attention to them." But this same man admitted that the dream could act as a vision experience and guardian spirit for others, whom he called dream shamans, saying:

We must be dream shamans, like P., to know what these dreams mean. Only the one who knows, who gets a vision with it, is all right. You can get more of this from P. He's an old man. He's about the oldest man here. He believes his dreams are true. When he dreams about the peccary, it means something bad. When he dreams about deer, it means something good.[2]

[1] There are two kinds of "death dreams." To dream of the death of living persons is made psychologically acceptable by interpreting it to mean the opposite. But dreams of the return or the sight of the dead are among the most harrowing of experiences.

[2] It is interesting that the good omen, deer, an animal much sought by the hunter, should be contrasted with the peccary, an animal that most Chiricahua will not taste.

Fortunately, the dream shaman to whom reference is made has given an account of his powers:

I have been guided during my entire life by dreams. They have helped me against sickness and against danger. My first dream came when I was but eight years old. In those days there were few white men here and no such thing as a railroad. I dreamed that I was riding on a black cloud. When I awoke in the morning, I said nothing, but I always remembered the dream. When the railroad came, I knew that it must have been a train on which I had ridden in my dream. This was a prophecy, and, although it was my first dream and very long ago, I have always remembered it.

I never think about dreaming before I go to sleep. The dreams always come unawares, and, whenever there is danger ahead, I dream a warning. Whenever someone is sick, I dream of what plant to use as medicine. In case of danger I used to see the enemy leader face to face, and he would tell me when the battle was to occur. In sickness I would actually see the plants to use. All my dreams have come true. I consider myself lucky and ascribe my present age to dream help. I have been in many battles, but my dreams have told me what to do, and so I have never been wounded. I tell my close friends about my dreams and help them too. I must be a shaman or I couldn't dream this way.

I can dream and see who is a witch too. Once at Fort Sill, in a dream I saw a bunch of men walking along over rocks and chewing them like bread. I knew they must be witches, because who else would chew rocks? I couldn't recognize the men because their backs were toward me, but I knew they were Chiricahua.

The most vivid dream I have had occurred when I was traveling with a group. One night I dreamed that there was a great number of soldiers coming from the east. Their leader rode at the front of the troop and came directly up to me. I asked the leader where his men were going, and the soldier answered that they were coming right to the point where the Chiricahua were, that they had orders and had to come. The leader spoke his own language, but I understood nevertheless. That ended the dream, and I awoke.

The next day, in the morning, we saw a large group of soldiers coming from the east. Before they got near we mounted and rode to a near-by mountain. From the mountain we watched the soldiers and noticed that they stopped right where our own camp had been. They made camp and stayed until noon. So everyone saw that my dream came true. The soldiers were too many, so we didn't attack them. Besides, the leader didn't tell me in the dream that we would fight; otherwise there certainly would have been a battle.

The last dream I had was about my grandson. He had been to school and had caught tuberculosis, and, when they thought he wouldn't live, they sent him back here. They took him to the place where his other grandfather lived. At that time I lived there too.

I prayed for the boy every night for a week. After the week was over, I had a dream. I dreamed that a huge deer was approaching the place where the boy lay.

It came from the east and kept approaching him, then backing away, approaching again, and backing up, and kept doing this.[3] I tried to chase the deer away with a stone, but it wouldn't leave. After the dream, the boy began to get well at once. I believe that, when I dream about a deer acting in such a manner, the sick one begins to get well and is safe. After the boy began to rise from his bed I kept praying for him, and he got better and better. He regained his appetite and got well.

Not only does this man use his own dreams for revealing the future and for curing but he is consulted when someone who is not a dream shaman has a disagreeable dream: "Not long ago D. had a bad dream, and since that time he has been meeting with P., and P. has been singing for him."

Not all persons who enjoy a special knowledge of dreams use them on behalf of clients:

I am guided by dreams. That is the only reliable information. I get special knowledge and wisdom in dreams. It is the power of the dream that carries me away and shows me the truth. Other people do not generally know about my power. It is just personal with me. I do not give general advice.

Still, this man's dreams served more than purely individual interests when he learned through them that his brother was in danger:

A long time ago I had a dream telling me that my brother and I were going to be killed in the morning at the time the sun is up just a little and things warm up. The dream told me that the troops were close and that a certain man was causing evil influence over us [sorcery] and was going to cause us to be killed in battle. The way to avoid it, I was told, was to go off before sunset to a spot where the sun, when it rises, first strikes a certain hill. During the dream it seemed that someone was shaking me by the hair and trying to rouse me.

I awoke, went over to my brother who was camping near by, and told him about it. My brother said, "No, I don't believe in these dreams. I have dreamed pretty bad things myself, and often thought I was going to be killed, but I always came out all right." I pleaded with my brother, but it did no good.

I went back to my camp, and my wife went over to my brother and advised him to do as I directed. But my brother told her, "No, he is just dreaming; that's all."

I went up to the place alone and did what had been directed in the dream. I walked in the sunlight to all the directions, beginning with the east and moving sunwise. Then I prayed a little and went back. Soon the enemy came and the battle started. My brother and another man were the only ones killed.

[3] The masked dancers use this same technique in curing (see p. 274).

COSMOLOGY AND SUPERNATURALS

Ritual, poetry, and prayer often refer to the time "when the earth was new" or "when the earth was created," yet there is no tale that describes the event. Parents, in talking with their children, credit Life Giver with the creation of the universe, but they offer no details and expect that faith in this deity will be later supplemented by interest in some more concrete manifestation of supernatural power.

Ideas concerning the relations of the earth, the heavenly bodies, and the forces of nature are often associated with personal supernatural power or with folk beliefs:

We did not discuss whether the world was round or flat. The old people used to say that the sun is as large as a mountain. I think that the sun and moon are in fixed position and that the heavens move. There are men who get power from the sun. They have songs and prayers directed toward the sun. It is thought that the sun goes into the sky at an eclipse. The moon does this too.

During the summer rainy season the sun has a moccasin string made of rotten material, and it breaks and breaks. The constant rain makes it rotten. That is why we have a long day; he cannot move fast. But during the winter the sun uses yucca fiber for a moccasin string and goes pretty fast, for he does not have to pause much to bother with his moccasins.

The moon is as big as the sun. Darkness interferes with the moon; therefore, we do not get so much light from the moon. The stars are thought to be pretty big too, as big as the moon or sun but set back farther. We notice that some are fixed and some travel, but we do not distinguish the two kinds by name.

A sun shaman would know all about the sun. But I'm no authority. I can only tell you what I've heard. I don't think that what I know amounts to much. I know that different men are telling stories in different ways. They may say that what I say isn't so. That's why I don't want to go into details.

Consultations with other members of the tribe revealed some disagreements in details but left a similar impression of the unorganized state of the cosmology.

Feminine qualities are attributed to the earth, and one informant definitely stated, "The earth is thought of as a woman." Moreover, in all ceremonial contexts the earth is called by a term that is said to mean "Earth Woman."[4] But, except to a few

---

[4] Dr. Hoijer claims that he cannot analyze the word to give this meaning literally and says that it is an instance of folk etymology.

shamans who obtain supernatural power from our planet, the earth is not personified, nor does it appear as a supernatural in the myths.

What attention is given to the sun, stars, and constellations by those who do not claim supernatural power from them is for the practical purpose of computing the passage of time and the change of seasons.

Much more determinate is the place of thunder (or lightning):

This is what I have heard about the lightning and thunder. I don't know what kind of people they are, but they are people. My parents and even older people used to tell me that they were just like humans in appearance. Some of them are good people and some are bad, just as people are here on earth. A good thunderstorm passes over with a good time for all. It does no harm; no one gets struck. But the bad ones go along hitting people, knocking down trees and destroying things. They say that the homes of these people are in the clouds. Thunder People is what they call them.

Lightning is the arrow of the Thunder People. I hear ceremonial songs, and in them they mention the "arrows of lightning." Not in my father's time or my grandfather's time did the Chiricahua make arrowheads of flint that were good to kill anything with. The flints they used are found around and are called "lightning's arrow" or "thunder's arrow." Some people say that they were made by men, but some Chiricahua say that flints like these are shot during a thunderstorm by the Thunder People.

. . . . They are persons and you can get power from them. They have children; they are just like regular people. Any of them can cause you to be struck by lightning. . . . . The Thunder People send lightning to punish some. Or, if someone did something bad to a man who "knew" Thunder, he could send lightning to avenge himself.

The flash is the flight of the "arrow," and the noise is the shouting of the real person, the one who is back of lightning and thunder.

At one time, runs a tale, the Thunder People acted as hunters for humans and with their arrows killed all the game the tribe could use. Ingratitude moved them to withdraw their support. It is important to court no risk of offending these well-armed inhabitants of the sky:

During a thunderstorm we go, "*piš, piš,*" in imitation of the bird called *piše* [nighthawk]. This bird, a speckled one, flies around on cloudy days near evening. It swoops and darts around so fast that it is hard even for lightning to hit it. Therefore, we use its call. It is just like making believe that we are that bird during the lightning, and then it is hard for it to hit us too.

Another thing to do when the lightning flashes is to make a spitting noise and say, "Let it be well, my brother, Lightning," or to say, "Strike high, my brother." Thunder you call grandfather when it hits close. When lightning is very close and sounds just as if it is going to tear up the ground, you say:

"Continue in a good way;
Be kind as you go through;
Do not frighten these poor people;
My grandfather, let it be well;
Don't frighten us poor people."

Sickness induced by or through Thunder is frequent, and special practices and curative rites have grown up to cope with such disorders.

Through the mythology an association is established between water and lightning. In most versions of the birth of the culture hero, his mother is impregnated by Water, but in one variant Lightning strikes at the divine woman four times and thus causes her to conceive Child of the Water. Another version, after describing the impregnation by Water, relates that Lightning tests the hero, discovers him to be his son, and later helps him conquer a giant.

Another myth tells of a quarrel between Thunder and Wind concerning their respective abilities. They separate, to the great detriment of the earth. Finally a meeting is arranged, and, with Sun as mediator, they agree to labor together once more. As an aftermath:

The breathing of the thunder created four persons, and these were sent out in the four directions, and they were told that, whenever the earth trembles, they should come to the center. Lightning and Wind used their power to make the earth as it was before, with green grass and the proper amount of water.

The existence of the earth, the heavenly bodies, and natural forces sets the stage for the appearance of the animals of the mythological period. These animals look and talk like men. Coyote, usually a trickster with few redeeming qualities, turns benefactor for a short interval by stealing fire from those who have hoarded it and spreads it throughout the world. But, by opening a bag which he has been told to leave untouched, Coyote looses darkness. This is acceptable only to the night prowlers and fierce animals; the birds and the small harmless creatures desire daylight. The moccasin game—a game of the hidden-ball variety—is arranged to determine whether day shall come; the victors are to dispatch the vanquished. The side of the birds wins, and the horizon to the east brightens. A few of the losers escape—the snake, the owl, and the bear—and these are still considered dangerous creatures.

During this epoch Coyote makes death inevitable for mankind by throwing a stone into the water and declaring that, if it sinks, living beings shall ultimately die. Coyote's behavior during this prehuman horizon creates a "path" that man has been obliged to follow. All that man does "Coyote did first." Gluttony, lying, theft, adultery, incest, and all the other faults and foibles were introduced by Coyote and have become inescapable for those who "follow Coyote's trail."

Next are introduced White Painted Woman, Child of the Water, and Killer of Enemies. White Painted Woman has existed from the beginning. Killer of Enemies' place in the time sequence is less certain; he is variously described as a brother of White Painted Woman, an older son, a twin brother of Child of the Water, and even, in one variant, as the husband of White Painted Woman and therefore the stepfather of the culture hero. In the most representative versions he appears as an older brother of Child of the Water, already grown when the culture hero is born.

During this period White Painted Woman and Killer of Enemies share the earth with human beings and with monsters who prey upon the human beings and prevent them from thriving. One of them, a giant, carries his depredations to White Painted Woman herself and consumes a number of children she attempts to rear. Finally she is impregnated by Water and gives birth to Child of the Water, who is protected from Giant by being hidden under the earth and by other stratagems. Child of the Water grows with miraculous speed, and soon the brothers are prepared to hunt together. On the hunt they encounter Giant, and Child of the Water slays his colossal foe. This is the first adventure of a series during which he destroys the other monsters: the giant eagles, the dangerous buffalo bull, and the antelope which can kill with its glance. Child of the Water forces those he conquers to agree to be of use to man henceforth. From the feathers of the monster eagle he creates the birds which exist today. Once the survival of mankind is guaranteed, the supernaturals prepare to leave for sky homes. But first White Painted Woman and Child of the Water instruct the Chiricahua in the girl's puberty rite, and Killer of Enemies frees the game animals from an underground "animal home" in which they have been kept by Crow.

As a result of Christian influence and white contact, certain accretions to this world-view have taken place. One of these is a story of a flood. This theme has been incompletely synchronized with other mythological events. Some informants place it before the moccasin game and the existence of human beings; others say it occurred after the creation of man. Some are inclined to omit it altogether.

The tale of the creation of man is another episode which seems to have been recently added. In keeping with the feeling that actual deeds are to be attributed to the culture hero rather than to Life Giver, it is said that Child of the Water shaped people from mud or produced them from a cloud. Giving this supernatural the role of creator imposes its difficulties, however, for in the most stable portions of the mythology he is said to have been brought forth to rid the earth of the monsters which were harrying mankind. Consequently, the creation story rarely becomes an integral part of the account of the exploits of the culture hero.

According to one tale, Child of the Water creates the white man at the same time as the Indian. In the division of the goods of the earth, Child of the Water chooses for the Indian (the Chiricahua), and Killer of Enemies for the white man—the former selecting the bow and arrow, the forested mountains, and the wild foods; the latter choosing mineral-rich lands, the gun, and agricultural food staples. In keeping with this pattern of Indian-white representation, Killer of Enemies is uniformly considered the less heroic of the two brothers and is actually described as craven on occasion.

Missionary teachings concerning the importance of the Bible have been registered in the folklore too. A man, sometimes named Herus (perhaps a corruption, through the Spanish, of

Jesus), comes into possession of a book. Its loss will result in the captivity and misfortune of his people. At his death the book is burned, according to custom, with the rest of his possessions, and the dire results foretold come to pass. Stories of this man and of another who followed him and had a like adventure (Kantaneiro)[5] have a distinctly biblical flavor.

There are two other sets of supernaturals—the Mountain People and the Water Beings. The Mountain People are of more importance than any supernaturals so far mentioned, with the possible exception of Child of the Water and White Painted Woman. They are not mentioned in the stories of the period when the animals spoke like people but appear in a separate series.

There are people in the mountains who are just like us. They are not masked dancers, but they make masked dancers just as we do here. Those they make can take off their masked-dancer costumes and dress as we do. We hear the people drum in there and we hear the masked-dancer performance too. We hear words in there when we listen at cliffs or mountains, but we can't see the people. We call all these people in there Mountain People. They live in these mountains and have many children. There are girls, boys, women, and old men there. The real masked dancers are the masked dancers of these people.[6]

Two kinds of Water Beings are mentioned. One, a beneficent supernatural, is called Controller of Water:

He is some man, not of this earth. He is the one who controls the water. I hear of him in the songs, the ceremonial songs. In those songs and in prayers they talk of Water Controller who sits at the water gate and stops the water. They hold up their hands and sing, "Controller of Water, please give us a little water." He lives up above somewhere. He is only mentioned in the ceremonies that belong to different people. Some sing that his shirt is of clouds of different colors. Some say that he wears a shirt of abalone.

He holds the rain. He lets it loose or shuts it off. You sing to him if you know his song. If people believe and learn his song, they can get rain.

[5] In 1909 M. R. Harrington, who was gathering specimens from Chiricahua Indians in Oklahoma for the museum expedition supported by Mr. George G. Heye, obtained a story which associated Kantaneiro with the Mountain Spirits (see M. R. Harrington, "The Devil Dance of the Apaches," *Museum Journal* [Philadelphia], March, 1912, pp. 6–9).

[6] The name "Mountain People" will be used to refer to the total population of mountain-dwelling supernaturals; the term "Mountain Spirits," to those of the Mountain People who act as dancers. It is the Mountain Spirits who are impersonated by the masked dancers of the Chiricahua.

More feared is Water Monster, who sometimes appears in human form and sometimes as a large serpent. He is responsible for drownings, and "when anything disappears at the water, they suspect Water Monster." "He is a swallowing monster. He would just swallow people up, and they'd disappear. There is a spring near here where they say there is a Water Monster. At Whitetail there is a spring like this. Even horses go there and never come out."

THE SHAMAN AND POWER

The personnel of shamanism.—In the great enterprise of traffic with the supernatural there is no hierarchy of religious leadership:

There were not a few shamans. Supernatural power is something that every Chiricahua can share. Most of the people have some sort of ceremony, little or big.

Shamans aren't ranked: each person knows a different thing, so no one is better than another. If you have the ceremony for a certain thing, you have it; that's all. If a shaman can't help you, he just can't cure you, and you get someone else.

One thing, like the power to make someone run fast, is enough to make you a shaman. The possession of any ceremony makes a person a shaman. A little rite makes you a shaman just as much as a long elaborate one.

Yet individuals whose cures are consistently spectacular and whose prophecies are often verified do achieve more than average renown:

Those well known for their ceremonial work were usually pretty well off. They depended on ceremony for a livelihood to some extent, but they went along on hunts and did all the work that the others performed too. When men came back from raids with booty, they were given many gifts. People went out of their way to help them.

At a time of strife the shaman whose ceremony pertains to the thwarting of the enemy may gain markedly in prestige:

The shaman whose work has to do with war had a strong part in politics and could rise to a position of power. But ordinarily a man with another ceremony is just like anyone else. Geronimo got political power from the religious side. He foresaw the results of the fighting, and they used him so much in the campaigns that he came to be depended upon. He went through his ceremony, and he would say, "You should go here; you should not go there." That is how he became a leader.

But it must not be overlooked that a person's supernatural experiences are often conditioned by his special abilities. Those who excel in warfare, for instance, are likely to attribute their success to supernatural help and to seek evidence that their actions are divinely guided. There consequently takes place a convergence of prowess in war and "power" for war.

Women are not barred from the acquisition of supernatural power. "Women can have any power. I knew a woman who had power from the Mountain People. She directed the making of the dancers, just as any man does. She died at Fort Sill." Few ceremonial privileges are denied to a woman. She may not impersonate a Mountain Spirit or use the sweat lodge. But "there are many women shamans, and they are as powerful as men. Women are capable of conducting ceremonies on an equal footing with men."

The time of the acquisition of supernatural power.—Mundane knowledge alone is not considered a full guaranty of a satisfactory life. "The Apache has help for everything against which he has to contend." "We have shamans for all purposes. There is a ceremony for nearly everything in life. There are ceremonies for sickness, love, hunting, war, and so on. All these are recognized."

It is understandable, therefore, that every individual should anticipate the time when he will gain strength beyond his own or any human resource. The need for such assistance is sometimes felt very early in life. It will be remembered that a dreamer to whom reference has already been made placed the first dream to which he attributed importance at about his eighth year.[7] Another whose dream assumed ceremonial significance likewise experienced it during childhood:

When I was a young boy, I had this experience and I was told that I would live to be an old man. Old age was promised to me, and I got it. The power told me, "You shall see your country again, but you shall be alone." I have lost my family, all except two boys. The power told me, "When you get old, you can tell about the ceremony." That is why I tell you this.

In another account two children, "a girl about seven years old and a boy a little bigger," acquire power.

[7] See p. 192.

Despite these several instances, to obtain a ceremony before or at the age of puberty is the exception rather than the rule. Since most children are without supernatural protection of their own and are, furthermore, particularly susceptible to certain kinds of "evil influence," their parents and other close relatives assume responsibility for them and provide them with amulets, arrange crisis rites, and hire shamans for them when necessary.

But whether or not an individual has formerly been concerned about supernatural aids, he seldom ignores them after he enters into the marriage relationship, for now he must afford supernatural protection to others, just as it was provided for him. Time after time, when supernatural power approaches someone and asks what is desired, the person is represented as replying, "Something good for my children in this world," or, "Something to help my family."

Encounters with supernatural power, then, can occur at almost any moment in an individual's life, but relations with power and the use of power are essentially adult pursuits, of immediate survival and social value to the newly married in their hope for a stable and fecund union.

Supernatural power obtained by direct experience.—No matter how eager a man is to acquire a ceremony, the first gesture is always attributed to the power, for power requires man for its complete expression and constantly seeks human beings through whom "to work."

It seems that these powers select for themselves. Perhaps you want to be a shaman of a certain kind, but the power doesn't speak to you. It seems that, before power wants to work through you, you've got to be just so, as in the original time. You've got to believe in things as in the old days and carry everything out.

Not only does power come unbidden but it has more than one way of making itself manifest:

Some hear it; the power speaks to them. Power usually comes in a voice to the one who is getting a ceremony. The songs and words are from the power that gives the ceremony. A person doesn't fast or prepare for it. It comes on him. Sometimes it appears to a person in a vision. F.'s vision went around the dwelling like a blessing.

Solemn obligations and even serious dangers attend the acceptance of supernatural power. Therefore, the first meeting with the power source is often a testing of opposing forces.

Suppose I was going to become a shaman tonight. The power would have many ways of letting me know. I would have to meet the power and follow its directions. It might say, "Well, S., you get up on that mountain over there about noon. I will let you know just what I want you to do."

It's just like anything else; flattery has to come in with this power. This power will be boasting about me. It will say, "I can't find a better man than you are. I like your ways. There are many men here, but I can't find a better one. You are the very person for me. I want to give you something to live by through this world, because you will meet with many difficulties. This ceremony from me will help you, and you will live well. I will speak to you up on the mountain tomorrow at a certain time. Have nobody with you. Come by yourself."

I might get this message right in my own camp. It doesn't have to come when I'm sleeping. I might be wide-awake. They say the power sometimes wakes you up when it wants to speak to you.

I might reply to the power when it comes, "I'm a poor fellow, and there are many other people here good enough for that. Let me alone. I don't want your ceremony." . . . . It is said that some fellows have done that. They claim it is more dangerous to take it than to refuse it sometimes. They say some power might help you nicely for several years and then begin a lot of trouble. You might have to sacrifice your friends. Then if you refuse you might get killed yourself.

But, if I am not afraid and am interested in this power and this ceremony, I will go up the next morning. Then it will appear in the form of a person or as a spirit. "Well," it will say, "you will be a shaman and have power from the sun."

Before this I don't know what the rules of sun power are. There may be some rules that I may not like. I may not be the person who can agree with it. So it tells its plans to me, how good it will be for me and how much it likes me, and I have to decide.

Disinterest or sorrow, as well as distrust concerning the "goodness" of the power, may also act as grounds for refusal:

At Fort Sill there was a man whose eldest son died. Shortly afterward the father was sitting by a campfire and something sat with him. It spoke with him and told him it had come to tell him something. He asked who it was, and it told him it was Buzzard. Buzzard told him to consider what he was being told, that it wanted to give him power so that he would be able to see things that otherwise he could not see. He was promised that he would be wise and would know everything going on in the world and that he could find anything lost if he took this power.

The man refused to accept this power. He said, "If you were going to give me

your power, why didn't you come before my boy died? I needed it then; I suffered. Now I have nothing to live for. Your power is of no use to me now."
And he told Buzzard to go back to the place from which he came. Then Buzzard
disappeared.

But in most instances the offers of supernatural power are
accepted. The source of power may approach in a dream or, if
the person is ill or overwrought, in a vision. But dreams of the
acquisition of power are not classified with ordinary dreams and,
indeed, are not interpreted as dreams at all. Of the experience
with the buzzard just recounted, the informant said, "This was
no dream either, because a man can tell the difference." If a person is asleep when supernatural power attempts to contact him,
he considers that the power awakens him and that what follows
is a real occurrence.

Power first makes its presence known by the spoken word, by
some sign, or by appearing in the shape of some bird or supernatural. Whatever its first guise, it later assumes a human-like
form and converses with the chosen individual. If the person approached is responsive, the details of the ceremony which he is
thereafter to conduct are revealed to him, usually at the supernatural home of the power, within or near some well-known
landmark.

This "holy home" is of the greatest religious significance to the
shaman. He describes its beauty and wonder in the story he tells
his patients of the origin of his rite and sings of it in his songs. It
is a concrete evidence of his experience. If he feels that his power
is dissatisfied with him or that it is deserting him, he journeys to
this place to pray and to receive some reassuring sign.

The first trip to the holy home is the means, often, by which
the power tests the faith of the novice and determines whether he
is the kind of an individual through whom it should work.
Frightful animals guard the portals through which the candidate
is conducted; insecure bridges, steep inclines, and forbidding
elders challenge his way. But, if desire for a ceremony is strong
enough, he reaches the very center of the power's abode and
gains the knowledge for which he has come.

Here are revealed to him the songs, prayers, and ritual gestures of a ceremony. He learns what functions the rite can perform, what ceremonial presents to request from those in whose behalf it is exercised, what restrictions to impose on patients, what design elements, what paraphernalia, what sacred substances to employ. He may be advised to wait a certain number of months or years, or until he receives some signal from his power before using the ceremony. Therefore, "even a man's wife may not suspect he knows the ceremony" until the auspicious moment arrives.

After the ceremony has been learned and the understanding with the power source has been established, the new shaman is conducted to the point from which he started, or he finds himself suddenly transported there.

The nature and sources of supernatural power.—Supernatural power is, in the largest sense, the animating principle of the universe, the life-force. Again and again, shamans have terminated a discussion of the authenticity of power by exclaiming, "It is alive! It speaks to me!"

Since it is the office of beneficial supernatural power to perpetuate life, it must find ways in which to heal, warn, and guard mankind. These mediums are the familiar channels—the animals, the birds, the personified supernaturals, and others. The manner in which some of these channels themselves contribute to life and health is self-evident. Venison is a staple necessary to maintain life. Therefore, supernatural power working through the personified essence of the deer is a logical source of a ceremony to make the deer obedient to human needs. Or, since the mountain lion is a mighty hunter, power obtained by contact with the personification of this animal may be useful to the same end.

But the maintenance of well-being is not alone a matter of procuring food. Inimical forces and creatures must be counteracted. When, for instance, someone has been bitten or frightened by a snake, a snake shaman is hired to use a ceremony derived from a supernatural experience with Snake to force the reptile to repair the damage it has wrought. This lends a homeopathic flavor to the ritual practices, in which a snake ceremony is expected to cure snake sickness, a horse ceremony is used for anyone thrown from a horse, and a deer rite is employed to bring luck in the hunt. However, the horse shaman may feel that his ritual can do other things besides procuring new horses, finding lost ones, and healing those injured in mishaps with horses. The logic of some of these extensions is not always self-evident.

The medium through which supernatural power appears to a person is always considered by him to be "alive" and capable of active communication with him. But this does not mean that only animate beings, in the ordinary sense of the word, are considered as possible sources of supernatural power. Any object or force of the external world is potentially animate for the candidate for supernatural power. Moreover, some object which is alive and communicative for one person need represent no such qualities for another:

> Some say that the earth talks to them. They get their ceremony from that. Some say the wind has life. Some say the mountains, like the San Andreas, have life. Anyone who gets power from it says, "That mountain talks to me." The old people tell stories that show that all things have life—trees, rocks, the wind, mountains. One believes that there is a cliff where the Mountain People stay and that they open the cliff and talk to him. I have heard old men say that trees, rocks, and mountains have life.

An instance of the latitude permitted in such assertions is the case of a man who claimed to receive special knowledge from his own anal flatulence. This evidently acted more as a sign, comparable to muscular tremor and the dream, than as a true ceremony. Yet a number of informants have seen in this man's ability a variety of supernatural power. At any rate he is alleged to have used it in games of chance.

In spite of such novel developments, the revelations of power tend to cluster about certain familiar animals, natural forces, plants, and supernaturals.

There is no definite arrangement of powers in order of efficacy. Power derived from "a little thing"—an insect, for instance—may prove to be of inestimable value. And, since the effectiveness of power depends so much upon the relations between the shaman and the source, the same kind of power—from lightning, let us say—may be considered appreciably stronger when practiced by one person than when used by another.

The relation between the shaman and his power source.—The prayers, songs, and material elements of a ceremony are not in themselves effective, and the simulation of power is most hazardous:

I might make headdresses the way my father does and imitate him, but I wouldn't have his ceremony. It wouldn't do me any good. I couldn't cure anybody with it, not even myself if I was dying.

Power is dangerous if you try to use it and don't know how. Then you go crazy and jump into the fire or jump off a cliff or stab yourself or lose yourself so that you die wandering around the mountains.

A certain man's wife was jealous because he danced with a girl at the social dances. She used a ceremony on him so that he would never dance with this girl again. But she had never learned this ceremony properly. It was her father's ceremony, and she imitated what she had heard, but she didn't know enough to do it right, and her husband went crazy.

The ritual details are important not because they cure in themselves but because the power, as soon as a shaman begins his rite, is expected to recognize its own songs and prayers and to honor its pledges. Often, after the opening events of a ceremony, a shaman will pause for some word or sign and then reassuringly tell his audience, "My power hears me."

In order to maintain the good will of his power, the shaman must observe its rules. The person who fails to live up to his part of the power relationship agreement runs the risk of alienating the power and inviting retaliation.

The old men told us that if the power likes you and wants you, when you take up the ceremony you learn it fast. If power doesn't want you, you'll never learn it. It is hard and there are often many rules. If you violate them, power gets after you. It's like taking an oath. You take an oath to the power, and then, if you break it, power gets after you and your family.

If a shaman makes a mistake, it won't affect him or his family. But the power he represents gets after him and calls him down. "I never told you to do it that way!" it says. Then the power gives him another chance. If the shaman always makes mistakes, he may get sick and die, for the power gives him up. If you disobey your power, something will happen to you. It is dangerous. A man who does his ceremony wrong all the time might be killed when at war; his power might let this happen.

Power is bitterly resentful if its ceremony is conducted in a slovenly or erroneous fashion, for this is evidence of little interest and faith.

It must not be thought that a shaman is concerned with his power only at times of ritual or when he is in communication with his supernatural guardian. This relationship invades every realm of interest and activity. One man, who has a ceremony from Lightning, tends to interpret everything possible in terms of it. He even sees a lightning symbol in the zigzag lacing of the child's cradle, a point that no one else seems willing to concede. Elsewhere I have indicated how the nature of a man's ceremony and power source may even affect the manner in which he relates traditional legends.[8]

In the course of a rite a constant interchange between the power and the shaman takes place. "A shaman with masked dancers does not paint them just the way he wants to. Every time he wants to paint, a picture comes before his eyes and tells him what to paint."

The shaman is the custodian of the songs and ritual with which he has been intrusted. It is his obligation to see that they are not inappropriately used. "If a man has a ceremonial song and his power has told him to sing it a certain way, he doesn't want anyone else to sing it, and he will tell him it's wrong if he tries."

It not infrequently happens that the power and the shaman discover that on some specific issue they have contrary aims or interests:

The old people say that a shaman often falls out with his own power. Many stories have been told about that, all of them true. After many years, the power will ask some shamans to sacrifice some of their best friends or the very ones they love best in the family. That's what they say.

There was one man who was a war shaman. He was well protected by his power. Once he had his own group of men ready to go into battle. Usually before going into battle, he would sing for his men and pray for them so that nobody would get a wound. This time he was praying for his men who were going into battle. All his warriors were sitting around him that night. He had never kept

[8] "Three Types of Variation and Their Relation to Culture Change," in *Language, Culture, and Personality; Essays in Memory of Edward Sapir*, pp. 146–57.

anything about his ceremony secret from his warriors. He always told them, "Go right in and fight. Nobody's going to get killed or shot. Go right in. That's what my power says."

That night during his ceremony for the next day's battle his power told him, "Tomorrow I'm going to take two of your very best men during the battle." It called them by their names, the two best warriors.

So right there he told them, "You two men are to be killed tomorrow. That is what my power says." Then he kept on with his ceremony. He was angry with his power.

But his power said, "This must be done. I have helped you and have done everything you asked for up to this time. Now you must do what I tell you."

This man answered his power, talking so loud that everybody heard it. They say he waved his hand over his men to cover all of them. He said, "These men and their families, I love every one of them. I want to see them as long as I live. I will not let you have any of them. I will not agree with you. I must tell you that right now." He was very angry.

His power said, "It must be done." And he told it, "It's not going to be done!" He was fighting it.

The power told him again, "It must be done." And he said, "If you think it must be done, take me. Then you can do whatever you want after that. Take me first. If that's the kind of thing you want me to do, take your ceremony back right now. I don't want it. I want to do only good things with it. When I have to pay [you] men, I will not put up with it any longer."

I think this argument ended by the power's saying, "If you don't want anything to happen, don't go into that battle tomorrow." The power is strong in this story. That's the way the old people tell it.

Since the value of a ceremony depends so markedly upon the intimate personal relations between the shaman and the supernatural source, anything that interferes with the clarity of purpose of the shaman gravely weakens the rite:

The only thing the old man told me was this: "The older you get, the weaker you become with your ceremony. Your mind is weak. Your praying is mixed up. You get the lines in the wrong-order in the songs and prayers. Your voice is weak in praying. Your voice is feeble and you can't sing as you used to. You can't have a good vigorous talk with your power any more."

And because the efficacy of power is so completely linked with this mutual confidence, any rupture of this relationship may result in the withdrawal of supernatural support from the shaman:

Sometimes the power of the shaman just goes, all at once. E. is a member of the Central Chiricahua band. I knew him when I was a boy. I lived right in the same place. He is my cousin (our fathers were brothers, sons of the same mother). E. lost his power over twenty years ago. Maybe he misused it. Maybe the power didn't want to use him any more. When they don't get any response from the power during prayer or the ceremony, they know the power has gone. If things are working well, a shaman will get a response to prayer; he will hear a voice. . . . . I know many people here who used to be shamans but are not now. If power begins to weaken, nothing can be done about it; it just goes and can't be kept strong.

Another informant, however, felt that waning power might be restored to the shaman:

Any shaman, even if he has had strong power that spoke to him, may feel that it has deserted him. Then he goes out to a lonely place and calls on his power. He puts pollen on his forehead and chest and prays. He never tells what he says to his power, but it may come back to him then.

The transmission of ceremony.—It is also possible to gain supernatural power and a ceremony by learning it from another. How can the transfer of power be reconciled with the emphasis laid on the close association of the shaman with the power that has spoken to him? No inconsistency is involved; these two basic methods of acquiring ceremonies have been skilfully blended in theory and practice. To the question, "Could a man go to one who had power and learn his power from him?" an elderly informant replied:

That is hard. Wind said to lightning, "See that mountain over there. If I want, I can split it in two pieces." Lightning answered him, "I also can split that mountain in two pieces." They both had power to do the same thing, but the power of the wind is not the power of the lightning. Neither is one man's power the power of another man.

Still, if you go to an old man and this old man teaches you the observances over and over, and if the man's supernatural power is pleased with you, you can obtain the power that the old man has. But if the source of the old man's power does not want you, nothing you can do will help. The old man goes out alone and asks his power, and, if it is pleased, pollen is put in your mouth. Then, no matter how many songs there are, you learn them all without difficulty.

He [the shaman] does not lose power by sharing it. But he usually does not share it until he is too old to practice much longer or is going to quit.

The same subject is treated in another statement:

Many of the ceremonies are passed along. They go from father to son and from one relative to another, although they can go to those who aren't relatives too. About half the ceremonies in use are got in this way. But even if a person wants to learn the power and the shaman is willing to teach him, often he cannot remember the prayers. When a man is handing down power, if the one he is teaching cannot learn the prayers and the rest of the ceremony in four days, it is a sign that power does not want to come to him. But if the man learns easily, he is the type of person for the work, it shows. It is not a thing that the shaman has entire say about. He must consult the power, the source from which he gets his ceremony. The shaman chooses, but it must please the power.

Of the final act of the transfer, it was said:

He told us we would have to stay up with him for four nights and learn it. Then the last night, the last thing he will do is to put pollen in our mouths four times, and the fourth time the power will come to us.

Since the power could have rejected him, the student feels that he has been approved. The power, pleased with the new incumbent, appears to him, speaks to him, and performs all the services for him that it rendered his instructor. One who has learned a ceremony, if he is a more forceful and religiously minded person, may actually come to know the power better than his predecessor.

Sometimes the shaman who teaches another his ceremony does not insist on payment. More often, some payment is required or, nevertheless, proffered. In learning some ceremonies, the person "in training" must submit during the period of instruction to certain food and behavior restrictions. "If the new shaman does not follow the rules laid down by his instructor, he will lose the power."

There is no obligation to accept instruction from a shaman who is eager to give it. "I was approached by a man a long time ago who wanted to transfer his power to me. I told him, 'No, I am afraid of it.' Sometimes a person will want to hand down a ceremony, but no one will take it because it is so dangerous."

Personality differences of shamans.—Some individuals are definitely "ceremonial people." They claim the right to conduct a number of rituals obtained by personal vision experience, by instruction, or in both ways. "R. has all sorts of power in different ways; he's just full of it," was a remark made of one man. Of another great shaman, his son said:

My father knew Goose, Bear, Wolf, Lightning, and many other things. When he received his power, the last man in the cave [holy power home] said, "All these are under you."

I never knew how many things my father did know. He said to me once, "I can't tell you. I'd like you to know it all, but some things I cannot tell. I could take you where I went in the cave, but you might not 'make' it." And he laughed.

The possibility of multiple powers leads to interesting ramifications. One shaman, after some reverses, may decide that two of his powers are hostile toward each other, and he may feel obliged to discontinue the use of one of them. Another may be assured that his power source and another "work well together" and so may attempt to secure a complementary rite. One informant felt, for instance, that "Wind and Thunder go together," and he organized his own ritual life in terms of this precept.

Personality differences and differences in interest are sharply evident. "Often men have more than one power. Some fellows have many; some just don't care about it at all. Several men may know the same thing, and one may know several things." Very nearly all adults are eager for supernatural guidance, but many see in their power merely a personal monitor or carry on ceremonies for the benefit of their immediate families only.

Some are suspected of having this power or that but refuse to give any satisfaction to their questioners. The power itself may have forbidden revelation of the connection or may have advised that the knowledge be withheld for a certain time. Consequently, curiosity about undeclared power is always rife. A newly worn feather or amulet arouses all kinds of speculation. A favorite device, when a person is suspected of ceremonial knowledge which he has not divulged, is to discuss the matter with him when his inhibitions are at low ebb. In a case of this kind "the man gave away the fact of his power while he was drunk, and the other got him to perform the ceremony for him."

Sometimes, to help a friend or a relative, a person who thinks his rite might prove effective reluctantly "gives himself up." One man performed a snake ceremony before a selected group but asked them to say nothing about it. When I interviewed him, he pleaded profound ignorance of the snake rite. Since I could not very well confess that he had been betrayed to me, there was no way to elicit the desired data.

Theoretically, no shaman is obliged to accept a call for assistance that he does not wish to honor. In practice, however, it is very difficult to turn away the sick person or his relatives, particularly if the request is attended by a prescribed ceremonial gesture, is expressed in language of great humility, or if relationship terms are employed in the asking.

An individual who shows initial reluctance to demonstrate his ceremonial knowledge may achieve signal success as a result of his first public venture. He is then likely to lose his shyness and to accept cases at frequent intervals. There are others who are more than willing to earn the rewards that come to a successful practitioner. They wear conspicuously amulets suggestive of their power and are ready to tell about their vision experiences and their ceremonial triumphs. They accept any reasonable case and make of their rituals a dramatic display.

The functions of supernatural power.—Besides its general function as a guardian spirit, the most frequent use of supernatural power is in the diagnosis and treatment of disease. There is no separate class of diagnosticians or shamans who consult their power solely to learn the cause of illness and the identity of another practitioner to cope with it. But sometimes "a shaman can tell you beforehand whether he can do you any good." If there is doubt concerning the cause of the sickness and the pertinence of a particular ceremony, a pragmatic attitude is assumed:

Both R. and A. sang for me. They kept singing because they did not know what I got sick from. If what they know is the right thing, it cures it. R. sang lightning songs, for he knows that too. He sang for nine days. It usually lasts four days, but if you don't know what a man is sick from, you keep on until you find out sometimes.

During the curative rite, when the shaman is receiving instruction from his power source concerning the best method to combat the sickness, he often obtains additional information. Some of it is of a prophetic nature, picturing the future state and fortunes of his patient. This is considered cogent material to introduce, especially if it suggests that the sick person will recover. Sometimes the predictions shed light on the affairs of some of the onlookers too. This acts as testimony to the effectiveness of the power and to the close understanding the shaman has with it. Such prophecy has its therapeutic function, too, for the religious zeal of all present is important in the successful outcome of any rite.

Supernatural experiences often bring to those who undergo them special abilities and techniques which may be used quite apart from any rite. It is not unusual to hear that a person possesses great bodily strength because his ceremony comes from Bear, that one who "knows" Bat is an excellent horseman, or that a man's speed and endurance date from his acquisition of power from Goose. It is often claimed that one who knows sun and moon power is able to look down upon distant events. Of a certain man, it was said: "When he went a long distance, he sang a song. In it were the words 'Near, near.' Then he got there sooner. He had songs for going a long distance and a short distance."

Another office of supernatural power is to bring success—success in war and raid, in hunting, in love, in games, and in many of life's endeavors. The degree to which it has guided his efforts to acquire stock and to deal with the enemy was related by one man:

Power told me that I was to get something if I went out on the raid. If I go out and look for something, my power gives me the ability to get horses and mules. The power sends me out and tells me, "You are going to get this."

My power told me that the enemy was coming. It told me, "If you want the enemy to see you, they are going to see you. If you want to see the enemy, you will see them. If you don't want to meet the enemy, they will swing around the other way."

The location of lost persons and lost or hidden objects is an important service performed by supernatural power. Usually power guides the shaman's hand in the direction of the object or person to be discovered. The ceremonial procedure, designated "it moves the arms about," is employed also in locating a foe. Usually the shaman stands, praying and singing, with arms extended, while the supernatural power moves him in the fateful direction. In ceremonies to find missing persons shamans use articles of clothing belonging to the one sought. Songs, prayers, or ritual acts carried on over the garments exert a controlling influence on the lost individual.

There are other ceremonial means of finding the enemy:

A shaman who got his power from a star could locate the enemy by making a cross of ashes on his left hand and holding it up to the star, the morning star. This was much used in war. Sometimes the cross was traced in pollen, or abalone shell was held aloft in the hand. Then a flash of lightning in the direction of the enemy appeared.

Fugitives can be found and halted by ceremonial methods too:

A young man killed his wife and ran away. Her relatives were looking for him. Finally they found his track. They brought a ceremonial man to it. "I'll make him come back," he said. He knelt down, put pollen on the man's track, and prayed and sang. Then he put his hand in the track and turned it. "He can't get away. He will be back," he said. In two days this boy came to his stepfather's camp. They were waiting for him and caught him.

Of great consequence is the function of power in weakening the enemy and in providing invulnerability from attack:

One time they all saw the enemy coming, and the enemy saw them. The shaman said to the people, "I am going to make them disappear, and we shall disappear from their view also." Then he told the people to go behind a hill so they couldn't see the enemy. He alone stood on top of the hill.

After about twenty minutes the shaman told them all to come up again. When they came up, there were only cattle grazing around where the enemy had been. The shaman told the men to herd the cattle, drive them to the river, and shoot them and eat them there.

When it became apparent that the Mexicans and Americans were menacing invaders, the ceremonies to influence the enemy were extended to cope with them:

C. was going into Chihuahua. He wanted to go to a certain Mexican town. He knew the ceremony of Cloud and started to perform it. Cloud told him not to use it but to use the ceremony to influence the enemy which he also knew. So he did. Then he went right into the town.

The mayor was surprised to see him come. "Aren't you afraid? Don't you know we kill all of you Indians?" he asked C. "I'm not afraid. What should I be afraid of? I have done nothing against you," C. replied. And no harm came to him.

. . . . K. got into some trouble. He had to run away to Oklahoma. He came back afraid, for the agent had said he would fix him when he got hold of him. So he hired a woman to pray for him and influence the white man.

She walked up the road behind him praying. Then she said, "All right, go ahead and see the agent." Then she turned off the road. K. went right on to the office. The agent did not seem angry with him. In fact, he was glad to see him. It surely does influence them!

Supernatural power further protects the warrior against his enemies by making him invulnerable to their arrows and bullets.

The control of weather and natural events are other objectives of ceremonialists:

There is a ceremony to bring rain when it is very dry. Then we get rain by calling on White Painted Woman and Child of the Water. The world is White Painted Woman. The thunder is Child of the Water. Sand, a whitish sand from Old Mexico, is used in this ceremony to call the rain. It is blown to the four directions. Also Lightning is called on when the sand is blown, and a blowing noise, "Hoo, hoo!" is made. In the prayer there is mention of the number of days it should rain.

I have a ceremony which, if carried out on the desert, would cause a sandstorm. But this would be uncomfortable for the people, and so I dislike to do it. It is a prayer. I used it when men were going to make a raid for horses so that they could get away without being detected. I throw sand into the air, blow against it four times, say the prayer, and it causes sand to blow around so thick that you can't see.

The length of day or night can also be controlled through power:

When he was on the warpath, Geronimo fixed it so that morning wouldn't come too soon. He did it by singing. Once we were going to a certain place, and Geronimo didn't want it to become light before he reached it. He saw the enemy while they were in a level place, and he didn't want them to spy on us. He wanted morning to break after we had climbed over a mountain, so that the enemy couldn't see us. So Geronimo sang, and the night remained for two or three hours longer. I saw this myself.

MEDICAL PRACTICES

The nonritual treatment of ailments.—Though it is true that most of the ceremonies deal with ill-health, it does not necessarily follow that all sickness must be treated ceremonially. An individual may become sick through surfeit or through want; he may weaken himself by overexertion; he may suffer injury because of carelessness or needless daring. Advancing years bring their infirmities; old age "can kill you." "There are several ailments you can get by not taking care of yourself, by foolishness—such things as tuberculosis and venereal diseases." Of course, in any particular case, the reasoning may be reversed, and a malevolent person or force may be blamed finally for the trouble.

For therapeutic purposes bloodletting is sometimes practiced without any ceremony:

Bleeding is done to humans for pain in the arms or for rheumatism. A skilled man is obtained to do it, not necessarily a shaman. He opens the vein on the back of the hand. This is not done on the legs, but just on the arms. . . . . Old Man P. used to cut veins on people when their arms ached. Sometimes he even cut a vein in the head.

Bloodletting is used for fatigue also, but to a limited extent:

Blood is sometimes drawn from the legs in order to relieve fatigue. We use prickly-pear cactus or something with spines to draw the blood. I have done this and got relief quickly.

The bone of a broken arm is set, and splints (flat pieces of sotol wood) are bound on it with buckskin or rawhide strips.

Frostbite is treated with pitch and grease: "One of my relatives, a man, froze the bottom of his foot. He took pitch [probably piñon pitch] and grease, put them together, and rubbed them in. It is good for it."

Massage is used for an illness said to be caused by a shift in the position of the intestines:

When you get hungry or sick, your intestines come up toward your chest. Then whoever is taking care of you should take something warm, rub you with it and push the entrails down. When they go down to their place, take something and tie it around the chest to keep them down. I did this a few days ago. I used my belt. My wife rubbed me first. You can hear the intestines go down.

A buckskin truss which a ruptured man made for himself has been described.

For rheumatism, grease and red ocher are mixed, warmed, and tied over the aching spot. A stone or a shell is sometimes heated and pressed on the painful joint. Such a stone or shell may also be pressed to an aching ear or any paining spot.

To relieve a toothache: "S.'s mother uses the awl that she makes moccasins with. She gets it hot and puts it in the hole in the tooth."

Even sleepwalking is often dealt with naturalistically:

When a person has the habit of sleepwalking, they make him sleep with some-one. They tie him to this one with a rope. Then he can't get away without wak-ing the other up. I was this way, and they did it with me. They tied me to my brother. One man was this way when we were in Old Mexico. He took a lance and ran over a cliff in his sleep. Another fellow climbed up a tree. They called to him, "What are you doing up there?" Then he woke up.

Despite these instances of the nonceremonial care of ailments, a short account which contains a number of elements inspired by ritual practices indicates how arbitrary is any division of the religious and secular treatment of disease:

You can burn charcoal on your arm or leg to kill pain.[9] You do this when you have a pain all the time. Take wood and burn it to charcoal. Then light a small piece of it again, one about the thickness of the lead in a lead pencil. Blow on it until it burns at one end and moisten the other end or the place on the arm where you are going to put it. Then stick it on. Let it burn out. Don't watch it as it burns. Some do it four times around the place where it hurts.

Here we have the fighting of like by like, the restriction against watching the flame, and the feeling that the procedure should be repeated four times; yet the sufferer does not have to possess a ceremony in order to give himself the treatment.

The method for curing ivy poisoning and red-ant stings obviously borrows from the psychology of ritual also:

My people knew about poison ivy and how to recognize it. If I touch poison ivy, the blisters break out, because I am sensitive to it. But perhaps you are not. Then my father and mother will call you over, because, though you touch it, it does not bother you. You don't have to be a shaman or know anything special. You come and rub anything on—it might be dirt. You say, "Now this person is just like me. Leave him alone. Go away. I'm watching him." It's the same with the sting of the red ant or any stinging thing.

Sweat-bathing.—Another practice that stands midway between therapeutics and ritual is sweat-bathing. Many who have used the sweat bath consider it a means of keeping fit and are little concerned with its ritual extensions. "I used to do it just for a general tonic," explained one informant. Even when the sweat bath is thought of as a cure for deformities, it is to the heat and the massage that the benefits are usually attributed. Said one commentator: "The sweat bath was the custom since the beginning. Maybe it was supposed to be a ceremony, but since then it has been wearing off."

[9] This method is similar to the tests of courage popular with young boys (cf. p. 69).

PLATE IX

FRAMEWORK OF THE SWEAT LODGE

The person who agrees to erect a sweat house is not a true shaman, nor are the rights which are now transmitted from individual to individual explained as a result of some past power experience. Thus, one informant was of the opinion that Child of the Water "gave the custom." And yet the right to build a sweat house is a special prerogative, claimed and controlled by relatively few men.

Not everybody can make a sweat bath. Just certain men can do it—men to whom the knowledge has been handed down. Such a man builds it or directs the building of it. All the while it is being built he sings and prays for it. He handles every movement in connection with it ceremonially, just as he was directed to do when the right was handed down to him. He is present when the sweat bath is used. He is the one who chants the prayer part of the song when the men are inside, though all who are in there join in the refrain. He is usually quite an old man. He sets the rules. You can't just come in and go out as you please. It might be in this man's "way" that you have to stay in there through a certain number of songs. Then you have to do it.

The sweat bath is used for good health, for long life, and to cure sickness. It is usually built near water, and when the songs are finished everybody rushes out and plunges into the water. Very old men who can't do that sit down on the bank and splash water on themselves.

An account of the erection and use of the structure may place the practice in perspective:

Sweat-bathing is for health and good fortune. Deformed people do it a great deal and are massaged when they come out. Usually a sick or deformed man pays one who knows how to put it on, but no special kind of payment is given. Others are invited. But often the man who knows how will just put it on for the benefit of the people. When the announcement is made, many men want to take the sweat bath. Everything else is laid aside. This is a special occasion. Women don't take sweat baths, nor boys before the racing [boy's training] age.

The sweat house could be made any time of year, but it is usually done in the summer. It is dome shaped like the regular house, only smaller. It is about four and a half feet high and about six feet in diameter. The framework is of oak, tied together at the top. The outside is covered with brush and with skins. No smoke hole is left at the top. The door faces the east. On the inside, close to the door and on one side of it, there is a pit for the hot rocks. The man in charge directs the making of this sweat house.

In the morning a person who is sick or deformed and who is going in there prays in his own way. He may say, "I am sick in this manner. I want to get well, and so I am doing this in the right way."

Often they begin about midmorning. Twelve is the most allowed in at one time. About four to six men usually go in at once. They wear just a loincloth. Before they go in, pounded piñon needles or pounded juniper may be rubbed on their bodies by the man in charge. All the men wear sage tied around their heads while they are in there. And they take a drink in which four pieces of mesquite bean have been put. Each man has to bring a stick to scratch with. He cannot scratch his body with his fingers.

Four big rocks are heated outside and then brought to the pit inside with a forked stick. Water is brought. The men are sitting in a circle but leave an open space to the east. Then the water is sprinkled on the hot rocks. Anyone who is appointed can sprinkle water on. One man sits outside and operates the door cover so that the heat does not escape. The man in charge is always in there. He prays in there and leads the singing. Special songs are sung, songs that mention the sweat bath, the earth, and the sky. Usually four songs are sung over and over. All who are inside sing.

The men try to stay in there about an hour. Then they come out and bathe. Some young fellows run a race, too, while they are still warm from the sweat bath, to enable them to become good runners and to make them long winded. That is their belief.

Sometimes the men go in four times during the day. But some can't stand it. K. went in once. The heat was so great that he didn't go in a second time. Sometimes they just go in once and it's over. They rub themselves well with their hands when they come out. Sweat-bathing like this keeps men in good physical condition. It isn't done right away again. They would wait at least fifteen days before doing it again. There is no use for very old people to go into the sweat house. Their lives are spent.

Herbalism.—Plants are used in the majority of cases, whether the manner of combating the illness be ceremonial or purely secular. "There are all kinds of roots and weeds and herbs, something for everything; nothing was left out." Some plants are considered so "strong" and so "ceremonial" that only those who have supernatural sanction and directions for their use dare apply them. Other plants, usually administered in nonritual contexts, appear in ceremonies if the supernatural power so orders.

Incensing with the smoke of burning juniper and piñon boughs is mentioned repeatedly:

My people take piñon and juniper, put the boughs together, and burn them. They do it inside the home and keep the members of the family there until they can't stand it any longer. This burning makes a lot of smoke, and they stay there until the tears come from their eyes. Then they won't catch a disease that is around. They do this if there is a great deal of disease around.

Various rectal ailments are treated with medicines administered through an enema tube:

The Chiricahua use the enema tube in cases of the passing of blood, for hemorrhoids, or for long-continued stomach trouble. The tube is of carrizo or elderberry wood. It is used on both men and women. The medicine, made from plants, is a liquid and is poured in. Then the one doing the curing blows into the tube. After the tube is taken out, a powder made of pulverized dry plants is placed in the rectum and around it. Last some grease mixed with red ocher is rubbed around the anus.

For blood in the stool, the root of cinquefoil is ground up and mixed with water; the decoction is drunk. It is also applied externally to aching parts of the body. Apache plume (*Fallugia paradoxa*) is used as a laxative, while for diarrhea cudweed (*Gnaphalium decurrens*) is recommended. "Boil the flower if you want to take it for diarrhea. Then dry it. It keeps dry all the year around. Pick it toward fall when it blooms. Drink it like a tea. Drink it first and eat afterward."

A cure for mumps and for swellings on the neck draws upon sympathetic magic. "If you have mumps or lumps on the neck, get a plant with a bulb, burn it to ashes, put the ashes on the place with grease, and tie it up."

Oak root is shaved, soaked in water, and used as an eyewash.

A number of pungent plants, among them sage and *Hilaria cenchroides*, serve as remedies for colds:

For headache, crush and smell strong flowers and plants. Do it when the nose is dry and you feel that you are getting a cold. But do not use them as snuff; do not breathe it right up. Sage is crumbled, mixed with tobacco, and smoked in cigarettes for colds. They also boil it, strain the liquid, and drink it.

The most widely used medicine for headaches, colds, and coughs is the root of osha (*Ligusticum porteri*):

Mix it with tobacco and smoke it for a cold. Chew it for a cold or cough too. Grind it up, mix it with water, and rub it on the affected part, on the nose if that is stopped up. If this doesn't work, boil some and drink the water. It may cause vomiting, but it is good for a chest cold. For headache, grind it up, mix it with water, and rub it on the forehead.

The screw bean (*Strombocarpa pubescens*) is a highly considered specific for ear trouble. "Grind it up. Put a little salt and water with it. Soak it up with some absorbent material, and then squeeze it into the ear."

Excessive dandruff has its remedies. "We use plants for this, two or three different kinds. We burn them to ashes and rub the ashes on with grease. The sap of trees is good for this too."

We see, then, that for minor ailments well-known plants are used without ritual. If pain or sickness persists, an herbalist may be hired who sings and prays while he gives the medicines.

My small boy hurt his arm, and it didn't get better for a long time. I heard that F. was good and had medicine for such things. So I got him. He sang a song first. Then he put some of the medicine on the boy's arm. It cured him too.

Toothaches are sometimes treated by a similar combination of prayer and medicine:

There was a person who knew something about teeth, and he gave an herb that was used for toothache. He prayed in addition, and the toothache was cured.

But in some illnesses which require dosage with herbs the medicine must be given with more formality. Such a malady is venereal disease. The medicine, which is made from the pounded and boiled roots of the locust tree, must be tendered to the patient by one who has special knowledge concerning its preparation and ritual.

A certain young fellow got gonorrhea. The boys used to joke with him a great deal about it. I don't think his mother ever knew what was the matter with him. He just said he was sick. I remember that he approached my father and asked if there wasn't some Apache remedy for the disease. My father said there was, and, of course, there is. I don't think my father had the ceremony that goes with the root, however, and could not have treated him anyway. But my father told him that part of the treatment was that the sick man had to bring the girl before the man who gave the treatment, or the disease could not be cured. The sick man refused to do this. He didn't want to tell on the girl. So my father said that he could do nothing for him in that case.

Of venereal disease another informant said:

We have a ceremony for venereal disease. When there is a hard boil down there, they recognize that it is very serious and hard to cure. When it breaks, they have a medicine to put on it. They use a ceremony and drink medicine. When a person is very sick from venereal disease and a shaman is carrying on a ceremony to save him, an herbalist, a man or woman who knows what plants will help this sickness, may be called in at the same time. In fact, the shaman may advise this. His power may tell him that someone who knows a good plant is needed. I know cases where a man is pretty sick with gonorrhea and they get him well.

Illnesses peculiar to women are treated by a combination of herbalism and ceremonialism often:

If menstruation stops and the woman is not with child, it is a serious disease called "blood is in her." It can cause a woman to die. For this "flint medicine" is used. This is a lightning-riven twig. The wood is chipped off, boiled in water, and the medicine put in a bowl or cup. Whoever gives it marks it with pollen, performs a ceremony with pollen, and then it is drunk. Just people with special knowledge can perform the ceremony.

For pain at the monthly period and for an excessive flow of menstrual blood, this medicine is also given. Sometimes scrapings from a flint or "thunder arrow" are added before it is taken.

So great a scourge is tuberculosis that plants considered effective against it assume much importance, and their use is accompanied by a great deal of ritual. The most highly esteemed specific for this disease is "narrow medicine," *Perezia wrightii*:

"Narrow medicine" is powerful. It is a root which is ground up and put into water. It is not boiled. Water is put in a shallow basket which is lined with pitch to make it watertight. Then the medicine is added to the water, and four hot stones are put in. It is necessary to use four. It foams up when it is heated. There is a prayer, and a cross of pollen is put on the medicine. Then pollen is held to the four directions and put on the head and back of the patient. A cup of the medicine is taken and held to the directions four times. Then the patient drinks. This is good for tuberculosis. Lots of people get well from taking it.

After taking the medicine, the patient lies out in the sun and gets heated up. He vomits up all the tuberculosis. If he doesn't vomit, he has to defecate. It works either way. Sometimes you see the tuberculosis worm alive and about a half-inch long. Then the patient starts to regain his health.

This herb has been in use a long time. My great-grandmother used it. If the patient is not too far gone, it works. It is given only once or twice. If you take much of it, it makes you weak. It is very expensive. You give a great many things for it—even a horse.

If the person giving it does not know the secrets of it and puts too much in, the patient will go crazy and kill himself. If you don't know the secrets, even though you know the right amount to give, it will hurt you. Tuberculosis is usually treated by old women who know a good deal about herbs.

ORIGINS OF DISEASE

Contaminating animals.—Ailments which do not yield to ordinary herbal remedies or to decoctions ritually administered are thought to have been contracted from unclean animals or from animals or supernaturals capable of sending disease when offended, defied, or instigated by malevolent forces. It is to combat sickness of this kind that the intricate curing ceremonies are reserved.

There are different ways in which the disease reaches the individual:

Here are three ways that you can get sickness from an animal or from some other source. One is by getting scared. This is typical of owl disease. It is the thrill of terror, the moment of cold fright, that is really the entrance of the evil influence into your body. You might have such an experience and not be sick for months. Then, when you get sick you remember. You say, "Ah, that is when it happened, when I was so frightened." Another way is by smell, odor. Bear and lightning sickness may be spread in this way. Another way is touch. Contact with hides of the evil animals such as the bear, wolf, and coyote will give you the disease.

The greatest caution is observed toward animals and forces which can do so much harm:

If a Chiricahua tells a story about a bear or any animal or thing that can sicken him, at the end he says, "I'm talking about pollen and all kinds of fruit. Let everything be as good as ever." He makes believe that he isn't talking about that animal.

Formerly the Chiricahua would seldom say the regular word for bear. They would call it "mother's sibling." It doesn't like to be called by the regular word. It gets after you when you say that. Bear is also called "wide foot" and "large buttocks." It likes to be called "ugly buttocks" too. We call the thunder "grandfather" and the snake "yellow flowers." We spit when lightning flashes.

Of the animals which are unreservedly dangerous to those who do not "know" their supernatural power, the most important are the bear, the coyote, the snake, and the owl.

Bear.—The general attitude toward the bear, the manner in which bear disease is contracted, and some of the symptoms of the ailment are described by one man as follows:

The bear, like the coyote, causes evil influence. It is killed only in self-defense, for no bear meat is eaten and we are afraid to skin a bear. If you come in contact with the track of a bear, or a tree where a bear has leaned, or bear manure, or if you sleep where a bear has sat down, or if you come in contact with a bear by smell or touch, you can get sick.

The smell is very important. As soon as it gets in a person through smell, that person is under evil influence. If a person does not come in contact with a bear but is scared by a bear, it causes sickness too. The condition of fright that a man gets in causes his sickness.

A person suffering from bear sickness gets run down. It seems like he is smelling that bear all the time. At night he is always dreaming that he has hardly got away from a bear that is chasing him, or something like that. . . . . Bear sickness often shows up in a deformity, in a crooked arm or leg.

Should the path of a bear be accidently crossed, an attempt is made to deceive the bear about it. "If you have to cross the tracks of a bear, you say, 'It was a year ago.' It is the custom to say that to make it appear that it happened a long time ago, so the evil influence will keep away."

Specific symptoms equated with the characteristics of the bear mark the onset of bear sickness:

When a man is sick from bear, he acts like a bear. First he gets a pain all over his body. Then his mouth is twisted, and he bites. His whole face twists. His body swells.

Long ago at Fort Stanton two men got sick from bear and died. These two men were out. It was snowing. There was a big pine tree. A bear had been there. The two men slept there all night. They got sick from it. Their arms went behind their backs, and they growled like bears. I saw them when they were sick. They tried to bite me.

A long time ago, when I was a child, I was playing in a cave where a bear had lived. Pretty soon I got sick. I got tired, wanted to lie down, and foam came out of my mouth as it does from the mouth of a bear when he is tired. They had a ceremony performed for me, and I got better. The shaman sang, and I got well that same night.

Coyote, wolf, fox, dog.—The coyote, if he is molested, can, at the very least, bring bad luck or an accident:

Our dog ran ahead [after a coyote]. Suddenly the dog doubled his tracks and ran right in front of S.'s horse. The horse went over as S. tried to avoid the dog, and S. fell and hit his head. He didn't come to for a long time. We were far away from anyone, and I didn't have any water. All I could do was sit there and hold his head and fan him with my hat. By and by he came to. That's what the old men say about coyotes; they say that Coyote is bad and that something always happens to you if you go after one.

More serious is a disease, marked by deformity, which Coyote is capable of causing:

When a person has it, his face gets lopsided with the mouth pointing one way. Or he gets cross-eyed, or his legs or hands get cramped. There is a disfiguration somewhere. You can get it from a coyote—from touch or fright or smell, or from crossing its tracks. We kill coyotes sometimes, but we don't touch the skins.

Eye defects, particularly, are attributed to coyote sickness. "One man whose eyeballs turn up told me that his eyes were all right until he used a coyote skin for a rug. Since then his eyes have been bad."

The coyote shares his evil reputation with the wolf and the fox. Most informants class the three together and claim that the ceremony that will cure sickness from one of them will serve for illness brought by the others. There is a definite feeling that the fox is the least dangerous of the trio and that the coyote is the most baneful. The appearance of a fox, however, is taken as an omen of impending death: "Gray Fox . . . . is connected with death. If at dark Fox goes near some camps, that means that someone in that group is going to die."

In the following discussion the nexus between wolf sickness and the evil influence of the coyote is made clear:

The wolf, coyote, and fox . . . . bring bad luck and make you sick, even if you only touch them or smell their breath. Such contact deforms a person, making him cross-eyed, turning his lips, and making him twitch. At Fort Sill an old lady had her dog follow a wolf. The woman went after the wolf in order to help her dog, and she pulled the wolf, which was in a hole, by the hind leg. She became ill. She began to get cross-eyed and to shake, and her lips became crooked. Geronimo was living then, and he sang over her and cured her.[10]

Of dogs the people say: "We didn't have dogs in the old days. Dogs make a lot of noise. The Chiricahua were on the run and couldn't have them." "We have had them only since contact with the whites." Evidently the dog was at first greatly feared:

The dog was classed with the coyote, wolf, and fox. We felt that all of them could cause you trouble. We wouldn't touch the skin of a dead dog. When you have a disease from a dog, the saliva comes down as it does with a mad dog. You get a little crazy and go, "Aaaa!"

[10] Geronimo's coyote power ceremony (pp. 40–41) is probably what was used on this occasion.

Now that the people lead a more settled life and raise stock, there is a real need for dogs, and the feeling against touching them no longer exists. But they are still regarded with some suspicion. "It is not liked if a dog sits on his haunches before you, looking the other way. It's a bad sign. For some reason, dogs are not allowed around the hoop-and-pole game grounds either."

Snake.[11]—There is, of course, some danger of bites from rattlesnakes, but it is not this alone that is feared. The bite, in fact, is treated ceremonially like any other manifestation of snake sickness. When a snake is accidentally encountered, it is accorded the greatest respect and is referred to by a relationship term:

If a person who does not "know" Snake sees one, he says, "My mother's father, don't bother me! I'm a poor man. Go where I can't see you. Keep out of my path."

You always want to be patient with the snake, and whenever you happen upon one you want to give it good words. Say, "I want to be friends with you, so you must not do anything to hurt me." Whenever you talk to it, say, "My mother's mother, I don't want to see you anywhere I go. You must stay out of my way. You must remain in the ground. There are many people on this earth traveling everywhere."

It is not surprising that the snake, which sloughs its skin, should be held accountable for serious skin ailments of all kinds:

Snakes have evil influence. The snake has the power to make you sick if you handle him. He causes your skin to peel. The snake is an animal, but at the same time he has a supernatural influence about him that is very bad and very powerful. All snakes are classed the same way.

We are not so much afraid of the snake as we are of the owl or the coyote which we can't fight back. But we don't like to handle snakes or the shed skin of a snake. It causes sores on the inside of the lips, on the hands, and on the skin all over the body. Sometimes blisters break out. It might cause this right away or sometime later.

Swelling appears as a symptom in a specific case of snake sickness:

[11] The eel is called by the same name as the snake and is classified with the snake.

On the banks of Medicine Creek at Fort Sill I went fishing. I left my cap on a bank. I went back to the village. The next day I went to look for my cap. I found it and wiped off the sweat from my face with the cap.

The next day my face was swollen. My relatives did not know what was wrong. They consulted an old shaman, a woman. She could trace everything from her singing. She said prayers and sang four songs over me. No one knew what was wrong. While she sang, she saw a cap on a bank. It was mine. While she was looking at it, she saw something moving and coiling around inside the cap. My relatives asked me about my cap. I told them what had happened. Then the old lady knew what had happened. A water moccasin had got into my cap.

There are many ways of contracting the disease:

A person gets sick by being bitten. . . . . The sloughed skin of the snake will also cause the sickness. If I pick up the skin where I am weeding, it causes death too. A person can get sick from being scared by a rattlesnake. . . . . A person gets sick from smelling the snake. If a person lies where a snake has been, he gets sick from that.

Mention of the snake is usually avoided except in invective: "The snake is used in quarreling. Sometimes people say, 'I wish a snake would bite you!' " But this, too, has its dangers:

If a man says in anger, "I hope a snake bites you," he will get sick from snakes. He has a bad mouth. Before this the snakes have not bothered him, but he's got a bad mouth, and it's bound to make him sick.

The fate of an impious man who defied the precepts for commercial gain is told today:

Every spring white spots used to come around that man's mouth. It happened right up to the time of his death. This is because he did things against the Chiricahua's way. He went around and fooled with rattlesnakes. Many people living here have seen what would happen to his mouth every spring.

He used to catch rattlesnakes and skin them and sell the skins. He was a strong man, and he used to grab them in the back of the neck and strangle them to death. Then he'd skin that snake. He'd take out his knife and cut it open. He'd put one end of the skin in his mouth, with the blood and fat all over him and streaming down his face, and he'd pull at it to separate the skin from the rest. He used to call to other people, "Come here! Get hold of this!" But no one would go near him. After that he got sick from it and got these white spots every spring. The Chiricahua doesn't want to have anything to do with snakes. I know I don't even want to look at a rattlesnake.

Even animals are susceptible to the malignant influence of snakes:

We had a good sheep dog. She found a nest of small snakes and ate them. Then she got so mean we couldn't do anything with her. We were afraid of her. She wouldn't obey and would come running at you. We had to shoot her.

Owl and ghost.—Fear of the owl, initially communicated to children by the very panic of their elders, grows in intensity with the passage of time. It is said: "Coyote and the snake are about the same, but the owl is most dreaded." "The Chiricahua are afraid to say anything about owls or to tell stories of owls." Nor can the presence of an owl around camp be treated with indifference:'

If an owl hangs around your camp, you can take a burning stick from the fire and throw it in the owl's direction. Some would shoot at these birds. But a man who had power from that bird wouldn't shoot at it. He would be praying to it. He would know what it was around for.

When my wife and baby and I are in sheep camp and the owl begins to hoot, we don't like it. My wife often asks me to chase it. Sometimes a little child gets scared. We don't like an owl around when children are sleeping.

A typical reaction to the sight of an owl is that of the old woman of this narrative:

My sheepherder is a Shawnee Indian. Not long ago he killed an owl and brought it into my camp. We didn't notice what he was doing. An old woman was there. It was about twenty minutes before she knew what it was. She thought it was an eagle at first. Finally she asked me what it was, and I looked and told her it was an owl. Then she blew up and began to scold. "Throw that thing away! It's going to cause you evil influence," she said. I said, "Not me, but that fellow who is handling it." "Yes, you, for you have it in your camp," she answered.

The owl is so greatly feared because it is the form assumed by another agent of disease and malevolence; it is the materialization of the ghost:

Once I was riding along with Old N. and we heard an owl. N. was a brave man, but he got so scared he nearly fell off the horse. I said, "Why, that's only a bird!" "Don't say that!" N. told me. "It's a ghost. It comes out of the grave and it goes back."

The proper destination of the shades of the deceased is the underworld, where it is hoped they will continue another existence oblivious of the living on the earth above. Their materialization as owls can indicate only an evil purpose:

The owl represents the spirit or ghost of a person who was bad during his life and continues to be vicious after death. He works by entering the body of an owl and exercises evil influence in this way. Those who were desperate in life, such people as murderers and those who were given to jokes of a rough nature, are the ones likely to assume such a form after death.

This is what I heard in my young days—I remember my father telling me of it. Our belief is that, when the Chiricahua who has been a bad one dies, he turns to an owl. We believe that the bad ones go right into the owl at death, at once. The others who were good through life go to the underworld.

Since the owl is the ghost of a malicious human being, its hoot is interpreted as a dire warning:

I'm not so much afraid to kill an owl or even to handle it; it's the call! When I was in sheep camp, I listened closely and it seemed to me that it was talking the Chiricahua language. Some say they hear it say, "I'm going to drink your blood!" My wife says it sounds that way to her. Some say it sounds like, "I'm one of your relatives." To me it sounds like, "I'm a Mescalero." Some believe that dead relatives are in the form of the owl. They don't want to hear it. It's not the owl itself which is the dead person, but the voice. The owl always fools around the place where a person has died.

These "words" of the owl can cause sickness through fright:

If you hear an owl, you know a ghost is near by, for the owl is connected with the ghost. The ghost uses him, goes into his body. Owls talk the Chiricahua language. They say different things to different people. To me it seems like they are saying, "All your people are going to get killed." The call of the owl is very powerful. It can get into your body and cause trouble.

Most people, feeling that direct reference to evil invites its appearance, are unwilling to speak of owl or ghost sickness. Therefore, because ghosts and owls are both particularly active at night, the malady which they bring is most often designated "darkness sickness."

An actual encounter with an owl is a harrowing experience:

The Chiricahua are afraid of the owl. It is because the owl stays around the place where people have died, and when it comes it is a sign that someone is going to die. Many people, when they hear the call of the owl, get frightened and faint. My wife went through an experience with the owl. About a hundred paces from her my wife saw a person in black. This person was walking toward her. When it got close, it changed to an owl and flew at her. When it flew up, it tried to sit on her head. She fought off the owl, and it flew away. I wasn't at home at the time. When I came home my wife was still trembling. I knew a ceremony toward the owl, and so I performed it and made her well again.

When you are frightened by the owl, your heart begins to flutter; your heart gets weak and you fall down. I can pray for a person who has been frightened like this and, even though his heart is beating only a little, can restore him so that he gets up again.

Another story, so well known that it has been recorded from four different informants, concerns the return of a woman's ghost to her former home:

A man and his wife lived out at Whitetail. About two years ago the wife died, and the husband continued to live at the same location, though he didn't use the place in which she had died. One night he heard a knocking at the door. Then something was calling him by name. He went to the door but could see no one. This happened for three nights. He was very frightened. He kept his gun ready.

There was a full moon the fourth night. He had gone to bed. He thought he heard a rapping on the window. He looked and was pretty sure he saw his wife's face. He tried to talk to her. He said, "Come in at the door; if you have anything to say to me, let us see each other face to face." But no one came in.

After a while he heard the rapping again. This time he shot, and he heard groans. He was afraid to go out until morning. When he went out the next morning, he found a dead owl lying by the window. The next day he told the story. He knew he wouldn't live long after that, and he didn't last long. He could have gone to an owl shaman, but he didn't care much about going on living after that.

It is evident that owl sickness is but one aspect of ghost sickness. But, though all owls are ghosts, the ghost need not take the form of an owl to frighten or harm the living. A whistling sound at night, when nothing at all is visible, is attributed to ghosts. This has given rise to a rule: "No whistling is permitted at night, for then the ghosts whistle back to you and scare you." There are ways of protecting one's self when the whistle of a ghost is heard:

When you get scared you get sick. If you go out on a dark night, you tie a small amount of ashes up and carry this. Put some ashes on your face too. When you hear a whistle at night, take some ashes and throw them in the direction of the whistle, and then the ghost gets frightened and doesn't scare you or bother you any more. Put ashes under your pillow too.

The shade may call attention to its proximity by other audible means:

A young man was walking up a canyon with a girl in the moonlight. He heard a horse coming, trotting along. He thought it was somebody from the camps, and, because it was late and he didn't want to hurt the girl's reputation, he didn't want to be seen with her. So they went up on the side of a hill. He heard someone laughing and talking on the other side. He told the girl to stay where she was and went to the edge and looked down. Nothing was there. It was impossible to block a clear view on this road. No one could go back or forth without being seen. He didn't tell the girl about it, for he didn't want to scare her.

I know this man well, and he is pretty reliable. I said to him, "Maybe it was just a horse." He said, "No, I could have seen a horse from that mountain."

This boy married the girl he was with on this occasion. She died. She didn't live long after that—only four years. It's funny! Ghosts come around the Chiricahua all the time. That's why we believe in ghosts.

Occasionally, the ghost is neither seen nor heard but makes itself known in some other way:

Sometimes a ghost throws a stone at a person and makes fun of him. My cousin, my wife, and her sister were going up a canyon to a ranch. It was toward evening. They were being drawn by a pretty lively pair of mules. My cousin sat in front and my wife in the back of the wagon. As they were going around a cliff, they saw a stone come through the air. It was thrown under the mules. The way it came proved that it could not have rolled. Three neighbor boys lived around there, but they were away that day. The mules were frightened and nearly tipped the wagon over. It must have been a ghost that threw the stone. No one else could have done it.

There are times when the ghost is discernible as an amorphous black or white object:

One day, after I was married, I was riding my mule back from Whitetail. My young brother-in-law was with me, and we got lost in the woods and could not get out before dark. We got into a canyon neither of us knew. And up among the trees I saw something white. I didn't think anything of it, but in a few minutes I saw it again. Still I thought it was a wild white horse or a bare patch of earth. Right then my mule began to balk and rear. I couldn't do anything with her. I got off and called to my brother-in-law, but it was a long time before I could lead that mule out of the canyon. Finally, we got our directions and got home.

I rode up to the camp and called to my wife to take the mule. I was so weak I could hardly get off. I couldn't even tell her what was the matter. She had to help me in, and I was just ready to die. My mother-in-law knew a great deal, and she said, "He is sick from darkness." . . . . I said to my young brother-in-law, "Did you see anything white when my mule shied?" But he hadn't seen anything at all. So he didn't get sick.

A footprint may be the only tangible evidence that a ghost has paid its unwelcome visit:

This happened to S., and he was a good Christian then. He was asleep by a window. It was at the time of a big snow. That night someone knocked at the window. S. and his wife heard it. At first they paid no attention. Finally S. called and asked who was there. He received no answer. They went to sleep. In the morning they went to the window and saw a track there. S. started to follow it. The trail led to the mountain. He followed it for a while, but he got tired and came back. Tracks like that usually lead to graves.

The greatest misfortune of all is to see the ghost in human-like form and to recognize the actual features:

I have heard stories of persons who have seen the dead. Those who see things like that die within a year. A certain man's wife died. At that time he was well. After her death he saw his wife; she came back and talked to him. She said, "It is a better world where I am. Come on." This man took sick and died a short time afterward. There is no way to protect yourself or prevent your death when a thing like this happens.

Most often it is in dreams that the dead are distinctly seen:

Ghosts appear also in dreams, in sleep. That is the worst form, I guess. You really see them in a dream. I get like that. The door opens and they get closer and closer. I want to get up and fight, but I can't move. I can just say, "Ah!" The Chiricahua say this is ghost sickness. It can make a person very ill. It's a sign of trouble with evil ghosts if you do that too much, and you have to go to a shaman about it.

Sometimes at midnight or toward morning while you are asleep, you dream that a person is choking you. It might be a dead person, a relative gone a year or two ago. If it happens for another night or two, you must go to a ghost shaman. If you see a dead person in your sleep, you are not going to last long, they say.

A dream in which his recently deceased friend appeared before him was described by a much-shaken informant:

This morning about four o'clock I dreamed of Old P. standing at the door. I woke up frightened and grabbed my wife. Maybe he came back because I sang his ceremonial song. The very night that P. died I dreamed he came to me. I didn't tell my wife because she would have been frightened. But they don't bother me much. I have my cross,[12] and they stay away. P. claimed that he knew nothing but Yusn and Child of the Water.[13]

[12] The cross of the Silas John cult, a modern religious movement which draws in part from aboriginal religious ideas, in part from Christianity. The cross, made of algerita wood, is worn to ward off evil and witchcraft.

[13] The informant here is trying to reassure himself. Since Yusn and Child of the Water are beneficent supernaturals, he is proving to himself that his departed friend can be up to no mischief.

Ghosts are often outspoken concerning their intentions and their death wishes. "I dreamed last night of C. who is dead. C. said to me, 'Why don't you hurry up and die?' I replied, 'I don't die because I don't know any false ceremony.'"

Dreams of dead blood relatives and affinities are not infrequent. "I dreamed of one of my relatives by marriage who is dead. I dreamed that she came back and held my grandchildren in her arms. . . . . If anyone dreamed about his dead relative nearly every night, he would cry every day. It makes his heart feel very bad."

The most terrifying dream of all is that in which one accepts food from a deceased relative, for such acceptance, as has already been noted, is a sign of immanent death.

Frequently a person recovering from a serious illness, during which he has lapsed into unconsciousness, tells those about him that he has been to the underworld. In one such case, an old woman is said to have visited the camps of her dead kin. Two young relatives met her and warned her not to accept food at her father's home if she wished to get back to the earth. Though she was urged to partake of the food, she refused and was able to reach the upper world and return to her body once more. The same theme is encountered in another of these tales:

Once a man who was very sick and out of his head went to sleep. He visited the other world and saw his friends and relatives through a kind of partition. He was offered food that was all laid out and marked with pollen as it is on the fifth morning of the girl's puberty rite. His guide, though his relative and friends urged him to eat, told him not to take the food, as he could not return to this world again if he ate it.

The symptoms of darkness sickness usually present a picture of extreme terror:

If you feel numb around the heart and in the chest, if, when you go to bed, as soon as you close your eyes, something scares you and you get a bad headache and vomit, that is ghost sickness.

Ghost sickness is one of the easiest illnesses to tell. . . . . It affects the person from the heart to the head and is considered very bad. The one affected has a breakdown. He is afraid to go out in the dark. He is nervous and afraid of the dark. When it gets dark he vomits. Even little children get it.

Sudden loss of consciousness is almost always attributed to the evil influence of a ghost:

A person with ghost sickness loses strength and consciousness. A boy got a ghost spell in the afternoon. Before he reached the house he fell to the ground. He got stiff as a board. They ran over to see what was the matter. They rolled him over on his back. His mouth was twisted. His eyes went up. They picked him up and took him home. They poured cold water on him. After that he came to his senses and got up. He was still weak. He got another spell. His mother went out to see a man and brought him over to the house. This man went to work. When he got through the boy was all right. Since then he has been happy.

The disposal of a corpse has its dangers, for "ghosts don't go right down to the underworld; they stay around the place where they died for a while."

That is why the Chiricahua doesn't want to live in the place where a person has died, or to handle clothes or bedding that were used by the dead person. If you have an experience with a ghost near a place where a certain person died, you know it is that person who is bothering you.

According to one informant, at least, even the ghost which has made its way to the underworld "has the power to come up and go to the place where it died." Yet "you have to go if a close relative in your own family or your wife's family dies. The group you are in comes to help—to help around camp, to help bury the dead, to help burn up things."

Strangers to the deceased may be exposed to comparable jeopardy accidentally. A man may unwittingly camp for the night at a spot which he later discovers to be the deserted scene of a death. If his sleep is troubled by a terrifying apparition, he will suspect that he has stayed too near a burial place.

The inclination of the ghost to linger around its corpse or its grave and to revisit the site of its demise explains the insistence upon hasty burial, the avoidance of graves, and the departure of the bereaved from their former home. It also accounts for the destruction of the personal possessions of the deceased which are thus freed for use in the hereafter. If this rule is violated, the ghost may come back to claim what is his and to punish those who have withheld his property. Moreover, ghosts may be encouraged to appear if the affectional threads that bind them to the living are not severed. Therefore, it is dangerous to keep the dead in mind through excessive grief. "Calling the name of a dead person any time is dangerous, but it is especially so after dark." It is an insult to speak the name of the deceased before his kin.

It is obvious that relatives and close friends of the deceased, particularly the former, are most likely to suffer from ghost experiences: "If one is a friend or relative of a dead person or in any way associated with him, there is a fear of his ghost."

Precautions during and after the death rites will not totally eliminate ghost sickness. We remember the man who thought that he was being persecuted for singing a deceased tribesman's ceremonial song and the man who, in a dream, defied the ghost which sought his death, telling it that he would not die because he knew no false ceremony. It takes no great insight to infer that these two men had clashed over the validity of each other's claims of supernatural power. In other words, the fear of the return of the ghost is not unrelated to rivalries of everyday life. The more free from friction relations have been with an individual, the less likely is dread of his ghost to materialize.[14] This was definitely in the mind of the informant who said: "I don't think my father's ghost would come back to bother me. No, my father was a sensible man. He wouldn't do a thing like that. Only those who were trouble-makers in life would bother you that way."

The ghosts of enemy peoples, particularly Americans and Mexicans, can cause an illness much like that produced by Chiricahua ghosts but differing from it in some particulars.

When you just go out of your head and want to bite your tongue, and you get scared and numb all over the back and chest, that's sickness from the white man's ghost.

. . . . A white man's [American's] ghost can make you sick. You can always see the ghost that makes you sick [in white man's ghost sickness]. To see an In-

[14] For a socio-psychological interpretation of these fears of the ghosts of relatives and also of the power of living kin see Opler, "An Interpretation of Ambivalence of Two American Indian Tribes," *Journal of Social Pscyhology*, Vol. VII (1936), and "Further Comparative Anthropological Data Bearing on the Solution of a Psychological Problem," *ibid.*, Vol. IX (1938).

dian ghost is fatal, but to see a white man's ghost makes you very sick, and you see white men all the time. . . . . Before the Americans came, we had Mexican ghost sickness a lot, especially when we took guns from them.

Unlike the Chiricahua ghost, the white man's ghost does not utilize the body of the owl to further its designs.

Bat, gopher, turtle.—The danger from the bat derives from its bite:

If a bat bites you, you had better never ride a horse any more. All the Chiricahua say that. If you do ride a horse after being bitten, you are just as good as dead.

B. never rode, because if a bat bites you, you shouldn't ride a horse. He never got into a buggy or an auto either. He would walk for miles.

To touch the gopher or to be bitten by it can cause illness. "In 1886 I shot a gopher. I thought it was dead, but it wasn't and it bit me. My arm swelled up, and it looked like gopher holes were in it. The Chiricahua say the gopher is bad. You can get sick from it."

An indication that the ordinary man hesitates to touch the turtle was obtained: "My people were afraid of the turtle and wouldn't touch it. Only a man who got power from it would handle it."

Red ant, vinegarroon, black water beetle, centipede.—A number of insects are considered dangerous, and among these are the red ants:

They say you can get sick from ants in the same way you can from the coyote [i.e., as a result of its inherent evil influence]. On some people, when the ants sting the hands, they swell up. Mine don't. They bite me, and it hurts a little but never swells up. There are songs and a regular ceremony for ants. . . . . All Chiricahua children are taught not to urinate into an anthill.

One of the most feared insects is the vinegarroon:

K. is suffering from a peculiar Indian disease. It comes from an insect bite, from the bite of the vinegarroon. The disease is marked by a circle of red dots around the body from the point where the person is bitten. In K.'s case he has such a row of dots running around his chest. If these dots meet and form a complete circle around the body, the person dies. K. has been having several people sing for him.

Later the stricken man died, and another informant observed:

> If the vinegarroon gets in your clothes or urinates on you, red marks come out on your body, and if they go around and meet, it kills you. K. was affected by it. He claimed it got in his clothes. It usually breaks out on your shoulder.

A small black water beetle is held accountable for a well-nigh fatal sickness which results when it is swallowed accidentally. Great care is taken, therefore, to see that the drinking water contains none of these insects. Even horses are not exempt from this illness: "If you swallow one, it will kill you. I have seen horses swallow it and die. I don't know any cure for it except to ask some shaman to sing for you."

To be bitten by a centipede causes alarm, for "after it stings you, you'll live one day for each leg it has. I've never heard of a cure for this."

Crow, eagle, buzzard, parrot.—A number of birds besides the owl are considered possible sources of peril, and prominent among these is the crow. One man warned against carrying crow feathers and added, "They say it makes you sick to touch its droppings or anything from it." The opinion is supported by other testimony:

> The Chiricahua doesn't use crow feathers for arrows. Crow is one of the worst of all. The sickness you get from Crow is worse than sickness from any other bird its size. In the old days the Chiricahua wouldn't kill a crow. They didn't like the crow to fly around. They were afraid to imitate it just as they were afraid to imitate the call of the owl. The crow is not connected with dead people like the owl, but when the crow comes around they say it means that someone is going to die; they think it is a bad sign.

A certain ambivalence in attitude toward the eagle exists. Eagle feathers are prized for use in ceremonial contexts. But, because eagles "catch lizards and snakes," the people "can't eat the kill of the eagle" (this taboo extends to the kill of hawks as well) and "are afraid of them, wouldn't touch them." It is primarily contact with the talons or bill of the eagle that is feared.

The negative reaction has left its impress on a story of a boy who climbs a cliff, finds an eagle's nest, and brings down an eaglet. He rears the bird and teaches it to hunt for him; but when he first reaches home with it, the people say to him,

"Throw it away! It will make you sick!" A similar attitude is reflected in this statement:

When you are sick the shaman may tell you that you have slept on an eagle feather or something like that which has made you ill. You could get sick from the eagle. And there were people [shamans] who knew about that.

Lots of people even felt that it was a bad sign to have an eagle fly around the camps in the old days. When birds are supposed to be wild and to live out in the mountains, they shouldn't come around where people live. It looked to the Chiricahua as if they were being sent when they did come, as if they were a bad sign.

But there are also those who express no fear of the eagle. "Eagle feathers are thought to give a person strength. The eagle is not regarded like a coyote [i.e., inherently evil]." Moreover, eagles are trapped and killed for their feathers, and eaglets are occasionally reared in cages until they can be plucked.

In general an unfavorable overtone and some fear mark comments about the buzzard:

Some are afraid of the buzzard. I remember that, when I'd go to pick up a buzzard feather, my father would call out, "Drop that feather!" Most Chiricahua do not think much about buzzards until they have a ceremony performed over them and a shaman gives them some directions about it, such as not to let the shadow of a buzzard fall upon them, or something like that. But these restrictions are not true for every Chiricahua; they are not general.

Another bird that is viewed with circumspection is the parrot:

The Chiricahua were not very familiar with parrots. Once in a while they saw them in Mexico. Only a few people have seen the parrot. They know it mocks you, and they don't like to be around it. They are afraid of it. They say, "Why is it that a bird imitates people? There must be something to it." I have heard people say, "If a bird talks, there must be a witch in him."

Horse, mule, spider, Thunder People, Mountain People.—There are a few creatures and supernaturals which are to be feared only if they are somehow offended. The horse and the mule, the spider, the Thunder People, and the Mountain People comprise this list. Of the first two, it is said:

If you mistreat a horse, if you hit it on the head repeatedly, it may take revenge on you. It will cause you to get sick. Then you must go to a shaman who specializes in the ceremony of the horse. The mule is bad if you mistreat it; it will cause you to be sick too. The man who knows the horse cures both kinds of sickness.

The "sickness" brought by the horse is the injury suffered in an accident for which a horse is held responsible.

If the spider or its web is not molested, there is no need to worry about this insect. But, as an informant explained, "We are all taught not to kill spiders. The spider has power and can do harm if angered."

The Chiricahua will not walk into a spider web. They call the strands of the web sunbeams and say that, if you damage these, Sun will make a web inside you and kill you. The spider web is connected with the sun because it looks just like a sun as it hangs there.

If you kill a spider, the same thing will happen. If you do kill a spider, there is a rule to follow. If I should kill one, I'd say what I have heard many older people say, "The president killed you." Or they name a white man or someone they don't like—anyone as long as it is not themselves. It's a lie but they do it. They put it off on someone else. This is done, too, when you kill any dangerous insect, like a beetle or a centipede. The danger in killing or injuring a spider is that the next spider will miss the one you killed or hurt and come and harm or bite you.

The most obvious evidence that the Thunder People are displeased with an individual occurs when he is actually struck by lightning. However, fright is again a powerful sickening agent: "The scare harms you." Lightning is said to be accompanied by an odor which comes from the powder or smoke that arises where it strikes. This powder, if it is inhaled, manifests itself in the ailment recognized as "lightning sickness."

The smoke or dust causes harm as well as the fright. This settles in the body. Lightning sickness affects you inside the body; it affects the stomach. When a person has lightning sickness, he vomits and has a little fever. His feet and hands are cold. He feels sickly and is in poor health generally. Then he should go to a shaman and have a lightning ceremony performed; the sooner the better for him.

A young man described his illness after lightning had struck close to him:

It was so close that I had breathed in all the lightning powder. About two weeks after that I began to be sick. I couldn't eat, and they took me to the hospital. I was sick to my stomach all the time. . . . . I didn't get any better before I went home. My mother-in-law said right away to my wife, "He has the lightning sickness. That powder he breathed in from the lightning has settled in his stomach and turned to frog spittle [i.e., the green growth on stagnant water]."

Since it is so dangerous when lightning strikes near by, everything is avoided that might "draw" it:

When I was little I was told not to have anything red around when it was raining. Even in camps we used to stick red things under something so they wouldn't show. We consider it dangerous to have red things out during a storm. It is because they draw lightning. Red is connected with lightning. And today the Chiricahua do not like anything red to be around when it rains, like a red blanket. It is covered up or taken off the bed.

During a thunderstorm the Chiricahua refrain from eating, even though the food is prepared and waiting. Eating during a storm causes much lightning, it is thought. Even if nothing else happens, a person who eats during lightning will lose his teeth.

A paint [pied or spotted] horse is dangerous during a thunderstorm. If you are riding one at such a time, you get off.

It is dangerous to have a little fawn around in the rainy season. If they find one, they get scared and let it go, for lightning is likely to strike you if you keep it.

The Mountain People are ordinarily pitted against disease, but they may themselves cause sickness if their rules are ignored. "The Mountain Spirits may cause you to become disfigured. That is why the masked dancers do not touch each other. Many are afraid of this sickness." Insanity may be regarded as punishment for omission of necessary ritual gestures during the masked-dancer preparation: "If the masked-dancer headdress is put on without ceremony, it makes you crazy; you see the Mountain Spirits all the time."

Menstrual blood.—Menstrual blood is dangerous for males, and girls are taught to dispose carefully of pads worn during the flow. The illness suffered by a man or a boy as a result of contact with menstrual blood is always described as rheumatism or malformation of the joints. The most serious form of the malady is contracted from union with a menstruating woman. "The Chiricahua are afraid to have intercourse with a woman during her period. It makes them misshapen and deformed. They become unable to straighten their arms or legs. I heard of one man who did this. This man was pointed out to me. He was deformed in this way."

SORCERY AND INCEST

The duality of power.—If an illness is long continued, the explanation that it has been caused by a certain animal or force may not satisfy the patient, his relatives, or the shaman. The symptoms, for instance, may point to bear sickness, but then the question will arise: Why did the encounter with the bear occur? Time after time the answer is sought in the machinations of a malevolent human agent. "A witch may cause it. A witch may cause any animal to attack you or make you sick." Whatever befalls a person, and even what he is forced to do, may be interpreted as the work of witches. One commentator defined sorcery as "making an individual do something evil by the power of some animal or spirit." There is little sickness which cannot be attributed ultimately to sorcery.

A witch can cause evil influence through the bear, the snake, or through almost anything.

The way they tell it, some know Sun. One who does might sing and say, "Sun, get that man sick," and it obeys him. He is a witch. Then someone else with stronger power and good power sees it and tells you that someone got you sick from Sun.

From such statements we infer that a good many individuals are suspected of using for evil those same sources of supernatural power and the same intimate relations with their monitors that others manipulate for legitimate purposes. "All disease can be caused by the supernatural power of witches. Both men and women are witches. Witches get power in the same way as shamans. They are people who have power which can be used for good or evil but is used for evil."

The dual nature of supernatural power leads to a widespread suspicion of religious practitioners: "There are lots of ways to know a witch from a shaman, though most people who have much power will have both kinds." Often there is great indecision in the public mind over the place of a given shaman in relation to these polarities:

The truth is that a person is a shaman if he uses his power for good, and a witch if he uses it for evil. A person will never admit using it for evil. You have to guess by what happens; you have to use your own judgment. Therefore, there are a good many people who look at the same person differently. Some people have told me that S. is a witch. Others think he is all right. Some tell me that B. is a witch, in fact, quite a few think so. Others consider him a shaman. On the other hand, J. and R. have power, yet I have never heard of anyone suspecting them of being witches.

Since a person can use power for good and evil and it depends on the individual, a man could be a shaman at one time and a witch at another. Sorcery is power used for evil; benevolent power is used for good. It may be the same kind of power. A witch can use pollen and do the same things that the shaman does. He does not have to arouse suspicion. There are many ways of working sorcery.

Yet there are often signs of witchcraft, things that would not be used by a shaman, such as . . . . hair or a piece of a man's clothing. If I saw these, I would know right away that it was witchcraft. Witches usually have bones of animals or something like that with which to work.

Great secrecy surrounds the use of ceremonies for evil ends, but a shaman whose power is beneficent may be able to detect witchcraft:

That witch business is always carried on in secret. It's such a thing that a person doesn't come out and tell about it. He wants to carry on his ceremonies in such a way that no one will catch on to it. It's usually found out when a shaman sings and performs a ceremony over one who is sick. He tells you then that such and such a person is performing a ceremony that makes you sick.

So firmly fixed is this idea of the duality of power that sorcery is described as being obtained and perpetuated by the same procedures as have been noted for beneficial power:

A witch learns his work in just the same ways a shaman does; he may learn it from a man who had it, or he may be told how by his power.

Witchcraft is often handed down to close relatives whose nature is that way. Whole families are sometimes suspected of witchcraft. The witch's secrets may be handed down, like the shaman's.

Of a man who claimed to have refused an offer of evil power, it was said, "That's what he told me, but I doubt that he refused it. Some say that he is a witch. Everybody knows his father was a witch."

The motives, scope of activity, and methods of the sorcerer.—In some cases it is not considered necessary to seek for causes of sorcery beyond the basic misanthropic nature of the witch. "These people don't want to see anyone happy; they don't want to see people laugh; they like it when there are many deaths."

"These people hate their own children; they hate their close relatives."

But in most instances of alleged sorcery, the motive of the witch is narrowed down to some quarrel or thwarted design:

One man suspects M. of being a witch. His wife used to be good friends with her. She used to be over at M.'s all the time. Then she died, just after those two women had a falling-out of some sort. That's the way they work. You have hot words with a person. Then you die from some little accident. The person is under suspicion after that.

The greed of the sorcerer and the danger of denying him his desires is a recurring theme:

If you suspect you are witched, you must think over everybody that you have refused anything to or to whom you have not freely given something he admired. Perhaps someone said to you, "What a nice Navaho rug!" But you didn't give it to him. He witched you. That's why Indians don't plan to live nicely and have good things around. They'd only be running into danger from witches.

Rejected marriage suits may stir the malice of witches. "A young woman might die. They would say that a man who had been refused by her before her marriage had done this to her because he couldn't have her himself."

There is no personal misfortune, no public disaster, that may not ultimately be construed as the work of a witch. Impotence is sometimes attributed to sorcery, and witches are accused of interfering with domestic tranquillity:

When I married, I lived near my wife's parents. A year later my wife had a baby and it died. About two months later she began to act as if she wasn't the same person at all. She was mean, and there was trouble all the time. I came away and lived down here, but my mother-in-law liked me and knew that I was trying to do the right thing. My wife had been witched. They took her to a shaman, and he saw what the matter was and cured her. About a month after she was cured I went back to her. She was just like her old self again.

Of difficult childbirth, it was said: "When a woman is having a hard time in labor, if her husband finds out for sure that a witch is responsible, he will go out and kill him."

At the other end of the scale is widespread sickness:

There has been much sickness around here, a lot of pneumonia. So last week my father painted masked dancers to find out what it was from and how it was going to end. He had the masked dancers perform right up there by his camp in the afternoon. They had a big fire going in the middle of an open space. While my father was singing and the masked dancers were working, their leader got a message. He found out that it is something that has settled here. He found out it is because the people don't get together, because they talk and work against one another [witchcraft] that the disease has settled among us. My father told the people that, when they act right toward one another and are no longer like this, the disease will all go away.

Many techniques, some of them subtle and surreptitious, are known to the sorcerer:

The way a witch influences you may start with little things. He may merely cause you to prick your finger, and all your trouble starts from that, or he may give you a stomach ache which continually grows worse. A witch has the power of evil influence with all his body parts, even with his sexual organ or his anal flatulence. He uses these as "arrows" to shoot the one he is getting sick. The women who are witching you with venereal disease, if they see you from a distance, open their vaginas toward you and go clockwise in a circle saying what should happen to you.

Sometimes witching is done with hair or with a rib and hair done up in buckskin. That is their arrow. It is a human rib and human hair that they use. They shoot these objects into the body of the one they are making sick. They usually have four such objects. A witch often works with the remains of dead people. One falls under suspicion of being a witch if he hangs around a grave. Few shamans try to take objects out of a sick person's body which have been placed there through evil influence. It is dangerous and most shamans are afraid.

Sometimes the glance, the thought, or the speech of a witch will cause evil influence. And a witch can often work through having some body part of the man whom he wants to harm, such as hair or nail parings.

A witch may have made his ceremony and said his words beforehand. Then he comes over to you and brushes against you, pushes you, plays with you, or steps on you—making believe all the while it is an accident or in fun. Thus he uses evil influence on you. A witch may even make marks on the ground and work with them.

An object of witchcraft is described in a tale of a witch brought to bay:

At Fort Sill a person once came out of his house and lost his purse. Somebody found it, and inside was his object of witchcraft. The name of the loser was D., and the finder was K., both well-known people. K. thought he had found money and opened the purse. To his surpise he found this object. It was a bone, two inches long, scraped fine, pointed on one end, and with a notch at the other, like an arrow. At the notch there was green coloring. On the side was a peculiar design.

K. did not give back the bone. D. looked for it in vain and soon he was unable to talk. He became very sick, was in awful condition, and died in a few days. Before he died, his wife had got sick and died. Before she died, something told her that her husband had witched her but that he would pay for it soon with his own life. The source that had given D. his power punished him. Maybe it didn't want him any more. A man always dies when he loses his objects of witchcraft.

The belief that a witch can accomplish his evil intentions by the power of the spoken word makes it very difficult for an accused person to defend himself adequately. One night while a man was sleeping there appeared before him first an old woman and an old man, both naked, then a young girl and a boy, also unclothed. They ordered him to put out his tongue, which they proposed to cross with pollen, and told him that thereafter anything he said should befall a person, "like wanting him to be killed, would happen that way." This man drove off his tempters, exclaiming, "Go away! Leave me alone! I'm a poor man. If it doesn't do good for my people, I don't want it." Concerning the lesson of this visitation, he added, "That's why a witch will say, 'All right, if I'm a witch, find it; take it out and I'll admit it.' You'd have to take his tongue out. You can't find it on him, but it's there."

A witch may take advantage of any situation to carry out his purposes. "It causes confusion in the tribe, that witch business. If they were out in the wilds and cowboys or Mexicans killed some of their best men, someone might hold a ceremony and say a witch did it. Many times when a person got sick or died, someone was blamed."

So resourceful are witches that a constant guard against the unexpected must be maintained:

One time C. and I were going along the trail to church. A small bow and arrow were lying there right in the path. C. said, "Someone is witching the trail because we always go through here. If we step on this, something is going to happen to us." He got sticks and carefully carried those things away. Then we went on.

Detection of witches; witchcraft and incest.—Not infrequently a witch betrays himself by his virulent or aberrant behavior:

A witch can be told by his language. If he makes a threat against another and it comes true, he may be suspected of being a witch. People who steal or habitually do mean things are witches.

Or his habits may be strange and may put him under suspicion. If you see a man on a high hill going through a strange ceremony, you can be sure he is a witch. A shaman would not go way out in the mountains and dance naked, as I have heard has been done. A shaman would perform his ceremony in the open and at home. Witches always go far out and do strange things.

There are people who are queer. They are seen doing things that are not right in this life, as if I should get out here and pray to the sun when I shouldn't. It would look bad. Or if a man is seen carrying bones of animals and trying to hide them; it is things like that which cause a person to be suspected of being a witch.

Not long ago my wife got up very early to make a fire. It was before anyone else was up. There, by the little road which runs past our camp, she saw a man waving a handkerchief to the four directions. This was after this man's wife died. My wife asked me what I thought of this. I said I thought it was sorcery. It was a queer thing for a man to do.

Even if you are not a witch but do something peculiar, you will fall under suspicion. For instance, one day I was whistling and doing some steps of the masked dancer just for the amusement of my wife and child. My wife said, "You had better stop. Someone may see you and think you are a witch." I was not dressed properly for the dance, and there was no music. It would have looked bad if someone had seen me. The Chiricahua has to be very careful. When a person is accused of being a witch, there is always some reason for it in his actions.

. . . . In one case I heard of, a woman who took all her clothes off somewhere around here and ran up a hill with her buttocks toward the camps was known as a witch. Once a man was seen entirely naked handling his sexual organ and saying some prayer. This is peculiar, and the man fell under suspicion. He was suspected of going through a ceremony to give someone venereal disease.

The possession of unusual amulets may also give rise to gossip:

They may have some beads or an arrowhead or something hidden under their clothes. Sometimes someone sees this. Then people are suspicious. Some may wear a little buckskin around the wrist or perhaps some little bones, or something like that, or maybe they have some hair. Some wear what they use openly and don't care if they are called witches.

The manner of dress may reveal the witch. "We were warned when I was a boy that witches never wear good clothes. That's

one way of finding them out. . . . . They say that a man is surely a witch if he is rich and yet doesn't wear clean clothes."

Though one informant asserted that "witches have a peculiar
odor, something like the odor of spoiled meat; if you smell it, it
may have a bad influence on you," others rejected this idea.
Sensitivity to elk meat provides a test: "If you are a witch and
eat elk, you throw up. Elk meat stays down in a good man."

It is not unusual for a trap to be laid for the sorcerer:

There was a fellow who was considered a witch. You know that tiswin or beer
that the Indians make out of corn. One shaman had a root which, if given to a
witch in this tiswin or in coffee, would kill him. It wouldn't do harm to any other
person. A man told me about this incident who was present when it happened.
It was thought that the man to whom this was done was a witch, because shamans had often pointed to him as the man who caused sickness. So this shaman
told several people privately that he was going to give the root to the witch in
tiswin this time. He told the other people to go ahead and drink the tiswin, for it
wouldn't harm them. When the witch came over, some of this root was put in
his tiswin. The witch went home and soon had stomach trouble. He died in a
few days. Other people drank the same tiswin and were all right.

The victim's guardian spirit may furnish information about
the attacks of the witch:

My children and my wife all died over at the hospital. They died because the
doctor can't help them in matters of witchcraft. I could tell by my dream that
my wife was witched. In my dream I heard a voice that told me. Sometimes the
witch appeared to me in my dream. But I could not stop it. I know who the
witches who killed my wife and children were. They are dead now. In my dream
I saw that some witches just talk, just go through a ceremony of words, and influence the people that way. Since that time I have not cared much about
dreams; I did not care to be notified any more.

Very often none of the devices enumerated serves to ferret out
the evildoer. "A man might be living with a witch and not know
it; it might be his wife." The witch who so skilfully masks his
identity is exposed only when a ceremony over a sick person is
held by a shaman powerful enough to learn the true cause. Accordingly, the most spectacular curing rites are those which constitute a battle, not against natural indispositions nor yet against
the evil influence of dangerous animals and forces, but against
the sorcerer.

The word "battle" is chosen advisedly. The entire contest between the shaman and the witch is phrased in terms of warfare. The sorcerer is said to "shoot" his victim with "arrows" (the witchcraft objects). Consequently, to intercept these arrows is literally to disarm the witch, and this is what the shaman tries to do. Then, with his good power, he attempts to shoot the arrows back into the witch. But if the shaman is not "strong" enough to accomplish this, he himself may fall ill, because the very witchcraft objects which he has extracted from his patient are now "sticking in him." Thus, the machinery of witchcraft, once put into motion, does not halt until some victim has been claimed—the object of the witch's ire, the witch, or the shaman. "The witch can take off the witching he has put on you, but he has 'given' your life when he put on the witching, and to take it off he must offer some other life in its place."

Only a self-confident ceremonialist will press a cure when he has ascertained that the primary cause is witchcraft:

A shaman has a good power and can make a sick person well, but if the person for whom he is singing is very sick and the sickness is caused by a witch, the shaman is very much afraid of that witch. Sometimes he can't get the sick person well, because the witch might be more powerful than he is. Or he might cure the sick person and then, if the sick person was witched, the shaman might die instead.

Nearly everyone is alarmed lest such evil influence sometime be directed against him. But no member of the tribe acknowledges mastery of sorcery or will say that he has ever employed a sorcerer. If rites purposely conducted to gain evil ends exist, they are conducted in secret. Some confessions from witches have been obtained, according to informants, but always as a result of duress and torture. Boasts of witchcraft accomplished and open threats occasionally occur, but without exception under the influence of drink. Of one man it was said, "Every time he got drunk he would tell someone, 'I'm a witch and I'm going to kill you.' So one time they killed him." These drunken threats do raise the possibility that there are individuals who believe that their imprecations actually harm those against whom they bear ill will.

One characteristic often attributed to the sorcerer is sexual aberrance. The stories of naked individuals displaying themselves come to mind in this connection. In the mythology, when Coyote is accused rightfully of having had intercourse with his mother-in-law, his rejoinder is, "That's witch talk." It will be remembered that one who neglects to hide from his avoidance relatives, or who is too familiar with the mate of a sibling or a cousin, runs the risk of being named a witch. Nor was it an accident that the tempters who offered a sorcerer's tongue were unclothed.

Incest is promptly equated with witchcraft. Of a person accused of marrying a close relative, an informant said, "In my opinion he must be a witch, and the tribe accuses him of that because he married a close relative. People are afraid of him." Another commentator declared: "In cases of incest, people say, 'They must be witches to do a thing like that.' I have heard several people who are accused of incest referred to as witches. They say, 'Even some witches wouldn't do that.'"

Public exposure and beatings are the mildest punishments meted out to those discovered in incest. Just as often the extreme penalty is demanded.

If two persons committed incest and were found out, a crowd would gather, and any headman would say, "I know those two had intercourse together; get them!" Everyone considered them witches, and they were burned. Incest sometimes goes before a council of people and sometimes the parents kill them outright. Usually the parents handle them.

If they are distant relatives and did not know they were related and find it out after they marry, they go apart. That has happened often, I have heard. But if they know it and everybody knows they are relatives and they marry anyway, in the old days they would kill both of them as witches. That's what N. used to tell us happened before there were white men and law.

A "love-death" story is told of a man who could not face the wrath of his relatives after misconduct with his sister:

In the old days there were a brother and sister, children of the same parents, who had been lying together. The people were suspicious of them for a long time. The young man thought that the old people knew about them, although they really did not. He knew that if they were caught, a terrible punishment would come, so he took this way out.

He cut a stick about nine inches long and began to whittle on it. He sharpened it at both ends. Suspecting that they were caught, the couple stole off and they lay together again, but the girl didn't see the stick that the boy had made. When they lay down, the boy put the stick at her belly, and when he pushed down, the stick went through her. Because it was sharpened at both ends, it went through him too, and they both died.

The people missed them, searched for them, and found them dead. In this case the parents were good and not witches, and that is why the boy killed his sister and himself.

In these days the charge of witchcraft is still made in cases of incest but not with as much effectiveness as formerly:

R. married C.'s daughter. C. and this boy's father were full brothers. C. didn't like it. He went to the boy. He told him, "Your father was my full brother. Why do you want to marry my daughter? People will call you a witch." He went to the agent about it, but he finally gave in. That's why there is so much trouble here now, they say. It's because things like this go on. The young people now are like dogs, like billy goats.

By the equation of incest with witchcraft, the gravest crime in the religious sphere and the most abhorrent act in the social realm have been combined. The charge of witchcraft acts as the dragnet which combs the society for the flagrant aberrant.[15]

Punishment of witches.—From the attitude toward those judged guilty of incest, the stern treatment of witches may be anticipated:

Sometimes personal revenge is taken on the witch. Every once in a while a witch is killed by the one he has been working against or by a dead man's relatives who find him out. Often they are shot. No one knows for sure who does it. . . . . The last case I know of happened twenty years ago. A man and his wife were shot as they came on horseback out of the canyon from the feast grounds where they had been working witchcraft.

[15] The data presented indicate the strong reactions of the majority of informants to incest and their equation of it with witchcraft. Some informants took a milder stand, however. Said one: "For incest between distant relatives, the punishment would not be so severe. A person might be whipped until he couldn't stand, but that's all. There is talk and disapproval, but after the pair are punished, the thing is forgiven and forgotten." Said another: "Not so much is thought about it if they are very distant relatives. They are whipped and insulted. This would not spoil their chance of marriage later on. A person who is pretty hard up is bound to get married sooner or later."

When the anger of the relatives is not immediately spent, or when the case involves many victims, a different course of action may be adopted:

In olden times when suspected persons came before the council because they were acting peculiarly, and extreme measures were taken, like hanging them up by the wrists and putting wood under as though to light it, they would sometimes admit that they were witches. This was often done. I have seen it. If a person confessed, they burned him alive. The witch has to own up and name the ones that he harmed. Even if he promises to remove the evil influence, he is burned. When they are burned they have no more evil influence. Sometimes they were shot though—any way to get rid of them.

As this indicates, the examination and punishment of the witch are frequently matters of public interest:

When something wrong which affects the whole group occurs, the leader calls in the people involved, or the important men, or even all the people. For witchcraft, a council of this sort would be held. The case would be presented, and the influential men would decide on the punishment. A man can't accuse another of witchcraft before the council unless he is absolutely sure of it.

Execution by fire is the accepted way to annihilate the sorcerer:

They find out from the shaman if a person is a witch. Then they force him to tell if he did it. His relatives have no comeback. They string the witch up by the wrists so his feet are off the ground. The witch has to tell whom he witched. The confession is good evidence. Sometimes he has to tell what he used in his witch ceremony, and it is taken away. I have heard people, when strung up to a tree by their hands, admit that they were witches. They never let them go if they prove it on them. Then a fire is built under the witch, and he is burned. Burning destroys a witch's power for future harm, but what he has already accomplished is not undone. Witches do not burn up quickly; they keep on living a long time.

Relatives are not likely to stand solidly with their kinsman when he faces a charge of sorcery. At other times a family can defend one of its members, for it will be pitted only against some other family group of comparable size. But since sorcery, unlike murder or theft, is a public offense, the witch's kin face an aroused neighborhood, and the odds are hopeless:

.... Even your own son will be punished the same way. The witch will insist on his side of the argument; his opponent may die within a short time. If your closest relative is a witch, he is grabbed by a crowd and burned. If the relatives object, they go right into the fire too.[16]

Fire and its derivative, ashes, are prophylactics against witches and ghosts. Objects of sorcery extracted from the body of the patient by the shaman are always consigned to the flames, where they explode noisily, giving assurance of the destruction of the witchcraft principle.[17] The same thing happens when the sorcerer's body is burned: "When he burns, there is a 'pop,' like a shot from a gun. It is the 'witchcraft' in him popping. At every burning I have seen there has been a 'pop.' "

That false charges of witchcraft can arise from motives of personal dislike is acknowledged. Sometimes those who doubt the validity of the accusation are silenced at the time, however, by the enormity of the imputations, the strident assurance and political influence of the inciters, and the prospect of defending an unpopular cause.

Some that they burned were witches, but it was not proved that they all were. H. was a war leader. He burned up several men and several women because he suspected they were witches. It's like this: Someone might come alone to him and say, "There's a man over there who is a witch." Just because one person had told him this, he would send men over there, take that man, bring some wood, and burn him alive. Often they tied witches to a branch of a tree by the wrists with the feet off the ground, swinging.

Punishment is in no way mitigated when the condemned witch happens to be a woman:

At a place in the Chiricahua Mountains, when I was a boy, I saw a witch woman burned. The people had gone to a shaman and had hired him to find out who was doing all the witching, for many deaths from witchcraft had occurred. The shaman had sung all night and had finally found out who the witches were. He told the people the witches were a certain husband and wife. He advised them to get rid of these two.

The couple had a young baby in the cradle at the time. While the shaman was

[16] Another reason why relatives shrink from aiding a witch will be developed later (see pp. 254–57).

[17] Only those things that are considered evil and dangerous are destroyed by fire. When I asked an informant his opinion of cremation, he said with feeling, "It would be sure to show hatred of a dead man. He is already dead. What's the use of burning him up?"

singing, the husband spied around to see what it was all about, and he heard that he and his wife were to be caught in the morning and punished. So he took his wife and baby and escaped over a mountain during the night.

The next morning the people went to the witches' camp, and they were gone. They began to trail them and they followed them up the mountain. They finally found the woman and baby in a cave, alone. The man had gone. They brought the woman and her baby back. Since the man had got away, they were satisfied to have the woman.

They questioned the woman and asked her to hand over her witchcraft [paraphernalia], thus giving her a chance. The woman said she was unable to do so; she admitted that she was a witch, but said that the power had split her tongue in the center and had put witchcraft there, so that whatever she mentioned happened. That was how she witched, she said; but, of course, she could give them nothing.

The people said, "Well, we've given you a chance. We would not have punished you if you had given us your witchcraft objects. But now we can't see a chance for you. You are in a bad way, and we have to punish you." Meanwhile they continued to question her. At the Chiricahua Mountains there had been a battle, and two good men had lost their lives. This should not have happened. Who was responsible for that? They asked her. She was scared and admitted that she was the one who had caused their deaths.

The people became angrier. They gathered wood and piled it under a tree. Then they hanged her on the tree by the hands so that just her feet touched the top of the woodpile. Then they set the wood afire. The fire flared up and burned the woman to death without her saying a word or crying.

While she was burning, they held her baby. The baby was very small, and nobody wanted to take it, and they didn't have milk for it. They thought it was better to kill it than have it suffer hardships when it grew up, so they threw it in the fire, although they hated to do it. The group felt good about having killed the woman, because a witch deserves punishment.

After this woman was burned, many people died anyway, because, as she burned, she may have been witching people. None of the leaders of that time or their relatives are living now, and it is odd. It must be due to witchcraft.

Sorcery, power, and kinship.—The evil pursuits of a witch are a constant threat to the lives of his relatives—an even greater menace to them, perhaps, than to outsiders:

A man may not be carrying out the rules of his power. The power says to him, "Now there, you stop that and do as I tell you." But if the man has a strong mind, he might say, "No, I'm going to keep on this way. If you don't like it, take your ceremony back." And if he continues to disobey, perhaps his close relatives are taken. But some keep on like this on purpose. They are witches and are willing to have their relatives die.

To this point the assumption has been that sickness is due to contact with something inherently injurious or to the plottings of the witch. But the last quotation suggests that power, too, may have demands of its own and is capable of vengeance. Power is not always a neutral, not always a force ready to act at the bidding of the shaman or the witch. It may aid the shaman, but only as long as it sees fit to do so, and at a price. It may sponsor the witch, but only to ruin him finally. The duality of power, then, must be read to mean not only that power can be used for good or for evil but that power itself may be good or evil.

Sometimes the evil intentions of power are discernible at first contact. "One can take or leave power. It is dangerous to take sometimes. Sometimes the ceremony that is offered requires some things that are not right. That is why some people refuse it." But power may even deceive the individual who aspires to enjoy its benefits. Many a practitioner has assumed that his power "is for good only" later to face a sad awakening.

He had some pretty songs! I sure liked them. But he told me over here one time, "Never sing them. They are witch songs, my friend. I never knew it for a long time, but I have found out since what they are." . . . . He doesn't sing them now. His power has run out.

Power which has seemed to be beneficent may finally demand that the shaman sacrifice a life to it.[18]

A shaman may succeed for eight or ten times, and then he has to pay for his success. The power, after working for him for a number of times calls on him for a sacrifice, saying, "I have let you work this ceremony so many times; now I want so many men." Then the shaman must pay with men. He is notified through a vision or dream. In the old days they sacrificed the best men in the tribe this way. They did it in battle. They sacrificed the ones in the front of the fight.

Sometimes a good man, when called on to do that, will say to his power, "You should have told me about this in the first place, and I wouldn't have taken the ceremony. This will make no better than a witch out of me. I refuse. You may do what you want." Often they lose their lives that way. Sometimes the power calls on them to sacrifice their own relatives, and they do. Sometimes they refuse. Many times relatives are afraid of a very successful shaman.

[18] In this connection the story of the shaman asked to sacrifice two warriors, introduced on p. 208 to illustrate a different point, will be recalled.

The last sentences are of particular importance, for they call attention once more to the special peril in which the relatives of a sorcerer are placed:

There is often a big penalty for being a very successful shaman. A shaman might do a lot of good, then the power demands that the life of a relative be sacrificed. If he does not agree, he pays with his own life; a trifling accident will cause his death. He allows the power to take his son, his daughter, his wife, or any other close relative. It causes them to get sick; it appears to be natural when they die. The power causes the sickness, and he permits it. The relatives of such shamans are afraid of them. The relative cannot defend himself. The matter is not made public. The shaman, when his time comes to die, can substitute a relative for himself. I have heard very often of shamans substituting a relative when their own time came to die.

I hear lots of talk about the fact that if a shaman has done a great deal of good, when the time comes for him to die, his power speaks and tells him to substitute a relative in his place. One old man told me that a relative approached him and wanted him to take a ceremony. He said to this relative, "Get out of here with your power! You will probably substitute me, and if you don't I don't want to have to substitute someone else." When you go to a man with much power and question him directly, however, he evades you. He says, "Well, if the power comes from some evil source, a person might do this." He never admits that he does it.

This fear of the power of a relative provides a source of wry humor:

I used to tease my uncle a lot. You know the Chiricahua think that, when a shaman's time has come to die, he pays out one of his relatives instead. He substitutes someone. It has to be a relative. I used to say to my uncle, "When your time comes, don't pick on me; let me die a natural death." That sounds very funny when you say it in our language. When I'd say this, he would just laugh.

But the subject is not always treated in such a genial manner. In the following instance traditional uneasiness is aggravated by a quarrel between father and son over the transfer of the older man's ceremony.

Close relatives of shamans become frightened sometimes because they are afraid the power may claim them. There is my father: I don't know what he knows. I'm afraid of him. He might witch me or harm me. The same with E.— I don't want to be around him. I don't want to be in sight of either of them. I don't want to be bothered.

Sometimes the man will let the power have its way. He will sacrifice one of his own relatives. Of course he's a witch then. After that he might mix bad and good. He might cure in a good way, but when the power demands a relative, he has to sacrifice one to protect himself.

You take my father: he must have had plenty of power in J.'s day. J. has told me how powerful he was with his ceremony. He was able to cure when he was younger. What he said always came true.

As a rule, after a while you can do bad things to your fellow-men among your own tribe more easily than you can do good things. I almost think it's easy for the old man to do those bad things, for they are easily done. In J.'s time the old man was doing good with his ceremony. But today he's a dangerous man to me. For the last several years I can't say he has done any good for anyone with his ceremony. Most of the people here call him and E. both witches today. E. has been standing by him because he is studying the old man's ceremony. Everybody knows it. The older people living here today say that, if you trace it down, there is no relationship whatever between the old man and E. But E. calls him brother. They have no proof that they are relatives.

THE GENERALIZED CURING RITE

Because of such factors as the diversity of the sources of power and the varying degrees of intimacy between the shaman and the supernatural force, no two ceremonies are exactly alike; yet all the rites conform to a general pattern.

Since many of the diseases are marked by well-defined symptoms, the sufferer is able to hazard a likely guess as to the cause of his illness and to seek a shaman equipped to cope with it:

A person makes his own choice. If he is pretty sure of what ails him, he takes his chance and goes to a shaman for a cure. A person has to use his own judgment. If he thinks it is a bear that made him sick, he goes to a shaman who knows power through the bear. The shaman will tell him whether this is the trouble or not soon enough.

Though there is a tendency to expect a rite from a particular source to cure sickness contracted through that same source, strong power usually can bring some relief to any malady. Therefore, the ailing person is as often concerned over the ability of the shaman as he is over the power source involved.

A sick man uses his judgment and goes to a shaman he thinks has most power. You can go to a shaman, and he can tell you beforehand if he can do you any good. Almost any good shaman can at least tell you what is causing the evil influence, though he might have to send you to someone who can help you.

The quest for a suitable shaman is sometimes a long one:

When you are sick, you tell the shaman what is the matter with you; you tell him your symptoms. If the shaman doesn't do you any good, you change to another. D. has been having a number of shamans sing for him.

The request for ceremonial aid is a delicate matter. Some shamans may be contacted for this purpose only during the daytime. If the sick person is able to do so, he is the one who visits the shaman; if not, a relative acts for him.

When C. came over he said, "Help me with whatever you know. I have tried others, but it seems as though I got no help out of it. Now I have come here to see you. I think there is hope, and today I want you to lift up my boy who is sick." . . . . C. called me brother. Just because C. was asking for help he called me brother.

Since the personal name is reserved for appeal and emergency, the need of the supplicant may be emphasized by its use:

If a person is very sick and is sent to a shaman, but is afraid the shaman will not take the case, he calls him by his name. I call this "to plead in the Chiricahua way." To do it you call the name of the person and then add, "I ask you to do this which I am to say." Then you tell what you want. This is a way of asking for help, particularly ceremonial help, but it is also used in cases of grave emergency or death too. It is always said with the name and shows that the person speaking relies on the person spoken to. It puts the person spoken to under an obligation. He can hardly refuse and not feel ashamed afterward.

The names of other members of the shaman's family may be mentioned also:

If a shaman is addressed by his name, he will be more likely to perform the needed ceremony. So that he can't refuse, you can say, "So-and-so, in the name of all your children, your wife, your whole family, I ask you to help me now." You can mention them by name. He can hardly refuse you after that.

Then, to show respect and faith, the supplicant "marks" the shaman "in the right way" with pollen. The usual manner is to trace a cross on the shaman's right foot, sprinkle pollen on other parts of his body, and finally draw a cross on his left foot. Often a ceremonial gift is placed on the shaman's foot at this time too, and the shaman picks it up to indicate that he will accept the case; or a cigarette may be placed on his foot, and he smokes it to express consent.

Before the ceremony can begin, and usually at the time of the request, ceremonial gifts are tendered the shaman. These are gifts to the power to assure its co-operation.

The shamans for different diseases get different presents first. Even today these can't be money. These are not given to the shaman. They are part of the ceremony. They must be given to complete the ceremony. For a ghost-sickness ceremony today one man wants a black-handled knife, a black silk handkerchief, a bag of smoking tobacco, and a wooden cross. After this and on top of this a further present might be given to the shaman, but these have to be given. . . . . His power always needs special things for a shaman to cure with, and you must have these ready.

These offerings are almost always four in number and are generally of such a nature that they can be directly employed at some stage in the rite. Among those which commonly appear are turquoise, abalone shell, eagle feathers, pollen, specular iron ore, unblemished buckskin, black flint blades, white shell, and obsidian. What is called for may vary according to the patient's sex. An unblemished deerskin, for instance, must come from a doe if the patient is a woman, from a buck if it is a man, and the head must be left attached with a piece of abalone or turquoise (again depending on the sex of the patient) tied between the ears. If possible, the gifts are logically associated with the kind of ceremony which the shaman controls.

I had a man who specializes on mules and horses castrate my mules. The old man made a ceremony of it. . . . . He said, "Give me a saddle blanket, a bridle, a little rope, and something else that is used for a horse. It doesn't have to be new. Give me something you don't want. I don't care how much it has been used. Just give me these to carry out the ceremony. Never mind other payment." He told me he usually gets paid besides, but he always gets these things to complete the ceremony. He made it pretty plain that his power wanted things that had already been in use on a horse.

For a certain rite of a shaman the ceremonial gifts are always the same, and, if the practitioner is well known, the requirements are public knowledge. In order to learn about the "way" of a lesser ritual figure, it may be necessary to make some inquiries. A visit to a relative of the shaman may prove useful, for example.

Once the shaman has agreed to perform his rite, he takes full command and announces where and when the ceremony is to take place. He is free to enlist the help of the sufferer's relatives and he may direct them to build a special shelter with the door facing the east or to gather paraphernalia and plants.

Many shamans, as a part of the ceremony, impose restrictions upon those who wish to watch the proceedings:

Some shamans don't allow barefooted people around when they are working, but not all are like this. Some don't allow you to scratch if you want to stay, but not all are like this either. Some tell you that you can't sleep while the ceremony is in progress. When we came to Geronimo's ceremonies he would warn us not to scratch or we would get a choking sensation then and there.

It is usually the close relatives, affinities, and good friends of the patient who are present. If the shaman is known for his dramatic performance, persons particularly attracted to religious spectacles also seek entrance. The shaman decides who may attend. Often fear of impiety or of witchcraft is a selective factor.

The ceremony ordinarily lasts four days, and the events open to the public take place on four consecutive nights, starting after dark and continuing until midnight. These are not inflexible rules, however. Food—often an abundant feast—is provided by the patient's relatives at the conclusion of each night's performance.

Every shaman has paraphernalia of his own which he uses in his rite. Many of these ritual objects have a logical association with the power source.

Usually, when a person gets power through some animal, he has four tokens of the animal with which he works—perhaps the hide, claws, tail, and paw. If his power is from lightning, lightning-struck twigs may be there. If the power comes from a bird, perhaps the tail feathers of that bird will have a place in the ceremony.

There are a number of ritual objects which appear in almost every ceremony:

A shaman has pollen, paints, herbs, and a drum. Eagle feathers are usually used. Some wear a cap or a vest of buckskin when they sing. Some have a tray basket at their ceremonies with pollen, paint, and eagle feathers in it.

Pollen, the symbol of life and renewal, is omnipresent on ritual occasions. Tule pollen is used most, but the power may request the substitution of pollen from piñon, oak, pine, sunflower, or, in later days, corn.

Besides the substances and objects already mentioned as ceremonial gifts to the shaman, many others, supplied by the shaman himself, may be used in the rite. Some of these are: white clay, red ocher, coral, rock crystal, opal, jaspar, gypsum, snakeweed, grama grass, the bezoar, the enema tube, and a decorated "age staff" upon which the shaman leans during his songs.

After all have come together, the shaman rolls a cigarette and blows smoke to the four directions:

He smokes ceremonially, sends the smoke up. First he puffs to the four directions. As he blows smoke to each direction he says, "May it be well." He might say as he smokes, "There are good and evil on this earth. We live in the midst of it. Let all be living in peace. I want nothing to harm us. We only want food and other good things."

An impromptu prayer calling upon the power source for aid is likely to follow the ceremonial cigarette:

This woman is in poor health. I want her to live. She has been searching for something good. This evening I hope that what is wrong with her life will disappear and that she will have a good life. Now I am going to tell you something. You must do right now what you promised me to do. Your power must go into the life of this poor woman.

At this juncture, that the patient by his belief and the audience by their "good thoughts" may please the power source and insure its co-operation, the shaman may describe the acquisition of his ceremony and its virtues. Another gesture implying faith is the reciprocal marking of the shaman and the patient with a sacred substance. Pollen is most often so used, but specular iron ore, red ocher, or white clay may be substituted. "Every shaman is known by his individual way of using pollen. Some put it to the four directions and up and down, some around the back of the neck and on the shoulders of the patient. Each man keeps his own way." The shaman may even mark everyone present in like manner, drawing the entire gathering into a spiritual brotherhood. The pollen, like all ceremonial objects or substances employed in the ritual, is held first to the cardinal directions, beginning with the east, and then moved in a sunwise circuit.

Some shamans next seek to learn whether they will be able to relieve the patient. One ceremonialist has, in recent times, looked at the sick person through a black silk handkerchief to determine this. Another draws the moon or a star with pollen on the palm of his right hand, and figures appear for him which permit him to prophesy concerning the outcome.

To determine the cause of the ailment and to learn what he must do to cure it, the shaman sings and prays. In this way he attracts the attention of the guardian spirit with whom the songs and prayers originated. He may sing without musical accompaniment, or he may beat time with a curved drumstick on the pottery drum that has been thus described:

Women make the pot. Men fix it to sing with and make the drumstick. The drum is a piece of buckskin stretched over a clay pot. Water and four pieces of charcoal, each the size of the end of my thumb, are put in. The charcoal is required for a ceremony. It makes the sound good too. The water is to keep the buckskin damp. The buckskin is wet and stretched over the mouth of the pot. It takes several men [to fix the buckskin in place]. It is sounded until it is right and then tied. Then four little holes are made in the buckskin. If this is not done, it will not be much of a drum. It helps the sound and is of ceremonial importance too. The drumstick is made of any kind of green wood that can be bent. Oak is sometimes used for it.

Less frequently the musical accompaniment is a rattle of some kind. Rattles of eagle claws and mountain-goat hooves have been mentioned for shamanistic rites. Occasionally, the shaman has an assistant who drums for him and aids him throughout the rite.

The songs are formal and unvarying for any one ceremony. The prayers tend to be extemporaneous, however, reflecting the need and the occasion. The song, and often the prayer, is divided into four parts or verses, all alike except for different associations of color and direction. The traditional color-directional association which is found in the mythology is black for the east, blue for the south, yellow for the west, and white for the north. Shamans take repeated liberties with this scheme, but for any one rite internal consistency is maintained. It is at the second or fourth verse of a song or prayer, or at the end of the second or fourth song, that the shaman ordinarily receives the message he awaits.

He may hear a voice, see a vision, or receive information in some other way. The sign is often for him alone; those around him know what is happening only when he interrupts his ritual after a visitation and addresses his power. Power may simply assure the shaman that the disease has been correctly diagnosed and that he need only complete the rite in its briefest form. For more serious illnesses, it may advise tests to determine whether the patient will recover, or it may suggest a plant remedy and give instructions for its administering.

Often medicinal herbs play a large part in the curing:

P. performed cures too. In his ceremony he would ask for it, the thing that would cure the sick person. You'd hear it on the roof. Then it was before you, a plant. He wouldn't take it up at once. He'd sing over it and talk to it first. When P. asked for it, it would come right through the crowd and land on the buckskin before him.

To produce some ritual object, to extract the "witch," or to demonstrate the potency of his supernatural source, the shaman may employ legerdemain:

Something I saw him do is more than anything I ever saw others do. As nearly as I remember, it was about 1888 when I saw B. go through his ceremony in Alabama. Word was sent out to meet in one place where B. was going to sing. A good many met there. It was a very pretty night, moonlight; everything was still. He called them all around. He spread a clean white sheet right out there. They lit some lanterns so you could plainly see any little bugs that walked on that sheet. He sat right there. He put a basket there. People crowded around watching him. I sat very close; I was pretty religious in those days. When something like this was going on, I'd be over there first.

Before he started he said, "Some of you people never believe anything. You people who want power, watch this." He took his shirt off and was naked from the waist up. He took a piece of turquoise about as large as your thumb and as green as could be. He said, "If any of you people can do what I'm going to do, I'll believe in you. I can do it. This is solid turquoise. Look at it."

So they passed it around. They handed it back to him. He held it out. While everybody was looking he put it in the center of the sheet, far from him. He knelt down on both knees. Everybody was watching closely.

He said, "You people don't believe in anything. There's a turquoise here. I'm going to pray first. As soon as I stop praying I'm going to start to sing. During the singing watch that turquoise closely."

He knelt down with arms outstretched. He prayed in a low tone. I couldn't hear all of it. He prayed to Yusn, Child of the Water, Cloud, and other things. He prayed for a long time.

Then he told us, "Watch that turquoise. It is going to be here in the center of my breast." And he held his arms outstretched with his hands open and began to sing. . . . . Between songs he told us to pray for our own good.

While he was singing, that turquoise disappeared. Everybody watched, and there it was right on his breast. And it started moving just like a little bug, going to his right arm, then moving up his arm, around his back to his other arm, and then back across the left arm to his chest. It was just like a little bug walking around on his back. And before you knew it, it was in the center of the sheet again. Everyone was praying. They believed there was something to him.

A shaman may also resort to such exhibitions to prove the hopelessness of a case:

My father looked at the boy. He took two eagle tail feathers and stuck them down the boy's throat. He wobbled them around. He took the feathers out, and big worms were there on the white calico. They were big and they were fighting. My father said, "They are hungry. That means no lungs are left. I can't do anything for you. If you had come earlier, I could have cured him. But it is too late." He burned up the worms. . . . . They took him [the patient] back. . . . . He died.

If the cause of the illness is found to be witchcraft, the shaman may be counseled by his power to continue his songs and prayers with greater intensity and thus defy the witch. At the proper time (usually the fourth and last night) and under the direction of his supernatural sponsor, he sucks out the object of witchcraft with his lips or a tube and spits it into the fire, where it "pops." As the sorcerer's "arrow" falls into the fire, the onlookers spit, thus symbolically ridding themselves of things unclean. Objects of many kinds are sucked from the bodies of patients: "A bone, a stick, horsehair, a needle, human hair, a little buckskin pouch, a spider—these are the kinds of things taken out."

The traits which have been described are the ones most frequently represented in a curing rite, but occasionally other modes of treatment appear:

A shaman may, after working over a sick person or sucking on the place that hurts, make a hissing noise to the directions, as though driving away the disease. This is called "to blow away from him." Some specialize in this.

. . . . They make steps of pollen just like those made at the girl's puberty rite and have the patient walk through. Anyone else who wants to can walk through after the patient finishes. They call it the trail of long life.

The ground drawing, too, may be an important feature of a particular rite. The one discussed below was used against epidemics as well as to foil the enemy.

I do not want to draw it because I do not know it. No one transferred the power to me, and it would not be wise for me to try it. This ground drawing was used in war too. Once it was used when I was there. A regiment of cavalry and a regiment of infantry were after us. This shaman drew the picture in pollen on the ground and left it there. Then we retreated to a hill. Both regiments turned off the trail and went back by a roundabout way, though the trail was plain, and they could have kept going. That is the way the ground drawing works. When it is used like this, the enemy is unable to follow. Something happens to the enemy always. They give up before they get to the place of the ground drawing, or they cannot pass it.

Death in a near-by home is the one event considered serious enough to halt a ceremony already started. "If there is a death in the camps, they stop any ceremony going on. They won't pray even. The ceremony has to be started over again. It can start the day after the person is buried."

Almost without fail, at the conclusion of a ceremony, the shaman imposes some food or behavior restriction upon the patient:

A Chiricahua, in the house of another, always asks if he can do anything before he does it. His host might have had a ceremony performed after which he was told not to let people smoke before him, step over him, or do any of a number of other things. We have to be careful not to disobey any of these things and cause sickness or harm to a friend.

The shaman restricts his patients. He tells some not to eat liver, entrails, heart, head, or not to let anyone step over them, or stand to the east of them when they are sitting down, or suddenly appear behind them. Or he might tell them never to let the shadow of a buzzard fall upon them, or, if someone gives them a piece of fruit and it drops, not to pick it up again and eat it.

Usually these restrictions are scrupulously respected:

One woman here was shot. She had a curing ceremony performed over her by one who specializes in gun wounds. He told her she must not eat deer meat, and to this day she will not do so. I know her well. Once I offered her deer meat, and she would not take it.

I went to visit C. I stood in front of him. He said, "Don't stand over me. Someone performed a ceremony for me and said that no one was to stand over me."

I never eat tongue myself. I had a ceremony performed over me when I was young, and at the end of it I was warned not to eat meat from the head of any animal.

A food taboo which becomes too irksome can be ceremonially lifted, however:

The shaman tells you sometimes not to eat tongue or liver. If you don't want to keep away from this, after four days you cook liver or whatever it was he told you not to eat. Then he comes and marks it with pollen, puts it toward your mouth three times, and the fourth time you eat it. Then it is all right. This removal of the restriction is called "one can eat it again."

At the conclusion of the ceremony the shaman may present the patient with a curative or protective amulet to hasten recovery and to prevent a relapse. This may be one of the four ceremonial gifts required by the terms of the rite, but more often it is something especial made by the shaman.[19]

Often the shaman gives the woman patient a piece of decorated buckskin to wear on her hair. A turquoise bead might be given a man and a piece of abalone shell to a woman. Sometimes a buckskin jacket or cap is made for the patient by the shaman. Sometimes it is a feather, sometimes a cross. The patient is directed to wear this after the ceremony so the disease will not come back any more. Bags of paint or pollen are sometimes worn for good luck after a ceremony. Different shamans give different things to wear.

Before the shaman departs on the fourth night, payment is made to him. Usually an understanding has been reached in advance. Sometimes the gifts are in view during the entire last evening, for supernatural power is well pleased when its ceremony is generously rewarded. More than the agreed amount may be placed before the shaman. Then, because the ceremonialist is grateful to the patient, he is expected to continue to pray for him and ritually protect him. In fact, some resentment may be felt when a shaman does not maintain interest in a case:

[19] In 1909, on the field expedition already mentioned, M. R. Harrington collected a large number of these amulets from the Chiricahua Apache. These objects are now in the Museum of the American Indian, Heye Foundation, in New York City.

PLATE X

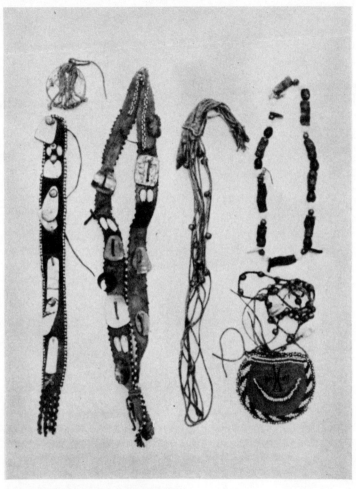

AMULETS

That shaman knows my wife is worse. He knows she got sick just before his boy died. We moved over there and had our camp near his. He didn't do anything. I've done a lot for that man. I gave him a steer when his daughter had her puberty rite. I've taken him other food. He thinks I should keep right on doing things for him.

Often the service that a shaman has rendered his client is the basis for closer friendly relations. Although the process is informal, this bond is an important one for many individuals. "There is no set rule that a cured patient is under obligation to a shaman, but sometimes a person himself feels that way."

Where a ceremony ends in failure, the shaman does not suffer irreparable injury to his reputation unless he has expressed himself too confidently concerning a favorable outcome. The result may be attributed to the fact that the shaman was not called in time or to the strength of an opposing witch. The ultimate effects of the rite are not always at once obvious, though it is hoped that the ceremony will pave the way for steady recovery. Should that recovery lag, it may be accounted for by the patient's carelessness in the wearing of the protective amulet, or by his failure to observe strictly the taboos. That a shaman may succeed in one case and not in another is conceded. To "try" the ceremonies of a number of practitioners before relief from some tenacious ailment is obtained has been the experience of a large percentage of adults at some time in their lives.

CEREMONIALISM IN ACTION; OBTAINING AND USING POWER

Mountain People.—The functions of the Mountain People and of their most important representatives, the Mountain Spirits, are well illustrated in the myths. One tale describes the curing of two children, one legless and one blind. Abandoned, these two try vainly to follow their people. The blind boy carries the cripple and is guided by his directions. Then the Mountain People appear and conduct the boys to their "home."

Many people lived in that mountain. They dressed all kinds of Mountain Spirits for these boys. They prayed and began to sing. There were women in the mountain too. The women made the sound, the cry of applause, as they do at the big tepee during the girl's puberty rite now.

By the ceremony of the Mountain Spirits the boys are restored to bodily perfection and are returned to their parents.

Another story tells of the flight of a man from a large force of traditional enemies. He runs, praying, toward a place known to be a home of the Mountain People. At his appeal, Mountain Spirits swarm from the cliff wall, surround the enemy, and drive them into a cave which then closes upon them. This myth emphasizes the protective role of the Mountain People who guard the tribal territory and defend the people from enemies and disease.

Another tale calls attention to the care which must be exercised during the masked-dancer ceremony and indicates the prominent place of the clown in the ritual. A shaman informs the people that he is going to paint masked dancers at a mountain far from the camps. He advises everyone, except the dancers and those who will assist him in preparing them, to stay on the flats below. Particularly does he warn parents to keep their children away from the place, and he reminds his hearers that they are not to call the names of the dancers when the performance begins. A little girl creeps up to the forbidden site, nevertheless, and mentions the name of an impersonator when the dancing starts. The shaman, immediately aware of what has occurred, tries to intercede for her with the Mountain People and finally conceals her under the fire. Soon Mountain Spirits come and displace their impersonators. On each of the first three nights a Mountain Spirit of a different color vainly leads the search for the miscreant. On the fourth night Long Nose or Gray One, the clown, heads the line and succeeds. For her impiety the girl is slain.

Another myth stresses the penalty for disrespect toward the Mountain Spirits and suggests the association between the masked-dancer rite and ceremonial defense against epidemics. Masked dancers are joined by two mysterious strangers who are superlative performers. The people seek to learn their identity. After the dance of the fourth night, riders stationed on swift horses pursue the two strangers. But the fastest mounts are outdistanced, a rock wall opens to receive the runners, and the mortals realize that they have pursued actual Mountain Spirits. "Not long after that disease broke out among them and killed many of them."

The Mountain Spirits are held in such fear and reverence that those who have no ceremony from them are hesitant even to discuss them. One man explained, "I'm not supposed to tell stories about the Mountain Spirits because it is dangerous for me," and another said: "In order to use another word besides Mountain Spirit in the stories, a term 'man from the mountains,' is used. This is put in the story a few times to show that the Mountain Spirits are held in awe and to prevent harm befalling the teller."

Masked-dancer ceremonies, though they may be later taught to others, always originate in a personal supernatural experience. The following account is a good example of the type.

My father is a shaman. He got his ceremony when he was a young man. It was this way. You know that Guadalupe Mountain over here. It is a religious mountain, a holy mountain. My father says that this place is the home of Mountain People. He says a spirit came to him and told him to go into that mountain. Someone talked to him, but he did not see anyone. It was outside the mountain that something, or someone, told him to enter. That was the first time anything had spoken to him; he was getting his first power.

When he thought he heard a voice telling him to go into the cliff, he turned around and started to enter the mountain. The cliff opened like a door. He says that the clown met him at the door. The clown said, "Follow me," and they came to the first outside door. Near by was a great rock turning around and around. They call it by a name that means "rock that swings around together." My father says he was frightened, but the clown told him, "Don't be afraid. You must go through four doors, all different. Don't be frightened because the rock is acting this way." Then he said, "Sh! Sh!" pointing his forefinger at the rock, and the rock stopped. He told my father to follow him. They went on.

They came to the second door. There were two great snakes there, twisting and squirming, and biting at each other. They were guarding the door. They were not really biting each other, just trying to. They were not allowing anyone to pass. The clown said, "Do not be afraid of them." The clown went ahead, and my father was close behind. The clown said again, "Sh! Sh!" pointing his forefinger at the snakes, and the snakes stopped twisting and biting.

So they passed the snakes and went on to the next door, the third door. Here there were two big mountain lions, one on either side of the door. They were trying to keep everyone from going through that door. They had their mouths open, and when they saw my father they were just wild. The clown said, "You must not be afraid; they are not going to hurt you." The clown went on ahead, and when he came to the mountain lions, he again pointed his finger, saying, "Sh! Sh!" and they quieted down. My father and the clown went through the door.

Then came the fourth door. There was nobody in there at the door. All these doors were rock. At the fourth door the guide again repeated, "Sh! Sh!" and the door opened. When my father got into the fourth room, it was just as if he were in high mountains.

After the last door had opened, my father looked about a hundred feet away. There was one old man sitting over there. The guide said, "That man is going to talk to you now, and you want to be very careful. He is the leader in this place. We are going to walk right up there, and he is going to ask you some questions in a rough voice, but don't be afraid. Now he sees you coming with me."

So they started to walk up to that old man. He was sitting in a big chair in an open place. He was an old, old man, with garments over his head and all around him. The clown told my father, "When I take you up there I am going to leave you, and he will talk to you. Don't be afraid. He is a kind man."

The clown and my father reached this old man. Then the clown said, "Ready!" and disappeared. This left my father standing there alone before that man, and that old man sat up looking angry. My father was standing right in front of him.

Then the old man said to my father, "What do you want in here? You have no business in here." Then my father was frightened. "You tell me what you want. You are not allowed in here; humans from outside are not allowed in here."

But my father said, "I want to live long in this world, and I want to be blessed. I want to live to be an old man."

"All right, you mean it, do you? You think you are going to be afraid?"

My father said, "I will try not to be afraid; that is not what I am looking for. I am looking for something good for myself and for my children, so that they will have some blessings. I have wanted to go into some holy place like this one I am in now. Will you help me?"

The old man said, "All right. I have talked roughly to you, but I will do what you say. I am a kind man. I have control of this whole mountain." Then my father says he saw some hills all around there.

The conversation went along like this with my father and the old man. "What kind of power do you want?" the old man asked him. "I have some very strict rules, so strict that if you fail, you are going to die. They will harm you, and if you fail them you are going to lose your life or some of your family. I tell you that beforehand. What kind of a shaman do you want to be?"

My father answered, "I can't tell unless I see what you will give me." He wanted to be shown.

The old man said, "You just wait a minute."

Then he got up. He could hardly get up; he was a very old, old man. He walked behind a little hill in there. He came back and took his seat. Then my father said he could hear things ringing, drums, and singing just like the masked dancers dancing—Apache drums and singing. He heard it in the east as if many dancers were coming. And then they came in from the east, the clown leading them. Many Indians dressed in buckskin and Mountain People came, dancing. Then they stopped right where he was. All kinds of birds, animals, and snakes came behind the Mountain People.

The old man told him, "These are the ceremonies I have here. Which do you want? Pick out the one you want and don't make a mistake."

When the old man finished speaking, my father said, it seemed that it was the privilege of those animals and Mountain People to say what they wanted to him. One little bird came up to my father and said to him, "I am the greatest power on earth; take me." Then the eagle came up and said, "I am the greatest power here; take me." Then the animals came up, also the snakes, and said the same thing.

My father says he thought of it from the beginning, of how the old man said not to make any mistake. So my father turned around and thought, "These little birds are too willing, and these others are too willing. There are others sitting over there. I must not make a mistake."

He saw that the Mountain Spirits were the leading ones in there. So my father hesitated and thought, "Well, the clown and the Mountain Spirits haven't said anything to me."

They came around with a drum, with turquoise and a pollen cross on the drum. "The clown and Mountain Spirits say nothing, but they are good," my father thought. So my father turned to the old man and said, "I will take the Mountain Spirits."

That is the way it is today. Just as soon as he chose the Mountain Spirits, all the rest were ordered to go back. Just the Mountain Spirits were left. After all the birds, snakes, and animals were gone, there came many Indians, all dressed just like Chiricahua Apache. They started singing. My father has told me, "I was going through the performance. I got all the songs and designs. For four days I made masked dancers with a different design every day on each one." My father was learning the ceremony.

The old man said to him then, "You have done well. You did not make a mistake. I was watching you. The birds, animals, and snakes asked you to choose them, but you did right to choose the Mountain Spirits. They are the most powerful, the best thing here. Now you are going to stay here and have a good time for four days."

My father says that after this the Indians gathered, and they began to dance just as they do at the girl's puberty ceremony. White Painted Woman ran just as the girls do now. So my father in four days learned the whole thing. My father called the mountain "Holy Mountain." He says that he gets messages from these people whenever he holds his ceremony. When he wants to know how to cure a man, they come and tell him. He says they talk. He stayed another four days and four nights there.

After four days the old man asked him, "Do you have what you want?" My father said, "Yes."

He said, "You didn't make any mistake."

My father answered, "I hope not."

The old man explained, "This is a good thing for you. The Mountain People will take care of you all your life. You can hand the ceremony down to anyone you want to. You can do anything you like. If the ceremony is given to your child, you will not have to ask for any ceremonial gifts; but if it is passed on to other people, then you can ask for gifts. But if you love someone else, you can hand it down to that one without gifts."

The Mountain People gave him directions. "You cannot sing these songs for nothing." So today my father is hard to convince on that.

After the four days, when this old man had told him he had what he wanted, the Mountain Spirits had all gone. Then the clown came. The old man ordered the clown back. The old man told my father, "That is all. I am through with you. Everything is all right. I hope you have a long life in this world. You may go home and use the ceremony according to what the Mountain People want you to do."

The clown had to take my father back through the mountain. They had to come back through those doors. They came again to the big mountain lions. The clown said, "Sh! Sh!" and told my father to come right behind him. They returned to the snakes. The snakes tried to stop them. The clown said, "Sh! Sh!" and then told my father to come right behind him. Then they reached the last door, that great rock swinging around and around. The clown stopped there and said to the rock, "Sh! Sh!" and to my father, "You come right behind me." And they went through. Then they came to the cliff. The clown said, "Sh! Sh!" again, and the whole thing opened like a door. The clown started to walk down the steep bluff. He said, "You must come behind me." My father says when he first went up there the spirit lifted him up suddenly, but now he had to follow the clown down or stay where he was. He did not think he could walk down the cliff but he followed the clown, and they walked down easily.

The clown said, "Here are four things I am going to give you." He gave him a little eagle feather, a very fine feather, and said, "This is one." He held something in his hand and said, "This is a small round turquoise with a hole in it. That makes two." He put the feather through the turquoise. He said, "If you are going to sing for a sick boy, the parents of the boy or his other relatives must give you a turquoise with an eagle feather like this. If he really wants to get well and believes in you, he must also give you a live thing, a horse or a cow, or anything you want, but it must be alive. The turquoise and eagle feather are used only in curing men and boys. The other gifts, which girls and women must give you, are the changing abalone and pollen. They must be tied in this way: the pollen must be in a little buckskin bag, and the string must be put through the hole in the abalone and tied in this way."

The curing rite in which masked dancers appear conforms to an easily recognized pattern. Its salient features are well described by one who has acted as an impersonator on many occasions.

If a sick man wants a ceremony of the masked dancers put on for him, he has to feed the helpers, the ones who dance. And the shaman has to be paid a whole lot. I've danced for my father's ceremony. His ceremony doesn't have to be at night. If it's nice weather, it might be during the day. He can paint any number of masked dancers—two or four, but not one; there must be more than one. It's hard work to dance like this. I'd rather not do it. They go there and dance around that sick person for four or five hours. I'd rather get out on the feast grounds and dance [at the girl's puberty rite]. I get more pleasure out of it. This other is tiresome work.

This is the way I have seen my father do his ceremony. Let us say I am a pretty sick man. I ride up on my horse. I come in with my turquoise and an eagle feather through it. I have pollen in my hand in a buckskin bag. I take some of the pollen in my right hand. I hold it up to the east, then I turn to the south, then to the west, then to the north, sunwise. I say, "My father (whether the shaman is my father or not), I hope with what you know I can get relief." I say to him, "This is your power," and I place a cross of pollen on his right foot. The shaman is sitting with his fingers touching his knees. Then I take my pollen and bring it up to the knee, then to the fingertips, down the left leg again, to the left foot, where I again make the cross with pollen. I still have the turquoise and eagle feather in my right hand. I either tie it to the buckskin string on his right moccasin or else just put it on there and he will pick it up.

Then I will be standing before him and say, "There is my horse standing just as I got off him, with my bridle, saddle, and blanket. I am a poor man. I want to live. I have given you all I have." Then I sit down.

Maybe he will not say anything for a while. I look as sick as I can so he will take pity on me. I am waiting for his answer. Finally he says, "All right," if he wants to take the case. He knows I am sick and have to be attended to right away. He says, "Bring your blankets and stay here."

He has to have a brush hut, and he must use two kinds of trees, juniper and spruce, to make a corral. It is up to him to fix the corral, or he can ask my parents or relatives to help him. I will be outside in the brush hut.

Now the shaman goes out and gets four young men to act as masked dancers. He comes back with them. My relatives are all working on the corral. They leave an open space facing the east, another doorway facing the south, another facing the west, and one facing the north. They make a fireplace in the middle of the corral.

I am taken into the corral. While my relatives are finishing the corral, the shaman is painting the masked dancers in the brush hut. I come in and await instructions. The shaman is with the masked dancers. He sees that everything is all right.

The shaman and the masked dancers come into the corral from the east when they are ready to begin. The shaman will be singing songs and may be dancing a little. The masked dancers are following him. He goes to the fire, walks around it clockwise, then goes on and comes back to the east. He tells the masked dancers to go around the fire four times and worship the fire four times. The masked dancers trot once around the fire. Then they back up and advance toward the fire again. They do that four times, and at the fourth time they make their call. They repeat the same thing, going around the fire once, but stopping this time at the south. They worship the fire in the same way from the south, west, and north.

The old man says to me, "Put your blanket right there." Then he goes to his masked dancers. He says, "There is a sick man over there. He wants to go through this ceremony." He tells me he is going to bring the masked dancers in to me. He says, "Are you able to sit up?" I answer that I am.

He says, "Have you pollen?" I reply, "Yes, I have it." I have some pollen in an open buckskin bag in my left hand. I have another turquoise with an eagle feather through it.

The shaman stands with a drum. I am facing the masked dancers. The shaman tells me, "All right, go ahead and put the pollen on the masked dancers."

I do this the same way I did it to the shaman. The leading masked dancer is dancing. I make signs to the directions, and the leader has to lean down so I can put the pollen on him. I put the turquoise on the leading dancer too. Then he stands aside and I do the same thing with the pollen to the next masked dancer. He then stands aside and I put the pollen on the remaining dancers.

Now the shaman asks, "Are you able to stand up?" And I answer, "Yes."

He says, "Maybe it will be good for you to stand and let the masked dancers work on you." So I stand up.

Then the shaman asks, "Where is your pain! What is ailing you?" And I tell him it looks as though I am very sick in my legs.

"On which side?"

"This side."

Or I may have a headache all the time that nothing can cure. If this is what I say, he tells the masked dancers who are standing there, "This man has not been relieved of his headache. Now I want you men to work on him. He is going to stand here."

He tells the masked dancers to come to the front of me. He is singing. He wants me to stand and let the masked dancers work on me. Many Chiricahua are watching me. The masked dancers begin to dance back and forth four times. The fourth time the leading dancer will shake his sticks with a weaving motion and cross them on my forehead. And pretty soon he takes hold of my hair on both sides and pulls as hard as he can, gives a cry, and lifts me up. He blows away the sickness to the east, south, west, and north. Then the masked dancers go around me once and stop on the south side. Then they come back to me and go through the same thing from the other directions. Then they go out of the corral.

The shaman asks me if I am tired and want to sit down. I say I would like to sit down, so they bring my blanket into the corral. I am sitting in the center alone.

When the masked dancers hear the drumming and singing start again, the leader begins to wave his sticks and dances around the corral four times, the fourth time stopping at the east. This blesses everybody in the corral.

The shaman tells the masked dancers to come in. The dancers face me. While the singing and drumming are going on, they dance around me four times. Then the shaman stops them.

He says, "All right, go around the fire once." While the singing is going on, they start to dance. Every once in a while the dancers blow to the directions to blow the disease away. They go around the fire once after they get through with me. All the time the singing is going on. Then the masked dancers go through the east door. Then they come back, dance around the fire, and go through the south door, dancing and blowing things away. They repeat the same thing through the west and north doors. They do all that has been described for four days or nights.

On the second or third night, if the shaman wants to see whether I am going to get well, he takes the abalone and comes up to me where everybody can see me. He sings and prays and holds up the abalone. Four times he puts the abalone against my forehead, and, if it sticks there by itself the fourth time, I am going to get well. If it falls off, I am not going to recover. He also uses a feather. He tells me to open my shirt, takes the feather, and points the quill end at my chest, over my heart, four times, so that everybody can see it. If it sticks on the fourth time, there is hope of my living. He uses either the abalone or eagle feather or both. I have to open my shirt, and the feather is put right on my heart. If they both drop off, he says, "I can't help you." But he can't stop before the fourth night, even though the eagle feather and abalone fall.

If these things fall or if I am getting worse, he talks and shakes his outstretched hands to his power. He talks to the Mountain People, who promised to help him. He says, "I have been paid for doing this and now you have got to help me." Sometimes tears run down his face and he cries, "I am going to make this man well! Even if the power does not help him, I am going to cure him!" He is angry and fights it out with the power that has made him a shaman.

The shaman does not tell everything that is going on. His spirit or vision may tell him that it can't do anything for me, but he fights it out with the spirit or vision.

I may get well before the fourth night, but if I am really sick, I may not get well for some time. The shaman tells me whether I am going to get well or not, and he tells me that I must follow certain rules. For instance, for a headache I must not put a knife in a cooking pot.[20] If I violate the rule, the disease will come back on me again. Or he may tell me to have the door of my house to the east. If I don't do this, if I violate this rule, the Mountain People will know whether I have done this or not, and the disease will come back to me.

It is up to the sick man to make gifts, anything he wants to give. After the fourth time the sick man is taken back to his own camp. In cases where the feather drops or the abalone drops, after the shaman leaves the man, he will keep on praying until the man gets well anyway.

A Mountain Spirit shaman can also perform his rite without any dancers. If there is a sudden emergency, if the full ceremony would be too costly for his patient, or if he cannot find enough dancers, he uses only the headdresses which the dancers customarily wear, placing them against the body of his patient and gesticulating with them to the directions to send the sickness away.

Many ceremonies cure the sickness of individuals, but the prevention of epidemics is a signal function of the masked-dancer rite. "When I hear of disease coming, I paint them and tell them to chase the disease away with the sticks," said a Mountain Spirit shaman. "When sickness is around, the masked dancers and the clown are made on a hill and then come to the people below, making fires on the way down. In this way they keep sickness away."

It is at such times that the clown, who merely acts as messenger and funmaker at the girl's puberty rite, may come into his own:

The old man always told us that the clown was the most powerful of the masked dancers. He said, "People think that the clown is just nothing, that he is just for fun. That is not so. When I make other masked dancers, and they do not set things right or can't find out something, I make that clown and he never fails." Many people who know about these things say that the clown is the most powerful.

At times of danger or epidemic another masked dancer, Black One, is sometimes made:

There are different grades of masked dancers. There is the clown, and he is dangerous. Then there is Black One, and he is supposed to be very dangerous. Black One wears nothing but feathers on top of his mask. He is painted black.

[20] There is a general prohibition against stirring food with a knife.

He does not make a noise like the other masked dancers and does not mix with the others. Any others that touch him will be harmed. Just one is made. He wears juniper boughs on his arms. Sometimes he carries sticks.

The one who is dressed to stand for Black One does not have the wooden frame above the buckskin face mask. He just has feathers in a bunch at the top of the mask. He wears a buckskin mask, all black. He is colored black all over. He carries spruce in his hands, and spruce is tied to each arm too. He wears a skirt of woven yucca which comes down long. He doesn't dance. Black One is just made for something bad, to keep everything bad away.

All three types of masked dancer may appear in the same ceremony to stave off epidemics:

It was during the World War when the "flu" was first coming this way. D. called all the people together. He was going to keep it away. He made the regular masked dancers and also Gray One [clown] and Black One. He wanted to pick out the best man for Black One. He tried to pick me out, but I said, "I don't know the ways of Black One, and I might make a mistake, and things might not turn out right." So I was one of the regular masked dancers instead. S. and I were the regular masked dancers, and R.'s boy was Black One.

The people were very quiet when this was going on. They said that we were two of the best dancers ever seen. We had a good clown there. He said, "You fellows certainly put on a good dance." Black One said he saw nothing but fruit and flowers around the fire, so D. said, "All is well."

D. told the people then, "Don't say anything bad about this sickness. Don't mention it, or it will come back."

For a while no one died. Then someone mentioned it, and the sickness began to come again. D. took us up on a high hill. The wind was blowing dust from the east. D. pointed to it and said, "That wind is bringing sickness back. I'm certainly sorry, but I can't help it. I told you about it. I warned you of it. Now it's too late." And it was true. The sickness came back, and many died. F. made his masked dancers, but it did no good.

This sickness died down. Then it came a second time. The second time it came, D. did not make his masked dancers. He didn't make Black One or any of them. He said, "All of you were safe. There was no sickness. I helped you. I told you what to do. But now it's coming back. I can't stop it."

When the sickness was on its way the first time and D. made his masked dancers, I went over to his camp. Many were camping around his place. He had his masked dancers there, and the people stayed around the masked dancers and marked them with pollen. All these people camping around him kept well.

In this ceremony it was Black One through whom the Mountain People transmitted their message. But this is not always the case. Most often it is the leader or one of the members of the regular masked-dancer group who receives the word of the super-naturals.

Some men when they dance say they see visions from the singing and praying of the shaman. I never did. I never saw a thing. Y. did though. It was in 1903 down at Fort Sill. There was smallpox. Lots of Indians were dying. We danced for four nights, from four in the afternoon until one or two at night. That was the hardest work I ever did. And you know, we never got that smallpox! It was all around. The Comanches had it. They were dying in Lawton, but we never got a case.

When the old man painted us he said, "Now one of you men is going to see a vision. I don't know which one it will be, but it will be one of you." I doubted it. I was a fool in those days. I didn't care. I just danced for a good time. Y. was the leader.

I watched Y. when he got the vision. This was the first night. The old man said someone would get it that night. We started out to dance at about four o'clock in the afternoon. The old man said it would have to be started while the sun was still up. There was a big crowd; Comanches, everyone was there. They put pollen on us dancers. We started dancing. We had to do what the old man told us. We had to go four times this way and that, and around the people. I was watching Y. He began going fast, shaking, running out to the woods and back.

About three hours later we rested for a while. We were smoking. Y. said, "Fellows, the old man said someone was going to see a vision, and I saw it. But that's all I'm going to tell you. I'm going to tell it to the old man, and if he wants to tell it to you, all right." Later I heard him tell the old man something, and the old man said, "That's good!"

Masked-dancer ceremonies conducted for the public good are usually undertaken in response to requests from a number of people: "We asked R. to put on a ceremony for us, but he is too weak. So another man and I have been trying to get F. to make masked dancers for a long time. He did it the other day."

A number of protective masked-dancer rites have taken place in recent years. One, held to prevent the penetration of sleeping sickness, is described by a man who attended it.

Yesterday F. held his ceremony to keep away sleeping sickness. I didn't feel so good when I came back yesterday, so I went over. I thought that perhaps F.'s masked dancers would help me. The masked dancers performed once in the day and once in the night. He painted four regular masked dancers and two clowns.

The grounds were fixed this way: there were four spruce trees set up, one in each direction, and a fire was built in the center. To start the fire, they first put up the sticks like a tepee. The singers came in from the south and went around the fire clockwise four times. Then they took a place to the east of the spruce, facing the sunrise. Then F., the shaman, went around the fire once. Then he called to the masked dancers, "Now it's your turn."

They came in from the east and advanced to the fire and back four times. On the fourth time they gave their call. They did the same thing from every direction. Then they went around the fire four times, then around the outside of the trees four times. After that they came in from the east and stood in a single file facing the fire. Then F. told the people to paint the masked dancers. It took a long time. The dancers knelt so the children could reach them, putting their sticks on the ground.

This started about one o'clock in the afternoon. The night ceremony lasted until morning. Later F. gave a little talk. He said that he didn't think the sickness was going to spread this far but that it was best to make the ceremony to make sure anyway.

The masked dancers not only act to keep illness away but "they can find out what the trouble is when people are sick." If witchcraft is discovered, the impersonators may have to expose the sorcerers. "The dancers should not point with their sticks at the spectators unless the shaman tells them to look for an evildoer. Then they point him out. Usually the leader of the dance group is used for this."

Even the control of the weather is not beyond their function. On several occasions when the performance of the masked dancers at the girl's puberty rite was threatened by stormy weather, I have seen the shaman gesture to the directions with a headdress in order to drive the clouds away.

A myth tells of the freeing of animals from the subterranean land where they were kept by Crow. There is the present belief, perhaps a corollary to this, in "animal homes," places within caves or mountains where the game is hidden. An example will indicate the type of "animal home" story that is common.

About eight or nine years ago there was a big snow at Whitetail. E. was hunting deer over there. He was on horseback. A deer jumped in front of him, and he started after it. He saw it disappear in a cave. Then he came on and met us. He told us, "The old people tell us that the animals come from caves in the mountains, and I believe them now." He told us the story of the deer he had chased.

Two others went to that cave with him. They followed the trail and found a hole there. They dropped a stone, and it sounded as though that hole were very deep, so they came back. People tell of homes of the mountain sheep like this too. They see the holes and the trails of the sheep going to them. I have heard of homes of animals in Hot Springs country too.

In this tale and in many others there is no attempt to link the animal home with the Mountain People, but in a description of the place where the first moccasin game was played there is a hint of such a nexus. "At the bottom of this mountain is a hole, a cave. In there the Mountain People live. Inside, it is about eight feet square. There is nothing but deer tracks there. The ground moves there."

It is evident from some descriptions of the Mountain People that they are considered not only the denizens of a given mountain but also the custodians of the wild life ranging in the vicinity. Often the power-acquisition stories have the "holy homes" of the Mountain People richly populated with game animals. The most unequivocal statement on this subject came from an Eastern Chiricahua who said:

All the animals, horses, sheep, come from the mountains. The Mountain People keep them. They take them in at night sometimes and let them out to graze here on earth during the day. R. killed a big buck here. It was cut [castrated]. That shows that the Mountain People make steers too.

Anyone who is in the vicinity of a home of the Mountain People, whether he has power from them or not, sprinkles pollen toward the holy place and prays, "Protect us from enemies and do not let harm befall us while we are near you." Those who are in need are advised to appeal to the Mountain People: "A man who made masked dancers said, 'Any time you are in trouble or in danger from animals, pray to the Mountain People, and they will come from the mountains and protect you.'"

Life Giver, Child of the Water, and White Painted Woman.—
The nebulous and remote Supreme Being is definitely not the source of any particular ceremony:

If a man felt that he was having bad luck, he might go out and ask Life Giver to help him. A man might get a ceremony of some kind at such a time in answer to his prayer, or he might just be helped out of his present trouble. If he gets a ceremony that will help him right along, that ceremony will come from some other source, like lightning or an animal, and not directly from Life Giver. But his prayer to Life Giver starts it.

When a person has a special ceremony, from Lightning, for instance, he will pray directly to Lightning and will not call on Life Giver. But many feel that Life Giver is answering through this other source. Life Giver is an old conception.[21] The very old Indians pray this way. Some old Indians who don't know the first thing about Christianity the way the preacher speaks of it, pray this way. . . . . We think of Life Giver as a spirit of no particular sex. We do not attribute deeds to Life Giver. No pollen would be thrown to Life Giver.

Child of the Water figures prominently in religious traditions and ritual. However, it is believed that his work was largely completed when he departed from earth. Though he once busied himself prodigiously with the affairs of man, now he is almost a sky-god, magnificent and rather remote. Occasionally, someone believes that Child of the Water has "talked" to him. One informant was certain that this supernatural was reaching him through the medium of dreams, for instance.

For ceremonial purposes White Painted Woman is the feminine counterpart of Child of the Water, and the time of her direct impingement upon worldly affairs, too, is at an end. Perhaps the most important use of this supernatural in rites now is a symbolic one. For instance, in a certain lightning ceremony the earth is referred to as White Painted Woman. This symbolism proves to be a dramatization of the legend of the birth of the culture hero. Just as lightning strikes the earth today, so White Painted Woman lay down "while the lightning flashed four times and acted as a man to beget Child of the Water. This is why the three are connected, and to this day White Painted Woman is mentioned in the lightning ceremony."

The ideological association between the earth and White Painted Woman is found in more than one context. "In any

[21] Despite this insistence on the antiquity of the conception of Life Giver, a good guess would be that the present position of this deity is a response to European doctrine. The word that has been translated Life Giver can be literally rendered "the one because of which I live." The individual still refers to his personal supernatural power source by that same linguistic form or a slight variant of it. Life Giver is apparently a symbolization of supernatural power as such, the reservoir from which particular power grants and ceremonies flow. The European influence in this greater personalization of diffuse supernatural power can be inferred from the synonyms for Life Giver, which are Yusn (from the Spanish *Dios*) and "He Sits in the Sky."

political speech or religious speech . . . . the world or earth is called 'Earth Woman.' This really refers to White Painted Woman. The real way to say 'all the people of the earth' is to say 'all the people on the top of Earth Woman.' ''

A shaman once had a girl impersonate White Painted Woman to symbolize the feminine principle:

He chose a little girl, nine or ten years old, and marked her and told her to come up and give food to the patient. Then he prayed again. Then the little girl picked up the food and first gave the patient the soup . . . . marked with pollen and an herb. She picked up the spoon which the man had marked with pollen, but the ceremonial man made four motions with her hand to the mouth of the patient, and then said, "You give him all he wants. It won't hurt him."

. . . . The shaman said, "That part of the ceremony I performed where I took the girl to feed the man—she was part of the ceremony. . . . . She knew the power of Woman; that's why I used her. Woman, White Painted Woman, is the power I was using. If the patient had been a woman, I would have used Child of the Water [i.e., a boy].

Thunder (lightning).—Sage is a most generally used prophylactic against lightning sickness. A spray of it is usually worn during rainy weather, and some is hung up in the form of a cross in the home. Cudweed is another plant for which similar properties are claimed. But, in spite of all safeguards, lightning sickness does occur, and a ceremony to cure it exists.

I received my ceremony through a dream when I was a young man. I just lay down and dreamed that I heard a voice, and the words of my songs were repeated. The giver said these words of the song in my ear while I slept. I believe that this power came from Thunder.

I have cured boys around here. I tried to perform a ceremony on my daughters when they were sick, but they did not want it. They did not allow me to do it, and they died. They did not believe in it. I performed this ceremony for my son. The white doctor said there was no hope. I said to the doctor, "If there is no hope, I would like to take him home and be by his side when he dies." I took him home and performed the ceremony for four nights. The boy began to get better at once. The doctor was very surprised when he saw the boy around again. He said, "I didn't expect to see you well and around!" This was about seventeen years ago.

My ceremony cannot tell who a witch is.[22] I have no power over that. If I do

[22] It is a comment on the degree of individuality among practitioners to note that another lightning shaman who believed that most witches were more powerful than shamans said, "The one exception is the man who gets his power from Lightning or Earth Mother. He has control over the witch."

not get a man well, I know that the man is mistaken about his trouble. If I get a person well, I usually get other payment besides the ceremonial gifts. For the ceremonial gifts I must receive a horse, a piece of turquoise with an eagle feather stuck through a hole in it, and an unblemished buckskin, these four things. They must be given before the ceremony starts. I have the feathers on my hat and the turquoise I wear through the ceremony.

The ceremony can take place in the day or the night, but it has to be continued for four days or four nights. If a person got struck or frightened by lightning in the afternoon, the ceremony would begin in the afternoon. I try to begin it at about the same time of day or night that the experience with lightning occurred.

First of all in my ceremony I smoke. I blow the smoke to the four directions, calling each by its color name. Then I call on Thunder and say, "Before you did this to him, this man's body and spirit were in a healthy condition. Now he is sick. I plead with you to breathe some of your spirit into this man, to make him over as he should be."

I have to have medicine for the sick person too. To make this medicine I take wood from a tree which has been struck by lightning, burn it, take the ashes, and put them in cool water. Scrapings from abalone shell are put with it too. With the ashes I make a lightning design (a zigzag) on the four sides of the cup. And I make the lightning design on the man's face, running it into the mouth. I pray, and while I pray I raise the cup upward four times, then toward the patient three times, and make the patient drink on the fourth.

Then I begin with the songs. This is my first song:

> He in the sky who is holy,
> He who is Black Thunder
> Who put up the earth,
> He zigzags down with life
> To impart life to her body;
> He in the sky who is holy,
> Black Thunder, my father.

This same song is sung to the other directions; the color terms alone change. At the end of the second song I push the chest, back, and sides of the patient with my hand four times and then blow the evil influence away. While I am singing, I am asking help of my power.

After the four songs I pray again. This last part changes to suit the occasion. Then the ceremony for this one day or night is finished. This power of mine comes from Thunder. Thunder power carries you to old age.

I have a hat that goes with this ceremony. I was ordered by a dream to make the hat. I do not use the hat in the ceremony or use it at all. I was told in my dream that the hat would just be for luck in the ceremony. But the hat belongs to Lightning; it belongs to this ceremony. It is copied after the old way.

I lost this hat one time. Later I was walking with four men. We were hunting deer. I saw a deer and ran to head it off. When I got to the point where I thought the deer would pass, I saw one of the men waving, telling me that the deer had gone back. It was raining a little. I started to go back. I went a long way looking around. It started to rain again. I began to look again. Close by, the lightning struck. I went to the place where it had struck and found the hat. This caused me to believe in my ceremony more than ever.

There is one other function of the lightning shaman, the making of amulets of various kinds to be worn as a protection against lightning and lightning sickness.[23]

Some say Lightning talks to them. When the lightning strikes a place, these people can go to the east of a pine tree that was struck and take a piece of wood. They shape it like this [a crude resemblance to the human figure with some features poorly indicated] and put it on them. They wear it suspended by four strings. The painting is done with a blue mineral and black specular iron ore. If this is made for a person, he won't be hit by lightning, and he won't be frightened by lightning.

Plants.—Occasionally, a plant is personified and becomes a source of ritual. One plant, now much used for wounds, revealed itself in a vision experience to a man who was wounded in battle and fell on it. The plant pushed him upward four times and spoke to him, telling him to chew the root, to rub some of it on the injury, and to put the unused leaves back in the ground. The man obeyed directions, recovered, and was able to reach his home and introduce this remedy.

A plant, as well as an animal, acted as supernatural guardian for a successful raider:

This happened long ago. The enemies used to know many ways to stop you, to make your legs ache so you couldn't get away with horses. My father was down in Mexico with a band. They drove away a good herd of cattle, burros, and horses from the Yaqui.

The Yaqui came on the trail. One of the men of the Yaqui knew a ceremony and was working against the Chiricahua. The Chiricahua had seen cacti thrown on their trail, and now they knew what it was for. They got cramps, their legs hurt, and they couldn't go fast. They were in danger, for the Yaqui were catching up.

For his raiding work my father mixed Wolf and Cactus [a small variety of hedgehog cactus type] together. They asked him to sing and he did. He found

[23] Among the ethnological specimens collected by M. R. Harrington from the Chiricahua Apache at Fort Sill, Oklahoma, in 1909 were a number of lightning fetishes.

out what had been done against them. He saw that the enemy had used cactus with a spider's web. This makes the toes twist [gives cramps] and makes the men fall off their horses. My father found it out and let them have the worst of it. He went to the edge of camp and "shot" four cactus plants on the back trail. They had no trouble after that.

Antelope and deer.—Deer and antelope ceremonies have as their primary function the securing of game, but other uses for such power exist, such as the employment of the deer ceremony in love rites. The usual deer ceremony is direct in intent and execution. It consists in prayers and songs to Deer the night before the hunt, bespeaking the singer's need, and instructing the animals to give up some of their hide and meat. The ritual may include placing a certain grass under the pillow the night before the hunt, refraining from mentioning the ordinary names for game animals during the expedition, or observing other rules. Often the mountain where the hunter intends to seek his kill is named in the songs.

The test of a deer or antelope shaman's relations with his power source is the success with which he can predict when, where, and in what quantity the game may be obtained. For some shamans the ability to produce or to find game almost at will has been claimed.

Many knew about deer, but A.'s father knew more than the rest. One man wanted to bet with him [about which one knew more on this subject]. The great man did not want to bet. "I don't know anything about deer," he said. The other begged him to bet. "All right," he said then, "I'm going to make a deer come to that oak. I'll make him eat of it. I'll shoot him there. You do the same to the other oak with another deer. If you can do it, you know as much as I do." But the other refused. . . . . "I don't mean that. I mean that we should go out hunting to see who kills a deer first." "No, that has nothing to do with power. Now you want to change the bet." But the other man backed down.

The individual with a deer or antelope ceremony uses it in many ways. He prepares the deer and antelope heads used in stalking game and sings over them to imbue them with the benefits of his rite. Because his practical experience is augmented by supernatural knowledge, such a shaman is requested by parents to instruct their sons in hunting. Moreover, since good fortune on the hunt is of constant importance to all grown men, those who do not possess such supernatural help, when they have been unsuccessful for any length of time, go to a deer or antelope shaman and hire him to perform his ceremony on their behalf.

The concept of animal homes is frequently encountered in connection with hunting rites:

A long time ago they made arrows of lightning for the Indians. There was one little cloud up in the sky, and the lightning from there killed a deer. All the time the Indians used to eat antelopes and deer killed by lightning.

One time a bunch of men just like these Indians around here got together and were talking. They said, "If we have lightning to kill things, pretty soon there will not be anything left on this world." So the old men talked about making arrows out of carrizo. They took this reed which is hollow and put inside it a foreshaft with a mark like a crawling snake.[24] They could shoot with it then. They did not have guns in those days. The Indians had bows and arrows in those days, but they could not kill anything. The lightning would kill things for them before this, but they could not find any game. Now the lightning would not help them any longer.

One time they were almost starving. One man went out hunting and was trailing some deer tracks. It was flat all over and there was a little hole out there with deer tracks around it, but the man could not find the deer. He was looking around where the deer tracks were and he saw a man coming out of the hole.

The man said to him, "What are you looking for? You have been looking for a long time and you don't find anything."

The hunter said, "I am looking for deer. Their tracks are fresh around here, but I can't find them."

The other man said, "Deer? What do you mean by saying 'deer'? I guess you must mean my horses." Then this man added, "They were here this morning and I just put them in the hole a little while ago." And then this man told the hunter, "I will give you some ceremonial power and from now on you can see the deer and you will have plenty to eat." This is why Indians can now kill deer.

When the hunter went back to camp that night, the others asked him where he got the power to kill deer. They kept on asking and asking, but the hunter would not tell them, for the man at the hole had told him not to tell, saying, "Even if you come to other camps, don't tell or you won't get anything to eat from me." But the Indians kept on asking and after a while the hunter got angry and told them. And from that time on they were starving again.

Before continuing to another story which emphasizes the importance of these animal homes, it is necessary to introduce a belief relating to the hunt:

[24] This refers to the fluting on the arrow.

The old people are still afraid when the deer goes in a sunwise circle around them and runs to the east. They say that when this happens a person has to follow the deer and he turns into a deer. Several times when I've been hunting they have run around and nearly made a circle. Then the thing to do is to get ahead of them or shoot them. This fear of being circled is for deer or antelope.

The account in which the concept appears is as follows:

A young man went out with his bow and arrows to hunt antelopes on the prairies. He found a bunch of them. He was wearing an antelope mask and got close to them with it. He was trying to get close enough to shoot with the arrow.

They started to run before he got close enough to shoot. They ran in a sunwise circle around him and came back to the same place. Then they ran to the east. He ran after them. The antelopes ran out on the plains to a place where there was a little hill. Underneath the hill was a hole. They went in the hole, and this man went in too. He changed into an antelope.

The boy didn't come home. Two days passed and then his father and kinfolk trailed him. They saw where he had stood, where the antelopes had circled him, and where he had run after them. They trailed him to the hole and saw his track there in the fine dust.

They went home and hired a man who knew Antelope. A group came back with him to the hole and he sang. He tried to make the boy come back. He sang and prayed for four nights. The next morning the young man came up. He told them to go away from the hole. They did.

Then he said to his father, "I can't come back. You've got to get used to being without me. Do not think of me any more. The reason I don't come back is that I have many children now. I can show you my children. I can't leave them." He called his father to the hole. "Tell the men to wait for you. You can come in my home with me."

The father said, "All right," and went down in the hole with his son. He told the men to wait for him.

They went into a place like this earth. There was a sun in there and mountains. The young man showed his father many little antelopes and deer. That's what he meant by his children. He called the place in there Antelope Home. It is like summer there always, and the ground is covered with fine, soft dirt.

The boy told his father many things. Then he came up on top with his father. He told his father to go home with his friends. He said to his father, "Maybe one year from now, maybe three years from now, I'll come to you again. When you are hunting antelopes and you see one big one behind, that will be I. If you want to kill two or three, I'll help you, for when you come I'll smell you and let you come close."

It is the one who claims special help from Deer who uses it in ceremonial contexts most often, but the deer is so important that it is of use to others as well:

If you have a good deer dog, burn deerskin and make him inhale it. Then he becomes a good hunter. I had a sick hunting dog. I tried everything. The dog was going down. I hated to lose him. So I got deerskin and rags and burned them together and made the dog inhale the smoke. He got well too. I tried it the last thing.

Buckskin, especially from deer which have been caught in head nooses or otherwise killed without damage to the hide, is in great demand for ceremonial gifts and for the making of amulets. "It is the holy hide, used for ceremonial purposes. It is supposed to come from a strangled deer, and the skin is supposed to be unblemished. Child of the Water used it so on earth; that is why."

When a hunter kills a deer, the carcass, the hide, and even the offal are treated according to prescribed rule, but, since all hunters observe these usages, a description of them is deferred until hunting methods are treated.

Bear.—A vision journey which resulted in the acquisition of a bear ceremony is described by the son of the man who became a bear shaman:

My father went across the plains twice, and the second time he slept at a place just beyond the White Sands. He usually found his tribe in the foothills at Hot Springs.

The second time, when he was sleeping at the place, something came to him. It was close to the springs. He was a little up the hills on a rock. He built a fire and went to sleep. He made a mattress of grass.

Close to morning he was sleeping there. He was sound asleep. It touched him and told him to awake. It had something to tell him. He pushed the cover off his head, and there sat a silver-tip bear. It spoke in a human way to him and told him it was time for him to get up and that he was about to get something to know and to travel by.

He got up. He knew that a door was open to him. He just walked right in, into the rocks. He was led into a room, and the bear changed itself into the form of a human and told him to follow wherever he went.

And so he showed him through the gate where the striking rocks were working, hitting against each other all the time. But they went through. Then they came to a place where four points of rock went back and forth. They also walked through that. They came to another rock that was rolling and was in the form of a round ball, just like a hill. It hit the bank on the other side all the time. But they walked over it and didn't even notice it strike the bank. Then they came to the swinging rock door, and it worked as in many other places.

Then they came to two big bears, black and white, at a gate. My father's guide told him to go on and they went through. On further they came to two big snakes, a black one and a white one. But they went through. This time something they never had seen before was present in the cave. It was the wolf, the big timber wolf. There were two, a black one and a white one. The wolf spoke to him, but he went on.

Then on further they came to two geese, a black one and a white one. When they saw my father, they tried to fly, but they came to the ground all the time because they felt pretty good. They said, "We know you. We have known you all the time." That's what the geese said.

Everything went smoothly until they started to cross a place where there were two moving logs used for a bridge. After my father crossed this bridge, he came into another more beautiful place. He asked the guide what this place was. He told him that it was the home of Summer[25] right there, but he passed through that place and then went to a crossing where a spider had a web for a bridge. He also crossed this without trouble.

Then he came to a still more beautiful place. Very pretty flowers were growing there. All of these spoke. He asked what this place was, and the bear told him that this was the home of the flowers and the herbs used for curing men all over the world. "This is Medicine's home."

He went on. Then came the humans. The humans were working out in the fields. They ran toward him and tried to show him many [supernatural] things. He paid no attention to them.

Then he came to a place where there was nothing but beautiful women. There were girls only there, dressed like White Painted Woman, who had just gone through the puberty ceremony. The girl's ceremony was shown him there. That was the home of the girl's puberty rite. But he paid no attention to this either.

On he went. He came to another land, and you could hear the drums beating steadily. It was even more beautiful. There were different kinds of Black Ones and Mountain Spirits there with different markings. It all belonged to the girl's puberty rite. The man said to him, "If you want to be the leader of the Mountain Spirits, you can take those four Mountain Spirits there. They are used in every way. They are the leading Mountain Spirits, stronger than any you saw in any other caves." There were twelve there altogether. His guide said, "You can use only four a night. If sickness is in the country, you can use them." But my father said, "No," and went on.

Then he was led out into the further end, and out before him was a big man. There were four tables. The man showed him all, but my father said, "No, I want to go to one stronger than you."

The man said, "No, they usually go no farther. This is the best." But my father said, "No," and wouldn't take any of it.

He went into another room, and there in the middle sat another man with a chair that turned either way. From him shone all kinds of light. And all around him was green fruit.

[25] The personification of summer is not unusual in these stories.

The man studied my father. He said, "There is no human who has come this far, passing the first man. What do you come for? You see many fruits here, and there are things here that are valuable above all. What you ask for your own good, for raising your children, I will give you."

My father said, "I come for one that is strongest. Are you the strongest?"

"No, there are two above me."

Then my father went on. He came to another man who was shining with a yellow light before him. The light made it appear as though the wind were blowing pollen from the trees around him, but it was not. This man also knew that my father was not going to stop there. So he brought before him two yellow horses with white tails. And a sort of wagon was there.

My father got in the wagon[26] with a guide, and they came to a gate, a big white gate. Everything was as white as could be, even the trees and fruit. Even the faces of the people there shone, and before him he saw all kinds of things. He bowed down four times, and the fourth time he was before a man in a big white chair who had a white staff in his right hand. This man was the last one. This man asked him how he got in and such things as that. My father told him all.

"We had better be moving," the man said, "for it is getting daylight."

So he listened and said "Yes" to everything my father asked him. Everything my father wanted, he got.

"I hate to see poor people sick. I hate it when people are walking along the road poor and without horses. I want to know what is best to do for them. You can give me what you think is best."

This man sang and performed what was given my father. And it raised him as though he had wings. There was nothing but clouds around him. Before him everything shook, and there was lightning and thunder. Much was shown my father, terrible things [witchcraft] and how to stop them.

The man handed him a staff. You'll always have this. It will speak itself. It must never be lost." He told him what was best. And this, they say, was the power of Bear.

After this he knew all the people and their ways and their thoughts, and what was going to be done, and what was going to happen to them. Afterward he did much healing, even for the whites and Mexicans. He was known in Comanche country and by the Navaho.

The curing ceremony which stemmed from this experience was recalled by the same informant:

He held a bear ceremony for four nights to heal the sick. That's as long as he would continue it. He cured many diseases through it. He used it once on a severe case of pneumonia, the worst case of pneumonia I ever saw. This was right out in the hills. The girl had hemorrhages with it. I thought she was going to die.

[26] Note the elements of European influence in this story.

My father sang the songs of the bear and found out what had to be done. He was told that a mixture of different herbs had to be given right away. That was to stop the bleeding. They got the strongest herb first. This one was pointed out by the bear. My mother went and got it, and that night it was given to the girl in four doses. It was given in pollen, and the bowl was lifted to her head four times, then to her lips four times, and she drank it from the side that was marked with pollen.

The next thing was to get after the pneumonia. The girl was stronger now. My mother mixed up the second dose of the same medicine they had given her before. They thought the second dose would surely stop the hemorrhage for good. They gave the medicine to her four times again.

Then my father started in. He took the right front paw of a bear, warmed it, and put it on her chest where it pained most. Then he took a bowl and put it to her chest. He sucked. Blood and pus and suds came out and foamed up. He did that four times. They had real good medicine for the pneumonia. It was the blazing star.[27] It was ground fine, mixed with grease and water; then they rubbed her with it and wrapped her up with some of it on her chest. They tried to make this ceremony short because she was weak.

The second night it went the same way. My father sang two songs. He marked her with pollen. He used the bear paw, putting pollen on it first. He sucked pus out of her again. It came out easily this time.

Now he waited two days before doing anything more for her, but he had my mother continue to give her medicine. He saw that the girl was gaining and getting well.

The third night he started in, he didn't know whether to suck or not. "There is no use to suck. Let me look at her," he said. After singing he looked and saw there was just a little pus left. "I don't think it is necessary to suck again," he said. But he asked the bear. The bear said he had better take it out because that little bit might get bigger. So he sucked it out. Before he sucked he always marked the place with pollen and put pollen in his mouth.

The girl said she could breathe much better. She said she wanted to get well quickly. She prayed all through the ceremony. That's why she got well so quickly. Then the fourth night of the ceremony came. It was a short ceremony this night. The girl was getting along nicely now. They just gave her the medicine.

Another account of the acquisition of a bear ceremony is of special interest because the final paragraph suggests the use together of multiple powers:

A long time ago a group of men went far south looking for horses and cattle. All the party except one man got killed, and, in trying to make his way back, he got lost. In those days they dressed in a buckskin loincloth and buckskin jacket.

---

[27] Two plants commonly known as blazing star are *Liatris punctata* and *Mentzelia multiflora*.

When they were cold they made a fire, pushed the ashes away, put grass on the hot ground, and slept there. It kept them warm. This man had nothing with him to eat, and the rain came and the buckskin got wet and stiff. It became very cold, and he nearly froze.

He went to a hole in a cliff for shelter. Then he heard a sound above, and he went up there. He saw a great cave between two rocks. He went in and found a mother bear and two little bears in there. Bear looked at him and he talked to Bear. "I'm about to die. Give me something to eat."

Bear said, "Come in."

He went in. The bear rapped on the stone wall, and a door opened. In there was a room with a fireplace. The bear woman had a shallow basket in there, and it was filled with acorns and wild fruit. She pounded it up nicely and gave it to him. He sat by the fire and warmed himself and ate. When this man got back to his people, he told them that bears were just like human beings. "They talk like us and live as we do. When they go out they turn to bears," he said.

When he had eaten, the bear said, "My husband is mean. I don't know what he will do to you. Sometimes he gets after me. But he is very fond of these children. Take one of my babies and put it in your lap when my husband comes and maybe he won't hurt you."

About dark Bear came. As soon as he came under the cliff he smelled man. He got angry and growled like a dog. His wife heard him and told the man to take the baby on his lap. Big Bear came in looking angry but didn't say anything when he saw the child on the man's lap. The woman said nothing.

Then Bear said to his wife, "Did you feed this man? Where did he come from?"

His wife said, "He came in here nearly dying. I fed him and warmed him."

Bear sat down and said nothing. Then he began to question the man. "Do you want anything more? You can have more." He acted like this because of the baby.

"I've had plenty."

"Do you want to stay overnight?"

"Yes."

So they put the man in another room that opened when they rapped on the wall. The next morning they opened the door and told the man to come out. They gave him a good breakfast of all kinds of Indian fruit and meat.

"I've had enough," the man said when he had finished.

Then Bear told him, "Go on top of this hill and you'll find a cave there. In it is water. Wash yourself and then get some good-smelling weeds, mix white paint with them, and rub them over your body and face. It will make you smell better. You smell bad; I noticed you all night."[28]

The man did as he was told. He went to the pool and bathed and swam.

[28] This is simply a reversal of the notion that the smell of bears is offensive and dangerous to human beings.

Then he mixed weeds and white paint and put it over his body. He came back, and Bear said that he didn't smell him any more.

Then Bear told him to take a good rest. "Meanwhile I'll go over and hunt up your people."

He stayed at Bear's home four days. Four days later Bear got home again. He lay down. "I'm very tired," he said. "I found your people far away. To-morrow we'll start out, and I'll take you to them."

The next morning the man started out with the father bear. They walked all day. About evening they came close to a mountain.

"Where do you want to stay?" Bear asked.

"In a hollow place," the man said.

"No," the bear told him. "It's better on top. It's warmer up there."

They went to the top and stayed there overnight. In the morning they started again. The next day toward sundown they went on top again. The next morning they started and walked all day. At night they went on top again. They carried dried beef with cooked fat and berries in it. The fourth morning they arose before sunup.

"Maybe we will find your people before noon," Bear said. "Then I'll go home."

About noon they found many Indian camps. Bear said, "There are your people. I'm going home now. After this if you or your children get lost, don't be afraid of Bear. Go to Bear's home." Then Bear went home, and the man went into his camp.

He found his wife and children cutting their hair off. In the old days they sometimes cut the hair short and sometimes cut it all off for mourning. They had killed all his horses and thrown away all the things he owned.

That bear had given him a ceremony with songs and prayers when he was in that cave. Then, when he got back to his people, he helped them when they got sick. When he healed sick people, he took a circular piece of rawhide, covered it with buckskin, and painted Bear, Lightning, and Buffalo on it. That was because Bear had told him that Lightning and Buffalo were his friends and their powers all worked together. He would make this for people and put a buckskin cord on it and later give it to them to wear.

Coyote, dog, wolf.—Details of a typical coyote ceremony have already been given[29] and need not be repeated here.

While sickness can be contracted from a dog, at least by a child, a coyote or wolf ceremony is thought sufficient to remove it. A certain amount of ceremonialism has grown up around dogs, but these usages are for the benefit of the dogs and not to cure ailments they have brought.

[29] See pp. 40–41.

When you want to train a dog to be a good hunter or watchdog, burn an eagle feather for it.

I wrap up an eagle feather in cloth with the kind of flies that bother animals. I burn this and throw a blanket over the dog's head so he can inhale the smoke.

If meat is rubbed on your feet and then given to a dog, that dog will stick by you and be a good watchdog. It will love you and guard you.

This is the way to make a dog good for trailing. Cut up four pieces of meat, spit on them, rub them on your moccasins to get some soil from there on them, put the meat in the dog's mouth, and talk to him, giving him instructions just as you would a boy.

Another way is to take a section of deer meat from the place where it swells between the two hoofs. Put this with the feather of the buzzard or crow. Put this to the windy side of the dog. Light it and make the dog inhale, saying to him, "May you keep the trail." We use the buzzard and crow because they fly all over and never miss a dead object. We use the deer meat so the dog will go after deer.

A friend told me to chop up a little rattlesnake into four parts and to give it to a dog with his meat. This is to be done when you want a fierce dog. It makes him fierce all right, but it is too dangerous. The dog is hard to handle then, even by the owner. The dog gets too mean, like a mountain lion. But if a man is far out alone and is afraid, it might be done.

There is a certain prickly pear that is called "dog medicine." It is a general tonic for a dog. You put it into his mouth whole.

The wolf has been known to offer a ceremony and special aid:

He smoked and prayed and went to bed again. He slept a little while and then was waked up again. Before him sat a big timber wolf, white as snow. It was the most beautiful creature, he said, he ever saw. He wanted to touch it but was afraid to. Then Wolf took its paw and touched him and told him he needn't be afraid. So he touched the wolf. The fur felt very soft and fine and warm. He touched the four legs of the wolf, then touched his own legs and said, "Let my legs be as strong as yours."

The wolf spoke to him and said, "I've seen you. . . . . I came to you myself. I will add what I can to the strength of your legs. You have done the right thing. . . . ."

Horse (*mule, burro*).—A characteristic horse ceremony was obtained by a man who was raiding for horses:

Two men started south from their home. On the way a horse spoke to one of them and gave him a ceremony. It happened this way. They were raiding for horses. They got to a town south of Tucson and found some horses there. They began to drive them off. At a certain place they stopped to rope horses to ride.

They had to run the horses up the side of a mountain and were at the top. One of them caught a gentle horse and got on it. The other roped a wild one, and when he was about to get on, it pitched with him and threw him off. He lay there as though he were dead. Only his throat moved a little.

The man who was left sat there crying. He didn't know what to do. He had a little buckskin pouch of pollen tied around his waist. There was one old sorrel horse standing near by. He marked the forehead of the horse with pollen and asked the horse to help him restore his companion. He led the horse to the man, from the east, and the horse put his nose to the man four times and neighed. In the same way he led the horse to the injured man from the south, the west, and the north, and the horse acted the same each time. Then the injured man began to stir, and he got up and asked what had happened. The sorrel horse went back to the herd then.

Later this sorrel horse talked to the man it had cured. It told him where the two men should camp that night on the return journey. They followed this advice. The horse told him where to camp for the second night too. This was at an open place, but the horse said, "Do not be afraid even though it is out in the open." They camped in that place and were not disturbed. The third night the horse told him that they should camp at a place called Sand House. On the fourth night the horse told him that they should stop between two mountains.

Then the horse spoke to the one it had cured. It told him, "I'm old and I'm no longer strong. I'd like to take you back to the place where you live, but I can't make it. A man who is thin can make it back to his home. But horses are different. We have to be fat and strong. So after you start out tomorrow you are going to miss me. But don't look for me. I am going back to my home. But I'll tell you now just how to continue your journey, where to stop each night, and where your relatives are now."

And the horse told him, "I give these songs to you. You will be a shaman through the horse. If anyone falls off a horse and is injured, you can heal him with these songs. These songs will cure even if bones are broken. And here is some medicine to use for those who are hurt inside.[30] But if the large cords at the back of the neck are broken, the ones which hold up the head, this ceremony will not be able to restore the person."

The men continued the journey as the horse directed and got back safely to their people.

How this man effectively used the ceremony he thus obtained is the subject of another narrative:

A leading man rode out with others to get horses that they had tied out somewhere. The rest came back, but this leading man was still missing. His family were worried. Then someone saw his horse standing on a ridge. It was saddled,

---

[30] Possibly "horse medicine" (*Eriogonum jamesii*), of which it is said, "It is a plant used in the horse ceremony. It is chewed for luck with horses. Give it to horses, too, when they are sick."

but the man was not on it. A group went out to look for him. They found him in a gully, unconscious and badly hurt. He had started from one hill to go to another where he had a horse tied to a tree, when the horse he was riding stepped into a badger hole, stumbled, and threw him.

They put him in a blanket, and four men, one carrying each end, brought him home. They asked the man who had learned the ceremony from the horse if he would bring the leader back to life. He said he would do it.

He told the people to get four poles like those which are used for the ceremonial tepee of the girl's puberty rite. The shaman had the people make a tepee, one big enough so that the horse could get in. He had them bring the injured man in there. The doorway was to the east, and for a covering to it the shaman hung up a big buckskin with the head downward and touching the ground. They brought the horse which had caused the accident around facing the door and took the rope off him.

The shaman, who was in the tepee, sang one song. The horse did not move. The shaman went on to his second song. The horse just stood there and made no sound. The shaman sang his third song. The horse stood in the same place. The shaman grew angry now. He spoke to the horse and said, "Why don't you cure this poor man? You are the only one that can help him. You had better do it without delay." The son of the shaman came out of the tepee now. He was angry too. He said to the horse, "You have done enough harm. There is no use thinking more evil things. You'd better neigh and do what you are supposed to." He hit the horse in the mouth.

Then the horse began to walk to the tepee by itself. The horse stopped at the door, put its nose under the buckskin, pushed it up, and walked in. Then the horse approached the man from each of the four directions in sunwise order and neighed each time. Then it left the tepee. The shaman sang his last song.

In these songs the parts of the horse are given names, and the saddle and saddle blanket have different names too. The back of the saddle is called the evening star, the sides of the saddle are called clouds, the saddle blanket a cirrus cloud, the saddle strap lightning, the saddle horn the sun, the cinch the rainbow, and the buckle the moon. The forehead of the horse is called abalone and the ears are the whirlwind.

When the last song was over, the man who had been lying there got up and asked what had happened. He was all right after that.

A celebrated cure achieved by a woman shaman of the Eastern Chiricahua band is of particular interest in that the use of the "big tepee" has encouraged the practitioner to extend the analogy and to draw upon a number of the features of the girl's puberty rite:

I saw an old woman who knew the ceremony of the horse. She died long ago. She had songs for the bridle and for every part of the horse. She had many horses, and all were nice and fat because she knew songs for them. She would take wild horses and saddle them up. They were always gentle to her. When anyone fell off a horse and got hurt, they went to her and she cured them. I'll tell you what she did one time. I was so little I can't remember what was done in there, though I saw it. But my folks and others remembered and told me.

One time a young man got a bunch of horses. With the others there were wild horses and mules which had never been saddled or roped. He tried to get one wild horse out of that bunch. He roped it and put the halter on it. He staked it out for a while. Then he turned it loose on a long rope. He watered it and tried to pull it back. It tried to get away. It circled him two or three times and then started to run. The rope caught on his legs and he was dragged over a rough place. Finally the rope broke and he lay there. His face, arms, and legs were skinned. He was unconscious.

They picked him up and carried him to his tepee. Then his people went to this woman and asked her to sing over the man. She came and looked at him. "He's pretty much bruised up," she said. She didn't want to do it. But they begged her. At last she said she would.

She started to work. I was there, just a little fellow then. She said, "I want a bridle, a saddle blanket, a saddle, and a whip." She asked for those four things because her power told her to. They gave these to her. She started to sing. First she told the father of the boy to rope that same horse. He did.

"Tie him close to the tepee."

They tied the horse near by, under a big tree. She had them tie the head so that the horse couldn't eat grass or drink water. "If that horse eats or drinks during this ceremony, the boy will get worse," she said. She sang over this young man four nights. She sang from sunset to sunrise for the four nights. The horse had nothing to eat or drink for the four days and nights.

They were in a tepee like the one the Mescalero have. The last day at sunrise she told them to take the cover off and leave nothing but the poles standing. Then she told them to clean up the inside. The sick man was lying there. She painted the sun on the palm of her hand with red paint and pollen. She sang and rubbed it off on the man's face. Then she turned the horse loose. She took the rope off. Everybody got away. The horse began to paw the ground and neighed four times. Then it started toward the man. The horse went in there. The woman said, "Take the blanket off that man," and they did so.

The horse licked the man all over and rubbed him all over with his nose. Everyone watched. The horse was on the east side and it pawed there. Then it went to the south side and pawed the ground. And it did this in turn to the west and north. Then it went around the man four times and out to the east. It looked around for other horses. It saw some and ran to them. Then this man's senses began to come back to him and he got well.

A less elaborate ceremony, performed in an emergency, was described:

It happened at Baharito. We were driving a bunch of wild horses. T. had the gentle horses and some of us younger men were running the wild ones. P.'s horse got his foot in a hole. The horse fell with him. The rope was caught around P.'s knee and he lay like dead with his mouth open when we came up. After the horse fell, it got up and walked a little ways and stood there. I was going to P., but Old T. said, "Get away and don't touch him."[31] So we went away and talked of other things.

T. went to the east side and walked toward him, praying softly to himself. I could not hear what he said. He touched him, kicked him four times under the foot, put pollen in his mouth, and told him to get up. And P. did. T. went back to where the horse fell and got dirt from four tracks and put it in P.'s mouth. Then he got saliva from the mouth of the horse and put it all over P.'s clothes.

In recording ceremonial songs, the details of another horse ceremony were learned:

This is R.'s horse ceremonial song. We were driving horses to Whitetail where we were going to brand them. This happened at Whitetail Spring. There were only three horses left in the corral. W. went across. Two others were in there roping horses. The three horses started at once and knocked W. down. He was nearly dead; he didn't come to for three or four hours.

Then R. worked on him. That's how I heard this song. He sang more than this one song, but I just caught this one. If you ever get hurt from a horse, it will fix you up. He used some herbs in his ceremony too. . . . .

These are the words of the song:

> The sun's horse is a yellow stallion;
> His nose, the place above his nose, is of haze,
> His ears, of the small lightning, are moving back and forth.
> He has come to us.
> The sun's horse is a yellow stallion,
> A blue stallion, a black stallion;
> The sun's horse has come out to us.

The horse ceremony is of great importance also in taming wild horses and in securing fresh horses on raids. When it is used for these purposes, the rite is confined principally to songs and prayers.

Some knew how to sing before going on a raid. They sang to corralled horses, so the horses would give them good luck.

Before leaving for raid or war, they often have a ceremony conducted by one who knows the ceremony of the horse. This is so good horses will fall into their

---

[31] After a mishap with a horse, recovery is speedier if the injured person is not touched until a horse shaman takes charge.

hands, so that their horses will be strong and carry them through, and so that all in the party will have good luck.

Gambling is a serious enterprise, and horse-racing is one of its important forms:

A horse shaman performs a ceremony over race horses used for gambling. I have seen horses worked over like this. Horses which have been taken care of by a horse shaman in this way always have an eagle feather tied just where the tail bone leaves off. The owner of the horse usually gives the horse shaman something that has to do with a horse for his pay—a saddle, a blanket, a bridle, or something like that.

Anything fast, like the coyote, the fox, the wind, or clouds, should be used in songs to make a horse run fast.[32]

When a valuable horse is to be gelded or is injured or sick (though "if a horse has been witched, you can't cure it"), the owner is likely to consult a horse shaman.

T . . . . . knew the ceremony of the horse. He knew a lot about the sickness of this animal. I saw him castrate them. People brought the horses to him to castrate. He treated horses that couldn't pass water and some that were going blind too.

But often the owner, though he is not a horse shaman, injects some ceremonialism into his care of his horse:

If a horse can't pass water, we have a little ceremony for it. Take a rope, hit the horse on the back with it, and tie a knot in the rope. Do this four times. Say prayers meanwhile. Don't hit the horse hard enough to hurt it. Then trot the horse a few hundred yards and bring it back to the same position.

When a horse gets blind, they cut the vein leading down from the eye that's getting bad. The horse gets well then. This is done to sheep now too. I have done it to both. If a horse is sluggish, it is given a root called "black medicine" which is put in oats or mescal or something the horse likes.

We practice bloodletting on a horse which is lazy. Then we put turquoise on the cut.

Horses that are scary and jump sideways are fixed with eagle feathers. These are tied on the mane or to the bridle. Then the horse doesn't get scared. I did it like that at Whitetail myself.

[32] The hummingbird is used as an aid in racing too: "Its feathers help in making a man or a horse speedy."

As various domestic animals have become more numerous, the horse shaman has seemed to be the logical person to cure them and is now thought of as the one who "knows a lot about [domestic] animal sickness." "These are the ones who take care of the diseases of animals; they have a general knowledge of animals."

There is some difference of opinion concerning the material benefits of a horse ceremony to the horse shaman himself. The story of the woman horse shaman whose horses were sleek and fine seems to bear out the statement of an informant who said, "Some persons have a ceremony from the horse and have fit horses all the time." But the opposite view is held by others. "I think that N. had power from the horse. His horses were poor. Some people say that a man with a horse ceremony has pretty poor horses. He can help others but not himself."

Wild goose.—An excellent example of the special abilities which a shaman may acquire because of the characteristics of his supernatural guardian, is power obtained from the wild goose:

During the old times when Geronimo was around doing mischief, the Chiricahua used to get a band of ten or twelve and go to the Mexican border and drive cattle home. A certain man got tired and was left behind. It got to the point where they couldn't help him, so they left him behind. They thought he would catch up. He was tired, hungry, discouraged, and had given up. He was thinking all sorts of unpleasant things. It was pretty bad.

All at once Goose appeared to him and said, "What's the matter?" He said, "I'm in a bad fix."

Goose said, "All right, I'll give you a certain ceremony, and you must obey. You must follow my directions exactly."

He gave the man four songs. The goose spoke of feathers; it told him he had to rub them on his right side. Goose is long winded and goes for many days. Goose said to him, "I will give you my endurance."

It happened that way. He caught up to the others. Everyone was surprised. The man was able to pass over broad flat lands without being tired out after that. The one who told me this story says that he had this man sing over him; then he won an important race.

Nighthawk.—An informant tells how he was cured by the power of Nighthawk in a rite jointly conducted by two shamans:

Old Man D. and T. knew the ceremony of the nighthawk. I saw them perform it several times. They sang together. Both knew the same thing; one learned it from the other. T. learned it from D.

Once I was sick with a bad case of kidney trouble. I went to the agency doctor, and he told me I couldn't get well. He said that I'd have trouble all the way through and that one day it would kill me. One side of my face and one side of my body were swollen. I got out of that hospital. Then, because they were distant relatives of mine, these two men sang for me and told me not to be worried, that I was going to get well. P. was there, S., B. and his wife, and some other people, the relatives of my wife. We were not alone.

When they started to cure me, they first smoked. Then they used pollen, marking me on the face. Then they marked the faces of all who were present with pollen. I did it back to these two men, marked their faces with pollen, and the other people did it too. There were quite a few people present. The people always like to listen. Some heard there was going to be singing and just dropped in.

Then they started to sing. During the singing one of them was always drumming. Sometimes it was one of them, sometimes the other. They sang about the nighthawk, calling him Great Old Man Nighthawk, and asking him what it was best to do to get me well. They used feathers of the golden eagle. One had two of them sewed together and attached to his hand all the time.

Their power talked to them any time they asked him something, and they asked him questions right in the songs. Then they would look at each other and talk. One would say, "Do you hear that?" The other would answer, "Yes." But we couldn't hear a thing. Sometimes they got a message, but they would tell me they couldn't say anything about it until morning. They carried on the ceremony at night only for four nights.

When they first sang, Nighthawk spoke to them and said that they didn't have to be frightened, that I'd be going along all right in a few days. I had been laid up during February, March, and April. This was in late April.

Next Nighthawk told them that there was a woman present who knew herbs and that it was best to have her use certain herbs on me. This was my own mother. They directed her in what to do, according to the word of their power, and she went out and gathered all the best herbs.

All during their ceremony they learned many things about my future. They told me that in the future I was going to have land and own everything and have children too. They said the first was to be a boy, and it was. And they said, "You are not only going to have this boy but girls too. In the spring you are going to plow. You will look up and see just one little cloud. And it will open and rain first on your place." And it all really came true. In the spring I was plowing back of East Mountain. It rained first on my place. It did this for several years.

The ceremony helped me a great deal. D. told me not to eat liver until I got real well. By May, after the last snow, and when the birds first began to come, I was well. And so I think the power of the nighthawk was certainly strong.

Owl.—When individuals are first troubled by the call of an owl or by thoughts and dreams of the dead, there are measures they may take, even though they lay no claim to a ceremony from the owl. A man who was gathering wormwood (*Artemisia frigida*), one of the plants known as "ghost medicine,"[33] explained: "Sometimes when you feel nervous and don't sleep well, you fumigate the house with this. People use it after a funeral." Others tell of self-treatment that "could be tried by anyone."

For trouble with ghosts I use "ghost medicine" and also ashes. I put a cross of ashes on my forehead at night. The Silas John cross is used too. I used it last night. A black-handled knife under the pillow is good for this too.

By scarring your nose with a live coal, you keep ghosts away. You take a burning stick, wet it at one end, fix this end on your nose, and let it burn down so that it scars your nose. Then the ghost will fear you and keep away. Ashes can be put on the nose to keep away ghosts too.

But, though self-purification often succeeds in dispelling persecution, in a residue of cases the attacks are so acute that there is no recourse except to consult an owl shaman. The ghosts are of two kinds—those of enemy peoples and those of tribesman (often of deceased relatives). Correspondingly, there are owl shamans whose rites are effective against enemy ghosts, and there are those whose ceremonies banish tribesmen's ghosts.

Most cases of enemy-ghost sickness result from battles.[34] "If a man who had killed an enemy thought he couldn't stand the haunting, he went to a shaman who used an owl ceremony on him." "If you have enemy-ghost sickness, you take a black silk handkerchief, a cross, and a knife and give them to one who knows songs for this. Then he can work for you. I've seen it

[33] Others are squaw weed (*Senecio filifolius*) and sage (*Artemisia filifolia*).

[34] It is unlikely that enemy-ghost sickness was ever very prevalent. Despite general dislike of the sight of the dead, the ghosts of those known or continually opposed in life are more likely to be feared than are the ghosts of persons who fall under the general classification of "enemy." Some individuals evidently had very little apprehension concerning the enemy dead. One old warrior said, "We had little fear of killing at war. War was just a kind of sport. Few had fear of the dead enemy." Another man, when he was asked whether one who killed a member of another tribe was in danger, seemingly discounted the supernatural risks altogether, for he replied, "Yes, the enemy might plan a raid to avenge the death of the man he killed."

happen. Of the Chiricahua, R. is the only one now that knows the enemy-ghost ceremony."

Since the more usual type of ghost sickness results from persecution by the shade of a departed acquaintance or relative, the period immediately following a death is a trying one, and a preventive rite may be performed:

The Chiricahua, if someone dies, may call in a shaman to perform a ceremony. The day after the dead person is put away, this shaman will go through a ceremony for them. The members of the family of the dead person look ragged. They have put on their oldest clothes and cut their hair. The men and women of the family have taken a little hair off, but from the children they have taken all the hair off. They have burned up the clothes they wore before the death. They move camp in any direction and go anywhere. Perhaps other people sympathize with them and give them something. Then the shaman comes over and sings for these people. This is to keep the ghost away. He goes through the ceremony he knows. Some shamans paint the faces of the mourners red; some use white paint. Each shaman has his own way.

Most ghost ceremonies, however, are conducted to cure ghost sickness that has already been contracted. An owl shaman has supplied an interpretation of his own ceremony and an explanation of how he obtained it.

I cannot tell how my great-grandmother got this ceremony, but my grandmother got it from her. My grandmother cured many. She could only cure those who were sick from the owl or whom witches had made sick through the owl. Owl sickness just affects a person from the heart to the head. The Mexicans killed my grandmother a long time ago. I got the ceremony from a strong memory. I kept in mind what she did.

After my grandmother died, an owl nearly killed a little child. Other people knew that my grandmother had known about Owl. They guessed that I might have the power too. So a certain woman came to me for help and asked me to try this ceremony. I went to her home with her. I cured that child the same night. I found that the power of my grandmother wanted to work through me too.

Now I can pray and I am able to get sick people well. My power can be used only at night though. When I hold my ceremony, if it doesn't work after two nights, I give up, for something else is wrong. . . . . Or perhaps a witch prevents the cure. Some witches have great power, sometimes more than I have. I can only try to help a person for two nights. Then I have to give them up. The person has to go to a more powerful shaman then, for some are more powerful than I am. I cure through song, prayer, and strong belief with the ceremony of the owl.

If an owl has scared a person into unconsciousness, someone comes for me, and I go to the person's camp for two nights. Those who want me to work for them have to give me a black-handled knife.[35] That is the rule: without it I cannot work. They give it to me before the ceremony. When my ceremony can help, even though an owl has frightened a person and he is unconscious the first night, he is supposed to get all right the second night.

I work with ashes. That is part of the power. My grandmother used ashes and nothing else. Before I do anything else I dip my hand in ashes and make a sign of the cross with the thumb and the first finger of my right hand. Then before praying I rub ashes on the patient. I mark the patient with ashes on the forehead, the top of the head, and the breast.

Then I roll a cigarette. The sick person must puff toward the east. In case the person is unconscious, I do it for him. Then I pray to the directions and send his sickness away. On the patient's head there is something that I can see. I see it that way on a sick person. And I see it on the breast of the sick person, something that sticks out.[36] I paint the body of the patient with pollen, on both shoulders and back, going around clockwise. I say prayers to the directions too. I talk to the darkness [owl].

In my prayer to the east I say, "Let no one come back from the east to bother this poor person again." I say this so all bad luck regarding the owl will fly away from the patient. Talking to the owl, I say, "You are the one who has done this. Never do this again."

At the south I say, "The downy feathers of the owl must not come back to harm this person again. Stay away from this person altogether, because you are the one who harmed him."

Next I turn toward the west and say, "This person doesn't want to eat. He has something on his breast. Therefore do not allow anybody to come back to harm this sick one. You are able to restore him as he used to be. For your own sake and his, help him to get up again."

I speak to the north now, and I call on darkness too. "Make this person strong. Help him eat again. Give him life again. And never do this again. Let him live to an old age in this world."

I pray for just a little while, just as long as these prayers last. Then I start the songs. The first song mentions the east and the south. The only words are, "East, in its head, you listen." This is repeated four times. Then I turn to the south and sing, "South, you listen." The second song just repeats, "West, you listen; north, you listen." After these songs everything evil from the heart to the head comes out. The third song mentions the flint cross. I make a low humming noise four times at the end of this song. The fourth song says, "In the

[35] Probably a long black flint or obsidian blade preceded the black-handled knife as a ceremonial present for this rite.

[36] The materialization of ghost sickness as a shapeless black or white object has been mentioned before. The inference is that this is really the ghost or the owl, and sometimes it is said to assume the shape of one or the other.

morning early, it goes to 'Cut-Grass-Sitting.' " "Cut-Grass-Sitting" is the name of a place. It is called on because the song [ceremony] started from there. It is a place in Old Mexico on the other [west] side of the Rio Grande.

Then I pray again, saying, "By tomorrow morning may all evil disappear and go to the east. May all the sickness that was above the heart in this person go to the west. From now on let him eat again." After this the patient says to me, "I was sick. Now I am well. I never knew you. Now you have made me well. I am well again. I am as I was before. If something like this happens to me again, I will appeal to you."

After the four songs and prayer the ceremony is over for the night. I do this for two nights. The songs and prayers are the same each night. I tell the sick person to put the black-handled knife under his pillow for the two nights so he won't get scared. And I tell him, "Don't eat tongue or liver."

Summer tanager.—Nothing is said in the following tale of a curing ceremony from the tanager, but it is evident that the bird acted as a guardian spirit:

J. M. tells this one. During his war days when he was young, there was a boy he used to go with, just a young boy. This boy always sang like the summer tanager, that entirely red bird. One time this boy camped out alone and was lost from the group that was out raiding for horses. He was left at a water hole. They were to pick him up on their return. Instead of picking him up, they went right by and left him. He was crying there, for he had little to eat.

While he was crying, something lit in the tree above him. He paid no attention, for he was still crying. Then this bird came to him and touched him on the head. "Don't cry. I have come to show you many things and to lead you to a good country where you will be happy always. All your people are worrying about you because you haven't come back. The ones who left you are already at home. They brought a good bunch of mules and a herd of horses. But there are a few horses and mules left, the ones that they lost on the way. Take them and drive them back. I will go with you. Take my tail feathers. They will talk to you and warn you of danger.

"The ones who left you here are saying wrong things about you to your family. They are saying that you are dead. Your family is going to wait four days and then cut their hair. So be back before four days. I'm going to lead you. Turn this horse loose, catch the others, ride the black one first, then the second day ride the gray horse. There will be seven horses (yours will be the eighth) and two mules."

The boy was shown that he could see at night and see through mountains, and whenever he asked a question it was always answered. He always had the feathers ready in his hand so he could talk to them. The tanager also turned into a man and rode with him.

Before sunrise of the fourth day the people at camp saw someone coming.

The men got weapons ready. They went out to kill whoever was coming and to take the horses away. They saw two men coming, but only one rode up.

The boy's father met him and asked, "Who was the other man?" The boy said that he was alone. They did not believe him.

Reptiles.—How one man obtained a snake ceremony which he used with signal success years later is related in the following account:

They say this man knew snake power better than anyone in the tribes around here. On his hat he wore the rattlers of a snake and two eagle feathers. No matter how badly a person was bitten, he never held his ceremony in the day, but always at night. He said he could cure snake bite on humans or horses.

This is how he got his power. He thought a bush was burning and went to see whether it was and what had started it. He found that the bush was not really burning and saw a big snake move from it. The snake was one such as had never been seen anywhere. It had red and white stripes, yellow streaks on its side, and very red eyes. The way it was throwing its tongue out was like a fire burning. The man started to speak to it, but the snake didn't say anything to him. So the man went off.

That night he camped out in a lonely place, for his home was very far away. The raiding party he had been with was scattered by a band of soldiers. He had only one blanket. He built a fire, roasted a rabbit, and, after eating it and saying a few prayers, went to bed.

He was sound asleep when all at once something touched him. He threw the blanket off his head and looked around but didn't see anything. He thought it might have been a branch fallen off the tree under which he was sleeping, and he started to cover up again. But he heard a sound, like something rubbing against the tree, and a second time something touched him. He threw off the covers. Nothing was in sight. He was about to go to sleep for the third time when the thing came again. He paid no attention and tried to go to sleep. The same thing happened for the fourth time, and he thought he heard someone come down from the tree. He was pretty sure some man was playing a trick on him. It didn't seem to frighten him a bit. He heard a voice, but he just kept his head covered. He tried to recognize it, but he did not know the voice. He stayed still as the voice came closer.

The fourth time it spoke, the voice said, "Wake up! Get up! Someone is coming to see you. You've been asking for me. Here I am. What do you want?"

The man knew it was some kind of power, and, as he looked up, rubbing his eyes, he saw a large snake. He started to cry out but changed his mind. The snake told him not to be frightened, that it had come for a good purpose, to help him out and give him good things which he needed. He said, "Very well," and before Snake could speak again he marked it with piñon pollen.

Then the snake asked him what he wanted. The man said, "I want many good things, for I like to help others."

The snake said, "I'll show you where these things are. Stand up and come with me."

He looked at the snake again, and there was a handsome man, dressed in Indian clothes. He carried a rattle made of a wild gourd decorated with eagle feathers and with the feathers of many other birds.

A door opened in front of them on the side of a big rock. The sun was shining in there, and it looked like daylight. Inside they had to pass a big crevice, too wide to jump. A single spider had spun its thread across. The man asked, "How do we cross?" and the snake said, "I'll lead you. Follow me." The man said, "Two of us can't cross on that thread; it might break." Snake said, "Come." They both got on and stepped across. The man seemed to be walking on a wide board; the web felt stiff. It never bent or sagged.

After crossing this place, they came to another door. It was thrown open, and a stronger light shone ahead. A great black snake was in their path. It had a large mouth, and it rose up and struck at them. But the man was told to come ahead, and so he stepped in front of the snake and continued.

Then they came to a blue snake with white eyes. From its mouth came flames. They had to cross in front of this snake, and it bit at them. The man stopped, but his guide told him to come, and he passed right in front of it.

Now they came to another place. A door opened and a still stronger yellow light shone out. At the entrance was a yellow rock and a great yellow snake was coiled on it, striking at them. The snake moved and rolled around. The guide stepped right on top of the snake and told the man to follow.

Then they came to another big door. The guide spoke, and the door opened to them. Inside there was still more light, and it hurt the man's eyes. But his guide touched his eyes, and he could see again. There was a great white snake with a big white tongue there, rolling in their path. The tip of the tongue looked like fire, but there was no heat to it at all. The snake didn't seem to pay any attention to them. The guide told the man to continue. They had to crawl through the coils.

Finally they came to the place where there was a man sitting. He was in charge of all these snakes and was very powerful. This one spoke to the Chiricahua and said, "My child, where have you come from? No man has ever entered this place. Why have you come? Who brought you and who showed you the way?"

The Chiricahua said, "That man brought me. You have power of all kinds and that's why I've come. I want the best you've got to help me and my people."

The other replied, "I have many things here that you want. Those things I show you, you can take. If you don't see them, tell me the things you want most."

The Chiricahua said, "I wish to have the power Yusn gives, and Child of the Water, White Painted Woman—things like that."

The man said, "I don't give that power, but I can ask for this for you. I am going to give you power. Wait here until I get back."

He walked away to a table made of rock and prayed. The clouds darkened, lightning flashed, and it thundered, and the whole place seemed to shake. In a little while this man came back and gave the Chiricahua something that stood for his power. He took this thing and thanked the man.

The one who gave the power said, "I'm glad you've come here. Do not tell others about this for four years. We will let you know when to practice it."

At that the Chiricahua thought he was stepping out of one door, but he was right at his bedding. There was nobody there. He heard the birds start to sing, and he got right up. It was morning.

This power never spoke to him until four years were over. One time his child was sick and he wanted to help his boy, but he had not been spoken to yet. He prayed in different ways. He did his best but he couldn't do much for the child, who kept getting worse all the time. Finally he hired a San Carlos Apache who knew a ceremony. This man held a ceremony for four nights. The power which the San Carlos knew told him that the father was going to have a ceremony to heal, but that he could not use it yet. This San Carlos Indian said to the father "Your power is stronger than mine. You hired me and you can cure the child yourself. But I will do my best to help you, for you believe in me." He helped him that much and the child got well.

One night, a little more than a year after this, he was wondering why the power had not spoken to him yet, when something struck his tent and shook it. It hit the tent from the four directions, from the sunrise first and around to the north. Then the tent moved way up in the air, it seemed. It did it four times that night.

The next day he was going after his horses to water them. He hunted and hunted for those horses until close to sundown. He was tired out and started to go back when a whirlwind came up, went to the four directions, came toward him, and disappeared. As he stood there he heard a voice calling him by his own name. "You have been thinking of me all night. The things you have seen are to tell you it's time for you to practice the power you received in the holy place where you have been. You've lost your horses and have been walking all day. Your horses are a little way up the right-hand canyon. Soon they will come up and shake their heads and rub against you. You can take them to water."

His horses came and he watered them and turned them loose. He got back to his tent and thought of his power. He took out the object given to him in the holy home and marked it with pollen of the cattail. Then he lifted it up to the four directions and prayed with all that was in him. His wife and children watched but did not know what he was doing.

He was being shown by his power what to use in his ceremony and what to avoid. People who had power were shown to him in groups. One group had less power, another more. He saw himself with the group that had greatest power. He was shown a big eagle flying toward him, about to pick his children up. His power told him that this did not mean that the eagle was going to take his children away but that they would have power of some kind when they got older.

Above him he saw different people, whites and Chinese, and others. He knew they had power, a different kind of power. Among his own people he saw people who had the same kind of power he had; they were healers and shamans.

While it is not impossible for a snake ceremony to counteract other ailments, it is most often used to cure snake sickness:

At Hot Springs there was a woman who was kin to me. She was just a little bit of a woman, but she knew the ceremony of the snake pretty well. During the time we lived at Hot Springs, P., my brother, and I went out to shoot birds with our arrows. We went to a prairie-dog town. My brother, who was older than I, was watching birds, and he ran into a snake. The snake bit him on the kneecap, and he couldn't walk. He fell right there. P. ran to tell our family, and I stayed with him.

As soon as he heard what had happened, my father went to get this woman. They came and carried my brother to camp in a blanket. He sweated and sweated.

Then the old woman came over. She said, "Well, I'll try it." First they had to give her turquoise, and she told my brother to mark her. He marked her foot with a cross of pollen and went around to her shoulders, chest, head, back, and down the other side the way they do. Then she could begin.

She put pollen on the boy and put it to the directions. She put some in his mouth and made a cross of it where he was bitten. Then she sang. She used no drum. . . . . She sang snake songs. The boy lay in front of her. She started in the afternoon and sang until sundown. She sang like this during the day for four days.

After she sang her songs she called on the biggest snake, the most poisonous kind. She said to it, "I want you to take your poison back. Put it back in your heart. I have sung your song and said your prayer and have done just what you told me to do. Now I want you to do what I say and not bother this poor boy." She didn't suck the wound. After calling on the snake she laughed. "The boy will be all right," she said. "Snake hears me."

The swelling went down, and he got well. She told him, "You will never be bitten by a snake again."

During the ceremony she said many things about snakes. She said that Snake has legs, four of them, but that no one except those who know Snake can see them. They are of turquoise, made like a ball, and he rolls along on them. That's why Snake likes turquoise. When a man is sick from Snake, the first thing he must do is give her turquoise. A woman must give her white stone. She said that Snake likes turquoise and pollen. He likes to eat pollen. She said that she could take pollen and put it there and sing, and a snake would come from the grass and eat it.

I saw her perform many ceremonies. Sometimes she would sing and rub saliva on the place where the person was bitten, and the swelling would go down right away.

At the conclusion of most snake ceremonies, as in the case of other rites, food and behavior restrictions are imposed:

You must not stir boiling meat with a knife or use the knife as a spoon. If you should lie down flat on your back with your legs crossed, no one should step over your legs. A rope must not be used on a person who has been bitten. In using a rope you must not string it out toward your camp or house. You must always go out the door of the home or tent, not out of the sides. In quarreling you must use no words that have anything to do with the snake. You must not eat the marrow of leg bones. You must not eat meat from the breast of an animal.

Often the patient, after an attack of snake sickness, is given a protective amulet:

After you go through a snake ceremony, the shaman may make a bandoleer for you to wear, or give you a stone to wear, or make you an arm band, if you are a man. For a woman he may have a beaded strip which she should wear in her hair. These will make the patients immune so that the snake cannot harm them again.

Fewer data exist concerning the place of other reptiles in the ceremonialism. Of the gila monster it was remarked, "I hear it mentioned in the ceremonial songs of old Chiricahua, but that's the only way it's used now that I know of," and of the turtle: "Some shamans use the shell for the giving of medicine. B. gave me some in one. He marked the shell with pollen and gave it to me four times. They say that the turtle shell cannot be hit by lightning." The lizard appears in the myths as a helper of Child of the Water and the small animals in their triumphs over the monsters, and it is considered a potential source of supernatural power.

Weapons.—The ordinary protection afforded by weapons is enlarged, in certain cases, to include supernatural help as well, and a set of songs and prayers known as "ceremony from the gun" (the same word means gun or bow) has arisen. Sometimes this ceremony is called "ceremony against the enemy."

Old Man S. was with Geronimo's bunch all through the war. . . . . He has power from the gun, they say. They say he used to get out on the bank; all the soldiers shot at him and couldn't hit him. One who went to shoot him might fall down or drop his gun; then S. would kill him instead. Another man told me he knows a gun ceremony. He, too, went through all the wars safely. Geronimo is said to have known this ceremony. He never got hurt either. Something always

PLATE XI

United States National Museum

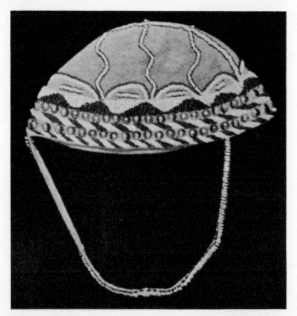

Denver Art Museum

CEREMONIAL HATS FOR PROTECTION IN WAR

happens to your gun when you try to shoot at such a fellow. Your gun jams, for instance. The one who knows this ceremony can fix it for someone else so that, when he is shot at, he will be missed.

The shield is always ceremonial and belongs to this kind of power. When you see a man with a shield, you know it was made for him by a ceremonial man in connection with a war ceremony. It's not like a bow or a sling. It's not just a weapon. Anyone couldn't have this. The shield is called "that which I hold up" in a ceremonial way. It is the same with the lance. You could only get it from a man who had the right to make it. It is not just a weapon.

I think I'm going to learn the gun ceremony from an old man now. I got him when he was a little full and asked him if he knew anything he would show me. He said, "Yes, I know Gun." He told me it would be easy for me to learn, that it was mostly some prayers and songs. He showed me some of it right there. In these songs and prayers the parts of the gun are given certain names. The wooden stock is called the earth. The metal barrel is called the moon. The little screws that hold it together are called whirlwind. This is true of all gun ceremonies. I'm going to see him again and learn more about it.

The preparation of shields and designed garments to be given to the client as protective amulets receives constant mention:

In connection with the gun ceremony there were circular buckskin head coverings. These were carried but not worn often. Actually, a man wore a strip of buckskin or cloth or a handkerchief around his head in war. Just the war shaman and those to whom he gave them had the hats. Most of the time the hat was just rolled up and tied to the quiver.

The shamans of the war ceremony made hats. These went with the shields; they were made by the same men. These hats were of buckskin. Some were round and decorated all around the rim. Some were colored black and white and were designed with serrated figures, four-pointed stars, and lightning symbols. Sometimes a jacket was given to the person to wear.

A protective ritual formula, allegedly first executed by Child of the Water before his conflict with the giant, was described by an informant who is reputed to know the gun ceremony:

Spit on the palm of the left hand. Dip the first finger of the right hand in the saliva and make a cross with it on the left foot, thigh, forearm, and cheek. As the crosses are made, call upon the four Thunders: Black Thunder, Blue Thunder, Yellow Thunder, and White Thunder.

Then recite the following prayer, "Black flint is over your body four times. Take your black weapon to the center of the sky. Let his weapons disappear from the earth." This prayer, with only the colors changed, is repeated four times. Then rub the first finger of the right hand horizontally across the lips four times.

Now the bow and arrows (or the gun) are held against the chest, pointing first downward to the left, then upward to the right. At the same time face the east and pray. The weapon is next worked over the right shoulder, across the back, and down to the left hand.

Then the bow string is run through the mouth, and some of the "juice" of the string is sucked off. This is spit into the palm of the left hand, and crosses are made with the juice as before. Then the prayer is repeated.

Sacred places and summary.—Besides the homes of the Mountain People, places with markings on the walls or on rocks may be considered sacred. "I have heard the old men tell of one cave which has the sun, moon, stars, and Mountain Spirits on the walls. . . . . They pray when they see this."

There are also wayside shrines and places of offering:

It is a pile of rock and stones about four feet high and eight feet wide. There are four holes in the center. The foundation is east and west, and the holes are running toward the east. You pick up a stone or leaves and hold this to the four corners—east, south, west, and north—while you pray. Then you drop what you have in the hole. It's asking a blessing. They take this to be a holy place.

We were on a trip by horse and we came to one of these. The older people told us younger ones what to do. We were on horseback. We rode around the left side of the shrine and dropped the stone in and then came right back. We could have done it on foot too. I have heard ceremonial songs, a long time ago, mention these shrines. The name means that rocks churn about in this place.

One informant ascribed the origin of sacred shrines to the mythological figure, Kantaneiro, who "told the Indians to do this for long life and good luck."

These shrines are now used primarily as a place of contemplation and prayer by persons starting on a perilous trip:

There is a ceremonial place on that mountaintop. The people go there before they leave on a long or dangerous journey. It is believed that, if you go to the place and drop a stone on the pile already there or throw on a sprig of a juniper tree, you will return safely.

In a society where shamanism is so broadly construed, to be sure that every possible rite is represented in a collection, it would be necessary to have the perfect confidence of everyone in the community and to work with every adult. What has been presented is admittedly only a sampling. Comments and stories pertaining to ceremonies obtained through supernatural experiences with Water Monster, Fire, Haze, Cyclone, Star, Moon, Sun, Cloud, Badger, Bat, Beaver, Mountain Lion, Wildcat, Bush Tit, Crow, Eagle, Hawk, Hummingbird, Yellow Warbler, and insects have been excluded because of considerations of space. But if the pattern, the range of power sources and ceremonies, and enough of the individual behavior to leaven the whole have emerged, the purpose has been achieved. It is interesting that, despite theoretical catholicity, the kinds of ceremonies obtained are, in practice, delimited by the concepts of disease and by the most vexing problems of existence. Thus, while power may be obtained from a wide variety of supernaturals, natural forces, animals, and the like, it is from a relatively small number of these (such as the game animals and the dreaded creatures which must be placated) that most rites actually come.

SKEPTICISM

Accounts of ceremonies usually come from the shaman himself, from his relatives and friends, or from a patient he has successfully treated. Therefore, what is said will in most cases reflect the sentiments of the believer. But any member of the tribe can be, on occasion, a sharp critic of supernatural claims. This was so clear to one shaman that he told his audience: "Many of you people don't believe in what I'm doing. You think I'm a fake. I tell you to your faces that many of you will be willing to be this man when you see how I restore him."

Criticism and skepticism are not likely to appear in stories of the acquisition and use of power, but they are revealed in casual conversations. For instance, when I asked an informant to identify another man for me, he described him as a shaman who had attempted to cure his wife of a swollen throat and had failed.

The attitude of respect for a basic pattern, tempered by doubt in regard to any individual claim which seems extravagant or unfounded, is illustrated in a "ghost" story:

One man was telling me that when he was coming home from hunting, between dark and dawn, he saw two big eyes looking at him. He got pretty frightened. He didn't want to shoot at it because he didn't know what it was. So he ran way around and approached it from the other side. When he got there he saw it was a cow. He said that if he had been like many Indians he would have run away and said it was a ghost. That's how most of this ghost business turns out. Three-fourths of it is just something natural, if you stay around to find out. Of course, there are some experiences with ghosts that are real.

Precedent for a sense of proportion in respect to the claims and motives of would-be shamans is found in the traditions. A tale is told of a woman who boasted of her ability to determine the whereabouts of the enemy by means of her supernatural power. One night, when the people feared a surprise attack, they asked this woman to perform her rite for them. She went about the inside of the windbreak in which they were clustered, solemnly moved her arms around, and assured them, "There is nothing. It is good all over." But in giving them this encouraging message, she leaned too far over the windbreak, and enemy soldiers who had crawled to it pulled her over and made her captive. The others, warned by her fate if not by her ceremony, fled under cover of darkness.

Another story has to do with a visitor who is asked to use his ceremony to find some missing tribesmen. He sings, shakes as though influenced by some invisible force, and is led into the brush. Returning, he asserts that a fully equipped horse must be tethered at a distant point to the east if his power is to continue the search. This is done, and again the man sings and is led into the darkness by his power, this time to the west. The others wait a long time for him to come back. Finally a hard-headed member of the group exclaims, "I'll bet he went over to the horse!" This, indeed, is the case; the pretender has made off with the finest horse in the encampment.

Religiosity is thus tempered with a saving humor and distrust which act as brakes upon unreasonable claims. In a setting where each person is allowed wide latitude in the acquisition of power, the threat of public ridicule is a force in the maintenance of the pattern. The individualistic principle itself becomes a curb. Any person may claim extraordinary supernatural experiences, but any other person may equally question the validity of the assertion. Each shaman knows that there are those who believe in the efficacy of his rite and those who do not and that it is wise not to swell the number of the latter by radical departures from established custom.

In keeping with the principle that ceremonialism should be confined to recognized values, undignified religious excitement is cause for humor rather than for praise.

This is sometimes called "religious excitement" or "religious ecstasy." It is the same as what is called "crazy ceremony." This is when a person goes through violent clapping of the hands involuntarily when in a religious ceremony. . . . . Some people get so excited in a ceremony that they shake all over or hit one hand on the other. I knew such a woman when I was young. Some go "Ah, ah, ah, ah!"—just gasp all the time. I knew one woman, part Chiricahua and part white, who acted like this when the masked dancers performed. The Chiricahua believe that you get this way when you take religion too seriously. Some Chiricahua think this is funny.

The motives of the shaman may be questioned:

A woman shaman got all this poor woman's possessions. She was treating her for a long time. She kept asking for things. Finally she said that the sick woman would have to come to her camp to be cured. C. said when he heard about it that, if she went, she would never come back. And he was right.

Outright charges of fraud are not uncommon:

That man was never known as a shaman. He just picked up those songs from anywhere and changed them. Now he uses them for ceremonial songs. I was out at Whitetail with my wife. He was sleeping in the next room. His son-in-law was out there. (This was when his daughter was still alive.) I heard him making those songs up. He'd sing it in different ways. He'd sing, "My song makes everything well." Now he uses it for a ceremonial song. After practicing he'd come in where I was. I'd sing those words, and he'd just stare at me. He wanted to make a church song;[37] then he turned it into a ceremonial song. They say that he is crazy now and that his songs don't mean anything. No one knows where he got them or what right he has to them.

Even when the patient recovers, the shaman may receive but grudging credit from his critics. Of one apparent cure, an informant said, "It is hard to tell why he got well. Maybe the man was ready to get well anyway, or maybe G. cured him."

[37] Songs patterned after old Chiricahua types musically but expressing Christian sentiments have lately been composed for church use.

MAINTENANCE OF THE HOUSEHOLD

HUNTING

IN THE securing of sufficient food the preoccupation of the man is properly with the hunt. "They think they are doing enough by going around hunting all day and getting food together." Except for participation in occasional rabbit surrounds, women are not encouraged to show concern for matters pertaining to the hunt. "Women never go out hunting because they aren't strong and able to get around," it was explained; but another comment suggests that the idea of appropriate male and female spheres is quite as important a consideration.

The Chiricahua don't like to see a man go out hunting with a woman, whether they're married or not. It's considered a disgrace. One man used to do this. He was so jealous he didn't like to leave his wife alone. The Whitetail people saw him going out hunting with his wife, and they criticized him and laughed at him.

Since the deer is the most important game animal, a hunting trip, unless it is otherwise stated, may be assumed to have as its goal the securing of venison. Whether or not a specific ceremony precedes the hunt, certain precautions are always observed:

There are two things you cannot do before you go hunting. One is to eat onions. The other is to chew osha [*Ligusticum porteri*]. The deer will smell you if you do. Suppose you are going hunting tomorrow morning. You can't eat them tonight then. You can't even dig them the day before you are going out to hunt. But the Chiricahua eat onions with deer meat when they come back from the hunt. They use the onions raw while they are eating the meat or they boil the onions with the meat.

When you are going hunting you take care not to clean yourself up. Perhaps you have been eating the meat of some animal and therefore have been rubbing the grease and marrow of the long bones on your face, legs, and arms. You keep this on. And you don't put anything else on yourself that may smell; nothing sweet-smelling like perfume [i.e., "Indian perfume," such as mint] can be used at this time.

Fasting immediately before the hunt aids the chances for success:

Another thing about the hunt according to the old Chiricahua ways: The older men would always give this advice to the younger. "Don't eat before you go out on the hunt," they would say. "Even though you have plenty in camp, don't eat in the morning before you go out. Go out and hunt with an empty stomach. Then Yusn will pity you. Perhaps you will not see anything to shoot though it is late in the day. You'll be empty, hungry, an object of pity. But if you go out with a full stomach, you'll hunt all day and won't get anything. As soon as you make your kill and come back with it, you can eat all you want."

The crow is associated with the hunt. A tale relates how animals were kept hidden by the crows until Killer of Enemies, with the help of Coyote, freed them during the absence of their keepers. The crows returned just in time to see their animals escape, and in their anger called the names of the waste products which form their usual fare. "So the human beings get all the best part of the meat, and the crows get what is left." On the basis of this story, the appearance of a crow just before the hunt is accepted as a favorable omen:

Well, suppose I am planning to go out hunting tomorrow. Crow might be very happy, flying around my camp. Then I might say, "Well, Crow, I'm going out hunting tomorrow and if I kill a deer you'll get the entrails, so help me." The crow must be connected in some way with hunting, but I've never heard how. But that's the way of it.

The attitude of the hunter should be one of reverence and generosity:

If I am going hunting with you, before we start out you might tell me, "If I kill two deer for you, I'm going to kill a good fat one and it will be mine." You must not show your selfishness in any way. If you say anything like this and walk all day and get no deer, you know what is the cause of it. You brought it on yourself. And even if you have killed several deer and you say something like this, you'll have bad luck later on. It'll make it bad for you.

The attitude against optimism is emphasized particularly in one of the rules of the hunt.[1] "The Chiricahua don't allow baskets around the hunt. To bring them means that you are overconfident that they are going to be filled up. It spoils your luck."

In late fall, when the deer are fatter and the hides better,

---

[1] One elderly informant, an Eastern Chiricahua, claimed to know nothing of this rule.

hunting activities are intensified, but this industry continues through the year whenever need commands and weather permits. "The Chiricahua killed any kind of deer—bucks or does, blacktail or whitetail, any time of year." Ordinarily, the hunter leaves for the chase alone or with one or two companions. Sometimes as many as ten men will travel together to a site where the game is known to be abundant, but then each goes his own way. The individual character of the hunt is evident from the following description:

In the evening, before going to bed, I think about where I am going to hunt. So in the morning I wake up at dawn and rise eager to be off. I may prepare myself something to eat, yucca fruit or mescal or perhaps some meat, fresh or dried, and eat it. I don't eat much, for my mind is on hunting; if I don't eat before going, it doesn't matter, for, when I make my kill, I eat. . . . . I leave alone invariably. Some of the men prefer to hunt in pairs, especially if they go on horseback, but I wait for nobody and go early, alone, because the deer are not wise in the morning.

If I have the luck to kill a deer close to camp, I carry it back home and butcher it and skin it myself at home. The neighbors come around, and I give them parts of the meat. If I kill a deer far away, I butcher the animal out there, skin it, wrap the meat tightly in the skin to keep the crows from getting at it, and hang it on a tree so that the animals can't get it. Then I go home and return with my horse and fetch the meat. I return to camp then with the meat, and everybody is proud of me, and all are happy. I give meat to all who come around; among these are women without husbands, who are very eager for meat.

If I am unsuccessful on the hunt, I keep going as late as possible, until dark, and manage to get home by dark. If several men hunt together, they might plan to stay out all night; but, if hunters don't plan it, they always get home by dark so that nobody worries. After coming home in the evening when I have been unsuccessful, there may be nothing to eat, but I have to stick it out. That's pretty hard, but I'm man enough to stand it until morning. Though I am unsuccessful, no one makes fun of me.

Sometimes there was no food, and we suffered much; in the old days the Indians could stand hunger, and they would tie a cord around their waists pretty tight.[2] If I have no luck hunting, I would go off to hunt like this every day until I kill something; but, if I have good luck, I can lay off for two or three days. I enjoy hunting, but when I have meat I may or may not feel like going hunting.

Most of the deer secured are killed with the bow and arrow. (This refers to the time before the introduction of firearms, of

---

[2] It is believed that this reduces the discomfort of hunger.

course.) Sometimes, especially when the hunter is mounted, the deer are run to exhaustion, roped, and strangled. An unblemished skin can be secured in this way, or the hunter might stab the tired animal in the throat or in some spot where an incision would be made anyway in skinning.

Arrows used on the hunt are occasionally treated with poison which has strong magical properties:

Get some animal blood. Then take the sharp prongs of plants like the prickly-pear cactus and pound them up with the blood. Allow this to spoil. Put it on the arrow point. Whatever you shoot with it dies. It does not spoil the meat though. It acts the same on humans. It acts like this because the plants used have prickers.

A favorite aid in stalking is a deer-head mask, a device contributed by Killer of Enemies:

We stalk deer wearing the head and horns of a deer. The head is mounted on a circular stick which rests on the top of the hunter's head. The features of the deer are filled in with grass, and the skin is tied together at the sides so the mask will stay on. The hunter sneaks up on the deer from the proper side, so the wind will not warn them of him. He acts like a grazing deer. He stoops over and rests on a stick which he holds in the left hand. In the right hand he holds his arrows. In this way he walks slowly to the deer until he is near enough to shoot an arrow. He doesn't wear the body skin of the deer as a disguise, but he puts on something that is pretty near the color of the deer's body. Some careful men could come within six feet of the deer in this way.

Sometimes, to draw the deer to him, the hunter employs a further stratagem: "They have whistles made of a leaf to call the deer. They can do it with any leaf held horizontally along the lips. It sounds like a small deer, and the mother comes."

Whenever possible the hunter tries to hit his prey in the flank, for then "the running motion makes the arrow work farther up." In the myths this technique is used by Killer of Enemies and Coyote.

Though it is common "for each man to hunt for himself" or for two or three to join forces, occasionally a larger number start out together. This permits a relay method of hunting; men are stationed at various points along a course, and deer are started in this direction. Fresh hunters are able to enter the chase at intervals and finally run down the tiring game. By much the same method, deer can be directed toward a "cliff or steep place so that they will have to stop or go down. Someone is stationed below to shoot them if they go down." There is no enthusiasm for running game, however, for it is said to make the meat "darker" and "slimy" and like the flesh of an old animal.

If a hunter is alone and kills a deer, he skins and butchers it immediately,[3] a task which must be done according to prescribed rules:

The Chiricahua have their way for hunting. They follow rules according to the way Child of the Water hunted when he was on earth. He always put the head of his kill to the east. And he never walked in front of it to the east; he never walked past the head when he was skinning or butchering. He never straddled the deer or walked across the carcass as the whites do when butchering a cow.

First skin the side that is up. Begin at the face, cutting down the middle. Continue down the neck and along the center of the body and along the inside of the forefeet and back legs. Always cut through the middle of the joint so there won't be any baggy place when the hide is tanned. Pull the skin off the legs and keep cutting and working it off the rest of the carcass. When the skin is off the top side, cut the flesh along the side, break the ribs, and remove the entrails so as not to spoil the meat. Then turn the carcass over and skin the other side. Cut the sinews so that the lower leg joints are not stiff. They look too much the way a dead person does if they are stiff.

When the skin is entirely freed, a further ritual action takes place; this is sometimes simple, sometimes rather elaborate:

When I skin a deer, I brush the body with the skin in the four directions.

After the hide is off and the carcass is lying there, we twice lay the hide on reversed, with the front end of the hide on the back part of the carcass. Then we talk to the deer and say, "When you see me don't be afraid. May I be lucky with you all the time." This is done twice. In that way you have good luck with the deer and see them all the time.

To complete the butchering, the legs are cut off, the backbone is severed at the neck and below the ribs, and the remainder

---

[3] One informant said: "The wolf call is used in hunting as a signal if you want help after you have made the kill." But another informant thought it would be used only in special cases: "I do not think that calling like a wolf at a kill is general for the Chiricahua. I have been with old men when they killed deer, and they did not do it. A man who knows the ceremony of the wolf might."

is cut into convenient sections. One man tells of his care to keep the meat of the right side separate from that of the left side until the butchering is concluded, but this seems to be personal with him.

If a hunter is on foot and far from his camp, it is likely that he will be able to take only part of the kill back with him:

> If you are on foot and can't take it with you, you put the meat in a heap, place the hide over it, and say to the animals, "This belongs to Yusn; leave it alone." Then you hang it up in a tree by means of strongly spliced yucca strings. You hang it high enough so that animals cannot reach it. Then you put what you are going to take home in the hide. After reaching home, you go right back after the rest and bring it in.

Another man mentioned a similar procedure, though he invokes a different supernatural:

> You put part of the kill in a tree if you can't carry it all at once. It is tied there with strings made from the yucca leaf. There is a little prayer that is used at this time. You say, "This belongs to Hedos."[4] He was the "first man," sort of a religious man. He did this every time he made a kill. Now the Chiricahua do it.

Crow is remembered with an offering. "Then I take the entrails out, put them to one side, and say, 'This is for you, Crow; make me lucky, and we'll have this kind of food all the time. I leave this for you every time.' "

Certain parts of the deer must have special care if good fortune in the hunt is to be maintained:

> As a general rule you must take the head home. Somebody might give you bad luck with it if you leave it there. You can do anything you want with it when you get it home, hang it up or anything. You must take the hoofs too. You can do what you want with them when you get them home too. Everybody is directed to do this.

A particular act also attends the bringing-back of the horns of a buck. "They take a slit of the entrails of a buck and tie it on the right horn. I was with M. hunting. He killed a deer and did this. I asked him why, and he said, 'For luck.' "

---

[4] This is the same supernatural character whose name was given before as Herus (see p. 198). The name is very unstable and has been recorded as Hados and Eyos as well.

The rules of the hunt require generosity:

The first man who comes up to you when you kill a deer is entitled to the whole deer, no matter who he is. You say to him, "Go ahead, help yourself. Leave what you want for me." He can leave half or take most and leave you a little. You can't say anything. He can take the skin and all. The Chiricahua always feels this way. A poor fellow is out here hunting because he needs meat. If I kill something and he comes over, I share with him. That's the feeling of all the hunters. If you have already butchered a deer and have it on your horse carrying it into camp and meet someone, it is different. Then you give him whatever you want to. It's up to you.

An etiquette of reasonableness and shrewd utility governs these privileges, however. In no case of which I have a record has more than the hide and half the meat been taken. Often the hide alone or the meat only is accepted. A man who is well supplied with meat and skins may even politely decline the gift, for he knows that acceptance constitutes an implicit claim against him when the situation is reversed.

When two men are hunting together, "it's up to the man who makes the kill to give the hide to the other if he wants to." So automatic is this response that a man who kills a deer while he is in the company of another hunter is said "to kill it for" his friend. "When you are out and you kill a deer for another, he skins it."

The ideal of selflessness in obedience to rule is sometimes difficult to maintain, particularly when hunting companions have a common need of buckskin:

I've heard jokes about hunting. This is one funny story. Two men were hunting together. Both were good shots. They saw a deer close by, a big deer. Neither of them could have missed it, it was so close. Each man knew that he wasn't entitled to the hide if he killed the deer. Each said to the other, "You shoot him." Each was making up all kinds of excuses for not shooting. One said to the other, "I've shot many deer for you, so you could get the hides. Now here's a chance for you to kill one for me, and you don't do it!" The other said, "You can kill that deer, and then I'll get the hide." Meanwhile the deer ran away, and neither of them got it. That's the story I've heard. They laugh when they tell this story.

The strength of the obligation of generosity can be inferred from this account, in which a man, despite his selfishness, is offered a share by the successful hunter:

C. told me what happened another time. He said, "I saw a big buck in the bushes. I shot him, and the deer just dropped down. So I went over there and put my knife in its throat so it would bleed. Then I had to get my horse that I had left a long ways behind. This happened in a canyon, and, when I shot, A. was over there and heard it.

"While I went back after my horse, A. got to my deer. He dragged it about fifty yards away into some other bushes. I got back to the place where I had left the deer, but I couldn't find it. I followed the track, but every now and then he had lifted up the deer, trying to make me lose the trail. All the time I was trailing I thought no human would do a thing like that. I thought it must be a bear. So I got off my horse and loaded my gun and followed it in the brush, down the hill.

"Pretty soon I saw something black. It was moving in the bushes and I couldn't tell what it was. I was just a little way from it, maybe twenty yards. I saw the black hair; I thought it was a bear. So there I was. I wanted to see where his head was, for I wanted to shoot him in the ribs. I followed him with my rifle, ready to shoot.

"Then A. stood up and said, 'Phew!' I had almost shot that fellow! I walked up to him. I asked him, 'Why is it you took my deer? Why is it you didn't butcher it up there where it was but carried it down here? I almost shot you. I almost took you for a bear.'

"Then A. told me, 'There's your deer; take it then!' I said, 'Go ahead; take what you want. I'll take the rest of it.' "

Then A. took the hide and C. got what was left. C. said, "I was pretty good about it and let him have what he wanted."

When three men are hunting together, and one shoots a deer, his companions run for the fallen animal, and the first to touch it has the privilege of skinning it and keeping the hide. To the others usually go portions of the meat.

It is customary to help the widows and the aged. If there are many such individuals and meat is scarce, the hunter may have little meat left upon his arrival at his own home:

If you go through the camps with a deer, they take it from you. You can't say anything. It's hard to refuse those who haven't any meat. That's the Chiricahua way. They take the hide and the meat; they take what they want. I used to sneak in at night. That's what some do.

Another informant feels that the distribution of food is governed by a more spontaneous generosity. "When a man returns from the hunt, the proceeds are his own. He doesn't have to give anything, but even if a lazy man wants food, he would not refuse him."

The proper care of the meat and the skeletal parts of the deer must be kept in mind until the animal is entirely consumed. It is forbidden to "take the meat when it is hot and blow upon it," for such action is likely "to blow the deer away." "We don't just throw the bones away. We are careful. We put them in a nice pile. They say if you throw the bones, it throws the deer away. You won't see any more deer when you are out hunting." Other safeguards are employed for individual ends:

Other things, like handling the meat a certain way, or not giving away certain parts, are done mostly at the direction of ceremonial men. If your luck has been bad and you've hunted all week without killing a thing, you might go to some man who has songs for this and ask him to help you. He will give you some restriction or rule on your hunting. That's how these things start.

The game animal next in importance to the deer is the pronghorn or antelope. Separate hunts to obtain antelopes are less frequent, however; often such hunts wait upon a chance encounter which reveals the presence of the antelopes. In general, the same usages, ceremonial and practical, which mark the deer hunt are true for the antelope hunt. The solitary hunter makes considerable use of the antelope-head mask. "They fix the antelope head for hunting. They take all the bone out, leaving only horns and ears. Only a man with ceremonial knowledge will do it, they say. They call hunting with a mask of this kind 'he slips up to it.' "

Stalking antelopes is even more time-consuming and difficult than approaching deer:

The antelopes live on the flats. They are harder to get near than deer. They are hunted like deer, with a mask. The hunter wears a jacket painted like an antelope skin. He has a stick in one hand. He imitates the walk of the antelope. If a herd of antelopes is seen in the distance, the hunter works up to them. It takes two or three hours sometimes, for it is necessary to advance slowly, acting just like the animals. The grass is tall, and the hunter keeps his head just above the grass.

The relay chase is used to secure pronghorns, too:

A group of about ten men sometimes goes off on horseback to hunt antelopes. When the antelopes are sighted, one bunch scatters the antelopes toward the other men who are strung along on horseback. When one horse gets tired, another man takes up the chase. Sometimes they rope the antelopes. Then they kill them by slitting them under the leg or throat where you have to cut anyway when skinning.

Then there is a surround in which mounted men participate:

When the herd is sighted, they scatter and approach it, making a big circle. Two or three men run in toward the antelopes and get them started. Then the circle closes in, and the hunters shoot or rope the animals. The men are about a hundred yards apart. Special horses, two-year-olds which are trained for hunting, are used.

Another animal which is occasionally hunted, but not as seriously as deer or antelopes, is the wapiti, or "American elk." These are few in number throughout some parts of the tribal territory (the Southern Chiricahua claim that there were none in most of their range), and the meat, perhaps because the people are less familiar with it, is not so greatly esteemed. The Central Chiricahua say that "there were plenty of elks" where they lived, however. Elk horns are too heavy to attach to masks, and informants say it is not necessary to use the heads anyway, for the elk "is not as smart as the deer and is easier to get."

The meat and the skins of the mountain sheep and the mountain goat are used when they can be procured. These animals are not numerous or easy to get, however, and are of limited importance in the economy.

Wood rats supplement the meat diet:

The Chiricahua hunt those big rats and eat them. Two men go to a nest. One pokes a stick in; the other waits at the other end and shoots when the rat comes out. For this they use a small arrow the same as is used for birds. It is all wood, with a sharpened point. When they get a good many rats, they pierce the legs and carry them home on poles over the shoulder. Sometimes to get them a person pokes into a hole and hits them with a stick when they come out.

Opposums, considered "the best meat in the rat class," are found in Southern Chiricahua range and are shot with bows and arrows.

Cottontail rabbits are hunted and eaten, but for some reason many persons are reluctant to eat jack rabbits:

Many won't eat jack rabbit, though they will eat cottontail. I don't know why exactly. They say cottontail meat is better. It's between the taste and the looks.

The jack rabbit is supposed to have a bad taste. I never have eaten it, but I have eaten cottontails. In Oklahoma the other Indians ate jack rabbits, but most of the Chiricahua didn't. We eat the cottontail though. I like it. It has saved me many times, that rabbit! Cottontails are good.

The dislike for jack rabbit is not unanimous, apparently, for a member of the Eastern band asserted, "The Hot Springs people eat cottontails and jack rabbits."

Rabbits are hunted assiduously by boys who are still too young to seek larger game. Grown men shoot them when other game fails and fresh food is required at once. Sometimes a communal rabbit hunt or "rabbit clubbing" is arranged.[5] Rabbits and other small furry creatures are sometimes dislodged from burrows by means of long sticks. "They use a stick to get small animals out of holes. You catch the end of it in the animal's fur and twist. Then pull out. Any kind of wood or stick will do for this. Rabbits mostly are pulled out this way. Sometimes they get away."

Only a few are fond of prairie-dog meat:

The prairie dog is sometimes eaten. Some do it for health, but others don't like it; they are afraid of it, as they are of fish. They don't like the looks of it, I guess. As I understand it, very few eat it. No one warned me against eating it, but I just haven't done so. My father has mentioned eating it, but very few of the older people do. They say that prairie dogs eat snakes, just as hogs do. They don't say you can get sick from the prairie dog as you can from the snake, but the Chiricahua just don't like it much.

Squirrels sometimes serve to replenish the larder. They are seldom hunted by grown men, but the boys hunt them and thus demonstrate their ability to add to the household's resources.

Although peccaries are found in some parts of the tribal range, the members of at least two of the bands—the Eastern and Central—will not eat this meat because "the peccary eats snakes." A Southern Chiricahua band member, however, tells of hunts in which the wild hogs are rounded up like rabbits and shot down with arrows. The hunters surround a brushy place, for "the peccaries are found where there is a lot of brush; when on the flats they always make for the brush." The same informant said,

[5] For a description of this see p. 76.

"The unborn of the peccary is eaten also. One pig has lots of them."

That the wildcat was formerly eaten is both affirmed and denied. One informant classed it with wolf and fox and said, "We don't like the meat; also it is forbidden and might kill us." It is possible that some individuals used it for food. Everyone wants the skin, and so the animal is killed whenever opportunity offers.

A number of informants have agreed that mountain-lion meat is edible. In addition, the hide is the favorite material for the quiver. Consequently, no opportunity to shoot a cougar is overlooked by the hunters.

Infrequently the chance was afforded to hunt bison. One account tells of a long trip to a point north and east of the present site of Albuquerque and of success in hunting bison there. Occasionally one was found in the vicinity of Hot Springs and was secured by the people of that region. But bison were entirely absent from the greater part of the territory.

In the historic period wild cattle became abundant and were supplemented by domestic stock obtained on raids to the south. The stock introduced by the Europeans became important very early:

Long ago there were cattle which we hunted and used. The old people say that there were some wild cattle and wild horses, wilder than deer. I don't know where they came from. Many ate burros and mules in those days; many ate horses.

Before the Americans came, a few Chiricahua had cattle, and, of course, there were some with many horses. In wars with the Mexicans they would sometimes steal cattle, and that accounts for the presence of cattle among the Chiricahua. They'd herd the cattle to a river and let them stay around there and increase. Five or six or a dozen men who made the raid would divide the cattle among them, and then the cattle belonged to them personally. Then these men might have enough meat so they wouldn't have to hunt any more for a while.

Many animals are hunted only for their fur. Among these are the badger (from which a skin bag for holding piñon seeds and acorns is made), the beaver, and the otter.

Birds are much more significant as a source of feathers than as food:

We don't like the turkey for food because it eats insects. We think it is nasty. When I was at Fort Apache my relatives used to tell me, "Don't go around white soldiers, don't go around Chinamen. They'll feed you hog meat and turkey meat, and these eat nasty things, anything at all." I never heard that turkeys eat snakes; but they eat worms and nasty things. The Chiricahua hardly even eat quails. When they get hungry, some just have to eat birds like the dove. They may eat these when they have to, but they don't like to do it.

That all are not of one mind concerning the inadvisability of using the turkey for food is suggested by other statements, however. Said a member of the Eastern band: "The Hot Springs people eat turkey all right. Some other Indians say it lives on bugs and won't eat it, though."

Evidently the effort made to get turkeys varies too. According to one informant: "They are shot with arrows when they are seen, but they are not hunted; there is no special trip to get them." From others, though, come accounts of organized attempts to flush them: "A group of men goes along a creek to scare turkeys. Another group will be about one-half mile away on the other side where they think the turkeys will fly when frightened. They wait there and when the turkeys appear, shoot them with arrows and club them."

Most informants agree that the dove is edible. One man, before singing the "dove song" of the moccasin game,[6] told a story that seems to support this:

The dove used to talk. It was making a nest. Then it said it was going to paint its legs red. "Here in this nest that I build, my little ones will increase. I will go out and look for something to eat for my young ones. Anyone who kills me will be obliged to eat me." It painted its legs red so as to be easily recognized. Since then these birds have been used for food.

Small birds, such as snowbirds and sparrows, are the targets of boys who are perfecting their skill with arrow and sling. Often the boys build a fire and roast and eat their kill at or near their base of operations. Rarely, except in times of dire want, do adults set out on bird hunts. Occasionally, mounted men chase quails to exhaustion and thus secure them in quantity. Some shoot ducks and geese for food, but not everyone will do so, for

[6] See p. 453.

the same division of opinion concerning their suitability exists as in the case of the turkey. One person, for instance, insisted, "The Chiricahua never eat duck. They just don't like it. I never hear them say why." Yet another man just as positively stated, "The Chiricahua eat ducks, quails, geese, doves, turkeys, and prairie chickens."

Birds are desired for their feathers, and oval or peaked blinds are constructed to catch them: "The bird blind is shaped something like a tepee—the poles slant up together. You put sticks on the top of it so the birds come and sit on it. You can shoot them easily this way."

Eagle feathers are in great demand, and the hunter is always on the lookout for an eagle which has so gorged itself that it is almost helpless: "Sometimes a man is lucky and comes upon an eagle when it has eaten so much that it can't get off the ground quickly. Then the man runs at it and hits it with a club. The eagle is that way—it will eat so much that it can't fly."

Eagles are also deliberately trapped:

Anyone can kill an eagle and use the feathers for arrows. When they find a dead animal, they put snares around the carcass to capture the eagle. They make an Indian trap. They use sinew, making loops with it which draw up tightly [slipknots] when the eagle steps in one and moves. The carcass or the meat that is used is tied down to a big rock so that the eagle cannot get it easily but must walk about a lot. These knots are all around, covered with grass. They are attached to sticks or brush. When the eagle is caught it is killed with a club, hit on the head. The eagle is not left alive intentionally, but if you hit it and think it is dead and then after it is plucked it gets up again, you leave it alone. Anyone may put out one of these traps.

One informant, a member of the Southern Chiricahua band, claims that eaglets are sometimes taken from a nest in the absence of the parent-birds, and he describes a cage in which they are reared until the feathers are ready for plucking: "They were caught on a mountain slope close to the present Arizona line. They were caught when they were small and were raised. We never caught grown-up ones. People climbed trees to get them."

The eaglets, according to this testimony, are kept in a large cage, approximately ten feet high and thirty inches wide, made of branches tied together with rawhide strips. This cage is secured to four stout poles which are sunk into the ground. Inside, near the top, are perches on which the eaglets may rest.

An Eastern Chiricahua band leader had three eagles in one house. Then another was built. There were two in there. The little eagles used to go out and come back. They ate lungs. They fought like dogs. When they had had enough to eat, they went to the top. Eagles that are raised are never killed. After they have pulled the feathers off, they let them go.

One other informant recalled having seen eagles in captivity but sharply reduced the size of the cage employed from that pictured in the preceding account. The practice of capturing eaglets alive and raising them must be quite rare, however, for a number of other elderly commentators denied knowledge of it. One man explicitly stated: "We didn't keep eagles in a cage. Many were afraid of them and wouldn't touch them. We couldn't raise them. We were moving all the time, staying three days or so in one place. That's why we stored our goods in cave caches."

It is possible that some individuals of the Southern Chiricahua band or members of some of its local groups make an attempt to secure fish and eat them:

My people eat fish. There was a certain river in Mexico where my people came. There they would lift rocks in the water and shoot the fish they found there with arrows. When they were traveling they just put the fish on the coals and broiled them. They also used to boil them in water. They ate fish eggs, but they ate no shell fish at all.

Another informant, an Eastern Chiricahua who lived close to the Rio Grande, explained that those with whom he lived fished whenever they could and ate any kind of fish.

It may be, therefore, that the dislike of fish reported by many informants is to be correlated with unfamiliarity with this kind of food and the distance from any possible supply. The intensity of the repugnance and the willingness of many to equate the fish with the snake, suggest something stronger than mere unfamiliarity, however. It is more likely that the Southwestern taboo on fish was beginning to influence the Chiricahua markedly and that the alleged similarity between the fish and the snake afforded a convenient rationalization.

In an attempt to explain why his people made so little use of fish a Chiricahua acquaintance said:

It is true that the old Chiricahua wouldn't eat fish. They say of fish, "They are slippery and slick just like snakes, and they are relatives to the snakes. They are relatives to the lizards and all the nasty ones." It looks just that way to them. And toads and frogs and tadpoles are classed with snakes. The Chiricahua wouldn't eat them. They never ate fish until they got to Fort Sill. Even now I don't like such things. I get a headache from them. I'm not used to such food, and it doesn't agree with my stomach.

I was up at the Ruidoso River for two years as a guard. I had to look at the passes, and those who didn't have the right ones I chased out. Those campers would bring fish to us every day. The fish were cleaned and fried. I would say to my wife, "Let's try it." We'd try a little, and then we'd have to throw it away. There were those poor fellows running themselves ragged every day trying to catch those fish, and here we were throwing them away just as soon as the people left! Even canned fish doesn't agree with me. My wife can't eat it either. There was no mention of sickness from fish though. I never heard any ceremonial songs about that. Many Indians eat fish now; they go around and fish.

A similar frame of mind is revealed in another account:

People did not fish when I was a boy. Fish was not eaten; it was not an Indian food in the old days. We classed fish with the snake and thought it could bite. We thought it could cause evil influence. There was no ceremony connected with it though. It is only since contact with the whites that fish is eaten. Formerly we had no separate names for different kinds of fish.

A younger man reaffirmed this last statement and added, "We younger people distinguish different kinds of fish. We call catfish 'fish with whiskers' and perch and bass 'fish without bones,' for instance." This young man went on to say:

It is perhaps true that P.'s group might have eaten fish. They were nearer water. At Fort Sill (1894–1913) about one-third didn't eat fish still—this many at least. The old folks didn't care if the young people ate fish. I ate it. I could eat it right next to old men who didn't eat it, and they wouldn't scold. A father would not object if his son ate it, but he would object if his son ate bear meat.

It is undoubtedly true that, since fish is not so definitely an animal of "evil influence" as the bear or the coyote, its use as food is more likely to be left to individual taste. Nevertheless, if the incident that follows is taken as a guide, the young man probably underestimates the animus of many of the older people toward fish:

The old people won't eat fish or pork. Some won't eat pork yet, and few will eat fish. If my mother eats a little pork, it makes her sick right away. She won't have fish around at all.

Once my brother brought a can of sardines to camp. He was going to open it for lunch. My mother didn't know what he had and she brought out a plate for him to put them on. She asked him what it was. He didn't want to tell her. He held the can behind him. Then he brought it out and opened it up and spilled the fish on the plate my mother was holding. She looked at it. She didn't know what it was. It looked funny to her. She asked my brother, and he told her.

You know how those old people are. She gave a yell and threw it. It landed right in the lap of the old man. The old man just sat there and looked at it. The plate was lying there in the dirt. I nearly died laughing. My brother was angry. He said, "What did you throw them away for?" She said, "If you bring me something bad like that again, I'll throw it right in your face."

"The frog is not eaten; it is classed with fish." "The frog is classed as a snake. We do not eat it. If you do, it will make you walk like a cowboy [i.e., will make you bowlegged]." An informant who apparently equates frogs with snakes said: "I killed frogs and sold them to the [American] soldiers, but I never ate them myself. There were eels in the creek near Fort Sill. B. used to catch them. The soldiers bought them, but the Indians wouldn't eat them."

One voice was raised in appreciation of frogs' legs as food. The Eastern Chiricahua informant, previously quoted, who claims that his people ate fish, added: "They ate frogs' legs too. The meat tastes like chicken and is good."

THE ECONOMIC INTEREST IN RAID AND WAR

For men, raiding approaches hunting in economic significance. In fact, these two pursuits may be said to be rival industries:

The man who has a deer ceremony either does not go on raids or does not spend too much time on raids, so he will not lose his luck with deer. If you are too successful on raiding parties and bring back lots of booty, you become unlucky with deer; you don't see the deer and become a poor hunter.

This statement embodies a psychological and practical truism: The man who becomes engrossed in raid and war very likely has only limited time and interest to devote to the chase.

The raid is a recognized and integral aspect of the economy. This finds expression in the songs. The words of a round-dance song, for instance, repeat: "The wagon goes along, they say, they say." This has been interpreted to mean: "The Chiricahua are out by themselves. They see a wagon. They are glad because they know their warriors will bring in the spoils."

Glory and enhanced status may be the by-products of the raid, but the immediate aims of those who organize such expeditions and participate in them are direct and practical:

One party after the other went out. They went on raids because they were in need. They divided their booty among the poor in camp. Sometimes they traded it to the well-to-do. Sometimes the horses were traded for a woman [in marriage]; they were given to the girl's parents.

When the people are poor and need supplies, the leader says, "We must go out and get what we need." It is volunteer work. Whoever is in want of food and necessities goes. The leader heads the party, which is made up of men only. Women never go on raids.

E.'s father was a great leader. He helped the people many times when they needed things. One time he prophesied that they were going to take a lot of booty near a certain hill. He told the people that a provision train with food and goods of all kinds would pass there. They went there, and the wagons passed by, and they got the goods.

In the speech of a leader, who is about to direct an expedition, the raid is also pictured as a stern economic necessity:

You love your homes and children. But we are going to leave them. Forget them. We do not know what is going to happen. Prepare your weapons. . . . . Do not be afraid. We want to accomplish something for our camp; for our people are in need. . . . .

Since raid and war are viewed as industrial pursuits, unwillingness to participate in them is attributed to indolence rather than cowardice:

If a man wouldn't go to war, it was because he was generally lazy, just too lazy to get around, and his mind watery. Another person might have to push him around to get him to do anything. People who don't go to war are just lazy people; that's all. There may have been some industrious men who did not go to war because they were cowardly—but, of course, these men would never tell why they would not go to war if this was the reason. I suspect there were some who were afraid to die. You couldn't tell for sure. It was usually blamed on laziness.

There is no absolute terminological distinction between the raid and a war expedition. Both are aspects of behavior which is described by a single term meaning "they are scouting about" or "they are raiding here and there." The unifying element again appears to be the interest in the spoils. "There is no difference between the raid and war; they are going to bring back whatever they can either way."

But there is a difference of primary intent which does distinguish the raid from the war expedition. The members of the raiding party have as their sole objective the garnering of horses, cattle, or unguarded possessions of the enemy. They do not go in numbers; they do not seek a bloody encounter. Descriptions of typical raiding parties emphasize the business-like procedure and the pacific attitude:

> As few as five or six would be in the party. About ten is the most that would go. Usually, but not always, one who had power connected with war was along. It was just according to how it happened. Each man took a robe or two along. Each took along a little food in a bag tied to his belt. Often no food was taken along, and the man killed something to eat on the way. Water was brought in a little bag made of entrails, which was carried in the hand. One of the party would bring along a fire drill which was carried in the quiver. The cattle were freely roaming. They drove them off. If they were discovered by the owners of the cattle, they would usually run away without fighting.

> When they are on a stock raid, they don't want to be seen. They sneak around. They are careful; they avoid meeting troops or taking life. It is different from a revenge party.

> A raid is organized by some leader. He decides. In the morning and in the evening he gets on a horse, or stands, and speaks to the people. He calls for all men who wish to go. The war dance is not put on just for a raid for booty. When they go out looking for a fight, they dance the war dance. The booty of the raid is divided as soon as it is obtained. If three men drive off just a little stock, they would keep it all perhaps, though they could give some to others if they wished. If there are many men on a raid and a great deal is driven off, it is evenly divided among the men. The leader of the expedition sometimes gets even less than the other people from the proceeds of the raid. He is supposed to be generous like that.

But, very often, raiders who do not contemplate an actual conflict, find themselves involved in one before they reach home:

> If we were raiding against Mexicans, a party would go down near the enemy's village and stay a short distance away while a few of the men went down and stole horses and cattle. Then, with these possessions, the party would start back. If the soldiers overtook us, there would be a battle.

It is when a raiding party is intercepted, or when disastrous retaliation on the camps follows a raid, that a real war party is formed:

Sometimes when the Chiricahua are on the raid, the enemy kills some of their principal men. The people whose relatives have been killed notify the leaders, warriors, and everybody—the entire encampment. Even though they are in sorrow they notify these friends to have a war dance. Following it they are going to go after the enemy, no matter where they have gone. All the warriors agree to it. Then they have a war dance that night for a few hours. The warriors bring their equipment, knives, bows, guns, and all the weapons they are going to fight with.

The atmosphere on this occasion is very different from that which marks the preparations for a raid:

During the war dance they show what they are going to use when they meet their enemies. This dance means that they are going after all their enemies, everyone except their own tribe members, any other enemies there are. It doesn't have to be the ones that killed their men. They go after anything, a troop of cavalry, a town. They are angry. They fight anyone to get even. When they go out this way, they fight to win. When they are out, they might meet the same enemy who killed their people. Then they turn for home after they have killed all their enemies.

But whether the occasion is a raid for spoils or a punitive expedition demanded by bereaved relatives, attention is likely to be directed to the enemy possessions:

They bring in the captured equipment—guns, saddles, ammunition. When the warriors come within sight of their camp, they all begin to shoot. Then everyone is happy.

When the news comes to camp that a victorious war party is returning (a scout is sent ahead with the news), everyone is excited because there will be things to distribute, and they say, "Let us beat the drum and sing to greet our heroes." The dancers are in two groups; one bunch eats while the other goes on with the dance.

When the men went to Mexico and fought, they would bring back booty of all kinds—blankets and horses. Then they have a dance which can take place in the day or night as soon as they get back. They dance around the fire and the scalp, if any was taken. Then the women dance with the men in the social dancing.

Before this the men dance, and they call off the names of the brave men who were down in Mexico. The men shoot off guns when a name is called. Then the man called makes up his mind and goes and brings blankets and things and puts them there. He tells the women to help themselves. Sometimes he kills a cow or a horse for them. This is done mostly for women who have no men to take care of them. Sometimes the man will just throw out things to the people.

The war dance.—Despite the identical designs on the enemy's goods, the war party differs from the raiding expedition in preliminaries, personnel, and tenor:

Only when they go out for revenge and fighting do they have the dancing beforehand. A relative who wishes a revenge party goes to the leaders and head men and asks them to use their influence to get one up. A large group would go, usually on foot. . . . .

All big war parties are undertaken to avenge deaths. The relatives of the father of the dead person or of his wife will get it started and try to enlist as many as possible. If they are important people, it will be a big party. . . . . As many as volunteered would go. Relatives of the dead man would agitate for the party, and if there was a leader among them, he would be in charge of it.

The war dance is a dramatization of warfare itself and a pledge on the part of the individual warrior to participate in the action and to acquit himself bravely:

All the leading men notified the others that they were going to have a war dance that night and that they were going after the enemy the next day. "Fierce dancing" is what they called this.

All the Indians gathered that night. They didn't tell men that they must go. They don't say, "You must go, and you and you." These Chiricahua feel as men on their own. If things like war are going to happen, they themselves have to show they are manly. It is left up to the individual to decide.

They brought a hide. They had a drum there, a pot covered with buckskin. They went through the thing that has been handed down in tradition from the original time. They know how to go through the performance; it doesn't have to be told. Those who were going to dance put their moccasins on and made themselves just like fighting men in war. They had long hair, so they tied it in place with a headband. Some who had long hair that came down the back tied it back there in the middle so it wouldn't get in the way. The Chiricahua man wears a long and wide loincloth which comes down in front to a place just above the knee and further down in back, near to the ankle. For this dance they brought the back flap through the legs and the front one around too and tucked them into the belt. They don't have to do it if the ends are not in the way, but they want to make themselves as "free" as possible.

What I saw was this. The upper parts of their legs were naked. The shirts of those who wore them flopped around. Some wore cartridge belts as bandoleers. Some carried guns.

The dance always starts with four men. Four men came from the east to the fire, just as the masked dancers do. They marched abreast in line, not one behind the other. They went around the fire four times like this. Then two got on the south side and two on the north. The singers and the hide that was being beaten were on the west. The four faced each other in two pairs. They danced in place. They danced toward each other, changed sides, turned around, and went back. They did this four times. Then the fun began. Then they sang and everyone shouted. The women from all over made that noise as they do in the big tepee. Now it was anyone's chance to dance who wished to. They didn't crowd forward at first though.

The other men were dressed just like those first four fellows. They don't paint their faces or decorate themselves especially for the war dance; they come in just plain. Now whoever wanted to dance got out there. They had guns. They put cartridges in. They shot. They said by their actions, "This is the way I'm going to act in the fight." They put cartridges between their fingers. Some put as many as they could in their mouths.

Some men did not dance. They signified their intention of going to war by coming out during the singing and marching around the fire once. It means, "I am going out."

The men doing the dance did not shout. They just made a noise softly under their breath, like, "Wah! Wah!" You can't shout in the war dance or in war. The belief that has been handed down is that, if you shout in battle, many of you will be killed. Those along the sides shout though.

The dance went on. At every song a new set of men came in and the others went out and stood at the side. There were prayers going on over there. Everyone along the side was praying during the dance. When a principal man's name was called, he got out with his men. They get out in squads, sort of.

When just a few were left who hadn't come out, a few fellows who had talked bravely when drinking tiswin, they were called on in the songs by name. All the rest had been dancing and had shown that they were going out. Then they called these last ones by name. They said in the song, "You, So-and-so, many times you have talked bravely. Now brave people at Casas Grandes (or Chihuahua) are calling to you."

If a person who is called like that doesn't come out and make good his boasts, he's considered no man at all. But few men would hold back when they were called like that. They come out the first thing when they hear their names.

When all who were going to the war had danced, every one of them got in there and they all went around the fire four times together, shooting as they went. Then it was all over.

This dance is also a profound religious experience for the man who takes part in it. "Some who had a spear, hat, and shield made for them through a ceremony danced with them," thus making a plea for success and personal safety in the coming conflict. The dance proceeds with prayer and ritual:

We dance one night and start the next morning. Everyone going on the party had to dance for power. Men puffed smoke to the four directions and prayed: "May I kill an enemy. May I get food."

The war dance lasted for four nights. We danced and prayed for good luck—not to have fun. We wanted to see our enemy and have a victory. This was a very strong ceremony. We asked our supernatural power to let us have the Mexican general or president. We called him by name for four days so that we would capture or kill him. We were always after him and prayed to get him.

The principal singer of the war songs, a patriarch whose supernatural power is connected with raid and war, acts as another link between this dance and the ceremonial complex. A knot of male singers (women do not sing for the war dance) intone the refrain, beating on a piece of rawhide or on pottery drums, and this shaman chants the half-sung, half-spoken prayers. In these prayers, when the other voices are stilled, he calls upon the individual to demonstrate his manliness. One war-dance song contains these words (any name can be substituted for the one that is used here):

> Geronimo, they say to you,
> You! You!
> They call you again and again.

Inspired by the ceremonialism of the occasion, the chosen man responds:

The shaman is on the side of the circle of seated warriors. He calls in his song on such-and-such a warrior to dance. . . . . He calls on one man after another until all are dancing. . . . . When the shaman calls, there is no backing out. I don't care if the odds are against him, a man goes out if he is called upon. He is frenzied, beside himself. It is the power, the prayers, and not just the man.

The use of the personal name acts as an exciting challenge to the warrior:

In the war dance the singer actually calls a man's name. He pretty near has got to go then. He's got to make some kind of a showing. "So-and-so, get up and go to the enemy!" He's got to act when he hears this. He can't very well stay back and keep his self-respect. When we appeal to a man to help, we use his name.

. . . . Not all come out at once. They name a man. This is in the song. They say, "You are a man! Now you are being called. What are you going to do when we fight with our enemy?" Then the man gets out and dances. Or, if he doesn't want to dance, he walks around the fire once to show that he is game.

I saw a war dance in 1883 at Fort Apache, when Chiricahua scouts were going after Geronimo. They called all the people together in a big open space. . . . .

Then the singer called a certain man by name. He said: "C., you are a man. You are known to be a great warrior. You have fought your enemies in close battle. We are calling you to dance." As soon as he said this, C. had his gun ready. He sprang out there, shooting into the air. Then they kept singing and called another name and another until four or five were out there dancing.

The women were at the war dance. But they didn't dance or mix with the men. They stayed about six or eight yards away in a circle around the fire. They made that noise they make in the big tepee at the girl's puberty ceremony. At this war dance the women are all called White Painted Woman. A woman can't be referred to by her own name here. And the men are all called Child of the Water [except when they are named in the song].

Not all men are equally persuaded by this dramatic summons to arms, however:

One fellow refused to fight the Mexicans because he had nothing against them. Hearing the remark, another man started to spear him, but two or three others stopped him. The objector sat down and actually cried. The rest of the group was angry with him. They told him it would have been all right if the other man had speared him. They told him, "You shouldn't say such things! The Mexicans aren't that way and would like to kill you." They all hated him and wouldn't allow him to go to war because his feelings toward Mexicans wouldn't go well in war.

The "fierce dancing" of the warriors is usually followed by social dances in which the women also participate. The first of these is the round dance, named, for this occasion, "they show resentment against the enemy." "It is done in connection with the war dance before they go out on a war party. It takes place after the war dance but the same night. The people are in a bunch with the women on the outside. They go around the fire in a circle. The circle dance is for everybody." After the round dance come the very partner dances which take place during the nights of the girl's puberty rite, and these occur in the same relative order as on that occasion.

There seems to be some variation according to the scope and seriousness of the enterprise in the number of nights these dances continue before the war party starts. One view is expressed in these statements:

They perform the war dance just at night before a fire. They dance all night for four nights. These have to be successive nights. The "fierce dance" comes first. Then there is social dancing until morning. The people sleep during the day.

The leader called all the men together and held a council. If they decided to go to war, they would have a big dance. Before going on the war path the Chiricahua had a four-day war dance.

Whether this is a concession to the sacred number rather than an exact description is difficult to determine. At any rate, a one-night dance has already been twice mentioned, and the possibility of shortening these preliminaries is suggested in other comments:

They generally put on a war dance for two nights and then go out. They wait a day and leave the morning of the fourth day. They do this to get rest and sleep so that they will not have to sleep on the way.

The war dance is carried on at night. It is done for four nights, sometimes two. Then they go. Usually the men rest up a day before starting out.

These excerpts suggest that the expedition need not start the morning after the conclusion of the war dance, and this is supported by a direct statement: "The men do not have to start out immediately after the dancing. They set a day. It may be the fifth or sixth day after the dancing starts."

The preparation for war; war practices.—Sometime between the announcement of the expedition and the departure of the group, those who plan to go put their fighting gear in order. The standard equipment is the self-bow, arrows, wristguard, war club, and a stone knife. A few bring spears and shields as well. After white contact, firearms appear.

The arrows prepared by the warrior are entirely of hard wood or have a cane shaft into which is affixed a hard-wood foreshaft. The tip is sharpened and fire hardened. Three feathers guide the arrow in its flight. Occasionally, arrow poison is employed. "We use it in time of war. To make it we use deer's blood and mix this with plants believed to be poisonous. This mixture is allowed to rot and then is put on arrow points." Variations of this formula occur. One calls for the addition of poisonous insects to putrifying liver; another is a mixture of deer stomach, blood, and thorny plants pounded together and allowed to spoil. Of the action of such poison, an informant declared, "A man hit with an arrow dipped in this turns black."

The bow and arrows are fitted handily into a well-made bow cover and quiver:

When the Chiricahua are on the march and are not using their arrows, they carry them so that the feathers come over the top of the right shoulder. When they are fighting, they reverse the bag so that the feathers come under the left armpit, and they can be snatched out of the quiver with the right hand. For a left-handed person it is just the opposite. Sometimes the quiver is carried over the chest so it will be more handy.

Few men carry shields, for their manufacture is associated with the ceremony obtained from weapons:

They wear the shield on the left arm (if right-handed). It is held over the arm by one or two straps, whatever is convenient. There is no buckskin cover for the Chiricahua shield. If I wanted to make one, I'd have to make it plain. To get it designed properly I have to go to a man who knows how and I have to pay him. A thing like this is made by a shaman, and you have to pay for it no matter how little it is. The man I go to uses his ceremony for my protection and puts on his design. Most shields have just a few feathers in the center and are of painted cowhide. There is buckskin around the edge only. They are very plain.

Spears, too, are most often made and decorated, either for themselves or for others, by shamans with "power of weapons." Before European contact, spears were essentially lengths of sharpened wood. Later, knives and bayonets were attached to the ends. Because the use of the spear brings the warrior within a few steps of his foe, fighting with this weapon is the kind of action expected of war leaders or those who aspire to that status. The spear rose in favor during the time of strife with the Mexicans:

I remember back to the time when the Mexicans and other enemies used guns that I guess they call breechloaders.[7] The Chiricahua were using arrows, war clubs, and spears then. The spear was used when the enemy was taking time to load his gun. The Mexican used to have that big gun. He would shoot once, and the Indian who was a good runner charged him and pushed the spear in him. The Mexican didn't have time to reload.

[7] Probably the informant is thinking of a muzzle-loader.

After the fast-loading gun with cartridges already fixed was in use, you had to be very quick and a good warrior to use a spear. Not everyone used spears. Just a few were brave enough to use a spear that close.

Before the beginning of the journey constant measures of a religious nature are taken. Amulets are procured; protective caps and jackets are made or refurbished; shamans are consulted concerning the probable outcome of the expedition. "The leader goes to a shaman and says, 'You know something. Help us. What will happen?' Then the shaman sings and prays and he tells the people to go on, that they will have success." Sometimes the prophecies of the shaman are not so reassuring, however. "Before they leave camp they might all go in a body to the shaman. He conducts his ceremony, and if he feels that the raid will not come off safely, he says so, and the party does not go out."

Raiding and warfare are the special interests of those who have supernatural power to find or frustrate the enemy. Therefore, one or more shamans are fairly sure to accompany any large war party. Not infrequently the leader himself is a man renowned for his religious attainments as well as for his military prowess. During the entire course of the journey the advice of those who claim revelations in regard to war are treated with respect. Even if the party does not include eminent shamans, the rank-and-file warriors do not fail to come ritually prepared: "Each warrior carries a bag of pollen. Pollen is given to him with other herbs if he gets sick [during the war expedition]."

The entire encampment gathers to watch the departure of the group. "They start sometime in the morning. When they are going for a real fight, everyone sees them off. When the men leave in the morning, the women give their call of applause."

The women, especially the wives of the departing men, have certain obligations during the absence of the warriors:

The women are careful about keeping the woodpile neat while the men are gone. The wood should be placed one way and should not be scattered, and the children should be kept off it for fear they will throw it around, and then the man will be lost. There are no other restrictions on the women when the husbands are out fighting. Some women pray when their husbands are out. Some are as religious as anything, but this praying is not general. During raids or wars the women had to be good and behave carefully so as not to give bad luck to the man. All of a man's relatives were under this restriction.

When a very prominent man with many relatives has been slain, or when an attack on an unguarded camp has aroused great anger, caution is forgotten. "When we are at war and out for a fight, we go right to the trail and face the enemy in the daytime. We are not particular."

Once a San Carlos Indian cut off a Chiricahua's head, and it led to much trouble and an outbreak. J. was right in the particular Chiricahua bunch when it happened.

Some Chiricahua had been away from the reservation. The U.S. army men had been after them and had offered twenty-five dollars for every hostile Chiricahua's head brought in. This bunch of Chiricahua decided to come in. They came close to the agency and were eating there. They put J. on a ridge to watch and stand guard. Finally J. was relieved by another boy, a good-looking young Chiricahua. A few minutes later, as he was sitting on the ridge with his gun across his knees, looking in the opposite direction, a San Carlos Indian crept up behind him and shot him. As soon as he shot, he was on this boy with his knife and cut his head off.

The rest of the Chiricahua came up and saw what had been done. They were as angry as could be. They found out who had done this and went down to his camp to get him. But he had been warned and got away. His wife and several children were there, though, and they killed them and left them lying right there. They went out and began shooting into other near-by San Carlos camps. They were so angry they didn't care what they did. Then they made for the hills. And so there was another outbreak.

But ordinarily rage is tempered by reason, and the war party moves in a disciplined way:

When they start out they have two men ahead and two behind; they have scouts on every side. When they are ready to camp for the night, they send scouts ahead and in the directions to look for the enemy until dark comes. Early in the morning they do the same. These scouts come back and report.

On the march "the men of each cluster [extended family] stick together near their own leader." But, generally speaking, each person is responsible for his own welfare:

Each individual usually takes his own provisions with him. He takes some mescal and dried meat which he carries in a buckskin or hide bag attached to his shoulder strap [bandoleer]. The fire drill, if he has one with him, can be carried in this bag too. He carries water in a container made of the intestines of animals. He just ties the ends to keep it shut. He doesn't carry a water jar, because they are clumsy and because when it gets warm the water gets a pitchy taste. Some might go on horseback and some on foot. Each man cooks for himself; each man eats what he has. If they capture horses from the enemy, each man ropes the best horse he can.

The leader or a shaman sometimes decorates the faces of the members of the group:

There is no special way of face-painting for all warriors. Some leader like Geronimo who has special power might decorate his men as his power directs him. Geronimo used to mark his men on the forehead, the sides of the face, and across the nose.[8] It was his own way though and not the way of all the Chiricahua.

Attached to the party sometimes are novices, though there is a tendency to encourage their attendance on the less hazardous raids instead:

Just the young boy, the novice who is fourteen or fifteen years old, takes a stick and reed for scratching himself and for drinking water. They have to use the sacred language while they are out. These boys have to use this kind of talk around camp too as long as they are novices. On the warpath or raid the men call the novice Child of the Water.

On the journey the shaman's advice is a powerful influence in determining the decisions of the leader:

Any big war party will have a shaman along to tell them how to get success. He tells them whether to go to the open country or whether to keep back in the hills where the enemy are. They don't have to take any certain shaman along on a war party. There is sure to be some regular warrior along who has power.

Of the time and manner of attack on enemy camps, this account has been given: "We usually attack early in the morning. We are quiet when we go to attack. We fight in hand-to-hand action, and the individual can advance or retreat according to his chance and how the fight is going. In the battle the men obey the leader."

The role of the leader in the actual conflict is a central one:

Before the engagement each leader would talk to his group and encourage them. He would go before them in battle and perform great feats to spur them on. After the engagement he had to lead his men to safety and water.

---

[8] One informant gave a secular reason for the face-painting: "The white paint on the faces of Geronimo's men was to mark them in battle so they wouldn't kill their own men."

The shaman and the leader entered right into the fight. In a battle the leader and the shaman would each be on one flank of the men. The leader would detail two to go out in front. If the enemy should begin to charge them, the leader would order all his men forward immediately. The leader takes the front and the shaman the rear, urging the men forward.

The position of the shaman at this time is not due to reluctance to risk combat with the enemy. He falls behind "to perform his ceremony and prevent injuries." This ceremonial function may even overshadow in significance leadership of the more warlike type, for ceremonialism is injected into the military action from beginning to end. In a description of a specific war party which he accompanied and in which he and his kin avenged the death of a relative, an informant reports: "When the war party was ready to attack, the shaman prayed, turned to the four directions, then faced the warriors, and ordered them to charge."

Should the warriors find themselves in jeopardy, they resort to strategy, as in this method of rendering Mexican firearms ineffective:

During the battle the Chiricahua used bows and arrows and spears but had no rifles. The Mexicans were not afraid of bows and arrows, so the Chiricahua leader would send two Indians into the open, just out of range. These two men would try to avoid the bullets; they were protected by the shamans and were never shot. The reason they sent these two men out was that the Mexicans' rifles would become heated after a while and they would not be able to shoot straight. I saw this happen often, for I was at war nearly every month.

After the two Chiricahua had been in the open for perhaps half an hour, they would go back to the line of warriors. Then all would charge the Mexicans and kill as many as a hundred. Often the Indians would kill all of their foes; those on horseback might get away, but never those on foot. The only way the Mexicans could beat us was if some Chiricahua men were scouting and the Mexicans made a raid on their home camp in their absence.

When hard pressed, the warriors are capable of arranging traps and ambushes:

Suppose there were forty or fifty men out on the war party. The enemy is right after them. They get to a brushy place. They all go straight ahead and then they divide, and part come back on the side in the bushes. The enemy goes right on. The Chiricahua ahead begin shooting. Then when the enemy turns, the Chiricahua in their rear and on the side begin to shoot. They did this many times. They always have a couple of scouts behind and on the side and a couple ahead in the roughest places, looking for signs of the enemy. These are the fastest men.

Another trick is like this. If the enemy is right on their trail and is catching up to them, they get into the roughest, most rocky place they can find. Two Chiricahua scouts stay behind and show themselves to the enemy while the rest conceal themselves. These two act as though they didn't know the enemy is there. They get in range of the enemy. They act as if they had no idea the enemy is in sight. They go toward the place where their own men are. They are watching though, and are ready to jump and run as soon as the enemy shoots at them. When this happens they will be running toward their own men. These Chiricahua see them coming and let them pass. But the enemy comes after them, and before they know it they are in front of the Chiricahua weapons. This has been done several times, they say. They have to plan what to do beforehand to accomplish it.

In the thick of battle the use of the name again operates as a solemn claim:

If we are having a fight with Mexicans, or are in any other kind of battle, and everybody runs away from me and leaves me with the enemy shooting at me, it is all right to call a man's name to get help. Maybe P. is the last man and he is starting away and is about to pass me. I call him by his name and say, "Don't leave me here alone with these people!" Then he would say, "Well, that's my name," and he would turn around and begin to fight again. That's how the name is used. If you call his name, it is almost impossible for a man to leave you. In time of peace a person doesn't like to be called by his name.

If superior numbers are encountered or if the fight is turning out badly, the warriors disperse:

Sometimes they scatter out and agree to meet at a certain place on a certain day. A small group goes this way and another goes that way. They run on rocks as much as possible so that their tracks will not be seen. They say, "Go on rocks so your tracks will not be fresh. Keep off soft ground."

A person hides his tracks by jumping from rock to rock and from bunch of grass to bunch of grass to get away from those who are following. Another thing he does sometimes is to take grass and rub out his tracks with it so they won't be noticed at some places where they are too plain.

Signs on the trail or other devices may be necessary in time of war:

Sometimes they tie a piece of something on a tree and then on another so that they can be trailed by friends who are looking for these signs. The pieces may be a whole day's journey apart. But the Chiricahua is looking for it as he goes along, for the agreement has been made, and he knows what the sign will be. Or they might agree that a stone pointing in a certain way will be a sign. Lines on the ground are also made to indicate which way they are turning on the trail. Dropping a stick in the direction in which you are traveling is another way.

The wolf howl may be simulated by the members of a scattered party. "The warriors would call to each other with the wolf howl. When the Mexicans were our enemies, we used to howl to each other in this way so that the enemy would not know who we were."

The smoke signal, too, is used to some extent:

If a group agrees that when they get to a certain place they will make a smoke signal, the others watch for it. None is made except on agreement. It has to be used during the daytime. Sotol is used to make these smoke signals.

For signal smoke a fire is built, and damp wood and grass are put on; this makes a smoke that can be seen for great distances. Whenever the Chiricahua see smoke from a long distance, they know something is happening. The smoke always means something, usually that there are enemies or that there is an epidemic. If it means the first, the smoke is from a mountaintop. If it means sickness, it comes from a camp in the valley.

According to another informant, the smoke signal can be used to determine whether members of an approaching group are friends or foes:

If one party of men sees another in the distance, it lights a fire to the right of it and sends up one column of smoke. This means, "Who are you?" If the other group builds a fire to its right and sends up one column of smoke it means, "We are Chiricahua and friends." To send up the smoke, they put wet grass on the fire and throw a rock on top. The weight of the rock makes the fire burn fast. Then you scatter the fire quickly to stop the smoke.

Finally, the smoke signal serves to acquaint the home camp of the war party's safety:

If, when the warriors leave, they are not certain at just what time they are coming back, the people who are left behind must look for smoke at a certain mountain or canyon that they name. These people have to have a scout looking for this smoke. For instance, they say they will be back in fifteen days. The days pass, and they are not back. Then those left behind look for smoke from that day on at the place they mentioned.

After the introduction of the mirror, some use was made of it for signaling in times of strife:

We used a mirror. Quivering a beam toward strangers and then casting out a long beam from you means, "Who are you?" The others reply, "A friend," by directing the beam toward themselves and then in a circle toward you. Flashing downward with the beam means, "Come." Flashing to the right means, "Go right," to the left means, "Go left."

One of the chief benefits of star lore, apparently, is to help raiders or warriors find their way about:

I can't tell you much about the stars. I never paid much attention to it. But you take a man like L.: he's been out at war many times. He has had to go by the stars. He knows all about them and what direction they are moving in.

Timekeeping devices are important to the warriors and to those awaiting their return:

Suppose you had promised someone to be somewhere in a certain number of days. You'd have to start at the right time to get there. So every morning you would throw a stone in a certain place and keep count of them. In this way you would know when to start. Or you might do it with marks on a stick. I have heard of doing it with beads on a string too. A few, maybe one or two out of the whole tribe, kept time by beads.

When a war or raiding party scatters, some individuals may lose their way, and they are likely to suffer from lack of water. Certain aids are therefore taught to everyone:

We are taught, when thirsty and without water, to put a dry stick or stone in the mouth. I have done it lots of times. It starts the saliva and helps you. We melt snow for water when we find some in the mountains. Different kinds of cactus are used when we are in the flats. We chew the inner parts of the cactus for thirst. No matter how hot the weather is, that is always cool. Barrel cactus saved many people too. To get the water you knock the top off. There is water in there; it's like a watermelon. To get the water, you have to squeeze the pulp. And we get rain water from mescal. This plant holds water [in the basal leaves]. The animals get water from these. The deer and horses drink from them. In the south the big ones grow. To drink, the man uses a reed or something hollow if he has it and sucks it out.

In emergencies, improvised footgear must sometimes be made. "When the Chiricahua were caught out on the raid or at war and their moccasins gave out, they took grass and tied it to their feet with two or three strips of yucca."

The warrior has little respect for a senseless sacrifice of life, but when he is brought to bay he is capable of furious resistance:

When a Chiricahua is cornered and desperate and thinks the end has come, he tears off his shirt and headband. He tears off all his clothes but his loincloth, and he goes right into the thick of it. Sometimes he fights so hard that he gets away.

The wounded constitute a major problem of war:

If anybody is wounded on the warpath, they try to bring him back. But it is often far, and they often die. If they get back, herbs will be used on the wounds, and the shaman will sing. . . . . Cures might be worked on the warpath if there was somebody along who knew how.

Scalping and the taking of captives.—Scalping is a very recently acquired custom and one for which there is limited enthusiasm. A number of spokesmen flatly denied that scalping is a practice of their people:

The Chiricahua never scalp. They never bother with them. They don't like them. It looks as if it is against their religion.

I don't think scalping is the habit of the Chiricahua, for I have not seen many try it. It looks as though a few saw other Indians do it and tried it.

Retaliation for atrocities visited upon them is the explanation most often given by those who admit that some scalps were taken. The Mexicans are frequently blamed for the development of this form of revenge:

The Mexicans used to take scalps. They started it first—before the Chiricahua. They used to take scalps, including the ears, and sometimes they took the whole head. The Chiricahua would make peace with the Mexicans. Then the Mexicans would give them liquor, get them drunk, take them in their houses, and cut off their heads. Then the war would start again.

Scalping is used as a last resort on a man who has made a great deal of trouble for the Chiricahua. Such a man, when finally caught, would be scalped and "danced on." He was scalped after he was dead. The whole scalp was taken off. In the dance the pole is in the center with the scalp on top, and they dance around it. The scalp is thrown away at the end of the dance. This is used mostly on Mexicans who did awful things against the Chiricahua.

While the Mexicans were undoubtedly the special object of Chiricahua hatred during this period, the data indicate that the scalping of members of other groups did sometimes occur. But, in any case, scalping was never carried on extensively:

They scalped enemies. They did it to the whites. They put the scalp on a stick and hold it up and dance. . . . . They put it on a tree after the dance and let it dry and rot away.

The Chiricahua do not take the scalps of all the fallen enemies; but they take just one scalp, that of the man they believe to be the leader. Then they all go home with the stock that they have captured. They take this one scalp home with them.

At home the hair of the scalp is tied onto a stick, and one man holds this stick upright with the scalp at the top of it. They have a dance around this scalp, lasting four days. The reason for the dance is that it is revenge for their dead, and they are proud, thinking that they are even with the other side. The widow, mother, and sister of a dead warrior feel proud when they see the scalp. They feel that they are even with the other side, and they take part in the four-day dance. They dance the round dance.

There is no interest in accumulating scalps; instead there is a fear of them. "They just let the scalp stay there until it wastes away; they don't do anything to it. Those who handle the scalp usually burn the 'ghost medicine' so the ghost won't bother them in any way."

All specific accounts of the scalp dance, incidentally, are from members of the Eastern band, neighbors of the Mescalero Apache and nearest to the Plains and its influences. Persons from other bands deny that they shared the custom. Said a member of the Central band: "I have never heard of a scalp dance among my people. I have been asking the old people. All say the Central Chiricahua do not do this." And from a man of the Southern band comes the statement: "We did not scalp or display a scalp at this time or any other. We are afraid of the blood and the ghost of the man. We didn't want to have anything to do with it."

Prisoners are taken in battle for a number of reasons:

When they capture a prisoner they always question him and get what information they can. If he won't give it, they usually kill him right there, or else they take him back to camp for the women to kill. Grown men are never kept alive to be married into the tribe or enslaved. A mature man is dangerous, and they kill him. But a young boy of four, five, or six is adopted into the tribe. He becomes a real Chiricahua and later marries into the tribe. Children like this are captured when their father and mother are killed. The Chiricahua take the children to increase the tribe, and they are treated like other children. When the

Chiricahua attack a village, they don't kill the women and children much, but let them run away.

The violent end of adult male captives at the hands of vengeful women has been described by several informants:

The Chiricahua treated Mexicans in a rough way when they were captured, but they didn't treat Americans like that. These Chiricahua were more the enemies of the Mexicans than of any other people on earth, because the Mexicans treated these Chiricahua in a nasty way.

They say they used to tie Mexicans with their hands behind their backs. Then they turned the women loose with axes and knives to kill the Mexican prisoner. The man could hardly run, and the women would chase him around until they killed him.

But usually they had to ask the head man whether he wanted it done. Then, even if he didn't want it done, the warriors could vote on it, and, if he was overruled, it would be done anyway. Usually the people whose relatives had been killed wanted it to be done. They wanted to have their way about it.

When a brave warrior is killed, the men go out for about three Mexicans. They bring them back for the women to kill in revenge. The women ride at them on horseback, armed with spears.

Women captives are rarely taken; when they are, there can be no sexual interest in them:

When Chiricahua men are on the raid or warpath and they capture Mexican women or women of other tribes, they don't do anything to them. They are afraid to have sexual intercourse with them, for they say, if they do, their luck will be spoiled. They can't do it. But the Mexicans did it every time they got Indian women.

Even after arrival in the camp, it is considered improper to mistreat the women captives sexually. "The Chiricahua do not force a woman captive. If you can make her love you, all right. But she is not mistreated."

The only captive really desired, then, is the small boy:

Our warriors would try to catch a young boy. They don't bother with women and older people. All the prisoners who were brought back and lived with the Chiricahua that I know about were males. At first they have to act as servants. They have to eat as servants. Some escape after a while. Others stay.

It is taken for granted that they belong in the group; they become members of the group. The feeling of captivity wears off in time. Such a boy can marry into the tribe later, and his children are accepted as members of the tribe. The captive is brought up by the man who captures him. He calls the man father and the woman who adopts him mother.

The victory celebration.—With their booty, the captives, and the scalp, if they have taken one, the warriors journey homeward as rapidly as possible. "When the men come into sight, all the women gather and give their call of applause." If horses or cattle have been obtained, these are distributed, and "everyone who took part in the war gets his share." Each warrior keeps the personally obtained enemy possessions which have fallen into his hands.

A victory is celebrated in dance, song, and feasting. "There is a big fire, and they dance all night and for four days and nights. Some hardly sleep for the four days, they are so proud. All the warriors are dressed as they were in the fight, and some of them wear a hat that they use in battle."

The dances now performed parallel those which took place before the start of the war party. The first of the set is the "fierce dance." "They have the same kind of war dance they had before the men went out. They have this first and then have social dancing." Again the men are called upon by name, this time to show how they acquitted themselves in the struggle:

In the songs that follow, the singers tell what the man dancing did. They say, "So-and-so, you did a great thing. Come out and show what you did." Then this man whose name is called comes out, and he shows in action what he did. He doesn't say anything. Those fellows who sing were in the fight. They saw what he did; they tell it in song. Some are too lazy to do anything more than go around the fire once when they are called like this. The war dance the night of the return is the same as before going out.

After the warriors have received recognition, general dancing takes place. "Not only the warriors but all the people who feel good dance. They dance the circle dance, the couple dance, and toward morning the men and women line up in opposite rows, and the two lines go back and forth together. All is just a good time."

The first of these dances in which all those present take part is the round or victory dance, this time called "they come in with the enemy." It is during this dance that the scalp is displayed by some of the groups. When this occurs, it forces no great shift in psychology or content:

The round dance takes place after the war dance at the return of the party. It can come at day or night. The dance is to show that they hate the enemy. The men are in a knot in the center and go around the fire with drums, singing. The women are in a circle outside facing toward the men. They dance in a sunwise circle. The men go around too. They sing songs about raid and war, like:

> Whatever you have brought back with you,
> Give me some of it.

This is a sample of the songs sung; they have to do with what happens on the warpath. Another of these songs tells of one who got out on a war party and then got separated from the others. In the words it says:

> I've been wandering around,
> Wandering around;
> When I got home,
> Everyone had moved.

The partner dance, in which the woman is free to choose a male partner, follows the round dance, just as it does the nights of the girl's puberty rite. Again the women are paid by the men who have danced with them. One informant claims that the obligation to pay the dance partner is fundamental to the victory celebration, when the men are in possession of booty; and that the gift-giving following the dancing of the puberty rite is an outgrowth of this custom. "The only time men paid for social dancing in the old days was when they returned from the warpath," he asserts. "They did not pay for dancing with women during the puberty ceremony in the old days."

In the fourth dance of the night, as at the girl's puberty rite, a line of men and another of women face each other and alternately approach and separate.

A Southern Chiricahua informant mentioned one other dance which he claims sometimes took place at a victory celebration. This he calls "holy singing walk." As he describes it, a single line of individuals, with men and women alternating, extends spokelike from the fire and swings around it sunwise: "They dance this when they come back from a war party, after the 'fierce dance.' There are no partners to it. Religious songs go with it; this is more of a religious dance."

There is no evidence that conventional morality is totally discarded at this time, but there are suggestions that more freedom than usual is allowed:

The dancing may go on for two, three, or four days. There is much feasting. Some people are eating, others are dancing. There are many marriages during this period. The Chiricahua, when they were captured and taken to Mexico, noticed that, when the Mexican people had a big victory, they always celebrated by dancing and marrying and having a good time. To get even with them, the Chiricahua turn their victories into a celebration and a dancing and marrying time. Many young men take advantage of the occasion.

Thoughts of death are not permitted to interfere with the happy mood: "Dead warriors are not mentioned in the songs, and the deaths are in no way formally announced. When the war party returns, the members state the news of the casualties privately." There is no general purifying rite for those who have come in contact with corpses during the fighting. The use by some of "ghost medicine" to stave off evil effects is "an individual matter; they don't do it in a bunch."

THE GATHERING AND UTILIZATION OF WILD FOOD PLANTS

The responsibility of exploiting the wild-plant resources of the region falls to the women:

While the man is hunting, the woman gets up before sunrise, builds the fire if the man hasn't already done so, and cooks the morning meal, using meat if there is some, vegetables if not. Then she goes out to gather seeds or plants, leaving the small children with another woman. She gathers yucca fruit, piñon nuts, or whatever is in season and carries it all home to prepare.

Gathering, preparing, and storing fruits and vegetables provide a continual round of labor as the women follow the natural harvests:

In spring they go out for mescal. They keep going for it for some time. They get plenty of it and store it up. By the time that is done they can go out after the first acorns and bring them in and store them in bags. Then the yucca fruit and the sumac berries and other things are ready.

The preoccupation with the growth of wild plants is reflected in the attitude toward the seasons and in the names of the principal time periods. Besides the four seasons, six time periods, beginning with the first signs of spring, divide the year. Their names, in order, are: "Little Eagles," "Many Leaves," "Large Leaves," "Large Fruit," "Earth Is Reddish Brown," and "Ghost Face." "Little Eagles" refers to early spring; "Many Leaves" covers the period of late spring and early summer; "Large Leaves" is midsummer; "Large Fruit" (some call this period "Thick with Fruit") designates the harvest time of late summer and early fall. By late fall the hills assume a color for which the term, "Earth Is Reddish-Brown" seems appropriate. Dread of the lifeless winter is expressed in the name, "Ghost Face." The entire year is called "one harvest." "Ten years ago would be ten harvests ago." Periods of time shorter than the six divisions with descriptive names are reckoned from new moon to new moon. "You say so many days from the beginning of the new moon," or, "So many new moons ago."

If food is to be gathered near home, the woman takes her large burden basket and works alone or with her daughter or sister. "They have a little jug to carry drinking water in while they are away from camp. Often they stay out all day. They eat any time they care to." When a long journey is necessary, a larger party of women will set out together. "They go in groups of six or so and keep their finds separately." Should the destination be so distant that the group cannot hope to return for some days, men or youths go along to protect them and to assist in the heavy work.

Through most of the winter and until mid-spring the household must depend on stored vegetables saved from the preceding year. But in the spring the narrow-leafed yucca sends up a central stem which is gathered while it is still green, tender, and without blossoms. Lengths of the stalk are placed on a bed of embers and roasted until they are soft. The charred outer surface is peeled, and the stalks are eaten without further preparation. Thicker stalks are sometimes roasted in an underground oven. A hole is dug in the earth (one is described as four feet long and three and a half feet deep) and a fire is kindled in it. Stones are heated by placing them on top of the burning wood, and the oven is lined with them. The woman peels the pieces of stalk, pounds them or cuts them in half, places them on the stones, covers them with dampened grass, and heaps a mound of earth over all. If she does this in the morning, the food will be thoroughly steamed by evening.

After the stalks have been cooked this way, they may be sundried and kept for some time, even for a year, in a parfleche. When they are wanted, they are soaked in water to soften them and eaten. Or they may be eaten immediately after they have been baked—often pounded—while they are still soft, with fruit from the broad-leafed yucca or some other fruit. This stalk is not the favorite vegetable, but it becomes important when other food is scarce.

Available at this time also are the white rootstocks and the tender lower portions of the shoots of the tule. These are boiled with meat or made into a soup. "We boil the root with a soup bone as some people do turnips." The root is sometimes dried and stored.

By now the clusters of white flowers of the narrow-leafed yucca are in bloom. These are gathered and boiled with meat or bones. Any surplus is boiled, dried, and stored. The buds of still another variety of yucca (unidentified) are opened and dried. During the process they must be impaled on sticks "as you dry peaches; you cannot put them on a hide because they would stick to it. . . . . These are used to sweeten drinks." The drinks are various kinds of "tea" to be discussed presently.

Not long after this an important food, the agave, century plant, or, as it is more commonly known, the mescal, is ready. The stalks, before any blossoms appear, are cut and roasted or pit baked like yucca stalks, but much more important as a food is the lower portion or crown. If the women live far from the place where mescal is plentiful, they make a long trip to obtain it, establish a temporary camp, and prepare it there before returning home. When many crowns are to be baked, a large pit must be dug and many rocks transported to it; therefore, men sometimes accompany the party to assist with this heavy labor. Whether men are present or not, the women are in charge of the proceedings:

When the stalks are just coming up and are going to blossom, we go to a place where the mescal is plentiful and dig a pit in about the center of the region in which we are going to get the plants. They are big and heavy, and we don't want to carry them farther than we have to. If men are along, they dig the pit while the women start bringing in the plants. There has to be plenty of wood too and some big flat rocks. If the plants are scattered and a long way from the pit, the woman uses a horse to carry them in.

The woman has an oak stick about three feet long, sharpened at the end like a chisel. She drives this at the lower part [at the stem below the crown], pounding it with a rock, and it [the crown] rolls out. Then she turns the plant over and cuts off the outside leaves with a broad stone knife. Enough of the outside is cut off to expose the white underpart. Then she brings it to the pit.

The pit is round, seven feet or more across and three or four feet deep. This hole is lined evenly with rocks. Then a big pile of wood is brought. This is put into the hole in criss-cross layers, first a layer one way and then a second layer the other. It is built up like this until the pit is just about full. Then more rocks are put on top of this wood. Fire is touched to it—from the east side first, then from the south, then from the west, and from the north. Then the woman who did this prays. They let the wood burn to ashes. Then they put the mescal in. Each woman will leave a leaf on her mescal heads in a certain place so that she can tell her own. Wet grass goes on top of the mescal, then dirt until no more steam comes out.

The smaller mescal they put in during the late afternoon and let them go all night. Sometimes they are ready the next day. To make sure, they take one out, and, if it is not ready, they put it back and let them all go for a while. How long it takes depends mostly on the size. The ones which grow to the south are larger. The largest ones take four days. Usually they take about two days.[9]

"The botton part of the mescal, the part that is put in the oven, has to be eaten at once unless it is to be dried and preserved. It will spoil if it is not dried." Therefore, the leaves, called "wings," are peeled off and put in the sun to dry, and the softer centers are pounded into thin sheets and spread out in the sun. Juice, drained from pounded mescal suspended over a receptacle, is poured on the dried mescal sheets and forms a preservative glaze.

When the mescal is sufficiently dry and cool to transport, the homeward journey begins. Sometimes the "heads" are carried,

[9] One informant, a Central Chiricahua, told of a method of baking mescal without digging a pit. According to him, rocks are heated and scattered on the level ground, the mescal crowns are put on them, and fresh grass and dirt are piled over all. This "oven" has the appearance of a mound.

on horses, in loosely woven, traylike containers made of yucca, and the sun-drying is done at home. Most of the mescal is stored in the sun-dried, caked state. When a part of a dried crown is to be eaten, it is soaked in water until it softens. It may be mixed with juniper or sumac berries, piñon nuts, or walnuts for variety. The leaves have a pithy, inedible center, but the inner surface of each has a soft layer that is chewed or scraped.

Ordinarily, the woman goes out several times to gather mescal, for she must have enough for general use and for storage. Since each operation—the trip to the place where the plants grow, the roasting and drying, and the return journey—requires several days, this is a busy period. By the time the mescal stalks have flowered and the plants are unfit for use, summer is at hand, and other foodstuffs have made their appearance.

In early summer the locust tree is in flower. The woman picks the blossoms and boils them with meat or other foods, or she boils them in water, dries them in the sun, and puts them away. Then, when she wishes to use them, "she can cook them over again." The first of a number of varieties of wild onion is ready, too. Onions are eaten raw or boiled with other vegetables and meat. Later at least two other kinds are gathered. In the early part of the growing season, too, especially when other food is scarce, the woman strips off the bark from the Western yellow pine, scrapes its inner surface, and heaps together the soft, sweet material.

Though most of the sumac berries are not ripe until late summer and fall, one variety is ready now: "It [*Rhus microcarpa*] has a small red berry which is picked and brought back. The berries are spread out, and the good ones are picked out, washed, and put in the sunshine to dry. After being ground, they are mixed with mescal, and the mixture does not spoil."

From midsummer on, in certain localities, the berries of the one-seeded juniper ripen:

They have a reddish tinge when they are ripe and fall to the ground. The women pick them up and put them in sacks or burden baskets they bring with them. When they are very ripe, they can be eaten raw, or, if they are still very hard, they can be boiled just enough to make them soft. Another way to use them is to boil them until they are quite soft and then mash them with the hands to get the seeds out. What is left is boiled down until just a thick juice is left. This is used more for health than food, although it is considered a regular food. It has a laxative effect, and we eat it as the white man eats prunes. It has a pleasant taste; you can eat a great deal of it, and it won't do you any harm.

In midsummer, too, the first of the edible seed-bearing plants are ready. The woman gathers the seeds by running her hand through the tops and dropping the seeds in a hide receptacle. Threshing is accomplished by working the seeds around manually in the sack. To winnow them, the seeds are poured from a tray basket to an outstretched hide below. The seeds are boiled and eaten or ground on the metate with the mano and reduced to flour from which bread is made.

Now such fruits as raspberries, strawberries, and the earliest of the wild grapes can be gathered. All these are eaten fresh. Grapes are sometimes dried and preserved, and raspberries may be crushed, dried, and kept in caked form.

In the mountains in late summer the woman finds such varied fruits and plants as the chokecherry, the mulberry, a species of potato (*Solanum jamesii*, Torr.), and wood sorrel. Chokecherries are eaten raw when they are very ripe and not infrequently are dried, ground, and stored. Dried chokecherries are soaked in water and eaten without further preparation. Potatoes are boiled and eaten soon after they are gathered or are dried, stored, and ground into flour for making bread. Mulberries are served fresh or caked and preserved. Wood sorrel is eaten raw or cooked with other greens. Another potato-like food (*Ipomoea lacunosa*) is available at about the same time. "It is like a potato in taste. It's white and looks like an onion, but it doesn't taste anything like an onion. It's about half the size of an onion. These are eaten raw. You can keep them for a couple of weeks."

During the same period, in the lowlands, such plants as the nipple cactus and the pitahaya yield their fruit. Of the latter, the more important of the two, this description is given:

This cactus is like the giant cactus, but smaller. It grows in Old Mexico. The plant is taller than a man. The fruit is as large as a man's fist. When the pod opens, it is ready to be picked. It is ready about the middle of August. The fruit is red and is eaten raw. The fruit is dried near the place where it is picked and after it is dried it is piled into burden baskets and brought home. Some of it is eaten fresh, but most of it is dried in the sun, caked, and stored. It never gets really dry; it is always sweet and sticky. Sometimes the fruit drops to the ground, and there are many ants in it when you pick it up.

At lower elevations the yellow fruits of the screw bean or tornillo are one of the first of the fall foods to mature. These sweet pods are eaten raw or are washed, dried, and ground into flour for making bread.

For those groups whose territory extends well to the south, the fruit of the giant cactus is available at approximately this time:

We eat the fruit raw when it is ripe. The women take a long reed stem or a pole and pick the fruit off with it, for it grows high on the plant. They cake some of it as they do mescal and yucca fruit. It never gets real dry; it is always sweet and sticky. It is ripe about the last of August and in September. When you eat it, you eat the seeds and all. The seeds are small, like those of figs.

Between the ripening of other foods, the last of the sumac berries are picked. No sooner are these stored than the broad-leafed yucca or datil fruit is ready:

When the Chiricahua are in the hills, they prepare yucca fruit for winter food. They gather it in the fall, in the latter part of September here [at Mescalero, New Mexico]. It is a pinkish color on the outside when it is ripe. It is good to eat raw when it is ripe. When it is very ripe, it doesn't have to be roasted. It is just cut open, the seeds are taken out, and it is spread out in the sun to dry. It will keep all winter then.

But most of the fruit is picked before it is quite ripe. The women gather a large amount. They roast it on the coals. When the fruits are black on top, they are taken off, and the burned outside is peeled off. They are split in two, and the seeds are taken out. The fruit is then put on a hide and pounded. Then they put it over a container in a basket and let the juice run down. They can drink this juice or pour it over the fruit again. It makes the yucca fruit soft and sticky. After that they spread the whole mass out to dry in the sun. If rain comes, they have to cover it up. It gets dry in the sun in two days. While it is drying, they take sunflower blossoms and put them on to make it pretty. They pray while they do it.

When it is dry, this fruit can be stored. It will keep like a cracker. During the fall the women put piles of it away for emergency or for the winter. When it is wanted, it is made ready for use by soaking and is then used alone or mixed with other things.

In the mountains at this season are gathered the sweet red berries of the algerita. When these are cooked a little, they soften to the consistency of a jelly. A portion of algerita berries is dried and kept for winter use. Currants are picked whenever the women, in foraging, come upon them. Hawthorne fruits are utilized when they are found in abundance, but the dependence upon them is slight. The berries of the alligator juniper ripen in the fall and are at once added to the household stores.

Ready at this time also is the fruit of the prickly-pear cactus:

When the fruit is ripe, while it is still on the plant, it is first cleaned of spines with a brush of stiff grass. It is then picked off with tongs of wood made by bending a branch on itself. While it is still held in these tongs, it is again brushed with the grass. Then the woman puts the fruit in her burden basket, and when she has many of them she takes them home. The fruit can be eaten fresh, or it can be dried and saved. It must be preserved by drying or eaten at once.

To dry the fruits, she splits them, takes the seeds out, and leaves them in the sun. They dry quickly if the sun is strong, but during rainy weather it takes a long time. After the seeds are removed, the pulp is mashed sometimes, and the juice that runs from it is put over the fruit again. It is kept in this caked form, for the layer of juice acts to preserve it. If it is thoroughly sun dried, when it is wanted for use, it is usually boiled. Sometimes soaking it in water without boiling will soften it enough for eating.

Sometimes the fruit is mashed, the pulp is thrown away, and the juice is kept for a drink. It is drunk while it is fresh and is considered healthful.

The mesquite beans are now large and ripe in the lowlands. These beans are used in a number of ways. The woman grinds them to flour on the metate and from this flour makes what can best be described as a pancake. Or she prepares a kind of sweet, thick gruel by boiling the beans and working the softened mass with her hands. She also cooks the whole beans with meat; then the seed coats are spit out when the food is eaten.

Walnuts, one of the important products, are sought at this time:

The Chiricahua use wild walnuts. They carry them around in a parfleche. When they want to eat them fresh, they just pick up those that have fallen on the ground. If the nuts have been there for a while and are dry, they just crack them and eat them. If there are many of them, they save some. In the winter they sit and crack nuts and give them to their children.

But if they want to mix them with other things, like mesquite beans, they do it differently. Then they gather them green, and each woman cuts a long stick, six or seven feet long, just heavy enough so that a person can sit there all day long hitting the nuts and hulling them. One woman will be sitting with hers spread out on the ground before her; another will be a little distance away. They have to do this near water, near a creek, and wash them. Next they spread them out to dry for many days when the weather is good.

Then in wintertime they use the nuts with mesquite beans or mescal. They sit there and pound the nuts with a stone, shell and all, just as fine as possible. The mesquite beans are boiled and strained. For a strainer they use sticks that cross or a branch that has many twigs. This catches nearly all the coarse material. Then they put the nuts in but do not boil the mixture any more. It is ready to eat then.

When this is finished, you can dip in there with your bowl and hold it to your mouth and drink it like soup. This food is used nearly always at the girl's puberty rite.

It's just the opposite from chewing tobacco. When you chew tobacco, you spit out the juice and leave in the coarse stuff; when you eat this, you swallow the juice and spit out the coarse stuff.

An Eastern Chiricahua added to the above that his people boil the meats of walnuts as well.

The nuts of the Western yellow pine are not large enough to gain much attention: "We don't pick them much; just a few now and then." Of much more importance are the seeds of the piñon pine. "When the outside shell is still green, the women pick many of them, heat them, and then, when they are shaken or stroked, the little nuts come out. Some ripen on the trees by themselves, open, and the nuts fall to the ground. The women pick these up too."

The women parch the piñon nuts for a few minutes until "they get a little darker; then they will keep." There are a number of ways of utilizing the seeds. They may be cracked with a stone and the meats eaten alone, or the meats, when a sufficient quantity of them is shelled, "are mixed with yucca fruit which has been baked on coals; it makes good eating." As in the preparation of walnuts, the seeds, shell and all, may be ground fine on the metate and mixed with other foods. Mesquite beans, mescal, yucca fruit, and sumac berries have been mentioned as other foods with which they are combined.

The acorns of both the Gambel oak and the live oak are valuable foods, for the acorn is used in a kind of pemmican:

In the autumn the women wait until the acorns are ripe and fall to the ground. Then they gather many of them and bring them in. Some people leave them in sacks just as they are when gathered and later crack the shells with their teeth and eat the nuts.

But some roast the nuts a little, crack them, and put them out in the sun to dry. Then they use the nuts with the dry [jerked] deer meat and some fat. First they pound the dry meat on a rock and mix it with a little fat. Then they take the acorn meats and pound them up fine. After that they mix the meat and the acorns together. They shape it like meat balls, and these keep all winter. If they are camping in any place, they can have it for any meal. When it is made this way it is all ready to eat at any time. You eat it just as it is. Because it is all prepared, it is a good thing to take on a journey. When a big group is on a journey and a child is hungry, they give it some of this.

During the summer and fall the women gather various greens for flavoring stews and soups. Lamb's quarter is one of these. It is cooked with meat or bones, chili, and onions. Locust pods, the white seeds of the anglepod, the seeds of the unicorn plant, and still other varieties of wild potatoes and onions are procured at this time.

A number of grasses and other plants (among them dropseed grass, tumbleweed, pigweed, spurge, and sunflower) are harvested for their seeds. Most of these are hand threshed as previously described, or a large amount of the seed-bearing tops is cut, put on a hide, dried, and beaten with a stick. The largest stems and leaves are picked out by hand, and the remainder winnowed "by letting them fall to a hide from a tray basket." The same end may be attained by "tossing the seeds in a hide; then the leaves are blown away."

To obtain sunflower seeds in quantity, the woman fills her burden basket with the flowers and later lays them out to dry at home. When the plants are thoroughly dried, the seeds can easily be shaken out. Or, if the seeds are very ripe, the back of the sunflower head is shaken or is given a sharp blow with a stick, and the seeds fall into a burden basket which has been placed under the plant. These seeds are ground up and are added to meat dishes to form a gravy, or they are made into flour for bread baked in hot ashes. Sunflower seeds and other seeds are often placed with hot coals in a tray basket and "worked around" until they are parched.

In the fall when the tule is yellow with pollen, the tops of the plants are cut off, brought to camp, and dried. Then the dry tops are shaken or struck over an outspread buckskin. Pollen is gathered, without special ceremony, from other plants and from trees by shaking them after placing a piece of well-tanned, uncolored buckskin to catch it. Buckskin is always the proper receptacle. It is said that "pollen would go through cloth," but more important is the feeling that "it would be wrong" to use anything but buckskin for pollen bags and containers.

From early spring to the onset of winter, the woman gathers fruits and vegetables which grow at different elevations and in different areas. She does not keep at this task steadily, for she has many other duties. But she must be ready at the report of a good natural harvest to leave at once for the region where it is. Often it is near by; but many times the site is so far distant, and the work ahead so time-consuming, that the entire household goes with her and sets up a temporary camp. Using this as a base, the husband hunts while his wife gathers the wild crop that has drawn them there. Not infrequently more than one household or an extended family consisting of a number of households temporarily leaves the larger encampment or local group on such an errand. Thus, in order that the woman may obtain the various foods in the order in which they mature, the household remains a mobile unit, ready to detach itself from the local group at short notice and to rejoin this group or another just as easily.

While the women are foraging, they are on the lookout for beehives:

Honey is found in the stalks of mescal, sotol, and the narrow-leafed yucca. The bee deposits the honey in the stalk. The bee which does this is a big yellow one. The women search for honey in these stalks. They gather it in the fall. They split the stalk to find it. It's like candy. I used to be great for honey!

Honey is also obtained from a large yellow bee that nests in the ground. To secure this store, the device of allowing the bees to emerge one by one and killing them as they come out is employed. A ceremonial touch is given the unearthing of these ground hives. "When the Chiricahua come upon one of these nests, they mark a big circle and say, 'May you be as big as this.' Then they open it up."

When hives are discovered in trees or in logs, a smudge fire is used to smoke the bees out. The co-operation of a man skilled in the use of the sling is required when hives are found among the rocks in cliffs. "He throws at it with a sling and brings it down. The bees leave the hive. Then the people go and get the honey. We put honey in drinks and eat it with bread." The bees which nest in the cliffs and bluffs are described as smaller and darker in color than the others. Sometimes a hive is wrapped in a hide and brought home before it is opened.

THE COOKING AND PRESERVATION OF MEAT PRODUCTS

The woman is not only responsible for the preparation and storage of the food which she herself collects but is expected to take charge of the meat which the man contributes to the household:

A man hunts and butchers the game. He brings it in to the woman. After that it's her job to take care of it.

I never heard of a man cooking when his wife was around in the old days. He doesn't now either. Getting water is a woman's job too. I don't see any men doing it even now. The same is true of getting and cutting wood. The men sit around and smoke and tell stories when they are at home.

Certain parts of an animal are seldom eaten. Ritual restrictions placed upon individual members of the household must be kept in mind too:

Some people ate pancreas a long time ago, I believe. I'm not sure. Now they don't do it. Some shaman started telling people not to eat this and that, and now they can hardly eat anything from the inside, it seems.

The Chiricahua does not like to eat any meat from the head.

It is dangerous to eat the heart. As a general rule the Chiricahua do not eat the heart of an animal. I think to myself, "Well, I don't know what there is to it, but I won't do it because it looks dangerous." My wife won't do it either.

Ceremonial considerations, too, govern the consumption of eggs, particularly for women:

We always ate eggs. Some women won't eat eggs for fear of getting children, however. But this is according to the shaman's directions. We eat the eggs of the quail and duck.

Those who do eat eggs prefer them boiled or roasted in hot ashes:

Some people eat the eggs of the quail, the duck, and other birds. A good many quail eggs are found together. The eggs are boiled, or a fire is made, the ashes are pushed aside, the eggs are put in there, and the ashes are put back over them.

Most meat is prepared by broiling over an open fire or by boiling, though some of it is pit baked. In the common broiling processes the meat is suspended over the coals with a stick held in the hand, or it is placed on top of the hot coals and turned at intervals. Sometimes it is cooked by placing it on a flat rock which borders a hot fire, while another rock, lying perpendicular to the first, holds in the heat. The most choice portion of meat is the fat part "on top of the ribs" next to the skin.

The favorite method of cooking wood rats, rabbits, and prairie dogs is to bury them in hot ashes before skinning them, and then to skin and eviscerate them when they are well roasted. But one informant, in describing how rabbits may be cooked, said: "Throw the whole rabbit on the coals. When it is partly cooked, take it off, skin it, take out the insides, and put it back on the coals to finish." Rats are sometimes skinned and cleaned before being roasted in hot coals. Wood rats and rabbits are also boiled, but this is a less popular mode of preparation.

Mountain lion or peccary meat, when it is prepared for those who will eat it, is roasted or boiled in the same manner as deer, antelope, or elk meat.

For those who have no aversion to eating any part of the head, it is cooked in a heap of hot coals or is steam baked in a small pit: "My people put the deer head in the fire, cover it with ashes, and let it cook. They break the eyes first. That is their way. It is done for good luck." The pit-baking method resembles the way in which mescal is prepared:

When the head is used for food, one way to fix it is to dig a hole, line it with rocks, and build a fire in there. It makes lots of ashes. Put the head in on top of the ashes and grass on top of the head. Sprinkle the grass with water and cover with dirt. Let it roast a day or a night. Usually the tongue is taken out first.

Sometimes the feet, liver, and entrails are placed in the earth oven with the head and are cooked with it for a day or a night.

The pit is used, too, for cooking fetal deer and antelopes, which are considered a delicacy. "The unborn of deer and antelopes are good eating. The meat is soft and has a good taste. We don't steam grown animals in an underground oven. But we do do it to a deer not yet born. This can also be prepared like any other meat, however."

Although the intestines are not so well liked as other parts, the hunter usually brings them home:

The intestines are much better if the animal is fat. We don't care much for the intestines anyway if we have plenty of other meat. If the hunter is loaded up on returning from the hunt, he does not bother with the intestines, especially if the animal is not fat. When he brings the intestines home, the hunter turns them over with the other meat to the woman who is going to cook it. She takes the outside off, working downward and squeezing out any waste left as she does so. Then she cooks them without washing them. Now the young people turn them inside out and wash them.

Intestines are cooked over the coals. Another good way to cook them is to stuff a piece with meat and fat. The woman puts sticks through each end so the filling won't come out. Then she puts it on a hot stone by the fire to cook. The windpipe of an animal is stuffed in this same way too. But the intestine is used just in an emergency when food is scarce. Now when we kill a sheep we throw away the intestines. We save only the liver and sometimes the heart from the inside.

Liver is usually thrown on the coals of an open fire and roasted. Sometimes a sort of "blood sausage" is made. The hunter fills the paunch with the blood of the animal he has killed and brings it home. Then the woman "adds fat and onions and puts it in the coals or in a pot, cooking it until the blood gets thick and tastes like liver. She punctures the stomach so it won't explode. She puts in some of the little red chili peppers that grow in the mountains of Old Mexico. These are small, like marbles." When it is not used in this way, the stomach is seldom eaten:

"The stomach isn't often eaten. Now when we butcher a cow, the stomach is thrown away."

Birds that are considered edible are most often boiled. Turkeys are eviscerated, plucked, and then boiled, for instance.

It is the woman's task, also, to preserve any surplus meat by "jerking" it:

She takes the thick parts, cuts them thin, and hangs them up to dry in the sun. To use the meat after it is dried, she pounds it up with a stone. It can be mixed with fat then and eaten like this without being cooked. Or even without the fat it is used on the march and in emergencies. When the people are in no hurry, this pounded meat can be added to soup, boiled in water, or fried. It will soften when boiled in water. This dried meat, in strips or in pounded form, can be kept in caches or carried in sacks. Jerked meat, when the people are camping in one place for a time, is laid over the higher limbs of a near-by tree.

THE PREPARATION OF BEVERAGES

The preparation of beverages, both alcoholic and nonalcoholic, is classified with cooking and is, therefore, the task of the woman. Of tiswin-making it was said: "A man would never make tiswin. It would lower his standing. One man used to make it, but he was a roughneck, and didn't care about his standing. He lowered himself many times."

The juice of the prickly pear is occasionally drunk, but "for health" rather than for quenching thirst. Drinks which are compared to commercial coffee and tea are described:

In those days when coffee was scarce, some people used the bark of different trees, such as oak [Gambel oak] to make a drink. Some used a plant for tea. It is better than the tea you buy. The English name for it is lip fern. It grows all around here. There is another plant [cota] that is used for tea too. To make it, some is just broken into convenient pieces, put in a pot, boiled, and the water drained off. It is about the same color as store tea and tastes much the same.

Alcoholic beverages are made from mescal, sotol, mesquite, and, more recently, from maize and wheat. Tiswin, the maize drink, is the only one of these beverages which is made or consumed in appreciable quantities. The people have become very fond of this mild beer, and the services and company of a woman who can make it well are in constant demand.

It is possible that all these alcoholic beverages were inspired by the customs of Mexican Indians and the Spanish-speaking peoples to the south, as is suggested in this recipe for a sotol drink:

There is a story that the Mexicans were making a drink out of sotol. I don't know whether the Indians used to make it or not, but I guess they did because I used to hear the old men say that it makes a good drink. To make it, roast the crown of sotol in an underground oven just as mescal is roasted for food. Then mash it up. Squeeze the juice out. Let the juice stand, sometimes in a hide in the ground, until it ferments. If the weather is warm, it does not take more than a day after it is standing. Then strain it, and it is ready to use.

In much the same way a drink is made from fermented mescal juice:

Roast the mescal in a pit just as if you were going to eat it. Pull off the outer leaves and cut the soft inner part into small pieces. Pound them, put the pounded mescal in a hide, and bury the hide in the ground. Cover this and let it ferment for two days. Then take it out and squeeze it by hand and mix the juice with some water. It will bubble for a day or two, and then it is ready. It gets strong.

The drink from mesquite beans is no more difficult to prepare:

The women know how to make a drink out of mesquite beans by boiling them, draining off the water when they are soft, mashing the beans, and letting the material stand and ferment.

The favorite drink, however, is tiswin, or "gray water," a weak corn beer. The maize used in its manufacture was obtained by trade or theft from Mexican Indians, Pueblo Indians, and white settlers before reservation days. Tiswin is considered the most nourishing of the beverages and is often spoken of as a food, because its mild stimulation when taken in moderate quantities has helped many a person withstand the rigors of travel and want. "Many used tiswin for food in the old days. Many even gave it to children when they didn't have anything else to feed them." Tiswin is also considered the appropriate beverage to serve during any social occasion.

To make tiswin the woman takes mature corn and shells it. She wants it good and dry to start with. She soaks it in water all night. In the morning she puts grass in a long trench, puts the corn kernels on top of this, and lays another layer of grass over it. On top of this she may throw some dirt, or she may just put a blanket over the trench. Each morning she sprinkles the corn kernels and each evening she sprinkles them just a little too. She does this for ten days or two weeks. The kernels begin to sprout, and when the sprouts are about an inch and a half long, she takes them out. She grinds them between two stones and makes them fine. She goes over them twice more.

The ground corn is put in water then and boiled until half the water is gone. It takes four or five hours to boil it down to where it should be. The container is filled to the top with water again and the brew is boiled until it is a little way from the top. The woman strains off the liquid now, lets it cool, and puts it in a water jar or gourd. Some cover the jar to make the tiswin work faster.

Different women have their own ways of fixing it from this point on. Some put aside some roasted mescal to ferment. Afterward they squeeze out the juice and mix it with the tiswin. Nowadays some add ground wheat. The woman who is making this tiswin grinds some wheat and puts it in the jar. She sprinkles it on top with a circular, sunwise motion. She speaks to it as she does so, saying, "I want you to make it good and not for fighting. I want everyone who drinks you to be happy, not angry."

In an hour the contents of this water jar is bubbling, moving around. If the tiswin is put in the jar in the evening, by late afternoon of the next day, when it stops bubbling, it is ready.

The corn and wheat sediment at the bottom are taken out. This material at the bottom is called "waste." It is always squeezed and the liquid from it saved and drunk by the woman who makes the batch.

After the tiswin is ready it will keep about a day and a half. It will be too sour for drinking after that. The taste is salty. It has a tendency to make you put on weight if you drink too much of it. There are many ways of fixing tiswin. Some shave oak root and put pieces of this in to make it strong. Some put mesquite beans in for the same reason. Now they even put yeast in to make it strong.

There is a proper manner of drinking tiswin, and its effects are, of course, well known:

We eat, all right, before we drink tiswin, but not too much. I learned this from B. and some other old men. I have noticed, myself, that if I eat a big dinner and then drink tiswin, I get hardly any effect. And you haven't got room enough to drink if you eat a big meal. Pretty soon you feel sick and can't drink. The two things are fighting in there, and something has to be done. But when you get through drinking you sure can eat! I've noticed that B. can eat about half a steer after drinking tiswin.

That tiswin surely cleans you out! It makes you drunk all right, but it's corn, and it feeds your body. And for two or three days afterward it makes your urine just as white and clear as can be! It must do something to purify the urine. And it acts like castor oil too; it cleans you right out.

THE STORAGE OF FOOD AND SURPLUS POSSESSIONS

Only a limited amount of preserved food can be carried in parfleches and sacks. The rest must be cached. "In those days we had no place to store things when the women had dried a great deal of yucca fruit, mescal, and berries. So we took this food to a hole in the rocks, to a little cave."

These caches are in rocky caves. I've never known them to make one in the ground. This is their secret supply. They can roam around away from this place and come back toward it when they are hungry. Then they get out just so much. They often have valuables in there—extra baskets and other things. An individual household might have its own cache, or several camps of related people might put their goods in together.

This is the way it is fixed on the inside. First a layer of rocks is put down. Then a great deal of oak brush is laid on the rocks. The parfleches are laid on this. Inside each parfleche are layers of food, layers of mescal or yucca fruit, each layer separated from the others by grass. Sticks are placed between the parfleches. The entrance is closed up with rocks and then plastered with mud so the room is sealed and airtight. Then they fix the place over with grass and dirt. You can hardly tell it from the solid mountainside. Food will keep it there for a year or so.

Perhaps they are camping a long way from that cache and they run low on food. They can send a man after some of the provisions then. He closes up the entrance again just as though nobody had ever been there.

Food is not considered an individual or personal possession. The successful hunter sends his wife to her parents with the game he has procured, or a large share of it. Most often the women of the extended family prepare the food from combined stores and hide any surplus in one cave cache.

The disposition of the stored food after the death of the woman who was responsible, in whole or in part, for gathering and preparing it, is a clue to the concept of joint ownership. One of the most solemnly respected death customs is the destruction of all objects which belonged to the deceased or were intimately associated with him. But:

If a woman has some food stored up like that and she dies before she uses it, many times it is used afterward. It is not considered her personal property.

The cached food belongs to the relatives as well as to the one who puts it away, but only to the family and the relatives of the woman. If the family is dying out, more distant relatives are told about the cache, and the secret spreads out in this way, so the stores will be of use to those who need them and will not go to waste.

AGRICULTURE

No attempt was made to cultivate crops until very recent times. One, and perhaps two, of the three major subdivisions or bands raised no crops at all until the modern reservation period. The oldest Southern Chiricahua informant stated categorically: "My people did not practice farming. The Indians had many plants which were given to them [by nature] and did not have to farm. They moved around too much also." The Central Chiricahua were little more inclined toward agriculture. One of them observed, "I do not think the Chiricahua ever planted before they came under the influence of the whites." In 1873, shortly after the establishment of a reserve for the control of the Central and Southern Chiricahua, the first agent reported:

In regard to the future prospects for farming operations by these Indians, I would state that I have conversed with Cochise and many of his head-men upon this subject repeatedly, and I am of the opinion that it will require some little time to bring them into the traces and make them submit to this exaction, which must eventually be required of them. They have never been an agricultural people, and claim that they do not know how to farm.[10]

But it is possible that the example of neighboring peoples who cultivated the land may have led to experiments on the part of individual families, as this statement of a Central Chiricahua suggests: "Even in Old Mexico, the Chiricahua tried to farm a little."

The Eastern Chiricahua, who seem to have had earlier friendly relations and trade contacts with the Spanish-speaking townspeople, began to farm even before the modern reservations were established. By 1869, according to government reports, the leaders of this band were complaining that they were being driven from lands where they used to plant.[11] Testimony from informants corroborates these old reports: "These Eastern Chiricahua Indians farmed before the whites came. They tell about

[10] *Report of the Commissioner of Indian Affairs*, 1873.

[11] *Ibid.*, 1869.

the big ditches they used at Hot Springs." "We've had corn as long as I can remember." "The Eastern Chiricahua planted corn even in the old times." "All the groups of Eastern Chiricahua planted." Maize was undoubtedly the first vegetable raised. "When I was young," recalled a very old man, "we never had any cultivated vegetables except corn. Later others came from Old Mexico."

The influence of the Spanish-speaking peoples to the south in the impetus toward agricultural pursuits is admitted:

The Eastern Chiricahua raised corn, pumpkins, potatoes, onions, chili, and watermelons. We had a good deal of contact with Spanish towns. We learned to speak Spanish, and the Spanish people showed us how to raise these things. We got the seeds from the Mexicans too. We got big hoes from them or traded them from the whites.

The Eastern band made good use of the intervals of peace:

If a Chiricahua had a Mexican friend, he would get corn as a gift, and the Indian might give a horse or something else to the Mexican. We planted at Hot Springs as well as in Mexico. We received corn up here, as well as in Mexico, from the Mexicans living around. The Indians used to be good friends with the Mexicans often. When I was small I used to play with Mexican children. They gave me the name the white people call me by now.

The techniques of cultivation in use among the Eastern Chiricahua are described by an informant:

We planted corn, cantaloupes, and watermelons. No squash or pumpkins were planted at first. Some Chiricahua never had pumpkins or squash until 1885 or 1886, except what they could get from other peoples.

We used irrigation. We dug trenches from a stream to the farm and stopped these irrigation ditches with dirt when we wanted to block them. When the corn was big enough to hoe, we went out in the woods and made a hoe of bent root. Later we had hoes from the Mexicans. To make the holes for the seeds, we used just a pointed stick. The men worked in the fields; the women worked in the fields too, but mostly men did it.

Although this informant feels that agriculture is a legitimate activity for men, another disagrees, saying: "Planting was considered a woman's job. That is the way I feel. At Fort Sill men had to do it." "Men, women, and boys assisted," according to a third spokesman. Evidently, the division of labor in agricultural work was not clear cut.

Another account from an Eastern band member adds to the picture:

We lived by hunting, fishing, and gathering plants. But we planted corn in May, too, with Mexican hoes that were traded up. The people kept camp near their farms then, tending the corn, watering it, and weeding it. Men and women both did the planting and other work. If the man was busy or off hunting, the woman would do it herself. Corn is a favorite food, because it can be used in a good many ways.

The Chiricahua picked up the trait [of planting] long ago in Mexico. Only some of the families planted corn, but they could share their crop with their neighbors. Only about six or seven families out of the hundred in a big encampment[12] might plant corn, and each family would do it on separate land. Others would help in the work on one of these plots, and then the owner would share the crop with them. The seeds came from the Mexicans, and many didn't plant partly because they didn't have seeds.

We also got beans, chili, squash, and watermelons from the Mexicans, and the Chiricahua learned to plant these. The Chiricahua never specialized on plants— each person who grew any, grew them all in his space. Some of the planted areas were as large as thirty acres, but there were no lines between; everything was free.

If some didn't want to plant, they could hunt. Then they would give their neighbors meat, and the farmer who had a great deal allowed anyone to take what he wanted. There wasn't any buying of things.

A more detailed description of the manner in which corn was planted by the Eastern Chiricahua is the following:

The corn is soaked all night. Then two or three kernels are dropped in a hole. They say the soaking makes it grow faster. Some plant the corn kernels deep. This is when they are not soaked. When you soak them, you don't bury them so deep. Beans and pumpkin and watermelon seeds are soaked first too.

Agriculture never became so important that its symbols were richly represented in religion or mythology. Occasionally, it is advised that the corncob be put back in the husk to insure an abundant future crop, undoubtedly an extension of the custom of replacing the unused part of a medicinal plant. There is an association of the katydid with crop-raising: "The katydid is an insect the Chiricahua will not kill. We say it helps the crops grow. We pray to it to help the crops grow." In discussing the

---

[12] It is doubtful that encampments of one hundred families ever existed in pre-reservation days. The informant's estimates of population and of the size of farms seem excessive in this statement.

various pollens used ritually, an informant included corn pollen and remarked. "You can get some pollen from corn; they used some of this a long time ago."

As in the case of other food products, it is the woman's task to cook and preserve the corn:

They would build a big fire and bring in load after load of the corn in sacks. Three or four women would work together. They would sit there and shuck corn and put it in the fire and let it get brown on top. Then they would throw it to a place where another woman sat. She would take the ears, cut off the kernels, put them on a clean hide, and throw away the cobs. Then they spread it out in the sun to dry. They would leave the corn out there for a week or two until it was very dry. They can carry that corn around then, and it won't spoil. It will keep for a year. They don't have to keep it in a cool place either. They store it in parfleches and use it in winter.

In the winter when the snow gets to be two or three feet deep, a man goes out and kills game and brings it in. Then they can use the dry corn with meat and bones, letting it boil together for three or four hours. It surely makes a good stew! We're using it right now, for we stored up last summer's corn. This dried corn is used at almost every puberty rite now too.

The dried kernels are also roasted or parched:

I saw my people cook corn in a shallow basket many times. They put several pounds of corn in the basket with some hot coals and keep working it around. The corn kernels split, and then they take them out and fill it up again.

Another corn dish reflects the influence of Mexican towns-people:

The Chiricahua never boiled the corn in the husks. They stripped off the husks. They cut off the corn kernels and piled them up. They ground the corn on a rock, using a big stone in the hand [mano and metate]. In those days flour was hard to get, and they made bread out of the ground corn. They used the corn husks to make a sort of tamale. They put some corn meal in a cornhusk and wrapped it up, tying it with a thin strip of cornhusk. Then they put it in water to boil with meat and bones. If they had chili, they put it in with the corn meal.

In season the corn is eaten fresh:

When they had the green corn, they cut the end off after husking it, broke it in two, and put it on to boil with bones or meat. In summer when the corn was ripe, they went out and brought in lots of it.

HOME INDUSTRIES OF WOMEN

In addition to her other tasks, the woman must furnish those things essential to the proper running of the household:

Men can carry wood, but they think it is woman's work. The women make their own rope out of hide, a special rope. It is about five yards long and of hard rawhide. They soften it with brains just enough so they can tie it. The women use this rope for getting wood.

When a woman is going to get some wood, she doesn't carry great logs. She gets thin pieces of brush and sticks about three feet long and makes them into a bundle about a foot and a half thick. She ties the bundle at either end with this rope, leaving a rather long loop between. She puts the wood in a bundle on her back, and the rope comes over her shoulders and across her chest, or else just across her forehead.

A man could use this rope if he wanted to—to hobble horses for instance. But the rope is put where the woman can get it any time to carry wood. The man uses it only if he needs a rope in a hurry.

The woman must keep on hand a plentiful supply of water for drinking, cooking, and washing. She brings it from a near-by spring or stream in a pitch-covered basketry jar.

Tanning and the use of hides.—"Tanning the hide is always considered woman's work. Men never do it." In the mythology, when Woodpecker wishes to deceive Coyote and make him think he is a girl, he scrapes a hide after the fashion of women. Yet certain realistic concessions are made. "Sometimes a man helps if it is a hard job, a big hide; he helps stretch it because it takes great strength."

The fresh pelt is treated in this manner:

First the woman who is doing the tanning scrapes off the flesh with a sharpened deer bone or a sharp-edged stone. (At present she uses a scraper with a toothed metal blade.) Then she soaks the hide in water for two or three days—not too long or it will spoil. To soak the skin, she uses a basin formed of some stiff hide. Then she takes the skin out of the water and wraps it around a pole. She leans this pole against a tree so that the hide will not pull away. Then she scrapes downward with a sharpened horse rib and takes the hair off. She uses a rib near the neck because it is wider there.

When all the hair has been removed, she puts some grass on the ground and lays the skin on top of this grass with the inner side facing upward. She pegs it out here in the sun to dry for two or three days. If it is lumpy or too thick in places, she works it over with a rough stone to even it up and to soften it at those places.

The process of transforming the scraped hide into buckskin has been thus described:

To turn it from rawhide to buckskin, the woman uses deer brains. She boils the brain just a little, just steams it, and then works it with her hands. As she works it, she puts warm water with it. Then she puts the hide in and works it until it gets soft. She takes it out and hangs it in the sun to dry a little. Then she wrings it out and starts to pull and stretch it.

She holds one end of it on the ground and stretches it by pulling at the other end. She works it all over and on both sides as it dries. If she starts early in the morning, she gets through about noon with this stretching. Once in a while she stops and lets it dry some more. By the time she is finished, it has turned to buckskin. Deerskin, antelope skin, and elkskin are treated in the same way.

Some women apply deer brains and fat directly to the hide before it is soaked in the water.

In cold weather when the tanned skin is not needed at once, the hide may be rolled up and put aside pending a milder season:

The skin should be made soft in summer. If it is worked in cold weather, you have to keep going and can't stop at any point until it is all finished, or it will not be a smooth job and will show where you started in again. In warm weather, though, it doesn't matter when you work on it. You can just pick it up any time and do as much as you want to on it and then lay it aside and pick it up again.

When thick rawhide is wanted, the method differs:

To get hide for moccasin soles, the woman begins just the same way as she does in making buckskin. She takes the hair off in the same way. But then she just lets the hide dry and uses it. Since it is for moccasin soles, she wants it thick, so she does not stretch it out with pins. If she wants to tan it, she will stretch it out; then it gets thin.

It often becomes necessary to re-work buckskin:

When you once turn hide to buckskin, you want to be very careful how you handle it. If you get it wet in one place, it's going to be hard there all the time. Then it has to be softened with a rough rock. After a rain, women will take buckskin moccasins or clothes, dry them, and then work them over with a rock. But the buckskin never gets as good as it was before.

If the rawhide bottoms of a pair of big overlapping moccasins wear out, they take off the soles. The uppers are sure to be dirty and hard near the soles. They may be torn where they were sewed. Then they take the moccasins and bury this hard part in damp ground. They sprinkle a little water on top of the ground, just enough to keep it damp. They leave the buckskin in the ground for a half-day or a little more. Then it is damp and soft and can be worked. They do this so that they will be able to stretch it and work it to fit the new bottom. I have seen this done many times.

When a skin is to be used as a robe or a blanket, still another procedure is followed:

When a hide is to be used for a blanket, the hair is left on. Deer and mountain sheep pelts are prepared like this. The inner side is fleshed carefully and pounded to soften it. Deer brains are rubbed on this inner side, and the blanket is worked until it is soft.

When they have those skins with hair on for blankets, they use them any way according to the weather. In cold weather they put the fur side inside.

Making saddle bags is also one of the woman's tasks:

After the hide is removed, the woman stakes it out in the sun. Sometimes she has grass under it, sometimes not. The hair side is underneath. She leaves it there until it is dry. Then she takes it and puts the hair side up. She has a sharp tool with which to scrape off the hair. Then she fleshes it. After scraping it, she rubs it with the brains to make it soft. She doesn't soak it in water at all. Now she cleans, cuts, folds, and sews it. Then she cuts a slit in the middle and puts dirt in on each side. When the hide is entirely dry, she takes the dirt out. A bulge is left on each side where the dirt was. Then it is ready to be put on the horse.

The parfleche or flat hide container is a recent acquisition, and its use has not penetrated to all sections of the tribe. Southern Chiricahua informants say that the parfleche was not made by them, and some Central Chiricahua report that it was not found in their group. One Central Chiricahua informant was much incensed, however, at the suggestion that the parfleche he described might have been inspired by Mescalero examples:

The Chiricahua had the parfleche, as I have told you. In fact, it originated with the Chiricahua. These Mescalero never went around or found out anything! They stayed right here year after year. They got the parfleche from the Chiricahua. I was with the Chiricahua when they were going from Fort Apache to Florida [1886]. Some of them had parfleches then. I saw parfleches in my own home.

The Central Chiricahua parfleche is very simply made. The fact that cowhide seems to be the only material used in its manufacture points to its recent adoption:

In the old days we had parfleches. The woman made them, and it is hard work to make one. She has to scrape off the flesh from the inside of the skin and scrape a little of the fur off the top. She has to work around and around, and pound and pound it until she gets it the way she wants it. First she pounds it all over, or it will be too thick. Then she pounds it more where she is going to fold it.

She cuts it the size and shape she wants, so that when she folds it over it will come out even. It is made by folding the cowhide over. You fold it over once, and then again, and then from the ends. The end pieces go on top usually. Some fold the ends in first and then fold the sides. There is no one way of doing it. Next the woman cuts out a cowhide rope and ties it, first the long way and then the short way. That's all there is to it.

You can store things away in it and keep it in a cave, or you can carry it on your pack horse. Bushes and rocks won't hurt it. Rain won't hurt it, because it is made out of cowhide. I've seen some with fur on and some without fur. The Central Chiricahua never put designs on the parfleches. They have them all sizes. I never saw any that were not made of cowhide and never heard of any that were made of anything else.

The Eastern Chiricahua lavish more care upon the manufacture of the parfleche. Two side pieces are made to fit over the bottom, and then the two end pieces are brought over and laced. All the fur is taken off, and designs, "as on the bow," are painted on the outer surface. One informant stated that men cannot be present when a woman is working on a parfleche, an interesting example of the strong feeling for the sexual division of labor.

This feeling extends into the artistic field, and the character of the decoration on painted or incised objects is determined by the sex of the worker. "Men draw things, such as animals, people, and freehand figures. Women do not. I would feel that it was out of place for a woman to do this. She doesn't even paint a star. She would just make certain patterns [conventional designs]. She can do this at any time."

Other hide objects besides parfleches are made by the woman. Awl cases and pollen bags are fashioned from buckskin. Bags to hold piñon nuts and acorns are made of badger skins. These are hung in the home, as much for their beauty as for their utility. The woman also cuts plate-shaped pieces of rawhide to be used "like the shallow woven bowl." In addition, she prepares "a container of rawhide, having the shape of a burden basket, but only half as large" to be used as a water carrier.

The quiver and the bow cover are so intimately associated with masculine activities that it is considered essential for a man to have some part in making them. The woman prepares the skin, the man cuts out the pieces to be used, and the woman sews them together.

The women color buckskin with a number of dyes of their own making. Dark brown is obtained from the juice of fresh walnut hulls, crushed and pressed. The buckskin is soaked in a mixture of the walnut-hull juice and water and is then re-worked to softness. Red is secured from the boiled root and bark of mountain mahogany. When this dye is lukewarm or cool, the buckskin is put in it and is left overnight or for a day; later it must be re-worked with a stone until it is pliable. A yellow decoction is made by soaking algerita roots. The buckskin is left in the dye until it is yellow and is afterward pounded and softened. Yellow ocher is sometimes applied to the entire surface of a buckskin; as the color wears away, more ocher must be rubbed on.

Sewing is essentially the concern of the women, though men on the raid will do repair work. For thread, the woman needs sinew. Therefore the hunter, when he butchers an animal, always removes the sinew from the loin very carefully and presents it to his wife. Sinew from any large game animal is acceptable, though that from the deer is considered best. In recent times sinew from the horse and the steer have come to be widely used. With an awl made from the sharpened leg bone of the deer, the woman punches a hole in the skin she is sewing, moistens the end of the sinew, and runs it through the hole.

Basketry.—Basket-making is one of the many tasks for which the woman supplies both the materials and the labor, and she possesses a large fund of knowledge concerning substances and techniques. She rarely uses cottonwood, since it breaks too easily. She does not use willow unless no other materials are available. She knows that, if she gathers stems in the spring, she will have to let them dry for some days but that, if she takes them in the winter, they are dry enough to use almost at once.

The woman makes a coiled tray basket with sumac stems for the foundation and yucca leaves for the sewing material and designs it with yucca of various colors:

To turn the yucca yellow, put dry grass among the leaves in the yucca plant while it is standing in the ground; then set fire to the grass. The fire and smoke

PLATE XII

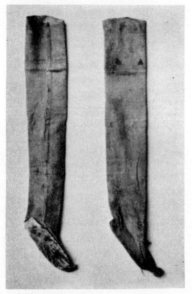

United States National Museum

b) BURDEN BASKET

United States National Museum

a) MOCCASINS

Claremont Colleges Museum, Thomas Miles, photographer

c) WATER JARS

turn the leaves yellow. Then cut what you want. When you want the leaves green, cut those on the outside fresh and use them just as they are. The inner leaves of the yucca plant, the ones near the stem, are white, and they can be used to give still another color.

The ruddy tendrils found at the roots of the narrow-leafed yucca are worked into baskets for contrast and design. The outer covering of the seed pod of the unicorn plant provides a black substance. The sewing materials for the ceremonial tray basket used in the girl's puberty rite come from these pods.

Tray baskets act as containers for dry foods and "for any little thing, like nuts." They are used in parching seeds, in winnowing, and in a variety of other ways.

The large burden basket is twined, and the withes employed are from the sumac or mulberry. The designs are seldom more than bands of color woven with strands that have been soaked in dyes similar to those used to color buckskin. Often the bottom is covered with buckskin or rawhide from which fringe and pendants hang.

The water jar is in reality a pitch-covered basket. It also is made by the twined technique and is usually of sumac, or less frequently of mulberry. A hide or wooden handle is affixed to each side. Jars for tiswin are usually larger than those for carrying or holding water:

In the making of the water jar, the woman does it all from the beginning. She makes a woven basket. Then she gathers pitch. The only pitch used is that from the piñon tree. If it is in a hard lump on the trunk, she breaks it off; if it is sticky, she uses a piece of wood. She places it in a basket and brings it home, first laying some kind of grass or leaves in the basket so that the pitch won't stick to it. She puts the pitch in a pot and heats it until it gets soft.

When the pitch is soft enough, she pours or transfers it to the inside of the water jar she is making. She has a heated stone in there too and moves the basket around, so that the pitch spreads evenly. While she is putting on the pitch, she doesn't allow any other person near the fire. She must be there by herself. But, when she is weaving the basket, others can be around.

Sometimes she puts pitch on the outside, sometimes not. To put pitch on the outside, she has a stick with a piece of buckskin on. She dips this into the hot pitch and rubs it on. Then she lets it cool for a while; but, when it is still a little warm, she dips her hand into water and smoothes the jar to make it look nice. Sometimes before putting the pitch on the outside, she rubs the surface with red ocher. It looks pretty then, because the red shows through the pitch. A woman can carry a water jar the same day it is finished. When the pitch has cracked and the jar leaks, she repairs it by putting hot stones in it. Then it comes together again. We use oak leaves or good clean grass to cover the opening. The oak leaves give a good taste to the water if they are used as a cover, we think.

Pottery and household utensils.—I have not been able to find a single existing example of the ceramics of these people. But women did mold pots at one time. The methods employed by his relative are reported by one informant:

, My aunt used to make clay pots. She got red clay, a sticky kind, and ground it between two rocks, ground it fine. She had water at her side and kept putting her hand in to make the clay sticky. She worked the clay. She said she had to grind the clay fine or it would break.

First she made the bottom. She made a ball and pressed it down flat. Then she'd take a pinch of it and roll it out to a long piece and put her hand in the water to make it smooth. She built it up by putting these pieces on, bringing them around the way the sun goes. She rested the pot she was making right by her side on the ground. She smoothed it as she built it, sometimes with her hand dipped in water and sometimes with a flat paddle that she dipped in water. Sometimes she rested the pot she was making right in her lap, sometimes on the ground by her side. Sometimes she made big ones, sometimes little ones.

Then she broke open the little round cactus that grows in clusters [nipple cactus] and rubbed a piece of it on the outside and the inside of the pot. This is sticky. Then she put the pot out in the sun to dry. If the sun was out, it would dry enough to handle and be put in the fire in two or three hours.

Then she built a fire. She used any wood and let it burn down to ashes. Then she put the pot in and kept turning it. She would strike it to see if it was done. She turned it so it got done evenly. The pots were dark brown when they were finished, but some clays made them lighter.

Sometimes she made several at once, of different sizes. She never painted or designed them. Not many women made them. In the big group in which I lived my aunt and two others made them. These women who made pots allowed men to watch while they worked.[13] They never ground up the old pots and put the old material with the new. I saw these women make olla-shaped pots, low bowl-shaped ones, and some that were like a pitcher. My aunt never painted or designed any of them.

Another account adds some interesting details:

Women were the pottery-makers. They went to a place where the animals would come to lick the salt and took clay from there. They rolled this clay with their hands into a long rope and wound this up, coiling it around and around in

[13] This was denied by another informant, who said that men could not be present when women were working on the parfleche or the pot.

the shape of a pot. When the pot was built up, they usually smoothed it, inside and out, by rubbing water over the surfaces.

For the baking, oak was burned to red-hot coals, a pit was dug in these coals, and the pot was placed in the pit and covered completely with coals. It was left so overnight. In the morning the pot would be brittle and would make a sound when tapped.

Over such a pot buckskin would be stretched and tied with sinews for a drum. Such pots were also used to boil things in. The pots were never decorated. When people haven't anything of importance to do, pots are decorated. Very often, however, the coil marks were left on the outside.

Another account indicates that some women, at least, decorated their handiwork:

Women make the pots. The pots are used for cooking and also for pottery drums. A special one is made for a drum, but its general shape is like that of the cooking pot.

This is the way a woman makes a pot. First she gets clay and sifts it until it is fine. Then she mixes it with water. She works it to the right consistency. Next she rolls some between her fingers and makes a coil. For the bottom she smooths off a flat piece of clay with a rock. She builds the pot up from this with the coils. She works on a level place on the ground. She takes a smooth stick or stone and smooths off the inside and outside as she works. She adds water to the clay when she needs it to make it softer.

Then she builds a fire. Any kind of wood is used for the fire. She places the pot in the fire and keeps turning it. When it gets red in the fire, when it is dried out, she takes it off, for it is ready then. Pots as big as two feet high and over one foot in diameter were made.

Some have designs on them. This is done with a stick when the pots are still wet [incising]. Some that I saw had three bands of wavy lines marked along their sides.

Nothing is added to the clay, but to give it a shine the juice of the prickly-pear cactus leaf or that of some gummy and prickly plant is squeezed into water and applied to the pot before it is fired.

The women made pots, drums, cups, and plates of clay. Cups, too, were built up with the coil. They had these cups when I was little and before. The Chiricahua had pottery from the time when animals were people. They got it from Coyote.[14]

Some women were recognized as the best pottery-makers and were expected to supply pots for others. They traded them for buckskin, meat, and other

[14] No Chiricahua Coyote tale was recorded that would justify this statement. However Coyote is credited with obtaining fire, bow wood, and arrow wood for the people, and, by extension, the origin of pottery may be attributed to his efforts.

things. They agreed on some reasonable settlement. Some unmarried women got along this way. Men did not assist in pottery-making.

According to another recital, a vegetal binder was actually mixed with the clay in some instances:

Get red or dark clay and grind it on a metate. See that no pebbles or sticks are in it. Then get a low-growing cactus plant. Split it and boil down some of it. Get the juice from it, mix it with the clay, and work it until it gets to the right consistency. Just work the bottom from a lump and then build the side out of coils. The inside is smoothed out with the hands. The outside is smoothed with the hands too but is finished with a bone. Handles are sometimes put on the sides.

Pots are sometimes designed. They are not painted but are incised with the fingernail. One design is a series of circles connected by a line. Another is a band across the pot with vertical lines on it. Sometimes they put a saw-toothed design on. They also make a clay water jug with lines running around it.

When it is the right shape, they leave the pot in the sun to dry. Often this takes several days. They strike it with a stick to hear whether it makes the proper sound. Then they know it is ready to fire. They build a fire. When it has burned down some, they put logs over it. They put the pots on the logs and keep them there for about an hour and then turn them.

Different shapes are made. There is a tall cooking pot. After it is used for a while it turns black. You can boil things in it. It is never decorated at all. The shallow ones are used for drinking, and some shallow ones are made large enough for food containers or frying pans.

In addition to the vessels already described, the woman makes dippers, spoons, and various receptacles of gourds, wood, and leaves:

From Old Mexico we get gourds for carrying water. We use them as dishes too, and you can drink from them. But you can't use them for cooking. The little gourds from the United States are too small and are not strong enough for use.

The bole from the oak tree is hollowed out and used for a vessel or dipper. We use the growths from the walnut tree too, or from any tree that has them. I've seen my aunt use them many a time. For a spoon we make a hollow at the end of a stick. Broad yucca leaves are used for spoons too.

To grind seeds and to pulverize foods that are to be preserved, the woman uses a mano and metate:

Not many women make grinding-stones. They find some which have been left by a people called "the ancient people." These were not Chiricahua, according to the story. They lived in Old Mexico in cliffs and stone houses. We also call them "those who live on top" and "[square] house people." These metates are too heavy to carry along. But we take the mano which is ready made and carry it along often. Then the woman uses it on a flat rock or one with a shallow depression.

Some metates are fashioned by the women for themselves, however:

These metates are about two feet long and one foot wide. They have a little depression which the woman makes by pecking it out with another stone and then rubbing it smooth. A woman has just one grinder on which she grinds the same food several times if she wants to make it finer.

Some women carry these all the time. It all depends on how often we move and how far we are going. The mano used with this grindstone is about six or eight inches long, just long enough so that a woman can work with two hands. Chiricahua women kneel when grinding. We have no grinding songs.

A pounder of animal bone, or one of a stone selected because its shape conveniently fits the hand, is another utensil with which the woman equips herself.

Housebuilding.—The woman not only makes the furnishings of the home but is responsible for the construction, maintenance, and repair of the dwelling itself and for the arrangement of everything in it. She provides the grass and brush beds and replaces them when they become too old and dry. With a stiff grass broom or with a leafy branch, she sweeps out the interior if that is necessary. However, formerly "they had no permanent homes, so they didn't bother with cleaning."

The dome-shaped dwelling or wickiup, the usual house type for all the Chiricahua bands, has already been described.[15] But a "peaked" home of brush, roughly resembling a conical Plains tepee in shape is also made. Said a Central Chiricahua informant:

Both the tepee and the oval-shaped house were used when I was a boy. The oval hut was covered with hide and was the best house. The more well-to-do had this kind. The tepee type was just made of brush. It had a place for a fire in the center. It was just thrown together.

Both types were common even before my time. For the girl's puberty rite the tepee type was used. Ten or more poles are used in the tepee. The number depends on the person who makes it. It is woman's work to do it, though sometimes the men would help a little.

[15] See pp. 22–23.

A house form that departs from the more common dome-shaped variety is recorded for the Southern Chiricahua as well:

A house with sides that go up to a point has been used as far back as I can remember. When we settled down, we used the wickiup; when we were moving around a great deal, we used this other kind. No certain number of poles was used for this type. The poles were never carried along. For the girl's puberty rite my people used the tepee. I can remember this was used back when I was eight or nine years old.

This alternate house type with slanting sides was a hastily constructed and very temporary dwelling among the Central and Southern Chiricahua and is hardly comparable to the permanent home of the Plains Indians. Among the Eastern Chiricahua, however, the tepee was more common and was better made, though it never became the favored form:

A few of the Eastern Chiricahua had a tepee like that of the Mescalero. Sometimes it was made with a three-pole base and sometimes with a four-pole base. The three-pole base was more common. In my day it was cloth covered, but the old people talk of them and say that, before the whites and the Spanish were here, hides were used. But most of the people of my group used the round house.

The Eastern Chiricahua didn't drag the poles of the tepee when they moved. They put them on the front of the saddle, as many as they could carry, and then went back for the rest. Usually they just discarded them though. They could always make new ones.

In addition to these regular house forms, both men and women, when they were away from home, made windbreaks by "crossing some sticks and throwing brush and leaves against them."

HOME INDUSTRIES OF MEN

Weapons and tools.—Foremost among the man's tasks when he is at home are the making and the repairing of weapons.

The favorite wood for the bow is from the mulberry tree. Oak, locust, and New Mexico maple are also acceptable. The self-bow is the only type made. It is usually three to four feet long, "the length of two arrows."[16] Almost always it has a single curve, though double-curved bows are made occasionally.

[16] These would be the "short" or hardwood shafted arrows. For arrow lengths see p. 390.

After the craftsman has cut a branch, split it, and shaped and smoothed the wood, he lets it season. When it is dried to his liking, he "greases the wood and pulls it in every way until it is slick and shiny." The wood is bent over the knee or over a tree and tied. Then it is put in hot ashes and watched so that it will not burn. After it cools it keeps its shape. The bow wood is kept tied and allowed to dry for over ten days after this treatment with heat. When the double-curved bow is made, the heated bow wood is bent between two young trees growing close together.

The outer surface is usually painted a solid color; on the inner surface the maker puts a design by which his handiwork is known —a star, a cross, serrated lines, parallel lines, or a naturalistic figure. This may refer to his supernatural power or may be simply a decoration or an identification mark. The dyes used are vegetable or mineral substances made permanent by mixture with juice squeezed from heated yucca leaves. Though the bow is never backed longitudinally with lengths of sinew, it is often wrapped with sinew. Usually, however, this is not applied until the bow has been weakened by use. Horse hair is used, but less frequently, as the reinforcing agent.

When the bow is to be sinew wrapped, animal hooves and horns are boiled for two days, and the glue thus obtained is rubbed on the wood at the places where the sinew will cover it. Then the moistened sinew is wound around the bow, usually at the middle and at places on each side equidistant from the center. Glue is rubbed on the outer surface of the wrapping too, and the bow is left to dry. Occasionally, piñon pitch is substituted for glue. "The pitch is put on the sinew warm, and the bow is worked and bent back and forth to spread the pitch and work it in."

Sinew from the loin or the leg of the deer is saved for the bow string. The man soaks the sinew in water, separates it into strands, and rolls three of them together on his leg to form a string. The warrior or raider will have an extra string with him in case the one on his bow should snap. One informant claimed that the tough fiber from the mescal leaf, rolled on the thigh and carefully tied, makes a bow string that serves well in emergencies and is even regularly used by some.

To release the arrow, the archer holds the string between his thumb and first finger and assists with his second finger. When the bow is not in use, it is left unstrung. In the hands of a strong man this weapon is quite effective.

[My uncle] made powerful bows. At one hundred yards he could kill a deer instantly. At fifteen yards he could send an arrow through a deer.

A good shot would be one that would send the arrow about a hundred yards with accuracy. The bow worked as fast as the gun in the old days. Formerly, before someone could load the magazine of a gun, you could shoot three arrows from the bow.

For hunting birds and killing pack rats, men fashion smaller bows of the same general construction. Boys who are learning how to use weapons are given these smaller bows.

In any important undertaking a man carries from thirty to forty arrows, and he likes to keep a reserve supply at home. Much time and care, therefore, go into their making and repair. An entire month may be spent on a full set of arrows. The arrows are of two kinds: those of carrizo or reed into which a hardwood foreshaft is fitted and those with the entire shaft of hardwood. For the latter, Apache plume, mulberry, mountain mahogany, or *Fendlera rupicola* is chosen.

When the man gathers arrow wood, he cuts it into appropriate lengths, peels off the bark, scrapes it, and allows it to dry from three to five days. The shaft is straightened between the teeth or is pressed against a heated rock and then is decorated with bands or stripes of black, blue, or red paint. On the upper portion of the shaft, at about the middle of the area which will be covered by the feathers, a narrow band of green or red is often traced.

Tail or wing feathers of the red-tailed hawk, the eagle, the buzzard, or the turkey are next affixed to the butt of the shaft. Turkey feathers, however, "can't stand rough treatment and are used mostly for the arrows used in practice or for boys' arrows." Each feather is split in half and trimmed, and the white substance is scraped from the quill. Three feathers are used, five- or six-inch lengths being arranged equidistant from each other and bound on the shaft with wet sinew. Sometimes a little piñon pitch is applied to the shaft at the point where the sinew will cross.

One feather is put on at a time, and the tops of the feathers are affixed to the shaft first. The first feather is held in place, and the sinew is wound around its top and the shaft once. The second feather is put in position and secured at the top with one strand of sinew also. Now the third feather is put in place, and the sinew is wound around it and the shaft many times. Then the arrow is put aside that the sinew may dry and tighten. When the craftsman is ready to resume work, he fastens the bottoms of the feathers to the shaft with sinew.

Flint arrowheads are used when they can be found. There is very little chipping of arrowheads. A single informant speaks of pounding slate and using the most likely pieces for arrowheads. Another, an Eastern Chiricahua, tells of seeing "flints used as arrowheads and one rock used to shape and chip another" during his youth. But the majority of commentators agree that their tribesman made no consistent attempt to manufacture flint arrowheads:

The pieces of flint are found already shaped. The legend goes that the animals and the birds made them and used them in the fight against each other for daylight.

The Chiricahua did not make stone arrowheads and beads. They found them. There were many of them in their country. They can be found in anthills there, the hills of the red ants. White shell beads are found there too.

The arrowheads we have are found. They are said to have been made by a people who lived here before the Apache. . . . . These people are called the "ancient people" [Pueblo]. I don't think these people were here even in the memory of the old men. It must have been before that.

Fine long blades and points found throughout the tribal range are also considered by some to be arrows of the Thunder People.

When flints are to be affixed, the shaft is split, the arrowhead is inserted, and the shaft is tightly wrapped with moistened sinew. More commonly, however, no flint is used; the wooden tip of the arrow is simply sharpened and fire hardened. Often the arrow is fluted. With a sharp stone, the arrow-maker scratches three channels along the shaft in line with the feathers or makes a spiral groove upon it. Zigzag incisings, one on either side of the arrow, occasionally are etched instead "because the arrows of Child of the Water, when he fought the giant, were like that."

The respective merits of the two basic arrow types were discussed as follows:

Some arrows are made short, some are made a little heavy, and some are made light. My father says that in order to shoot a long way you should take a short arrow. For short distances he uses the long arrow with a shaft of carrizo. I think an arrow made with a wood shaft is better than a reed [carrizo] arrow. Of course, those reed arrows are good for shooting birds and for other light shooting.

If the shaft is of reed, the arrow has a hard wood point. In the old days they were tipped with any wood hard enough to go into the animal, but I never knew men to put on a stone arrowpoint. Instead they seasoned their arrows until they were very hard. Many times I have seen my father sitting over a charcoal fire heating the end of an arrow until it was just as hard as steel. He'd look at it and sharpen it. I have never seen them chip stones for arrows.

When the shaft is to be of reed:

The man goes to the streams and gets some reeds before they grow too tall. He cuts them green and fresh. They become hard as they dry. He straightens them between his teeth and lets them dry for about two weeks. Then he puts the hard foreshaft in, fastening it with piñon pitch and binding it with wet sinew. It gets tight when dry. About two inches or a little more of the foreshaft goes into the reed, and about the same amount is left sticking out.

The carrizo arrow is usually about thirty inches long; the type with the shaft entirely of hard wood is a few inches shorter. The length and stoutness of the bow are adapted to the size and strength of the man, and the arrow must be of the proper size so that "it is not too short when the string is pulled back."

In addition to the methods of straightening arrows which have been mentioned, the use of discarded potsherds for the purpose has been described: "Take a reed arrow and get it hot. Put grease on and rub it with a piece of discarded pottery which has been heated too. This straightens it. I used to do it in Arizona."

On the child's arrow or on the arrow used for hunting birds and small game, one long feather may be wound spirally around the shaft for a distance of approximately eight inches. Often such arrows are left without any feathers at all.

PLATE XIII

b) War Club

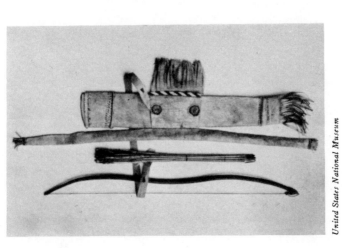

a) Bow, Arrows, Bow Cover, and Quiver

A man must not only be able to make arrows but to use them effectively. In times of peace he keeps in practice by frequent competitions with his fellows. "If a man is expert, he can shoot one arrow, then shoot two more into the air before the first one comes down." Significant personal differences are found in the ability to make and handle bows and arrows. Some men are acclaimed as experts; others are credited with fair performance; while still others are rated decidedly below average.

The quiver and the bow cover are usually made at the same time and of the same material; they are always attached and are both called by the same term, literally "arrow container." Mountain lion skin is the favorite material for the quiver because it is thought that "it makes a man lucky." The fur and the tail are left on, and the finished product is called "quiver with tail." Deer, antelope, otter, and wildcat pelts, with the fur either scraped off or left on, are also used for quivers. Recently hides of cattle and horses have been used, usually without the fur. One informant asserted that the skin of a fetal calf makes a good quiver.

The man cuts a wristguard out of rawhide for himself. This laces up the back of the left wrist and has a projecting piece which protects his hand against the impact of the bowstring.

For a spear a man selects a sotol stalk or a young spruce, scrapes and dries the wood, and sharpens and fire-hardens the tip. Such spears are about seven feet long. The shaft is usually painted in one or more colors, and two eagle feathers are attached near the point. After contact with Europeans, metal knives and bayonets were inserted to make a still more deadly weapon. In battle the spear is never hurled, and it is used by the warrior only when he is on foot.

The round hide shield is connected as much with ceremonialism as with actual defense. It, too, may be a recent acquisition:

Just those with power have them. The man with power prepares these hides himself. He uses the hide from the shoulder region of the animal. He makes it just big enough to protect his chest and face.

First he takes the hide off. Then he scrapes all the flesh from it. He does this with a knife, a steel knife. (They made this shield only from the time they had steel knives and not before.) Then he rakes together sand and builds a fire on it. When the sand is thoroughly heated, he rakes the coals away and pegs the hide down over that place. Then he scrapes the fur from the outside and pegs it down again in another place that has been heated first. Now he takes it up and cuts the hide to the size he wants his shield to be. He makes two holes and ties on a handle big enough to grasp. Sometimes he has another handle so that his arm can be fitted in too. Some men design their shields with sun symbols or other things and paint them various colors.

Many shields are without buckskin covers and have the design painted on the rawhide. One of these which I collected is painted with yellow ocher and has a black morning-star design. More elaborate and Plains-like shields are not unknown, however.

Some shields are covered tightly with buckskin; the designs are painted on the buckskin. The buckskin is sewed onto the hide. Holes are driven through the hide for the purpose of fastening the cover on. There are tail and inner wing feathers of the eagle around the edge, and there are two more eagle feathers in the center. The eagle feathers mean that the maker has power. Just a few men had shields.

To give a shield marked convexity, a wet hide is pressed into a shallow hole in the ground and left to dry there. Buffalo hide is said to have been the material liked best in former times, but the supply obtainable must have been very small. Almost all the shields which informants had made or had seen made were of cowhide.

The warrior may prepare another weapon, the war club. A round stone, the size of a man's fist, is covered with rawhide and connected by a short length of flexible rawhide to a wooden handle. The handle is often covered with buckskin. A loop is provided at the end of the handle for the hand. A horse tail or, after the introduction of cattle, a cow's tail is often attached to the end of the handle too. Such clubs, or "stone carriers," are sometimes painted red or black, especially along the handle. While they vary in length, the average specimen seems to be approximately twenty inches long from stone to handle end.

Less frequently another type of war club, really a hand ax, is made. A grooved stone ax head (more often than not of ancient Pueblo manufacture) is inserted into a handle which has been split to receive it. Pitch has been applied to the inner surface of the split, and the stone is held in place by sinew bindings on either side of it. Often an animal tail is attached to the end of the handle. An ax of this type, without the tail or any decoration, may serve around camp as a household tool.

The man makes for his own use a sling, a diamond-shaped piece of rawhide, pounded a little and thus softened, with four perforations through the median line of its width. A rawhide string is attached to each side, one with a loop at the end and the other without any. Because of the perforations, the sling can be folded over a stone about two and a half inches long and one inch thick. The loop is placed on the middle finger of the right hand, and the free string is held between the thumb and first finger. The sling is drawn back and whirled just once. As it comes forward the unlooped string is released, hurling the stone.

There are slings of two sizes that the Chiricahua carry. One is for things close by and is short. The other is a long one, for long-distance shooting. You can get to be very accurate with a sling. You never whirl the sling around a lot, as the stone might come out and hit someone. It just goes back once, and then you let it go. You can hurl a stone a hundred and fifty yards with it. It can be used for hunting birds or deer alike.

Finally, there is the stone knife, chipped with another stone. "They used to chip off the hardest rock they could get and use it for a knife." This knife may have a shoulder jutting from the handle end so that it can be tied to the belt or waist, or it may be carried in a rawhide sheath made by the woman.

A man makes a long rope from a piece of buckskin or rawhide by cutting it in a continuous clockwise circle from the outer rim to the center. To form an especially strong rope, he braids several strands of rawhide together. Such a cord or one braided from horse-tail hair makes a serviceable bridle. By shredding yucca leaves and braiding the tough strands, he makes a durable rope which also can be used for tying and hobbling horses or for a bit and bridle.

"Anyone could build a fire. Whoever woke up first did it. A woman can use the fire drill." Yet the fire drill is made by the man and is employed by him most frequently:

We take a little stick of wood about eight or ten inches long. It has to be good solid wood and dry. It might be juniper or sotol. It is shaved thin—to about the thickness of a pencil. It does not come to a real point at the lower end but is rather blunt there.

We have a flat piece of wood made of sotol stalk or yucca. It is thin. When it is to be used for the hearth, it has to be about one and a half inches wide and about eight to ten inches long. The one who is going to work the drill makes a little hole or notch in which to put it at the start, so it won't slip around. This little hole can be at the center or at the edge. If the drill goes right through the hearth without a fire being made, the person can start a new notch.

We go to a juniper tree and get the bark, the dry bark, and get some dry grass too. We keep these tied to the set and keep the whole thing dry. When using the drill, we put the grass or shredded bark around the hole, and some of it in the hole too. If we can't get a fire quickly, we put just a pinch of dirt or sand in the hole. As a man twirls the drill between his hands, the smoke comes up. Sometimes the tinder blazes up. If it doesn't blaze but you see that you have a good spark, you take the stick out of the hole, push the grass close together, and blow on it until you get your fire.

All you need is two sticks and your tinder. These two sticks are wrapped together and carried around, for these are the matches of the Chiricahua, you know. They are carried in a bag tied to the belt or in the quiver when the men are on a journey. Dry manure is used to catch the spark sometimes. Some men can get a fire in a very few turns, but some blister their hands trying to do it and give it up.

The designation of sotal and yucca as male and female, respectively—a concept which figures in the construction of the cradle—is extended by some (but not by everyone) to the parts of the fire drill:

The same distinction between the "he" and the "she" is made when talking about the fire drill. The bottom part is supposed to be made out of the "she," the yucca stalk [narrow-leafed yucca],[17] and the top part, which is spun between the hands, should be made out of sotol, the "he."

There are other ways of making and preserving fire. Sparks from flints can be caught in dry pulverized pith of such plants as the elderberry.[18] The flints and the powder are often carried in a buckskin bag, attached to the belt. In wet weather, when it may be difficult to rekindle a fire, a slow fuse of shredded juniper bark tied with yucca leaf strings proves useful:

[17] As the description above shows, this convention is not always respected.

[18] Probably the use of flints and pyrites to make fire followed European contact.

PLATE XIV

Museum of the American Indian, Heye Foundation

a) Fire Drill, Hide-Scraper, and Knife Sheath

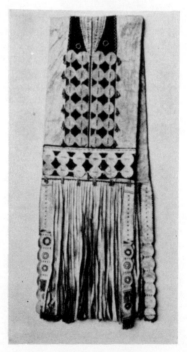

United States National Museum

b) Saddle Bag

If it rained we had a slow-burning fuse that kept a fire going. And when it burned to the end we lit another from it. Thus we kept a fire burning at a rainy time. To play safe, we usually took these fuses along with us in case of emergency, especially if it looked like rain.

Since the operation of the fire drill is considered hard work, whenever there is a chance of getting fire by other means, these are attempted first. It is not unusual, for instance, to send some member of the household to a neighboring camp to borrow fire. He "carries a hot coal between two sticks and runs back to his camp. Mesquite wood will burn the longest when carried this way."

Equipment for the horse.—There is a tendency to associate the horse with the man and his affairs. Women obtain horses by gift and in payment for services, particularly ceremonial services, but the majority of the horses remain in the possession of the men:

Caring for stock is man's work. Men round up the horses and cattle. When a horse is to be loaded, the woman gets the pack ready, but the man does the loading. Men make the saddles, and they saddle the horses for themselves and their wives. The women know how to saddle horses, however, and can do it when necessary. A woman might saddle a gentle horse. A widow has to saddle her own horse.

It is the business of the man to furnish the equipment needed in making use of the horse—the saddle, stirrups, bridle, bit, and quirt.

The saddle, which is modeled after European examples, has a cottonwood framework. Tree forks are whittled down to form the front and cantle. On the front a projection is left for the horn. Two flat boards are lashed between these forks, one on either side, to form the saddle skirts. Wet hide, often with the fur left on, is stretched over this frame and laced into place. As it dries, it contracts and fits securely. When metal tools came into use, the pieces of the frame were joined still more solidly by burning holes through the wood with a red-hot metal punch and drawing rawhide laces through them.

The man also makes a pack saddle, little more than a pad or frame of grass or hide bundles. He makes, too, rounded oak stirrups, a rope bit which is tied under the horse's mouth, and a bridle with reins attached to the bit and tied together at the end. The quirt, of braided rawhide, is a foot and a half or more long and is fringed at the tip. The handle ends in a loop by which it is suspended from the wrist or held. Yucca-rope hobbles are made; they are tied to the saddle when not in use.

If the horse has a sore foot and goes lame, its owner makes a rawhide pouch with a drawstring at the top and ties this over its ailing hoof. Since these "horse moccasins" are always said to be made of cowhide, perhaps their use is recent.

The horseman likes to have a mountain lion skin or some other fine fur to throw over the saddle bag "to make it look nice. The Mexican people did this, so the Chiricahua did it too."

The rider mounts from the left side of the horse, putting his left foot in the stirrup and throwing his right leg over the horse's back. If the horse is not in the habit of running away, the rider, when he stops anywhere, throws the reins over its head to the ground.

Rafts and boats.—When rivers or rain-swollen streams have to be crossed "if there are just a couple of men on horseback, they hang on to the manes of the horses, and let them swim with them." But if groups of people must cross bodies of water, the men make rafts:

When we were coming east and got to the Rio Grande and it was high, the men took logs about twelve feet long or so and tied cross-pieces to them. It makes a raft about three or four feet wide. They had a rope attached to it in front. The best swimmers pulled it along. The rope was around their bodies, or they pulled it with their teeth sometimes. Some good swimmers would be in back to help push. One person would sit on the back to keep the front of it out of the water. Others who couldn't swim or who couldn't swim well would hang on to ropes along the sides. Possessions, sick people, or old people could be brought across water in this way.

One Eastern Chiricahua informant described a bullboat which the men make: "Sometimes when there are no big logs around, they take a rawhide and put sticks crossways inside it. Then they tie the ends up. In this way they make a boat and go across with that."

Not all individuals display an equal willingness to engage in every task that has been described. Shiftless persons have to be exhorted to better efforts by their spouses, relatives, and friends. Concerning a man whose laziness is proverbial, an informant remarked: "I heard his wife begging him to get out and work. She said, 'We're hungry. We haven't anything to eat.' I never was lazy like that man."

The strong group loyalty of kin, and the feeling that food should not be withheld from the hungry, save the family of the unproductive individual from acute suffering. "They just live poorer, that's all." And, since both the man and the woman work, remissness on the part of one is often compensated for by the redoubled efforts of the other. Here it is that the relatives of the partner who is being imposed upon step in to prevent his abuse. The kin of a woman whose husband is economically worthless to them are likely to bring pressure upon her ending either in more significant contributions from the man or in a divorce. If the fault lies with the woman, the husband's relatives remind him of the more satisfactory way in which he lived before his marriage, and he feels that he has grounds for divorce.

Ordinarily, however, ridicule is enough to force the unenterprising into moderate conformity:

If there is a lazy man who doesn't work but lives off the others instead, they give things to him all right, but at the same time they talk to him, telling him that he's able-bodied and has a family and should help himself and hunt and take care of himself. They scold him and shame him and try to make him change. A man like that usually changes; there are lots of them. Many of them don't even go to war, but prefer to stay at home with the women. Some make excuses and act sick and do things like that so they won't have to work.

The products of an individual's industry, skill, and daring are, in theory at least, his own. The dwelling and the domestic articles she has made belong to the woman. How she disposes of baskets, water jars, and parfleches is strictly her business, and her actions are seldom disputed by her husband. The only limitation on her rights is that her own household be reasonably well equipped. Likewise, those things which a man makes or obtains are his own, and his wife may not dispose of them without his permission. But if he recklessly gives away all the booty he has earned in a successful raid and leaves his own family impoverished, he is subjected to stinging criticism at home and ridicule outside.

Trade is more likely to be intertribal than intratribal. "The women who didn't make their own pots got them in trade from the Pueblos and from the Navaho too. Those people came down with peaches and pots and things on burros and traded them for saddles and things we had." But some bartering does go on among tribesmen. "If a man wants a certain blanket, he offers something. If it is refused, he offers more until a deal is made." When something is needed for ceremonial purposes, a particular kind of feather, for instance, the one who has it is approached and offered whatever is required to induce him to part with it.

That trade is not further developed has been attributed by informants to the lack of emphasis on specialization of labor:

A good maker of bows cannot spend his time just making bows. Everyone makes his own bows and takes care of his own property. A woman who is widowed lives in a poorer condition; that's all. She does not get things she needs by trading.[19] There is not much specialization of labor. We were on the move all the time. The Mexicans were always after us. A person didn't have the chance to specialize on any kind of work and trade off the things he made.

Another barrier to great interest in trade is the solidarity of the kin group and extended family in material matters. The ease with which objects can be borrowed for legitimate purposes makes less important their actual ownership and their acquisition by barter.

And yet, in various ways, goods do pass from person to person. The wagering of property on games of chance, for instance, makes for a great deal of circulation of possessions of all kinds. Gambling is almost a major occupation for some individuals, and persons of all ages and both sexes show a lively interest in it. Much wealth changes hands, too, as a result of payment for ceremonial services. Because so many persons are involved in the

---

[19] But for evidence that pots were sometimes traded see pp. 383-84.

practice of ritual, the distribution that this fosters is constant and equitable.

It is gift-giving that largely takes the place of trade, though the difference is mostly one of phrasing. There is the feeling that exchanges should depend upon an implicit reciprocity to be worked out in individual relations rather than in terms of declared measures of value. One speaks of "giving" instead of "selling." But it is understood that generosity begets generosity and that a man loses nothing by kindness to his neighbors. Thus a father caps advice to his son with this admonition: "Do not be stingy and mean. Treat people right. Give half of what you have. Then you will be invited to feasts and get presents."

The openhanded individual builds up a fund of friends who will serve him in good stead whenever he needs assistance, material or moral. One informant told how a member of a certain family gave gifts to his wife. "Now they are our friends" was his comment. The implication is that some gesture on his part will be forthcoming later, for this is an almost inevitable consequence of friendship initiated in this way.

Reputation and social standing are significantly related to generosity, and, even if the individual gains no more than added prestige, he does not regret his philanthropy:

Gifts are given because we are sympathetic to one another. If someone needs food, we help him in a material way, for we feel that we are one people. We feel that way to a man who is poor. Giving is a great thing to the Chiricahua. A man can make a great reputation by giving.

Acceptance of a gift is felt by the receiver as a claim upon him to be adjusted in his own time and way:

You are ashamed to borrow a horse, a bow, or other things, for that shows that you are not a real man and have not been on the raid and obtained things for yourself. To start out, the young man would be given the necessities. Giving is a great thing with us. I don't think there was much selling in the old days, but there was always lots of giving.

Even now there is not much selling. I could walk up to any man and ask for a horse. Even though I don't know him well I have a good chance of getting it. I've been offered horses. C. offered me a horse, but I never took it. I didn't take it because I did not want to feel under obligation to him. He just offered it to show his friendship. This was done in the old days a great deal.

Prestige, obligations to relatives, and the general tenet of generosity perpetuate gift-giving even in situations where no return present is likely to be forthcoming. Nevertheless, these gifts set up currents of reciprocity which stimulate the exchange and circulation of property:

The Chiricahua's nature, the life of the old times that we have been telling about, was free. We gave gifts to one another and didn't ask anything in return. If a man liked you he would say, "I am going to give you a horse, or a ring"— like that . . . . free. To give is considered a good trait, to give without asking something in return.

MARITAL AND SEXUAL LIFE

PERSONALITY ADJUSTMENT BETWEEN HUSBAND AND WIFE

THE common term for mate, used reciprocally by husband and wife is "companion," or, literally, "one with whom I go about." Their joint concern in maintaining a home, rearing children, and securing the necessary household supplies requires close co-operation between them. Although men receive greater deference in public and women are subordinated to them in many ways, at home the feeling tone is usually one of equality between husband and wife.

Occasionally, in spite of the fact that women are considered more unstable than men, "easier to tempt," and more prone to quarrel over trivial things, the wife may be the dominant figure in an encampment. One extended family is continually referred to by the name of the wife of the founding pair, though the husband is living. In this case, the man is very retiring and so is generally ignored. Of another man it was said, "Now he is a slave to his present wife; she cusses him out anywhere."

That a wife is in touch with her kinsmen and has a haven available gives her an assurance in dealing with her husband which she might otherwise lack. If she is badly treated, she can escape to her parents' dwelling, and they will permit her to stay there. Then "the man has to beg for his wife from the outside, and he may or may not get her back."

Still, parents are often unwilling to involve themselves in the personal affairs of their married daughter unless the situation is truly desperate. One father, though he complained of his son-in-law's conduct, seemed in no mood to give his daughter help:

One time my daughter came in and began crying to me. She said, "That man beat me again. I am not going back to him! I don't want to live with him any more!" I told her, "I told you not to marry that man, but now that you have done it, you had better go over there and take your medicine."

No less important in determining a wife's social and domestic position is her economic usefulness. An industrious woman contributes so significantly to the family resources that the indispensable part she plays cannot be minimized by the men. Moreover, much of the wealth she creates belongs to her. Consequently, wives are well aware of their rights and do not accept abuse supinely:

Not long ago this man started beating up his wife. She just took him and rolled him under the bed. You know he is paralyzed on one side and is pretty near helpless when you get him like that. It was a low bed, and he got stuck there. He stayed there until another fellow came along and let him out. He was there calling to his wife to get him out.

An amusing anecdote better illustrates the usual independence of wives in their own homes:

Geronimo was very absent-minded. He would be looking for his hat and he would have it on his head.

One time when we were over to visit him, he was making a bow with a big knife. Pretty soon he began asking his wife where his knife was. All the time he had it in his hand, but we didn't let on. So there he was, scolding his wife and telling her to look for it for him. He was short and stout and pretty old by then, so he wasn't active any more. That's why he wanted his wife to get it for him. But she wouldn't look. She said, "You're old enough to look for your own knife."

Geronimo got pretty angry. "Boys, you see how she is!" he said. "I advise you not to get married." Finally he saw the knife in his hand. "Why, I'm nothing but a fool!" he said.

Important in the stabilization of many marriages are the respect and affection that grow through the years as a result of shared experiences. An elderly informant told of the long period of domestic happiness which he and his wife had enjoyed. Besides being a loyal and helpful mate, she had saved his life. Once when Mexican villagers were overhospitable to a group of Chiricahua, she suspected duplicity and accepted none of the food and drink offered. As she had feared, just as soon as her people were properly befuddled, a massacre began. But she remained clear-headed and managed to get her helpless husband to a hiding-place. The moral force that this exceptional woman exercised over her mate is generally recognized. More than once it was said of him, "That man never gets into trouble; he has a good wife." During my work with this man, his wife showed a lively interest and often assisted with useful suggestions and details. Not long afterward the man died, and she was truly a grief-stricken figure.

Another informant, despite the pose of male indifference, paid his wife a deserved compliment. Speaking of another woman with whom he had once been friendly, he said, "That woman was very pretty when I was a young man. I nearly married her, but I did right to marry my wife. She is a good little woman and has a good reputation."

At another time, when I inquired about a sound of wailing I heard, thinking that someone must have been newly bereaved, I was told, "No, that woman cries every once in a while like that for her husband who died many years ago. She has never married again."

One informant, irritated by insinuations that marriages among his people were not stable or satisfactory before American interference, exclaimed: "Some people think that, because the Chiricahua didn't have a license in the old days, their marriages were no good. But a man couldn't leave a woman for nothing. The Chiricahua had strict and high standards."

But no matter how satisfactory a marriage arrangement is, husbands and wives, as far as external symbols are concerned, are expected to take each other for granted and to demand no small attentions or extra considerations:

A man does not kiss his wife or relatives. We don't show emotion like that. Young people dance together before marriage and now some kiss before marriage, but not after.

The Chiricahua woman does not resent it when her husband goes off without saying goodbye or saying when he will be back, and there is no special greeting for a wife even if the man has been away several days. Yet these married people think just as much of one another as white people do. It's just their way of acting.

SEXUAL ADJUSTMENT

In speaking of the sexual adjustment in marital life, informants have emphasized the role of individual differences:

I was talking about this with my friend, H. At that time I was young. When I saw a woman I'd have an erection. "What makes that?" I asked him. He said, "I get that way too." But there was another fellow. We used to chum together. You couldn't make him get an erection. You could have five naked women in front of him and it wouldn't matter! It's all in the nature of the individual. I have noticed that lots of fellows don't care for women, and lots are worse off than I was. It's in the brain, in the nerves. It's like some who get to be cigarette fiends when they smoke. It's just their nature to feed their bodies.

These two fellows and I were together. H. and I used to go down to Lawton and go with girls. The other boy wouldn't do anything, though the girls were after him. He never even danced. Yet he's married now. He has only one child, a boy of about twenty.

In spite of the acknowledged individual differences, there is an accepted ideal of moderation in sexual life:

The Chiricahua is not willing to show a lot of feeling for the other sex. That is why our women are probably colder than women of other races. They would consider it shameful to lose control of themselves during intercourse.[1]

Sexual intercourse two or three times a week is considered normal for married people. In the old days even less than that, because men were away so much. Yet some men are so bad about this that they get their wife with a second child before the first one walks, and the oldest child does not get proper nourishment.

The young Indians tell me about intercourse with women of other peoples, with Negroes, Mexicans, and whites, and they are surprised at the activity of these women during intercourse. One fellow said, "Well, I went into a place to have intercourse with a woman, but she had intercourse with me!" We say that those who are too fond of this get old quickly, that a person ages rapidly if he is just like a hog about it.

In an autobiographical statement, the same pattern of moderation is pictured:

For the first three or four months I had intercourse every night with my wife; after that about twice a week; later on, after the first year, once a week or less. Now after eleven years of married life, when I'm home, about once a week. Once a week won't hurt a man, I guess.

But prudery and continence in the married person are just as heartily condemned and ridiculed as unbridled sensuality, as a humorous story indicates:

[1] Yet one informant expressed a contrary feeling concerning female sexuality, saying, "I've always heard that women are twice as eager as men, never getting enough of sexual intercourse."

They tell this story of a certain man. They say he was J.'s grandfather. He married and when he and his wife went to bed the first night, he just turned away from her. She didn't think much of it at first. Then he did the same thing the second night. Every night she thought he was coming to her, but he turned the other way instead. He did this for seventy-five nights, and then she left him.

BIRTH CONTROL, BARRENNESS, AND FERTILITY RITES

A childless marriage is considered a great misfortune, and sterility is an accepted cause for divorce. Sterility in a woman is sometimes attributed to a ceremony conducted over her in girlhood by envious or scheming adults.[2] But often a disappointed husband wonders whether his wife "has hired a man or woman who knows herbs and a ceremony to make her sterile, so that she won't be bothered by children:"

I have heard old people say that some women can perform a ceremony for another woman, and she will have no children no matter how many men have intercourse with her. Girls of about the age of puberty go through it, and older women who have too many children go through it too. They have a medicine to drink and a ceremony that goes with it that will prevent birth forever. Certain people practice this ceremony. It has to be paid for like any other ceremony.

Various methods for the prevention of pregnancy have been described. "Rock crystal is used as a medicine when a woman does not want a child. The rock is ground up fine, and some of the powder is put in a drink. There are prayers and a ceremony connected with this, but I do not know them." A certain variety of small prickly-pear cactus fruit, because it is rare and its fruits are said not to ripen, is magically associated with these practices.

Food or behavior restrictions imposed as a part of such ceremonies must be carefully observed. "If a woman is avoiding pregnancy by keeping away from some food or drink, such as honey, and breaks this fast, she will become pregnant." It is noteworthy that honey should be specifically mentioned as one of the foods prohibited if a woman wants no children, for beeswax is said to be "used ceremonially to cure sterility in women."

Because of the prevailing desire for children and the insecurity of a childless woman, fecundity ceremonies are of much more frequent occurrence. In one of these rites the practitioner cere-

[2] See pp. 80–81.

monially feeds one egg (now a hen's egg) and the testicle of a rabbit to her client each day. This is accompanied by the throwing of pollen to the directions and appropriate prayers. According to the account, "she does this a few days, and then the woman is with child."

A ceremony performed by an old woman resulted, one man and his wife feel sure, in the birth of their only child:

My wife was eager to have children. She didn't do anything about it at first. But four or five years after our marriage we had an old woman perform a ceremony over her. It was held at the camp of the old woman in the springtime of the year, when everything comes to life. The ceremonial woman blew smoke to the directions first. Then she used pollen. The ceremony was prayer mostly. My wife had to eat some chicken eggs.

Childless marriages are sometimes attributed to male sterility:

It's not only the rich blood [semen] of a man that causes him to have children. Yusn has made it that way. When it's going to be that way, it's going to be that way. I've heard some men say that, if Yusn doesn't want it to happen, you won't get children.

Informants have cited cases of the divorce of childless couples, after which the woman has remarried and borne children, while the second union of the man is as unproductive as the first:

Sometimes each blames the other if there are no children; a woman sometimes holds a man to blame for this and divorces him. Who is to blame is found out soon enough, for they marry others and prove the truth.

Such instances provide proof that "some men are unable to give children." The sterile man tries to overcome his misfortune. "A man might get treatment [ceremonial] for sterility too."

JEALOUSY AND EXTRA-MARITAL RELATIONS

To judge from the number of instances which have been reported, extra-marital affairs are not infrequent and usually lead to tension between husband and wife. "Jealousy and consequent quarreling are grounds for divorce. Jealousy is the foundation of divorce. Women are more to blame than men; they nag more." Despite this pronouncement, actual cases of jealousy seem to be quite evenly divided between the sexes. Of one man it is said:

"He had his house built far from the other camps because he is jealous. He has a young pretty wife and he doesn't want anyone around." Undue precautions which ended in divorce are attributed to another man. "N.'s first wife is married to another man now. N. was abusing her all the time. He even took her out hunting with him in winter when it was cold, he was so jealous of her, and he whipped her all the time." On one occasion a young married man was called aside by a woman. When he returned, he explained:

That woman was telling me that her husband is jealous of her. This morning I was going past the hospital and I saw her sitting on the steps. I said, "Hello, what you are looking so angry about?" She didn't even answer, so I went on. Her husband saw us there and is accusing her of fooling around with me, she says.

The women are no less critical of mates whom they suspect of duplicity. One informant lamented, "My wife got jealous. I could not stand it. I had nothing to do with other women, but she was jealous." A man in danger of becoming involved in an affair with a girl some years his junior soon found that his wife was closely observing his progress:

About five years after I was married I got into a little flirtation with a girl I had known when I was younger. She tried to attract my attention. She met me at the store. She would talk a lot to me. It was kind of an adventure to me. She was eight or nine years younger than I was.

My wife heard about it. This girl hinted around that she wanted me to go farther with her. I could gather this from the way she talked. She would ask me to see her at night. She would name a meeting place. I never met her. I kept a cool head. If I hadn't, I would have been in serious trouble.

This went on for about a month, until my wife spoke to me about it. Once when she got angry she told me what she knew. She asked me if I had met the woman. I told her, "No." The next time I saw the girl I told her she was causing trouble for me and to let me alone.

In explaining why a certain man declined an invitation to go on a trip, my informant remarked:

His wife probably isn't sick, but she is pretty unreasonable about such things and just doesn't want him to go. She is very jealous. He wants to be like most of the other men and go out a great deal, but he has to stay home to keep peace in the family. She imagines all sorts of things that are not true. He and his wife live near her mother. Once his wife made things so miserable for him that he left.

A blue-green alga (Nostoc) is used to combat suspected unfaithfulness:

It's found in the mountains, just on the ground. It's very scarce. It can be used both ways—on a man or on a woman. If you think your wife is unfaithful, you can make her smoke it with tobacco, and it will make her stop acting like that. I've had it for about eight years. I keep it in a buckskin pouch. My wife and I went and got it. We tried one day and couldn't find any. We went the next day and got a little.

Love magic is used also to keep or to regain the interest of a mate. A story is told of a man who stayed out on raids and war expeditions so long that his wife felt abandoned. Her mother, who "knew love charms," performed "a deer ceremony . . . . the kind used to get deer in a certain position, to charm a deer so that he will be at a place where you can get him easily." The husband, who was far away, became lonesome for his wife. That very day he started for home and, when he got there, begged his wife "to take him back."

Affairs, especially for women, are probably more common after marriage than before: "Unmarried girls are watched very carefully; married women aren't guarded carefully by the community." In all traditional stories of unfaithfulness and perversion the woman is described as the culprit.

An actual example of infidelity throws light on the behavior of individuals in these domestic crises. A man hears that his wife has become involved with a widower during his absence and hurries home:

His intention was to kill both of them or one of them the night he got back. He had a long knife. I heard this story the next morning. Somehow those two got word that he was looking for them and hid; they were warned and ran out to the mountains. The people wouldn't tell him where they went. He hunted for them all night. He looked in all the homes the next day. I talked with him myself but couldn't cool him off.

Meanwhile a bunch of the leading men got together. They didn't want trouble. They pleaded with him to let them go. Prominent men pleaded with him. The evening before the feast I was with him. The leading men called him over to a place near the feast grounds. They were all waiting for him. I walked over with him. The woman and the man he was after were hidden in another tent. The old men said, "Brother, nephew, we wish to talk with you." They called him all kinds of relationship terms. "Cool down," they told him.

"The only way I'm going to cool down is if you bring those two people before me, right here. I won't do anything to harm them now, but I want to talk with them before you men."

They didn't say "Yes" right away. Instead these old men said, "Are you sure you are just going to talk to them? We don't want trouble. We don't want you to kill those people or to kill yourself."[3] They had several minor arguments about it until they felt sure he would behave himself.

The husband told them, "Bring them in if you have them close by. I want to talk to them before you."

They brought the two in there. Men were sitting around. The woman came in crying, scared. The man came in and sat down. The husband was sitting over on the other side. He started to talk. "The pleading that these men have done for you is the only thing that is saving you two. I would have killed you both, or you would have killed me, if I had found you. If it wasn't for these men, I don't know where you'd be."

Then he said to his wife, "Are you marrying that man for love?" She wouldn't speak.

He spoke to the man. "Do you know what kind of a woman she is? She fights like a man. She's a mean woman, I'm warning you. She'll give you plenty of trouble. But now that you are going to take her away from me, you're going to keep her. If you get too much of her and give her up, or if you don't lick her enough and can't handle her, I'm going to beat up both of you. Small as you are, you are going to get beaten up many times! I've had many a fight with her. You two are not marrying for love. Now take her and remember what I say."

The man told him, "You can take my word for it, she won't make a slave out of me."

"She'd better not. You'd better not let her," the husband said.

As the traditional stories and this account indicate, the husband of a faithless woman is permitted to take drastic action if he feels strongly about the injury done him. It is the function of the leaders to dissuade him from violence, but their pressure is moral and not binding. A wronged husband who does not show some rancor is considered unmanly. "A man would at least pretend anger." The husband of the episode just recounted, in spite of his great display of fury, "didn't care. He married right away to a Comanche." If a husband does not seem to be very much ex-

---

[3] Suicide as a result of unfaithfulness and marital difficulties is not unknown. "If a man's wife was unfaithful and he killed her, he might kill himself." During the stay at Fort Sill a Chiricahua known as Fun took his own life after an attack on his wife in which he thought he had killed her. The woman recovered, however.

cited over such an affair, "sometimes his friends will try to inflame him." Thus the social pressure upon the husband for stern action is often almost equal to the efforts of the leaders to settle the matter peaceably.

The woman, since she is close at hand, is likely to be the first to feel the husband's wrath. A beating is the least punishment she suffers. If there is no one to intercede for her, her very life may be forfeit, or she may be subjected to mutilation:

A man never whips his wife without reason. If he finds out that she is unfaithful, he whips her, cuts her nose, or else kills her. He would have to have evidence of unfaithfulness and not hearsay, however. Treatment like this does not come for little things. For not obeying him, or for not working, a man would merely scold his wife, and he would do so in private. If the woman has committed adultery, the people think that what happens to her is her own fault and don't say anything about the punishment she gets.

The reason they cut the nose of a woman is to make her look ugly. She is marked so that no one will meddle with her. One woman who is still living has her nose cut like this. Her husband cut her nose out of jealousy and left her because she went with another man.

The husband is just as insistent that the man who has disrupted his home be punished:

After the husband has punished or killed his wife, he will go after the man and kill him. But the other, if he is wise, will run away and not return for years until it has blown over. I cannot remember a case where the man who is to blame has killed the husband instead. If that happened, close relatives of the husband would kill him.

Nothing leads more quickly to trouble between men than suspicion or charges of wife seduction:

This morning I went up to a place where a group of men were standing. I was right beside B. Pretty soon L. came. You could see he was angry. He placed himself right in front of B. and said, "Somebody was crawling around my camp last night and bothering my wife, and I just want to say that if I catch anyone around there again, I'm going to kill him." You could see he was talking to B. B. just hung his head. Then L. talked to B. directly and said, "If you ever come around my camp again, I'm going to kill you."

I saw there might be trouble, so I stepped between them. "Now don't get mad," I told L. "Don't get yourself into trouble."

PLATE XV

Laboratory of Anthropology of Santa Fe

WOMAN WITH MUTILATED NOSE

The birth of twins is considered evidence of unfaithfulness:

If any woman has twins, she is looked upon as having run with other men besides her husband. My sister is one of a pair of twins.[4] The other died a few days after birth. I think they were both girls. The older one died. I never heard my father say anything about it. One twin would not be kept. We believe that both could not grow up; one would die. They keep the boy if the twins are a boy and a girl.

Sometimes twins are born. Twins are considered unlucky. Twins cannot grow up; they always die. Unfaithfulness on the part of the woman causes twins. Sometimes one of the twins is stillborn.

If it is the husband who is philandering, his wife scolds him and complains to her close relatives. But the man is in no danger of a beating or of mutilation. Few wives take desperate action of any kind:

If the husband is unfaithful and is discovered by his wife, his wife may say to him, "Well, you love the other woman better than me; go and marry her." Or she might let it go and forget and forgive entirely. The women don't have power to do much to the men. A very mean woman might stab her husband at night or something like that. The people wouldn't blame her much, because it is the husband's fault. But only a very hard-up man would marry the woman after this; so that keeps women from killing their husbands.

However, a woman who is very much angered by her husband's conduct can send him away:

I heard the quarrel at the time. She told him, "You think you're going to have this woman and myself for your wives, and you think you're going to stay with this woman one time and with me another time. You think you're going to go back and forth between us two wives. You are mistaken! You might pull that on somebody else, but not on me. So you'll marry that woman. Go right ahead and marry her. Our married life is over; we'll quit here. You'll leave this house without anything and go and live with that woman." She sent him away.

It is apparent that both husband and wife are in a position to demand fair play and to take appropriate action. Enough feeling of self-importance and competence has been communicated to individuals of both sexes during the training period, so that no one is willing to accept humiliation as a matter of course.

The permanent disruption of a household involves the entire

---

[4] The informant is not here impugning the virtue of his own mother, since this is a half-sister, the offspring of his father's second wife.

extended family; therefore, the woman's relatives watch anxiously any developments which may deprive them of the services of a satisfactory son-in-law. Their tendency is to support the woman in minor disputes; but, when she is obviously in the wrong, they are just as likely to side with the husband and to remind their relative of her wifely duties:

> I feel sorry for that boy, my son-in-law. He's a good boy and steady, and I know he is trying to do the right thing. But my girl is not doing what she should. She's not keeping house in the right way and she is beginning to run around. She thinks I don't know it. I'm going to put a stop to it.

DIVORCE

The word for divorce can be translated "they walk away from each other." To divorce a person is "to throw him (her) away." The woman is ordinarily left in possession of the home which she has built, the household utensils which she has made, and her private effects. If the trouble has been long continued, the husband is willing enough to leave the encampment of his wife's relatives. He takes with him his personal possessions only; there is no return of marriage gifts at divorce.

The most common causes of divorce and the procedure have been summarized in these words:

> Unfaithfulness on the part of husband or wife, brutal treatment on the part of either, and nagging are causes for trouble and divorce. Laziness on the part of either, failure of the man or woman to do the proper share toward the support of the home, and excessive gambling on the part of the man are other things that lead to divorce. Barrenness on the part of the woman is sometimes given as a cause too.
>
> The one who intends to break it up just goes, taking what valuable personal belongings he has. It's about half and half; sometimes women divorce men; sometimes it's the men who leave. Divorce just consists of getting up and leaving.

Additional factors and details are given in another comment:

> Usually divorce follows if a woman cannot work well or if she is cranky and hard to get along with. Sterility is also a cause for divorce, and frigidity too, for men don't like that kind of a woman. Even if a woman is sweet and a good worker, a man could divorce her for sterility or for frigidity. If she is sterile, a woman might get on with her husband for a while, but he will soon divorce her. Pretty soon she'll be passed from man to man, and she isn't respected.

With divorce, each person takes his own belongings without fuss and goes to his and her old home. This did not often happen. The woman has little power to stop a divorce if her husband wants one. Even if she doesn't want a divorce her husband can get up and leave. If the woman wants to leave and the man doesn't want her to, he can try to hold her by force. But she can usually get away to her parents' home.

Impotence as well as frigidity may be an important factor in divorce decisions:

When a man can't get an erection, it is attributed to witchcraft. If it can't be cured, this might be the real reason back of a divorce.

If a woman marries an impotent man, she may stay married to him for wealth or something, but most likely they would separate.

After divorce, though a man must continue the avoidances and polite forms which his marriage brought into being, the material hold of his former wife's relatives is at an end:

If a man is determined to divorce his wife, or if she insists on divorcing him, the parents-in-law cannot very well stop it. All the obligations of the man to support the woman's family stop at divorce. He cannot be made to marry any sister or girl cousin of his wife at any time in the future.[5] But avoidances and polite forms go on. Both the man and the woman are free from each other and from each other's families as soon as the divorce has gone through, as soon as they have separated. They can each marry as soon as they wish again then.

The presence of children acts as a decided brake to divorce action. "In the old days it was pretty hard to get a divorce when there were children. It was not often done then."

If, in case of divorce, the mother's relatives are willing to contribute to the support of the children and the mother is willing to maintain her household, this is considered the best solution. Though there is no definite rule, there is the feeling that children should be under the care of the mother and her kin during their formative years. Babies who are not yet weaned always remain with the mother, and, in general, very young children are likely to stay with her. Sometimes older children, particularly boys, are claimed by the father. When the man can charge that the woman is at fault and has not been a fit parent, public opinion and the pressure of group leaders force acquiescence on the part

[5] For a discussion of the sororate see pp. 421–25.

of the wife and her relatives. Wealth may even decide the issue; where the relatives of the wife are poor and the man and his kin have greater resources, the husband may take a child with him at the dissolution of the marriage.

The divorced man returns to his parental home or stays with some close relative. Unless he is well along in years, he soon marries again.

The chief loser in a divorce action is the woman. For at least part of her sustenance she is now once more dependent on her own relatives, who, too, have lost economic assistance. Because she is now an experienced woman with a record of marital difficulties, it is unlikely that a new husband will offer presents to her parents. Should she fail to be married again soon, her reputation suffers. The word meaning "single woman who has been married before" (divorcée, widow) has an unsavory connotation. "This word would only be used to a single woman who was married before, and never to one who is single in the sense that she has not married at all yet. The word is more or less of an insult, and a person would not use it to a woman whom he respects."

Because unmarried girls are carefully guarded, the promiscuous women are usually divorcées and widows who have failed to remarry. From them the community and their kin do not exact the same high standards of conduct demanded of the unmarried girls: "At a drinking party there might be a young divorced woman, but it is very unlikely that any unmarried girl would attend. Young men attend though." Divorced women are thought more likely to have illegitimate children than the unmarried: "After a first marriage a woman might have children out of wedlock, but that kind of woman is not liked."

Marriage can be more easily contracted with a divorced woman than with a maiden. The waiving of marriage gifts has already been noted. Less pressure upon relatives and less persuasiveness are required in arranging such a match. The celebration of a military victory or the social dance of a puberty rite may even be the occasion for a very informal union with a divorced woman:

During the dance after a war party returns, it is all right to go home with a divorced woman. This kind of marriage is permitted. But it would not be done with a girl who had never been married. This could also be done during the social dancing at the tepee ceremony. These are people who have already been courting each other and talking together. It is just a good chance to do what they intended to do anyway.

SEXUAL ABERRANCE AND PERVERSION

According to an informant, "homosexuality is forbidden. The person who does this is considered a witch and is killed." Yet there is a suggestion of the violation of the canon in another statement. "I have never heard of two men having sexual relations together. I've heard about women doing it and about boys doing it to each other, but not older men."

One story of Lesbianism continually goes the rounds. "They say that there were two women at Fort Sill who lived together and had sexual relations together. They say someone once heard one of them ask the other, 'Is it sticky?'" Another informant who mentioned this incident placed it in the distant past:

I never heard of male homosexuality. I have, however, heard of Lesbianism. There was a case a long time ago, and the old men used to talk about it. There were two married women who ran off from their husbands and made a camp together for themselves. The people went to their camp and heard the two women talking. One was on top of the other, and one asked the other if she felt something sticky. The answer was, "Yes."

These women were laughed at and ridiculed. I don't know what they did after they were discovered, whether they continued to live together or not. I just heard the old people talk about this long ago.

If I should see two women behaving like this, I would feel ashamed of them if they had relatives. But if the women didn't have close relatives, I wouldn't feel so ashamed of them. The difference is that the women would bring shame to their relatives. The rest of the people might think they were so hard up they couldn't be married properly.

There are a number of women who excel in activities commonly considered the interests of men. Two such women, both now very old, were mentioned by several persons, and one in particular was singled out as a deviant from the ordinary feminine behavior pattern:

Every now and then a woman would be expert with the bow and could make arrows and a bow. This is exceptional though. Two women here could do everything like a boy when they were young. D. could ride well, make a bow and arrows, and was a real athlete. She has been married. Her husband died just a few years ago. She has never had children, but her husband was married before and had two children by his first wife.

These women, though they are more interested in masculine pursuits than the average woman, are not considered transvestites. All girls are urged to be strong and fast. It is simply accepted that these particular individuals have carried the requirement further than is strictly necessary. Their preoccupation with such things was confined primarily to their youth. They have married, have accepted the woman's role in all essentials, and in old age are not distinguishable in dress or behavior from others of their sex and years. The attitude of those discussing them is never one of ridicule or condemnation but rather one of admiration.

True berdaches are rare, and their emergence is definitely discouraged. The last one of whom I have a record died before 1880:

P. and S. had a brother who was like this. He never married. He died in Old Mexico. This man talked and walked like a woman, sewed clothes, and made moccasins. He didn't make baskets though. He went where the women were all the time. He hardly ever went where the men were playing at hoop and pole, and he himself never played it. Instead he played the stave game with the women. Such people were never treated with any great respect by us. We just laugh at them.

POLYGYNY AND SORORAL POLYGYNY

In a coyote story a white man whom Coyote deceives is said to have two wives. The polygyny with which this alien is credited is really practiced by some men of the tribe:

In the old way a man can have more than one wife. Of course, he isn't expected to take more than one wife if he can't afford it. If he isn't a leading man or a good warrior, he shouldn't do it. A common man is criticized for it. It is the wealthy men who have more than one wife. A man can have more than two wives. It depends on a man's position and whether he can provide for them.

When a man takes a second wife, it is usually a sister or relative of the first. But this is not always the case. Perhaps there are no more girls in that family, or there are none of the right age. If the women a man marries come from different families, he has to hide from both his mothers-in-law and keep up the avoidances and polite forms for the relatives of both those women.

There is no real ranking of wives, though the first, because she is usually older, might have more to say. The wives live in one encampment but in separate households. When a man has two wives, the one he married first is called "she who sits first." The second wife is called "she sits on her." It really means that she is going to help, to sit next to the other woman. That's how we feel about it.

N., a leader who died about ten years ago, had two wives at the same time. He had them right through the time we were at Fort Sill. The wives and children got along well. He had children by both women, and they lived in peace.

When there is more than one wife, the children of one call the children of the others *šik̓is* and *šilah*. If a second wife is the sister or cousin of the first, the children of one call the other woman "aunt" and are called "niece" and "nephew" by her.

If their father's other wife is no relative of their mother, they call her "stepmother."[6] The husband calls the children of both of these women "son" and "daughter." The real mother calls her own children "son" and "daughter" too.

If a man marries a second sister, he does not have to give more presents. If he marries outside his first wife's family, he does have to give presents though.

The subject of plural wives drew this statement from an elderly man:

Most men have one wife. . . . . The limit is about five. If a man can afford it, he might have more, because there is no rule, but the greatest number of wives I ever heard of is four or five, and the greatest number I've actually known about is only two or three. Just because a man marries the eldest of several sisters, he has no claim on the others. Of course, he might marry a sister of his wife if he is ready to marry again and both are willing.

When a man has more than one wife, the first wife is respected more than the others, providing she has children. She acts like the boss and can order the other wife around. If the first wife has no children and the second one has, the second wife would probably be liked better, and in time the first one might be divorced. If one of a man's wives dies, the other wife or wives help to raise her children. They are not adopted by anyone else.

Though all agree that sororal polygyny is preferable, there is some difference of opinion concerning the strictness with which the rule should be applied. A strong feeling for the custom is expressed thus: "A man can have more than one wife. If there is one available for him, he has to marry a wife's sister if he takes a second wife. He marries the oldest sister usually. They all live

---

[6] One term, a self-reciprocal, means both stepmother and stepchild, woman speaking.

in the same dwelling. If one has a baby, he sleeps with the one who has no baby."

The motive force toward sororal polygyny, of course, is the obligation which the man owes his first wife's parents. Should they permit him to marry a second wife from another family, they would, in effect, be agreeing to share his time and services:

If a man wants a second wife, he is not free to marry anyone who appeals to him. His first obligation and duty are to his wife's family. If his wife has any sisters or female cousins who are eligible, he would have to marry one of them rather than go outside the family. If he wants to marry outside nevertheless, he has to get permission from that family. He would never make such a request unless he suspected that the family does not care much about him anyway. Even if the wife's family does not have any eligible girls, as a matter of courtesy he should state his intentions and ask permission. The great obligation of a man to his wife's family guides him in all his actions. Therefore, the second wife is usually the sister of the first.

But, for one reason or another, it is often impossible to establish sororal polygyny:

Sometimes a man takes the sister of his wife as his second wife. But it does not always happen that way. It's pretty well divided. N. had two wives who were not sisters. Another man has two wives who are sisters. There are a good many cases where the women are not sisters. C. had three wives at one time. One is left now. They were not sisters. G. had four at one time; none of them were sisters.

Whether sororal polygyny can be arranged depends in large measure on the ages of the wife's sisters when the husband joins the family and on the relations which they initially establish with him:

If the sister of your wife wants to, she can hide from you. Usually she doesn't do this though. She can use polite form to you if she wants to. If she starts this, you probably will never marry her, at least while your wife is alive. Only a grown girl would use the polite form to you. Using the polite form is not a matter of liking a person only; it is a matter of respect. And when you have this respect relationship between you, you aren't going to get friendly and intimate to the point where she can become a second wife.

But if a sister of your wife is quite young when you marry and she doesn't use polite form to you and grows up around you, sees you without your shirt, and under all conditions, she isn't going to use polite form to you when she grows up. She is too friendly with you for that. Then you can marry her all right. . . . .

The manner in which interest in the wife's sister develops to the point where sororal polygyny occurs has been convincingly described:

I don't know whether I would marry my wife's sister, too, under the old conditions. It depended on a man's wealth, on whether he could support more than one woman. The intimacy grows up gradually. Maybe you get familiar with her in secret. Then it comes out into the open, and, if your wife thinks it is all right, you marry her sister too. That's how it was with a man I know of. Now he doesn't care. He walks to the store with that other woman [his wife's sister, his second wife].

The other day my wife and her younger sister were going to the creek for water. I went along. The sister did something, like poking me in the ribs. I picked her up and made believe I was going to throw her in the creek. My wife was pouring water down my neck. I didn't think anything of it because we are always cutting up like that. My wife didn't either. I thought no one was around. Then I noticed that a lot of people were watching. I felt pretty much ashamed and let the girl down.

Just to show you how it works: My wife had a sister, now dead, who used to want to go around and camp with us. I didn't know it, but after a while my wife told me that the people were saying that I had two wives. The old man, her father, heard of this first and didn't want the sister to go with us any more.[7] He told his wife, and she told my wife. My wife said she didn't care, that it wasn't so, but that even if it was so, it would be all right. You see the idea is still pretty strong. My wife's sister didn't care what they said either, and she didn't stop going around with us.

I think this is the way those double marriages came about in the old days. It was a gradual thing growing out of intimacy, and nothing was thought about it. It was possible because sisters were together so much, and an unmarried girl, if there wasn't any hiding or polite talk to interfere, would be around her sister's home and see her sister's husband all the time.

There seems to be no unalterable usage governing living arrangements when a man has more than one wife:

If there are two wives, sometimes each has a separate dwelling and sometimes not. All eat together if they are living in the same dwelling; if not, each woman and her children eat separately. The man divides his time between the women. The first wife has authority and the favored position.

According to the testimony of another man, the "wives live together in one camp, with the first wife having rights over the

---

[7] This man, the father, was himself practicing sororal polygyny at the time.

second woman." Another commentator, however, feels that separate households for wives is the more usual state, especially in
times of peace, although "sometimes in wartime they are in the
same house because of the danger." In all probability adjustments are made to needs and particular situations. The size of
the family and the degree of cordiality existing between wives
have much to do with the determination of living arrangements.

Leadership and wealth come with years and experience; therefore, a man is not likely to take a second wife until a good many
years after his first marriage. This may account, in part, for the
absence of serious friction between co-wives. The older woman
normally has shared her youth with her husband, has borne him
children, and has attained status and a good deal of control over
the family before the second wife enters the household. She often
welcomes the newcomer for the assistance the arrangement will
give her with the household duties. Sometimes it is at her insti-
gation that another wife is taken. Since only leaders and wealthy
men can afford to have more than one wife, polygyny is not widely practiced. No more than 20 per cent and perhaps only 10 per
cent of the men would be able to undertake such responsibilities.

THE SORORATE AND LEVIRATE

At the death of a wife or a husband, the surviving mate is
spoken of as "one who has become *ica*." The word *ica* does not
yield to linguistic analysis, but it has the force of "bound to" or
"under the control of." Those who exercise the control are the
relatives of the deceased spouse. Those to whom the surviving
partner is "bound" (in the sense that they may request marriage
of him or her) are the dead person's siblings and cousins of the
same sex. Of the terminological usage one informant explained:
"A man shouldn't say of another man, 'He is "bound" to me.'
He should say, 'He is "bound" to us,' meaning to the whole
family. But a man can be 'bound' to a woman." Another said of
the word: "When you say, 'She (he) becomes "bound,"' you
mean that the person is a widow or widower, but is not free."

The substance of the sororate and levirate has been defined
thus:

A man is "bound" to his wife's sister when his wife dies. The woman has the right in the matter. She approaches the man or not as she wishes. If the wife has a sister and a cousin, and the sister does not like him but the cousin does and asks him to marry her, he is obliged to marry her as if she were the sister, and the family considers it in the same light. If no one asks him within a reasonable period of time, the man can marry anyone he wishes.

It's just the reverse if a man dies and leaves a widow. Then one of the dead husband's brothers or cousins can ask her to marry him, and she cannot refuse.

The sororate.—As soon as a man's wife dies he becomes "bound" to his affinal relatives. Together they go into formal mourning. The attitude toward a well-liked and grief-stricken son-in-law is kindly. "After the death of his wife, a good man, in the old days, would not care for anything. He would not even care about making a living. But his wife's relatives would help him. They would see that he got the necessities." But should the widower be too light-hearted or show interest in any woman of another family, it is counted a grave affront to the departed and a serious breach of the respect owed her relatives. Those to whom the bereaved is "bound" are said to be "jealous," that is, watchful of his conduct.

As it functions, the sororate is a device for bridging quickly, with least disadvantage to the children of the deceased and to the extended family, the gap caused by the death of a married woman:

When S.'s sister, my wife, died, he called me [by the term meaning] "bound to" his family. I couldn't have called him this. It meant that I was not free from him, that if he had any more sisters he could make me marry one. But that was all the sisters he had. Now that I'm married again, he can't call me that.

If a man's wife dies, he will marry a woman to whom he is "bound." If his wife dies, a man is "bound" to her sister, and if she has no sister, to her unmarried cousins. If the dead woman has two unmarried sisters, he might be asked to marry either. The word *ica* means "belonging to."[8] In this case, where his wife has died, the man is "bound." He is not exactly forced to marry the woman to whom he "belongs," but her family wouldn't like it if he refused. They couldn't do much about it though. He would just violate that rule.

If a man is "bound" to a woman, it's up to her to act and show what she intends to do. He must not speak to her first about it, for he belongs to her, and it's her right. After a while she would come to him if she felt like it and say,

---

[8] While this informant's suggestion is good, it seems to me that "bound" or "bound to" is a closer approximation to the meaning of the term.

"Now you are 'bound to me.' If you are willing, we will get married." She would come to him personally. Then there would be no presents, no wait, no feast; they just begin living together.

But if she lets several years pass without asking him, it would be a sign that she does not want to marry him. In this case, he knows that they are willing to let him go, to let him marry outside that family.

The man usually goes and asks permission of his dead wife's family if he wants to marry out of it. Even if his dead wife's people have no more girls and he wants to marry again, he will have to let her parents know what he wants to do as a matter of courtesy.

The family of the dead woman cannot force the man to marry anyone other than a relative of his former mate, however:

If the dead wife has no sister, the man may be forced by his in-laws to marry whom they say, and he won't object as long as it is a relative of his wife. But if they have no relatives for him to marry and they suggest another girl, he isn't bound to obey.[9]

If there are two sisters of the dead wife left and they both want him, he takes the one he pleases. He practically always takes the older though. But it's the woman who has the say; if she objects to the man, he doesn't marry her, of course.

The degree of control which the family of the deceased exercises is further explained in another statement:

If the widower has nobody to stand up for his rights, his in-laws can make it tough for him and see that he can't marry anybody else if he won't marry his sister-in-law. He might marry her, however, and if they don't get along, they can divorce—and that is the man's chance to get free.

When a man's wife dies, the children usually go to a female relative of the wife to be cared for. Later, if the man marries again out of the family, he can get his children back. But if he marries out of the family, he can't get married again until a year or two after his wife has died. It depends on how soon her relatives will let him marry again. If you marry out of that family, you have to wait a long time. If a man loved his wife, he wouldn't want to remarry for a long time anyway. Only a bad one, a low-down cuss who was not brought up right, would remarry soon.

The long mourning and waiting period which must elapse before a man may marry someone who is not a relative of his first wife is again emphasized in another comment:

[9] But a sister by adoption may be considered a blood relative for these purposes: "If a girl adopted into a family has a 'sister,' at her death her husband would be 'bound' to this sister."

If a man whose dead wife has no eligible sisters or cousins marries outside the family too soon, his former wife's family resent it and call him down for it. This is thought to be very disrespectful to the dead and is considered very serious. He can't do anything like this before a year of mourning has passed. Often it is two years before he can get permission.

Soon after his wife's death a widower was approached concerning matrimony by an alien woman. In his own words:

I changed the subject as quickly as I could. It was only a short time after my wife's death, and I knew that I couldn't marry then, for my dead wife's family would take it as an insult. . . . . Then I told her, "Maybe I could think about such a thing later on. But here my wife has been dead only a little while, and her relatives would get mad at me if I married now, and then no good would come of it."

This same point is brought out in a criticism of a book purporting to be a life-history of Geronimo:

I know that there are lots of things in that book that Geronimo wouldn't like. For instance, he [the author] says that Geronimo married again a few months after the death of his first wife. Geronimo did not marry a sister or relative of his first wife; therefore, he could not have remarried that soon. The Chiricahua simply do not do that. I know that Geronimo didn't marry until long after the death of his first wife. The only way an Apache can marry again pretty quickly is if he marries one he is "bound to." But if he marries an outsider right after his wife's death, they sure criticize him!

Look at R. His wife died. He then married his wife's sister. He married about four or five months after his wife's death. No one thought anything against it. But if he had married that soon outside the family, they would have thought it was awful. After his first wife died he stayed camped near his mother-in-law. The mother-in-law and his present wife took care of the children after their mother died. Now the family goes right on. That's what this way of doing things is for.

The last part of this quotation introduces a significant point—the shortening of the mourning period to facilitate the remarriage of a man to a member of his deceased wife's family:

The dead woman's sisters talk over who should take the children, if there are any. If one is unmarried and wants the man, she marries him and takes the children. If a woman dies and leaves a widower, the dead woman's sister is supposed to ask the man to marry her. They marry in less than a month sometimes, though they might wait as long as a year. But some people don't wait long after the death of a brother or sister. This is all right if they marry the mate of the dead person.

The sororate does not become operative when one of a man's co-wives dies, even though the two women were not sisters. It is then considered that a man's obligations are to his surviving wife and her relatives:

N. was an Eastern Chiricahua. He had two wives. One died. The one who died had sisters, but they had no claim on him, because he had one wife left. He lived with this one wife until she died. This last woman had no sisters, so he lived on single for many years before he died. The "bound to" relationship does not apply when a man has more than one wife.

Theoretically, a bereaved man is supposed to accede without dispute to the wishes of those to whom he is "bound." But actually he or his relatives may resist these dictates, and, if his case is a good one, he succeeds in gaining his freedom:

If they offer me my sister-in-law after my wife's death and I don't like her, I do not go to my wife's family myself but I get a relative of mine whom I trust. I say to him, "My brother, my mother-in-law wants to give me her daughter, and you know what kind of a girl she is! Her sister was a very different sort of woman. I had a good home with her and I worked well. But with this girl it would be different. She would make trouble for me and perhaps I would make trouble for her. She runs around with men and doesn't work hard."

Then my friend will go to my mother-in-law's house and bring back word from her. If the old lady is convinced, she will say, "My son-in-law lived well with my daughter and we like him. This other daughter is not the right kind for him. He is sensible and is doing right. We would be glad to keep him in the family, but I don't blame him at all. I leave it to him." Then I am free to marry as I want to.

Just as often the man is willing enough to marry his wife's relative but waits in vain for the summons:

D. was married to T.'s oldest girl. This woman died. He wanted then to marry another girl of the family, the sister next in age to his dead wife. The old folks wanted to arrange it that way, for it was according to the old customs and D. was "bound to" them. But the girl didn't want to. This girl is dead now. There were no other daughters old enough. She considered him too old and ugly, I guess. The girl thought she could do better by passing up that old custom. It was up to them to give him a girl or to free him. The old people didn't want to force the girl, so they had to let him go.

So important is the sororate that it may override any restraints which avoidance or polite form has imposed:

If the wife's sister or girl cousin avoids a man and at the death of his wife she wishes to marry him, she could roll a cigarette, take a few puffs on it, and send it to him by a messenger with the words that after that they would not have to be ashamed before each other. If the man accepts the cigarette, he no longer has to avoid her and is free to marry her.

If she has not been avoiding him but was just using polite form to him, she could offer the cigarette herself, saying that thereafter the polite form would not be necessary. If he accepts it, all would be as before.

Even when the family to which a man is "bound" has no girl to offer in place of the deceased, the man must act with the greatest of respect until he is formally freed:

If his father-in-law has no more daughters, the husband will want to marry out of the family after a while. He will say, "I am young and I wish to marry. I respect you and your family, but you have no more daughters for me." He has to get permission to marry out. If the old man refuses permission, even if he has no more daughters, the young man will have to obey. The old man, the father-in-law, is the boss. When the young man gets permission he goes off to another encampment and marries there.

An excellent example of the spirit in which an understanding is reached and of the speeches that pass back and forth before the widower regains his freedom of action is provided in this account:

If, after my wife's death, my mother-in-law has any more daughters and she likes me, she will send one of them, and I'll marry her. But if she has only sons, and finally I feel that there is some other woman I want to marry, I talk to my brother-in-law, if he is old enough, and I say, "I have had a hard time, but now I want to marry again. You have no other girls for me to marry, and now I am ready to marry again."

Then he will go and tell his mother, and the next day he will come back and say, "What has happened has happened. It can't be helped. If we had anybody to give you, we'd give you a woman. You have been good to us, and we hate to have you part from us, but there is no help for it. We hope you will get a good girl and be happy." After this you are not under obligation to your mother-in-law.

The levirate.—The existence of the levirate does not give a man any extraordinary privileges with the wife of his brother or male cousin while these relatives are still alive:

In the right way a man is supposed to have great respect for his cousin's wife. You should leave your brother's wife alone and your cousin's wife alone too. They call you a witch if you do otherwise. Only when people get very old do they joke a little when they are related like this—people of R.'s age [sixty-five to seventy] might, but never the young people.

If a married man dies, however, his widow becomes "bound" to his family and particularly to his brothers and male cousins:

The woman then "belongs to" the dead man's brothers or cousins. She would be "bound" to them. The woman cannot marry for a long time after her husband dies, except to one of his relatives. But if none of them asks her to marry within a couple of years after the death, it is a sign that none of them wants to marry her, and she is free to marry someone else if she has the chance.

Even though the woman remains among her own relatives after her bereavement, cares for her children as usual, and need not have much direct contact with her former husband's kin, she owes them obedience and courtesy. If she fails in this obligation, they are not slow to show resentment:

G. married a Chiricahua man. She was a Chiricahua herself. Her husband died, and she was, therefore, "bound" to her husband's family. They did not have an available man for her. T., the only possibility, was already married. So she married a Mescalero Apache. She went around saying some pretty mean things about the family to which she was "bound." T. got pretty mad and said he was going over there and slit her nose.

This illustrates the point that a woman is directly responsible to her dead husband's family. A woman who went around with someone to whom she was not "bound" might have her nose cut. It was the right of the dead man's family to dispose of her and watch her conduct. Any of them can warn her of her conduct. If the husband has no brothers, a cousin will marry her. The age of the cousin does not matter. The oldest one does not necessarily marry her. Choice is what counts.

Should the widow's relatives-in-law choose for her a man she does not like, she and her kin must convince them that the marriage would be unwise. If the woman has been an unworthy wife, if none of the brothers or cousins of the deceased is interested in her, or if the dead man's relatives feel that her family was too harsh to him, the group to whom the widow is "bound" reject her.

There is the case of a single man whose married brother died. Then the dead man's wife was "bound" to him. She wanted to marry him all right, but he didn't want her. She waited a number of years, but he wouldn't have her. He knew she wanted him. People used to kid him about it. We would say, "Now she is 'bound' to you, why don't you go and marry that woman?" It would sure make him angry! A good many of the boys used to tease him. She finally married someone else.

THE ROUND OF LIFE

THE economic, ceremonial, and social practices which have been described provide a framework within which members of the tribe move. But the full reality is something more. The individual pauses to enjoy the result of his efforts, seeks to earn the good opinion of his neighbors, pays visits to his friends, and attempts to find satisfaction and laughter. His days are filled with many minor adjustments to other human beings. And all these responses are guided by a body of understandings and etiquette.

CAMP LIFE AND ETIQUETTE

Every encampment of any size, especially when there is any suspicion of danger, has a guard at night. The lookout "is not especially chosen. It is just anyone who feels like it and is willing to do it. There is no organization about it." When information concerning the enemy's movements demands that near-by groups of tribesmen be notified, "fast runners are sent" with the message. If the distance is great, the messenger rides a horse, because "horses are hardier and don't get hungry or thirsty soon."

When the people move from a camp site, certain precautions must be taken:

The fire pit is covered up neatly, and the brush beds are gathered up and put in a neat pile. They say that, if you leave the camp just as it was in use and simply pick up your blankets and go, the coyote, the crow, and other harmful animals and birds may come and urinate or defecate on the place. Then, because everything is arranged just as it was when it was occupied, the person it belongs to will be affected wherever he is.

A different reason for the care taken in breaking camp was offered by another informant:

When moving camp, the mattresses of grass, leaves, and branches are brought together and put all in one pile. The beds are not left as they were when they were in use, for, if some member of the family should die and the bed is not taken apart in this manner, it would be at the last camp site as it was when it was used by this dead person and would remind others of the user. This causes sorrow to friends and relatives.

There are a number of methods for reckoning time, so that movements and meetings may be planned and ceremonies performed according to a schedule:

During the day, time is judged by the shadows caused by the sun. It is noon when the shadow drops just under you. Some people place a stick upright in the ground and watch the movement of the shadow to figure out the time of day. Another way is to note how many fingers the sun is above the horizon. On cloudy days you have to guess at the position of the sun.

We notice the shortening of the days as winter gets near. As soon as the days begin to lengthen, we say, "It [the sun] has begun to move back upward."

During the night we tell time by the position of the moon and the morning star. In wintertime the morning star gets as high as halfway between the horizon and the zenith. When it is in this position, it is nearly morning.

The Big Dipper is used in telling time at night. "As its stars 'spin around' it is possible to tell the passage of the night by whether the cup is turned or not." "The Dipper turns around and faces down; this takes all night." Another group of stars consulted for the time of night is the Pleiades. "You can see it early in the evening in winter in the east. When it is high, morning is near."

Stars that appear at certain seasons are noted. "There is a star that is right straight up in the summer. We call it 'rock bed' after the rocks at the bottom of the mescal pit."

Members of the household usually eat two meals together, although sometimes individuals eat during the day as they get hungry and gather for an evening meal only:

We never followed the three-meals-a-day idea at home or away. Even in the morning there wasn't a regular meal unless there was meat that had to be boiled and eaten warm. Then we would eat together for convenience. Otherwise there was no system. Three meals a day is recent. At home, in everyday life, the women eat with the men, but at social dances and feasts they do not.

Each person helps himself from a common container, using his fingers for solid foods and a yucca-blade spoon for liquids. Though "it is considered impolite to make a noise while eating," it is permissible "to smack the lips to show that you are enjoying yourself when you are eating out."

Not only the stomach but the entire body should be "fed":

We put grease on the legs when we eat in order to "feed" them. It makes us good runners. After we eat fat meat there is grease on our hands, and we rub them on the legs and say, "Let me be a fast runner." Sometimes the leg bone of an animal is broken, and the marrow is rubbed on the lower legs, the forearms, the hair, and the face while this is said.

There are few special usages in departing from friends or in returning to them. A phrase "said at parting, by people who are very graceful in speech, to a friend, acquaintance, or relative" can be literally translated, "May we live and see each other again." Upon returning after a long absence, the formal manner of expressing pleasure and greeting is the embrace. "Friends and relatives embrace; if a friend does it, it means that he thinks a great deal of you."

Loneliness growing out of separations has a special treatment. "If you are lonesome, if you have lost someone, or if your daughter has gone away and you are worrying all the time, they put a basket over your head four times, and then you are all right. Now they use a bucket or a sack too."

There are no set phrases to be uttered when a friend is encountered in the vicinity of the camps. "We have no words like 'Good morning' or 'Good evening.' But when we meet a person, we have to say something. You can't call a person's name. You must be clever and say something appropriate to the occasion. You might start off by asking, 'Where have you been?'"

The question of greetings and salutations directs attention again to the proper use of the name.[1] The manner of its employment is well summarized in two statements:

The name is very valuable. Children are taught not to call a person's name when they meet him. My own name is "Making a Bed All the Time." When I

[1] That the name need not distinguish the sex of the bearer has already been mentioned (see p. 9). An incident illustrates the point. "A woman's name and a man's name are not distinguishable. If I hear nothing more than a name, I have no idea whether it belongs to a man or a woman, just from the sound or meaning. My wife mentioned a certain name. I thought she was talking about a certain man. One day I saw him pass by and I said, "There goes So-and-so

was a boy my relatives made a bed for me wherever we stayed, and so I got this name.

I will tell you under what conditions I would call a man's name. If someone in my family died and I wanted help, I would do so. I would go to someone, call him by name, and say, "So-and-so, my wife has died and I need help." The person would then be under obligation to help me all he could. If a man who is in need comes to me and calls me, I would help him at once. I would give what I could.

No matter how poor a man is, if he is called by name, he will do something about it. It makes a person very sad if someone calls on him by name and he is not able to help. If a man calls my name and asks me for something valuable, I will give it to him, because I know he needs it badly. A man is willing to do anything for another if he calls him by name. But if a man asks for something valuable without calling my name, I would consider it a joke, for, if the man really needed it, he would call my name.

If a man is very sick and is sent to a shaman, and he is afraid the shaman will not take the case, he will call him by his name. Also in war or in the war dance the name is used because it is a case of emergency.[2]

(using the name I had heard from my wife). My wife came and looked. 'Why, that's not his name!' she said. 'It belongs to his wife.' "

Because names have been reduced to initials throughout this study, a number of them are included here in translation to indicate their quality. Most of these could be borne by either men or women; a few, such as "Thin Old Woman" and "Red Boy" could not, for they denote sex.

Names of Women	Names of Men
Stepping on Water	Heavy-Set
Round Nose	Going about with Head Bent Down
One Who Has Sucked	One Who Yawns
One Who Stays at Home	One Who Chews
Streaming Down	One Who Peels It
Sleepy	One Who Checks the Horse
Walks into White Man	Not Quite Enough
Yellow Eyelids	Blessing with Pollen
Buckskin Shaker	Little Rabbit
Thin Old Woman	Coyote Has Sores
	One Who Tears Up Things
	Broken Foot
	Little Face
	Belt

[2] An instance of the use of the name in an emergency plea is introduced in one of the myths. Wind had hidden from the earth after a quarrel with Lightning. The rain fell unhindered. Finally, the bees were sent to find Wind and induce him to return to his duties. When they located him, "they called the name of the wind, for it was an emergency, and they called his name to his face."

The only other times a man will call the name of another to his face are when he is drunk or angry; a man in his right senses won't do it. But if a person is angry with another, he drops all reserve and calls the other's name freely, telling him what he thinks of him. You have to be careful about this, for it means a fight.

It is considered very impolite to call a man's name to his face. You might call his name when he is not present, but we think it impolite to call the name of a person who is with you. Not long ago I was by the roadside with a young fellow. An old man was riding past. This young fellow forgot himself and called the rider by name. The old man paid no attention and rode on. The young fellow felt pretty much ashamed.

An occasion when the name was purposely used to start a quarrel was described:

This boy came toward me, calling to me and using my name. "You think you're smart!" he told me. He used my name a lot. He did it with emphasis. Then we started to fight.

Very early the next morning, before I was out of bed, he came over. He had come to tell me that he was sorry for what he had done. He used my name this time too. This was a special occasion; that's why.

The proper use of the name is a potent factor in obtaining a favorable response to a request:

One time my wife and I wanted some medicine to keep. We were collecting lots of roots. We had a sack of them. We didn't know how the leaves of one particular plant looked, so we couldn't collect any. My wife heard that an old lady had this kind we wanted, and she asked me to go and get some.

I didn't want to do it, for I knew this plant was valuable to the old lady. She was a ceremonial woman and used some in her ceremony. But my wife kept bothering me until I went to the old lady's home. First I visited with her for a few minutes. You have to act just so to the old people. When I got there, she began to talk about things, about the weather. When you call on a person you haven't visited before, you are treated extra fine, for that person knows you want some favor.

I didn't want to ask her for it. I guess she thought I needed help. People come to her because of sickness. Finally, she asked me what I wanted. I started to say I didn't come for anything special, and then I had to say it; so I called her by name and said, "So-and-so, I am gathering some plants, just out of curiosity. I have some of my own, but I hear you have a plant used in a certain sickness. If you care to, I wish you would give me a sample of it."

I used the language that brings results. She gave me a handful of it. This medicine is for tuberculosis. It is called "narrow medicine" [*Perezia wrightii*].

When she gave it to me, she told me not to use it, for I didn't know the ceremony and would get into trouble.

Later on she met my wife. She told my wife that ordinarily she would not have given me that medicine, that it is very valuable and she doesn't give it away. But I had come like a gentleman. I knew the old customs and how to call her name. I wasn't like so many of the younger people. I had respect for the old customs, and so she gave it to me. Since then I have been pretty good friends with that old woman.

To avoid using names, teknonymy, nicknames, and age terms are resorted to in referring to individuals:

You often hear a person spoken of as the father of So-and-so, the mother of So-and-so. The reason for doing this is that it is an easy way to get around calling a person's name, especially before the person or his relatives. A younger person is spoken of through his older relatives too.

I don't know whether I have a nickname. A person's nickname will never be called before him. H. is known as "He Who Wears Glasses." If I say this, everyone knows who I mean. It is a good way of getting out of calling the real name. But though everyone uses it, I doubt that H. even knows about it, and he probably never will.

J. is called "Mexican." Everyone uses this. But he doesn't know it and probably would not like it. But this is not said for meanness. Even some who use polite form to him call him this.

"Old man" is not used like the English "Mr." We never would say "old man" and then add a man's Chiricahua name. The word refers to age or is used so that the name of a person can be avoided. A man goes to a camp looking for another man. He has to let the people there know what he wants. So he says to the wife or whoever is around, "Where is the old man?" They know who he means then, for he's looking for the man of the family.

Lots of people come around looking for my father-in-law. They don't call him by name, for it is very impolite to call a man by his name just for nothing. So they ask for "the old man." Of course, they might mean me if I were absent. My wife would have to take a chance in answering. She could guess pretty well by who it is. If it's someone I know well or go around with, she would know he was looking for me.

Persons or objects may be indicated by pointing:

If a man asks where another is, the person spoken to is more likely to point with the lips than with the hand. Now old people come in the store and point to objects on the shelves with their lips. Pointing with the hands is really for emphasis and is not considered polite. It should be done only in anger, when you might say, "That man over there!" and point.

A gesture of mock-seriousness is often seen:

If a person wants to give you a good talking to or wants to emphasize what he is saying, but is just joking, he puts his arms akimbo as he talks. If he pushes the joke too far, you also put your arms akimbo to indicate this. But then you are in earnest and not joking.

One fellow is always joking with me. When he sees me, even at a distance, he will put his arms akimbo as he comes toward me. Then when we meet he will begin to tell me just what he thinks of me. I kid back at him. I say, "Get that arm down!" and try to knock it down.

If a person is giving you a good talking to or a lot of unwelcome advice, you might say, "All right, go ahead and talk!" and you put your arms akimbo to show that the advice means nothing to you. Or if a person whose opinion you hold to be of little worth suddenly begins to give you advice, you show your surprise that he should talk that way to you by putting your arms akimbo. Then it means, "You've got your nerve!"

If a person takes this posture unconsciously, it is said that he is putting on airs or thinks himself great. This position is taken in imitation of someone who thinks too well of himself.

An informant described how amazement would be shown:

One time I met C. on the street. "Well," he said, "what's the news?" "There is no news," I told him. "As long as you fellows are satisfied under the government, there is no news. We ought to be free." C. clapped his hand over his mouth.

This story explains when the hand is put over the mouth. I know what C. was thinking. He was thinking, "Oh, what a speech!" It is a sign of amazement used when someone has done the unexpected and has taken you off your feet.

Another time several of us went to sheep camp. We were standing there with our sheep herder. Finally we started to go away. The sheep herder came after us and asked me, "Did you bring me any tobacco?" C. was supposed to take care of this, so I turned to him and asked, "Did you remember the smokes for Chapo?" He clapped his hand to his mouth and held it there a couple of minutes. What he meant was, "By golly, I forgot it!" This illustrates another use of the hand over the mouth.

There is a definite etiquette of visiting:

Suppose somebody is coming to my camp. When he is about fifteen feet away from the door, he clears his throat or coughs loudly to attract attention and let me know he is coming. If I am there with my wife and children, I say, "Here I am. Come in." And when the man sits down politely, the children are already in order. Of a person who walks right in without coughing, we say, "He is not polite."

Guests usually sit near the door when they come in, although there is no particular place for a visitor to sit. There are many people in there, so they sit

near the door most often because it is the most convenient and unoccupied place·
If there is a bed along one side of the home, a visitor doesn't sit there unless he is
called and told to.

When you have a visitor, you have to be very careful of how you act. In
passing in and out of the house, a person must not touch or press against another
person, especially against visitors and strangers. The visitor, in turn, must not
let the one who is passing touch him or press against him. To leave your home
when you have company is considered very impolite. If you have to leave, you
say, "I am going to walk there by you."

Great politeness is exercised in personal matters between visitors and host:

Suppose there are a number of people in my home. We are all interested in
some conversation. I'm telling stories or something like that. Perhaps one of the
visitors wants to go out and relieve himself. He has to excuse himself. They will
know where he is going if he just walks off. So he says, "I have to go out and tend
to that horse," or, "I've got my horse hobbled at the foot of the hill over there
and I want to chase him toward the water. He hasn't had water all day." Sometimes he hasn't even got a horse there. And another fellow sitting there says, "I
have to see about my horse too." And he goes off. Or a person will say, "Well, I
have to tend to something!" just as if he suddenly remembered something.

The women make excuses too. They say, "Where have my little ones gone?
I'll have to see where they are." That's the way I was taught when I was a child,
to make some good excuse.

When two men know each other well, though, if the wife and children are not
at home, one will just say to the other, "I am going out."

When visitors are speaking—and, indeed, when any serious
discussion is taking place—it is a mark of good manners to indicate attention and interest by murmurs of approval and interjec-
tions of encouragement:

If someone is talking in a social gathering or telling a story, to show that you
are interested and are a very polished person, you keep saying, "*he, he,*" at intervals. Or you might say "*do'a,*" which is just like saying, "Indeed!" or "Yes,
yes, go on!" Women say it slower, "*doya,*" and in a higher-pitched voice. You
hear the old people use it all the time.

During a speech by someone, to show that you approve, you nod your head
and break in on him, as whites would with applause, saying, "*ao, ao*" [the
affirmative expletive] or "Um, um."

HUMOR

When friends are together, teasing and bantering take place.
Misleading or exaggerated statements are followed by a wink "to

show that the person is joking," or a gesture may take the place of a wink:

The equivalent of a wink is to raise the right hand, palm forward, with first and second fingers up and the thumb over the fourth finger. You say something to a man which you mean only as a joke, like, "Your wife's coming." As he looks, you raise your hand in this way and motion with it toward him for the benefit of others, but, when he looks, you stop.

There are other ways to save face and turn the laugh on a companion:

One way to cover up embarrassment is to stick out the tongue. If you ask a man for something that you don't expect to get, you stick the tongue out when others are looking, but when he doesn't see you. Then, if he turns you down, you don't feel badly about it, for you have shown to the others that you are just fooling anyway and expect to be refused.

Much of the humor is broad and falls under the caption of practical joking. Putting plants that are irritating to the skin in the bedding of an unsuspecting individual is of this nature. Of one man, it was told: "H. is a great practical joker. You have to watch out for him. He might throw a box in your path. His father was like that, too, always playing practical jokes. You never knew what he was going to do."

But most of the humor is verbal. A man who is considered to be especially good company is described in these words by one of his admirers:

He's about sixty years old. He's very funny. When he gets in a crowd, he always keeps everyone laughing. He just takes the topic of the day or whatever someone is talking about and sees the funny side of it. At the same time he is talking sense. If you think about it, you can get something out of it too.

Imitations, especially of peculiar or foreign characters, are much appreciated. One informant, himself adept at this art, stated:

Some are very good at this. Some can imitate C. [an eccentric character], but I can't. His voice is too high-pitched for me. In Oklahoma I used to imitate a butler, just like I saw in the movies. I would make believe that I was waiting on my father when he wasn't looking, and, when he looked again, I would stop. He didn't know what my sister was laughing about.

Even the pun is not unknown. The term for "leader" is very similar to the word that means "to shake the head." A braggart who was telling a group about his ability as a leader was interrupted by a hearer who, deliberately pretending to have misunderstood, remarked, "Yes, we all know you can shake your head pretty hard!"

Another story that points to the quality of the humor is an account of nonchalance under trying circumstances. An old man on horseback was attempting to pass a knot of his friends with some show of dignity. Just then his horse bucked, threw him, and ran ahead. Instead of waiting for the mirth of the beholders, the man pulled out his tweezers the moment he hit the ground and with great unconcern began plucking his whiskers.

PARTIES, DANCES, AND STORY-TELLING

The preparation of tiswin is almost always followed by a party to which friends and neighbors of both sexes are invited, for the beer is made in relatively large quantities and sours if it is not used at once.

My first tiswin party came when I was about fourteen years old. It was during the summer. A woman who was noted for the good tiswin she made told me to tell my grandmother to come over that afternoon, for she had some tiswin. She invited me too. I went right over to my grandmother and told her. I went with her and attended that party. It was just a social occasion. I drank a lot and got to feeling good. I was not used to it, but I didn't get sick. It lasted about two hours.

They sit around and tell stories at these parties, laughing and talking. A man with a bad temper could not get in. It is considered very impolite to come in to a party without an invitation, but some get around this. They hate to miss it and find some excuse for coming there. One cup is kept going. The woman who gives the party does the dishing-out. A boy of about fourteen can attend. Usually a girl has to be a little older. After this I attended tiswin parties whenever I could.

Social dancing and singing sometimes add to the pleasures of a tiswin party. Even the women, when a certain point of gaiety is reached, may elect to act as singers, though this is not their customary role:

One time Mrs. S. and C.'s wife sang social dance songs. The men were all played out. One got the drum and the other helped her. In the old days the Chiricahua woman sometimes sang songs and used the drum too. They used to do it for the round dance. They would get around in a bunch and sing and drum.

Social dancing is recreation which all can enjoy equally:

We do not speak of a good dancer when referring to the social dancing. One person is not considered better than another at it. There is no chance to show off. The only dances in which the individual can show ability are the war dance and the masked dancing. Women cannot dance these. But people get real pleasure. out of dancing the social dances with someone they like.

To sing well for the social dance is a real distinction, however:

It seems to me that there are three different registers of singing found among these Indians. My voice is low; N.'s is high. If I put my hand to the side of my mouth, I can sing all night. But I can't last on the high ones.

The telling of myths provides another opportunity for those who live in close proximity to gather. The expert raconteur is highly regarded.

I was in the store the other day, and J. was in there talking to a group of men. He was talking about the old times. He told about a man who used to be very good at telling all kinds of stories. A group of men thought they would play a joke on him. They all went over there and told him that he had to tell all the stories he knew and that they were going to sit there and listen until he was through. They were going to give him his fill of telling stories for once.

This fellow was quite a joker. He said, "All right!" and he started in. They came there early in the evening. That man told stories all night and then kept on during the day until about four o'clock in the afternoon. Everybody else was all tired out, and he was still telling stories.

Another able story-teller, whose case is of special interest because his excellence as an entertainer evidently was his chief claim upon the respect and good opinion of his fellows, is likewise fondly remembered:

My father knew I. He couldn't fight; he was no account in war. But he was a great joker and story-teller. All used to gather at his camp to hear him. The old men laugh and talk about him yet. My father imitates him, using the left hand, for I. was left-handed. It sure is funny to watch. I. thought quickly. Even the old people surely liked him.

As a general rule the Chiricahua dodge around when they fight. Though I. never fought, he'd talk like this: "When you're in a fight, don't dodge—you might run into an arrow. Why do you fellows dodge around like that?"

He'd say things like this: "Do you see those hills? Those hills were small when I came through there a little while ago. They must have grown since. Do you see that mesquite tree? I was chasing deer. Notice that limb. The horse was going full speed for it. It looked as though I was going to get brushed off by it. Then I jumped one way and the horse went the other. I landed on the back of the horse again on the other side of the branch and we went on and killed the deer I was chasing."

When he was telling stories, if anyone acted as though he were going to go, I. would say, "Wait, we're going to cook something pretty soon." It might be noon and there would be nothing to eat in the camp at all. But he'd ask his wife, "Have you got anything to eat?" His wife was just as bad as he was. "Certain-ly," she'd say. "In just a few minutes, I'll get it ready." It would never come. After all of his stories he would turn to his wife and ask, "Now isn't that true?" She'd answer, "Yes, that's true."

He had only one woman. No other would have anything to do with him. Yet he would say, "When a woman gets angry with me, I go off. I don't cut her nose. I don't beat my wife. I don't say anything. There is always another woman ahead, I say."

I. once saved a large encampment, they claim. The children were thinking of going swimming. Enemies were near. I.'s camp was out in the open on the side of a hill. He called all the people, all men and boys, to listen to stories, and they all came. While he was telling stories, he saw enemies in the distance coming toward the camp. He saved them, every one. If he hadn't been telling his stories, the children would have been in swimming. The white soldiers came, but the Apache all got away.

Many times these sessions are arranged for the particular benefit of the children, for it is an integral part of their education to be properly versed in the tribal lore. Just as often no definite plans are made in advance, but the older people drift from casual conversation to a review of more traditional materials, and the children gather around to listen.

Sometimes in the evening we would all gather over at my grandmother's home. There would be my sister, my cousins, and myself. The old lady would tell us Coyote stories. At other times some old men used to come over to my uncle's place and tell each other stories of the old times. Then we children used to come around and listen.

The long winter evenings are the most acceptable time for story-telling. Indeed, certain myths and myth cycles, such as the legend of the hidden-ball or "moccasin" game played for day-light, and the Coyote trickster cycle, can be told only at night and in cold weather, when the snake and the bear are not abroad. The events and atmosphere of the evenings during which he listened to Coyote stories have been recaptured in this vivid account by an informant:

It is not an easy task to learn these stories. You have to be patient when the stories are being told. You have to listen very closely. You have to sit up at night when it's very cold, no telling how long, sometimes all night. When a funny story comes along, everybody is laughing. And at all other times you have to listen very closely and be quiet. As much as I have sat up and listened to the stories, I have to be reminded of some of them in order to get it correctly the way I first heard it.

When Coyote stories are being told, there is generally a big crowd present. The older people, before they told the Coyote stories, would say, "When you tell these stories, they make you very sleepy." When you get sleepy, they wake you up. They shake you or they tickle your nose with grass. I've been treated that way. But, if someone just can't keep awake, they let him go to sleep.

Both old men and old women could tell the stories. It would be like this. Some of these stories are very funny, and many times the boys of about fourteen years of age would get together and go to some old man's home and say, "Tell us Coyote stories."

But the Apache is very careful not to embarrass someone before whom he is ashamed, even when he is telling Coyote stories. If he comes to one of the stories that would embarrass anyone, he says, "I want to tell you, in case people who are ashamed before each other are here, that I am going to tell some very funny stories now." Of course, not every man will do this; it depends on the individual. A man like C. doesn't care what he says. But I remember that most people would be very careful at such times. Once my father was telling stories. My brothers were there, and my sister and my wife and some other women. Pretty soon he came to one of these stories. One by one we men went out and went into a shack next door. You probably noticed that just now I told my son-in-law to go into the tent next door, build himself a fire, and stay there. I just don't want him to hear me tell stories like that.[3]

When interested people, young or old, visit him to hear his rendition of the myths and tales, it is an opportunity for the narrator to display his hospitality as well as his abilities. He seldom allows his guests to leave without offering them food:

One time at Fort Sill seven of us boys came to N. About ten o'clock he said, "Make coffee for these boys. I don't know how long they'll stay. We'll have lunch about midnight." So we stayed and had a big lunch. That's what they used to do a long time ago, he said. N. knew the old ways. We stayed until three or four in the morning listening to old stories.

[3] No father-in-law avoidance is practiced in this case. Though the informant is a Chiricahua, his son-in-law is a Lipan. The Lipan do not practice avoidance of affinal relatives.

A really talented raconteur has at his command a seemingly inexhaustible fund of stories. Of the host of the occasion mentioned above it was said with admiration: "N. began at sundown. He told Coyote stories all night. He never finished them that night." For those who stay up all night to listen to him, the narrator is expected to have some gift. By keeping the audience up until dawn, he has "stolen the night" from them and owes them amends:

The old-time Indians used to give you a big present if you stayed up all night and listened to them tell stories. They used to kill a cow or even give a horse or saddle. I went over to C.'s place with my wife. We got tired and wanted to come home about ten o'clock. C. said, "Why don't you stay all night and win something? We'll give you a big pan of piñon nuts." But we were too tired and came home.

If the host does not have suitable presents on hand, he may feel uneasy about keeping his audience too long:

A while back we were over at T.'s camp and the old man was telling stories. We were willing to stay all night. But the old man stopped before the night was over and said, "I haven't got much here, and so I don't want to go too far. I'll give you what I have." He brought out some things. I took a pocketful of piñons and some tobacco and went home.

It is the story-teller's use of appropriate gestures, onomatopoeia, and asides—in short, his gifts as actor and dramatist, which lend luster to his reputation. In order to keep interest at a high pitch, he does not hesitate to tease the less attentive members of his audience:

Once the old man was telling the whole bunch of us Coyote stories. It was just the time when E. was having some trouble with his wife and his mother-in-law. The old man thought he would have some fun with E. He made believe he wasn't looking at E., but he was watching him out of the corner of his eye. When he came to a part where Coyote has some trouble with his wife or mother-in-law, if E. wasn't looking he'd motion toward him and say, "I guess it's this fellow." Everyone would laugh, and E. would look up. But by this time the old man would be looking the other way and going on with his story as though nothing had happened.

At first E. laughed too. He didn't know it was for him. But after a while he got suspicious. He kept his eyes on the old man. Then he'd get tired or look around, and just that quick the old man would do it again. E. was always just too late to catch him at it.

Then they came to the story where Coyote tells his mother-in-law to put her arm in the log after the rabbit because her arm is longer. Right there E. caught him. He jumped up. He cursed and said, "You just talk about me all the time!"

The old man laughed. "What's the matter? Why do you get mad? Was it you? Are you that Coyote?"

E. was so mad he walked out. The old man called after him, "You must have been that Coyote."

It was surely funny to watch E. try to catch the old man at it. The old man sat there whittling. Just as soon as E. looked away, he'd motion with two fingers and say, "I guess it's this one," and when E. would look up, there the old man would be, whittling away as before.

SMOKING

Smoking adds to the pleasure and relaxation when old tales are recounted. Before the distribution of trader's supplies, tobacco was very scarce. Consequently, it was used mostly for ceremonial purposes and was looked upon as a great luxury on social occasions. Boys were counseled not to smoke until after the training period, and it was thought unbecoming for women under middle age to use tobacco, except as ritual might demand it. The source and use of the wild tobacco are described as follows:

Before the white man's tobacco came in, the Chiricahua found their tobacco out in the woods or out in the Arizona plains. It grows in reddish soil. It is a low plant, and you cannot find a great deal of it together. The plants have white and yellow flowers and long narrow leaves, about four inches wide or less. It doesn't grow everywhere but just in certain places, and it is therefore hard to get. We pick it and let it dry out in the sun. Some sprinkle mescal juice on it and then let it dry. This wild tobacco is milder than the present tobacco we get. Often this tobacco is used with other plants. Sumac leaves are picked, dried, crushed, and put with it, and sage is too.

The tobacco we found was called "big tobacco." It was used for social purposes as well as for ceremony. It was passed around at private gatherings or at story-telling. But it was not so common. You just saw it here and there, because it was so scarce. Boys were not allowed to smoke, and just old women were allowed to smoke. When we fought Mexicans we took their tobacco. When the white man's tobacco first came in, it was pretty scarce. If you had a good horse, you would give it for one cigarette of the white or Mexican kind.

In the old way, when the tobacco is ready, they crumble it up. They use the leaf of the oak for a cigarette paper. They take the fresh leaf in summer, but sometimes they carry them in a bundle, one on top of the other. Every now and then they wet the leaves to keep them in shape. And they get cornhusks that they use. Many times I've seen old men sitting on the sunny side of the camps peeling cornhusks. They carry these in a bundle too. Even cornhusks were hard to get in those days.

To illustrate the value and scarcity of tobacco before reservation days, the following story was given with this introduction: "Someone told this at the store, and I heard one of the young fellows say, 'Oh, that's nothing but a lie!' But I can believe it, for I know how scarce tobacco was in those days."

Tobacco was very, very valuable in the old days. Just enough to make one cigarette was worth a horse, and horses were very, very valuable, too, then. Two old men were camped near each other. One had some tobacco and the other had none. The man who had no tobacco came over to the place where his friend was smoking. He sat there watching him smoke and hoping he would offer him some, but he did not. Then he hoped he would get the butt out of it, but he knew that this fellow smoked his cigarettes right down to the end. He was getting more and more eager for some, yet he hated to ask right out.

Finally, the one who was smoking said, "Well, it is late. I guess I'll go to sleep after this smoke." The man who had no tobacco could not hold himself in any more. He said, "Friend, give me just one puff of that cigarette before you finish it and I'll take it back to my camp, holding my breath, and I'll inhale it when I get over there in bed." And he did that. He held that smoke in his mouth until he got over in his camp and then he inhaled it, making noises showing his relief.

Tobacco is smoked in a small tubular clay pipe as well as in cigarettes. Men usually make these pipes, though women occasionally make them too. They are four or five inches long and cone shaped, tapering from the front to the end which is held in the mouth. To make these pipes, a thin coat of clay of the right consistency is spread over a wooden mold and is allowed to become partially dry before removal. Smoking completes the drying process. When the pipe is freshly filled with tobacco, it must be tilted upward to prevent the burning embers from falling out, but after it has been smoked for some time this is unnecessary. These pipes are never designed. Evidently they were never very common or numerous. "Some make pipes out of clay. But very few do this. These Chiricahua Indians never bother much about pipes. If they get hold of a cigarette, they smoke it, but they don't have many pipes."

A tubular pipe drawn by a Southern Chiricahua informant has a short projection or handle on the underside near the stem end.

All other illustrations secured lack this feature, however. A small pipe cut with a knife from soft limestone was described by another informant. Since this pipe resembles the modern American pipe and must be made with a metal knife, it is probably a more recent type. As a less durable approximation to the tubular clay pipe, blades of the broad-leafed yucca are rolled into the same shape and are used as long as they last. One informant said that he has also seen a length of reed filled with tobacco and smoked.

SPORTS AND GAMES OF ADULTS

Games and sports comprise much of adult recreation. The various arrow games already described in the section on children's pastimes—shooting for distance or for accuracy, sliding arrows, and the play which has been likened to blind man's buff—are popular with grownups as well. Men also play the bone or "heads and tails" game and the marble games.[4]

Competitions in tug-of-war and wrestling are frequently arranged. A variant of the usual tug-of-war is to fasten a rawhide rope around the waist of a very strong man. Three others hold the free end of the rope, along which knots have been tied to afford them a grip. The man to whom the rope is fastened is further handicapped by having a fourth member of the opposition attempt to hold him down. If he manages to arise, nevertheless, and to drag forward the three who are bracing themselves at the other end of the rope, he is the winner.

Keen interest is manifested in wrestling:

We wrestle a great deal. Some men are expert and are just like professionals. They even wrestle with men from other tribes who come here. Big sums are bet. The wrestlers start by holding each other around the middle. After they begin, tripping, twisting the arm, or anything is allowed. When one man is under the other, it ends. It doesn't matter which part of his body touches, as long as one man is off his feet and the other man is on top. Sometimes it lasts for hours.

Most contests of chance and skill involve gambling, and it behooves anyone who wagers seriously to have his luck ceremonially safeguarded:

[4] See pp. 50–53.

There is a ceremony for luck in games and gambling, for luck in the hoop-and-pole game, for foot-racing and other games. When a person has a ceremony for any of these, he is usually a "professional." He depends on it to win big stakes. Ceremonies like these are among the most secret ones, for a man doesn't want others to know too much about it and spoil his luck. You can get a man to talk about anything but this and witching usually.

Ceremonies for luck are mostly in connection with racing, the hoop-and-pole game, stave games, and the moccasin game, for these are the big betting games. Singing or ceremony for luck is not carried on for the ball game or shinny. They aren't betting games but are more for exercise, although, of course, people bet on them too.

Foot races in which both men and women participate, constantly occur:

We have races for short distances in which women as well as men run. Sometimes the women beat the men. Somebody paces off the race course. Instead of measuring by yards he uses steps. Two steps are like a yard; each time the right foot comes forward the man counts one. The track is one hundred of these "yards" long.[5]

During the race the runners are timed by counting. Old men sit at the finish line counting as the runners race. Each runner has someone counting for him. I saw two of the best runners race when I was a boy. The old man only counted to eleven, and the winner was over the finish line.

At the start of the race they don't crouch. They stand braced. The man who is starting them might say, "I'm going to count. When I say 'two,' go!" Or two men might walk toward the runners with a string or a stick. When the runner is touched, he starts off. When we are camping in a place where we are going to stay for a time, we would make a track. We clear a path. This is used for horse-racing too. Cross-country foot races take place once in a while also.

Horse-racing and the ceremonialism associated with it are discussed by an informant:

Horse races are generally started with a gun or by shouting, "Now!" Some horses would be back of the line facing the other way; some would be on the line

---

[5] Another unit of measure, "one stick," was described by an informant: "We measure by saying 'one stick.' This is the distance from the middle of the chest to the end of the outstretched middle finger. Both arms outspread equals 'two sticks.' Later these were called yards. A step of the right length was called 'one stick' too. Later 100 steps were considered 100 yards. In buying a yard of cloth now we are really asking for 'the length of one stick.' The actual length of the foot is used as a unit of measure too. To measure height you take a rope or stick and measure the person; then you put it down on the ground and measure off the feet."

Note that at least two attempts have been made to equate aboriginal units of measure with the American "yard."

facing forward. Most face the line, but some are trained the other way. We ride them bareback. Women do not ride against men, but they do race among themselves. There are cross-country horse races too. It takes one day's travel to cover the course.

Some sing for their horses. This is done at home before the race. Let us say a man's horse is going to run tomorrow. He is going to bet heavily on it. Then he will sing for the horse so it will win. Not everybody knows such a ceremony, but some know the songs. If you don't know songs, you might pay a person to sing for your horse. The same thing is done for runners in the foot races.

Shinny is one of the roughest and most taxing of the games:

To play shinny you have to have a stick about three and a half feet long which is hooked at one end. It is usually made of oak wood and the curved part is the root. The one who is making it heats it and ties it around at one end and lets it stay tied for a day or overnight, if it has been made in the evening. The next day it will be curved and will stay that way. Some players carry a second stick, a straight one, too, when they play. The straight stick is used for protection. It is used to ward off the other fellow's stick. Some play without this second stick though.

They usually knock off a piece of round wood for the ball. It is about half the size of a baseball when it is finished. Sometimes a buckskin ball of the same size is used. Any number can play on a side. Usually there are from five to twelve on a side. But there has to be the same number on each side.

A flat place a half-mile long or less is chosen. When there are ten or twelve on a side, they use a longer distance. The width does not matter except at the goal. But at the goal the ball has to go between two objects, usually trees, to count. This is true for both sides.

In starting the game they all march out into the center of the field. They just guess at the center. The two leaders meet in the center and hook their sticks like two boxers touching gloves. They spit on something flat and throw it up, and one of them calls, "Wet," or "Dry." The one who wins out on this can choose the side his team will play on. Each side scatters out and faces the other's goal.

The two leaders tell their men to get ready. They decide which of them is going to throw the ball high in the air between them. Or another fellow is there to throw it up. Players from the same side can be on both sides of the center to start, so that if their leader misses the ball at first and the other leader hits it, they can get possession of it.

When the ball goes up, the two in the center can hit it in the air as it is on its way down or wait until it strikes the ground. But it has to be hit with the stick. If I am one of these leaders and think that the other fellow will miss it in the air, I wait until he has swung and is off balance, and then I hit it from the ground to one of my men.

Once the ball is in play, they can advance it by kicking it or by hitting it with the stick, but they can't hit it with the hands. They try to hit it toward the other side's goal, and drive it across. They hit the ball any way, in the air or on the ground. Every time a goal is made it counts one.

The best runners always play this game. If they get away with the ball, it's a goner. Some get hit in the shins by mistake. There are no fouls. They try to hit each other's sticks when trying for the ball. They play until they get tired. They play that game all morning; sometimes all afternoon. Men thirty or forty years old played this game when I was a little boy. When I was just a little boy, I saw middle-aged men play this game and the ball game. Women played these games too. Some young women can outrun men. There were dangers in those days, and the women had to exercise so they could stand anything.

A popular game is one called "throwing objects in a hole." Two holes, each with an opening a little larger than the stones used, are dug, one at either end of a playing field about thirty paces long. Each player has two disk-shaped stones with which he throws for a hole. The stone nearest the hole earns its thrower a point. Should the two stones nearest the hole belong to the same player, he earns two points; otherwise only the nearest stone counts. To place a stone in the hole wins four points. If the player gets both stones in the hole, he scores ten. When two men each get a stone in the hole, neither counts. A third stone in the hole earns the thrower the usual four, however, and a fourth stone in the hole displaces the third, counting four instead of it. The contestants throw first for one hole and then for the other. The player to amass twelve points first is the winner.

The ball game, called "they who run" or "they slap the ball," has been mentioned briefly in connection with the play of children. But it is a game which adults enjoy as well.

If you want to see a really interesting game, you should see this ball game. There are two sides and each side has a captain. Each captain chooses four or more good, fast men. The ball must be made of buckskin stuffed with soft material, and it is about half the size of the baseball Americans use.

The players meet on the field and examine the ball to see if it is suitable to hit a person with. They mark out a big circle with a stick. This is called "he has come back" because a person is always trying to get back to it. It's like the home plate in American baseball. They are going to have three other rings, arranged something like the bases of the baseball field. They step the distance out to the first of these. It might be fifty or seventy paces away. They are not particular as to the distance. They make it the same distance to the second of these circles, and the same to the third. They are all the same distance apart. But these last three rings are not so big as the first one; they are just big enough for four or five men to stand in. The first of these smaller circles is called "where one stops first." The second is "one usually goes here second" and the third we call "one usually goes here third."

Suppose I am head of my team. We pick up a piece of flat rock and spit on one side of it. The other captain says, "You toss it. Which side do you want?" I take the dry side. Then the ball is rolled slowly between the two sides. At the same time the rock is thrown up. We watch to see whether the dry side comes up. If it does, all on my side run for the big circle, and the other side run to get the ball and try to hit one of us with it before we get in. If they do that, they will get in the circle first. If the rock turns up wet, they are the ones to run for the circle, and we try to hit one of them before he makes it.

Now my side is in. The head of the other side will talk to his men and place them out. The pitcher is very careful. If one of my men is outside the ring or partly outside it he can hit him with the ball.

The pitcher must stand before the ring. He must throw the ball underhand. The ball must be hit with the open hand. Some catch and throw the ball at the same time when batting, but this is a violation of the rule. Some do it so quickly you can't catch them at it. To count, the ball has to go forward.

I am the first man to hit it, say. I try to place the ball so that I can get to the first circle before getting hit. If I get hit by a man on the other side who picks it up and throws it at me before I get to the first circle, as soon as I'm hit I run for the ball. My team, as soon as they see me get hit, run out and try to help me. The other team, as soon as I am hit, run for the big circle. If I or one of my men gets the ball and hits one of them before he gets in the circle, my side is still in and can keep on batting.

If I hit it up high in the air and a fellow on the other team gets under it before it hits the ground, he can hit it away, and all on his side run for the big circle. It's just like catching a fly in American baseball; it puts my side out if they get to the circle safely.

But, if I hit it and make the first little circle, my second man is up. The pitcher watches me and tries to hit me when I am out of the circle. If my man hits it and someone on the other side standing near the circle where I am gets it, I do not have to run. More than one can get in one circle. So I stay there and do not take chances.

If we all get in the first little circle, the pitcher stands there and throws the ball straight up in the air, giving us a chance to run. We say, "Throw it up! You don't throw it high enough." So he throws it higher, and we run. He catches it and throws after us. Sometimes you make a couple of circles on a pitcher that way.

We play the game all afternoon, as long as we want to. We can stop any time. We keep track of the number of "runs" each side makes. One side puts marks on one side of the big ring, one on the other. If we all come in in a bunch, we each make a mark on our side. Sometimes fast girls mixed with boys to play this game. Lots of times they don't care about the score or the winner, but just try to stay in and hit the ball. This is just a pleasure game, not a gambling game, though a few might bet on it. This is a real old game. Old men seventy years old and older say it was played before their time.

The most important game which the men play is hoop-and-pole. It can be played only during the daytime. The equipment and the ceremonialism involved in its preparation have been described thus:

Different men make hoop-and-pole outfits, and they make them in different ways according to their ceremonies. But the hoop and the poles look the same no matter who makes them. If someone makes a hoop with the wrong number of "beads" on it, it is not any good. And the poles have to be exactly the same length.

The pole is sometimes made out of four pieces of wood bound together with sinew; sometimes out of three pieces.

Some men are well informed on the ceremony of the hoop-and-pole game. They are the ones who make the sets. They are the ones who play all the time and who are considered to have the best luck at it. They are always good players. They have the hoop-and-pole game songs. They do not sing these songs on the playing ground, but, if they are going to play on a certain day, they sing the night before. They go ahead and talk to the hoop and everything.

My father knows songs for this, but his voice is no good any more. I didn't learn them because my father said, "It's no good to learn one or two of these songs. If you mean it, you've got to really study it. You've got to learn all of them, and they take a long time. One or two might harm you; they might even kill you."

The right to these songs and this ceremony, which goes with the rite to make the set, is handed down. Just certain people know about these things. It is dangerous for others to try to make a hoop-and-pole set or to sing for their luck, though any man can play the game and gamble on it.

The manner in which the hoop-and-pole ground is arranged and the game is played is given in this summary:

This game of hoop-and-pole is very important and must be played on a ground arranged in a certain way. You have to have a grass bed about thirty feet long for it. There must be a rock right in the middle and one at each end to show the boundaries of the field. The field is covered with something real slippery, like pine needles, so the hoop will roll. The ground must stretch just one way, with the long way running east and west. At each end of the field there are ridges of grass. These lanes are called "that against which the pole is repeatedly thrown." They act as a guide to the distance the hoop should roll before the players slide the poles after it. The hoop can be rolled through these lanes or outside of them.

PLATE XVI

Museum of the American Indian, Heye Foundation

a) MEN PLAYING HOOP-AND-POLE GAME

Museum of the American Indian, Heye Foundation

b) HOOP OF HOOP-AND-POLE GAME; "MOCCASINS," BLANKET, BONE, STRIK-
ING STICK, AND COUNTERS OF MOCCASIN GAME

Only two play against each other at a time. When they start to play, one takes the hoop, and they walk to the center. Each man is holding his pole. These poles are long, almost as long as the playing field. One of the poles is colored red at the butt end. The one with the hoop rolls it toward the grass ridges, using an underhand motion. When the hoop is about to fall over, the men slide their poles after it. Each wants the butt of his pole to fall under the hoop. The butt of the pole is notched and marked, and each notched part which shows up under the hoop counts so much. The hoop is notched too, and it also has a knotted string tied across the middle. We call these knots "beads"; the biggest knot is in the middle.[6] You make something, too, according to the notches or the "beads" which cross the pole. All these notches have names. You agree on how much they should count before the game begins, and you agree how many points are needed to win.

The two men play from the center, first to the east, and then to the west. Only the winning throw is counted each time, and only one score, that of the man who is ahead, is kept. What he gets is added to his score and what the other fellow gets is subtracted from it. Men gamble a great deal on this game.[7]

In a real game of this kind you are not allowed to cross the playing field from the east while anyone is throwing. That's the rule. I don't know why it is, but they play it like that. And they don't allow any dog near the grounds where they are playing hoop-and-pole. Also it is strictly forbidden any girl or woman to go anywhere near the hoop-and-pole ground. Any woman who comes around will get swollen joints and pains in her legs. And it would sort of paralyze her. The women never come near the place; they go a long way to avoid it. If a woman even comes in sight, the men straighten up and hold the pole up straight until she passes out of sight. Women and children know where the ground is and keep away from it. There are a good many things to remember in this game. A man who is playing doesn't like anyone to step on his shadow. It makes him lose his luck.

Little material is forthcoming concerning the origin and mythological background of the game, but the words of one informant suggest an association between the pole and the snake:[8]

[6] One informant claims that there should be 50 "beads" on each side of the big "bead," making a total of 101. Another described a hoop which had 30 "beads" on each side of the big "bead." Evidently there are minor variations in the "ways" of the hoop-and-pole makers.

[7] When the trickster Coyote loses all his possessions in a gambling game, it is, characteristically, the hoop-and-pole game he is said to have been playing.

[8] When M. R. Harrington purchased a hoop-and-pole set from its Chiricahua maker in 1909, he was told: "The red paint on the wheel and on one pole represents a snake. Two men were arguing as to who had the strongest supernatural power. Finally, one took a snake and made a hoop of it to show his power. Not to be outdone, the other took a snake and transformed it into a pole. Then, as

The hoop-and-pole game was handed down from the animals when they were people. They used to play it. The hoop-and-pole game comes from the four-footed animals like the bear [i.e., the dangerous ones] and also from the snake. During the time the snakes were people they made the game. In ceremonies the pole is referred to as a snake. This is done in the snake ceremony.

The hoop-and-pole ground is as much a meeting place where masculine concerns are discussed and planned as it is a field of play. Here the men come together in easy companionship, free of the inhibitions imposed by the presence of women. It is little wonder that one commentator declared, "The hoop-and-pole ground is like a pool hall." An air of informality and good humor pervades the scene, and much jesting and story-telling are always in progress.

Often musical instruments, such as the musical bow, are played at this spot:

There is something we do around the hoop-and-pole game. A man takes a bow, just the regular fighting bow, and tightens it up. He puts one end in his mouth and hits the string with an arrow. Men enjoy doing this and are interested in it. They can make a sound like Chiricahua songs. A man can do this anywhere, but you see it mostly at the hoop-and-pole ground when the men are by themselves and enjoying themselves.

Another musical instrument, made and played by men, is frequently seen at the hoop-and-pole ground, although it is not limited in use to this place. This is the "wood that sings" or the Apache fiddle,[9] a hollow wooden cylinder about twelve to eighteen inches long with one sinew string stretched over its surface. The bow is approximately the same length and is strung with horsehair. A single peg controls the tension and pitch of the

---

the point was not yet decided, they devised this game and played, but still neither could win, for their power was equally strong. The people took it up and still play it, but consider it sacred."

Two other informants who were consulted, however, claimed to know nothing about a relation between the game and its parts and the snake.

[9] It is certain that these "violins" are modeled after stringed instruments introduced into the region by Europeans, but they have been made by the men of this tribe for some time now. One of the oldest members, a skilful maker of these instruments, stated: "We made it from the oldest times. I think it was the Chiricahua's own invention because it was common in my boyhood."

string, and the top of the body is perforated by a number of triangular or diamond-shaped sound holes, usually two opposite the peg and four or more at the other end of the instrument. The surface is ordinarily decorated with painted designs of tribal art pattern (stars, sun symbols, serrated lines, etc.), but, in addition, a scroll-like figure and floral motifs appear. Of the method of manufacture, this account is given:

I use any dead tree from which to make it. A good tree to use is the walnut. An older piece of wood makes a better tone. One end is usually a little wider than the other. The limb chosen should be a little longer than you want the fiddle to be. After cutting the limb off, I split it down the middle. Then I scrape out the inside of each piece with a knife. It is quite a job to scrape out these inside holes. Then I cut little holes [the sound holes] along the margin where the two pieces are going to meet on top. Now I scrape the outside and put on the decorations. There is no particular meaning to the designs I put on. Then I tie it together with deer sinew.

For the bow I use sumac wood. I warm the wood and bend it into place. I use horsehair from the tail for the bow. I used to make many of these for the soldiers. You play this as though you are using words and sing social dance songs as you play it. I used to go around here playing it and singing. I used to play songs in the store for the men on winter days not long ago when my voice was better.

Women are likely to be as engrossed in the stave game as men are in hoop-and-pole. Men occasionally join women to play it, but it is understood to be a woman's pastime.

This is really a woman's game as I understand it. I say this because it's a light game, a pastime for women. Women can't get out there and play with arrows like men. A few do, but not many. So the women play this while the men do other things.

Any man who plays this all the time is laughed at. But men play it once in a while, all right. I have seen men and women mix up and play it, play partners. Some fall in love this way. Mostly a bunch of women were playing it alone.

Not everybody can make the outfit. A person has to know how. There is power connected with it. A certain woman or man has to make the sticks and place the stones. Those who make them give these sticks to other people. The one who gives you the sticks tells you what to do so you'll have luck with this game. Some have songs they sing before a big betting game. When two sides are playing against each other, there is great excitement. Everyone wants to be the one to throw the sticks for his side. Valuable property (like mescal and horses) is bet. I never saw this played during the night, though I never heard that it couldn't be played then.

The equipment and method of play are described thus:

Round sticks are split and three six- to eight-inch lengths, round on one side and flat on the other, are selected. They can be painted black on the flat side, or a black or red stripe is put on instead. The round side is painted yellow or white.

On the ground they put forty small stones. They put down ten stones, leave a space, put down ten more, leave a space, and so on until the forty are arranged in a circle. The four spaces are called rivers, and there is one for each of the four directions. In the middle of this circle is a big square rock, usually (but not always) colored black on top. Each player, or a representative for each side, has a small stick to lay between the stones as a marker.

The player throws the three sticks on end against the center rock so that they bounce off. This player then moves his marker stick according to the score he has made. If the three flat surfaces are down, it counts ten. If they are all up, he makes five. One flat up counts one or two, according to what has been decided,[10] and two flat up usually counts three.

The players start from the east. If just two are playing against each other, one moves around in one direction, and one in the other. This is done if many people are playing and betting, but there are just two sides. If four are playing partners and there are two on a side, two partners go around one way, and two the other. But if a number are playing for themselves, they all go around the same way, sunwise. The idea is to get your marker stick around the circle first.

A person who makes ten gets another turn. Whoever gets into the water (whose marker falls on one of the big spaces at the directions) has to go back to the beginning. Also, if your marker falls in the same space as that of someone who is playing against you (not your partner), you pull out his stick and throw it to the beginning, and that person has to begin over.

There is a game like this played with four staves. The fourth one is longer than the others. The scoring is different for this game.

A third stave game, played without the circle of stones, was mentioned by one informant. Three staves, each uncolored on one side and painted white, black, and yellow, respectively, on the other, and one longer stave, black on both sides, are used. These are thrown on a rock four inches in radius. The object is to make the long black stave remain on the rock and to have the

[10] Many variations occur as a result of agreements before play starts. "Sometimes we play that a person has to go back to the beginning if he gets in the river, but we might agree not to do this. The way some play it, your partner, if he gets to the same place you are, throws you into the river ahead. And some make the rule that, if your opponent falls at the same place you are, if you are past the first river, you have to go back to the last river you passed, instead of to the beginning."

painted sides of the other staves fall uppermost. If the long stave crosses the center of the rock, it counts one hundred; if it stays on the rock but is at either side of the center, it is worth but fifty. Of the other staves, the yellow one counts twelve points if the painted side shows, six if the unpainted surface is up. The others earn an agreed amount if the painted surfaces face upward, but score nothing if the plain surfaces show. This game can be played by men or women but, like the others, is most often played by the women.

More tradition, song, and ceremony center around the moccasin game than about any other form of adult recreation. It is the only game with which a major myth is connected; it was the game played in the beginning of the world at the Mogollon Mountains when the birds were pitted against the four-footed animals and monsters to determine whether there should be daylight. The manner in which the game is conducted now is intended to be a faithful duplication of that first contest.

The moccasin game is played only in the winter and only at night, until daybreak. If they play beyond daybreak, they have to paint their faces black. The story of the first moccasin game is told just at night and in winter. They say, "If you tell this story in summer, you will see bad animals like the rattlesnake." You have to be careful about the songs of the game too. You can't sing them in the summertime, for a snake will bite you if you do. In the wintertime you can sing them in the day or at night. In the winter there are no snakes around; that's why.

Even snow has a song in the moccasin game. The people don't like to hear the snow song before the real cold weather. It brings snow, they think. They got after me because I sang it the other day.

Men and women join to make an exciting occasion of the game. Arrangements for playing it are informal. "If I wanted to have that game tonight, I'd say to someone, 'Let's play the moccasin game tonight.' I'd get my friends, and he'd get his. Each man wants to have good singers."

To play the game the members of the two teams gather and face each other on opposite sides of a fire that has been kindled at a level place. Each of the groups arranges a row of four "moccasins" in which the bone is to be hidden. "We usually do not use real moccasins for this game but just make four holes. After the bone is hidden in one of these, they are all filled at the top with grass." Often cylindrical sacks made of hide (later of cloth) serve as moccasins.

The rounded section of bone from the hip or knee of an animal is hidden. It is often blackened by being thrown into the fire before the start of the game. The other things required are a robe or blanket to be held up by those hiding the bone, a stick with which the person delegated to find the bone strikes the moccasin in which he thinks it has been placed, and counters which each side is trying to obtain. The stick is about two feet long and often is incised with carvings representative of birds which took part in the legendary game, such as the road runner and the turkey. The counters are strips of yucca leaf, six to eight inches long. Usually there are sixty-eight of them, worth a point total of one hundred and four. Sixty-four of the counters are plain and count one each; four of them are fringed at the end and are each valued at ten.

To determine which side shall hide the bone first, a bone or a stone which has been moistened on one side is thrown between two of the opposing players, and one calls "Wet" or "Dry." The side which wins this trial now orders the blanket raised, and one of its members hides the bone, while the others sing.

When they play the game, they sing the songs which the birds and animals who played it first sang about themselves. And the moccasins and the bone, too —each has a song about itself. These are the first ones sung. These songs are sung during the playing. The side hiding the bone sings while the hiding is going on and while the one who guesses for the other side is trying to make up his mind about which moccasin to strike. They sing loudly and try to confuse him in every way, but no drum is used. If a side is lucky with a song and the others are guessing wrong, they keep on singing that same one until the bone is taken away from them.

During the singing, members of the group dance in place.

When the bone is concealed, the hider calls, "Ready," and the robe is removed. A representative of the opposition comes forward to strike with his stick. If he hits the correct moccasin, he wins the bone for his side without any gain in counters for the other side. If, however, he strikes a moccasin to either side of the one in which the bone actually lies, four counters are taken from the central bundle and handed to the hider. And, if he strikes a moccasin two or more removes from the right one, the side of the hider gains ten plain or one fringed counter. Those who are hiding the bone keep it until a correct guess takes it away from them. Then the roles are reversed, and the opposition does the singing and hiding until it, too, must give up the bone.

As the game progresses, the players present, in character, the songs of the many beings of the mythic account. The song of a small bird is given in falsetto, while that of the slow-witted, lumbering giant is intoned in a gruff voice. These songs are often chosen with reference to situations in the current game that parallel events in the game of tradition. When one side is lagging, a song may be selected which was used to good advantage by the birds of the original game at a moment when defeat for them seemed imminent. This characterization and interweaving of mythological knowledge add interest to the game, and the fever of rejoicing and disappointment is maintained by lively betting, both on the final outcome and upon the individual plays.

When all the counters have been distributed to one side or the other, the losing side must pay the winner from its own store. When one side has taken from the other all its counters, it has won the game.

What has been described is the orthodox mode of play. But, as the game is sometimes played, a person who has unsuccessfully struck one of the moccasins, may be offered, or may request, another turn without a rehiding of the bone. If he succeeds this time, he wins the bone for his side and does not have to pay counters for the first wrong guess. Should he fail this second time, he pays heavily. In another variation, one who is guessing may elect to poke the moccasin instead of striking it. By this he signifies that he is trying not to select but to avoid the moccasin in which the bone lies. If he pokes three moccasins without result, he has found the bone by a process of elimination and obtains it for his side. In still another variation, a player may reach into the moccasin with his hand instead of striking or poking it with the stick. The hider may be allowed to conceal the bone on his person instead of in one of the moccasins:

Sometimes the one who is hiding the bone does not put it in a moccasin but under his arm. When he does this, it doesn't count against the other side if they fail to guess where it is. The hider is doing this just so his luck will come back to him. He does it when the other side has been getting the bone too easily. But if someone on the other side thinks you have got it hidden on you, instead of striking, the one who is guessing for the other side says, "You have it." Then you have to hand it over to him if he's right; your side loses the bone.

Another manner of play is to penalize upon discovery the one who conceals the bone in this way. "If a player, instead of hiding the bone in a moccasin, conceals it on his person, he will, if discovered, lose ten points for every move made by the opposing side before the discovery of the trick."

The moccasin game has given rise to several less elaborate forms of play of the same general character and bearing the same name:

When a few get together, we sometimes play with four heaps of sand and a marble. We follow the same way of counting as in the moccasin game, and we call this a moccasin game, too.

Then there is one game where a marble is hidden in one hand or the other, and the other fellow has to guess where it is. We don't keep moving our hands around when we are playing this. We just hide it and let the other side guess.

They also play a game in which a small stick is hidden behind one of the four fingers of the hand. All these are called moccasin games.

INVECTIVE

A curse is a grave affront because of the acknowledged potency of verbalism. The general respect for the efficacy of words has its roots in traditions of the early period of mankind's existence:

"At this time, anything that they said occurred in exactly that way. Anything of which one said: 'It is to happen so,' happened in just that way. For that reason one did not say just anything to someone. If one spoke in that way to someone one hated, it happened in exactly that way..... They spoke only in a very good way."[11]

After the flood there were many, many Indians [Chiricahua]. These Indians were very religious. They were careful how they used their language. They wouldn't ever dare to say, "I wish that dog would bite you," or, "I wish that coyote would get you." They wouldn't ever dare say things like that. They were afraid to tell lies.

[11] Hoijer, *Chiricahua and Mescalero Apache Texts*, p. 18.

This fear of the expression of evil wishes is an aspect of the belief that what is fervently voiced, for good or for evil, is likely to occur. It is a conception which gives point alike to the faith in the "good words" of ceremonialism and to the dread of "witch talk."

Invective is graduated from those exclamations and phrases which arouse mild resentment to those which are considered unforgivable insults. Rather innocuous, and directed as often at a situation as at a person, is an inexplicable cry of frustration, "Knife and awl!" "You're no good!" is likely to bring a more positive reaction if it is directed at a person. It is a stinging rebuke and challenge to be told, "You're no man!" Quite as insulting is it to tell a person, "You are trashy!" or, "Even though you are trashy, you ought to try to restrain yourself." Serious imprecations which rankle and are keenly resented have to do with death wishes and the underworld. "May an enemy [white man] kill you!" is one of these. The most common of this type is the malediction, "Go to the underworld!" "When some people get angry, they say, 'Go to the underworld!' It's just like telling a person to go to hell. That kind of talk is very bad and strong. People get killed for saying such a thing. You are considered to have a witch mouth if you talk like this."

Other curses have sexual or scatological implications: "A bad word is one that means 'your excrement!' If you use it to anyone, it will surely make him furious, and he might kill you for it." An incitant to physical violence is the threat, "I'll squeeze you so hard that I'll make your excrement move out!" An abusive phrase which was described as "the dirtiest cuss word in the Chiricahua language" inelegantly labels one's parents witches: "You for whom the witches copulated!"

But, in the eyes of many, the gravest insult is a combined curse and gesture, the ultimate in indignant response of a very angry woman:

If a woman gets very angry at anyone, she will double up her right fist with the palm up, put her thumb between the first and second fingers, and then open the fingers suddenly in the direction of another person, saying at the same time, "Smell this!" A man dreads this! It's just like shooting a man. It shows contempt. The word refers to her vagina.

But men, too, use this gesture and the same expression upon occasion, and it is still more vitriolic if one man levels it at another:

At Fort Sill in 1910 one man was swearing at another in every way. The other man said nothing that night. The next morning he came up to the one who had cursed him. He was making the woman's gesture of contempt. He said, "You spoke bravely last night. Now let's see what you can do."

They fought. The one who had started the trouble the night before went down. The one on top took dirt and sticks and grass and hit him on the mouth with them saying, "Now you won't use such bad language perhaps!"

When a person is goaded to action by insult or abuse, there is an exclamation that warns of the attack to come:

There is an expression of rage, "*ahagahe!*" It means that a man has stood for as much as he is going to. When you hear that, you know that the man is going for his weapon and will fight it out. The word has no literal meaning.

In keeping with their assertions concerning the greater peevishness of women in comparison to men, a number of male informants have insisted that women are quicker to make use of these inflamatory phrases:

As a general rule in the old days, Chiricahua men didn't curse. The women did most of the cursing. There were very few bad words. Then if you said, "You coyote!" or "Your excrement!" that was very, very bad. Cursing was brought in by the white people. Now the woman doesn't talk that way, and the man does. A big change, isn't it!

ANTISOCIAL CONDUCT

In the eyes of his fellows the moral person is one who heeds the social conventions and discharges his obligations in obedience to the tribal ethic.

Ceremonies for curing are religious. But these have nothing to do with morals. You can have a ceremony performed over you and drink and do what you please.

The Chiricahua religion is directed toward long life, good health, and things like that. In the Chiricahua way, I can't see how religion has anything to do with living right, as long as a person is not a witch and is not trying to use his ceremony for meanness. Religion might be a good thing all right, but I know from experience with my people that it didn't take that to make a person good.

Good conduct is the result of obeying the customs, and it is up to the person. It has nothing to do with religion. A man would come to a bad end in the old days because he violated the customs. It's just a matter of a man looking out for his own welfare. If you obey all the rules, you get along all right in Chiricahua society. But if a person doesn't take hold of the customs, if he cuts loose, if he doesn't treat other people right, he has no chance. Then others do not help him. He is alone. He is bound to come to a bad end and perhaps be killed. A person just has to observe certain things. They aren't laws—they are so strong we don't need laws. A person is supposed to keep certain customs.

These customs, the resentment evoked by their violation, and the rewards attending their faithful performance have constituted a large share of this narrative. Consequently, definitions of antisocial conduct have emerged in particular contexts. The measures·taken to correct children who misbehave and the penalties attached to premarital sex adventures, rape, witchcraft, incest, perversion, and infidelity have received such treatment.

Nothing has been said thus far about theft. Most possessions are so obviously personal and easily identified, or so readily made or procured, that theft is rare. But food and buckskins are occasionally taken.

If a person is known to be a thief, the one from whom something is stolen will take measures of personal punishment according to the value of what was carried away. If the thief pays back something valuable, it is acceptable; or a relative of his might pay it back. The whole group did not have to be called together for this. It could usually be straightened out between the two involved.

Nothing much is done in case of theft. If the thief is caught, he has to give back the property, and he is talked about and disgraced.

Theft is uncommon enough so that anyone who is guilty of it is viewed as an aberrant. The identification of witches as "people who steal" will be remembered.[12]

The reaction to murder is of an altogether different character. What happens if the murderer is an alien has already been discussed. When he is a member of the tribe, the bereaved relatives are scarcely less bent upon satisfaction. They may insist upon his surrender and death, even though refusal of their demands leads frequently to armed conflict and a feud between the families. Though the slayer's kin may elect to defend him, if, before they can act, the relatives of his victim catch him and kill him, they have no just cause for grievance: "If your relative is murdered and you kill the one who did it, it is all right. His family have no comeback. There is no meeting about it; it is no group

[12] See p. 247.

affair. If the killer is not given up by his family, usually a fight between the families takes place."

In another statement the rancor of the murdered man's kin and the possibility of struggle between the two families is mentioned, but the effort on the part of outsiders, and particularly of the leaders, to maintain the internal peace of the group is also stressed:

If they are not interfered with, the dead man's relatives take revenge. Sometimes a battle between the two families takes place. More often, though, the head men use their influence and succeed in preventing the fighting. They try to arrange it so the murderer or his family makes a payment to the family of the slain person or to his friends. There is no set payment for this. Horses or anything valuable that they have would be used.

Sometimes relatives of the slain person may be satisfied with physical punishment of the murderer which falls short of the death penalty:

A man killed my brother. He shot him in the head and the brain splattered. I came and asked him why he did it. He said, "Your brother is not the only one whose brain I'll splatter!" My heart burned. I said, "All right! We'll fight it out!"

We went to get guns. We came toward each other. He shot twice and missed. I just kept coming. I shot him in the left arm, and he said he had had enough. His arm was always stiff after that; he couldn't use it much.

If the slayer has been a constant trouble-maker and an embarrassment to his family, they may be unwilling to defend him further, particularly when he has evoked the anger of a powerful kin group:

In a case of murder the relatives of the dead man kill the one who did it if they can find him. Sometimes the killer's own relatives do not protect him. If he has been getting them into difficulties right along, in order to avoid future trouble in which many lives would be lost, they do not do much about it. They figure that they did not encourage him to do the killing, and it was on his own responsibility. If the killer has a wife and children, however, others try to prevent the family of the slain person from taking revenge.

But unless outside pressure and the influence of leaders conciliate the two families, the tendency is for the relatives of the murderer to shield him and for the others to insist with equal vehemence that they give him up. Out of such impasses grow feuds.

What prevents this from occurring, in most cases, is the flight of the murderer, who either leaves the region as soon as he realizes the consequence of his act or is advised by his relatives to stay away until bitterness against him has abated or compensation has been arranged. His family may be implicated in his escape to the extent of furnishing him supplies and keeping his destination secret. Sometimes it is impossible to conciliate the aggrieved family, and the exile is forced to remain away—to join some other band or even some other tribe.

But usually, as soon as he is safe, a strong movement for a peaceful settlement is launched. It is the duty of the group leader to lend his moral weight toward this solution. He tries to bring representatives of the two families together at a council where generosity is likely to be acclaimed. If the plan succeeds, an old and respected member of one of the families steps forward finally and says something like this: "Let us not have trouble. We eat the same food, walk upon the same earth, breathe the same air, and the same sun is over us. There is no reason why we should have trouble between us. Let there be peace." This truce is then solidified by the passage of valuable gifts to the family of the slain person. Now a spokesman for the murderer is free to voice his plea: "We all know our friend, and we are sorry for what has happened. What has happened cannot be helped though, and now our friend has given valuable presents, and we wish to take him back into our people. Let us go on living together and forget what has happened."

Yet the animosity often continues to smolder latently. A polite but unmistakable antagonism between two men, for instance, was explained in this way:

He has it in for L. It was his uncle that L. killed in Alabama. They got drunk, and somehow L. hit the other man on the head with a bottle. This case was supposed to be patched up, but it has never been forgotten. That's the way it is in lots of these cases. They can't get out of their minds what was done to their relative, and they look for some other excuse to start trouble.

In all probability the greatest deterrent to antisocial conduct is not the specific penalty for the offense but the concern over social disapproval. The influence of this factor is diffuse and difficult to trace in detail, but children and adults alike are exhorted to remember what others will say and think of their behavior.

POLITICAL ORGANIZATION AND STATUS

ALL members of the tribe, despite minor differences which exist between the bands, are aware of the linguistic and cultural bonds which identify them as one people and which distinguish them from other groups of the region:

In customs, speech, beliefs, and manner of dress we people over the other way [west of the Rio Grande] in Chiricahua country are very much alike. There may be slight differences in speech. [It is doubtful that these ever went deeper than some variations in vocabulary.] But we could always understand one another thoroughly. The fundamental things—beliefs and ceremonies—are the same. By these people I mean the Southern Chiricahua, the Central Chiricahua, and the Eastern Chiricahua.

This tribal tie is expressed in a number of ways. The three bands remain at peace with one another. Visiting between members of different bands, especially near the peripheries of the band territories, is a frequent occurrence. Individuals of one band are always ready to attend the puberty rite of the daughter of a member of another band. The social dance songs, with their repeated references to a woman or a man "from a far country," are further evidence of intercommunication. Marriages between members of different bands grow out of these social contacts. Quite often persons whose lives would be forfeit in their own band territory find a refuge in another district.

The right of members of one band to pass freely through the territory of another band was not challenged until the Americans became interested in controlling the activities of the Chiricahua:

We [the Eastern Chiricahua] were on friendly terms with the towns around us and we were causing no trouble there. But the Central Chiricahua and the Southern Chiricahua came around. They used to bring in horses stolen from the south, and they got us into trouble.

Some of our leading men said, "There are too many Southern Chiricahua and Central Chiricahua here. They are bringing in horses. They will get us into trouble." But our leader, Victorio, wouldn't do anything about it. He said, "These people are not bothering us."

Then a bunch of them came with some horses from the south. There were about seven in the bunch. They had stolen horses from the Pima Indians around Tucson. The Pimas told the missionary there, and he wrote to Washington. Soldiers came and took these men prisoners. They chained them and took them to San Carlos. Then they took all the Eastern Chiricahua band there. Those seven men were taken in wagons. We all had to come with horses.

Despite the peaceful relations and frequent social contacts between the bands, there is no political synthesis and scarcely any formal recognition of the tribe as such. There is no distinct tribal name. The word which serves to identify tribesmen also differentiates all Apachean-speaking peoples from others and is now used by the Chiricahua to distinguish Indians in general from Europeans and other non-Indian populations. Moreover, there is no organized leadership for the entire tribe; and no instances have been found where the three bands acted in concert to carry war to others, to repel invasion, or for any other purpose. The tribe is too widely scattered over its extensive, varied, and difficult terrain for united action. While individuals and families can cross band borders and be received as tribesmen, a concourse of the entire population is not practical.

The band, however, does achieve the political consciousness that the tribe lacks. It possesses a distinct name which has no other meaning. It is guided by a recognized leader (occasionally by more than one), assisted by a number of subordinates. The opportunities for interaction are much greater for members of the various local groups which comprise a band than for members of different bands. As this indicates, the band is a division of the tribe based on territory, including within its borders those local groups near enough together to unite for military action if the need arises or to co-operate for any important social occasion. The nature of the local group and that of the extended family have already been discussed.[1]

This segmentation of the society into social units graded in size and scope of activities implies a pyramiding of responsibility and leadership. It is the men who formally assume posts of authority, though "women attend councils and may speak if they have anything to say." The married man acts as the head of his

[1] See pp. 18-19 and 24-25.

household and answers for his wife, his daughters, and his unmarried sons. When he reaches middle life, after his daughters have married and he has sons-in-law to heed his wishes, he is the head of an extended family and gains in prestige. If anything very serious, such as a witchcraft trial, brings the members of a local group together, though all adults are present, it is these heads of extended families who monopolize the discussion and carry the decision. However, these representatives of extended families do not all stand on a par. They, and the families for whom they appear, vary in status and affluence. Of these elders, one is the recognized leader and a person who is expected to voice his views in detail and with conviction. It is loyalty to this local group leader and trust in his wisdom which holds the particular nucleus of families together.

There may be others present, men distinguished for wealth, bravery, or exceptional ceremonial knowledge, who are little less important in status than the leader. The leader needs their good will and support and seldom ignores their advice when their desires are obvious. These men may be considered the inner circle of the council, the advisers upon whom the leader leans heavily. "The heads of extended families are not necessarily leaders. They are often men of some influence though. C. was the leader of his little bunch, yet he was not recognized as a great leader. N. was both. The leader, however, is sure to be also the head of an extended family." Most of the others, because they are younger or more retiring, or because they represent families that are small, poor, or low in social position, add little besides their presence and their assent to what is decided.

To complete the picture, it is necessary to add that it is the most dominating of the local group leaders who heads the band. This distinction is not always clear cut. Sometimes the membership of two different local groups of a band each considers its leader superior. Then, when these two local groups join forces, authority is fairly evenly divided. Thus, while the Central Chiricahua of all local groups acknowledged Cochise as their leader, among the Eastern Chiricahua some preferred the direction of Victorio, others had more confidence in Nana.

To appreciate the mechanics of the elevation of a man to the office of leader, the conception of status must be understood. Distinctions of status dependent upon birth are recognized, although they are not rigidly maintained and are not uninfluenced by considerations of wealth and ability.[2]

When we say "people who are worthless," we are thinking of those who are not refined, who are of low birth. It is as if you said, "That person's line is no good." It always carries the idea of low birth. When a man gets angry at someone, he tells him that he belongs to this class; he uses it as an insult. But, no matter of what family a man comes, he isn't called this unless he is shiftless, lazy, and unreliable. Some are like that. Of some we say, "Their excrement juts out [because they are too lazy to wipe it away]."

Of another person we might say, "He is from his [good] people." This is used in the sense of descent from the families of leaders and the wealthy. Those of whom this is said are more respected. It is pretty clear cut, and there is not much doubt whether a person belongs to this class or not.

Another informant speaks of the same extremes of status designation but calls attention to the middle position which most individuals hold:

Those who have sprung from families of wealth and influence are said to be "the people of good birth." It is easy to recognize them. A ceremonial man's children would not necessarily come under this classification, for a ceremonial man could be very poor. The word "worthless" is applied to people who are just loose, ignorant, or of a very poor family. Most people are in between; they are respectable people and contribute to everything in a good way. But still they are not the descendants of leaders. There is no name for them.

The right to respect has to be validated by achievement and effort:

The word meaning "he is from his [good] people" is used of the descendants of the politically influential and wealthy. Still, of a man who comes of good blood but is worthless and a waster, they say, "He comes of good blood, all right; but he is worthless." The term is not applied to such a person. It is said only of descendants of influential or wealthy men who are themselves so. There isn't much question about it or any need for dispute. Whether you like a person or not, you have to recognize his importance and position. If my grandfather or uncle was a leader, I would come under this term. People would expect me to live up to it. The term includes strong people, people strong in social position or in war. But it has to be generally accepted. People have to have respect for you.

[2] Such distinctions have already been touched upon in connection with the rearing and training of children (see pp. 28–29).

A personal enemy might class you the other way, but you would be prominent enough so that his motive would be apparent.

The conception of status conditions the amount of deference an individual expects and the degree to which it is thought seemly for him to take part in public affairs:

I nearly had some trouble with B. Some of her sheep had got mixed in with L.'s and mine, and there was some question about range. She got angry right away and came over and began to talk about the fact that she comes from good blood. She was referring to her relationship to Mangus, a leader of the old times. She did this to remind L., who is related to a leader's son, that she is as good as he is.

Another man described an occasion when his father publicly rebuked him for voicing opposition to a leader, the son of a man of rank:

My father scolded me right there. He said, "You are not a leading man here, and yet you try to find out all these things. You should not put yourself in."

I got up again to answer him. I told them all, "I am not a leading man. I don't pretend to be. But I am here and I don't want to be misled. I defend my family."

It is from the group of well-born and politically conscious individuals that the leaders are drawn. But family origin, while it does confer status unless there is some grave personal disability, does not determine political rank:

If the son of a leader is qualified, it is easier for him to become a leader. But it doesn't have to work that way. It's queer; I don't know just how to explain it. But those who become leaders are smarter. They are willing to come out and say what they think. I notice it here. Some people get the idea that it is handed down from father to son or from one relative to another. This is not so. Ability in war and wisdom make the leader. It's easier to get to the front if you are a good fighter. Yet some people, though they were good fighters, never became leaders. So I think it is a matter of smartness more than anything else. The leader is not chosen; he is just recognized. A leader might have a son who is not much good. That boy would not be recognized as a leader then.

The leader has no absolute control. What the white man calls a chief is really only a natural leader. Because of his skill and ability, men look up to him. If his son is as good as he is, that boy is recognized as a leading man in time. Otherwise he is not looked on as a leader. S. has more influence than N. or G., though the fathers of both of these men were leaders. Even I have more influence than these men. That's the way it looks to me in regard to this leader matter. I think a man becomes a leader because he is a little smarter.

Clearly, whatever his antecedents, a man must show presence and a willingness to assume responsibilities if he is to be accepted as a leader:

I don't look on N. as a leader. His father was one all right. I don't believe others think of him as a leader either. I have never heard him speak in public. If he would stand up in public and talk, if he would take part in public affairs, he probably would be considered a leader. Often now I hear people say to him, "Why don't you do something? Why don't you take an interest in these things?" But he just doesn't care for it. There are two other men here whose fathers were leaders. But they are just common men now.

The man mentioned in the above excerpt has supplied his own interpretation of his status: "Some people call me leader because my father was a leader. But I don't take it that way. I'm just like a poor man. I have no horses, no cattle. I don't live in a good house. I live just the way [other] Indians live, in a camp."

"Sometimes a leader's son refuses the responsibility," but the expectancy is that he or a close relative will succeed the head man. It is assumed that the leader has given his young relative the benefit of his knowledge and has prepared him for the position by the most rigorous training:

A young man, the son of a leader, has no excuse for not knowing what his father knew. Therefore, a young man is expected to be able to take the job. He is expected to act like a young man no longer. He is expected to have lots of sense.

Someone teaches him how to lead his people, so that they will not be in danger of starvation, how to select well-watered sites for camping, where to go after deer, and how to lead men into battle.

The leadership idea came from Child of the Water. When he was on earth, he was a leader. The leadership is usually kept in the same family; it is just handed down. If a man's father, uncle, grandfather, or someone else in the family is a leader, the boy is in line to be one too. Then he is especially trained for this. He is instructed by his parents or grandparents to be a leader.

The son of the leader is the first choice when the leader dies or isn't active any more. Most of the leaders I knew were sons of leaders. The chief's children get special advice and act in a different way. Because he is trained in a good way right from the start, the leader's son usually turns out to be a real man.

It is customary for the leader to be a man of wealth too, for the backing of prominent relatives and the attention bestowed upon a young man of rank are likely to assure him more than the ordinary share of gifts and products of the raid. His marriage connections will probably also be of the best. The tie between leadership and wealth is a close one:

If a man gets a lot of cattle, all his friends and relatives want to help him and live off him; and so such a man is respected. Everybody wants to help him and be his friend. He may butcher an animal for the whole crowd occasionally. He becomes a leader. If he has many horses, all his friends use them; they thus put themselves under him, and he becomes their leader. A leader has to be rich anyway in order to give feasts. An important leader has four or five wives, and he takes care of them. In general, he has the best of everything.

Exceptional bravery sometimes elevates a warrior to rank even though his antecedents are ordinary:

A man who has done great deeds in war may be looked on as a leader when he comes back, even though he is not of a leader's family. A prisoner who has grown up with the Chiricahua and has accepted the life might even become a leader if he is brave and successful enough.

The functions of the leader are varied:

In case of war a leader heads the men when they go to battle. In time of peace he acts as adviser. He has charge of the group as far as camping, living conditions, and water supply are concerned. He advises the men about the hunt, where to go and how. Besides being an adviser and commander in war, the leader is also a peacemaker on occasion. If there should be a murder and the leader finds it out, he and some assistants saddle their horses, ride out among the camps, and work for peace so that there will not be any trouble. If the leader is not present when the act occurs, there may be a lot of trouble. The people try to fix it up peaceably; if not, trouble continues and there may be a long family feud.

The leader is supposed to talk to his people. He is supposed to be sympathetic and tell them how to live, sympathetic in the sense of giving out horses and valuables to those who need them. The leader is supposed to give something to eat to everyone who comes around. He has control in time of war. You can't disobey him. The leader advises the people to help the unfortunate, to give to those whose luck is bad. He advises against fights in the camps; he doesn't want any quarrels within the group.

He advises the people to be on the lookout all the time. He may request that a ceremony be performed by a shaman for the benefit of the men during a raid. If the leader is advised by the shaman as a result of such a ceremony to do this or that, he carries out what the power tells him to do. A man must be wealthy and have a big following to be a chief.

Nothing special is done when a man becomes a leader. People just take it for granted. He talks then. He gives speeches on public occasions.

The leader's effectiveness as a speaker is likely to prove a measure of his success. When he repeatedly fails to convince his followers of the necessity of the actions he counsels, his control simply dissolves:

The leader has to be a good man, a good talker. He takes charge of things. He always has much to say. When anything is pending, he is asked about it, and he gives his opinion. What he says is respected, and his advice is usually followed. His directions are followed when the men are at war. In case of a murder he advises what to do about it. If more than one local group is involved, the leaders have a meeting and decide what to do with the murderer.

The leader generally gets on a hill or a high place and gives advice to the people. He does this every day or sometimes just once in two or three days if there is nothing much to report. When there is a great deal of sickness in the camps, the leader may ask some shaman to hold a ceremony for the people.

Except for the greater respect paid to him and the fact that everyone likes him, the leader is treated like anyone else in the group. If the leader gets too old, he just drops out; another man is put in his place. Then he stays home and doesn't try to go out and direct things. If they have any dispute over the leader, if it gets so that a good many don't trust him, they just get a new leader in his place. The one who has been leader is just a common member of the group after that.

As the last quotation suggests, the authority of the leader is far from absolute; his position is little stronger than that of an adviser of excellent reputation:

A man called "leader" is respected all right. N. was a leader when I was young. If what N. advised when he was leader was in line with what the others considered their best interests, they followed him. The minute his ideas ran counter to those of the people he was directing, his ideas were not followed. He never had absolute control. No man would do what he said just because he said it. People always listened closely to what he said; they gave his words more attention than they gave to those of some ordinary man, but they didn't have to accept everything he said.

The word "leader" carries the idea of director or commander. It does give you the idea that the directions are to be obeyed. But in actual life this is not always true. We use the same word ["he leads, commands, directs"] when a man is giving directions at a ceremony or about a piece of work.

Consequently, the head man's rank is assured only as long as his direction is effective:

When the leader gets old, he may call the people together and say to them, "I have been your leader for a long time, and I am becoming old and feeble, even of mind. I want you to choose another who can do for you what I once did."

But most often nothing as formal as this takes place. The retirement of the leader is gradual. His son or some prominent younger man who works closely with him and has his confidence takes charge in an increasing number of situations where physical vigor is essential. The old man, on the other hand, devotes a greater amount of attention to affairs of the camp. It is only a matter of time before the former leader is satisfied to act as the honored patriarch and as "he who commands for the home," leaving to his successor the responsibility for major decisions and military action. Therefore the length of the leader's period of service can be said to depend to a large degree upon his health and the amount of assistance he himself requires. Many leaders hold their following unchallenged until their death because they remain clear of mind and commanding in manner despite advancing years. The hereditary rights of a leader are honored only as long as he can fulfil the promise of his birth:

If the group is dissatisfied with their leader, if they are tired of him and don't like him, they may just move away and camp elsewhere and recognize another leader. Then the former leader is left alone with his family. If a leader sees that such a thing is going to happen, he can, of course, give up his rights of leadership and remain with the group as an ordinary man.

Leadership, then, is a process in which birth and wealth have their place, but in which ability and personal magnetism are always the leavening factors.

Whatever a man's rank in society, as long as he is not senile, advancing years entitle him to increased deference. "A person is respected more in home life when he reaches his prime." This attitude is indicated in countless small details of everyday life. The older person, for instance, is permitted to open the conversation when two individuals meet. One young woman is criticized because she is "too forward with older people" and frequently takes the initiative in greetings. When friends embrace, the older acts first.

Whatever aged men and women do for the young is especially appreciated; the hope is that the actions of the elders may operate as a prayer to secure comparable long life for the child:

If a very old woman, though she is no relative to me or my wife, comes in here, she can pick up my child and call it, "my daughter's child." If there are more than the one around, she can call them by the term that White Painted Woman used to Child of the Water. This has been handed down from the beginning. I've seen many old women who have a kind heart for children do this. Old men can do it too. It's a religious way, sort of a blessing.

Also, certain of the prohibitions are less strictly applied to the aged. It will be recalled that very old people may joke in a mildly risqué manner with affinal relatives whom they had to treat much more circumspectly when they were young.

And yet, the consolations of age notwithstanding, this way of life is such a strenuous one that the episodes of action and daring of youth and middle age are the treasured moments in a career. The individual grows old reluctantly, with his eyes on the past, often with sad songs that recall his lost youth:

Many years ago I saw an old man sitting by the fire working. He sang this song then, and, as he sang it, the tears rolled down his cheeks. He was thinking back to the good times he had when he was a young man. It's really an old man's song. They just sit there in a pitiful way and sing it slowly. I can't sing it like that.

> When I was young, I took no heed;
> Old, old I have become!
> Because I knew that age would come
> To me, I took no heed.

But to those who live still longer there comes a time when life becomes a burden, when debility hems them in, and "they are not happy because they can't get around." Then, at last, the aged person must confess:

Well, I've seen my best days. I am old. I am a nuisance to the group, and if anything happens to me it's all right. When I was young, I saw happy days and I had a good time. Now I'll never see those days again. I'm old and useless and not fit for anything, not even to live.

DEATH, MOURNING, AND THE
UNDERWORLD

THE topic of death is sedulously avoided. The regular term for death is seldom used; the approved euphemism "he is gone" is employed instead.[1] When an informant was asked whether his people had any death songs, his emphatic reply was:

There are no death songs for the Chiricahua. Our war songs urge the men to go forward all the time. Death wouldn't be mentioned. If a Chiricahua man heard a word about death in there during a war dance, he would stop dancing. He would go to a man with a ceremony for war and have him sing his songs and find out what it meant. Some men would back right out as soon as they heard anything like that. They'd be afraid that the fight would turn against them if that bad word was said in there.

But, when death does strike, a formal pattern of thought and procedure exists to make possible the requisite material and psychological adjustments.

The data already presented concerning the owl, the ghost, and ghost sickness[2] have paved the way for a summary of the characteristics of the burial practices:

When a person dies, his close relatives pull their good clothes off. They tie any old thing around themselves to keep themselves covered and warm. It is sometimes a month before they dress in good clothes again. Members of the family cut their hair; the women wail; the men cry.

A few minutes after death (whether a man or a woman has died) a close male relative may go out of doors and shoot off a good many cartridges in the air. He doesn't shoot in any special direction. Any male relative can do it. I don't know exactly why it is done; no one seems to be sure. But I think that this has to do with the importance of the person who has died. It tells the rest of the people that someone of standing has died. N. was a leader. When his mother died, he

---

[1] In spite of the great terror surrounding death, suicides occasionally occur when life becomes unbearable. Individuals have committed suicide when captured by the enemy, when stunned with grief at the loss of a child or some other close relative, or as a result of marital strife.

[2] See pp. 14-15, 229-37, 301-5.

took a gun and shot into the air about fifteen times, right in succession. This was not done with arrows before the guns came into use. I'm pretty sure it dates from the time that guns came in. It may be connected with the shooting over the graves of dead soldiers by their comrades that the Chiricahua saw. Such shooting is not always done, but it occurs quite often.

The close relatives get the body ready for burial. A close friend might help, but it's hard to ask him. A person who lays out the corpse of a near relative does not mind so much, for he is supposed to do it, but you have a queer feeling if you lay out the body of one you are not related to. No particular relative has to do it. All those who are closely related to the dead person feel that they should help if they are called on. It can be men or women who do it. We don't like to do it, but it can't be helped. We are really a little afraid to handle bodies. Not long ago I had to handle a little baby when it died; I had to stay up and see it die. Many try to get out of it when they can.

The body is bathed, or at least the face of the dead person is always washed. The hair is combed, and red paint is put on his face to make him look nice. The dead person is dressed up in his best clothes for the burial. The burial always takes place in the day, on the same day that death occurred if possible. They bury the corpse quickly and far from the settlements—in the mountains, if they are near. They don't want children at a burial. Just a few older people who are needed go.

The best horse, the favorite horse of the dead person, is used. The dead person's robes or blankets are tied to the horse, and the horse is loaded with his belongings. His good saddle is put on the horse. Then the corpse is mounted on the horse and is held there by his relatives as the funeral procession makes its way up the canyon to the place where the burial is to be. As the funeral procession passes near the camps, the people cry for the dead man, if he was their good friend.

Out there the members of the burial party might strike a little natural depression at the bottom of a hill. They could use this as a grave. They wrap the body in a blanket or a hide, put a little brush under it and some on top, and put a few rocks on top if they are handy. Or they put down a layer of rocks, put the body on it, then brush and branches over, then leaves and dirt, and finally rocks on top until there is a small mound.

If they find a little cave or a hole in the rocks, that is used.[3] The body is put on the floor, and the entrance is blocked up with rocks and covered with mud to hide it and make it look like the side of the cliff. They aren't going to talk about the grave and tell where it is. They don't want anyone to know or think about it.

When a cave is not handy, they might scoop out a hollow grave and bury the body in a hole in the ground. A hide or logs would be put over the body to keep out the animals.

The body is always laid with the head to the sundown. The property they

[3] Interestingly enough, there is a term which means both "cave cache" and "grave."

brought is buried with the corpse. What they don't bury with him is burned or destroyed back home. All that a person had is destroyed. They say that whatever is thrown away with a dead person that belongs to him he carries to the underworld. They want him to have the use of these things in the other world. They don't want him to get there poor. They want to show that they do not hold property above their relative. And they don't want anything that the dead person had used a great deal to be around. It would only remind people of the one who died and bring them sorrow. Also they fear that the ghost of the person who owned the article will come back to molest the one who keeps it.

For the same reasons they kill the horse that has carried the dead person's possessions. It is stabbed in the throat or shot, at or near the grave. If a man has several horses, sometimes they kill them all; sometimes only his favorite horse or horses, the ones he actually used all the time. It is because a person used a thing continually and it is associated with him and reminds you of him that you don't want to keep it. People don't want to see his horse. Because he used to ride it so much, to have it around reminds them of the former owner. Besides they kill the horses so they will go with the dead person. The saddles are burned.

They don't have to kill all the horses of the family though. All the horses of a family are not thought of as belonging to one person, even to the man who is the head of that family. If a family has five or six horses, one is considered the property of a child, another of the wife, and so on. A man might not be considered to possess more than one or two horses of his own. These are his favorites and the ones he always used, and they are killed at his death. They cut the tails and manes of horses if any are kept at the death of a man.

Everything is buried or destroyed. If a woman's baskets or pots are not buried with her, they put holes through them. Nothing is left whole, for they don't want them used again, even by mistake. Usually for a man the only things that are buried with him are his clothes and weapons. Other things are burned.

The things he used in his ceremony are not kept either. Those things are destroyed. Sometimes they put them in the grave with the dead person. Some hang them on a tree. There was one woman who died at Fort Sill. She had a cross that she used in her ceremonial work. They put it in her grave with her. Then at night something like lightning would come out of the grave.

When the person died of old age, branches of fruit-bearing trees are used to cover the grave. When an old Indian dies, they bring branches of all trees that bear fruit. They put the limbs on top of the grave. They say, "Next season I hope there will be many of these trees." Young people call the dead out by name and say, "I hope that I will also grow old."[4] When a person dies in youth, his name is not called this way. When they bury a person, they brush off their own bodies with green grass and then put it on him in the form of a cross. Then they won't dream of him.

[4] This material was obtained from a Southern Chiricahua informant. A member of the Eastern Chiricahua band claimed to know nothing about the particular procedure.

> The burial doesn't take very long, and they come away as soon as they can. They keep away from that place; it is not revisited. Just witches are seen fooling around graves.

It is the intention of the members of the burial party and of the close relatives of the deceased to alter so completely the situation with which their dead kinsman was associated that nothing will remind them of him, and nothing they have or do will draw his ghost to them. They destroy not only all his property and all the objects which he handled or used to any extent but also gifts which have come from him. The members of the burial party and any others who have come into contact with the corpse bathe carefully and burn or "roll up and hide in the woods" the clothes they have worn during their unpleasant task. Most often, too, "the others change their clothes. They don't want to wear what they had on when the person was living and when they were going around with him." Other precautions are taken:

> Often after a death the person who has had contact with the body purifies himself by taking "ghost medicine," throwing it on a fire, making smoke from it, and sitting before the smoke with a robe. If the smoke is plentiful, no robe is needed. He then sits or stands where the smoke can get all over him—any way so the smoke goes all over. The hair is always washed after contact with the dead, and the clothes worn are burned or thrown away. Sometimes all the close relatives use the "ghost medicine."

In addition, there must be a further change in the appearance of the bereaved—the cutting of the hair:

> The hair of men, women, and children is cut when a close relative dies. The hair is cut once, to about ear length, and then it is allowed to grow out again. It is done for a parent, a brother or a sister, or a husband or a wife. For a man, the wife and mother are sure to cut their hair. Some sisters do, some do not. It is seldom that cousins do it, and the relatives of a dead person's husband or wife do not do it at all. Some adults only cut the ends of the hair.

Camp life must be reconstructed in a new locality and on a different basis. "Following a death we move camp. The relatives don't want to live in the same place. It doesn't matter whether the person died in the home or not. It is destroyed anyway. Usually it is burned. And they do not go back around that old camp site much either."

Because the name is so intimate a facet of the personality, one of the most rigid injunctions forbids the mention of the name of the recently deceased. If the dead person must be mentioned, a qualifying phrase provides a safeguard:

There should be no mention of a dead person. To mention the name of the dead reminds relatives of him and makes them feel bad; it only causes sorrow. Besides it might prove dangerous. To call the name of a dead person at any time is bad, and especially after dark.

We are instructed, in case it is necessary to use the name of the dead, to put a word after the name which means "who used to be called." Another way is to say "the one who used to be a relative of So-and-So." The avoidance of the name is not observed only before the relatives of the dead person. It is a general observance.

When an elder of the family, who has been in close contact with the children, dies, their names are changed:

The children of the family get different names then. The person who has died has called the children by this name that is being dropped; that is why they don't want it used any more. The older people don't have their names changed because of this, however.

If the relative who suggested one's name dies, that name is sure to be changed: " 'Little' was my first name. Later a name was given to me by my grandmother. When she died, it was changed."

When a person who is named after something of common reference dies, the people are reluctant to use the term for a long time after the death. "They are especially careful around the relatives." Circumlocutions and synonyms are employed until the danger period is past. Even the use of relationship terms is restricted because their utterance might stimulate painful memories or ghost anxieties:

If you have two relatives that you call by the same relationship term and one of them dies, you don't call the other by this term for a while. You call him by his name until the dead person is forgotten. Then you can use the relationship term to him again.

Those outside the relationship group in which a death has occurred must exercise the greatest care not to arouse the resentment of the bereaved:

What the relatives do not like if a person dies is to see in the next few days anyone wearing a red dress, a red shirt, a red headband, or red clothes of any kind. It hurts the feelings of those who have lost their relative to see this. If a death occurs near by, others take off their red clothes at once. It is because red is colorful and stands for a good time. If your relative dies and you see someone wearing red, you say, "Well, that fellow wore red when I was sad. When his relative dies, I'm going to wear red just for meanness." Fights and bad feelings can start from this; enemies can be made in this way.

And yet, in spite of all the determined efforts to obliterate the memory of the dead, a prolonged period of formal mourning is sanctioned:

For some time after the death of his wife a man will not dress in fine clothes or colors. And he won't go to social dances. He won't even be invited, because the people know he isn't thinking of such things. A woman will not attend the social dancing at a puberty rite, though it is held several months after her husband's death. She will wait about a year before she will go to such affairs.

Moreover, regardless of all warnings concerning the danger of excessive grief, some individuals find it impossible to repress their sorrow:

A woman may wail for a dead relative before sunrise for years after he dies if some special calamity has come which she thinks wouldn't have come if the relative were alive. Or she may wail when she sees a special friend of her dead son, or one who is of the same age and looks like him.

While the relatives are observing the necessary rites, the ghost of the departed makes its way or is led by other ghostly kin to the underworld, "a beautiful place beneath the ground, where a nice stream of water flows between banks that are lined with cottonwood trees, and everything is green." This home of the departed has been variously termed by informants "where the cottonwoods stand in a line," "ground that is streaked with red," "underground," "where they go off," and "where they go down." The last two names refer to the manner of reaching this subterranean paradise:

Our concept is down, a place beneath. When I was a child, many years ago, the Chiricahua never talked about where other Indians go at death. They just talked about where their own people, the Chiricahua, go. We think of a dead person going on to another life—of his whole body, as it was on earth, going to the other world. He is really transferred to that other world.

When a person is very sick and is unconscious, it is said that he is somewhere else, that his ghost has gone where the dead people are, to visit his friends. If he regains consciousness, it is because his ghost gets back again, and when he gets well he may tell where he was. Every once in a while someone has an experience like this. That is how we know where the place is and what it looks like.

For instance, when I was a little boy someone was very sick, more dead than alive. He peeped into the underworld. But he didn't quite go there. He came back and told what he saw. He described the entrance to it as a huge sand pile upon which people are dropped and which they are trying to climb. But the sand gives way, and they don't get to this world again. The underworld, according to this man, lies just below our present world.

When a person dies, he goes under the ground. He goes through an opening in the ground which is cut out like a window. Someone leads him to it so he can't miss it. There is tall grass all around it to hide it and make it look natural. When this opens, there is a great pile of sand, shaped like a tepee or cone, stretching down beneath. It is a far distance from the top to the bottom. Once a person is down there, it is almost impossible to get back. Once he is through the gate it is impossible for the person who is really dead to come back to life; yet some who are just very sick or in a death coma, but who later recover, can come back and tell about it. This big sand hill closes off the underworld for those who are there. If you are in the underworld and succeed in getting to the top of it, you will get back to earth and life. But it is almost impossible. Many try it. They get up so far, and then the sand rolls down with them.

The conditions of life in the underworld are pictured by one who claims to have glimpsed the place during a serious illness:

The same ways we have here are carried on down there too. Those people dance, eat, and sleep. A person down there can actually feel another in the flesh. The people remain the same age as they were when they died. I saw people as they were when they went. That is the way it is always seen. There is no sickness, death, pain, or sorrow there. Those who were good and those who were bad are down there together. I saw them all mixed together. The same places, the same sacred mountains, the same ceremonies exist there as here. It is just as though everything is transferred to a different country.

Always the emphasis is upon the perpetuation of customary activities:

There is no death there, but lots of good things to eat. Affairs go on in the same way, but better. Those who are there just go on living happily. Life means more. It is always the same life, the hunting, the raids, and all, as in the old days. There are the same puberty rite, masked dances, and sacred mountains. In the underworld they are just like a big community, but they are split up into the same groups as on earth. Each person is with his own group. And each does the same things he used to do when he was on earth. As the story goes, if you were an arrow-maker, you are there making arrows. If you were a good hunter, you are over there hunting. If you were a great warrior on earth, you are out at war.

And so, at the final point to which we have traced this culture, the underworld in which it has been faithfully projected, we take leave of the Chiricahua life-way.

APPENDIX

CHIRICAHUA KINSHIP SYSTEM AND TERMS

The following symbols are used in Fig. 2:

The triangle indicates male; the circle indicates female.

The sign of equality indicates marriage of the individuals between whom it is placed.

Vertical lines are generation lines and connect parent and offspring; horizontal lines connect collateral relatives of the same generation.

The appearance of a letter in more than one generation shows that the term which the letter represents is a self-reciprocal (e.g., the term for father's father [A] is also used of son's child [man speaking]).

St.f. means stepfather, *st.m.* means stepmother, *old.* means older, and *yng.* means younger.

TABLE 1

Chiricahua Kinship Terms

A*................	šìnálé	H...............	šìmá·'
B................	šìčìné	I...............	šìɣóyé, sìdài
C................	šìcóyé	J...............	šíḱà̇·
D................	šìčó	K...............	šìk'ìs
E................	šìtà·	L...............	šílà̧h
F................	šìdè·dé''	M...............	šíɣè', sìžâ·
G................	šìbé·žè'	N...............	šìyáčè'

* The letters ("A," "B," "C," etc.) refer to the relatives in Fig. 2. The terms listed under "I" can be used interchangeably, as can also those listed under "M."

479

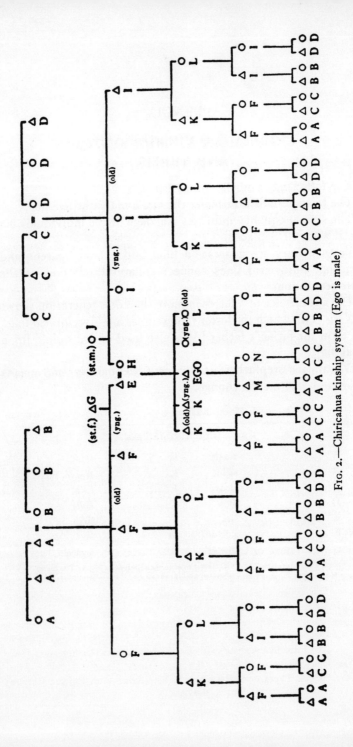

Fig. 2.—Chiricahua kinship system (Ego is male)

SELECTED BIBLIOGRAPHY

BARRELL, S. M. *Geronimo's Story of His Life*. New York: Duffield & Co., 1915.

BOURKE, JOHN G. *Apache Campaign in Sierra Madre*. New York: Charles Scribner's Sons, 1886.

———. *On the Border with Crook*. New York: Charles Scribner's Sons, 1891.

———. "Medicine Men of the Apache," *Ninth Annual Report of the Bureau of American Ethnology*. Washington, 1892.

CASTETTER, EDWARD F., and OPLER, M. E. *The Ethnobiology of the Chiricahua and Mescalero Apache*. "Bulletin of the University of New Mexico, Biological Series," Vol. IV, No. 5. Albuquerque, 1936.

DAVIS, B. *Truth about Geronimo*. New Haven: Yale University Press, 1929.

HARRINGTON, M. R. "The Devil Dance of the Apaches," *Museum Journal* (Philadelphia), VIII, No. 1 (1912), 6-9.

HOIJER, HARRY. *Chiricahua and Mescalero Apache Texts*. With ethnological notes by MORRIS EDWARD OPLER. "University of Chicago Publications in Anthropology." Chicago: University of Chicago Press, 1938.

OPLER, MORRIS EDWARD. "The Concept of Supernatural Power among the Chiricahua and Mescalero Apaches," *American Anthropologist*, XXXVII, No. 1 (1935), 65-70.

———. "Note on the Cultural Affiliations of Northern Mexican Nomads," *ibid.*, No. 4, pp. 702-6.

———. "An Interpretation of Ambivalence of Two American Indian Tribes," *Journal of Social Psychology*, VII (1936), 82-116.

———. "Some Points of Comparison and Contrast between the Treatment of Functional Disorders by Apache Shamans and Modern Psychiatric Practice," *American Journal of Psychiatry*, XCII, No. 6 (1936), 1371-87.

———. "The Kinship Systems of the Southern Athabaskan-speaking Tribes: A Comparative Study," *American Anthropologist*, XXXVIII, No. 4 (1936), 620-33.

———. "An Outline of Chiricahua Apache Social Organization," in *Social Anthropology of North American Tribes*, ed. FRED EGGAN. Chicago: University of Chicago Press, 1937.

———. "The Sacred Clowns of the Chiricahua and Mescalero Apache Indians," *El Palacio*, XLIV, Nos. 10-12 (1938), 75-79.

———. "Further Comparative Anthropological Data Bearing on the Solution of a Psychological Problem," *Journal of Social Psychology*, IX (1938), 477-83.

———. "A Chiricahua Apache's Account of the Geronimo Campaign of 1886," *New Mexico Historical Review*, VIII, No. 4 (1938), 360-86.

———. "Three Types of Variation and Their Relation to Culture Change," in *Language, Culture, and Personality: Essays in Memory of Edward Sapir,* ed. LESLIE SPIER, A. IRVING HALLOWELL, and STANLEY S. NEWMAN: Menasha, Wis.: George Banta Publishing Co., 1941.

———. "Myths and Tales of the Chiricahua Apache Indians." In press.

OPLER, MORRIS EDWARD, and HOIJER, HARRY. "The Raid and Warpath Language of the Chiricahua Apache," *American Anthropologist,* XLII, No. 4 (1940), 617–34.

Reports of the Commissioner of Indian Affairs, 1869, 1873, 1874. Washington, 1869, 1873, 1874.

INDEX

Abalone shell, 21, 40, 110, 131, 215, 259, 266, 272, 275, 283

Ability, influence of, in status, 465, 466, 467

Abortion, 147

Abstinence, in boys' training, 71

Acoma, 1

Acorns, gathering and use of, 363

Adultery, punishment for, 410, 411

Adulthood, at completion of novitiate, 139

Affinal relatives, terms for, 163–64, 185

Affirmation, 434

Afterbirth; disposal of, 8

Agave, gathering and use of, 356–58

Age: attitude toward, 62–63; prerogatives of, 470–71; and status, 63; stick, 116, 128, 261; terms, 432

Aged: bring good fortune to young, 470; as bugaboo for children, 30–31; ceremonial prerogatives of, 84

Agriculture: extent of, 374, 374 n.; influence of Mexicans in, 372, 373, 374; methods of, 373–74; recency of, 372

Algerita berries, gathering and use of, 361

Ambushing, 345–46

Americans, 215, 351, 462

Amulets: for children, 12, 37; for cradle, 11; for lightning sickness, 284, 284 n.; for war, 342; wearing of, following ceremony, 266, 293, 310

Anal flatulence, as source of ceremony, 206

Anglepod seeds, 363

Animal homes, 286–87

Animals: contaminating, 224; domestic, cared for by horse shaman, 300; game, killed by lightning for people, 286; of mythological period, 196

Animism, and supernatural power, 206

Ant, red: disease from, 237; stings, treatment of, 218

Antelope: ceremony from, 285; encirclement by, dangerous, 287; methods of hunting, 324–25; monster, slain by Child of the Water, 197–98

Antelope head mask, use of, in stalking game, 285, 287, 324

Anthill, urinating in prohibited, 237

Apachean-speaking peoples, 463

Arrow: child's, 390; feathering, 388–89; fluting, 286, 286 n., 389–90; lengths, 390, making of, 388–91; straightening, 388, 390

Arrow games, 50–52

Arrow poison, 319; used in war, 340–41

Arrow release, 388

Arrow-shooting contests, 391

Arrowheads, 389

Art, naturalistic, forbidden to women, 379

Ashes, 8, 283, 302, 304; as prophylactic against ghost, 231; as prophylactic against witchcraft, 253; for rash, 186; to stop muscular tremor, 188

Attendant, of puberty rite, 84, 90; nonshamanistic functions of, 84; selection of, 84–85

Avoidance: of affinal relatives, 160, 161, 164; behavior pattern of, 164–69; by choice, 170–72; continuation or termination of, 172–75; cousin,